The Perfect
BABY NAME

The Perfect
BABY NAME
A Proven Plan for Choosing a
Name You'll Love

· JEANINE COX ·

STERLING

New York / London
www.sterlingpublishing.com

STERLING and the distinctive Sterling logo are registered trademarks of
Sterling Publishing Co., Inc.

Library of Congress Cataloging-in-Publication Data Available

10 9 8 7 6 5 4 3 2 1

Originally published in 2004 by Sterling Publishing Co., Inc.
387 Park Avenue South, New York, NY 10016
© 2004, 2010 by Jeanine Cox
Distributed in Canada by Sterling Publishing
c/o Canadian Manda Group, 165 Dufferin Street
Toronto, Ontario, Canada M6K 3H6
Distributed in the United Kingdom by GMC Distribution Services
Castle Place, 166 High Street, Lewes, East Sussex, England BN7 1XU
Distributed in Australia by Capricorn Link (Australia) Pty. Ltd.
P.O. Box 704, Windsor, NSW 2756, Australia

Sterling ISBN 978-1-4027-2179-3

For information about custom editions, special sales, premium and
corporate purchases, please contact Sterling Special Sales
Department at 800-805-5489 or specialsales@sterlingpublishing.com.

To my wonderful husband, Lew, and beautiful children,
Oliver Max and Nadia Grace. Their ongoing enthusiasm and interest in this
project has kept it meaningful and fun.

Contents

Acknowledgments

Without the unique skills and creativity of my editorial and programming team, this book would not be.

Gratitude and thanks to Christine Beaudry, my long-time editor and friend. Her enthusiastic dedication to perfection is an inspiration to all of us.—Daughters: Erin Elizabeth and Lauren Elise

Thanks to Noel Hanlon, my technical guru, friend, and a soon-to-be exceptional father.

Thanks to my special Chinese friend, Ginger Yao. Her technical expertise and fluency in Mandarin are appreciated.—Daughter: Jocelyn Yao

Thanks to Fred Jonas for his technical expertise and reliable hosting services. —Sons: David and Zachary

Thanks to Kathleen Finnegan whose fluency in French and German was of significant value.—Daughter: Una; Son: Milan

Thanks to Lina Zaltsman, who created the world's most sophisticated baby-names software for us and helped with Russian names.—Daughter: Julia Beth; Son: Benjamin Leo

Thanks to Mariel Swiggard for her creative contributions as are evident in poems, quotes, and interesting facts regarding names throughout the book.—Daughter: Savannah Mae; Son: Alexander James

Thanks to Pauliina Vahaama. Her fluency in German, Persian, and Finnish added insight and accuracy to our database.—Son: Saam Erick

Thanks to Claire Matze. Her expertise and fluency in Arabic and Spanish helped pull the book together.—Sons: Gerard and Bernard; Daughters: Laura and Sabrina

Finally, special thanks to Meredith Peters Hale for believing in the project and helping to bring it to perfect realization.—Daughter: Sloane Florence

Other contributors:
Ayako Howard, Dr. Stanley Lieberson, Ed Lawson, David Courchane, Kathie M. Donohue, Chikage Windler, Jessica and John Peters, Jim and Laura Koumarianos, Sandra Connors, Shari Becker, Stephanie Torres, Joëlle Reidy, Isabel Cervera Díaz, and Hanna-Reetta Paasonen

Introduction

CONGRATULATIONS ON YOUR PREGNANCY! THIS TIME OF YOUR LIFE is nothing short of a magical voyage that lasts (give or take) nine months. While you anxiously wait for your son or daughter, you have a very important decision to make: What will you name your precious baby?

As generations have passed, we've learned from psychological studies, case histories, and experts in onomastics—the scientific study of names—about the overwhelming evidence that names and personalities are interwoven entities, and that what you name your child will impact his or her future. Many of our own parents believed that a popular name was the most desirable choice for a child because of a flawed yet well-accepted study indicating that kids with popular names do better in school. More recently, published research says that a child should have a unique name to stand out in this highly competitive world; likewise, namesakes, stereotypes, and spelling variations can be frowned upon. While this is interesting edification, what continues to be overlooked is that expectant parents have a natural, intuitive image of what their child may be and what name will suit him or her. Religious parents often choose a biblical name; more liberal or creative parents may go for something more unique, while conservative parents tend toward something popular but safe. So while it appears that the name defines the child, it's logical that parents naming a child with certain expectations and raising a child in a particular manner define or "stereotype" that child.

Fortunately, there's enough media exposure to a myriad of names in our increasingly diversified culture that perceptions and stereotypes are now skewed. While it's interesting to see what impressions are associated with a name, today's global society is less likely to judge people solely on their monikers. Today's classroom is filled with many ethnicities and thus, many old school "bad choices" are in every class roster. How can anyone in this society be concerned with name perception when the president of our country has frankly the funniest sounding moniker yet?

Despite this newfound openness in choosing a name, you still want to find a meaningful name for your child. After all, any important decision in life requires research and contemplation. But remember, only you have some inclination of what road your daughter or son may take, only you know what ideals you will set forth for your child, and only you will say, repeat, and abbreviate this given name thousands of times as you endeavor to raise your child into an exceptional person.

Here you will find facts (not opinions), reliable statistics, and polls gathered from various sources as well as fun exercises, inspirational quotes, and fascinating information on the history of naming babies. What you won't find is our judgment of what makes a name cool, trendy, good, or bad. You will be provided with all the information you need to come to that conclusion on your own; after all, you are naming your child for yourselves.

When it was time for my husband and me to name our first child, we did what many parents do and bought every baby-naming book we could find. While perusing the books and forming lists, we were also busy launching and developing BabyZone. com, the popular parenting site which quickly began developing tools to help parents name babies. Nine months later, we gave birth to Nadia Grace, and two years after that her little brother Oliver Max was born. Today, several years from my pregnancy with Nadia and the inception of BabyZone.com, my editorial staff and I have helped moms and dads name millions of babies. We've also gathered a plethora of baby-naming data from parents, experts, and public sources, and compiled stats via the Internet from millions of parents. Now, for the first time ever, we're publishing this unique factual content. Along with this data, I've added scores of lists, games, and guides to create this all-in-one inspirational book.

So, are you ready? Let's go name your perfect baby a perfect name.

A Baby by Any Other Name... Is Still Your Baby

If you hope to find the ideal name for your beautiful baby, simply said, you will. As an expectant parent that has chosen this book, you are undoubtedly determined to overturn every stone until you *do* find the right name. Naming your child is the first of many big decisions you'll make as a parent. To guide you, we've included an easy-to-follow, step-by-step program that will inspire you to find meaningful names, followed by a guide to help you narrow down your list of potential names. But before you get started choosing a name, here are a few important points to keep in mind.

Trust Your Instincts

We've all had that deep gut feeling that prompts us to make specific decisions, and allowing these instincts to guide you—rather than being persuaded by a barrage of opinions—offers you the best chance at picking the consummate baby name. To cultivate this skill (and yes, it is a skill), you need to get out of your own way and be open to anything. Give yourself time; you don't need to name the baby before his or her arrival. Many parents wait until they meet their baby to make a final name selection, especially if they have a couple of name favorites. Don't worry—your baby will not remain nameless because her parents were too undecided! A name *will* come to you, so have confidence, get informed, and enjoy the selection process. To quote

Deepak Chopra, "Trust your gut and your heart and your toes, too." Your baby's name could come from a person, place, thing, or idea, and it can be popular or unusual—it can be anything you want it to be, because it's not the name that makes the person, it's the person that makes the name. Your child's name, personality, and beliefs will be interwoven and mixed into a combination that is truly unique.

Name Dilemmas

While our handy lists and methods help add order to your naming process, there is no way to address every possible name dilemma expectant couples encounter. The most frequent predicament is that parents can't agree on a name. While some couples are so like-minded they easily agree on name choices, others agonize over this decision. Here are a few guidelines to help you overcome naming problems.

- See if you can begin the journey on common ground. Try agreeing on a strategy or process as opposed to a specific name. Think about what naming style you both *do* agree on—whether you're looking for a unique name, a biblical name, or a traditional family name, for example.

- Keep baby naming between you and your mate. Unless you have a very secure relationship with your parents or in-laws, it's usually best to keep their opinions out of the mix. The same goes for other well-meaning relatives and friends. One of the most common naming problems is that a relative or friend may feel she has ownership over a name you're choosing. What they don't know won't hurt them.

- Establish that both parents have the right to veto any name they absolutely do not like. After all, you want your mate to feel like an equal partner in this decision as well as many future decisions to come. Begin on common ground and name your child together.

- Think compromise. You have a first name and a middle name to work with, and if you're planning on having more children after this baby, you'll have additional opportunities for baby naming. If all else fails, try the "if it's a boy/girl—the mother/father picks the name" process. (However, avoid having one parent select the first name, while the other selects the middle name. Here the *compromise* tends to become the priority, when the *best name combination* for your child should receive precedence.)

A Word to the Mothers If you're pregnant, you are naturally hormonal! The father-to-be may have an opposing opinion about your favorite baby name selection, but remember, this is not a personal attack on you or your choices. Keep in mind, you're carrying this child, and Dad doesn't have much say in the whole pregnancy experience. Naming your child is one of the most meaningful decisions concerning your unborn baby that requires his input.

As desperate as you may be to choose baby's name, it is imperative that you and the baby's dad move into the realm of parenthood as partners. If this is his first child, be sensitive to the metamorphosis of the man becoming a father. Contrarily, if your partner seems ambivalent about the chosen name, consider that he is overwhelmed with the concept and still in "acceptance stage," or he may simply trust that you will do a wonderful—even better—job and is choosing to focus his time on your baby's college tuition fund! Whether he's opinionated or ambivalent, you *are* hormonal, so take it in stride!

A Word to the Fathers Some women begin dreaming of names for their unborn children as early as age three and grow up with favorite names or ideas of how they will name their babies. The expectant mom is also hormonal (I can't stress this enough!), and that means she is particularly sensitive to everything—especially conflict. While you may have some very strong opinions about baby's name, try to be sensitive to the mom-to-be. Often men want to avoid unique names for boys, but think of all the successful men with creative names today and try to keep an open mind, Dad.

A Word about Siblings There's a balancing act between keeping an older child involved in the pregnancy and not setting him up for disappointment because you didn't choose his name for the baby. If babies' siblings chose their names, there would be plenty of Disney characters checking out of the maternity ward—not to mention children's wonderfully creative invented name choices! Undoubtedly, kids will hear you discussing names amongst yourselves and will naturally have "suggestions," but make it clear from the beginning that naming baby is big business (tell them their own baby-naming story), and is a decision ultimately made by Mommy and Daddy. Do be sure to listen to your child though, because you never do know where that perfect name might originate—and if it does happen to come from a sibling, it can be all the more meaningful.

A Word about Grandparents (and Other Well-Meaning Friends and Relatives) Your well-intentioned parents and in-laws will inevitably have opinions about your child's name, whether it's concerning a namesake or a style of naming they find comfortable. Assess how much pressure they are capable of putting on you and make a decision to put the "rules" in place before discussing names with them. The rule may be that you are going to keep your name choices confidential until your baby is born, thus not allowing any outside influences. You will inevitably get unsolicited name suggestions from relatives and friends, which you can politely respond to with, "thanks for the suggestion, we'll keep that in mind" (whether you like the name or not!).

Naming a child after a beloved and possibly deceased relative is certainly a strong and sentimental desire, and something you may consider. Many parents who choose to incorporate a namesake do it in baby's middle name or find a variation of the namesake that suits their taste. If that compromise is not possible, keep in mind that no matter what name you choose, Grandma and Grandpa will fall in love with your little one at first sight and most likely forget there was ever an issue with the baby's name.

How to Use This Book: The Name Selection Process

To begin, all you need is a pencil, an eraser, and an open mind. Throughout the following chapters, you'll find various baby-naming exercises. Use these exercises with the corresponding workbook in the middle of the book. This workbook will keep you on track and communicating effectively with your partner. If you're single and pregnant, you can choose a close friend or relative to partner with or simply ignore instances where we ask your partner to step in and find a name solo. There are a total of ten exercises to be done as you go through the chapters and intermittently browse our name dictionary.

Feel free to return to the exercises or lists at any time throughout the process to add or remove names. The first exercise—which will most likely generate your longest list and the one you return to the most—is also where you can add names that "sound nice" if they don't fit into the other list categories. Keep in mind that the process is just that—a process, not to be rushed or forced, but to be enjoyed either on your own or as a couple.

About the Pronunciation Guide

You will note throughout the dictionary section that not all names include pronunciations. This cross-cultural collection of names encompasses many languages and dialects, and establishing the correct pronunciation of an ancient or ethnic name requires deep scrutiny. Our researchers cautiously included the pronunciation of names that could be validated by more than one reliable source. Likewise, pronunciations for the more recognizable, obvious names were not included in an effort to save space.

To preserve the legacy of these names and give you—the parents-to-be—access to the entire collection of names, we chose to include some names without the phonetic guide. If you're interested in the pronunciation of a name that is not included in this book or you think you know how to pronounce a name we don't have, please e-mail me at jeaninecox@mac.com.

Baby Name Pronunciation Guide

A cat, can
AH cot, con
AW fawn, bought
AY rain, cane
E wet, share
EE meet, mean
I bit, win
IE find, kite
O boat, blow, phone
OI boy, coin
OO moon, boot
OW out, gown
U but, fun
UW book, put
ə about (neutral vowel)

Exercise One: Positive Visualization

As you fantasize about your baby, take it a step further, and visualize who your child might be, what she might look like, and what her genetic code is. You have a sense for this child along with a special innate knowledge available only to you as parents. Now visualize the same person as a young adult, and then reach a little further and imagine her in a career or family setting. Begin thinking of names for this person, and as these names come to you, write them in the corresponding workbook space in back of the book. We recommend doing this for both boy and girl names, but if you're certain of the sex and want to focus all of your attention on a specific gender that is, of course, your prerogative.

Over time, feel free to add or remove names. We encourage both parents to work on this and all the exercises as a team but, at this stage, only the parent that added a name to the list can remove that name.

CHAPTER 2

Let the Names Begin

What to Consider When Choosing a Name

"A signature always reveals a man's character—and sometimes even his name."
—Evan Esar (1899–1995)

First Things First! Last Names

Good, bad, or just plain funny—your child's surname is the name you have the least control over, yet it is the most important consideration in choosing the right-sounding first and middle names. As your child grows and enters the workforce, his identity will no longer be as simple as a first name. He will be referred to by first and last or, if he chooses, first, middle, and last. When considering names, keep in mind that a lengthy, difficult-to-spell last name would be compounded by a difficult first name; likewise, a plain last name might be further diluted with a common or short first name. An easily picked on last name (Cox) could be toned down or up with the right or wrong first name. It could also fade into a complementary first name—Courteney Bass Cox—becoming a memorable identity. A quick study in alliteration (the repetition of initial consonant sounds in two or more neighboring words) can inspire some rhythmic name ideas.

Exercise Two: A is for Alliteration

Use this exercise to discover complementary first names based on your last name. Flip through the alphabetical listings of names that have a similar initial sound as your last name; for example, Smith should look at S and the soft-sounding C. If any names in these sections appeal to you, add them to your list.

Count Your Syllables

According to some experts, an important naming rule is to have an odd number of syllables between the first and last names. So Meredith (three syllables) could go with Beaudry (two syllables), and Grace (one) might link nicely to de'Angelo (four), but there are so many exceptions to the rule, perhaps it shouldn't be a rule at all. Some general guidelines to find compatible names include not picking a first name with many syllables if your last name also is multi-syllabic. And while you want your child's full name to be harmonious, you don't necessarily want it to rhyme. Although, I bet no one forgets Peter Streeter once they've heard his name! On the other hand, Kate Mates is definitely a questionable choice. Your child's name should be memorable but pleasant sounding.

Acronyms and Initials

When creating your lists, always write the entire name out including the surname. Look at the initials, ensuring that nothing offensive is spelled. Paula Ilene Gunther (PIG) or even more subtle initials like Phillip Ike Nathanson (PIN) could prove tortuous to a child with a particularly unruly bully in the classroom.

In 1998, Dr. Nicholas Christenfeld at the University of California studied death certificates from 1969 to 1995 and determined that men whose initials form nasty acronyms, such as ASS or UGH, die an average of 2.8 years sooner than those with meaningless initials. Men blessed with positive initials such as ACE, JOY, or GOD were apt to live around 4.48 years longer. Mysteriously, negative initials had no impact on women's longevity. Perhaps, that's because they can change their initials upon marriage. Coincidence? You decide.

Another obvious but noted consideration is the first and last initials. Victor Daniels (VD) could expose your child to teasing, while Brandon Browne could end up with the nickname "BB" or Jeffery Russell with "JR." While you do have some control over what your child may be tagged as a nickname, no naming strategy is foolproof. An ancient Hungarian proverb states, "A child with many names is a loved child." With that in mind, consider possible pet names or nicknames before the rest of the world does, because assuredly, your child will be much loved!

Exercise Three: The Acronym Game

Try using initials to spell a desirable acronym. Take the first letter of the baby's last name, and place it at the end of your acronym. Then spell desirable words with the first letters of first and middle names you like. For example, if your last name is Parker, use the P as the last letter to spell POP. Add a first name beginning with a P and a middle beginning with an O: Paul Oz Parker.

Chinese Lunar Calendar

Will you have a handsome baby boy or a beautiful baby girl? Try consulting the Chinese Lunar Calendar. A Chinese scientist discovered and drew this chart which was buried in a royal tomb about 700 years ago. The original is kept in the Institute of Science of Peking. The accuracy of the chart has been proven by thousands of people—in fact, it's believed to be ninety-nine percent accurate!

If you're a mother, look across the top of the table and find your lunar age (add nine months to your actual age) at the date of conception. Next, find the month of conception, located along the left side of the calendar. Follow the column and row, and see where the two intersect. If the box is blue, the calendar predicts you'll have a boy; white, you'll have a girl. For instance, a thirty-year-old-woman who conceived in January will give birth to a boy, according to the Chinese Lunar Calendar.

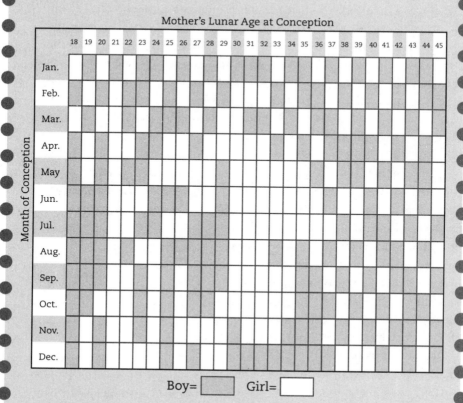

Mother's Lunar Age at Conception

Month of Conception

Boy=　　　　Girl=

So what if your favorite baby name spells something less than desirable? As caring, thoughtful parents, we don't want to expose our children to unnecessary ridicule. If your "perfect" name creates an unpleasant acronym or initials, or even a nickname you're not thrilled with, make sure you think through your decision and evaluate all of your priorities and options. Look at a spelling variation as an option, as well as using the mother's maiden name hyphenated with the last name. For every problem, there is a solution. An answer will come to you.

What about the Middle?

Consider the middle name your "insurance"—a name your child can default to or use with her first name to achieve a desired effect. It is also where you can go light if you have a formal first name or vice versa. Legally, you are not required to give your child a middle name, but we can't think of one good reason not to—a middle name helps add to your child's identity. An interesting trend in choosing a middle name is to use the mother's maiden name. So a David Nielson might become a David Howell Nielson. Since surnames are increasingly being used as first names, this option often works well and is especially meaningful if the mother doesn't have siblings to carry on her last name.

> "Any child can tell you that the sole purpose of a middle name is so he can tell when he's really in trouble."
> —Dennis Frakes

To Peek or Not to Peek

That *is* the question.

At around the twentieth week of pregnancy, many expectant parents are offered an ultrasound to check in on the well-being of their cute little fetus. At the same time, the question is raised: "Do you want to know the gender of your child?" This is a very personal decision that mother and father may or may not agree on. Couples that wish to wait appreciate the nostalgia of times gone by when ultrasound technology wasn't available and enjoy the anticipation leading up to the big surprise, thus creating "the moment." Many of these couples do not have a gender preference or are first-time parents.

Parents—and parents of children with a strong preference concerning their new sibling's gender—often choose to learn baby's gender, finding time to prepare themselves or their potentially "disappointed" children.

Finding out your child's gender has many other advantages, from choosing paint color and making clothing purchases to focusing on a particular gender in the name selection process. Keep in mind that while it is very rare, there are instances of boys playing hide and seek or being late bloomers, leading to a false gender prediction. So, even if you're expecting a girl, you may want to consider choosing a backup boy's name, and vice versa, just in case.

Unique vs. Popular Names

Once upon a time, not so long ago, there were a plethora of Lindas, Jennifers, Jasons, and Michaels in a classroom. Naming your child a popular name was so common that a child with an unusual name may have stood out negatively. The resulting confusion in the classroom (Stephanie "C," please!) prompted many parents

> "I sometimes think I was born to live up to my name. How could I be anything else but what I am having been named Madonna? I would either have ended up a nun or this."
> —Madonna

to give more conspicuous names to their children, adapting a belief that offering a child an unusual moniker inherently sets a premise of creative and unique expectations.

On the other hand, kids naturally want to fit in with their peers, and bestowing an easy to remember, familiar name has many advantages. "Contrary to the 'Boy Named Sue' idea that a nonstandard name will strengthen a child in adulthood, the more unusual a person's name, the harder it is for them to adjust," says Dr. Albert Mehrabian, a doctor of psychology and the author of *The Name Game*. However, looking at current trends, it may just be that "fitting in" means having an uncommon name. With more parents choosing "nonstandard" names in general, all names—previously popular, familiar, and even "old-fashioned"—have more room to be chosen and still considered fresh without being trendy or too popular.

Naming a Boy vs. Naming a Girl

In our society, parents tend to choose more unique or exotic-sounding names for girls. But our culture has had stricter rules for boys—strapping boys require strong, familiar names. Even parents inclined to choose a more unusual name for their son may ultimately opt to name him something "safe." While good, common sense is important in

Former champion alpine ski racer Picabo Street was "Baby Girl" Street until age two, when officials questioned her hippie parents about the blank on her birth certificate during a vacation to Mexico. The name has been explained in press accounts as being her favorite baby game and the name of a town near her Idaho home meaning "shining waters."

Exercise Four:
Get Descriptive

Write down adjectives that
define personal characteristics
most important to you. Now,
take these virtues and check
synonyms in a thesaurus for
possible boy and girl name
options, or search our name
dictionary for names with those
meanings. For example, "honest"
could lead to the name Candid
for a girl. If you can't find
anything in the thesaurus or
dictionary, try just listing names
that you naturally associate
with a characteristic.

the process of naming any child regardless
of sex, parents should keep in mind that
this is a new age of naming. Ethnic names
have infused our culture, and parents can
feel comfortable going beyond the norm.
Contrarily, with more ethnicities and larger
name pools in general, deeply rooted names
like David, Matthew, and Alexander are now
less popular, but still strong choices.

Another trend that has taken shape
over the last couple of decades is giving
unisex or traditionally male names to
daughters with an underlying intention of
helping them succeed professionally "in
a man's world." If this is something you
are pondering, also consider that young
children are very gender specific and may
not necessarily appreciate sharing their name
with another child of the opposite sex.

If you're naming a girl and are undecided, there are names like Samantha
("Sam"), Alexandra ("Alex"), and Andrea ("Andy") that can double under any
circumstances. On the other hand, many of the androgynous names are very
appealing. We have a nice list of unisex names on page 76 for you to peruse, but also
let your imagination work; as girls continue to dip into the pool of boy names, there
are many more options available to those expecting daughters. If you're expecting a
son, not to worry! Boys can still use names that have been given to the opposite sex.
Think Jordan, Cameron, and Riley.

Family Names

Keeping a name in the family has strong sentimental appeal. Turning to a beloved
family member or digging deeper into your genealogy can open the door to desirable
and extremely meaningful possibilities. Surnames are making a splash as good first
name options today, which expands your possibilities further. Popular names from
the past have hit the scene again, so open your mind to all those vintage varieties.
Do you have a Great Aunt Matilda but fear her name is too dated? "Tilly" makes a
cute familiar variant, and you're still using a family name. Or look to your mother's
maiden name for a special name for your child. I found Anthony, Relyea, Brook(s),
Zive, Hanlon, and Carston among my immediate list of family names that could
become first names.

Name Histories and Trends

At the turn of the century in North America, many names were inspired by the Bible or by British customs. At the time, very few name books were published, and those available were mostly etymological studies—not advice to help parents name their babies. In 1857, William Arthur's *An Etymological Dictionary of Family and Christian Names* was published in the United States, making it easy to see how names such as Mary, Elizabeth, Sarah, Joseph, and John were so consistently popular that they remained in the top ten throughout World War II and up until 1965. Other names such as Frank, meaning "free," William "the Conqueror," Henry, Margaret, Emma, and Alice were all borrowed from the British, while the Brits borrowed many of them from neighboring European languages.

In the mid-'60s, Mary was officially bumped from its number one spot by Lisa. In fact, by 1972, Mary had dropped out of the top ten names completely and Jennifer hit the scene. About this time, John was seeing competition with David and Michael, and names like Jason were appearing on the boys' list. Jennifer remained number one throughout the '70s and well into the '80s, with other less traditional names entering the mix such as Heather, Angela, Amy, and Jessica. Meanwhile, the boys danced around their biblical conservative mix while slowly adding a few additional biblical varieties such as Daniel and Joshua.

More recently, invented, vintage, and place names became more fashionable. Brandon and Tyler became two of the favorites for boys of the '90s. Jessica and Ashley replaced Jennifer in 1985 and were accompanied by up-and-coming names such as Sara and Brittney. Then in 1992 we saw Emily, a name that has remained on the top with other vintages such as Olivia and Emma. At the same time, place names like Austin and Savannah have entered the scene, opening a wide world of naming possibilities.

While looking to geography for names seems to be a newer trend, naming a child after a place is not an entirely modern concept. Medieval crusaders often took water from the Jordan River to baptize their children, and often these children (both boys and girls) would be dubbed Jordan. Later in history, Kimberley was first bestowed as a baby name soon after the town of Kimberley, South Africa, was besieged during the Boer War (1899–1902). Names of religious shrines like Loreto or Lourdes were commonly given to Catholic children—a tradition that continues today. Affluent English-speaking parents often named their children after the city in which they were born; Florence Nightingale is a prime example.

In general, all names, even our most popular, are now less popular per capita because of our vast name pool and increasing population. In 2003, the most popular boys' name, Jacob, was chosen for roughly 1.5 percent of the approximate two million boys born that year. Translation: If you name your son Jacob or Aidan, he may still be the only one in his classroom. Girls' names are even more eclectic, and with so many to choose from, popular vs. unique is no longer much of an issue.

> **Exercise Six:**
> **Place Names**
>
> Find out if a place important to you could work as a name for your child. Try answering the following questions:
>
> 1. Where did you meet your partner?
> 2. Where were you when you got engaged?
> 3. Where did you go on your honeymoon?
> 4. Where were you when you conceived your child?
> 5. What do you think is the most beautiful place on earth?
> 6. Do any special places or moments come to mind? Add them to this list.

Name Perceptions and Associations

Often when you hear a name an image will flash in your head, or it reminds you of an event, song, or time in history. You don't want to stereotype a person based solely on hearing her name, but you often can't help yourself. Some names carry a stronger stereotype than others, usually because there is a famous person we identify with that name.

Though you may want to discover how people perceive your favorite name, avoid being influenced by others' perceptions. Concerning yourself only with the stereotype you and your partner associate with a name is critical in choosing your perfect name; keep in mind that your child will define the name you choose! With the barrage of media in our culture, everyone is likely to have some perception of the name you select and you can't please everyone.

While you don't need to concern yourself with what others think, you should pay close attention to the perceptions you and your partner have. If your husband dated a Celeste that he never quite forgot, you don't want to choose that name. After you hear the name Jeremiah, do you sing "was a bullfrog"? That might get annoying. Even though your child will ultimately define his or her name, certain names may always carry a derogatory association for you or your partner.

CHAPTER 3

A World of Ideas

Baby-Naming Traditions Around the World

How did our ancestors and neighbors around the world find and celebrate their babies' names? Ethnic and religious customs can lead you to a strong, ethnically rooted, meaningful name.

Europe

If you were born in Elizabethan England (1558–1603), you may have been named by your parents just a few days after birth, at your baptism. Like many other newborns of the time, you were named after one of your godparents, carefully chosen for their higher socioeconomic stature. The pool of names considered acceptable during this time was significantly smaller than what we are used to today. Elizabeth, Anne, Joan, Margaret, Alice, Mary, and Agnes accounted for approximately 65 percent of all girls' names. Likewise, John, Thomas, William, Richard, and Robert accounted for approximately 60 percent of male names. When it came to naming a baby in old England, life was comparatively simple but somewhat boring. Naming options broadened during the

Exercise Seven: The Ethnic Challenge

Wouldn't it be nice to fall in love with a name that creates a connection between your child and his or her own heritage? Peruse the name dictionary for names specific to your or your partner's ethnic background. If you find something you like, add it to the list; it may just fit as a middle name.

classical revival period which brought in French and Italian imports, opening the door for more creativity.

Today, throughout predominately Christian Europe, you find similar baptismal ceremonies but various customs in adopting namesakes—that is, who your child will be named after. Orthodox Greeks have customarily named their babies after the fathers' parents. The French often use a child's middle name to pay homage to a set of grandparents, using both grandmothers' first names for a girl and both grandfathers' names for a boy. The Spanish, known for their traditionalism, have rigid rules even for today; the first-born daughter is named after the father's mother, whereas the first son is named after the father's father. Younger siblings are named after the mother's parents, and even younger siblings after aunts and uncles on the paternal side followed by the maternal aunts and uncles. Many other European countries also have customs of naming after the parents. In the common, patronymic style, the "Jr." wears his father's moniker. Likewise, but much less common, a girl may become her own mother's namesake.

The Americas

In the Americas, the earliest naming traditions we find are from Mesoamerican communities where a child may be named after the day on which she was born—a common tradition throughout many aboriginal communities around the world.

Native American

Native American naming traditions, some of which are still followed today, vary greatly from tribe to tribe and were often inspired by natural conditions, animals, and virtues. This is especially apparent in the Miwok tribe's use of water names, often chosen by the way the stream looked when the baby was born. The Southwest Hopis had a mystic tradition of placing an ear of corn, representing Mother Earth, next to the newborn. Twenty days after baby's birth, the corn was rubbed over his body while the baby, held to face the rising sun, was named when the first ray of sun hit his forehead. The Navajos attribute great powers to their names. A Navajo name is considered so precious it's only used during ceremonies, meaning a day-to-day conversation in a Navajo family may go

"**My name,** Apv-whilt-tin-toom, was given me by my adoptive Indian mother, Ella McCarty. Her Native American name was Am-toola (One Who Sits in the Circle). My name is a remembrance of a warm moment between us, when I said to her, 'You are like a mother to me.' She said, 'Apv-whilt-tin-toom . . . that will be your name . . . Like a Mother to Me.' So, she adopted me and sent me on the Naming Trail . . ."
—Kathie M. Donohue, Native American Genealogy Foundation

something like "Mother, go get Son." The Salish tribe follows a "naming trail" in which the name given to a baby by his parents at birth (usually a virtue or trait the parents hope for the baby) is eventually replaced at adolescence with another name that is given by the tribal leader at a ceremony called the Jump Dances. This name usually represents a talent or strength for which the child is known. Likewise, as an adult, yet another name might be granted, but this name would reflect expectations or something for the person to live up to.

The Puritans

While biblical names satisfied most Puritan American colonists in New England, some families of the Mayflower age chose to bestow their own virtuous names such as Charity, Joy, Mercy, Grace, Prudence, and Hope. In more extreme examples, parents derived slogans to send a very direct message through their child's name: "Fear-God," "Jesus-Christ-came-into-the-world-to-save," and "No-Merit," to name a few. One has to wonder about the conscience of a young lad named "If-Christ-had-not-died-for-thee-thou-hadst-been-damned." And what do you think "Sin-deny" did when he was caught dozing in church?

In many cultures, a name is chosen for a specific attribute the parents or society consider desirable. Ada (Hebrew), Alika (Nigerian), Anabelle (Latin), Belinda (English), Calista (Greek), Jolie (French), Jameelah (Arabic), Keely (Irish), Meili (Chinese), Nazneen (Persian), Omorose (Egyptian), and Wyanet (Native American) are just a handful of examples that all carry the same meaning—Beautiful.

Hawaii

If you're of Hawaiian descent, your "Inoa" (name) is your most prized possession. Traditionally, Hawaiians believed that an ancestral god will mystically send a name to a member of the unborn child's family. They look for this name in signs, visions, and dreams, and believe that if the specified name is not used, it will cripple the child. If a name is not chosen through the god, there are many different types of names—such as those given to trick evil spirits or known only in secret—and more than one name may be given to a child. Christian names are also used in Hawaii and have been altered to fit with the Hawaiian language, which doesn't pronounce many English sounds.

African American

African Americans have their own unique naming history and culture. In the days of slavery, a slave owner often renamed his slaves something not generally used by whites; Greek mythology names were commonly used (Daphne, Apollo, Nessus, or Diana) or a slave's full name was converted into a diminutive cognate of another white-owned name (Tom, Cas, Lil, Bo). Slave owners also granted biblical names in their attempts to convert slaves to Christianity. However, in an attempt to preserve their heritage, slaves often gave their children ethnically based names, which they used secretly in their communities. It wasn't until the Civil War that most African Americans had complete control in naming their children; with newfound freedom, slaves immediately bestowed previously prohibited names on their children (Moses, Abraham) and also changed their shortened names to the formal versions (Thomas, Cassandra, Lillian, and Robert).

African Americans also adopted the style of creating unique names, which took off even further during the 1960s as individual names, distinct from the white community, surfaced. Traditionalism and pride inspired them to look to their Muslim and African roots, to names like Muhammad, Hassan, and Ali for boys, and Shawana, Naajila, and Malaika for girls.

Mormons

Similarly, Mormons are known to create unique or uncommon names in a variety of ways, often combining parents' or grandparents' first names. So, Lewis and Amanda might result in Le'Anda. They also appreciate extremely unusual spelling variations, such as Kellee, Katlynn, Leee, and Alysoon. Could it be the Mormons that started the surname as first name trend? It seems they've been doing this for decades; we found Bowden, Doerr, and Rainey among surnames used for males. Mormons also love French sound prefixes ("La" or "De") and wouldn't hesitate to completely concoct a name: LaJune or DeBekka. Creativity is the name of the game for Mormon parents.

Muslim

Following tradition, Muslim parents may name their child on his or her birthday or at an "Aqeeqah." Held on the seventh day after baby's birth, this ceremony entails a sacrifice of a goat or sheep (two for a boy, one for a girl). The infant's head is then shaved and covered with saffron. It is important to Muslims to give their child a good name, determined by its meanings, which should be beautiful.

Jewish

A Jewish boy is given his Hebrew (as opposed to his secular) name at his "Bris" eight days after his birth, at which time he is also circumcised by a trusted Mohel. A Jewish baby girl receives a naming ceremony eight to fifteen days after birth that includes a public reading of the Torah. During the reading, the special "Mi Sheberach" blessing is said. The blessing begins with a prayer for the mother's health and continues with the giving of the baby's name—and a prayer that this new daughter should grow to be a wise and understanding person of goodness. Jewish people believe that you should name an infant after someone who was righteous in hopes that the child will emulate that person. The Eastern European, Yiddish-speaking Ashkenazic tradition is to name after a beloved departed relative, while the Sephardic Jews may name their offspring after a living person.

From Asia

China

What do a name and an egg have to do with each other? If you're in China, you might be invited to a "Red Egg and Ginger" baby naming party—a celebration held after baby's first month of life. The egg, considered a delicacy in ancient China, represents fertility and is dyed the color red for good luck. At the ceremonial feast, the baby's hair is shaved and gifts are presented to the new life. Today, modern Chinese families use brightly colored eggs as party favors at their adapted ceremonies.

Superstitious as they are, the Chinese wouldn't dare name a child before he is born! Instead they will give him a fake or "milk" name—something very undesirable, such as "mud face" or "excrement," that is meant to disgust evil spirits and trick them to stay away from the child. These names may stay with children throughout childhood. On the heels of the many childbirth practices they follow, the Chinese believe that each child is unique and should carry an individual moniker; however, this is becoming increasingly difficult for them to follow as the most populous country in the world.

> **In the Chinese** capital of Beijing, the word "Shu" (kind and gentle) is the favorite name for women.

Japan

In Japan, on the "Oshichiya" (baby's seventh day), family and friends congregate for a celebratory feast. Traditionally, the baby may be clothed exclusively in white, and an elegant "Shodo" (name plaque) with the child's name eloquently inscribed in Japanese characters on a special Japanese paper is hung on the wall. The festivities continue with laughter and eating—certainly a pleasurable celebration for new parents and a visual welcome to the world for their new baby.

India

There are many variations of the "Namakarana" naming ceremony in India. In the state of Maharashtra, you will walk in on a beautiful image of a baby in the cradle, decorated with flower garlands and surrounded by women singing hymns and gently rocking the cradle. The mother or a grandmother will then enter the room with a lit silver lamp and a small gold jewel for the child. Afterward, the baby is blessed with rice and a small dot of vermilion is placed on her forehead. Blessings are once again said, and the ceremony ends with the mother whispering the gods' names and then whispering the child's name in her ear. Finally, the name is announced to the guests.

Buddhists have their own Namkarana within the first three months of life or when it's thought that the baby can hear. During the event, a mother writes the baby's name on a banana leaf, which is then covered with handfuls of uncooked rice. The mother lays the baby on the banana leaf and whispers the child's name three times in his ear, after which the other relatives and guests do the same. A frequent practice among Hindus is to name their children after sages, saints, holy persons, deities, and the names of the incarnation of God. It is believed that by repeatedly calling such names, one is reminded of God.

Out of Africa

In many regions of Africa, naming ceremonies are extensive and elaborate, with special prayers recited by an appointed religious teacher. Usually, animals are sacrificed during these proceedings. Africans mostly choose names that denote the time ("Abena"—born on Thursday), something that represents the times ("Iniko"—born during troubled times), a physical characteristic ("Hassain"—handsome), or possibly the child's position within the family ("Delu"—the only girl).

As a Muslim African newborn, you will be told of God's greatness before you are shown the sun. Afterward your father will whisper "God is Great" immediately followed by your given name.

> *"Omoro then walked out before all of the assembled people of the village. Moving to his wife's side, he lifted up the infant and, as all watched, whispered three times into his son's ear the name he had chosen for him. It was the first time the name had ever been spoken as this child's name, for Omoro's people felt that each human being should be the first to know who he was."*
> —Alex Haley, *Roots*

If you are an Egyptian, you may learn of a special naming ceremony called the "Sebooh," held on the child's seventh day of life. As a guest of this event, you will find the baby dressed in white and placed in a sieve. The parents will slowly rock the sieve to symbolize acquainting their child with the motions of life. Guests chant, sing, and laugh as the child is placed on a white cloth on the floor with everyone surrounding her and scattering grains around her—symbolic of the earth's bounty. At this time, gifts are presented to the infant. The baby's mother may then sidestep the baby's body seven times to ward off evil spirits. Everyone's focus is on the mother's motions, as a knife is momentarily laid across the baby's body to ward off more evil spirits. The ceremony ends with the lighting of candles, which are given to attending children to bear in a procession led by the mother, who is carrying the baby throughout the home. She is followed by the incense bearer shaking a lantern-like incense burner releasing cleansing scents. This time-honored custom dates back to the Pharaohs but is still used throughout Egypt in Christian and Muslim homes alike.

Creating Traditions Today

It is a strong human force to mark life's mileposts through ceremony or festivity. Good decisions and achievements should be celebrated, and surely, you're dedicated to finding the perfect baby name, so certainly a celebration is in order! This is especially true since for most American parents today, the closest thing to a name tradition is a mailed birth announcement.

While we hope these customs throughout history and around the world have inspired you to add more names to your list, you may also want to consider creating a naming tradition within your own family.

Christian families, for example, may choose to announce their baby's name at his baptism or christening on the seventh day of life. While we don't recommend sacrificing animals or shaving the baby's head, you may want to look to the Japanese and have a calligrapher create a special name plaque for your son or daughter, or simply have the baby's closest relatives whisper her name in her ear (babies can hear at birth) in a peaceful and gentle setting. Likewise, the Chinese "Red Egg and Ginger" custom could be the theme of a welcoming party for your new baby. A naming ceremony can be performed by anyone and can offer a place for mothers and fathers to declare their commitment to being good parents within their circle of friends and family.

But, first we need to choose a name, so let's carry on . . .

CHAPTER 4

Suiting Your Style

Meaningful Lists

B y now your workbook section should be coming together with several lists of possible baby names. Throughout this book, we've empowered you to form your own naming style with self-confidence. Now, with both confidence and experience you're ready for the less structured exercise of choosing names by categories.

Biblical Names

If the idea of a biblical name with a sense of tradition appeals to you, closely analyze this list for possible name choices. Many of these namesakes, whether from the Old or New Testament, have incredible character and qualities parents find favorable for their children. You may wish to further research the figures behind the names (and some of their fascinating stories) or revisit your favorite scripture for a name choice.

Exercise Eight: Choose Your Lists

Select one or more of the following name types that have significance to you: Biblical, Nature, New Age, Shakespearean, Musical, Place, and Surnames as First Names. After you have decided which of these lists have meaning to you, browse those lists for more naming ideas; if you find any possibilities, add them to your workbook.

BOYS			
Aaron	Elijah	Jesse	Nehemiah
Abel	Elisha	Jesus	Nicholas
Abner	Elliot	Jhon	Noah
Abraham	Emmanuel	Joash	Obadiah
Abram	Ephraim	Joel	Oren
Achan	Esau	John	Paul
Adam	Eshton	Jonah	Peter
Ahio	Ethan	Jonas	Philip
Alexander	Ethnan	Jonathan	Reuben/Ruben
Ammon	Ezekiel	Jordan	Salomon
Amnon	Ezequiel	Joseph	Samson
Amon	Ezra	Joshua	Samuel
Amos	Felix	Josiah	Saul
Andrew	Gabriel	Josias	Seth
Aner	Gideon	Judas	Sidon
Anslem	Ira	Jude	Silas
Asa	Isaac	Kanan	Simeon
Asher	Isaiah	Kenan	Simon
Bartholmew	Israel	Kirk	Simri
Becher	Jabin	Lazarus	Solomon
Benaiah/Benayah	Jacob	Levi	Stephen
Benjamin	Jadon	Liam	Thaddeus
Cain	Jalon	Lucas	Thomas
Cainan	James	Luke	Tilon
Caleb	Jamin/Jaymin	Mahlon	Timothy
Canaan	Jared	Malachi/Malachy	Tobias
Chislon	Jaroah	Marcus	Zacariah/ Zachariah
Cyrus	Jashen	Mattaniah	
Damian	Jason	Matthew	Zaccheus/ Zacchaeus
Daniel	Javan	Matthias	
Dathan	Jedediah/Jedidiah	Micah	Zebediah
David	Jeremiah	Michael	Zebulon
Eden	Jeremy	Moses	Zephan
Eleazar	Jeriah	Naamon	Zion
Eli	Jericho	Nathan	
Elias	Jesiah	Nathaniel	

GIRLS

Abigail	Beraiah	Hannah	Merari
Adalia	Bethany	Hazael	Micaiah/Michaiah/ Mykayah
Adeil	Carmel	Hazaiah	
Adina	Celeste	Haziel	Michaela
Adriel	Cheran	Irijah	Michal
Ahira	Chloe	Izri	Milalai
Ahlai	Claudia	Jael	Naomi
Aiah	Dalaiah	Jane	Natalie
Aliah	Dana	Jannah	Rachel
Amzi	Danielle	Japhia	Ramiah
Anaiah	Deborah	Jemima	Reaia
Angela	Delaiah	Jesaiah	Reaiah
Anna	Delilah	Jesse	Rebekah
Annabel	Dinah	Jessica	Rhea
Ara	Easter	Jezliah	Ruth
Areli	Eden	Joanna	Sala
Arisai	Elasa	Judith	Salah
Asahiah	Elhanan	Kelaiah	Salome
Asaiah	Eliah	Kezia/Keziah	Sarah/Serah
Ashbel	Elika	Kirsten	Seraiah
Asriel	Elisabeth/Elizabeth	Leah	Shelah
Atarah	Elisha	Lydia	Shiloh
Athaiah	Esther	Lysias	Susannah
Athalia	Eve	Madaleine	Tabitha
Athena	Ezri	Magdalena/ Magdelena	Talia/Thalia
Azaliah	Faith		Tamar
Azaniah	Freya	Mahalah	Tamara
Azarael	Gabrielle	Mara	Tarah
Azaria	Grace	Mary/Maria	Tarea
Azriel	Gwyneth	Maryam	Trinity
Bela	Halliday	Melea	Zipporah
Belah	Hanani	Meraiah	

Nature Names

Is the great outdoors where you and baby will spend time? What natural elements represent who you are—and who your child may be? If you're looking for something feminine, browse through the flower names for some fragrant girl name choices.

Sun Names

Girls

Alaine (French)

Asia (Arabic)

Dawn (English)

Helia (Greek)

Kalinda (Hindi)

Lian (Chinese)

Solana (Latin)

Talayeh (Persian)

Boys

Arun (Hindi)

Ciro (Spanish)

Dinesh (Sanskrit)

Etu (Native American)

Helios (Greek)

Sampson (Hebrew)

Sol (Latin)

Earth Names

Adda (Welsh)

Ertha (German)

Kaia (Greek)

Meadow (English)

Tellus (Latin)

Tuwa (American Indian)

Adam (Hebrew)

Blair

Clay (English)

Ezebo (Egyptian)

Forrest (French)

Damek (Czech)

Mahkah (Native American)

Water Names

Assana (Irish)

Brooke (English)

Coral (English)

Dalis (Hebrew)

Eathelyn (English)

Edlin (English)

Fontaine (French)

Kallan (Scandinavian)

Lana (Hawaiian)

Lynn (English)

Oceana (Greek)

Sarila (Turkish)

Talulla (Native American)

Assan (Irish)

Cain (Welsh)

Calder (Scottish)

Callan (Scandinavian)

Dallas (Scottish)

Evian (English)

Kelsey (Teutonic)

Lisa (Native American)

Moses (Hebrew)

River (French)

Wade (English)

Fire Names

Girls

Adan (Irish)
Barbara (Greek)
Brande (English)
Bridget (Irish)
Edna (Celtic)
Fia (Italian)
Kai (Scottish)
Sarafina (Hebrew)

Boys

Aidan (Irish)
Ash (Hebrew)
Azar (Persian)
Edan (Celtic)
Eth (Irish)
Flint (English)
Ignazio (Spanish)

Air, Wind, and Sky Names

Aura (Greek)
Avira (Hebrew)
Ilma (Finnish)
Ambar (Hindi)
Lani (Hawaiian)
Loni (Greek)

Avirit (Hebrew)
Shu (Egyptian)
Dyaus (Hindi)
Nasim (Persian)
Rodor (Anglo-Saxon)
Uranus (Greek)

Girl Flower-Power Names

Azalea (Greek)
Aziel (Hebrew)
Brionna (English)
Calla (Greek)
Camilia (Latin)
Daffodil (Greek)
Daisy (English)
Dalia (Arabic)
Fern (English)
Ginger (Latin)

Heather (English)
Holly (English)
Iris (Greek)
Ivy (English)
Jasmine (French)
Laurel (Latin)
Leia (Hawaiian)
Lilly (English)
Linnae (Scandinavian)

Magnolia (French)
Pansy (French)
Peony (French)
Petunia (Native American)
Rose (Latin)
Violet (French)
Zahara (African)

New Age Names

If your eyes are focused on the stars, research your child's zodiac sign based on your intended due date. Obviously this can be somewhat risky given that babies are rarely punctual, so you may want to include an alternate sign as well. Look to your child's zodiacal element and go back to nature names on page 26 for compatible name ideas. Gems and flowers offer additional interesting possibilities, while lucky Hindi name sounds might inspire phonetically harmonious selections.

Zodiac Sign	Element	Gems	Flower	Lucky Hindi Name Sounds
Aries [Ram] (March 21–April 19)	Fire	diamond, ruby, bloodstone, amethyst, jasper	Daisy	chu, che, cho, la, lee, lu, le, lo, aa
Taurus [Bull] (April 20–May 20)	Earth	emerald, sapphire, quartz, diamond, agate	Lily of the Valley	chu, che, cho, la, lee, lu, le, lo, aa
Gemini [Twins] (May 21–June 21)	Air	agate, alexandrite, tourmaline, pearl	Rose	ee, oo, ae, o, va, vi, vu, ve, vo, ba, bi, bu, be, bo
Cancer [Crab] (June 22–July 22)	Water	pearl, moonstone, ruby, beryl, emerald	Water Lily	hi, hu, he, ho, da, di, du, de, do
Leo [Lion] (July 23–August 22)	Fire	ruby, amber, peridot, topaz, diamond	Gladiolus	ma, mi, mu, me, mo, ta, ti, tu, te
Virgo [Virgin] (August 23–September 22)	Earth	agate, carnelian, sapphire, peridot, jade	Aster	to, pa, pu, kh, tha, pe, pi, pi
Libra [The Balance] (September 23–October 23)	Air	opal, sapphire, aquamarine, tourmaline, blue topaz	Cosmos	ra, ri, ru, re, ro, ta, ti, tu, te
Scorpio [Scorpion] (October 24–November 21)	Water	topaz, tourmaline, bloodstone, opal, black pearl	Mum	to, na, ni, nu, ne, no, ya, ya, ye, yu

Zodiac Sign	Element	Gems	Flower	Lucky Hindi Name Sounds
Sagittarius [Archer] (November 22–December 21)	Fire	turquoise, lapis lazuli, topaz, obsidian	Narcissus	ye, yo, bh, bhi, bhu, gh, ph, dh, bhe
Capricorn [Goat] (December 22–January 19)	Air	garnet, onyx, black pearl, turquoise	Carnation	bho, ja, ji, ju, je, jo, kh, khi, khu, khe, khoo, ga, gi
Aquarius [Water Bearer] (January 20–February 18)	Water	aquamarine, hematite, jet, garnet	Violet	gu, ge, go, s, sh, si, su, se, so, da
Pisces [Fish] (February 19–March 20)	Water	amethyst, sugilite, aquamarine, bloodstone	Daffodil	di, du, tha, jh, ja, de, do, ch, chee

Shakespearean Names

Literature buffs, this list is for you! Peruse your favorite Shakespearean works for some unusual name choices used (and even created) by one of history's greatest and most prolific writers. Or recall your favorite book, poem, or play for potential name choices.

Play	Names	Play	Names
A Midsummer Night's Dream	Lysander Theseus Titania	Comedy of Errors	Adriano Aegeon Aemilia Balthazar Luce Luciana Nell
All's Well That Ends Well	Lafeu Rinaldo		
As You Like It	Adam Audrey Jaques Oliver Orlando Phoebe Rosalind Silvius	Cymbeline	Belarius Pisanio
		Hamlet	Barnardo Marcellus Ophelia Reynaldo
Barbara Pym: Less Than Angels	Aleric	Henry IV	Thomas
Henry V	Alice Michael	Richard III	Anne Thomas

Shakespearean Names continued

Play	Names	Play	Names
Henry VI	Peter Thomas	*Romeo and Juliet*	Abraham Juliet
King John	Arthur Peter		Paris Peter
King Lear	Oswald Regan		Romeo Rosaline Sampson
Love's Labour's Lost	Jaquenetta Katharine Maria Mercade Rosaline	*Taming of the Shrew*	Katharine Mariana Nathaniel Philip
Macbeth	Angus Lennox Malcolm Ross Seyton	*The Tempest*	Adrian Ariel Iris Juno Miranda Sebastian Stephano
Measure for Measure	Isabella Juliet Lucio Peter Pompey		
Merchant of Venice	Antonio Jessica Lancelot Leonardo Lorenzo Portia	*Timon of Athens*	Timandra Timon
		Titus Andronicus	Aaron Marcus
Merry Wives of Windsor	Robin	*Twelfth Night*	Maria Olivia Sebastian Toby Valetine Viola
Much Ado About Nothing	Antonio Beatrice Ursula		
Othello	Montano Othello Roderigo	*Two Gentlemen of Verona*	Antonio Julia Launce Silvia Valentine
Richard II	Thomas	*The Winter's Tale*	Paulina

Musical Names

Musically inclined? Relax to the sound of your favorite CD while you look through these names with melodious meanings. Or reflect on your favorite band, orchestra, or musician for other noted name ideas.

Girls

Alima	Understands dance and music
Aria	Melody
Cadence	Rhythmic flow of sounds
Cannia	Song
Carmen	Crimson song
Carol	Melody
Celia	St. Cecilia was a talented musician and patron saint of music
Chantal	Singer
Gala	Lovely voice
Harmony	Harmonious
Jazmine	A play on the musical style of jazz
Lyria	Variation of *Lyric*
Lyric	Words to a song
Melody	Melodious
Rena	Joyous song
Shira	Tune
Taraneh	Song
Viola	Instrument in the violin family
Yarona	Sing

Boys

Amadeus	The name of Wolfgang Amadeus Mozart, an Austrian composer considered one of history's best and most creative musical geniuses
Baird	Minstrel; a medieval musical entertainer
Hototo	The whistler
Leron	The song is mine
Rani	My song
Ron	My song
Shiron	Songfest

Place Names

In chapter two, we discussed how place names have become fun, common options for parents. The name of a place can also have very meaningful associations or a potential destination for a trip shared with your child. Browse our collections for a place name that might be perfect for your baby.

BOYS		GIRLS	
Aspen	Jordan	Abilene	Italia
Athens	Kent	Alabama	Jamaica
Bergen	Kerry	Albany	Jordan
Berlin	Leicester	Alma	Kimberley
Boston	Leith	America	Kerry
Brighton	Lester	Ashanti	Libya
Brooklyn	Lincoln	Asia	Loraine
Berlin	London	Aspen	Loreto
Cairo	Maldon	Bali	Lourdes
Camden	Marlow	Bethany	Lucerne
Carlyle	Milan	Bethel	Madison
Cayman	Nazareth	Beverly	Marseilles
Chester	Nevada	Britney	Martinique
Cleveland	Phoenix	Capri	Normandy
Cyprus	Rhodes	Chelsea	Odessa
Dakota	Ross	Cheyenne	Paloma
Dallas	Rudyard	China	Paris
Dane	Rugby	Clare	Rhodesia
Dayton	Selby	Dakota	Sahara
Denver	Sheffield	Devon	Savannah
Denzel	Siam	Dixie	Selby
Darien	Skipton	Eden	Seville
Devon	Spaulding	Florence	Shannon
Everest	Sterling	Florida	Shelby
Eyton	Tennessee	Geneva	Sinai
Holland	Texas	Georgia	Valencia
Houston	Tyrone	Guadalupe	Venice
Israel	Welsh	Gwyneth	Wyoming
Jericho	Whitby	India	Zamora
	Zaire		

Surnames for First Names

Appropriately, we have saved surnames for last! Surnames are a great way to find a
unique name.

Bestowing last names as first names has become increasingly popular for
children of either sex—take for example the recent use of Irish surnames for children:
Braden, Keegan, Kennedy, and Riley. Parents seeking to combine originality with
a sense of familiarity can find good options with surnames. Here are a few of our
favorites.

Abram	Brice	Dane	Evens
Adler	Bronte	Darwin	Everet
Albee	Bryce	Dedrick	Ewing
Alden	Byron	Devlin	Fairley
Alston	Cadby	Devon	Falkner
Anson	Caddell	Dewey	Farley
Archer	Cade/Caide/Cayd	Dexter	Farris
Arlo	Caidan	Dickins	Fenton
Arman	Calbert	Digby	Fielding
Ash	Calder	Dillon	Fischer
Ashton	Calvert	Dixon	Fitz
Aubrey	Calvin	Donnelly	Fletcher
Austin	Camden	Donovan	Flynn
Avery	Carsen	Doogan	Forrest
Baird	Carsten	Doran	Foster
Bartley	Carver	Dorsett	Frantz
Barton	Casper	Drake	Frasier
Basel	Chet	Drew	Frisbee
Baxley	Clemens	Drexel	Frye
Baxter	Clement	Duke	Gaige
Beaudry	Cole	Duncan	Galvin
Benson	Conan	Dunlap	Garland
Bernard	Conlan	Durwin	Garner
Blaine	Cortlan	Duval	Garrett
Blair	Cortland	Eames	Garvin
Blake	Costa	Eden	Gerard
Blane	Daine	Elias	Gibson
Boston	Dale	Elmer	Gillean
Bowden	Dallas	Elton	Gilmore
Bowen	Dalton	Ernest	Gleason
Brandeis	Damon	Erving	Glenn

Surnames for First Names continued

Grafton	Kallen	Nielsen	Stryker
Graham	Kameron	Norton	Sullivan
Grant	Karsen	Odar	Taft
Grear	Keane	Ohnstad	Taggart
Greig	Keaton	Oldham	Talbot
Grey	Keegan	Olsen	Talon
Grier	Kelsey	Otis	Tanner
Griffin	Kendall	Owen	Teagan
Gulbert	Kimball	Palmer	Thatcher
Gunther	Kipley	Parker	Tobias
Gustin	Kipling	Percy	Tomlin
Guthrie	Lamar	Peyton	Torrance
Hadley	Lane	Phillip	Travais
Hagen/Haygen	Langley	Piper	Trent
Halston	Larkin/Larkyn	Presley	Truman
Halton	Larsen	Preston	Tucker
Hanley	Loren	Quinne	Vance
Hanlon	Lennon	Radcliff/Radcliffe	Wade
Harley	Lesher	Raleigh	Wallis
Harmon	Lincoln	Randolph	Ward
Harper	Logan	Reese	Warren
Hartley	Lucas	Riley	Webster
Hayden	Lyndon	Rosen	Wesleyan
Heath	Macaulay	Ross	Wessley
Heyden	Maccoy	Rowan	Whitney
Hogan	Maddock	Royce	Willis
Holden	Maguire	Sanborne	Wilson
Holland	Mallorey	Sanders	Wrenn
Hudson	Manning	Sawyer	Wyatt
Humphrey	Markham	Sergent	Zale/Zaile/Zayle
Hunter	Marlin	Seth	Zive
Irving	Marlow	Shay	
Irwin	Marques	Sheldon	
Ives	Marshall	Sidney	
Jackson	Milan	Skyler	
Jaegar	Milton	Spencer	
Jansen/Janson	Mitchum	Sterling	
Jarvis	Nelson	Stetson	
Jensen	Neumann	Steward	

CHAPTER 5

Drum Roll, Please . . .

Making Your Final Selection and Loving It

So here you are, closing in on the baby-naming journey. While I am sure you've enjoyed your trip, the vacation is nearly over and a choice should be made—it's finally time to choose that perfect name. By now you may have a good idea of what your decision is, but even if you do, you will find the final phases of this guide are fun and enlightening while empowering you to make that selection with confidence.

Making Your Lists, Checking Them Twice

Before moving to the next phase, review your name lists, being careful not to have missed an opportunity to find another contender for a name. While this book aims to inspire, there is no exact formula to selecting your child's name. At this point, you want to feel that you've thoroughly explored all your options and you're excited by your collection of name choices—enthusiastically ready to begin the process of filtering down and discovering the right name.

Eliminating the Fear Factor

During this final phase, you should also keep in mind that many parents choose a name simply because of the way it sounds—especially with their surname and even middle name choice. So, if at the end of your nine-month journey, you "just love the way it sounds," then be secure in your decision because you've truly set all other issues

On the '90s hit TV series *Mad About You*, Jamie and Paul chose the name Mabel for their infant daughter—an acronym for Mothers Always Bring Extra Love.

aside and simply chosen what you feel is the most suitable name possible for your new family member.

Any anxiety that you have that your child may not like his name can be calmed by a study conducted through Mindworks—a forum for children in grades 1–12 to express their opinions. In the study, most kids said they liked their names and felt that their efforts and life decisions—not their names—would shape them. Even the few that didn't like their names said they appreciated the sentiment behind their names and would never consider changing them. Your young to school-aged child will most likely love his name as much as you love his name.

As a caution to new parents: don't be concerned if you find you're uncomfortable calling your child by her carefully selected moniker. For some parents, especially those that have waited until the last minute to decide on their baby's name, there is a very normal period of adjustment that shouldn't be interpreted as having chosen the wrong name. You will see—after a few short days, the name and child truly do become one.

The Process of Elimination

Up until now, you have been asked to work side-by-side with your partner compiling your lists; but now it's time to divide and conquer! So turn on your

Exercise Nine: Mom and Dad's List of Favorites

Both Mom and Dad should now spend alone time with the lists you've created together. Each of you should form "your personal list"—individually selecting names, both first and middle, that you compiled together from the various exercises and lists. (You'll find a separate list for each of you in the workbook section.) As you copy the names, try rating each one. *Absolutely Love the Name* gets a 10, and *Can Live with It* a 1, 2, or 3. Your lists should not exceed your top fifteen choices. You will also want to include notes on *why* you like the names on your list. You may love one name along with a certain middle name because it forms a snappy acronym, or it is a family name or, better yet, it is a family name *and* it sounds great with your surname. Whatever meaning your name choices have should be written in the allocated space in the workbook. These precious notes will be cherished by your child when they grow old so be sure that they're saved for future recollection.

internal dialogues, pull out your pencils and lists, and let's get started.

> ☑ Exercises: completed
> ☑ Thoroughness: checked
> ☑ Fear factor: eliminated

Now Mom and Dad, it's time to take a break. There's actually no rush unless you're eight centimeters dilated, and even if that's the case, remember to relish this time and enjoy your pregnancy and the process of naming your child. With that in mind, you may want to spend some time with your personal lists paying close attention to the reasons you chose the names. You might be surprised to see that this process can also be revealing to your priorities and parenting style. Did you find yourself giving higher rankings to religious or family names than you had expected? Now would be a good time to reopen the discussion of baby-naming priorities with your partner, reevaluating what's important to each of you. This is also a nice time to get intimate with your partner and even peek in on his or her list, because the fun will soon begin, and your "final cut" is next!

Exercise Ten: The Final Cut

If you haven't done so already, it's time to compare lists and, once again, combine efforts in the selection process. After comparing the lists you created in Exercise Nine, consider it "hitting the lottery" if a name shows up on both lists and immediately bring that name down to the "final cut" section of your workbook, on page 51. Follow up these agreed-upon first names with complementary *middle* names. Keep in mind, while the middle can be a good compromise, your priority is choosing the right names (both first and middle) for your child's last name. See page 11 for important considerations in choosing a middle name.

Next, Mom and Dad should now each choose their favorite first names from the opposite parent's list, and write these names in the allotted workbook space. (If you're doing this alone, you can simply select your highest-rated names.) For those first names that Dad chose, Mom gets to select her favorite complementary middle names, and vice versa.

You now have your final list of potential names for your baby. Whenever you're ready, choose your favorite first-and-middle name combination for each gender. A good trick to play on yourself when you're at this point is to think about how you will feel calling your child with these various names at a playground. Visualize your child coming when you call—does the name turn heads? And if so, does it matter? Does her name roll off your tongue? Does his name make you grin?

The Last Word on Baby's First Name

If this isn't smooth sailing so far, try rereading the section on working through name dilemmas in chapter one. As we've mentioned, naming your baby is not an exact science, and bending and flexing are absolutely in order. Because of your union, we hope you will glide through this process effortlessly and that by now congratulations are in order as you have both methodically and carefully chosen a meaningful name for your baby, but if you still have a few options in the mix, wait . . . Meet your little one and let him tell you which name to choose. Maybe *he* looks more like an Owen than an Oliver, or *she* more like an Erin than a Lauren.

And just for the record, if you've made it to the end of this book and put this much time and effort into naming your child, you will undoubtedly be the "perfect" parents to a young Mister or Miss (<u>fill in the blank</u>).

Baby Name Workbook

It's time to name your baby! The following ten exercises correspond with those found in chapters one through five. (Brief recaps of the instructions are provided for your convenience.) Pencils only, please, as I encourage you to add or erase names at any time throughout the process.

Exercise One:
Positive Visualization (see page 7)

Throughout your pregnancy, visualize who your child might be and what she might look like. Now visualize the same person as a happy young adult, and then imagine her in a successful career or family setting. Begin thinking of names for this person, and as these names come to you, record them below. **This is your primary ongoing collection;** you may add to this list throughout the process and refer to it as you complete the other exercises. You're just brainstorming at this point, so be as creative as you'd like!

GIRLS' NAMES	BOYS' NAMES

Exercise Two:
A is for Alliteration (see page 8)

Flip through the alphabetical listings of names with a similar initial sound as your last name, as well as similar sounds within your name. (Middle names are optional at this stage.) For example, Smith should look at S and C. If any names in these sections appeal to you, add them to your list.

GIRLS' NAMES		
First	**Middle** (optional)	**Last**
Example: Sandra		Smith

BOYS' NAMES		
First	**Middle** (optional)	**Last**

Exercise Three:
The Acronym Game (see page 9)

Use the first letter of your last name: __ (example: P for Peters)

What desirable three-letter words can it spell?

(Feel free to use phonetic, rather than actual spellings.)

<u>P O P</u> _ _ _   _ _ _   _ _ _

Now choose first and middle combinations that achieve the desired acronyms

---

GIRLS' NAMES

Example: Pamela _____ Olivia _____ Peters _____ = P O P _____

_____ _____ _____ = _____

_____ _____ _____ = _____

_____ _____ _____ = _____

_____ _____ _____ = _____

_____ _____ _____ = _____

_____ _____ _____ = _____

_____ _____ _____ = _____

BOYS' NAMES

_____ _____ _____ = _____

_____ _____ _____ = _____

_____ _____ _____ = _____

_____ _____ _____ = _____

_____ _____ _____ = _____

_____ _____ _____ = _____

_____ _____ _____ = _____

_____ _____ _____ = _____

Exercise Four:
Get Descriptive (see page 13)

Write down adjectives that define personal characteristics most important to you. Then look through the book for names with those meanings, or check synonyms in a thesaurus for possible name options. See pages 89, 174, 240, and 321 for lists of virtue names.

GIRLS' NAMES

Adjective	*Name*
Example: Honest	Candid

BOYS' NAMES

Adjective	*Name*

Exercise Five:
The Family Name Quiz (see page 14)

Try answering the following questions about your family for inspiration: (1) Which relative(s) has inspired you the most throughout life? (2) What is your mother's maiden name? (3) Is there a relative that has passed away that should be remembered? (4) Any other special family names? Add them to your list.

GIRLS' NAMES	BOYS' NAMES

Exercise Six: Place Names (see page 15)

Is there a special place in your lives that could be the perfect name? Try answering these questions: (1) Where did you meet your partner? (2) Where were you when you got engaged? (3) Where did you go on your honeymoon? (4) Where were you when you conceived your child? (5) What do you think is the most beautiful place on earth? (6) Do any special places or moments come to mind?

GIRLS' NAMES	BOYS' NAMES
Example: Georgia	Troy

Exercise Seven:
The Ethnic Challenge (see page 16)

Peruse the name dictionary for names specific to your or your partner's ethnic background. (These names could even be contenders for your baby's middle name.)

Mom's ethnicity: _____

Dad's ethnicity: _____

GIRLS' NAMES	BOYS' NAMES

Exercise Eight:
Choose Your Lists (see page 23)

Do any of the following categories of names have special meaning for you: Biblical, Nature, New Age, Shakespearean, Musical, Place, or Surnames as First Names? If so, peruse the various lists in chapter four, and write down any names that appeal to you. If a category doesn't appeal to you, leave it blank—or feel free to use your own name list strategy.

GIRLS' NAMES	BOYS' NAMES

Biblical

_____   _____

_____   _____

_____   _____

_____   _____

_____   _____

_____   _____

Nature

_____   _____

_____   _____

_____   _____

_____   _____

_____   _____

New Age

_____   _____

_____   _____

_____   _____

_____   _____

_____   _____

GIRLS' NAMES	BOYS' NAMES

Shakespearean

_____	_____
_____	_____
_____	_____
_____	_____

Place Names

_____	_____
_____	_____
_____	_____
_____	_____

Musical

_____	_____
_____	_____
_____	_____
_____	_____

Surnames as First Names

_____	_____
_____	_____
_____	_____
_____	_____

Other

_____	_____
_____	_____
_____	_____
_____	_____

Exercise Nine:
Mom and Dad's List of Favorites (see page 36)

Now it's time to start narrowing down your choices. Mom and Dad, separately go through the lists you created in the previous exercises—or look up new names, if you think the perfect one is still out there—and write your favorite names below (first names only at this stage). Include your reason for choosing each one. Then rate each name from one to ten.

MOM'S LIST		
Girls' Names	*Reason*	*Rating*
_____	_____	_____
_____	_____	_____
_____	_____	_____
_____	_____	_____
_____	_____	_____
_____	_____	_____
_____	_____	_____
_____	_____	_____
Boys' Names	*Reason*	*Rating*
_____	_____	_____
_____	_____	_____
_____	_____	_____
_____	_____	_____
_____	_____	_____
_____	_____	_____
_____	_____	_____
_____	_____	_____

DAD'S LIST

Girls' Names	Reason	Rating

Boys' Names	Reason	Rating

Exercise Ten: The Final Cut (see page 37)

Now, Mom and Dad, work together again. First, write down any first name appearing on both of your lists from the previous exercise. Then, put your heads together to choose a complementary middle name. (See page 11 for important factors to consider when selecting a middle name.)

GIRLS' NAMES	

Any name appearing on **both** lists   Favorite complementary **middle** name

_____

_____

BOYS' NAMES	

Any name appearing on **both** lists   Favorite complementary **middle** name

_____

_____

> *Note: If you're doing this exercise on your own,*
> *simply choose your favorite two names from your*
> *boys' and girls' lists and write them above.*

Next, compare your individual lists and select your favorite first names from your partner's list. For each first name that Dad chooses, Mom gets to choose her favorite complementary middle name and vice versa.

GIRLS' NAMES	
Dad's favorite first name from **Mom's** List	Complementary **middle** name
Mom's favorite first name from **Dad's** List	Complementary **middle** name

BOYS' NAMES	
Dad's favorite first name from **Mom's** List	Complementary **middle** name
Mom's favorite first name from **Dad's** List	Complementary **middle** name

Now that you've chosen the final contenders, it's time to pick the winner. Spend as much time as you need with the above list of names. For tips on making your final selection, see pages 35–37.

Girls' Names

AARDINA (ar-DEE-nah) Dutch: Earth
Nicknames: *Aarde*

AARONA (er-RO-nah) Hebrew: Singer; one
that teaches

AASE (O-sə, AH-sə) Norse: Tree-covered
mountain

ABAN (AH-bahn) Persian: Eighth month of
the Iranian calendar

ABAYOMI (ah-BAH-yo-mee) African: Bring
great joy (Nigerian)

ABBASEH Persian: Lioness

ABBY American: Nickname for Abigail
Abbie, Abbey, Abhy

ABDERA Greek: Place name of a town in
Greece

ABEDABUN (ah-beh-dah-bun) Native
American: Sight of day (Cheyenne)

ABELLA (ah-BEL-ah) French: Variation of
Ahelia
Abelia, Abelina

ABENA (a-BAY-nah, ah-BEE-nah) African:
Born on Tuesday
Abenaa, Abbena

ABEO (ah-BE-o) African: Her birth brings
happiness

ABEQUA (ah-BE-kwa) Native American:
Stays at home (Cheyenne)

ABHIRATI (AB-ər-AH-tee) Hindi: Mother
of five hundred children; a mother goddess

ABIA (ah-BIE-ah) Arabic: Great
Abeya; **Famous namesakes:** French author
Elisabet Abeya

ABIGAIL Hebrew: Gives joy, my father
rejoices. Abigail was the third wife of the
biblical King David and was described as
discreet and beautiful in form.
(Spanish) *Abegail*; (Gaelic) *Abaigeal*; (Irish)
Abiageal, Gobinet, Gobnait; *Abaigael, Abegayle,
Abhy, Abichail, Avagail, Avichayil, Avigail*;
*Abagail, Abbigail, Abigale, Abbigale, Abbigayle,
Abbigaile*; **Nicknames:** *Abbey, Abbie, Abby,
Abi, Gael, Gail, Gaila, Gayla*; **Famous
namesakes:** Advice columnist Abigail Van
Buren, First Lady Abigail Adams; **Star babies:**
daughter of Anthony Perkins

ABILENE (a-bə-LEEN) American: City in
Texas

ABIR (ah-BEER) Arabic: Fragrant or
numerous
Abeer

ABIRA (ah-BEER-ah) Hebrew: My strength

ABRA (AB-rə) Hebrew, Italian: Mother of
many nations; a feminine form of Abraham;
(Arabic) lesson
*Abarrane, Abree, Abri, Abriana, Abrianna,
Abrielle, Abrienne*

ACACIA (ə-KAY-shə) Greek: Thorny. In
Greek mythology, the acacia tree symbolizes
immortality and resurrection. Acacia wood
was used in the Bible to build the tabernacle
in the wilderness.
Acantha; *Akantha*; **Nicknames:** *Cacia, Casey*

ACCALIA (ah-KALL-ee-ah) Latin: Meaning
uncertain; possibly derived from Acca
Larentia, the mythological she-wolf who
nursed the twins Remus and Romulus

ACELINE (AH-se-leen) French: Noble

ACHALA (ah-cha-lah) Hindi: Constant

ADA (AY-də) Hebrew: Beautiful, adorned;

(African) first daughter; (English)
prosperous, happy
(Finnish) *Aada*; *Adah*, *Adda*

ADABEL Teutonic: Lovely or happy

ADAIR (ah-DER) Scottish: From the oak tree
ford; surname
Adaira, *Adairia*

ADALINA Teutonic: Diminutive form of
Adele

ADAMINA (a-dah-MEE-nah) Hebrew: Of
the red earth; feminine form of Adam
Admina

ADANYA (a-dahn-YAH) African: Her
father's daughter (Nigeria)
Adanna

ADAOMA (ah-day-oh-mah) African: Good
daughter

ADARA (ah-DAH-rah) Hebrew: Noble,
exalted; (Welsh) catches birds; (Irish)
from the ford at the oak tree; (African)
hope; (Arabic) virgin, unblemished pearl,
untrodden sand

ADDIE (AD-ee) English: Nickname for
Adelaide
Addy

ADDIENA Welsh: Beautiful
Addien

ADDISON English: Of Adam. This surname
was traditionally a male name but is growing
in popularity for girls.
Addeson, *Adison*, *Adisson*, *Addisyn*;
Nicknames: *Ad*, *Addie*, *Addy*

ADE Arthurian Legend: A mistress of
Lancelot

> *The young man waited impatiently for the lady to finish with the drugstore telephone directory. After she had turned page after page he said, "Madam, can I help you find the number you want?"*
>
> *"Oh, I don't want a number," she replied, "I'm looking for a pretty name for my baby."*
> —Bell Telephone News

ADELA (ah-DEL-ə) Latin: Variation of
Adelaide

ADELAIDE (AD-ə-layd) German, French:
Of the nobility; the wife of Emperor Otto the
Great and the name of an Australian city
(Latin) *Adela*; (French) *Adele*; (Spanish)
Adalia, *Adaliz*, *Adelaida*, *Alita*; (Dutch) *Aaltje*,
Aleta; (Polish) *Adelajda*; *Adalene*, *Adalyn*, *Adelia*,
Adelle, *Adelynn*, *Adilene*; **Old forms:** *Adelheid*,
Adelheide; **Nicknames:** *Ada*, *Addie*, *Heida*,
Heide, *Heidi*, *Addy*, *Del*, *Della*, *Delle*, *Lady*

ADELE (ə-DEL) German: Of the nobility, a
noble wolf; feminine form of Adolph
(English) *Adalbrechta*; (German) *Adalicia*,
Adalie, *Adaliz*, *Adalwolfa*, *Adelinda*;
(Teutonic) *Adal*, *Adaline*, *Adelicia*; *Adali*,
Adel; *Adelle*, *Edelle*, *Adela*, *Adelia*; **Old forms:**
Adellinde; **Diminutive forms:** *Adalina*,
Adelita, *Adette*

ADELINA (a-də-LEEN-ə) French: Of the
nobility; variant of Adelaide
Adeline; **Nicknames:** *Adele*, *Lina*

ADELITA (ah-day-LEE-tah) Spanish: Of the nobility, noble; a diminutive form of Adela. During the Mexican Revolution in the early twentieth century, adelitas were *soldaderas*, or female soldiers, who cooked for and washed up after the armies, cared for their wounded men, and fought bravely in battles alongside the soldiers. A vital force in the war effort, these women are memorialized in the famous Mexican song "La Adelita."

ADELPHA (ah-DEL-fə) Greek: Dear sister
Adelphe, Adelphie

ADENA (ah-DEEN-ə) Hebrew: Noble, delicate
Adina, Adinah, Adine; **Old forms:** *Adinam*

ADERYN Welsh: Bird

ADESINA (ah-DAY-see-NAH) African: Opening the way for more children. Often used after a woman has had difficulty conceiving.

ADHELLE Teutonic: Lovely or happy

ADIBA Arabic: Polite, learned, honest. Adiba stems from *Adab*, meaning *manners*, and synonymous with culture and literature.
Adeeba, Adeebah, Adibah

ADILA (AH-dee-lah) Arabic: Similar, bundle, equivalent; feminine form of Adil

ADIRA Arabic: Strong, powerful, wealthy

ADITI (ah-DEE-tee) Hindi: Free

ADMETA (ad-MEE-tah) Greek: Untamed

ADOETTE (ah-do-AY-tu, ah-do-ET) Native American: Large tree (Omaha)

ADOLPHINE Teutonic: Noble wolf; feminine form of Adolph
Adolpha

ADONIA (a-DON-ee-ə, a-DON-yə) Greek: Beautiful lady

ADORABELLA Latin: Adored beauty
Adorabelle

ADOREE (ah-dor-AY) French: Adored

ADORIA Latin: Glory
Adora

ADRASTEIA (ad-ra-STAY-ə) Greek: Unyielding; another name of the Greek goddess Nemesis

ADRIAN (AY-dree-ən) Latin, English: Dark; from the Adriatic Sea region
(French) *Adreanna, Adrienne*; (Italian) *Adreana*; (Dutch) *Adrie*; *Adra, Adrea, Adria, Adriana, Adrielle, Adrienna, Adrina*; **Star babies:** daughter of Harry Belafonte

ADSILA (AD-sil-ah) Native American: Blossom (Cherokee)

ADYA (ahd-YAH) Hindi: Born on Sunday

AEDON (ay-EE-dahn) Greek: Daughter of Pandareos

AEGERIA Latin: From the Aegean Sea
Aegaea, Aegates

AEGINA (AY-gee-nə) Latin: Mother of Aeacus, who, in Greek mythology, was the first king of Aegina. Aeacus was known for his piety and became a judge in Hades after his death.
Aeginae

AELDRA English: Noble

AEOLIA Latin: Daughter of mythological chariot-warrior Amythaon

AERONA (ayr-ON-ah) Welsh: Berry

AERWYNA English: Friend of the sea

AETHRA (EE-thrah) Greek: Mother of Theseus, the hero and king of Athens who slew the Minotaur

AETNA (EHT-nə) Greek: From Aetna; a volcanic goddess of Greek mytholocy

AFARIN (AH-fah-reen) Persian: Praise
Afareen

AFRA Latin: Roman nickname for African woman; the name of two early saints

AFREDA English: Friend of the elves
Aelfraed, Aethelwine, Aethelwyne; **Old forms:** *Aelfwine*

AFRICA (AF-ri-kə) American, Celtic: A continent. Parents may choose Africa as a name symbolic of their heritage. Africa is also the Anglicized form of Aifric, an Irish name popular since medieval times.
Affrica, Apirka; Affrican, Affrika, Affrikah, Africah, Afrika, Afrikah, Aifrica, Aphfrica, Apirkah

AFSOON (AF-soon) Persian: Spell

AFTAB (ahf-tahb) Persian: Sun

AFTON English: From the Afton River

AGALIA Greek: Splendor
Agalaia

AGATHA (AG-ə-thə) Greek: Good, kind; Saint Agatha was a third-century Sicilian martyr
(Greek) *Agathi*; (French) *Agathe*; (Spanish) *Agacia, Agueda*; (Irish) *Agate*; (Swedish) *Agda*; (Russian) *Agafiya*; (Hungarian) *Aggie, Agi, Agotha, Agoti*; *Agaue, Agave, Agna*; *Agata, Agueda*; **Famous namesakes:** English mystery writer Dame Agatha Christie

AGHAVNI (a-gah-HAV-nee) Armenian: Dove

AGLAIA (ə-GLAY-ə) Greek: Goddess of grace

AGLAUROS (ə-GLOR-əs) Greek: Mythological woman who was turned into stone by Hermes

AGNES (AG-nəs) Greek: Pure, chaste, innocent; a popular Roman martyr of the Middle Ages. See also *Ina*
(English) *Anessa, Anisha, Anissa, Annice, Annis*; (French) *Ynes, Ynez*; (Spanish) *Agnese, Ines, Inesa, Inez*; (Gaelic) *Aigneis*; (Irish) *Aghna, Una*; (Danish) *Agneta*; (Russian) *Agnessa, Agnia, Inessa*; (Czech) *Anezka*; (Finnish) *Anneetta, Aune*; *Agnella, Annissa, Anyssa*

AGRAFINA Latin: Born feet first
(Russian) *Agrafena; Agrafine*; **Nicknames:** *Fenya*

AGRIPPINA (a-grə-PIE-nə) Latin: Colonist
Agrippinae

AGUEDA (ah-GWAY-də) Spanish: Variation of Agatha

AHALYA (ah-hahl-yah) Hindi: Night

AHANA Irish: From the little ford

AHANG Persian: Harmony

AHAVA (ah-hah-VAH) Hebrew: Dearly loved
Ahave, Ahuda, Ahuva

AHELIA Hebrew: Breath
(French) *Abella; Ahelie*

AHELLONA Greek: Masculine

AHISMA (ah-hees-mah) Hindi: Gentle

AIDA (ah-EE-də) Italian, English: Reward, happy, helper. Aida is one who brings benefits and advantages and was the Prophet Mohammed's favorite wife. Verdi's opera bears the same name and is an epic classic tale of love, loyalty, betrayal, and courage. It tells of the love triangle between Aida, Amneris, and the soldier they both love.
Aidia; Ayda

AIDAN (AY-dən) Irish: Little, fiery; Aidan is a modern English spelling of the early medieval Gaelic name Áedán.
Adan, Adeen, Eideann; **Old forms:** *Eithna;*
Star babies: daughter of Faith Daniels

AIDEEN (AY-deen) Irish: Spelling variation of Etain

AIDOIOS Greek: Honored

AIFE (AY-fə) Celtic: A great female warrior of myth

AIFRIC (A-frik) Irish: Pleasant
Afric

AIKO (ah-ee-ko) Japanese: Child of love

AILA (IE-lə) Scottish: From the strong place

AILANI (ah-ee-LAW-nee) Hawaiian: High chief

AILEEN (ie-LEEN, ay-LEEN) Scottish, Irish: Light, from the green meadow. See also *Eileen, Helen*
(Greek) *Alina;* (Irish) *Aileen; Aileana;*
Nicknames: *Ailey, Aili, Ailia, Lina, Leena*

AILI German: Sweet

AILIN (AY-lin) Irish: Noble
Ailinn, Ailan, Ailyn, Ailynn, Aelin, Aelinn, Aelyn, Aelynn, Aelan

AILIS German: Sweet

AIMEE (AY-mee) French: Variation of Amy
Famous namesakes: Singer Aimee Mann

AINE (AWN-ye) Celtic: Radiance; the queen of the fairies in Celtic mythology
(Swedish) *Aina*

AINO (IE-no) Finnish: Only one; a character in the Finnish epic *Kalevala*

AINSLEY (AYNZ-lee) English: My own meadow
Ansley; Ainsleigh, Ainslee, Ainslea, Ainslie

AIRIC Celtic: Agreeable

AIRLEAS Gaelic, Irish: Oath

AISHA (ah-EE-shə) Arabic: Lively. Aisha was the Prophet Mohammed's favorite wife. Aish means *food, wheat,* or *bread;* it is symbolic of the sustenance of life. See also *Asha Ashia, Iesha, Myesha, Myeshia; Aishah, Ayeisha, Ayesha, Ayisha, Aysha, Eisha, Iesha, Ieshea, Iesha;* **Star babies:** daughter of Stevie Wonder

AISLIN (ASH-ling, ASH-lin) Irish: Vision; may also be a variant of Ashlyn
Aisling, Aislinn, Ashling, Isleen

AIYA Hebrew: Bird

AJEYA (ah-jay-ah) Hindi: Invincible or unconquerable
Ajaya

AKAKIA Greek: Guileless

AKANE (ah-kah-nah) Japanese: A red sunrise

AKEISHA (ah-KEE-shə) American: Contemporary name using the letter A and the name Keisha
Akeesha; **Nicknames:** *Keisha*

AKELA (ah-KAY-lah) Hawaiian: Noble

AKIKO (ah-kee-ko) Japanese: Child; light and bright

AKILI (ah-KEE-lee) African: Bright, smart (Tanzania)

AKIRA Scottish: Anchor

AKIVA (ah-KEE-vah) Hebrew: Protected
Akiha

ALAIDA Latin: Winged

ALAINA (ə-LAYN-ə) Irish: Fair, good-looking; feminine form of Alan or variant of Helen
(Swedish) *Gala*; *Alain*; *Alana, Alane, Alani, Alanna, Alannah, Alayna, Alayne, Allana, Allene*

ALALEH Persian: Buttercup

ALAMEA (ah-lə-MAY-ə) Hawaiian: Ripe, precious

ALAMEDA (ah-lah-MAY-dah) Spanish: Promenade; (Native American) grove of cottonwood

ALANA (ah-LAH-nah) Hawaiian: An offering

ALANE Celtic: Fair

ALANZA (ah-LAHN-zah) Spanish: Ready for battle

ALAQUA (ah-LAH-quah) Native American: Sweet gum tree

ALARICE (AL-ə-ris) German: Noble leader; feminine form of Alaric
(Teutonic) *Alaricia*; *Alarica, Allaryce*

ALASTRINA Celtic, Irish: Defends mankind; feminine form of Alastair and a variant of Alexandra
Alastrine, Alastriona

ALATHEA Greek: Mythological goddess of truth

ALAULA (ah-LOW-oo-lah) Hawaiian: Light of daybreak

ALAZNE (ah-LAHZ-ne) Basque, Spanish: Miracle

ALBA (AHL-bah) Latin: White
(Italian) *Albinia*; (Arthurian Legend) *Albiona*; *Albina, Alvinia*

ALBERTA (al-BUR-tə) German, Teutonic: Bright, noble; this feminine form of Albert is also related to the name Bertha.
(English) *Alberteen*; (French) *Albertina*; (Spanish) *Elbertina*; *Albertine, Albertyna, Auberta, Elbertine*; *Alberthine, Auberte, Aubertha, Auberthe, Aubine, Elbertha, Elberthina, Elberthine*; **Nicknames:** *Ali, Alli, Allie, Ally, Berrie, Berry, Bert, Berta, Bertie, Berty*; **Famous namesakes:** Singer Alberta Hunter

ALBERTINE (ahl-ber-TEEN) French: Spelling variation of Alberta

ALCESTIS (al-SES-təs) Greek: In Greek mythology, the name of a woman who gave her life to save her husband

ALCHEMY (AL-kə-mee) American: A power or process of transforming something common into something special
Star babies: daughter of Lance Henrikson and Jane Pollack

ALCINA Greek: Feminine of Alcinous, a mythical character that helped Odysseus return home. Alcina is also the name of a mistress of alluring enchantments and sensual pleasures in the Orlando poems. (Italian) *Alcee, Alcinia*; *Alcine*

ALCIPPE (al-SIP-ee) Greek: In mythology, Alcippe is the daughter of Aglaurus and Ares and mother of Daedalus by Eupalamus.

ALCMENE (alk-MEE-nee, ahlk-MAY-nay) Greek: Mother of Hercules (Latin) *Alcmena*

ALCYONE (al-SIE-ə-nee) Greek: In mythology, daughter of King Aeolus

ALDA German: Wise, elder, sometimes wealthy; variant of Aldo. See also *Aldys, Aleda* (German) *Aldona*; *Aldea, Aldis*

ALDERCY (ahl-DER-see) English: Chief

ALDONA German: Variation of Alda

ALDONZA (ahl-DON-zah) Spanish: Nice, sweet
Aldonsa

ALDORA Greek: Winged gift; (English) noble

ALDYS (AWL-dəs) English: From the old house

ALEANDRA Russian: Defender of man

ALECTA Greek: Honesty

ALEDA English: Winged

ALEEN Celtic: Fair, good-looking; variant of Helen or Eileen

ALENA Greek: Variation of Alena
Aleana; Alyna, Aleena, Alenna, Alenah

ALENE Celtic: Fair, good-looking; feminine variant of Alan

ALERA Latin: Eagle
Aleria

ALESANDESE (AHL-es-an-DEEZ) Basque: Variation of Alexandra

ALESIA (al-lee-see-ah) French: Defender; (Greek) helper
Nicknames: *Lee, Lisa*

ALETA (ah-LAY-tah) Spanish: Little wing; (Greek) truthful; mythological goddess of truth

ALETHEA (al-ə-THEE-ə, ə-LEE-thee-ə) Greek: Truthful; mythological goddess of truth
(Spanish) *Aletea, Aletia*; *Aletha, Aletheia, Alethia, Alithea, Alithia, Olethe, Olethea, Olethia, Olithia*

ALEV (ah-LEV) Turkish: Flame

ALEX Greek: Defender of mankind; a familiar form of Alexandra
Alyx; **Famous namesakes:** Actress Alex Kingston

ALEXANDRA Greek: Defender of mankind; feminine form of Alexander. See also *Alondra* (English) *Alexandrea*; (French) *Alexandrina, Alexandrine*; (Italian) *Alessandra, Alessia*; (Spanish) *Alandra, Alejandra, Alejandrina*; (Basque) *Alesandese*; (Russian) *Aleksandra*; (Czech) *Olexa*; (Polish) *Olka*; (Ukrainian) *Olesya*; (Hungarian) *Alexa*; *Alexandina, Alexandria, Alexandriana, Alexine, Alixandra, Alyssandra, Lexandra, Oleisia*; **Nicknames:** *Aleka, Alex, Alexia, Alexis, Alix, Drina, Lexann, Lexi, Lexie, Lexina, Lexine, Sandra, Sandrine, Sasha, Shura, Xandra, Zandra, Zondra,*

Zandra; **Diminutive forms:** *Sashenka, Shurochka, Sondra*; **Famous namesakes:** Actress Alexandra Paul, Educator Alexa Canady; **Star babies:** daughter of Mikhail Baryshnikov and Jessica Lange, Barry Gibb, Whoopi Goldberg, Dustin Hoffman, Christopher Reeve, Keith Richards

ALEXIS English: Nickname for Alexandra *Alexus*; **Nicknames:** *Lexi, Lexie, Lexy*; **Famous namesakes:** Actress Alexis Smith; **Star babies:** daughter of Ted Danson, Dennis Rodman and Annie Banks, Martha Stewart

ALFONSA (ahl-FON-sah) Spanish: Noble and ready or battle ready; this was the name of six kings of Portugal and kings of several ancient regions of Spain.
(German) *Alfonsine*; (Italian) *Alonza*; (Teutonic) *Alphonsa*; *Alonsa, Alphonsine, Alphonza, Alphosina*

ALFREDA English: Elf counselor; feminine form of Alfred; (Teutonic) oracle
Alfrida

ALGIANA Teutonic: Elf-spear, spear man; feminine variant of Alger or possibly Algernon
Algiane

ALGOMA Native American: Valley of flowers (tribe unknown)

ALI (ah-LEE, AH-lee) Arabic: Greatest; a variant of Allah, the Supreme Being in the Muslim faith; feminine form of same name
Alli, Allie; Aly; **Famous namesakes:** Actress Ali McGraw; **Star babies:** daughter of Robert Plant, Ruth Pointer

ALICE German, English: Noble, of the nobility; Alice is a variant of the old French name Adeliz, a form of Adelaide. Children of all ages know Alice as Lewis Carroll's heroine in *Alice's Adventures in Wonderland*; (Greek) truthful (Hebrew) *Alisa*; (Latin) *Alisia, Alycia, Alysha*;

(German) *Alison*; (French) *Alisanne, Alyson*; (Spanish) *Allyce, Alyce*; (Gaelic) *Ailis, Ailse*; (Irish) *Ailise, Allison, Allsun*; (Scottish) *Aileas*; (Hungarian) *Alisz, Aliz*; *Ailisa, Alicea, Alise, Alissa, Alisse, Allison, Allyse, Allyson, Alys, Alyse, Alyssa, Alysse, Alyssia*; **Old forms:** *Allis*; **Famous namesakes:** Author Alice Walker

---

> "Must a name mean something?" Alice asked doubtfully.
>
> "Of course it must," Humpty Dumpty said with a short laugh: "my name means the shape I am—and a good handsome shape it is, too. With a name like yours, you might be any shape, almost."
>
> —Lewis Carroll,
> *Through the Looking-Glass*

ALICIA Spanish: Noble; variant of Alice and Adelaide
Alecia, Alesia; Alycia, Alysha; **Diminutive forms:** *Lecia, Licia, Lisha*

ALIDA (ah-LEE-də) Latin, Dutch: Small winged one; (German) archaic. See also *Aleta* (English) *Alita, Elida, Elita, Oleda, Olita*; (French) *Allete; Aletta, Oleta*

ALIKA (ah-LEE-kə) African: Most beautiful (Nigeria)

ALIMA (ah-LEE-mah) Arabic: Knows dance and music, sea maiden, knowledgeable, delicate, a well yielding much water; stems from *eilm*, meaning knowledge; feminine form of Alim or Al Alim

ALINA (ah-LEEN-ə) Latin: Of the nobility; variant of Eileen, Adelina, and feminine form of Alan; (Celtic) fair. See also *Aleen* (Celtic) *Allena*; *Aleena, Aline, Allina, Alyna*

ALISON German: Variation of Alice *Allison, Allyson, Alyson*; **Nicknames:** *Ali, Allie, Ally*; Famous namesakes: Author Alison Lurie, Actress Alison Eastwood; Star babies: daughter of Tom Berenger, Heather Menzies and Robert Urich

ALISSA English: Spelling variation of Alice *Alisa, Alysa, Alyssa*

ALITA (ah-LEE-tə) English: Variation of Alida

ALIYAH (ah-LIE-yah, ah-LEE-yah) Hebrew: To ascend, to rise up *Aaliyah, Alea, Aleah, Alia; Aliya, Aliah, Aliye, Allia, Alliah*; **Famous namesakes:** Singer and actress Aaliyah Haughton

ALIYN Gaelic: Beautiful; feminine form of Alan (Teutonic) *Allys*

ALIZ (AH-leez) German: Sweet

ALIZA (ə-LEE-zə) Hebrew: Joy, joyous one *Aleeza, Aleezah, Alitza, Alizah*

ALKA (AHL-kə) Polish: Intelligent; (Hindi) youth

ALLA (AHL-lah) Russian: The goddess; from Allat, name of pre-Islamic Arabic goddess of fertility **Nicknames:** *Alka, Allochka*; **Famous namesakes:** Russian singer Alla Pugacheva

ALLAIRE (ahl-AYR) French: Cheerful, glad; variant of Hilary *Alair*

ALLEFFRA (ah-le-FRAH) French: Cheerful

ALLEGRA (ə-LEG-rə) Latin, English: Joyous *Alegra, Alegria; Allegria*; **Nicknames:** *Allie*

ALLURA English: To allure

ALMA (AL-mə) Latin, Spanish: Nourishing, soul; (Persian) apple; (Celtic) good; (Swedish) loving

ALMAS Arabic, Persian: Diamond, adamant *Almaz*

ALMETA Latin: Driven; (Danish) pearl

ALMUDENA (ahl-moo-DAY-nah) Spanish: The city. The Virgin of Almudena is the patron saint of Madrid.

ALODIA Anglo-Saxon: Wealthy; Saint Alodia was a ninth-century Spanish martyr (French) *Elodie; Alodie*

ALOISA (ah-lo-WEE-see-ah) German: Famous warrior; feminine form of Alois *Aloise, Aloisia*

ALONA (ah-LO-nah) Hebrew: Strong as an oak tree *Allona, Allonia, Alonna*

ALONDRA (ah-LAWN-drah) Spanish: Lark; a beautiful songbird **Nicknames:** *Ally, Al*

ALONSA German: Spelling variation of Alfonsa

ALOYSIA (ah-lo-EE-zee-ah) German: Famous fighting; (Teutonic) famous in battle

ALPHA (AL-fə) Greek: Firstborn; the first letter of the Greek alphabet

ALSATIA French: From Alsace, a region in France

ALSOOMSE Native American: Independent (Algonquin)

ALTA Latin, Spanish: Lofty

ALTAGRACIA (al-tah-GRAH-see-ah) Spanish: High grace; given in honor of Mary, mother of Jesus
Nicknames: *Alta*

ALTAIR (ahl-tah-EER, ahl-TAYR) Arabic: Bird, poultry. Altair is the name of the main star in the constellation Aquila, which is known as Orion in the western world.
Altaira

ALTHA English: Healer

ALTHEA (al-THEE-ə) Greek: Pure, wholesome
Althaea, Althaia, Altheda, Althia; **Famous namesakes:** Tennis star Althea Gibson

ALULA (Al Oola) Arabic: The first, number one; refers to firstborn child

ALUMA Hebrew: Girl, maiden, or hidden secret
Alumit

ALURA English: Divine counselor
Alurea

ALVA Hebrew: Exalted one; an Old Testament descendent of Esau

ALVAR English, German: Army of elves (Latin) *Alvita*; (Spanish) *Alvara, Alvarita*; *Alvarie, Alvera*; **Nicknames:** *Alvie*

ALVERA (AHL-ver-ah) Spanish: Speaker of truth; feminine form of Alvaro

ALWEN (AHL-wen) Welsh: From the River Alwen
Alwyn

ALYDA German: Archaic

ALYSSA (ə-LIS-ə) Greek: Rational
Alissa

ALZINA (al-ZEE-nə) Arabic: Adornment, feast, illumination. When used in a name, these attributes refer to Woman.
Alzena

AMA (AH-mah) African: Born on Saturday (Ghanaian); (Norse) eagle
Ami

AMABELLE (AM-ə-bel) Latin, French: Lovable; Beautiful or loving
Amabel, Amabilis

AMADA Latin: To love
(Spanish) *Amata*; *Amare*

AMADAHY Native American: Forest water (Cherokee)

AMADEA Latin: Loves God; feminine form of Amadaeus
Amadis

AMADI (ah-MAH-dee) Arabic: My pillar; (African) rejoicing (Nigerian)

AMADINA Latin: Worthy of God

AMAIA (ah-MAH-yah) Basque: The end

AMAL (ah-mahl) Arabic: Hope, trust, expectation
Amala

AMALIA (ah-MAH-lee-ə) Latin: Original form of Emily
Nicknames: *Lia, Maya*

AMALTHEA (am-al-THEE-ə) Greek: Woman who nursed Zeus

AMANDA Latin, English: Worthy of being loved. Poets and playwrights brought this name into popular usage in the seventeenth century.
(French) *Amadee*; **Nicknames:** *Manda, Mandalyn, Mandi, Mandie, Mandy, Mandy, Mandi, Manda*; **Famous namesakes:** Actress Amanda Plummer; **Star babies:** daughters of George Lucas, Donna Summer, Billy Bob Thornton

AMARA (ah-MAH-rah) Greek: Eternal; a form of Amarantha

AMARANTHA (AM-er-AN-thə) Greek: Unfading; refers to the Amaranth plant with dense bulbous green and red flowers. The plant is so named because the flowers retain their color even when dried.
(French) *Amarante*; (Spanish) *Amaranta*; *Amaranda, Amarande*; **Nicknames:** *Amara*

> *Amarantha sweet and fair,*
> *Ah, braid no more that*
> *shining hair!*
> *As my curious hand or eye*
> *Hovering round thee, let it fly!*
> —Richard Lovelace (1618–1658)

AMARIAH (ah-mə-RIE-ə) Hebrew: Yahweh; name of several Old Testament characters
Amarisa, Amarise

AMARILIS (ah-mah-REE-lees) Spanish: Variation of Amaryllis

AMARIS Hebrew: Given by God; (Spanish) child of the moon

AMARYLLIS (am-ə-RIL-is) Greek: Flower; poetically used to mean a simple shepherdess or country girl in *I Care Not for These Ladies* by Thomas Campion (1567–1620)
(Spanish) *Amarilis*; **Nicknames:** *Marilis*

AMBA (ahm-bah) Hindi: Mother. See also *Umayma*
Amhi, Amhika

AMBER English: A jewel-quality fossilized resin; derived via Old French and Latin from Arabic ambar; as a color, the name refers to a warm honey shade and was popularized by Kathleen Winsor's novel *Forever Amber*.
(French) *Ambre*; *Amberlee, Amberlyn, Amberlynn, Ambra*; **Star babies:** daughter of Simon LeBon, Neil Young

AMBERLY (AM-ber-lee) English: Ambrosia; immortal
Amberlee; **Nicknames:** *Amber*

AMBIKA (ahm-BEE-kah) Hindi: Goddess of the moon

AMBROSIA (am-BRO-zhuh) Greek: Immortal. In mythology, ambrosia is a food delicacy of the gods and immortal beings.
Ambrotosa, Amhrosine

AMEENA (a-meen-AH) African: Trustworthy (Swahili)

AMELIA (ə-MEE-lee-ə, ə-MEEL-yə) Latin: Industrious, hardworking. Amelia is the heroine of Henry Fielding's 1751 novel *Amelia*.
Famous namesakes: Aviation pioneer Amelia Earhart

AMETHYST (AM-ə-thist) Greek: A purple or violet gemstone. According to ancient Greek superstition, an amethyst protected its owner against the effects of strong drink.

AMIA English: Spelling variation of Amy

AMINA (ah-MEE-nah) Arabic, African: Trustworthy or faithful
(Persian) *Amineh*; *Ameena*; *Ameenah*, *Aminah*

AMIRA (ah-MEER-ah) Arabic: Princess; feminine form of Amir; (Hebrew) one who speaks
Ameerah, *Amirah*; **Famous namesakes:** Actress Amira Casar

AMITA (ah-MEE-tah) Hebrew: Truth

AMITOLA Native American: Rainbow (Unknown tribal origin)

AMITY (AM-i-tee) Latin: Friendship
(French) *Amite*; *Amitee*

AMMA (ah-mah) Hindi: Mother goddess

AMOR (ah-MOR) Spanish: Love
Amora

AMORICA English: Ancient name for Britain. In the Middle Ages, the Celtic nation of Brittany became known as Amorica, and was considered a center of Celtic culture in Europe.

Roscellinus of Amorica in Brittany (1050–1121) was the founder of nominalism in the Middle Ages, and instigated another approach to universals. According to Dr. C. George Boeree in his essay on the middle ages, Roscellinus was quoted as saying that the universe is just a vocal sound, or a word: "Only individuals actually exist. Words, and the ideas they represent, refer to nothing."

AMORITA Latin: Little loved one
Amoretta, *Amorette*

AMPHITRITE (am-fə-TRIE-tee) Greek, Latin: A sea goddess; aunt of Achilles

AMREI German: A blend of Anne and Marie

AMRITHA (ahm-REE-thah) Hindi: Precious

AMY French: Dearly loved
(French) *Aimee*; *Amia*, *Amie*; *Ami*; **Famous namesakes:** Actress Amy Irving, Singer Aimee Mann; **Star babies:** daughters of Robert Redford, Julie Andrews and Blake Edwards

AMYMONE (a-MEM-ə-nee) Greek: The mythological daughter of Danaiis

AMYNTA Latin: Protector

ANABEL Latin: Spelling variation of Annabel

ANAHITA (ah-nah-HEE-tah) Persian, Hindi: Immaculate, undefiled. This was the name of the Persian goddess of fertility and water. She was sometimes identified with Artemis, Aphrodite, and Athena.
(Armenian) *Anahid*

ANAIS (a-na-EES) French: Variation of Ann
Famous namesakes: French author Anais Nin; **Star babies:** daughter of Noel Gallagher and Meg Mathews

ANALA (ah-NAH-lah) Hindi: Fiery

ANALENA (ah-nah-LAY-nah) Spanish: Grace, favor; variant of Anna

ANALISA English: Blend of Anna and Lisa
(Latin) *Analiese*, *Analisia*; (Swedish) *Annalina*; *Analicia*, *Analise*, *Annalisa*, *Annalise*, *Annalissa*

ANAMARI Hebrew: A hybrid of Anna and Marie

ANANDA (ah-NAHN-dah) Hindi: Bliss

ANANTA (ah-NAHN-tah) Hindi: Name of a serpent

ANAROSA (ah-nah-RO-sah) Spanish: Grace, favor; variant of Anna

ANASTASIA (ah-nah-stah-SEE-ah, a-nə-STAY-zhə) Russian, Greek: Resurrection. The daughter of the last tsar of Russia, she was killed with the rest of her family and small dog by the Bolsheviks in 1918. In 1920, a Polish peasant girl with a striking resemblance to Anastasia claimed her identity. It wasn't until her death and subsequent DNA test that she was identified accurately as an imposter. Disney pictures animated this true story in the 1997 film *Anastasia*. (Greek) *Anastacia, Anastasha*; (Russian) *Nastasia*; (Czech) *Anastazie*; (Polish) *Anastazja*; (Hungarian) *Anasztaizia*; *Anastashia, Anastassia, Anastazia, Annastasia, Anstice*; **Nicknames:** *Asya, Nastia, Stacie, Stacy, Tasya, Tazia, Ana*, **Famous namesakes:** Russian ballerina Anastasia Volochova

ANASUYA (AH-nah-SOO-yah) Hindi: Charitable

ANAT (AH-naht) Hebrew: To sing
Anata, Anate

ANATH (ah-NAHT) Egyptian: Goddess of love and war, sister of Baal
Anat

ANATOLA Greek: From the east
Anatolia

ANCE Hebrew: Grace

ANCELIN (AHN-slin) French: Handmaiden
Ancelina

ANCYRA (an-SIE-rə) Latin: From Ankara

ANDEANA (ahn-day-AH-nah) Spanish: Leaving

ANDELA (AHN-dieh-lah) Czech: Variation of Angela

ANDENA English: A man's woman; variant of Andrea

ANDIE English: Nickname for Andrea *Andee, Andi, Andy*; **Famous namesakes:** Actress Andie MacDowell

ANDISHEH Persian: Thought

ANDRASTE Celtic: Victory

ANDREA Greek, French: A man's woman; feminine form of Andrew. This name may be considered particularly appropriate for Andrea Verrocchio, a Renaissance sculptor who taught Leonardo da Vinci and Perugino. (Latin) *Andranetta, Andrena*; (Greek) *Andreas*; (French) *Andree*; (Spanish) *Andere*; (Danish) *Anndrea*; *Andena, Andreana, Andreanna, Andreya, Andria, Andriana, Andrianne, Andrienne, Andrina, Aundrea*; **Nicknames:** *Anda, Andee, Andes, Andi, Andie, Andra*

ANDROMACHE (an-DRAH-mə-kee) Greek: Mythological wife of Hector (Latin) *Andromacha*

ANDROMEDA (an-DRAHM-ə-duh) Greek: In Greek mythology, Andromeda was the daughter of Cassiopeia and the wife of Perseus. This is also the name of a northern constellation named after the mythological figure.

ANE Hebrew: Prayer

ANEISHA English: Variant of Ann or Agnes

ANEKO (ah-nay-ko) Japanese: Older sister

ANESSA English: Variation of Agnes

ANEVAY (ah-ne-VAY) Native American:
Superior
Anevy

ANEZKA (ah-NEZH-kah) Greek: Gentle

ANFISA (ahn-FEE-sah) Russian: Blossoming

ANGA (AHN-gah) Swahili: Sky

ANGELA Latin, Italian: Messenger of God;
feminine form of Angelus
(Hebrew) *Erela, Erelah*; (Latin) *Angel*; (Greek)
Angeliki, Angelina, Angelique; (Anglo-Saxon)
Engel; (French) *Ange, Angelette, Angeline, Angilia*;
(Spanish) *Angelia, Angelita*; (Gaelic) *Aingealag*;
(Celtic) *Aingeal*; (Czech) *Andela*; (Polish) *Aniela*;
(Persian) *Fereshteh*; *Angelena*; *Angele, Angelee,
Angelene, Angeli, Angelisa, Angell, Angelle, Angelyn,
Anjali*; **Nicknames:** *Angie*; **Famous namesakes:**
Actress Angela Lansbury

ANGELICA Latin: Angelic; derived from
Angelicus
(German) *Angelika*; (Spanish) *Anjelica*;
Famous namesakes: Actress Anjelica Houston

ANGELINA Greek: Variation of Angela
Famous namesakes: Actress Angelina Jolie

ANGERONA (an-jə-RON-ə) Latin: In
mythology, the goddess who relieved men
from pain and sorrow

ANGHARAD (ahng-HAH-raht) Arthurian
Legend: Much loved; in Welsh mythology, the
lover of Peredur

ANGIE Latin: Nickname for Angela
Famous namesakes: Actress Angie Dickinson

ANICE Scottish: Variation of Ann

ANICHKA (ah-NEECH-kah) Russian,
Ukrainian: Grace
(Hebrew) *Aniki*; (Dutch) *Anika*; (Slavic)

Anica; (Finnish) *Annikki*; (Hungarian) *Aniko*;
Annikka, Annikke; **Famous namesakes:**
Swedish golfer Annika Sörenstam

ANIELA (ahn-YE-lah) Polish: Variation of
Angela

ANIQA (ah-nee-kah) African: Elegant; beautiful
Anica

ANISA (ah-NEE-sah) Arabic, Persian:
Friendly, social
Anysia; **Famous namesakes:** Hard rock artist
Anisa Murphy

ANITA Hebrew: Grace; variant of Ann
(Hebrew) *Anitra*; *Aneta, Anetta*

ANJEANETTE English: Gift of God's favor;
blend of Anne and Janet
Anjanette, Anjanique, Annjeanette

ANJOLIE English: Blend of Anne and Jolie

ANKA (AHN-kah) Polish: Grace; (Native
American) (Quichua) Eagle

ANKARA (ANG-kə-rə) Latin: From Ankara

ANKINE (an-KI-ne) Armenian: Valuable

ANKTI (AHNK-tee) Native American:
Repeat dance (Hopi)

ANN English: Graceful; a variant of Hannah
introduced to Britain in the thirteenth century
(Hebrew) *Ayn*; (German) *Antje*; (French)
Anais, Anne; (Scottish) *Anice*; (Swedish) *Annika,
Annike*; (Dutch) *Anke, Anki*; (Russian) *Anna*;
(Polish) *Ania*; (Finnish) *Anniina, Annukka,
Anu*; (Hungarian) *Anci; Ana*; **Nicknames:** *Anni,
Annie, Anya*; **Diminutive forms:** *Anechka*;
Famous namesakes: Fashion designer Ann
Klein, actress Anne Bancroft, writer Anne
Frank, author Anne Morrow Lindbergh, advice
columnist Ann Landers

ANNA (AHN-nah) Russian: Variation of Ann; (Native American) mother (Algonquin) **Famous namesakes:** Tennis player Anna Kournikova; **Star babies:** daughters of Bob Dylan, Peter Gabriel, Kirk Cameron, Tom Petty

ANNABEL Latin: Beautiful, beloved; considered an elaboration of Anna and Belle or a variation of Amabel (Irish) *Annabla*; *Anabel, Anabelle, Annabella, Annabelle*

> "And the stars never rise but I feel the bright eyes
> Of the beautiful Annabel Lee"
> —Edgar Allen Poe, *Annabel Lee*

ANNABETH English, Latin: Blend of Ann and Beth; in the Bible, a devout woman who saw infant Jesus presented at the temple in Jerusalem.

ANNA CRISTINA Swedish: Graceful Christian

ANNALIE (AH-ne-lee) Swedish: Graceful meadow (German) *Annalena*; (Spanish) *Analee, Analeigh*; *Annalee, Annali*

ANNAMARIA Hebrew: Grace or bitter; blend of Anna and Maria (Spanish) *Anamarie, Yanamaria, Yanamarie*

ANNASTIINA Finnish: Blend of Anna and the Swedish name Stina, which is a short form of Kristina *Annastina*

ANNBRITT German: Blend of Ann and Brigitte

ANNEGRET German: Blend of Ann and Margaret

ANNEKE (AHN-nə-kə) Scandinavian: Favor, grace; variant of Hebrew Hannah

ANNELI (AHN-e-lee) Swedish, Finnish: Graceful meadow; a pet form of Anna

ANNELIESE Hebrew: Grace or devoted to God; a blend of Anne and Lisa *Annaliese, Annelisa, Annelise*; **Star babies:** daughter of Kelly LeBrock and Steven Seagal

ANNEROSE German: Blend of Anne and Rose

ANNETTE French: Little Ann **Famous namesakes:** Actress Annette Funicello

ANNIE Hebrew: Nickname for Ann **Star babies:** daughters of Kevin Costner, Jamie Lee Curtis, Glenn Close

ANNIS Greek, Anglo-Saxon: Whole *Annys*

ANNORA Latin: Variant of Honora *Annorah*

ANOOSHEH (ah-NOO-she) Persian: Happy

ANORA Hebrew: Grace; (English) light

ANOUK (ah-NOOK) French: Grace *Annouk*

ANOUSH (ah-NOOSH) Armenian: Sweet-tempered

ANSA Latin: Opportunity; (Finnish) constant, also *trap* in the traditional Finnish meaning of the word *Anse*

ANSTACE Greek: One who will be reborn; derived from Anistemi, meaning *to stand up* or *to raise up*

ANTANDRA Latin: From the Amazon

ANTHEA (ahn-THAY-ah) Greek: Flower; Lady of flowers
Antea, Anthia; **Nicknames:** *Thia, Thea*

ANTICLEA Greek: In mythology, mother of Odysseus
Anticleia

ANTIGONE (an-TIG-ə-nee) Greek: The mythological daughter of Oedipus and sister of Priam

ANTIOPE (an-TIE-o-pee) Greek: In mythology, daughter of Asopus

ANTOINETTE (awn-twaw-NET) French: Variation of Antonia
Famous namesakes: French Queen Marie Antoinette

ANTONIA (ahn-TO-nee-ah, ahn-TON-yah) Latin, Italian: Praiseworthy; feminine form of Anthony
(German) *Antonie*; (French) *Antoinette*; (Italian) *Antonella, Antonietta*; (Russian) *Antonina*; *Antoinetta, Antonette, Antonique*; **Nicknames:** *Nella, Toinette, Toini, Toni, Tony, Tonya*; **Famous namesakes:** British author Lady Antonia Fraser; **Star babies:** daughters of Anthony Quinn, John Wayne

ANUNCIACION (ah-NOON-see-ah-see-ON) Spanish: Of the Annunciation

ANWEN (AHN-wen) Welsh: Very beautiful

ANYA Russian: Nickname for Ann
Star babies: daughter of Stanley Kubrick

AOLANI (ow-LAH-nee) Hawaiian: A heavenly cloud

APALA (ah-PAH-lah) Hindi: Endearing, beautiful; name of a legendary Hindu wise woman

APHRAH (AF-rə) Hebrew: Biblical place name meaning *dust* or *of the earth*
Afra, Afrah, Aphra; **Famous namesakes:** Writer Aphra Behn

APHRODITE (af-ro-DIE-tee) Greek: Foam-born. The Greek goddess of love, Aphrodite was born from the sea foam, married to the smith god Hephaestus. She became the mother of Eros (Cupid), among others.

APOLLONIA (ah-pə-LO-nee-ə) Greek: Belonging to Apollo. Apollo was the Greek god of sun, light, music, and poetry.
(Latin) *Apollonis*; (French) *Apolline*; (Scandinavian) *Abelone*; (Danish) *Abellona*; *Abellone, Apollina, Apollinaris*

APONI (ah-PO-nee) Native American: Butterfly
Aponee

APPLE American: Apple, a fruit
Star babies: daughter of Gwyneth Paltrow and Chris Martin

APRIL Latin, English: Opening up, evocative of the opening of flower buds in the spring; born in or belonging to the month April
(French) *Avril*; (Spanish) *Abril*; *Aprille, Apryl, Apryll, Averil, Averill, Averyl, Avriel, Avrill, Avryl*; *Aipril, Aprill, Averel, Averell, Averyll, Averylle*

APSARAS (ap-SAH-res) Hindi: In Hindu mythology, Apsaras are female spirits of nature akin to water or forest nymphs. They are considered beautiful creatures who are also talented artists and performers.

APULIA (ah-PYOO-lyə) Latin: Place name for the southeastern most region of Italy and the river Apulia

AQUANETTA English: The exact origin is unclear, but this is most likely a recently created name based on a feminization of the blue-green color aqua.
Aquanette

AQUENE (ah-KAY-ne) Native American: Peace

AQUILINA (ah-kee-LEE-nah) Spanish: Eagle
Akilina, Aquiline

AQUITANIA (a-kwə-TAY-nyə) Latin: Place name referring to a region in southwestern France or people from that region; the name of a transatlantic ship of the Cunard line so beloved that it earned the name Ship Beautiful

ARA (AHR-ah) Latin: Altar or place of prayer; the name of a star constellation south of Scorpius; (Arabic) brings rain; (Teutonic) eagle's wisdom

ARABELLA (ar-ə-BEL-ə) Latin, English, Dutch: Beautiful alter. See also *Orabella* (English) *Orabel; Arabelle; Arabel, Arabela, Arabele, Arbela, Arbell, Arbella, Arbelle, Orabelle;* **Nicknames:** *Ara, Bel, Belle, Bella, Ora, Orra*

ARABIA Latin: Place name referring to ancient country to the southwest of Mesopotamia, which in modern geography would include the Middle East and might reflect a family or cultural connection to that part of the world

ARACELI (AYR-ə-chel-ee) Latin, Spanish: Altar of heaven
Aracelia, Aracelis, Arcilla, Aricela; Aracely, Ariceli, Aricelly

ARACHNE (ə-RAK-nee) Greek: In Greek mythology, Arachne was a young girl whose pride in her weaving skills and attitude during a weaving contest prompted Athena to turn her into a spider. In Latin mythology, it is Minerva who transforms Arachne.

ARAMINTA (ar-ah-MIN-tə) English: Unclear origin and meaning; possibly invented by playwright William Concreve for his heroine in the 1693 play, *The Old Bachelor*; possibly a variant or blend of Amynta or Arabella
Araminte

ARCADIA (ahr-KAY-dee-a) Greek, Latin: A powerful bear woman; also a mountainous region of Greece
Arkadia, Arcaydia; **Nicknames:** *Kay, Cay*

ARCELIA (ahr-SAY-lee-ah) Spanish: Treasure, altar of heaven

ARCHANA (ar-CHAH-nah) Sanskrit: Honored

ARDA Hebrew: Bronze, strong metal
Ardah, Ardath

ARDEA Latin: From Ardea

ARDEN (AHR-dən) Latin, English, Celtic: Burning with enthusiasm, passionate and eager. Shakespeare set the romantic comedy *As You Like It* in the magical forest called Arden. The name also evokes the image of glamorous actress Eve Arden.
(French) *Ardella, Ardelle;* (Celtic) *Ardena, Ardene, Ardra; Arda, Ardeen, Ardel, Ardelia, Ardelis, Ardina, Ardine, Ardinia, Ardis, Ardyne, Ardys;* **Nicknames:** *Ardi*

ARELLA (ah-RAY-lə) Hebrew: Messenger of God, an angel
(Latin) *Arela; Arelle*

ARENA Greek: Holy one

ARETE (ah-RAY-te) Greek: Virtue, the Greek concept of striving for excellence in all aspects of one's life; unforgettably linked to singer Aretha Franklin
Areta, Aretha, Aretina; Oretha, Oretta, Orette; **Nicknames:** *Retha*

ARETHUSA (ar-ə-THOO-sə) Greek, Latin: In mythology, Arethusa was pursued by the river god Alpheus, who had fallen in love with her. Rather than give in to him, she begged Artemis to save her, which she did by turning her into a spring. Not to be defeated, Alpheus turned himself to water and united with her.

AREVIG (ahr-e-VEEG) Armenian: Like the sun

AREZOO (AHR-ay-zoo) Persian: Wish

ARGANTE Arthurian Legend: Name of a queen

ARGENTA Latin, Spanish: Silvery. The country Argentina was named after the precious metal explorers hoped to find there.
Argentia, Argentina

ARIA (AHR-ee-ə) Italian, Greek, English: Melody, generally referring to an elaborately done and beautiful song sung by a soloist in an opera; possible familiar form of Greek name Ariadne; (Teutonic) eagle, eagle's wisdom; see Ara
(English) *Ariette; Arietta*

ARIADNE (ah-ree-AHD-ne) Greek, Latin: Holy one; In Greek mythology, Ariadne is the daughter of King Minos who saves Thesus by helping him navigate the prison maze known as the Labyrinth.
(French) *Ariane;* (Persian) *Aryana; Arene, Ariadna, Ariana, Arianna, Arianne, Arriana; Ariagna, Arianie, Aryane, Aryanie, Aryanna, Aryanne*

ARIAN (AR-ree-ahn) Welsh: Silver; derived from Greek Arion, the mythological magic horse born to Poseidon and Demeter.

ARIANA (ahr-ee-AHN-ah) Welsh: Like silver; also a variant of Ariadne
Arian, Ariane, Arianna, Aryanie, Aryanna, Aryanne

ARIANWEN (ahr-ee-AHN-wen) Welsh: Silver woman

ARICIA Latin: From Aricia

ARIEL (AR-ee-əl, ER-ee-əl) Hebrew: Lioness of God, a biblical name for Jerusalem. Ariel is also Shakespeare's name for a mischievous spirit in *The Tempest* and Disney's lovable character in *The Little Mermaid*.
(French) *Arielle;* (Spanish) *Ariela; Areille, Arial, Ariele, Ariella, Ariellel;* **Nicknames:** *Ari*

ARIETTA (ahr-ee-ET-ə) Italian: Small melody sung by a soloist; variant of Aria
Ariette

ARILDE Teutonic: Hearth maiden
Arilda

ARISHA Russian: Diminutive form of Arina

ARISTA (ə-RIS-tə) Greek: The best. Arista is the name of a star in the Virgo constellation and of a major music recording company;
(Latin) ear of corn
(Persian) *Arissa; Aristella, Aristelle*

ARJEAN (ahr-ZHAWN) French: Silvery
Arcene

ARLEIGH (AHR-lee) English: Variation of Harley

ARLENE English, Irish: Pledge or oath; variant of names ending in –*arlene*, such as Carlene and Charlene. Arlene may also be a feminine form of Arlen or Charles
Arlyne, Arlana, Arleana, Arleen, Arleena, Arleene, Arlena, Arlenna, Arleta, Arlette, Arlina, Arline, Arlyn, Arlyne; **Diminutive forms:** *Arla*; **Famous namesakes:** Actress Arlene Francis

ARLETTE (ar-LET) French: A medieval given name; derived from a feminine dimunitive of Charles
Arleta, Arletta

ARLEY (AHR-lee) English: Unisex name, meaning bowman
Arlee, Arlie

ARLINDA English: Origins unclear, but probably a modern blend of Arlene and Linda

ARLISE Hebrew: Pledge, probably related to the name Arlene; feminine variant of Arliss
Arlyss

ARMENIA (ahr-MEE-nee-ə) Latin: Place name of country located in southwestern Asia, east of Turkey

ARMIDA Latin: Little armed one, little warrior

ARMILLA Latin: Bracelet, armlets

ARMINA German: Warrior maiden; feminine variant of Armand or Herman
Armilda, Armilde

ARNAUDE (ar-NOD) French: Strong as an eagle; feminine form of Arnold

ARNE (AHR-nə) German: Eagle
Diminutive forms: *Arnette*

ARNELLE English: Eagle strength; feminine form of Arnold
Arnalda, Arnolda

ARROSA Latin, Basque: Of the rose or of the rosary; variant of Rose
Arrose

ARSENIA Greek: Strong; feminine form of Arsenio
Arcenia, Arsania, Arsemia

ARTEMIS (AHR-tə-mis) Greek: Huntress and virgin goddess of the moon in Greek mythology; the equivalent of the Roman godess Diana

ARTEMISIA (ahr-tə-MI-zee-ə) Greek: Gift from Artemis, perfection
Artemia; Aretmasia, Artemesia

ARTHURINE English: Noble, courageous; a modern feminine variant of Arthur, which would confer meanings of stone and bear as well
Artheia, Arthelia, Arthene, Arthurene, Arthurette, Arthurina, Arthurine, Artia, Artice, Artina, Artis, Artlette, Artrice

ARTURA (ahr-TOOR-ah) Spanish: Noble or courageous; feminine form of Arturo

ARUNA (ah-roo-nah) Hindi: Radiant morning star

ARVADA Danish: Eagle

ARVANEH Persian: Wild violet

ARWEN (AR-wen) English: In J.R.R. Tolkien's *The Lord of the Rings*, Arwen is the daughter of Elrond and marries Aragorn to become the queen of elves and men. She is called Evening Star.

ARYA (AHR-yah) Hindi: Noble goddess

ASA (AY-sə) Hebrew: Healer; traditionally a male name; (Japanese) born in the morning; (Norse) goddess

ASAKO (ah-sah-ko) Japanese: Morning child

ASAL (as-al) Persian: Honey

ASDIS (AHS-dees) Norse: Divine spirit; Asdis was a character in Grettir's Saga

ASELMA Gaelic: Fair, divine

ASENATH (AHS-ə-nath) Egyptian: Gift of the sun-god. In the Bible, Asenath is Joseph's Egyptian wife and mother of his sons Manasseh and Ephraim.
Acenath

ASHA (AH-shah) African: Lively, woman, life; variant of Aisha; (Sanskrit) wishes; hope
Ashia

ASHILDE Norse: God fighting
Ashild, Ashilda

ASHIRA Hebrew: Wealthy or I will sing
Asheera, Ashirah

ASHLEY Anglo-Saxon: From the ash tree meadow; a surname and an increasingly popular girl's name in recent years
Aisley, Aisly, Ashla, Ashleah, Ashlee, Ashleen, Ashleena, Ashleigh, Ashlen, Ashlie, Ashly;
Famous namesakes: Actress Ashley Judd, Actress Ashley Olsen; **Star babies:** daughter of Howard Stern

ASHLYNN English: Possible variant of either Ashley or Aisling; possible blend of Ashley and Lynn
Ashlin, Ashlinn, Ashlyn, Ashlynne

ASHTON English: Town of the ash trees; surname
Ashten, Ashtyn; Ashtin, Ashtyn, Ashtynn

ASIA Greek, Latin: The rising sun; a Greek sea-nymph, daughter of Oceanus and Tethys, for whom the continent was named
Aja, Asiah, Azhah

ASIANNE Arabic: Plait, tress, braid; stems from El Assina

ASIMA (ah-SEEM-ah) Arabic: Capital of a country, town; also someone that one turns to for protection or help
Aasema

ASLI Turkish: Genuine, real

ASMA (ahs-MAH) Arabic: Prestige

ASMEE (ahs-mee) Hindi: Self-confident

ASPASIA (as-PAY-zee-ə) Greek: Welcoming, inviting. History remembers the fifth-century bearer of this name as the mistress of famed Greek statesman Pericles and as one of the most beautiful and educated women of her time.

ASPEN (AS-pən) American: Type of tree noted for heart-shaped leaves which flutter in the slightest breeze. Aspen is also a place name of a ski resort town in Colorado.
Star babies: daughter of Tyler England

ASTA Greek, Latin, Swedish, Finnish: Like a star, of the stars; possible diminutive for Augusta, Anastasia, or Astrid
Nicknames: Asteria

ASTARTE (ə-STAHR-tee) Latin: Phoenician predecessor to the Greek Aphrodite, mythology places her as goddess of war, passionate love, and fertility; (Egyptian) goddess of Syrian origin introduced into Egypt during the eighteenth dynasty.

ASTERIA (a-STEER-ee-ə) Latin: Like a star; variant of Asta. In Greek mythology, Asteria hurled herself into the sea after being abducted by Zeus. She became the island of the same name.

ASTHORE (ah-STOR) Irish: Loved one

ASTOLAT Arthurian Legend: In Arthurian legend, Astolat is the home of Elaine, who falls in love with Lancelot, but whose love is unrequited.

ASTRAEA (as-TREE-ə) Greek: Star maiden; Astraea was the daughter of Zeus and Themis, and a goddess of justice. When the gods abandoned earth, Astraea was the last to leave, becoming the constellation Virgo when she finally did.
Astrea

ASTRID Norse, Scandinavian: Divine strength. Popular since the Viking age, this name was borne by Astrid Lindgren, Swedish author of *Pippi Longstocking*.
(Teutonic) *Astred*; *Astlyr, Astrud, Astryd*; **Old forms:** *Astrithr*

ASTYNOME Latin: In Greek mythology, she is daughter of Chryses, probably fathered by Agamemnon, although her mother claimed Apollo was the father.

ASUNCION (ah-soon-see-ON) Spanish: Assumption; refers to the assumption of the Virgin Mary into heaven

ASVOR Norse: Wife of Asrod from Grettir's Saga
Asvora, Asvoria

ATALANTA (a-tə-LAN-tə) Greek, Latin: Immoveable; the name of a female athlete and huntress in Greek mythology who vowed never to marry a man unless he beat her in a race. See also *Atlanta*
Atalante; Atlante

ATALAYA (aht-ah-LIE-ah, aht-ə-LAY-ə) Spanish: Guardtower

ATARA (AT-ə-rə, ah-TAH-rə) Hebrew:

Crown, coronet; related to the word *tiara*
Atarah, Atera, Ateret; **Nicknames:** *Tara*

ATE (AH-tee, AY-tee) Greek: Blindness; she was the Greek goddess of rash decisions and irrationality

ATEPA Native American: Wigwam (Choctaw)

ATHALIA (a-thə-LIE-ə) Hebrew: The Lord is exhalted; Old Testament power-hungry wife of the King of Judah
Athaliah, Athalie

ATHANASIA Greek: Immortal
Atanasia, Atanasya, Athenasia

ATHDARA Irish, Scottish: From the oak tree ford

ATHELAS English: From J.R.R. Tolkien's *Lord of the Rings*, a miraculously nourishing bread

ATHENA (ah-THEE-ə) Greek: Female strength. Mythological goddess of wisdom and war, Athena is the daughter of Zeus but has no mother. She sprang forth from his head, fully grown and fully armed. Her symbol is the owl, and the city of Athens is named for her.
(Latin) *Athene*; **Famous namesakes:** Journalist Athena Desai

ATILDA English: At the elder tree
Athilda

ATIYA Arabic: Gift, present, allowance; feminine form of Atteya
Ateya, Atteya, Atteyah

ATLANTA American: Immoveable; variant of Atalanta and the capital city of the state of Georgia

ATOOSA (ah-too-sah) Persian: Name of a princess

ATROPOS (A-tro-pəs) Greek: In Greek mythology, Atropos was one of the three Fates, or Moirae, female deities who supervised rather than determined outcomes. Atropos was the fate who cut the thread or web of life.
Atropes

ATTHIS Greek: Mythical Greek princess for whom the city of Attica was named

ATTRACTA Latin: Drawn to, attracted; (Irish) name of a saint, healer, and co-worker with Saint Patrick in Ireland. Also called Araght or Taraghta

AUBINA Latin: White
Aubine

AUBREY (AWB-ree) French, English: Elf ruler, implying leadership with supernatural wisdom. Aubrey was originally a male name, only recently becoming popular for girls.
Aubree, Aubrie, Aubry, Avery; Aubary, Aubery, Aubreigh, Aubrette, Aubury; **Star babies:** daughters of Jimmy Connors, Bob Saget

AUBRIANNE French, English: Modern blend of the names Aubrey and Ann, possibly an attempt to endow the originally male name Aubrey with a more feminine sound
Aubriana, Aubrianna

AUBRIELLE English: Blend of Aubrey and Gabrielle

AUDE (OD) French: Old or wealthy
(Norse) *Aud, Auda*

AUDHILDA Norse: Rich warrior woman
Audhild, Audhilde

AUDNEY (AWD-nee) Norse: Prosperity, wealth
Audny

AUDREY (AWD-ree) Anglo-Saxon: Noble strength. Saint Audrey, one-time queen of Northumbria, was known for wearing fancy lace necklaces, which supposedly helped cause her death.
(French) *Audra, Audree, Audrielle; Audelia, Audene, Audre, Audrea, Audreana, Audreanna, Audria, Audriana, Audrianna, Audrie, Audrina, Audris; Audra, Audreen, Audry, Audrye*;
Nicknames: *Audie, Audri, Audi, Audy;* **Famous namesakes:** Actress Audrey Hepburn; **Star babies:** daughter of Faith Hill and Tim McGraw

> "I do not know what poetical is. Is it honest in deed and word? Is it a true thing?"
> —Audrey in Shakespeare's *As You Like It*

AUDRIS Teutonic: Lucky, wealthy
Audfis; Audrisa, Audriss

AUDUNA Norse: Friend of wealth; feminine form of Audun, the Westfjorder from *Grettir's Saga*

AUGUSTA Latin: Majestic; feminine form of Augustine
(English) *Austine;* (Irish) *Augusteen;* (Welsh) *Awsta; Agustina, Augustina, Austen, Austina*;
Nicknames: *Gussie*

AULIS (AW-ləs) Greek: Small port of ancient Greece where the Greek fleet sailed against Troy after the sacrifice of Iphigenia

AURA (AWR-ə) Latin: Gold, subtle light or glow surrounding a subject, also a variant of Aurelia; (Greek) gentle breeze
Aure, Aurea; Ora

AUREAR English: Gentle to hear, music
Auriar

Uncommon Unisex Names

Interested in a gender-free moniker? Here are a few of our favorite not-so-common recommendations:

Austin	Quinn
Avery	Raleigh
Bryce	Reece/Reese
Chaney	Rohan/Rowan/Rowen
Channing	Royce
Chauncey	Rumor/Rumer
Jansen	Sawyer
Kai	Scout
Kalen	Sean/Shawn
Layne	Skylar
Luca/Luka	Sloane/Sloan
Merle	Tate/Tait
Merrill/Meryl	Tayler/Taylor
Peyton	Teague
Piper	Tegan/Teagan/Teigan
Presley	

AURELIA (aw-REL-yə) Latin, Spanish: Golden; originally a Roman clan name (French) *Aurelie, Aurielle, Orane*; (Italian) *Oria*; (Spanish) *Aureliana*; (Hungarian) *Aranka*; *Aureline, Aurene, Auriel, Orali, Oralia, Oralie, Orelia, Orlene, Orlina*; **Nicknames:** *Aura, Ora*

AURELIE (o-ray-LEE) French: Variation of Aurelia

AURNIA Irish: Golden lady

AURORA (ə-ROR-ə) Latin: Dawn. Aurora was the Roman goddess of the dawn and the equivalent of the Greek goddess Eos. Aurora is also the name of the beautiful princess in many versions of *Sleeping Beauty*.
(French) *Aurore*; *Zorah*

AUSET (aw-set, ah-set) Egyptian: Another name for Isis. Most powerful of the female Egyptian goddesses, Isis was consort and sister to Osirus, mother of Horus, and is usually depicted as a motherly woman with arms wide open.
Aset

AUSTEN English: Spelling variation of Augusta

AUSTIN English: A form of the Latin name Augustine, meaning *majestic*. A name traditionally given to boys, Austin is becoming more common for girls.
Austyn

AUTONOE Greek, Latin: With a mind of her own. In Greek mythology, she was the daughter of Cadmus and Harmonia and the mother of Actaeon. In Roman lore, she is the mother of Palaemon by Hercules.

AUTUMN English: Born in the fall, seasonal name
Star babies: daughter of Jermaine Jackson

AVA Hebrew, English: Like a bird; possibly related to the names Aya and Aveline; (Persian) voice
Avah; *Avis*; **Famous namesakes:** Actress Ava Gardner; **Star babies:** daughters of Aidan Quinn, Reese Witherspoon and Ryan Phillippe, Heather Locklear and Richie Sambora, Mark-Paul Gosselaar

AVALLON (AV-ə-lahn) Welsh: Island of apples
Nicknames: *Ava*

AVALON Celtic: Celtic for island of the apples, Avalon is the magical island where the old and the new religions of England meet and overlap in legend. Legends of the island as a paradise probably pre-date Arthur, but the island is most famous as King Arthur's burial place and the place where he will return to earth.
Avaron, Avarona, Avilon

AVANI (ah-VAHN-ee) Sanskrit: Earth

AVASA (ah-VAH-sah) Hindi: Independent

AVELINE (ah-ve-LEEN) French, English: Nut, hazelnut, akin to Hazel
(English) *Avalee, Avelyn, Avlynn*; *Avelaine, Avelina*

AVENA (ah-VAY-nə) Latin: From the oat field
Avina

AVERA Hebrew: Crossing over, transgression

AVERNA Latin: Roman goddess queen of the underworld

AVERY English: Elf ruler, implying leadership with supernatural wisdom; also a variant of Aubrey

AVIANA English: Origin unclear; possible variant or blend of Ava, Anna, or Aviva
Avia, Avianna

AVIANCE English: Bearer of good news; modern blend of Ava and Ana.

AVICE (ah-VEES) French: Warlike

AVIRA Hebrew: Air

AVIS (AY-vis) Latin: Bird; variant of Ava and Aya; (English) refuge in battle

AVISA Persian: Clear water

AVITA Latin: Youthful

AVIVA (ah-VEEV-ah) Hebrew, Latin: Springlike, dewy and fresh, implies innocence and youth; feminine variant of Aviv
Avivah, Avivi, Avivit; Auvit; **Nicknames:** *Viv, Viva*

AVONLEA English: River meadow

AVONMORA Irish: From the great river

AVRIL (av-REEL, AV-ril) French: Variation of April
Averel, Averell, Averil, Averill, Averyl, Avrill; **Famous namesakes:** Canadian singer Avril Lavigne

AWEL (AH-wel) Welsh: Breeze
Awell

AWENASA Native American: My home (Cherokee)

AWENDELA (ah-wayn-DAY-lah) Native American: Morning

AWENITA (ah-way-NEE-tah) Native American: Fawn
Awinita

AWSTA (OWS-tah) Welsh: Variation of Augusta

AXELLE (ahk-SEL) German: Of peace; feminine variant of Axel

AYA Hebrew: Bird; possibly related to the name Avis
Ayla

AYAKO (ah-yah-ko) Japanese: Color, design; may refer to a colorful fabric

AYALA (ie-ah-LAH) Hebrew: Gazelle or hind (female roe deer), suggestive of a graceful, shy animal
Ayalah; **Nicknames:** *Aya*

AYAME (ie-yah-may) Japanese: Iris flower

AYANNA Hebrew: He answers

AYASHA (ah-ya-sha) Native American: Little one (Chippewa)
Ayashe

AYLA (AY-lah) Hebrew: Oak tree; possible variant of Aya. In literature, Ayla is the heroine of Jean Auel's *Clan of the Cave Bear*; (Persian) halo around the moon
(Persian) *Aylin*; *Aila*

AYLIN (Persian: IE-lin, Spanish: ie-LEEN, Contemporary: AY-lin) Persian: Variation of Ayla
Nicknames: *Lin*

AYN (IEN) Hebrew: Variation of Ann
Famous namesakes: Philosopher Ayn Rand

AYSEL (IE-sel) Turkish: Like the moon, like the moonlight

AZADEH Persian: Free

AZALEA (ə-ZAY-lee-ə) Latin: The dry earth; a beautiful flowering shrub closely related to the rhododendron
(Greek) *Azalia*

AZAM (AH-zam) Persian: Greatest, supreme
Aazam

AZAR (ah-ZAR) Persian: Fire, also September

AZARA Persian: Scarlet

AZARIN Persian: Like a fire
Azareen

AZELIA Hebrew: Aided by God; feminine form of Azriel
Azelie, Azriela

AZHAR (ah-ZAHR) Arabic: Flower, blossom, appear. El Azhar University is the world's oldest university and Sunni Islam's foremost seat of learning.

AZIMA (ah-ZEEM-ah) Arabic: Resolute, steady, determined
Azeema, Azeemah

AZIZA (ah-ZEE-zah) Arabic, African, Egyptian: Cherished, beloved
Azizah, Azizeh

AZRIELA Hebrew: God is my strength, God helps me; feminine variant of Aziel and Azriel

AZURA (ah-ZHOO-rə) Persian: Sky-blue
(English) *Azurine*; (French) *Azure*; *Azur*

BAB (BAHB) Arabic: Door, gateway

BABETTE (ba-BET) French: Diminutive form of Barbara

BADRA Persian: Full moon
Nicknames: *Badri*

BAHA Persian: Price, value

BAHAR (BAH-har) Persian: Spring

BAHATI (bah-HAH-tee) African: Lucky, fortunate (Swahili)

BAHIRA Arabic: Dazzling, brilliant, splendid, dazzled by sunlight; feminine form of Bahir
Baheera

BAHRAMAN Persian: Ruby

BAILEY English: Steward or law enforcer from occupation of bailiff; surname adapted to first name use
Bailee, Baylee, Bayley, Baylie; Baileigh, Bailie, Bayleigh; **Star babies:** daughter of Melissa Etheridge

BAKA (bah-kah) Hindi: Crane

BALARA Latin: Strong; variant of Valerie

BALI (BAH-lee) Contemporary: An Indonesian island

BALLARD German: Bold or strong

BAMBI (BAM-bee) Italian: Pet name for Bambino, meaning little child. Bambi is the fawn of Walt Disney's famous movie.

BANAFSHEH Persian: Violet

BANITA (bahn-ee-tah) Hindi: Woman

BANU Turkish: Lady
(Persian) *Banou*

BAPTISTA Greek: Baptizer; feminine form of Baptiste
(Italian) *Baptiste, Battista, Bautista*

BARANEH Persian: Rain; possibly used as a feminine variant of Baran
Baran

BARBARA Latin: Foreign woman, exotic; stems from *barbus*, meaning stranger. In Catholic custom, Saint Barbara is a protectress against fire and lightning. Barbie dolls are a household name throughout the world. (Spanish) *Barvara*; (Gaelic) *Baibin, Bairbre, Barabal, Barabell*; (Swedish) *Barbro*; (Slavic) *Varvara*; (Russian) *Varushka*; (Czech) *Barbora, Baruna, Barunka, Baruska, Varina*; (Polish) *Basha*; (Hungarian) *Borbala, Borhala, Boriska, Borsala, Brosca, Broska; Babara, Vavara; Babarra, Barbera, Varvera*; **Nicknames:** *Babita, Barbie, Basia, Bora, Borka, Vara, Varya, Wava, Bab, Babe, Babs, Bar, Bara, Barb, Barbs, Bora;* **Diminutive forms:** *Babette, Barbarina, Barbina, Varinka;* **Famous namesakes:** Journalist Barbara Walters, singer Barbra Streisand, author Barbara De Angelis, First Lady Barbara Bush

---

"A baby is a blank cheque made payable to the human race."
—Barbara Christine Seifert

BARRAN Irish: Top, summit

BARSIN Persian: Clover

BASILIA Greek: Regal, royal; feminine form of Basileios
Basilea, Basila

BASIMAH (BAH-see-mah) Arabic: Nickname for Ibtesam

BASTET (BAHS-tet) Egyptian: In Egyptian mythology, Bastet was a cat-goddess whose cult-center was at Bubastis in the Nile Delta. In the Late Period, she was regarded as a beneficent deity.

BATHILDA (bah-TIL-dah) German, Teutonic: Warrior woman, commanding, heroic
Bathild, Bathilde, Bertild, Bertilda, Bertilde

BATHSHEBA (bath-SHEE-bə) Hebrew: Daughter of the oath. Bathsheba was the beautiful wife of King David, whom she married after David had her husband Uriah killed in battle. She was the mother of Solomon. *Bethsheba;* **Nicknames:** *Sheba*

BATTZION Hebrew: Daughter of Zion
Battseeyon

BATULA Arabic: Virgin
Batoula

BATYA (BAHT-yah, bah-TEE-ah) Hebrew: God's daughter
Bitya

BAUCIS (BAW-səs) Greek: In mythology, she was the wife of Philemon. Though poor, they were a happy couple and, when tested by the gods, they were found to be generous and giving people.

BEA (BEE) Latin: Nickname for Beatrice
Famous namesakes: Actress Bea Arthur

BEATA (be-AH-tah) Latin: Blessed, happy
(German) *Beate*

BEATHA Celtic: Life
Betha

BEATRICE (BEE-ə-tris) Latin, Italian: Bringer of joy. Author Beatrix Potter is well remembered for the joy she brought countless children with Peter Rabbit and other classic characters. Beatrice is the name of literary heroines ranging from Dante's idyllic heroine in his *Divine Comedy* to Shakespeare's spunky protagonist in *Much Ado about Nothing*. (Spanish) *Beatrisa, Beatriz; Beatricia, Beatrix;* **Nicknames:** *Bea, Trixie, Trixy;* **Famous namesakes:** French actress Béatrice Dalle; **Star babies:** daughters of Alan Alda, Prince Andrew and Sarah Ferguson, Emma Samms and John Holloway, Paul McCartney and Heather Mills, Prince Andrew and Sarah Ferguson

> "But Nature never framed a woman's heart Of prouder stuff than that of Beatrice."
> —William Shakespeare, *Much Ado About Nothing*

BECCA English: Captivating, beautiful; variant of Rebecca

BECKY Hebrew: Captivating, beautiful, desirable, to tie or bind; variant of Rebecca

BEDA English: Battle maiden, female warrior

BEDEGRAINE Arthurian Legend: A surname; Castle and forest where Arthur fought his infamous battle against eleven kings *Bedegrayne*

BEHNOUSH Persian: Pleasant

BEILIN (bay-leen) Chinese: Treasure rain

BELEN (bay-LEN) Spanish: Bethlehem

BELGIN (BEL-geen) Turkish: Dear

BELINDA Latin, Spanish: Beautiful; (Italian) serpentine
Bellinda; **Nicknames:** *Bel, Bella, Belle, Linda*; **Famous namesakes:** Musician Belinda Carlisle

BELKA Russian: Squirrel; also Russian nickname for Bella

BELLAMY (be-lah-MEE) French: Handsome friend; possible variant of Isabella

BELLANCE Italian: White, strong, karmic or predestined; variant of Blanca, meaning white

BELLANGE (be-LAHNZH) French: Beautiful angel
Nicknames: *Belle*

BELLE French: Beautiful, fair, lovely one; an abbreviation of Isabelle. In the fairy tale, *Beauty and the Beast*, Belle is a young woman who teaches the enchanted Beast how to love and is rewarded handsomely for learning to see beyond appearances and trust her heart.
Star babies: daughter of Donna Dixon and Dan Ackroyd

BELLISSA Italian: Fair; lovely one

BELLONA Latin: Goddess of war

BENAZIR (BE-nə-zeer) Arabic: Incomparable. The assassinated prime minister of Pakistan, Benazir Bhutto was the first woman elected to lead a Muslim nation.

BENEDICTA (BEN-ə-dikt-ə) Latin: Blessed; feminine form of Benedict. See also *Benita* (Italian) *Benedetta*; (Swedish) *Bengta*; (Czech) *Benedikta*; *Benecia, Benetta, Benicia, Bente; Benedictine, Benoite;* **Nicknames:** *Bennie, Benny, Binnie, Binny, Dixie;* **Famous namesakes:** Opera singer Benita Valente

BENITA (be-NEE-tah) Spanish: Blessed; common variant of Benedicta

> "Why not say it? I'm bursting out of my cocoon . . . I looked out and heard all that cheering. And it was for me. And I loved it."
> —Opera singer Benita Valente, after twenty-five years on stage

BENTLEY English: From the meadow of coarse or bent grass; Bentley also evokes images of the luxury vehicle. This surname is traditionally a boys' name. However, as with many male monikers ending in "ley," this name is becoming more popular for girls.
Bentlea, Bentleah, Bentlee, Bentleigh

BERDINA (ber-DEE-nah) German: Glorious; (Greek) intelligent maid
Berdine; Berdeena, Berdinna

BERENICE (ber-ə-NIE-see) Greek, French: One who brings victory; spelling variant Bernice is referred to in the New Testament of the Bible
(Spanish) *Bernicia; Bernice, Bernyce, Berynice, Berrenice*; **Nicknames:** *Berny*; **Famous namesakes:** Writer Edgar Allan Poe wrote *Berenice*

BERKELEY (BURK-lee) English: From the birch tree meadow; Berkeley is also a well-known university in California. Originally a surname and traditionally a boys' name, Berkeley is increasingly used for girls.
Berklea, Berkleigh, Berkley

BERNA (bayr-NAH) Turkish: Young

BERNADETTE (ber-na-DET) French: Courage of a bear; feminine form of Bernard. Saint Bernadette was a French peasant girl who was visited by the Virgin Mary at a grotto near Lourdes.
(Irish) *Berneen; Berdine, Bernadea, Bernadina, Bernadine, Bernarda, Bernardina, Bernelle, Bernetta, Bernette, Bernita*; **Nicknames:** *Nadetta, Nadette*; **Famous namesakes:** Actress Bernadette Peters

BERTHA Teutonic, German: Sparkling, bright, splendid
(French) *Berthe*; (Swedish) *Berta*; (Hungarian) *Bertuska*

BERTILDA Teutonic: Warrior woman, commanding, heroic; variant of Bathilda

BERYL (BER-əl) Greek, English: Beryl stones have been historically associated with good luck, eternal youth, and strength. Traditionally pale green, including emeralds and aquamarines, beryl gemstones may also be red or colorless. This birthstone is associated with the astrological sign of Gemini.
Beryla, Beryle; **Nicknames:** *Berri, Bery*

BESS English: Nickname for Elizabeth
Bessie; **Famous namesakes:** Singer Bessie Smith

BETH Hebrew: House; a diminutive of Elizabeth and Bethany. Beth is remembered fondly by generations of readers as the gentle, loving sister in Louisa May Alcott's *Little Women*.
Betsey

BETHAN (BETH-ən) Welsh: Consecrated to God

BETHANY (BETH-ə-nee) Hebrew, Aramaic: A village near Jerusalem where Jesus raised Lazarus from the dead; a possible variant of Beth and Ann
(Spanish) *Bethania; Bethanee, Bethani, Bethanie, Bethann; Bethaney, Bethannie, Bethenny, Betheney, Betheny*

BETHEA (BETH-ee-ah) Hebrew: Maid-servant of Jehovah

BETHELL (BETH-əl) Hebrew: House of God
Bethel, Betheli, Bethelle; Bethuel, Bethuna

BETHIA Hebrew: Daughter, follower of Jehovah
(English) *Betia; Bitia*

BETHUNE (bə-THOON) Hebrew: House of God; variant of Bethell

BETJE Dutch: Devoted to God

BETSY English: God is my oath; a nickname of Elizabeth. Students of American history remember Betsy Ross, a seamstress and flag maker during the American Revolution who is often, and with little evidence, credited with sewing the first Stars and Stripes.

BETTE (BET) French: God is my oath; a familiar form of Elizabeth
Famous namesakes: Actress and singer Bette Midler, actress Bette Davis

BETTINA (be-TEE-nah) German: Nickname for Elizabeth

BETTY English: God is my oath; a variant of Elizabeth
Famous namesakes: Actress Betty White, activist Betty Friedan, First Lady Betty Ford, cookbook author Betty Crocker

BEULAH (BYOO-lə) Hebrew: To marry, claimed as a wife. In the Bible, Beulah is a name symbolic of the heavenly Zion.
Beula

BEVERLY English: From the beaver stream or meadow; a surname and place name of Beverly Hills, California. Traditionally a boys' name, Beverly is now more commonly used for girls.
Beverlee, Beverley; Beverle, Beverlee, Beverlie, Beverlye, Bevlyn; **Nicknames:** *Bev, Buffy, Verlee, Verlie, Verly, Verlye;* **Famous namesakes:** Singer Beverly Sills; **Star babies:** daughter of Sidney Poitier

BEVIN (BAY-vin) Irish: Fair lady, melodious one; an Anglicized variant of Bebhinn
Bebhinn

BEYONCE (bee-YAHN-say) American: Unknown
Famous namesakes: Singer Beyoncé Knowles

BHADRA (bah-drah) Hindi: Auspiciousness unto thee

BHARATI (bah-rah-tee) Hindi: India, being maintained; feminine form of Bharat

BHUMA (boo-mah) Hindi: Earth

BIA (BEE-ah) Greek: Goddess of force; winged enforcer for her father Zeus
Bya, Beeya; **Nicknames:** *Bee*

BIANCA (bee-AHN-kah) Italian: White, shining; variant of Blanche
Bianka; **Star babies:** daughter of Jean-Claude Van Damme

BIBIANA (bee-BYAH-nah) Latin: Animated; (Persian) lady
Nicknames: *Bibi*

BIENVENIDA (bee-EN-vay-NEE-dah) Spanish: Welcome

BIJOU (BEE-zhoo) French: Jewelry
Star babies: daughter of John Phillips

BILGE (beel-GAY) Turkish: Wise, intelligent

BILINA (bee-lee-nah) Aramaic: Iris of the beautiful eyes

BILLIE English: Nickname for Wilhelmina
Famous namesakes: Singer Billie Holiday, tennis star Billie Jean King; **Star babies:** daughter of Carrie Fisher

BINAH African: Dancer

BINDI (BIN-dee) Sanskrit: Drop; auspicious sign on the third eye
Star babies: daughter of Crocodile Hunter Steve Irwin

BINTA African: With God

BIRDIE English: Bird, like a bird; contemporary name referring to our fine feathered friends and their characteristics and talents
Birdena, Birdine, Birdy, Byrdene

BIRGIT (BEER-git) Scandinavian: Variation of Bridget
Nicknames: *Britta*

BISA African: Greatly loved

BITA Persian: Unique

BITHYNIA (bə-THIN-ee-ə) Latin: An ancient kingdom in Asia Minor

BLAKELEY Anglo-Saxon: From the dark or pale meadow; surname traditionally used for boys but, like many English names ending in "ley," is increasingly popular for girls
Blakelee, Blakely, Blaknee, Blakeney, Blakeny; **Nicknames:** *Blake*

BLANCHE (BLAWNSH, BLANCH) French: White
(Czech) *Blanka*; *Blanch*; **Famous namesakes:** Publisher Blanche Knopf

BLANCHEFLEUR French: White flower

BLANDINA Latin: Mild, fair-haired, blond
(French) *Blondell, Blondelle, Blondene*; **Nicknames:** *Blondie*

BLESSING English: Consecration
Bletsung

BLISS Anglo-Saxon, English: Intense joy; a name used since medieval times
Blisse, Bliths, Blyss, Blysse; *Blysse*

BLITHE (BLIETH) English: Cheerful, lighthearted
Blythe; **Famous namesakes:** Actress Blythe Danner

BLODWEN (BLOD-wen) Welsh: White flower
Blodwyn

BLOSSOM English: Blossom, flower
Star babies: daughter of Kacey Ainsworth

BO English: A name made popular by actress Bo Derek; (Scandinavian) commanding; (Chinese) precious

BOADICEA (bo-di-SEE-ə) Anglo-Saxon: Victorious. A queen of the Iceni when the Romans invaded Britain, Boadicea was beaten in an attempt to intimidate her people. She became a fierce enemy of the Romans until their more organized forces finally captured her.
Bodiccea, Bodicea, Bodicia, Boudicea

BOBBI English: Modern diminutive of Roberta and Barbara
Famous namesakes: Family therapist, author, and personal historian Bobbi Fischer; **Star babies:** daughter of Whitney Houston and Bobby Brown

BODIL Norse, Danish: Commanding battle
Bodile, Bothild, Botilda

BOGDANA (bawg-DAH-nah) Polish: God's gift; feminine form of Bogdan
Bohdana; **Nicknames:** *Bogna*

BOHUSLAVA Czech, Ukrainian: God's glory; feminine form of Boguslaw

BOLANILE (bo-la-NEE-lah) African: Finds wealth at home

BOLBE Latin: A mythical nymph

BOLIVIA American: Place name for a country in South America

BOLOUR Persian: Crystal

BONITA (bo-NEE-tə) Spanish: Pretty little one

BONNIE Scottish, English: Pretty, charming, beautiful; This Scottish term is likely a derivation of the French word *bon*, meaning *good* or *nice*.
Bonni, Bonny; **Famous namesakes:** Singer Bonnie Raitt, speed skater Bonnie Blair

BOUSSEH Persian: Kiss

BRADLEIGH (BRAD-lee) English: From the broad meadow. This surname has been adapted to widespread first-name use.
Bradlea, Bradlie, Bradly, Bradney

BRANDY English: A type of alcoholic beverage used as a given name; possibly a variant of Brandeis or Brendan
Branda, Brande, Brandee, Brandi, Brandice, Brandie, Brandilyn, Brandyce, Brandyn; Brandais, Brandea, Brandess, Brandye, Branndais, Brannde, Branndea, Branndi;
Famous namesakes: Actress Brandy Ledford

BREANDAN Gaelic: Little raven

BREENA Gaelic: Fairy palace; also variant of Brianna and Sabrina
Nicknames: *Breen*

BRENDA Teutonic: Sword; a feminine form of Brendan; (Gaelic) little raven
Famous namesakes: Actress Brenda Vaccaro

BRENNA Celtic, Irish: Raven, black-haired; also used as a variant of Brenda
(English) *Brynna*

BRETT English: A person from Britain or Brittany. Brett is derived from a French surname and was co-opted by the English as a first name for both girls and boys. Lady Brett Ashley is the heroine of Hemingway's *The Sun Also Rises*.
Bret

BRIALLEN (bree-AL-en) Welsh: Primrose
Briallan

BRIANNA Celtic, English, Irish: Strong or ascends; feminine form of Brian
Breanne, Briana, Briann, Briannah, Brianne, Briannon, Brielle, Brienna, Brienne, Brina, Bryana, Bryann, Bryanna, Bryanne, Bryna; Breanna, Briana, Breana; **Diminutive forms:** *Brea, Bree*; **Famous namesakes:** Journalist Bree Walker

BRICELYN English: Spelling variation of Bryce
Bricelynn, Brycelyn, Brycelynn, Bricelin, Bricelinn, Brycelin, Brycelinn

BRIDGET (BRIJ-ət) Irish: Strength, power; Brighid is an ancient name borne by the mythological Irish goddess of poetry, wisdom, and song, as well as Ireland's fifth-century patron Saint Brighid. See also *Zytka* (German) *Brigitta*; (French) *Brigitte*; (Italian) *Brigida*; (Spanish) *Brigidita*; (Portuguese) *Brites*; (Celtic) *Brigid*; (Irish) *Brighid*; (Welsh) *Ffraid*; (Scandinavian) *Birgit, Britt, Britta*; (Swedish) *Birget, Birgitta*; (Polish) *Brygida*; (Finnish) *Pirjo*; *Brigetta; Bridgett, Bridgette, Brietta, Brigette*; **Nicknames:** *Biddy, Bidelia, Brid, Bride, Brit*; **Diminutive forms:** *Gitta*;
Famous namesakes: Actress Bridget Fonda, Model Bridget Hall, French actress Brigitte Bardot

BRIELLA English: Exalted beauty

BRIGANTIA Celtic: Bright light; Celtic goddess representing healing, awakening, and rebirth

BRIGHTON English: From the bright town; Brighton is a seaside town in southern England. A surname traditionally used for boys, Brighton may become more gender neutral in the future.
Bryton

BRIGITTE (bree-ZHEET) French: Variation of Bridget
Famous namesakes: Actress Brigitte Bardot

BRINLEY (BRIN-lee) American: Virtuous, princess
Brinleigh, Brinlee, Brinlea, Brinlie, Brynley, Brynleigh, Brynlee, Brynlea, Brynlie, Brynnley, Brynnleigh, Brynnlee, Brynnlea, Brynnlie

BRINNA (BRIN-ah) German: Warrior; superior sword
Briyna, Brina

BRIONY (BRIE-ən-ee) English: Botanical name, a flowering perennial vine with heart-shaped leaves and a root used in some folk medicine; variant of Bryony

BRISEIS (bri-SAY-is) Greek: Captive maiden given to Achilles
(Spanish) *Brisa, Brisha, Brisia, Briza*

BRIT Celtic: A person from Britain or Brittany. Brit was derived from a French surname. In recent history, the name Brittany has become so popular that many do not realize that Brit was the original, not a nickname.

BRITANNIA Latin: A poetic name for Great Britain; also variant of names Brit/Brittany
Britania, Brittannia

BRITTANY English, Celtic: A native of Brittany (originally the ancient duchy of Bretagne in France) or Britain. The surname Brit became a given name, Brett, in the English language and in recent history has given rise to longer and more feminine-sounding variants.
(Norse) *Brit*; *Brettany, Britani, Britney, Brittaney, Brittani, Brittania, Brittanie, Brittanya, Brittnee, Brittney, Brittni*;
Nicknames: *Bret, Brett, Bretta, Brette, Brite, Britta*; **Famous namesakes:** Singer Britney Spears

BRONISLAVA Czech: Protecting glory; feminine form of Bronislaw
Branislava; **Nicknames:** *Bronya*

BRONTE (BRAHN-tay, BRAHN-tee) English: Surname, probably derived from the Gaelic word meaning *bestower*
Famous namesakes: Authors Emily, Anne, and Charlotte Bronte

BRONWYN (BRAHN-wen) Welsh: Fair raven or white-breasted. According to Welsh myth, Branwen is the sister of Bran and wife of Irish king Matholwych.
Brangwen, Branwen, Branwenn, Branwyn, Bronwen; *Bronwin*; **Star babies:** daughter of Angela Bassett and Courtney B. Vance

BROOKE English: Near the small stream. Once a first name originally used for boys, Brooke is now used often for girls as well, especially when spelled with an "e" at the end.
Brook, Brooklyn, Brooklynn, Brooklynne; **Star babies:** daughter of Chynna Phillips and William Baldwin

BROOKLYN English: Small stream, bringing forth, and a borough of New York City; variant of Brooke
Brookelyn, Brooklynn; **Star babies:** daughter of Donna Summer

BRUNA (BROO-nah) German: Brown, dark-haired; feminine form of Bruno
Brune, Brunetta

BRUNELLE (broo-NEL) French: Dark-haired
Brunella

BRUNHILDA (broon-HIL-dah) German, Teutonic, Norse: Armor-wearing warrior maiden. The mythological Brunhilda is one of the Valkyries.
Brunhild, Brunhilde, Brunnehilde, Brynhild, Brynhilde; **Nicknames:** *Hilda, Hilde, Hildie, Hildy*

BRYCE (BRIES) Latin: Son of a nobleman, though *child* of nobleman makes more sense for girls with this given name which was once reserved for boys. It is now used for both genders *Bricelyn*; *Brice*; **Star babies:** daughter of Ron Howard

BRYLEE (BRIE-lee) American: Noble, strong, meadow
Bryley, Bryleigh, Brylea, Brylie

BRYNNA English: Variation of Brenna
Brinna

BRYONY (BRIE-ən-ee) English: Botanical name for a flowering perennial vine with heart-shaped leaves and a root used in folk medicine
Brione, Brioni, Brionna, Brionne, Briony, Bryani; *Bryoney, Bryonie*

BUENA (BWAY-nah) Spanish: Good

BUFFY American: Nickname for Elizabeth

BURCU (BOOR-joo) Turkish: Sweet scent

BURGUNDY (BER-gən-dee) American: A region in France famous for its wine; also a color name, referring to a deep red

BYHALIA (bie-HAL-ee-ah) Native American: White oak standing (Choctaw)

CADENCE Latin: Rhythmic flow of sounds
(Italian) *Cadenza*; *Cadena, Cadencia, Cadyna*; **Nicknames:** *Cadee, Cadi, Cadie, Cady, Kady*

CADHA Scottish: From the steep place

CADHLA (KIE-lah) Irish: Beautiful

CADIE (KAY-dee) English: Nickname for Cadence
Cadee, Cady

CAELA (KAY-lə) Gaelic: Slender

CAELESTA (kie-LES-tə) Latin: Heavenly
Nicknames: *Caelia, Caeli*

CAIETA Latin: In Roman mythology, the wet nurse of Aeneas

CAILIN (KAY-lin) Irish: Girl; variant of Colleen
Caelan, Caileen, Cailyn, Caylin

CAIRO (KIE-ro) English: Cairo is a place name for the capital of Egypt.
Star babies: daughter of Beverly Peele

CAITLIN (KAYT-lin) Irish: Pure, innocent; variant of Catherine
Caitilin, Caitlyn, Caitlan, Caitland, Caitlinn, Caitlyn, Caitlynn, Catelyn, Catlin, Catline, Catlyn, Kaitlan, Kaitleen, Kaitlin, Kaitlyn, Kaitlynn, Katelin, Kateline, Katelinn, Katelyn, Katelynn, Katlin, Katlyn, Katlynn, Katlynne;
Nicknames: *Cait, Caitie*; **Famous namesakes:** Musician Caitlin Cary

CALANDRA (kah-LAHN-drə) Greek: Beautiful one or name given to a lark
(French) *Calandre*; (Spanish) *Calandria*; *Calyndra*; **Nicknames:** *Calla, Calli*

CALANTHA (kə-LAN-thə) Greek: Lovely blossom
(French) *Calanthe*

CALEDONIA (kal-e-DO-nyə) Latin: From Scotland
Star babies: daughter of Shawn Colvin

CALIANA Arabic: A castle or tower; Caliana was a Moorish princess for whom a splendid palace was built in Spain.
Kaliana

CALIDA (kah-LEE-də) Latin: Ardent, warm, or loving; (Greek) the most beautiful
Callida; **Nicknames:** *Calla, Calli*

CALINA Russian: Snowball tree

CALINDA Hindi: The sun; variant of Kalinda; (English) most likely a modern blend of names such as Carolyn/Calandra/Cassandra with Linda

CALLAGHAN (KAL-ə-han) Irish: Strife
Callahan, Ceallach

CALLEN Gaelic: Powerful in battle
Calynn

CALLIA Greek: Beautiful voice

CALLIE (KAL-ee) Greek, Gaelic: Most beautiful; pet form of Callista and other names beginning with Cal–
Kahli, Kalli, Kallie, Kallita, Kally; Cahli, Calli, Cally

CALLIGENIA Greek: Born of beauty

CALLIOPE (kə-LIE-ə-pee) Greek: Beautiful voice; describes a mythological muse for epic poetry and a musical instrument filled with steam whistles
Kalliope

CALLISTA (kə-LIS-tə) Greek: Most beautiful. In mythology, Callista was tricked by Zeus and as a result gave birth to a son, Arcas. Hera transformed Callista into a bear, and when she was almost killed by her hunting son, both were transformed into constellations, creating Ursa Major and Ursa Minor. Callisto is also a moon of Jupiter.
Calissa, Calista, Calisto, Calliste, Callisto, Calysta, Kallista; **Nicknames:** *Cali, Calla, Calli, Kallie*; **Famous namesakes:** Actress Calista Flockhart

CALLULA Latin: Beautiful

CALVINA Latin: Bald; feminine form of Calvin
Calvinna

CALYBE Latin: A mythical nymph, small hut

CALYCE Latin: In Greek mythology, Calyce was the mother of King Cycnus.

CALYPSO (ka-LIP-so) Greek: Hidden; the mythological sea nymph and daughter of Atlas who beguiled Odysseus for seven years. Calypso is also a West Indies style of singing.

CAM (KAM) Vietnamese: Sweet orange

CAMBRIA (KAM-bree-ə) English: Place name originating from the Latin word for Wales
Kambria; Cambrya, Kambrya; **Nicknames:** *Cambrie*

CAMDEN Scottish: From the winding valley; a surname adapted to first name use, and a place name of a section of London.
Camdyn, Kamden, Kamdyn

CAMELIA Latin, English: Evergreen tree or bush with white or red roselike blossoms known for their beauty and fragrance
Camella, Camellia, Kamelia, Kamella

CAMEO Latin, English: Portrait, usually of an elegant woman, carved on a shell or jewel
Cammeo; Kameo; **Nicknames:** *Cami*

CAMERON Gaelic: Crooked nose; the name of a great Highland clan
Kameron, Kamren, Kamron, Kamryn; Camryn; **Famous namesakes:** Actress Cameron Diaz, actress Camryn Manheim

CAMILLA Latin: Possibly indicates the beautiful ceremonial girl who assisted in ancient pagan rites. See also *Kamila, Milla* (French) *Camille*; (Polish) *Kamilka, Kamilla*; (Egyptian) *Kamilah; Camile, Cammi, Kamille, Kamlyn*; **Nicknames:** *Milja*; **Famous namesakes:** Prince Charles' wife Camilla Parker-Bowles

The Way of the Warrior

Want to arm your child with a name he or she can take into life's daily battles?
Here are some names meaning "brave" or "strong."

Boys' Names

Aitan (Hebrew)
Albern (English)
André (French)
Andreas (Swedish)
Armstrong (English)
Arnold (Teutonic)
Arseni (Russian)
Artur (Celtic)
Baldwin (Teutonic)
Beamard (Irish)
Balen (Latin)
Bern (Scandinavian)
Bernhard (German)
Cathal (Irish)
Durango (Spanish)
Emory (English)
Ethan (Hebrew)
Everett (English)
Farrel (Celtic)
Garet (English)
Gifford (English)
Harding (English)
Hartman (German)
Helmut (German)
Honovi (Native American)
Jabari (African)
Karl (German)
Ken (Japanese)
Maynard (Anglo-Saxon)
Merrick (Teutonic)
Prewitt (French)
Reginald (Teutonic)
Reinhard (German)
Riley (Gaelic)
Songaa (Native American)
Tracey (Anglo-Saxon)
Urho (Finnish)
Valiant (English)
Oz (Hebrew)
Zytka (Polish)

Girls' Names

Adira (Hebrew)
Allona (Hebrew)
Arthurine (English)
Artura (Spanish)
Bernadette (French)
Briana (Celtic)
Bridget (Irish)
Caci (Gaelic)
Carla (German)
Caroline (Latin)
Isa (German)
Karel (Czech)
Kemina (Spanish)
Magnilda (German)
Mathilda (French)
Maude (French)
Melicent (Teutonic)
Millicent (German)
Nadette (German)
Nadina (German)
Naja (African)
Nalda (Spanish)
Nina (Native American)
Raina (Teutonic)
Ricarda (Spanish)
Tarsha (Native American)
Tyra (Scandinavian)
Valentina (Russian)
Valerie (Latin)

CAMPBELL (KAM-bəl) Scottish: Crooked mouth; name of a famous Highland clan **Famous namesakes:** Journalist Campbell Brown

CANAN (jah-NAHN) Turkish: Beloved

CANDACE (KAN-dis) Latin: Dazzling white; Candace was also an ancient hereditary title used by Ethiopian queens. (Greek) *Candance*; (French) *Candide*; *Candice, Candida, Candiss, Candyce, Kandace, Kandice, Kandis, Kandiss, Kandyce*; **Nicknames:** *Candi, Candie, Candy, Kandee, Kandi, Kandy, Kandie*; **Famous namesakes:** Actress Candice Bergen

CANEADEA (KAHN-ee-ah-DEE-ah) Native American: Where the heavens lay upon the earth, the horizon (Iroquois). The country name, Canada, may be derived from this name. *Canada*

CANENS Latin: A mythological nymph, Canens was the wife of King Picus and the personification of song.

CANNIA Latin: Song

CANTARA (cahn-tah-rah) Arabic: Bridge

CAOILFHIONN (KEE-lin) Gaelic: Slender and fair

CAOIMHE (KEE-va, KWEE-va) Irish: Beautiful

CAPRICE (kə-PREES) Italian: Fanciful, whimsical; derived from the Italian word capriccio *Kaprice, Kapricia, Kaprisha*; **Nicknames:** *Kapri*

CAPUCINE (kah-poo-SEEN) French: Nasturtium *Capucina*

CARA (KAHR-ə, KER-ə) Italian: Beloved, darling; (Celtic) friend (Spanish) *Carisa*; (Scandinavian) *Carita*; *Carissima, Carrissa*; *Carah*; **Nicknames:** *Cari, Carina, Carinna*

CARALISA Latin: Beloved.

CARDEA (KAR-dee-ə) Latin: The mythological goddess of thresholds and protectress of hinges

CARELLA Latin: Beloved. *Caralea, Caralee*; **Nicknames:** *Cari*

CAREN English: Spelling variation of Karen

CARESSE French: Endearing, tender touch *Caress, Caressa, Carressa*

CAREY (KER-ee) Welsh: Near the castle *Cary, Karee, Kary*

CARIDAD (kah-ree-DAHD) Spanish: Variation of Charity **Nicknames:** *Cari*

CARILLIE Latin: Beloved.

CARINA (kə-REE-nə) Latin: Keel; one of the five stars in the Orion constellation; (Italian) little darling *Carena, Cariana, Carine, Carinna, Carrina, Caryna, Karina*

CARISSA (kə-RIS-ə) Greek, Italian: Beloved; very dear person *Karessa, Karisa, Karissa*

CARLA German: Strong; also a familiar form of Carolyn (German) *Karla*; (Irish) *Carleen*; (Scandinavian) *Karlee, Karlin*; (Contemporary) *Karlesha*; *Karleen, Karleigh, Karlen, Karlene, Karlyn*; **Nicknames:** *Carly, Karley, Karli, Karlie, Karly, Carlie*; **Diminutive**

forms: *Carlita*; **Famous namesakes:** Actress Carla Gugino, singer Carly Simon

CARLEEN Irish: Variation of Carla
Carlene

CARLIN (KAHR-lən) Irish: Little champion
Carlinn, Carlyn, Carlynn, Karlin, Karlinn, Karlyn, Karlynn

CARLOTTA Italian: Variation of Charlotte

CARMELA Hebrew: Garden, orchard, vineyard; Mount Carmel in Israel is considered a paradise.
(Italian) *Carmelina, Carmeline*; (Spanish) *Carmelita, Carmina*; *Carmella, Carmelle, Karmel, Karmelit, Karmelita, Karmelle, Karmit*; **Nicknames:** *Carmel, Carmencita, Melita*

CARMEN Latin: Song. Carmen is well known as the main character in Bizet's opera, *Carmen*, based on a short novel by the French author Prosper Merimee. A beautiful gypsy, Carmen becomes entangled in love affairs that lead her to a tragic ending.
(Spanish) *Carmita*; *Carmia, Carmin, Carmina, Carmine, Karmen, Karmia, Karmina*; **Famous namesakes:** Singer Carmen Miranda; **Star babies:** daughter of Robert Plant

CARNA Latin: The name of at least two figures in Roman mythology: the goddess of bodily organs and a nymph with power over door handles

CARO (KER-o) English: Nickname for Caroline

CAROL Gaelic, English: Melody, song; feminine form of Carl
(English) *Carolan*; (German) *Carola, Karola*; (French) *Carole*; (Spanish) *Carrola*; *Carolanne, Carroll, Caryl, Karol, Karole*;

Famous namesakes: Comedienne Carol Burnett, singer Carol King, actress Carole Lombard

CAROLA (ker-OL-ah) German: Variation of Carol
Karola

CAROLANN English: A blend of Carol (song) and Ann (graceful)

CAROLINE Latin: Strong. Caroline is the feminine form of Carolus (manly), which is the Latin form of Charles. See also *Carla, Carol* (German) *Karolina*; (Italian) *Carolina*; (Scandinavian) *Karoline*; (Finnish) *Karoliina*; *Caralyn, Carilyn, Carilynne, Caroliana, Carolyne, Carolynn, Karlin, Karlina, Karline*; *Caraleen, Caraleena, Caraline*; **Nicknames:** *Caro*; **Famous namesakes:** First daughter Caroline Kennedy Schlossberg, Princess Caroline of Monaco; **Star babies:** daughter of Katie Couric

CAROLYN English: Little woman; variant of Caroline
Karalyn, Karalynn

CARRIE English: Familar variant of Carol, Carla, and Caroline
Caree, Carree; **Star babies:** daughter of Dick Van Dyke

CARRINGTON English: Origin is not entirely clear, but it refers to a town; English surname
Carington

CARSON English: Child of Carr; a name originally for boys, now used for both genders
Carsyn, Carsynn, Carsen, Karson, Karsyn, Karsen, Karcyn, Karcen; **Famous namesakes:** Writer Carson McCullers

CARYS (KAH-ris) Welsh: Love
Karis; *Karis*; **Star babies:** daughter of Michael Douglas and Catherine Zeta-Jones

CASEY (KAY-see) Irish: Vigilant; (Greek) familiar form of Acacia
(English) *K.C.*; *Cacey, Caci, Cacia, Casee, Caycee, Kacee, Kacey, Kaci, Kacia, Kacie, Kacy, Kasey, Kasie, Kayce, Kaycee, Kayci, Kaycie*

CASPERIA Latin: Second wife of Rhoetus

CASSANDRA (kə-SAHN-drə) Greek: Helper of men. In Homer's epic poem *The Iliad*, King Priam's daughter Cassandra foretold the ending of the Trojan war, but her warnings were tragically ignored.
(Spanish) *Casandra, Kasandra*; *Cassandrea, Cassaundra, Cassondra, Kasondra, Kassandra, Kassondra*; **Nicknames:** *Cassi, Cassie, Cassy, Kassi, Kassie, Casey*; **Star babies:** daughter of Charlie Sheen

CASSIA (KA-shə) Greek: Cinnamon; Hebrew variant Keziah was one of Job's daughters in the Bible
(Hebrew) *Keziah*; *Kassia*

CASSIDY (KAS-i-dee) Irish, Gaelic: Clever or curly-headed
Caiside, Kassidy; **Star babies:** daughters of Maurice Banard, Kathie Lee and Frank Gifford

CASSIE English: Familiar form of Cassandra, Cassiopeia, Cassidy, and similar names
Cassi, Cassy, Kassi, Kassie, Kassy

CASSIOPEIA (ka-see-o-PEE-ə) Greek: In Greek mythology, Cassiopeia was the mother of Andromeda. According to legend, both women are now constellations.

CASTA Latin, Spanish: Pure, modest one

CASTALIA Greek: According to Greek mythology, Castalia was a nymph loved by Apollo. A spring of water was named after her as the sacred fountain of the Muses.

CAT (Ka) Irish: Nickname for Catherine

CATALINA (kah-tah-LEE-nah) Spanish: Variation of Catherine

CATARINA (kah-tah-REE-nah) Italian: Variation of Catherine

CATH Welsh: Cat

CATHERINE Greek: Pure, innocent; a traditional female name having variations in many languages and used since the third century AD. Early Latin forms Katerina and Caterina became Katharine and Catherine.
(German) *Katharina, Katrin*; (Italian) *Catarina*; (Spanish) *Catalina*; (Portuguese) *Catrina*; (Gaelic) *Caitrin, Catriona*; (Welsh) *Catrin*; (Norse) *Trine*; (Scandinavian) *Katrina*; (Swedish) *Katarina*; (Danish) *Katrine*; (Dutch) *Tryn*; (Basque) *Catalin*; (Russian) *Ekaterina*; (Czech) *Katerina*; (Polish) *Katanyna*; (Finnish) *Katariina, Katri, Katriina*; (Hungarian) *Katakin, Katalin*; *Caitriona, Catalyn, Catarine, Cateline, Catharina, Catharine, Catherin, Catheryn, Catheryna, Cathlyn, Cathrine, Cathryn, Katalina, Katalyn, Katarin, Katarzyna, Katerine, Kati, Katilyn, Katina, Katine, Katlyn, Katriana, Katriane*; Nicknames: *Cat, Cate, Cathi, Cathia, Cathie, Cathy, Catia, Catlee, Cattee, Kajsa, Kat, Kate, Katie, Katiya, Katja, Katy, Katya, Kit, Kitty, Riina, Trina, Karen*; **Diminutive forms:** *Catrinetta, Catrinette, Kätchen, Katica, Katyenka, Katyushka*; **Famous namesakes:** Russian empress Catherine the Great, French actress Catherine Deneuve

CATHLEEN Irish: Spelling variation of Kathleen

CATRICE (cat-REES) English: Modern blend of Catrina and Patrice; derived from the Latin word *catarata*, meaning *waterfall*

CATRIONA (ka-TREE-na, ka-TREE-o-na)
Gaelic: Variation of Catherine

CAYENNE (kie-EN) English: Biting; the
name of a very hot pepper

CECILIA Latin: Dim-sighted, blind. Saint
Cecilia, the patron saint of music, was blind
and a talented musician. See also *Sheila*
(English) *Cecily, Cicely, Cicily*; (German)
Silke; (French) *Cecile, Cecille*; (Gaelic) *Sighle*;
(Scandinavian) *Silje*; (Czech) *Cilka*; (Finnish)
Silja; (Hungarian) *Cili*; *Cecelia, Cecilee,
Cecilie, Cicilia, Zezili, Zezilia*; **Nicknames:**
Ceil, Cele, Celia, Celie, Cece; **Famous
namesakes:** Model Cecilia Chancellor; **Star
babies:** daughter of Vera Wang

CEDRICA (SED-rik-ə) English: Chief, battle
chieftain; feminine variant of Cedric, a name
of Celtic origin
Cedrina; **Nicknames:** *Cedra*

CEINWEN (KAYN-wen) Welsh: Lovely,
blessed

CELANDINE (SEL-ən-deen) Greek: A
swallow
Celandina

CELESTE (sə-LEST) French: Heavenly;
from the Latin name Celestia
(French) *Celesse, Celestiel, Celestine*; (Spanish)
Celesta, Celestina; *Celestia*; *Celestyna*

CELIA Latin: Of the heavens; familiar form
of Cecilia

CELINA Greek: Heavenly; Greek goddess
of the moon, one of seven mythological
daughters of Atlas transformed by Zeus into
stars of the Pleiades constellation

CELINE (sə-LEEN) French: Gem from
heaven. See also *Celina*
(Greek) *Zelena*; (English) *Zelene*; (Spanish)
Selena; *Celena, Celene, Celenne, Celicia,
Celinda, Celinna, Salena, Salina, Selene, Selia,
Selina, Xalina*; **Famous namesakes:** Singer
Celine Dion

CELLA (CHEL-ah) Italian: Nickname for
Marcella

CELOSIA (see-LO-zee-ə) Greek: Burning

CENDRILLON (sen-dree-ON) French: Of
the ashes
Cinderella

CENOBIA (say-NO-bee-ah) Spanish:
Variation of Zenobia

CERDWIN (KAIR-dwin) Celtic: The mother
goddess

CERELIA Latin, English: Of the spring,
fertile; possible variant of Cyril, which means
lady
Cerella, Cirilla, Sarelia; *Sarilia*

CEREN (jer-EN) Turkish: Young gazelle

CERES (SIR-eez) Latin: Goddess of the
harvest and love for children in Roman
mythology, equivalent to the Greek goddess
Demeter

CERIA Italian: Form of Cyrilla

CERIDWEN (ke-RID-wen) Welsh: Blessed
poetry; the name of a Celtic mythological
poetry goddess

CERISE (sə-REEZ) French: Variation of
Cherry

CESARINA Latin: Long-haired; feminine
form of Caesar
Kesare

CHABA Hebrew: Life, a primitive root

CHAHNA (chah-nah) Hindi: Love and light

CHALINA (chah-LEE-nah) Spanish: Form of Rosa

CHALIPA Persian: Cross

CHANAH Hebrew: Spelling variation of Hannah

CHANDRA (CHAHN-drah) Sanskrit: Of the moon
Candra, Chanda, Chandaa, Chandara, Chandi, Chaundra

CHANEL (shə-NEL) French: Surname used as first name; popularized through the fame of French haute couture designer Gabrielle "Coco" Chanel
Chanell, Chanelle, Channelle, Chenelle; Shanel, Shanelle

CHANNA (chah-nah) Hindi: Chickpea
Nicknames: *Chan, Shan*

CHANNING English, French: Of uncertain origin, possibly related to French meaning *canal* or indicating a church official. The spelling is suggestive of a paternal meaning such as Chan or Cana's child.

CHANTAL (shawn-TAL) French: Song, singer
Chantae, Chantalle, Chantay, Chante, Chantel, Chantell, Chantelle, Chantrell, Chaunte, Chauntel

CHARDAE (shahr-DAY) French: Nickname for Charlotte

CHARIS (KAR-is) Greek: Grace and beauty
Carrissa, Charissa, Karis

CHARISH English: Held dearly, beloved

CHARITY Latin, English: Benevolent

goodwill and love; a theological virtue
(Spanish) *Caridad*; *Chariety*

CHARLA English: Nickname for Charlotte

CHARLAINE (shahr-LAYNE) French: Variation of Charlotte

CHARLENE English: Variation of Charlotte

CHARLISA French: Manly; feminine form of Charles

CHARLIZE (shar-LEES) French: Variation of Charlotte
Famous namesakes: Actress Charlize Theron

CHARLOTTE French: Strong, a feminine form of Charles and the name of many Queens in history, including wife of King George III of England, after whom a major city in North Carolina is named. It is also the name of the clever and kind-hearted arachnid heroine of E.B. White's *Charlotte's Web*.
(English) *Charlene*; (German) *Karlotta*; (French) *Charlaine, Charlize*; (Italian) *Carlotta*; (Spanish) *Carlota*; (Irish) *Searlait*; (Russian) *Sharlotta*; *Charlayne, Charleen, Charleena, Charlena, Charlette, Charline, Charlyn, Charlynn*; **Nicknames:** *Chardae, Charla, Charlee, Charli, Charlisa, Charly, Lotta, Lotte, Lotye, Sharlene*; **Diminutive forms:** *Charlita*; **Famous namesakes:** French actress Charlotte Gainsbourg, Welsh singer Charlotte Church, actress Charlotte Rae, Author Charlotte Brontë; **Star babies:** daughters of Jane Birkin and Serge Gainsbourg, Pierce Brosnan and Cassandra Harris, Sigourney Weaver, Amy Brenneman

CHARMAINE (shahr-MAYN) French, English: Feminine form of Charles; Charmain was one of Cleopatra's attendants in Shakespeare's *Antony and Cleopatra*.
Charmae, Charmain, Charmayne, Charmine

CHARO (CHAHR-o) Spanish: Nickname for Rosario

CHARUMATI (char-oo-mah-tee) Hindi: A beautiful mind, one who is wise

CHARYBDIS (kə-RIB-dəs) Latin: A deadly whirlpool characterized as a female monster in Greek mythology

CHASTITY Latin: Purity; a virtue name
Chasity, Chastina, Chastine; **Nicknames:** *Chasta*

CHASYA Hebrew: Sheltered by God
Chasye

CHAVA (HAH-vah, CHAH-vah) Hebrew: Life
Chabah, Chaka, Chaya, Chayka; **Famous namesakes:** Singer Chaka Khan

CHAVIVA Hebrew: Dearly loved
Chavive

CHELINDA Arthurian Legend: Tristan's grandmother
Chelinde

CHELSEA (CHEL-see) English: Seaport. The word itself is derived from an Old English expression meaning *landing place for limestone*, which likely refers to the docks in the Chelsea district of London.
Chelsa, Chelsee, Chelsey, Chelsi, Chelsie, Chelsy; Chelsey, Chelsy, Chelsi, Chelsa, Chelsee, Kelsey; **Famous namesakes:** First daughter Chelsea Clinton; **Star babies:** daughters of Tom Berenger, Steven Tyler, Rosie O'Donnell

CHER French: Spelling variation of Cherie
Famous namesakes: Singer and actress Cher

CHERELL (sher-EL) French: Spelling variation of Cherie

CHERICE (sher-EES) French, English: Dear one, beloved; variant of Charish, Cher, and Cherie
Cherese, Cheresse, Cherisa, Cherise, Cherisse

CHERIE French: Dear one; darling
(French) *Cherise, Cherrelle; Charee, Cher, Chere, Cheree, Chereen, Cherell, Cherelle, Cheri, Cherina, Cherine, Cherree*; **Nicknames:** *Cherita*

CHERILYN English: Modern blend of Cheryl and Lynn
Cherilynn

CHERINE (sher-EEN) French: Spelling variation of Cherie

CHERRY Latin, French: Variant of Charity; (English) cherry fruit, bright red
(French) *Cerise; Cherri, Cherrie*

CHERYL English: Modern English variant of the French name Cherie (dear one); possibly a blend of Cherie with Beryl or Meryl
Cherrell, Cherrill, Cheryll; Sheryl, Sherill; **Nicknames:** *Sherri, Sherry*; **Famous namesakes:** Actress Cheryl Ladd

CHEYENNE (shie-AN) Native American: A name given to a tribe of the Algonquians by the Sioux, Cheyenne is derived from a word meaning *unintelligible speakers*, but a truer meaning might be *strangers* or *foreigners*.
Cheyanna, Cheyanne, Chiana, Chianna

CHI (CHEE) Vietnamese: Tree branch

CHIARA (kee-AH-rə) Italian: Variation of Clara
Nicknames: *Chiarina*

CHICA (CHEE-kah) Spanish: Pet name meaning little girl

CHIKA African: God is supreme (Nigerian)

CHIKAGE (chee-kah-ge) Japanese: Thousands of views or vistas
Famous namesakes: Japanese actress Awashima Chikage

CHIKAKO (chee-kah-ko) Japanese: Child of wisdom

CHIKO (chee-ko) Japanese: Close child, pledge

CHINA English: Asian country; fine, delicate porcelain
Chyna, Chynna; **Famous namesakes:** Singer Chynna Phillips

CHIQUITA Spanish: Pet name meaning *little girl*

CHITRA (CHI-trə) Hindi: Bright, picture

CHIYO (chee-yo) Japanese: Thousand or intellect, generation, or lifetime

CHLOE (KLO-ee) Greek: A young green shoot
Cloe, Khloe, Kloe; **Star babies:** daughters of Candice Berger and Louis Malle, Tom Berenger, Olivia Newton-John

CHLORIS (KLOR-is) Greek: Blooming, greenish; a mythological goddess of flowers or spring
Cloris; **Famous namesakes:** Actress Cloris Leachman

CHRISTABEL Latin: Beautiful Christian; see Christina
Christabella, Cristabel, Cristabell

CHRISTAL Scottish: Variation of Crystal

CHRISTINA Greek: Christian, follower of Christ; feminine form of Christian
(German) *Kristin*; (French) *Christine*; (Spanish) *Crista, Cristina, Cristine*; (Gaelic) *Cairistiona*; (Irish) *Cristin, Cristiona*;

(Scandinavian) *Stina*; (Swedish) *Kerstin, Kristina*; (Polish) *Krysia, Krysta, Krystka, Krystyna, Krystynka*; (Finnish) *Kirsi, Kirsikka, Kristiina*; (Hungarian) *Kriska, Kriszta, Krisztina*; *Christan, Christana, Christanne, Christeen, Christeena, Christen, Christena, Christene, Christiana, Christiane, Christianna, Christyn, Chrystina, Cristen, Cristyn, Kristen*; **Nicknames:** *Chrissa, Chrissie, Chrissy, Christa, Christi, Christie, Christy, Chryssa, Chrysta, Chrystie, Crissa, Crissie, Crissy, Cristie, Cristy, Crysta, Krista, Tiina, Tina*; **Famous namesakes:** Poet Christina Rossetti, actress Christina Ricci, tennis star Chris Evert, actress Christina Applegate; **Star babies:** daughter of Maria Shriver and Arnold Schwarzenegger

CHRYSANTHE Greek: Golden flower; feminine form of Chrysanthos
(Spanish) *Chrysann, Crisann*

CHYNA English: Spelling variation of China

CIANA (chee-AHN-ah, see-AHN-ah) Italian: Variation of Jane

CIARA (KEER-a, KEE-ar-a) Irish: Dark-haired one; feminine form of Ciaran. Irish nun Saint Ciara established a monastery at Kilkeary in the seventh century.
Ceara, Chiara, Kiara, Kiera; Keara

CIBIL Greek: Seer; variant of Sibyl

CICELY (SIS-ə-lee) English: Variation of Cecilia
Famous namesakes: Actress Cicily Tyson; **Star babies:** daughter of Sandra Bernhard

CILLA (SIL-ah) Latin: Nickname for Priscilla

CIMBERLEIGH (KIM-bər-lee) English: Spelling variation of Kimberly

CINDERELLA (sin-də-RE-lə) English: Of the ashes, from the French name Cendrillon;

Cinderella is a beloved fairy tale told in more than 3,000 versions around the world.

CINDY English: Familiar form of Cynthia and Lucinda
Cinda, Cindel, Cindi, Cindia; Cindee

CINNAMON Greek: Sweet reddish-brown, aromatic spice
Cinamon, Sinamon

CIRCE (SUR-see) Greek, Latin: The mythological sorceress who tempted Perseus and changed Odysseus' men to swine; derived from the Greek word *kirke*, meaning *bird*

CIVIA Hebrew: Spelling variation of Tzviya

CLAIRE French: Clear, bright; variant of Clara
Famous namesakes: Actress Claire Danes;
Star babies: daughter of Oliver Platt

CLARA Latin, English, German: Clear, bright, from the Latin word clarus. See also *Claire* (Latin) *Clarine*; (Greek) *Clarrisa*; (English) *Claressa*; (German) *Clarinde*; (French) *Clarinda, Clarisse*; (Italian) *Chiara, Clariee*; (Spanish) *Clarisa, Clarita*; (Swedish) *Klara*; *Clair, Clare, Clarice, Clariss, Clarissa, Clarissant, Klarissa*; **Nicknames:** *Clarette*; **Famous namesakes:** Musician Clara Schumann, actress Clara Bow, Red Cross founder Clara Barton, politician Clare Booth Luce; **Star babies:** daughter of Ewan McGregor

CLARABELLE English: Bright and beautiful; a blend of Clara (bright) and Belle (beautiful)
(French) *Claribel, Claribelle*

CLARETA Latin: Clarity, distinguished

CLARICE (kla-REES) English: Spelling variation of Clara
Claris, Clarise, Clarisse, Claryce, Klarice, Klaryce

CLARIMOND German: Brilliant protectress
Clarimonda, Clarimonde

CLARISSA English: Spelling variation of Clara

CLAUDIA Latin: Lame; feminine form of Claudius. In the Bible, the name is mentioned in one of Paul's letters to Timothy.
(English) *Claudelle, Claudine*; (French) *Claude, Claudette*; (Italian) *Claudina*; (Danish) *Clady; Klaudia*; **Famous namesakes:** German model Claudia Schiffer, actress Claudette Colbert

CLEANTHA English: Glorious woman; derived from the Greek *kleo*, meaning *fame* or *glory*

CLEMATIS (klə-MAT-is) Greek: A climby floral vine

CLEMENCE Latin, French: Clemency, mercy; Clemence was the mythological Roman goddess of pity.
(French) *Clementine*; (Spanish) *Clementina*

CLEMENTINE French: Variation of Clemence
Star babies: daughter of Cybill Shepherd

CLEONE (klee-O-nee) Greek: The mythological daughter of a river god
(Irish) *Gliona*

CLEOPATRA (klee-o-PAT-rə) Greek, Egyptian: Of a famous father or glory of the father; Cleopatra was a queen of ancient Egypt and mistress to Julius Caesar and Mark Antony, two great Roman leaders. Her story has been immortalized in several works, including *Antony and Cleopatra* by William Shakespeare.
Nicknames: *Cleo*

CLEVA English: Lives near the hills, cliffs; feminine form of Cliff, Clive, and Clifford

CLIANTHA Greek: Glory
Clianthe; Clyantha, Cleanthea

CLODAGH (KLO-dah) Irish: Name of a river in Tipperary, Ireland

CLORINDA Latin: Renowned
Clorynda, Klorinda, Klorynda; **Nicknames:** *Clory*

CLOTHO Greek: A goddess of Greek mythology and the youngest of the three fates

CLOTILDA (klo-TIL-də) German: Renowned battle
Clotilde

CLOVER English: Clover, a wild flower
Old forms: *Claefer*

CLYMENE Greek: Famous one; the name of several women in Greek mythology, including the mother of Atalanta and the daughter of Oceanus and mother of Atlas
Clymena

CLYTIA (KLIE-tee-ə) Greek: Lovely. In Greek mythology, Clytia was a sea nymph who was in love with the sun god. Upon her death, she became a sunflower and now always turns her face toward the sun.
Clytie

COAHOMA (ko-ah-ho-mah) Native American: Panther, cat (Choctaw)

COCHETA (sho-CHAY-tah) Native American: Stranger

COCO French: Made popular by French haute couture designer Gabrielle "Coco" Chanel
Star babies: daughters of Sting, Kim Gordon and Thurston Moore, David Arquette and Courteney Cox Arquette

CODY English: Pillow
Codea, Codee, Codey, Codi; Kodee, Kodie, Kodey, Kody

COLBY English: Dark-skinned or from a coal town
Kolby

COLETTE (ko-LET) French: Dark; a diminutive form of the masculine name Cole
Collette, Kolete, Kolette; **Famous namesakes:** French actress Colette; **Star babies:** daughter of Dylan McDermott

COLLEEN Irish: Girl, derived from the Gaelic *cailin*. Curiously, Colleen has been commonly used for many years in the United States and England, but is not at all common in Ireland.
Coleen, Colene, Collena, Collene; **Famous namesakes:** Actress Colleen Dewhurst, Australian author Colleen McCullough

COLUMBA Latin: Dove. Saint Columba was an Irish missionary who reintroduced Christianity to Scotland. Two female saints also had this name. See also *Columbine*
Famous namesakes: Third-century martyr Saint Columba of Sens

COLUMBINE (KAHL-əm-bien) Italian: Dove; also a beautiful plant known for its unusually shaped flower and its medicinal properties

CONCEPCION (kon-sep-see-ON) Spanish: Common reference in Latin American countries to the Virgin Mary and the Immaculate Conception
(Italian) *Concetta, Conchetta*

CONCETTA (kon-CHE-tə) Italian: Variation of Concepcion

CONNELLY Irish: Love, friendship; a popular surname

CONNEMARA (kah-nə-MAHR-ə) Irish: Place name of a scenic region in Ireland

CONNIE English: Nickname for Constance
Famous namesakes: Journalist Connie Chung, entertainer Connie Francis

CONSOLACION (kon-so-lah-see-ON) Spanish: Consolation

CONSTANCE Latin: Constancy, steadfastness
(Italian) *Constantia, Constantina, Constanza; Constanze, Konstanza, Konstanze*; **Old forms:** *Constancia*; **Nicknames:** *Con, Connie*;
Famous namesakes: Actress Constance Zimmer

CONSUELO (kon-SWAY-lo) Spanish: Consolation
Consuela; **Nicknames:** *Chela, Consolata*

CORA Greek: Maiden, from the coral of the sea. See also *Corinne*
(Latin) *Coraline*; (Greek) *Coralin, Coralina*; (French) *Coralie, Corette; Coralia, Coralyn, Coreen, Coreene, Coretta, Corisa, Corissa, Correen, Correena, Corrissa*; **Nicknames:** *Corri*; **Famous namesakes:** Activist Coretta Scott King

CORAL Greek, English: Sea coral

CORALIN Greek: Variation of Cora

CORAZON (ko-rah-ZON) Spanish: Heart
Famous namesakes: Philippines president Corazón Aquino

CORDELIA (kor-DEEL-ee-ə, kor-DEL-yə) Latin: Warm-hearted, loving. In Shakespeare's *King Lear*, Cordelia is a princess noted for her unwavering honesty and her undying devotion to her father; (Welsh) jewel of the sea
Nicknames: *Delia*

CORELLA Greek: Maiden

COREY Irish: From the hollow
Cori, Corie, Corrie, Corry, Cory

CORIANDER English: Spice

CORIANNE English: Modern blend of Cori (Cory) and Ann
Coriann, Corianna, Corrianna, Corrianne

CORINNE (ko-RIN) French: Maiden
Corine, Corrine, Korine, Korinne

CORINTHIA (kə-RIN-thee-ə) Greek: Woman of Corinth

CORISSA English: Spelling variation of Cora

CORNELIA Latin: Horn; feminine form of Cornelius
Cornella, Kornelia, Kornelie; **Nicknames:** *Nelia, Nella, Nellie, Nelida, Nelly*

CORONIS (cor-O-nis) Greek: Crow; the mythological mother of Asclepius

CORRINA Latin, Greek: Maiden; variant of Corinne
Corina; Kor; **Star babies:** daughter of Amy Grant and Vince Gill

COSETTE (ko-SET) French: Victorious; the name of one of the main characters in Victor Hugo's *Les Miserables*. The beleaguered and romantic Cosette is the daughter of infamous refugee, Jean Valjean.

COSIMA (kə-SEE-mah) Greek: Cosmos; infinite stars
Kosima; **Nicknames:** *Cosie*

COUNTESS English: Title name; the feminine equivalent of Count

COURTNEY French, English: Courteous or from the court
Cortney, Courteney, Courtlyn, Courtlynn; **Famous namesakes:** Actress Courteney Cox Arquette

CRESCENT French: Increasing, growing
Creissant

CRIMSON English: A shade of red

CRISANNA (kree-SAH-nah) Spanish: Variant of Chrysantus

CRYSTAL Greek: Ice; a brilliant clear glass of high quality
(Greek) *Kristel, Kristell*; (Scottish) *Christal, Christel*; *Khrystalline, Kristabelle, Kristalena, Kristalyn, Krystabelle, Krystal, Krystalyn, Krystalynn*; **Famous namesakes:** Singer Crystal Gayle

CYAN (SIE-an) English: Greenish-blue color

CYBELE (SIB-ə-lee) Greek: An Asian mythological nature goddess worshiped as the Great Mother of the Gods, Cybele was later identified with Rhea by the Greeks, and with Maia and Ceres by the Romans.

CYDNEY English: Spelling variation of Sydney
Star babies: daughter of Chevy Chase

CYMA (SIE-mə) Greek: Flourish

CYNTHIA Greek: Woman from Cynthos; Cynthia was a name of the mythological moon goddess Artemis, referring to her birth on Mount Cynthos.
(Italian) *Cinzia*; *Cinthia, Kynthia*; **Nicknames:** *Cyndee, Cyndi, Cyndy*

CYPRESS (SIE-prəs) Latin: A coniferous tree, usually evergreen and known for durability

CYPRIS Greek: From Cyprus; feminine form of Cyprian
(Italian) *Cipriana*; *Cyprien, Cyprienne*

CYRA Persian: Sun or enthroned, feminine variant of Cyrus

CYRENE (sie-REE-nee) Greek: In Greek myth, Cyrene wrestled with a lion, which endeared her to Apollo. He took her away to Africa and built a city for her that now bears her name.
Cyrena, Kyrene

CYRILLA (seer-IL-e) Greek, Latin: Lordly; feminine form of Cyril
(Italian) *Ciri*; (Spanish) *Ceri, Ceria*; *Cyrillia*

CYTHEREA (si-thə-REE-ə) Greek: From the island of Cythera; another name for Aphrodite, who rose from the sea near Cythera and was worshipped there
Cytheria

DACIA (DAY-shee-ə) Latin: From Dacia (near Rome)

DAERE Welsh: Friend
Dera

DAFFODIL (DA-fə-dil) Greek: Springtime yellow flower with a trumpet-shaped central crown

DAGANYA Hebrew: Ceremonial grain
Old forms: *Daganyah*

DAGMAR (DAHG-mahr) German, Scandinavian: Glorious day
Dagna; **Old forms:** *Dagomar*

DAHLIA (DAHL-yə) Norse: From the valley. The dahlia flower was named in honor of Swedish botanist Anders Dahl.
Daliah, Dalyah, Dallia

DAHNA Italian: Variation of Dana

DAINA (die-ee-nah) Lithuanian: Song

DAISY English: Day's eye; a flower name; a slang term for someone who is deemed excellent or notable. In F. Scott Fitzgerald's *The Great Gatsby*, the title character is hopelessly in love with Daisy Buchanan. *Daisey, Daisi, Daisie, Daizy, Daysi, Deysi*; **Star babies:** daughters of Markie Post, Lucy Lawless

British television chef Jamie Oliver chose two delectable names for his daughters: Poppy and Daisy.

DAKOTA American: Allies; name of a group of tribes more familiarly known as the Sioux *Dakoda, Dakotah*; **Famous namesakes:** Actress Dakota Fanning; **Star babies:** daughter of Melanie Griffith and Don Johnson

DAKSHINA (dahk-shee-nah) Hindi: Competent

DALE English: Lives in the dell or valley; originally a surname (Norse) *Dalr*; (Dutch) *Dael; Daelyn, Dalena, Dalene, Dalenna, Dayle*; **Nicknames:** *Daly*; **Famous namesakes:** Actress Dale Evans

DALIAH Hebrew: Tree branch, gentle (Arabic) *Dalia; Daliyah*

DALILA (dah-LEE-lah) Spanish: Variation of Delilah; (African) gentle (Tanzanian and Swahili)

DALIS Hebrew: Drawing water *Dalit*

DALLAS Scottish: From the field with the waterfall; a village in Scotland and a major city in Texas *Dallis; Dalles*

DAMARA (dah-MAHR-ah) Greek: Gentle. In Biblical reference, Damaris was the educated woman who heard Paul speak at the open-air supreme court of Athens. (Latin) *Damaress; Damaris, Damariss*

DAMARIS (DAM-ə-ris) Greek: Spelling variation of Damara

DAMAYANTI (dah-mah-YAHN-tee) Hindi: Subduing; in Hindu legend, the name of a beautiful princess

DAMIANA (dah-mee-AHN-ə) Greek: One who tames or subdues; feminine form of Damian (French) *Damia, Damiane, Damien*

DAMITA (dah-MEE-tah) Spanish: Little noblewoman

DANA (DAY-nə) English: From Denmark; variant of Daniel or Donna; (Persian) wise (Italian) *Dahna, Dahnya; Daena, Daina, Danah, Danna, Dannah, Dayna*; **Nicknames:** *Daney, Dania, Dannalee, Dannia, Danya*; **Famous namesakes:** Actress Dana Delany

DANAE (də-NAY) Greek: Mythological daughter of Acrisius who became the mother of Perseus when Zeus appeared to her as a shower of gold; also a variant of Danielle *Danay, Danaye, Danea, Danee, Denae, Denay*

DANICE English: Spelling variation of Danielle

DANIELLE Hebrew: God is my judge; feminine form of Daniel (Italian) *Daniella*; (Basque) *Danele*; *Danelle, Danetta, Danice, Daniela, Danila, Danita, Dany, Danyelle*; **Nicknames:** *Dani, Danise, Danit, Danitza, Dannee, Dannell, Dannelle, Danni, Dannon, Danya, Danylynn*; **Diminutive forms:** *Danette*; **Famous namesakes:** Author Danielle Steele; **Star babies:** daughters of Jerry Lewis, Donna Dixon and Dan Aykroyd

DANIKA (DAN-i-kə) Slavic: Morning star *Danica, Dannica, Dannika*; **Famous namesakes:** Actress Danica McKellar, racecar driver Danica Patrick

DANNON English: God is my judge; variant of Daniel and Danielle

DANTINA English: God is my judge; a blend of Danielle and Tina

DANYA (DAHN-yah) Hebrew: Nickname for Danielle; (English) from Denmark; variant of Dana and form of Danielle

DAPHNE (DAF-nee) Greek: Bay tree or laurel tree. The mythological and virtuous Daphne was transformed into a laurel tree to protect her from Apollo. *Dafne, Daphney*

DARA Hebrew: Wisdom. The biblical Dara was a male descendant of Judah, who was known for his wisdom; (Gaelic) oak tree *Darah, Dareen, Darissa, Darra, Darrah*

DARACHA Scottish: From the oak

DARBY Norse: From the deer estate; (Irish) free man

DARCY Irish: Dark; (French) from the Arcy (Oise River) which flows into the Seine (French) *D'arcy; Darcel, Darcell, Darcelle,*

Darcey, Darchelle, Darci, Darcia, Darcie; **Famous namesakes:** Ballerina Darci Kistler

DAREEN Hebrew: Spelling variation of Dara

DARERCA Irish: Name of a saint

DARIA (DAHR-ee-ə, DAHR-yah) Persian: Rich; feminine form of Darius. Saint Daria was martyred with her husband Chrysanthus under the Roman emperor Numerian. (Russian) *Darya, Dasha; Darian, Darianna, Dariele, Darielle, Darienne, Darrelle*; **Star babies:** daughters of Gregory Hines, Brian Wilson

DARISSA Hebrew: Spelling variation of Dara

DARLA English: Nickname for Darlene

DARLENE English, Anglo-Saxon: Darling; from the Old English dearling, possibly used on occasion as a variant of the male name Darryl *Darel, Darelene, Darelle, Darleane, Darleen, Darleena, Darlena, Darlina, Darline, Darolyn, Darrellyn, Darylene, Daryll, Darylyn*; **Nicknames:** *Darla*

DARNELL English: From the hidden place **Nicknames:** *Darnetta, Darnisha*

DARU (DAH-roo) Hindi: Pine

DARYL (DER-əl) English: From a French surname and place name, D'Arel (from Arielle in Calvados) *Darrill, Darryll; Daryll*; **Famous namesakes:** Actress Daryl Hannah

DARYN (DER-ən, DAR-ən) Greek: Gift

DASHA (DAH-shah) Russian: Variation of Daria

DAVENEY (dah-ve-NEE) French: Name of a town and castle in Flanders; also a rhyming variant of Daphne

DAVINA Hebrew: Cherished, beloved; feminine form of David
Daveen, Davia, Davianna, Davida, Davinah, Davine, Davinia, Davita, Davitah, Davite, Davonna, Davynn; **Nicknames:** *Davi, Davy, Vida*

DAWN English: The first appearance of daylight; daybreak
Dawne, Dawnika; **Nicknames:** *Dawna*; **Diminutive forms:** *Dawnelle, Dawnetta, Dawnette, Dawnielle*

DAYO (DAH-yo) African: Joy arrives

DEARBHAIL (DER-vahl) Irish: True desire
Derval, Dervilia, Dervla; **Famous namesakes:** Irish harpist Dearbhail Finnegan

DEBORAH Hebrew: Bee. Deborah was a biblical prophetess and heroine of Israel. Her victory song is in the Book of Judges.
Debora, Debra, Debrah, Debralee, Devery, Devora, Devorah, Devoria, Devra, Devri; Nicknames: *Deb, Debbie, Debby, Debi, Devi*; **Famous namesakes:** Actress Debbie Reynolds, actress Debra Winger, journalist Deborah Norville, musician Deborah Gibson

DECIMA Latin: Born tenth
Famous namesakes: British opera singer Decima Moore

DECLA (DEK-lə) Irish: Full of goodness; feminine form of Declan

DEE English: Abbreviation of names beginning with the letter *D*

DEEANNA English: Valley; feminine form of Dean or possible variant for Diana
Deana, Deane, Deann, Deanna, Deanne, Deeana, Deeann, Dene, Deneen, Denia, Denni

DEFENA English: From Devonshire

DEHEUNE Celtic: Divine one

DEINA (DAY-nah) Spanish: Religious holiday
Deiene

DEIRDRE (DEER-drə, DEER-dree) Celtic: Melancholy. In Celtic legend, Deirdre died of a broken heart.
Dedre, Deedra, Deidra, Deidre, Deirdra; **Nicknames:** *Dee*; **Famous namesakes:** Actress Deidre Hall

DEKA (DEE-kah) African: Pleasing (Somali)
Dekah

DELANEY (də-LAYN-ee) Irish: Descendant of the challenger; Delaney could also be derived from the Norman surname *De l'aunaie* meaning *from the alder grove* in French.
Famous namesakes: Actress Kim Delaney; **Star babies:** daughter of Martina and John MacBride

DELARAM Persian: Quiet-hearted

DELBINA Greek: Flower
Delbin, Delbine

DELICIA (də-LISH-ə) Latin: Delightful, gives pleasure
(English) *Delight*; (French) *Delice*; *Delicea, Deliciae, Delisa, Delisha, Delissa, Delit, Deliza, Delyssa*

DELILAH (di-LIE-lə) Hebrew: Desired, seductive. The biblical Delilah tempted Samson into revealing the secret of his strength.
(Spanish) *Dalila*; *Delila*; **Star babies:** daughter of Lisa Rinna and Harry Hamlin

DELLA German, English: Bright, noble. Della is a short form of Adelle, Adeline, and Adelaide, today seen as a name in its own right.
Dell; *Delle*; **Famous namesakes:** Singer Della Reese

DELMA German, Spanish: Noble protector
Delmi, Delmira, Delmy

DELMARA (del-MAHR-ah) Spanish: Of the sea
Delmar, Delmare

DELPHINA (del-FEE-nah) Greek: From Delphi, dolphin. Thirteenth-century French Saint Delphine is the patron saint of brides. (French) *Delphine; Delfina, Delfine, Delphia;* **Famous namesakes:** French actress Delphine Delage

DELTA Greek: Born fourth, fourth letter of the Greek alphabet

DELU (DAY-loo) African: The only girl

DELYTH (DEL-ith) Welsh: Pretty

DEMAS (DEE-məs) Greek: Popular
Demos

DEMETRIA (de-MEE-tree-ə) Greek: Of Demeter; the Greek goddess of the harvest and fertility, and mother of Persephone
Demeter, Demetra, Demitra, Demitras, Dimetria, Dimitra; **Nicknames:** *Deetra, Deitra, Demi, Detria;* **Famous namesakes:** Actress Demi Moore

DENA (DAY-nah) Native American: Valley

DENDERA (DEN-der-ah) Egyptian: From Dendera, a small Egyptian town on the Nile
Denderah, Dandarah

DENICA English: Avenged; a blend of Deana (divine) and Dina (from the valley)

DENISE (de-NEEZ, də-NEES) French: Derivative of the Greek name Dionysus (the god of wine and revelry); also feminine form of Denis
(Spanish) *Denisa; Denice, Deniece, Denissa, Denisse, Dennise, Denyse*

DENISHA African: Wild

DENIZ (deh-NIZ) Turkish: Sea

DEOCH (DYUK, JUK) Celtic: Mythical princess of Munster

DERBY English: Deer town

DEREKA (DER-ik-ə) English: Gifted ruler; modern feminine variant of Derek, derived from Theodoric
Derica, Dericka, Derrica

DERORICE Hebrew: Free
Derora, Derorit

DERRICA (DER-ik-ə) English: Spelling variation of Dereka

DERYA (DER-yah) Turkish: Ocean

DESDEMONA (dez-də-MON-ə) Greek: Unlucky; Shakespeare's leading lady in *Othello*, Desdemona is a faithful, loving wife who dies for her love. A satellite of Uranus is named for her.

"Those that do teach young babes/Do it with gentle means and easy tasks."
—Desdemona, in Shakespeare's *Othello*

DESIREE (dez-ih-RAY) French: The one desired
(English) *Desire;* (Spanish) *Desideria; Desarae, Desaree, Desirae, Desirat, Dezirae;* **Old forms:** *Desirata*

DESMA Greek: Oath

DESTINY English, French: Fate, fortune
Destanee, Destine, Destinee, Destini, Destinie;

Destiney; **Star babies:** daughter of Billy Ray Cyrus

DESTRY American: Feminine variant of a French surname usually used for boys
Star babies: daughter of Kate Capshaw and Steven Spielberg

DEVA (DAY-vah) Hindi: Superior

DEVAKI (day-vah-kee) Hindi: Black

DEVERA Latin: Truth; Roman goddess of brooms used to purify ritual sites

DEVERRA Latin: Goddess of birthing

DEVI (DAY-vee) Sanskrit: Divine. Devi is a mythological Hindu title relating to Shiva's wife who is known by different names according to her exercise of power for good or ill.

DEVIKA (day-vee-kah) Sanskrit: Little goddess; from the mythological Hindu Devi

DEVIN (DEV-in) English: Poet, poetic; possibly related to the Latin word for *divine*. The variant Devon is a county in England noted for beautiful farmland.
Devan, Devana, Devanna, Devon, Devona, Devondra, Devonna, Devonne, Devyn, Devyna, Devynn

DEVONY Irish: Dark-haired
Devinee

DEVORIA Hebrew: Spelling variation of Deborah

DEVOTA Latin: Devoted

DEXTRA Latin: Adroit, skillful

DHANA (dah-nah) Sanskrit: Wealthy
Dhanna

DHARANI (dah-rah-nee) Hindi: Earth

DHARMA (DAHR-mah) Hindi: Ultimate law of all things. In certain religions, such as Buddhism and Hinduism, dharma is the essential nature of all that is, of the cosmos, and of each of us. Dharma is closely linked to the concept of karma.

DIAMOND English: Of high value, brilliant; can refer to the precious stone
(French) *Diamante*; *Diamanda, Diamonique, Diamontina*

DIANA (die-AN-ə) Latin: Divine. An ancient Roman goddess of the moon, Diana was noted for her beauty and swiftness
(French) *Diane*; (Hawaiian) *Kiana*; *Deona, Deonna, Deonne, Di, Diahann, Diahna, Dian, Dianna, Diannah, Dianne, Dyana, Dyann, Dyanna*; **Famous namesakes:** Princess of Wales Diana Windsor, actress Diahann Carroll, actress Diane Keaton, actress Dianne Wiest, journalist Diane Sawyer; **Star babies:** daughter of Veronica Lake and Andre De Toth

DIANDRA Greek: Flower of God; also a botanical term for flower with two stamens
Deandra, Deondra

DIANTHA (die-AN-thə) Greek: Heavenly flower
Dianthe

DICE Greek: Justice, to slice; numbered cubes used in board games

DIDO (DIE-do) Greek: The legendary founder and queen of Carthage, Dido was the subject of Henry Purcell's opera *Dido and Aeneas*.
Famous namesakes: British musician Dido

DIEGA (dee-AY-gah) Spanish: Supplanter; feminine form of Diego

DIGNA Latin: Worthy
Digne

DILYS (DIL-is) Welsh: Sincere, genuine
Dylis, Dyllis

DINAH Hebrew: Judged. The biblical Dinah
was Jacob and Leah's only daughter.
(Spanish) *Dinora*; *Deena, Dena, Dina,*
Dinorah, Dynah; **Famous namesakes:**
Entertainer Dinah Shore

DINARA (dee-NAH-rah) Russian: Breath
Famous namesakes: Russian tennis player
Dinara Safina

DIONE (dee-o-NEE, dee-AHN) Greek,
English: Divine queen. In Greek mythology,
she was Zeus's mate and the mother of
Aphrodite.
Diona, Diondra, Dionna, Dionne; **Famous**
namesakes: Singer Dionne Warwick

DIONYSIA (di-ə-NI-zhee-ə) Latin, Greek:
Named for Dionysus, god of wine
(Spanish) *Dionisa*; *Dionysie*

DIRCE Greek, Latin: Mythical mother of
Lycus

DISA (DEE-sə) Greek: Twice or double;
(Norse) spirited

DITA (DEE-tah) Spanish: Variation of Edith

DIVINA Latin: Divine one
(Celtic) *Divone*; *Devina, Devona*; **Nicknames:**
Deva, Diva

DIVSHA Hebrew: Honey
Divshah

DIVYA (DEEV-yah) Hindi: Divine

DIXIE English: Refers to the French word
for ten. Dixie is also a term for the southern
states below the Mason-Dixon line.
Famous namesakes: Actress Dixie Carter

DOANNA English: American compound of
Dorothy and Anna

DOCILLA Latin: Calm

DOLI (do-lee) Native American: Bluebird
(Navajo)

DOLLY English: A vision, gift of God; pet
form of Dorothy
Famous namesakes: Singer Dolly Parton,
First Lady Dolly Madison

DOLORES Spanish: Sorrows
Delora, Deloras, Delores, Deloris, Deloros;
Nicknames: *Lola, Loleta, Lolita, Lolitta, Lola,*
Dee, Dee Dee; **Diminutive forms:** *Dolorita*;
Famous namesakes: Actress Dolores Fuller,
actress Delores del Río

DOMELA Latin: Mistress of the home
(Gaelic) *Domhnulla*; *Domele*

DOMIDUCA Latin: Mythical surname of
Juno, a goddess in astrology

DOMINA Latin: Spelling variation of Donna

DOMINIQUE (do-mee-NEEK) Latin,
French: Of the Lord, belongs to God. A
feminine variant of Dominic, this French
spelling is used primarily for girls.
(Spanish) *Domenica, Dominga*; *Domenique,*
Dominica, Domitiana, Domitiane; **Famous**
namesakes: Gymnast Dominique Dawes,
gymnast Dominique Moceanu, singer
Dominique Eade; **Star babies:** daughter of
Michael Caine

DONALDA (do-NAHL-də) Gaelic: Ruler of
all; feminine form of Donald

DONATA (do-NAH-tah) Italian, Latin: To give

DONNA (DAHN-ə) Italian, Latin: Lady, a
respectful title and female equivalent of Don

(Spanish) *Dona*; (Gaelic) *Donia*; *Damina, Domina, Donella, Donetta, Donica, Donielle, Donisha, Donnalee, Donnalyn, Donya*; **Nicknames:** *Don, Donni, Donnie*; **Famous namesakes:** Singer Donna Summer, actress Donna Mills, actress Donna Reed

DONOMA (do-no-mah) Native American: The sun is there (Omaha)

DONYA Persian: World
Dunya

DORA Greek: Gift; familiar form of Dorothy, Doris, and Theodora
(French) *Dorine*; *Darynn, Darynne, Doralia, Doralice, Doralie, Doralis, Dordei, Dorelia, Doretta, Dorinda, Doryne*; **Nicknames:** *Dorie*

DORALICE Greek: Heroine of a Russian fairy tale by Straparola

DORBETA (dor-BAY-tah) Spanish: Reference to the Virgin Mary

DORCAS (DOR-kəs) Greek: Gazelle; the biblical woman who abounded in good deeds and gifts of mercy
Dorkas

DORE African: Gift

DOREE (dor-AY) French: Golden
D'or, Dior

DOREEN Irish: Moody, sullen; variant of Dora
(Greek) *Dorienne*; *Dorene*; **Old forms:** *Doireann*; **Nicknames:** *Doire, Dory*; **Famous namesakes:** German actress Doreen Jacobi

DORIAN (DOR-ee-ən) Greek: Of the sea, descendant of Dorus of Greek myth and a variant of Doris
Dorea, Doria, Doriana, Dorianna, Dorianne, Dorien, Dorrian

DORICE (DOR-is) Greek: Spelling variation of Doris

DORIS Greek: Gift. Doris was the mythological daughter of the sea god Oceanus and the mother of fifty sea nymphs. *Doree, Dorice, Dorisa, Dorris*; **Nicknames:** *Dori, Dorri, Dorrie, Dorry, Dory*; **Famous namesakes:** Actress Doris Day, author Doris Lessing, actress Doris Roberts

DOROTHY (DOR-ə-thee, DOR-thee) Greek: A vision, gift of God. The character of Dorothy in L. Frank Baum's *The Wonderful Wizard of Oz* learned that there was no place like home. (English) *Dorit, Dortha*; (German) *Dorothea*; (Spanish) *Dorotea*; (Gaelic) *Diorbhall*; (Russian) *Doroteya*; (Polish) *Dorota*; (Hungarian) *Dorika, Dorottya, Duci*; *Dorita, Dorlisa, Dorote, Dorothee*; **Nicknames:** *Doll, Dollie, Dolly, Doro, Dorte, Dottie, Dot, Thea, Tea*; **Famous namesakes:** Figure skater Dorothy Hamill, author Dorothy Parker, author Dorothy Sayers, activist Dorothea Dix

DORY English: Nickname for Doris
Dori, Dorri, Dorrie, Dorry; **Famous namesakes:** Singer Dory Previn

DOTTIE English: Gift of God; pet form of Dorothy

DRAGOMIRA (drah-go-MEER-ah) Slavic: Precious, peaceful

DREW Scottish: Brave; the feminine of the familiar form for Andrew
Famous namesakes: Actress Drew Barrymore

DRISANA (dree-sah-nah) Hindi: Daughter of the sun

DRUCILLA (droo-SIL-ə) Latin: Strong; feminine form of the Roman family name Drusus
Drusilla; **Nicknames:** *Dru*

DUANA Irish: Dark; feminine form of Duane
Duayna, Dubhain, Duvessa; **Old forms:**
Dubheasa; **Nicknames:** *Du*

DULCIE (DUL-see) Latin: Sweet, sweetness.
Dulcinea was the name created by Cervantes'
literary character Don Quixote for his
idealized lady.
(Spanish) *Delcine, Dukine, Dulce, Dulcina,
Dulcinea; Dulcea, Dulcine, Dulcy*; **Old forms:**
Dulcia

DURGA (DOOR-gah) Hindi: Unattainable.
In Hindu mythology, this is the name of a
fierce goddess.

DUSANA Czech: A spirit or soul; feminine
form of Dusan
Dusan

DUSTY English: Fighter; a pet form of the
male name Dustin
Dustee, Dusti; Dusti, Dustee; **Famous
namesakes:** Singer Dusty Springfield

DYANI (die-YAH-nee) Native American: Deer

DYLLIS (DIL-is) Welsh: Spelling variation
of Dilys

DYMPHNA (DIMF-na) Irish, Gaelic: Bard, poet
Old forms: *Damhnait*

EABHA (AY-va) Irish: Breath of life

EADA English: Wealthy
Eadda; Ead

EADLIN Anglo-Saxon: Princess

EADWINE English: Wealthy friend; an
Old English name compounded from *ead,*
meaning *rich* or *happy,* and *wine,* meaning
friend

EALASAID (ee-la-say-d) Gaelic: Devoted to
God; Gaelic variant of Elizabeth
Elasayd

EALGA (AYL-ga) Irish: Noble. Ireland is
sometimes referred to as Inis Ealga, "the
Noble Isle," which is the source of this
unusual name.

EARIE Scottish: From the east
Eara

EARLENE English: Noble woman, shield;
feminine form of Earl
(Spanish) *Erlene; Earla, Earlena, Earline;
Earleen*

EARNA English: Eagle

EARTHA (UR-thə) English, German: Earth,
the planet, soil in which to grow
Ertha; **Famous namesakes:** Singer Eartha Kitt

EASTER Anglo-Saxon: Goddess of the dawn;
a fitting name for a little girl born on Easter
Eastre; **Old forms:** *Eostre*

EAVAN (EE-van) Irish: Fair, beautiful; an
Anglicized variant of Aoibheann, the name of
Saint Enda's mother
Aoibheann, Aoibhin

EBBE (E-bə, E-bee) Swedish: Strong,
flowing tide; variant of Esbjorn
Ebba

EBERTA Teutonic: Intelligent
Ebertta; **Nicknames:** *Ebe*

EBONY (E-bə-nee) Greek, English: Black or
a dark hardwood
Ebonee, Eboni, Ebonique

EBRILL (EB-ril) Welsh: Born in April
Ebril

ECE Turkish: Queen

ECHO Greek: Sound. Echo was a mythological nymph who faded away until only her voice was left.
Ekko

EDANA Irish: Fire; feminine form of Aidan
Edelina, Ediline; **Nicknames:** *Edee*

EDDA (ED-dah) German: Pleasant; refuge from battle
Eda; **Old forms:** *Hedda*

EDEE English: Nickname for Edana

EDEEN Scottish: From Edinburgh

EDEN (EE-dən) Hebrew: Pleasure, delight; the biblical paradise home of Adam and Eve
Eaden, Eadin, Edin

EDINA English: Wealthy; possibly a variant of Edwina; (Scottish) from Edinburgh
Edine

EDITH English: Prosperity, goodness, and wealth. Edith was a fashionable name in the nineteenth century.
(Anglo-Saxon) *Edit*; (Italian) *Edita, Editta*; (Spanish) *Dita*; (Teutonic) *Edyte*; *Edyt, Edyta, Edyth, Edythe*; **Famous namesakes:** British writer Edith Sitwell, Author Edith Wharton, French singer Edith Piaf

Why not be oneself? That is the whole secret of a successful appearance. If one is a greyhound, why try to look like a Pekingese?
—Edith Sitwell

EDLYN English: Noble or princess
Edlen, Edlin, Edlynn, Edlynne; **Nicknames:** *Edla*

EDMUNDA German: Wealthy defender
(English) *Edmanda*; (Anglo-Saxon) *Edmonda*; *Edmee*

EDNA Hebrew, Celtic: Pleasure, delight; derived from the same word as the biblical Garden of Eden
Edra, Edrea

EDOLIE Teutonic: Good humor
Edolia

EDUARDA English: Rich benefactress

EDULICA Latin: Mythical protectress of children

EDURNE (e-DOOR-nay) Basque: Snows

EDWINA (ed-WEEN-ə, ed-WIN-ə) English: Rich in friendship; feminine form of Edwin
Edwinna; **Nicknames:** *Winnie*

EFFIE Greek: Fair flame; Abbreviation of Greek name Euphemia

EGBERTA English: Shining sword
Egbertina, Egbertine, Egbertyne

EGERIA (i-JEER-ee-ə) Latin: A water nymph

EIDEANN Gaelic: Spelling variation of Aidan

EILA Irish: Nickname for Evelyn

EILEEN Irish: Shining light; variant of Aileen
Eileene, Eilena, Eilene; **Old forms:** *Eibhlhin, Eibhlin*

EILWEN (AYL-wen) Welsh: White, fair

EILY Irish: Light
Old forms: *Eilidh*

EIRA (OI-ra, IE-ra) Welsh: Snow

EIRICA Scottish: Ruler

EIRLYS (AYR-lis) Welsh: Snowdrop

EKATERINA (ye-kah-tye-REE-nah)
Russian: Variation of Catherine
Katerina; **Nicknames:** *Katia, Katusha, Katya*;
Famous namesakes: Rumanian gymnast
Ecaterina Szabo, Russian skater Ekaterina
Gordeeva

ELAHEH Persian: Goddess

ELAINE French: Shining light; Old French
variant of Helen. In Arthurian legend, Elaine
was a young maiden who was in love with
Lancelot. She was also the sister of Sir Percival
and the mother of Sir Galahad.
(Irish) *Elan*; *Elaina, Elayne, Ellaine, Ellayne*;
Star babies: daughter of Veronica Lake and
John Detlie

ELANA Hebrew: Oak tree
Elanah, Elanie, Elanna

ELATA Latin: Glorified

ELBERTE (el-BUR-tə) English: Noble or
glorious; variant of Alberta
Elberta, Elbertyna

ELDORA (el-DOR-ah) Spanish: Gilded,
golden
Eldoris, Eldreda, Eldrida, Eldride; **Nicknames:**
Elda, Elde

ELDRID Norse: Fiery spirit; also a variant of
Aldred

ELEADORA Greek: Gift of the sun

ELEANA Latin, Greek: Daughter of the sun.
See also *Elena*
(Spanish) *Iliana*; *Elayna*

ELEANOR (EL-ə-nor) Greek: Shining light;
variant of Helen
(French) *Eleonore*; (Italian) *Eleanora, Elenora,
Elenore*; (Gaelic) *Eilionoir*; (Irish) *Eilinora*;
(Swedish) *Ellinor*; (Finnish) *Eleonoora*;
*Eleanore, Eleonora, Elienor, Elinor, Elinore,
Elnora*; **Nicknames:** *Ella, Ellie, Leora, Nora*;
Famous namesakes: First Lady Eleanor
Roosevelt; **Star babies:** daughter of Diane
Lane and Christopher Lambert

> *"Woman are like tea bags;*
> *put them in hot water and*
> *they get stronger."*
> —Eleanor Roosevelt

ELECTRA (i-LEK-trə) Greek: The fiery sun.
Electra was the mythological daughter of
Agamemnon and a central character in three
Greek tragedies.
Elektra

ELENA Greek: Light; variant of Helen
Star babies: daughter of Sam Neill

ELETA Latin: Chosen
Electa, Elekta

ELETHEA English: Healer
Elethia, Elthia

ELFREDA (ehl-FRED-ə) English: Elf
strength
(English) *Elfrieda*; (Teutonic) *Elfrida*;
Nicknames: *Elfie*

ELGA Teutonic: Spelling variation of Helga

ELHAM Persian: Inspiration

ELIANA (el-lee-AH-nah) Hebrew: My God has answered; (Latin, Greek) daughter of the sun (Greek) *Elianne*; (German) *Eliane*; *Elianna*, *Lianna*

ELICA German: Noble; a variant of the old German name Alice

ELIDA English: Variation of Alida

ELIKAPEKA (E-lee-kah-BE-a) Hawaiian: Variation of Elizabeth

ELINA (e-LEE-nah) Spanish, Finnish: Shining light; variant of Helen

ELIORA (el-ee-OR-ah) Hebrew: God is light; feminine form of Elior

ELISAMARIE French: Blend of Elise and Marie

ELISE (ay-LEES, e-LEES) French: Consecrated to God; abbreviation of Elisabeth (English) *Ilyssa*; (German) *Ilyse*; (Spanish) *Elisa*; *Elicia*, *Elisha*, *Elishia*, *Ellesse*, *Ellyce*, *Elyce*, *Elyse*

ELISKA (EL-izh-kah) Czech: Variation of Elizabeth

ELISSA (ə-LIS-ə) Greek: Devoted to God, from the blessed isles. Elissa is another name for the mythological Dido who was Queen of Carthage; (English) variation of Elizabeth *Elysa*, *Elysha*, *Elysia*, *Elyssa*, *Elysse*

ELITA Latin: Chosen one; familiar form of Carmelita

ELIVINA English: Good elf

ELIZA (i-LIE-zə) English: Nickname for Elizabeth *Elyza*

ELIZABETH Hebrew, English: God is my oath. Elizabeth was the mother of John the Baptist in the Bible. Today, Elizabeth is one of the most frequently used names in England. Royal namesakes include Queen Elizabeth I and Queen Elizabeth II.
(French) *Elisabeth*; (Italian) *Elisabetta*, *Elizabetta*; (Scottish) *Elsbeth*; (Scandinavian) *Elisabet*, *Elizabet*; (Danish) *Ailsa*, *Lisbet*; (Dutch) *Liesbeth*; (Russian) *Elisaveta*, *Lizaveta*; (Czech) *Alzbeta*, *Eliska*; (Polish) *Elzbieta*; (Ukrainian) *Yelysaveta*; (Hungarian) *Erzsebet*, *Orzsebet*; (Hawaiian) *Elikapeka*; *Elizaveta*, *Elsa*, *Lisabet*, *Lisabeth*, *Lizabeth*, *Lyzbeth*; **Old forms:** *Elisheva*, *Elspeth*; **Nicknames:** *Ailsie*, *Bess*, *Bessie*, *Bessy*, *Beta*, *Beth*, *Betsey*, *Bette*, *Betti*, *Bettina*, *Bettine*, *Betty*, *Buffy*, *Eliza*, *Elli*, *Els*, *Elyza*, *Elzira*, *Ilsa*, *Ilse*, *Libby*, *Lilibet*, *Lilibeth*, *Lise*, *Liz*, *Liza*, *Lizbet*, *Lizbeth*, *Lyza*, *Sissy*, *Telsa*, *Lizzie*; **Diminutive forms:** *Liesl*, *Liezel*, *Lisette*, *Lizette*; **Famous namesakes:** Queen Elizabeth of England, actress Elizabeth Taylor, cosmetics executive Elizabeth Arden, entertainer Liza Minelli

---

"When I received this [coronation] ring I solemnly bound myself in marriage to the realm; and it will be quite sufficient for the memorial of my name and for my glory, if, when I die, an inscription be engraved on a marble tomb, saying, 'Here lieth Elizabeth, which reigned a virgin, and died a virgin.'"
—Elizabeth I (1533–1603),
    British monarch

ELKA Hebrew: God has created; feminine form of Elkanah

ELKE (EL-kə) German: Noble; variant of Alice
Famous namesakes: German actress Elke Sommer

ELLA German: All, complete; also familiar form of Eleanor and Ellen; (English) a beautiful fairy woman
Elle; **Famous namesakes:** Singer Ella Fitzgerald; **Star babies:** daughters of Gary Sinise, Kelly Preston and John Travolta, Annette Bening and Warren Beatty

ELLAMAE English: Blend of Ella and Mae

ELLECIA English: Variant of Elias

ELLEN English: Light; a variant of Helen (Greek) *Eleni*; (Italian) *Elene*; (Irish) *Elleen*; (Welsh) *Elen*; (Scandinavian) *Elin*; *Ellena, Ellene, Ellyn; Ellene*; **Nicknames:** *Ellee, Ellia*; **Diminutive forms:** *Ellette*; **Famous namesakes:** Comedienne Ellen DeGeneres, actress Ellen Burstyn, actress Ellen Barkin

ELLERY (EL-ə-ree) English: Joyful, happy; surname
Ellary, Ellerie, Ellarie

ELLICE (EL-is) Hebrew: The Lord is my God. The Tuvalu Islands were formerly known as Ellice Islands
Ellis, Ellisha; **Famous namesakes:** Painter and sculptor Ellice Endicott

ELLISON English: Variant of Elias, the Greek form of Elijah
Ellisyn

ELLORA Hindi: The name given to the cave temples of India.

ELLY English: An abbreviated form of Eleanor and Ellen
Elli, Ellie

ELMA German: God's protection; (Greek) friendly

ELMAS (EL-mahs) Turkish: Diamond

ELMINA Teutonic: Intimidating fame
Elmine

ELMIRA English: Noble

ELODIE (ay-lo-DEE) French: Variation of Alodia

ELOINA Latin: Worthy

ELOISE (EL-o-eez, ay-lo-EEZ) French: Renowned in battle; French variant of Louise. See also *Heloise*
(Italian) *Eloisa; Eloisee, Heloise*; **Famous namesakes:** Actress Eloise Howe

ELSE (EL-sə) German, Scandinavian: Noble maid; also a familiar form of Elizabeth (Spanish) *Elsa; Ilse*; **Old forms:** *Elsje*; **Nicknames:** *Elsie*

ELSHA German: Noble

ELVA English: Nickname for Elvira

ELVIRA Spanish: Truth, white, or beautiful (English) *Elvyne*; (Anglo-Saxon) *Elwine*; (Irish) *Elvinia*; (Polish) *Elwira*; *Elvena, Elvera, Elvia, Elvine, Elwyna*; **Nicknames:** *Elva, Elvie, Elvin*

ELVITA (el-VEE-tah) Spanish: Truth

ELZIRA Hebrew: Nickname for Elizabeth

EMBER English: Anniversary. Ember day is a day in Lent devoted to fasting and prayer.

Ember can also be used as a rhyming variant of Amber.
Emberly, Emberlyn; Emberlee, Emberley, Emberleigh, Emberlie, Emberlea, Emberlynn, Emberlin, Emberlinn

EMBLA (EM-blah) Norse: From an elm; the first woman in Norse mythology

EMELIA (i-MEE-lee-ə, i-MEEL-yə) Latin: Industrious, striving; variant of Amelia (Teutonic) *Emiline; Emelin, Emelina, Emilia*

EMELINE (EM-ə-leen) French: Variation of Emily

EMERALD English: Green gemstone; the birthstone for May
(French) *Emeraude;* (Spanish) *Esmeralda, Esmerelda, Ezmeralda, Esma; Esmeraude;* **Nicknames:** *Esme, Meralda*

EMERSON (E-mər-sən) German: Surname; son of Emery
Emersyn, Emercyn; **Star babies:** daughter of Teri Hatcher

EMESTA Spanish: Serious
(English) *Earnestyna;* (German) *Emestine; Enerstina, Enerstyne*

EMILY Latin: Industrious, striving. Emily is one of the most popular names in America and England.
(German) *Amalasand, Amalasanda, Emilie, Emmeline;* (French) *Amalie, Amelie, Emeline, Emmaline;* (Italian) *Amalia, Emilia;* (Teutonic) *Aimiliana, Aimilionia, Amialiona;* (Gaelic) *Aimil;* (Finnish) *Emmi; Amalija, Amelinda, Amelita, Amilia, Emalee, Emilee, Emmalee, Emmalei, Emmalyn; Emilee, Emiley, Emmaleigh, Emmalee, Emely;* **Old forms:** *Amalea;* **Nicknames:** *Emmy, Em;* **Famous namesakes:** Poet Emily Dickinson, etiquette expert Emily Post, author Emily Brontë; **Star babies:** daughters of Chevy Chase, Tatum

O'Neal and John McEnroe, Beau Bridges, Alex Trebeck, Gloria Estefan

*Hope is the thing with feathers
That perches in the soul
And sings the tune
without words
And never stops, at all.*
—Emily Dickinson

EMMA German: Complete, whole, universal; can also mean nanny
(Spanish) *Ema;* **Famous namesakes:** British actress Emma Thompson, poet Emma Lazarus; **Star babies:** daughters of Julie Andrews and Tony Walton, Christine Lahti, Eric Roberts, Wayne Gretzky and Janet Jones

"Emma Woodhouse, handsome, clever, and rich, with a comfortable home and happy disposition seemed to unite some of the best blessings of existence . . ."
—Jane Austin, *Emma*

EMMALINE (EM-ə-leen) French: Variation of Emily

EMMANUELLA (i-MAN-yoo-EL-ə) Hebrew: God is with us; feminine form of Emmanuel, a name used throughout the Bible for Jesus
(Spanish) *Manuela; Emmanuelle*

EMOGENE Latin: Spelling variation of Imogene

EMUNAH (e-MOO-nah) Hebrew: Faith

ENCARNACION (en-cahr-nah-see-ON)
Spanish: Reference to the Incarnation of Christ

ENDORA Greek: Fountain

ENFYS (EN-vis) Welsh: Rainbow

ENGEL (ENG-gel) Anglo-Saxon: Variation
of Angela

ENGELBERTHA (ENG-gǝl-BUR-thǝ)
German: Bright angel
(German) *Engelbertine*; *Engelbertina*,
Engleberta; **Nicknames:** *Engl*

ENID (EE-nid) Welsh, Celtic: Soul. Enid
is a heroine in Arthurian legend as the
immaculate wife of Geriant, a knight of the
Round Table.
Enit, Enite, Enyd

ENNA Italian: City in Italy
Ena

ENNEA Greek: Born ninth

ENNIS Irish: From Ennis

ENOLA (ee-NO-lah) American: A literary
character and sister of Sherlock Holmes; the
name is most recognizable as the bomber
Enola Gay

ENRIQUA (en-REE-kah) Spanish: Keeper
of the hearth, rules her household; feminine
form of Enrique, popular Spanish form of
Henry
Henriqua

ENYA (EN-ya) Irish: Spelling variation of
Ethna
Famous namesakes: Irish musician and
composer Enya

ENYO Greek: A mythological goddess of war
Nicknames: *Eny*

EOSTRE (EES-trǝ) Anglo-Saxon: Original
form of Easter

EPHYRA Latin: Daughter of Oceanus

ERELA (e-REL-ah) Hebrew: Variation of
Angela

ERENDIRA (ǝ-RAYN-deer-ǝ) Spanish:
She who smiles. Eréndira is an Aztec name
and character appearing in works by Gabriel
García Márquez.

ERIANTHA (e-ree-AHN-thǝ) Greek: Sweet
Erianthe, Erianthia

ERICA Norse, Scandinavian: Eternal ruler,
forever strong; feminine form of Eric.
The spelling variation Erika is popular in
numerous European countries.
(Finnish) *Eerika*; *Ericka, Erika, Erikka*

ERIENNE Gaelic: Spelling variation of Erin

ERIKO (e-ree-ko) Japanese: Inlet, cove, child

ERIN Gaelic, Irish: Peace; a poetic name for
Ireland
*Erienne, Erina, Erinn, Erinna, Erinne, Eryn,
Erynn*

ERIS (ER-is) Greek: Goddess of discord

ERITH Hebrew: Flower
Eritha

ERLINA Gaelic: Girl from Ireland
Erleen, Erlene, Erline

ERNESTINE (UR-nǝs-teen) English:
Serious, determined; feminine form of Emest
(Latin) *Ernestina*; (Spanish) *Ernesta*;
(Hungarian) *Ernesztina*; *Ernesha*; **Nicknames:**
Erna

ERRITA Greek: Pearl

ERWINA English: Friend of the sea
Earwyn, Earwyna, Erwyna; **Old forms:** *Earwine*

ESHE (E-shə) African: Life, energy (Swahili)

ESIN (e-SEEN) Turkish: Inspiration

ESMA Anglo-Saxon: Kind defender

ESMEE (EZ-may) French: Esteemed
Esma; **Famous namesakes:** Dutch actress
Esmée de la Bretonière

ESMERALDA (ez-mə-RAHL-də) Spanish:
Variation of Emerald
Esmerelda; **Nicknames:** *Esme, Meralda*

ESPERANZA (es-pe-RAHN-sah) Spanish:
Hope
(French) *Esperance*; **Nicknames:** *Espe,
Speranza*; **Star babies:** daughter of Bob and
Anna Sellers

ESTA Italian: From the east

ESTEE (es-TAY) French: Star; variant of
Estelle
Famous namesakes: Cosmetics executive
Estée Lauder

ESTEFANIA (es-tay-fahn-EE-ah) Spanish:
Crowned with laurels; feminine form of
Esteban, a popular Spanish form of Stephen
Estebana, Estefana, Esteva; **Nicknames:**
Estefani, Estefany, Estefanita

ESTELLE (es-TEL) French: Variation of
Stella

ESTHER (ES-tər) Hebrew, Persian: Of
debated origin and meaning, possibly star
or myrtle leaf. In the Old Testament Book
of Esther, a beautiful young Hebrew woman
named Esther marries the Persian King
Xerxes. As queen, she then risks her life to
save the Jews from persecution.

(Hebrew) *Estrela*; (Spanish) *Ester, Izar,
Izarra, Izarre*; (Irish) *Eistir*; (Finnish) *Esteri*;
(Hungarian) *Eszter, Eszti*; **Nicknames:** *Essie,
Hester*

ETAIN (AY-teen, AY-deen) Irish, Celtic:
Little fire. In Irish mythology, Etain was a sun
goddess and the lover of Midhir.
Aideen, Eadan

ETHEL (ETH-əl) Anglo-Saxon, Hebrew,
English: Noble
(English) *Ethelreda*; (German) *Ethelinda*;
(Hungarian) *Etel*; *Eathelin, Eathelyn, Ethelda*;
Famous namesakes: Actress Ethel Barrymore,
entertainer Ethel Merman

ETHETE (eth-e-te) Native American: Good
quality (Arapaho)

ETHNA (ETH-na, ET-na, EN-ya, EN-a) Irish:
Kernel. Saint Eithne was the daughter of a king
and one of Saint Patrick's followers. The name
variant Enya is likely best known in America
for the modern Irish musician and composer.
Aithne; *Ena, Enya, Ethne*; **Old forms:** *Eithne*

ETIENNETTE (ay-tyen-ET) French:
Variation of Stephanie

ETTIE English: Pet form of Etta, which is an
abbreviation of Henrietta

EUDOKIA (yoo-DO-kee-ə) Greek: To seem
well
(Latin) *Eudocia*; *Eudosia, Eudosis, Eudoxia*;
Nicknames: *Dunya, Dusya*

EUGENIA Greek: Well-born, noble;
feminine form of Eugene
(French) *Eugenie*; (Czech) *Evzenie*; *Eugena,
Eugina*; **Nicknames:** *Zhenya, Eug, Eugie*;
Famous namesakes: Actress Eugenia Silva,
artist Mary Eugenia Surratt; **Star babies:**
daughter of Prince Andrew and Sarah
Ferguson

EUGENIE (uu-zhay-NEE) French: Variation of Eugenia

EULA (YOO-lə) Greek: Nickname for Eulalie

EULALIE (yoo-LAY-lee) Greek: Sweet-spoken
(French) *Aulaire*; (Spanish) *Lala, Lali, Lalla*; (Hawaiian) *Iulalia, Ulalia*; **Nicknames:** *Eula, Eulah, Eulia, Lelia, Ula*

EUNICE (YOO-nis) Greek: Joyous victory, she conquers. In the Bible, Eunice was the daughter of Lois and the mother of Timothy, to whom Paul addressed two of his Epistles: Timothy I and Timothy II. She was a woman noted for being without hypocrisy.

EUPHEMIA (yoo-FEM-ee-ə) Greek: Well-spoken. Saint Euphemia was a virgin martyr. (Spanish) *Eufemia*; *Euphemie*; **Nicknames:** *Effie, Phemie*

EURYDICE (yoo-RI-də-see) Greek, Latin: Wife of Orpheus in Greek mythology. This name is derived from the blend of two root words: *eury* meaning *broad* or *wide*, and *dice* meaning *wood worm*.

EUSTACIA (yoo-STAY-shə) Greek: Fruitful, productive; feminine form of Eustace

EUSTELLA (yoo-STEL-ah) Greek: Fair star

EVA (AY-ə, EE-və) Latin: Form of Evelyn
Star babies: daughter of Susan Sarandon

EVANGELINA Greek: Bearer of good news
Evangela, Evangelia, Evangeline, Evangelyn

EVANIA (ee-VAHN-yə) Greek: God has been gracious; feminine form of Evan
Evanee, Evanna, Evin

EVANNA English: Spelling variation of Evania

EVANTHE (e-VAHN-thə) Greek: Flower

EVE Hebrew: Life. In the Bible, Eve was Adam's wife and the first woman. Eva is a name used in many countries throughout the world.
(Hebrew) *Evika, Evike, Ewa*; (Spanish) *Evita*; (Irish) *Aoife*; (Welsh) *Efa*; (Russian) *Yeva*; (Ukrainian) *Yevtsye*; (Persian) *Havva*; *Evia, Eviana*; **Nicknames:** *Evie*; **Famous namesakes:** Argentine First Lady Eva (Evita) Peron, performance artist Eve Ensler, actress Eve Arden, actress Eva Marie Saint

EVELYN (EV-ə-lin) English: Life; originally both a surname and masculine name, but became popular as a feminine name in the late nineteenth century
(French) *Evelyne*; (Italian) *Evelina*; (Finnish) *Eeva, Eevi, Eveliina*; *Eva*; *Evaleen, Evalina, Evaline, Evalyn, Eveleen, Evelin, Eveline, Evelynn, Evelynne*; **Nicknames:** *Eila*

EVERAINE English: Modern blend of a word name with a nature name.

EVERLYN English: Modern blend of a word name with the feminine suffix –*lyn*
Everlynn

EVETTE Latin, Hebrew: Living one; variant of Eve or Ivette
Evetta

EVIANA Hebrew: Spelling variation of Eve

EVIN English: Spelling variation of Evania

EVINA Scottish: Right-handed

EVONNA German: Variation of Yvonne
Evon, Evony

EYOTA (e-YO-tah) Native American: The greatest (Sioux)

FABIA (FAH-bee-ə) Latin: Bean farmer; feminine variant of Fabian, from the Roman family name Fabius
(French) *Fabienne*; (Italian) *Fabiana*; *Fabianna, Fabianne, Fabiola, Fabra, Favianna, Faviola*

FADILAH (fah-DEE-lah) Arabic: Virtuous, distinguished, superior; feminine form of Fadil
(African) *Fadhila*; *Fadila, Fadileh*

FAE English: Form of Faith

FAELYN English: Beautiful fairy
Faelynn, Failyn, Failynn

FAINA (fah-EE-nah) Russian: Bright

FAIRAMAY (FER-ə-may) English: Middle English; fair maiden
Nicknames: *Fay*

FAIREN (FER-ən) American: Beautiful
Fairyn, Fayre; Fairynn, Fayryn, Fayrynn, Faeryn, Faerynn

FAIRLY English: From the bull's or sheep's meadow; a surname and variant of Farley, with a more feminine spelling for girls
Fairlee, Fairleigh, Fairlea, Fairlie

FAIRUZA Turkish: Turquoise

FAITH English: Enduring belief that does not require proof. Faith is a virtue name that was commonly used by the Puritans.
(Spanish) *Fe; Faithe, Fayanna, Fayth, Faythe*;
Nicknames: *Fae, Fay, Faye*; **Diminutive forms:** *Fayette*; **Famous namesakes:** Singer Faith Hill

FAKHRI Persian: Glory

FALA Native American: Crow (Choctaw)

FALALA African: Born in abundance

FALLON Irish: In charge; surname used as a first name
Faline, Fallyn, Falon

FANCHON (fahn-SHAWN) French: Free; a common name in Brittany
Fanchone; **Nicknames:** *Fanny*

FANNY English: Nickname for Frances

FANTINE Latin: Childlike
Fantina; **Nicknames:** *Fanny*

FAQUEZA (fah-KAY-zah) Spanish: Weakness

FARAH English: Traveler, fair-haired; (Persian) happy
Famous namesakes: Actress Farrah Fawcett

FARICA Teutonic: Spelling variation of Frederica

FARIDA (FAH-ree-dah) Arabic, Egyptian: Unique, peerless; feminine form of Farid
(Persian) *Farideh*; *Faridah, Fareeda, Fareedah*

FARKHONDEH Persian: Happy

FARREN Irish: Adventurous; some spelling variants are also surnames
Farin, Farrin, Farron, Farryn, Faryn, Ferran, Ferryn

FARVA Persian: Precious

FARZANEH (far-ZAW-nah) Persian: Wise; feminine form of Farzan

FATIMA (FAH-tee-mah) Arabic: Captivating, sea fowl. Fatima was the daughter of the Prophet Mohammed and one of four perfect women mentioned in the Koran.
(Persian) *Fatemeh*; *Fatimah*

FAUNE (FAWN) French: Young deer; Fauna was the mythological Roman goddess of fertility and nature.
(English) *Fawn*; *Fauna*, *Faunia*, *Fawna*, *Fawne*, *Fawnia*

FAUSTINE Latin: Fortunate one; feminine form of Faust
(Italian) *Fausta*; (Spanish) *Faustina*; *Faust*

FAVOR English: Approval

FAWN English: Variation of Faune

FAYDELL English: Valley fairy
Faydelle, *Faedelle*

FAYE English: Nickname for Faith
Famous namesakes: Actress Faye Dunaway

FAYLINN English: Fairy kingdom
Faylyn, *Faylynn*, *Faylin*, *Faelinn*, *Faelin*, *Faelyn*, *Faelynn*

FAYOLA (fah-YO-lah) African: Walks with honor

FEE German: Fairy

FEECHI African: Worship God

FELDA German: From the field

FELICIA (fə-LEE-shə) Latin: Spelling variation of Felicity
Felisha, *Phylicia*; **Famous namesakes:** Actress Phylicia Rashad

FELICITY (fi-LIS-i-tee) Latin: Happy; feminine form of Felix
(French) *Felicia*, *Felicienne*; (Spanish) *Felicita*, *Felicitas*, *Felisa*; (Polish) *Fela*, *Felka*; *Falisha*, *Felecia*, *Feleta*, *Felice*, *Feliciona*, *Felise*, *Felisha*, *Felita*, *Filicia*; **Famous namesakes:** Actress Felicity Huffman

FEMI (FE-mee) African: Adore me (Nigeria)

FENNELLA Celtic: White shoulder

FERMINA (fer-MEE-nah) Spanish: Strong

FERN English: Botanical name for a green plant that loves shade; also a short form of Fernanda
Ferne

FERNANDA (fer-NAHN-dah) Spanish: Adventurer, traveler; feminine form of Fernando
Nicknames: *Anda*, *Nan*, *Nanda*

FERNLEY English: Fern meadow
Fernlea, *Fernleigh*, *Fernlee*, *Fernlie*

FIA Scottish: Dark of peace

FIACHINA Irish: Raven
Fiachra

FIAMMETTA (fee-ə-MAY-tə) Italian: Little fiery one
Nicknames: *Fia*

FIANAIT Irish: Deer

FIANNA Celtic: Comes from a legendary tale about Irish hero Fionn Mac Cool. Fianna was the name of his Celtic army of warriors.

FIDELITY Latin: Faithful
Fidela, *Fidelia*, *Fidelina*, *Fidelita*

FIDELMA (fi-DEL-mə) Irish: Anglicized spelling of Feidhelm, an old name of uncertain origin. Fidelma and her sister Eithne were early converts of Saint Patrick.
Fedelma, *Feidhelm*

FIFI (fee-FEE, FEE-fee) French: Diminutive form of Josephine
Star babies: daughter of Paula Yates and Bob Geldof

FILA Persian: Lover

FILBERTA English: Extraordinarily brilliant; feminine form of Filbert
Philiberta; Filiberta, Philberta, Philberthe

FILIA (FEE-lee-ə) Greek: Daughter; represents love between a parent and child

FILOMENA (fee-lo-MAY-nah) Spanish: Variation of Philomena

FINEENA Irish: Fair at birth; feminine form of Fineen

FINNEA Irish: Wood of the ford; also an Irish village
Finea

FINOLA (fin-O-lə) Irish: White shoulders; an Anglicized variation of Fionnghuala
Fenella, Finella, Finnguala; Fionnuala, Finoula; **Nicknames:** *Nola, Nuala, Nualla;* **Famous namesakes:** Actress Finola Hughes

FIONA (fee-O-nə) Irish, Gaelic: Fair; feminine form of Fionn
Finna, Fionn, Fionna

FIROUZEH Persian: Turquoise

FIRTHA Scottish: Narrow inlet of the sea

FISSEHA (fis-sey-HA) African: Happiness

FLAIR English: Style, verve

FLAMINIA Latin: Priest
Flamina

FLANNA Irish: Red-haired
Nicknames: *Flannery*

FLANNERY Irish: Nickname for Flanna
Famous namesakes: Author Flannery O'Connor

FLAVIA (FLAH-vee-ah) Latin: Golden or blond; from the Roman family name Flavius

FLETA English: Swift
Fleda, Flede, Flita, Flyta

FLEURETTE (flur-ET) French: Little flower

FLORA (FLOR-ə) Latin: Flower; the mythological Roman goddess of flowers and spring
(French) *Fleur, Flore;* (Spanish) *Flor, Florida, Florita;* (Gaelic) *Floraigh;* (Hungarian) *Florka; Floressa, Flori, Floria, Floriana, Florinda;*
Nicknames: *Florrie;* **Diminutive forms:** *Fleurette, Floretta;* **Famous namesakes:** Chinese actress Flora Chan

FLORENCE Latin, English: Blooming, flourishing. Florence is often thought of in reference to a beautiful city in Italy that is considered a cultural art center. Renowned nurse Florence Nightengale was named for this city of her birth.
(Italian) *Florentina, Florenza;* (Spanish) *Florencia, Florinia;* (Irish) *Blathnaid; Florella, Florentine, Florentyna, Florice, Floris;*
Nicknames: *Flo, Floor;* **Famous namesakes:** Athlete Florence "Flo-Jo" Griffith-Joyner, actress Florence Henderson

FLORIANA (flor-ee-AH-nə) French: Spelling variation of Flora

FLORIDA Spanish: Variation of Flora

FONTAINE French: Fountain, spring
Fontanne; **Famous namesakes:** Actress Joan Fontaine

FORBA Scottish: Headstrong; (Celtic) fields
Forbia

FORTUNE Latin: Fortune, good fate; Fortuna was the Roman goddess of happiness.
Fortuna, Fortunata

FRANCE French: Free one; also a place name for the country of France
Francia; **Diminutive forms:** *Francena, Francene, Francine*; **Famous namesakes:** French singer France Gall

FRANCES Latin: From France, free one; feminine form of Francis
(German) *Franziska*; (French) *Francoise*; (Italian) *Francesca*; (Spanish) *Francisca, Paquita*; (Teutonic) *Ziska, Ziske, Zissi*; (Slavic) *Fanya*; (Czech) *Frantiska*; (Polish) *Franciszka*; (Hungarian) *Franciska*; *Fanceen, Francille, Francina, Francique, Franze*; **Nicknames:** *Fani, Fania, Fanni, Fannia, Fannie, Fanny, Fran, Franci, Francie, Franki, Frankie, Franny, Franky, Frankie*; **Famous namesakes:** Actress Frances McDormand, actress Francis Conroy, actress Fran Drescher; **Star babies:** daughter of Kurt Cobain and Courtney Love

FRANCESCA (frahn-CHES-kah) Italian: Variation of Frances
Star babies: daughters of Martin Scorcese, Jason Leonard, Erik Estrada, Frances Fisher and Clint Eastwood

FRANCINE French: From France, free one
Famous namesakes: British television personality Francine Lewis

FRANZISKA (frahn-TSIS-kah) German: Variation of Frances

FREDA (FREE-də) German: Nickname for Frederica

FREDERICA German: Tranquil leader, peaceful ruler; feminine form of Frederick. Three years after founding Georgia in 1733, General James Edward Oglethorpe established Fort Frederica to defend the fledgling colony against Spanish attack from Florida.
(German) *Friederika*; (French) *Frederique*; (Swedish) *Frederika, Frideborg*; *Farica, Farika, Fredrika, Friederike*; **Old forms:**

Friedegard, Friedegarde; **Nicknames:** *Freda, Fredda, Freddi, Frici, Frida, Frieda, Frika, Frikka, Fritjof, Fritzi, Fritzie, Fryda*; **Famous namesakes:** Opera singer Frederica von Stade

FREYA (FRAY-ah) Norse: A noble woman. Freya was the Norse goddess of love and fertility for whom Friday is named, said to be the most beautiful of the goddesses.
Freja, Freyja, Froja

FRIEDA (FREE-dah) German: Peaceful ruler; feminine form of Frederick
Frida; **Famous namesakes:** Mexican artist Frida Kahlo

FRIGG (FRIG) Norse: Beloved. In Norse mythology, Odin's wife, Frigg, was the mother of the gods and the goddess of the earth, fertility, and love.
Frigga, Nerthus

FRITZI (FRITS-ee) German: Nickname for Frederica

FRONDA Latin: Leafy branch
Fronde

FUJIKO (foo-jee-ko) Japanese: Child of wisteria

FUKAYNA (foo-KE-ee-nah) Egyptian: Knowledgeable, intelligent

FULLA Norse: A name from Norse mythology of uncertain meaning. Fulla was one of the goddess Frigg's attendants.

FULVIA Latin: Blond

GABRIANNA English: Modern blend of Gabrielle and Anna

GABRIELA Hebrew: Variation of Gabrielle **Famous namesakes:** Argentine tennis player Gabriela Sabatini, writer Gabriela Mistal

GABRIELLE Hebrew, French: God is my strength; feminine form of Gabriel (Hebrew) *Gabriela*; (Italian) *Gabriella*; (Slavic) *Gabinka*; *Gabriele, Gabriell, Gavra, Gavriella, Gavrila, Gavrilla*; **Nicknames:** *Gabi, Gaby*; **Famous namesakes:** Volleyball player and model Gabrielle Reece

GADAR (GAH-dahr) Armenian: Summit *Gadara, Gadarine*

GAEL (GAYL) English: Joyful. Gael is an abbreviation of Abigail and a term for descendants of the ancient Celts in Scotland, Ireland, and the Isle of Man. *Gail, Gale*

GAETANA (gie-TAH-nah) Italian: From Gaeta (French) *Gaetane*; **Famous namesakes:** Italian mathematician Maria Gaetana Agnesi

GAHO Native American: Mother

GAIA (GIE-ə) Greek: The earth; mythological female personification of the earth and mother of the Titans **Star babies:** daughter of Emma Thompson and Greg Wise

GAILA (GAY-lə) English: Joyful; abbreviation of Abigail and a variant of Gael or Gail

GAIRA Scottish: Small one *Gara, Garia*

GALA Norse: Lovely voice, singer

GALATIA (gal-ə-TEE-ə) Greek: White as milk. In mythology, Pygmalion fell in

love with the statue Galatia and Aphrodite brought her to life for him. (French) *Galatee*; *Galatea*

GALE English, Norse: Joyful; abbreviation of Abigail *Gayle, Gaylen, Gaylene*; *Gael, Gail*; **Famous namesakes:** Actress Gale Sondergaard

GALIANA German: Haughty *Galiena, Galiene*

GALICE Hebrew: Fountain, spring *Galit*; **Nicknames:** *Gali*

GALILAH Hebrew: God shall redeem *Galila*; **Nicknames:** *Galia*

GALILANI (gal-i-lan-ee) Native American: Attractive (Cherokee)

GALINA (gah-LEE-nah) Russian: Calm, tranquil; feminine form of Galen **Nicknames:** *Galya, Galka*; **Diminutive forms:** *Galenka, Galochka*

GALKA Russian: Jackdaw; also a nickname for Galina

GALLIA French: From Gaul *Galla*

GAMADA African: Glad

GAMILA (ga-MEE-lah) Egyptian: Beautiful *Jamila*

GAMMA Greek: Third letter in Greek alphabet

GANDHARI (gahn-dah-ree) Hindi: Mythological Hindu princess known as a just and fearless speaker

GANESA (gah-NAY-shah) Hindi: Hindu god who removes obstacles

GANIEDA Arthurian Legend: Merlin's sister

GANIT (gah-NEET) Hebrew: Garden
Gana, Ganet, Ganice, Ganya

GARABI Latin: Clear
Garbi

GARABINA (gah-rah-BEE-nah) Spanish:
Purification
Garabine, Garbina, Garbine

GARAITZ (gah-RAH-eets) Basque, Spanish:
Victory

GARAN Welsh: Stork

GARCELLE (gahr-SAY) French: Tomboy;
probably derived from the French word
garçon, meaning *boy*
Famous namesakes: Haitian actress Garcelle
Beauvais

GARDE German: Guarded
Garda

GARDENIA (gahr-DEEN-yə) English: Sweet
flower blossom
Gardenya; **Famous namesakes:** Cape Verdean
singer Gardenia

GARINE (GA-ri-ne) Armenian: Name of an
ancient city

GARNET (GAHR-nət) English: A dark-
red gemstone named for the pomegranate
because of its color; from Old French *grenat*
Garnett

GARUDA (gah-roo-dah) Hindi: Sacred bird
that carries Vishnu

GAURI (GOW-ree) Hindi: Yellow or pale;
name of a Hindu goddess

GAVINA Scottish: White hawk; feminine
form of Gavin
Gavenia

GAY French: Joyful, light-hearted; variant of Gail
Gae, Gaie, Gaye

GAYLA English: Nickname for Abigail

GECHINA (ge-CHEE-nah) Basque, Spanish:
Graceful

GEIRBJORG Norse: Sister of Bersi the Godless

GELASIA Greek: Inclined to laughter

GELLA Hebrew: Golden-haired

GELSEY (GEL-see) English: A variety of
jasmine
Gelsi, Gelsy; **Famous namesakes:** Ballerina
Gelsey Kirkland

GEMMA (JEM-ə) Latin: Gem, a jewel
Gemmalyn, Gemmalynn, Jemma; **Nicknames:**
Gem

GENAYA English: White wave; variant of Jenny

GENEROSA (he-nay-RO-sah) Spanish:
Generous

GENESEE (JEN-e-see) Native American:
Beautiful, shining valley (Iroquois)
Gennisheyo

GENESIS (JEN-ə-sis) Hebrew: Origin.
Genesis is the name of the first book in the
Bible.
Genessa, Genisa, Genisia, Genisis

GENEVA English: Place name for a historic
city in southwestern Switzerland

GENEVIEVE (JEN-ə-veev) French: White wave
(Italian) *Genevra, Ginevra*; (Spanish) *Genoveva,
Ginebra, Ginessa*; (Russian) *Zenevieva*; *Geneve,
Genevie, Genevre, Genivee, Jenavieve, Jeneva,
Jenevieve, Jennavieve, Jenneva*; **Nicknames:**
Genny, Gen; **Famous namesakes:** Canadian
actress Genevieve Bujold

GENISTA (jə-NIS-tə) English: Broom plant

GENNA (JEN-ə) English: Spelling variation of Jennifer

GEONA Hebrew: Glorify

GEORGETTE French: Variation of Georgia
Georgetta, Jorjette

GEORGIA Greek: Farmer; Georgia is a feminine form of George and the name of a southern state
(French) *Georgette*; (Italian) *Giorgia, Giorgina*; (Spanish) *Jorgelina*; (Finnish) *Irja*; *Georgeanne, Georgegina, Georgiana, Georgianna, Georgina, Georgine, Jeorjia, Jorja*; **Nicknames:** *Gigi*; **Famous namesakes:** Painter Georgia O'Keeffe; **Star babies:** daughters of Harrison Ford, Jerry Hall and Mick Jagger, Harry Connick Jr.

> ### "Georgia, Georgia, the whole day through/Just an old sweet song keeps Georgia on my mind."
> —Stuart Gorrell's song, "Georgia on My Mind"

GERALDINE (JER-əl-deen) German: Rules by the spear; feminine form of Gerald
Geralda, Geraldina, Geralyn, Geralynn, Geriann, Gerianne, Gerica, Gericka, Gerika, Gerilyn, Gerilynn, Gerrilyn, Jeraldine;
Nicknames: *Geri, Gerri, Jeralyn, Jerelyn, Jeri, Jerilyn, Jerilynn, Jerri, Jerrilyn, Deena, Dina*;
Famous namesakes: Politician Geraldine Ferraro, actress Geraldine Page, opera singer Geraldine Farrar

> ### My sire is of a noble line, And my name is Geraldine
> —Samuel Taylor Coleridge, "Christabel"

GERARDA (jə-RAHRD-ə) German, Spanish: Mighty with a spear; feminine form of Gerard
Gerhardina, Gerhardine, Gerwalt

GERD (GERD) Norse: Enclosure, protection. In Norse mythology, Gerd was a fertility goddess.
(German) *Gerde*; (Swedish) *Gerda*; (Danish) *Gjerta*; *Gerta, Gerte*; **Nicknames:** *Gerdie*

GERMAINE French: Brotherly; derived from the Latin word *germen*, meaning a *sprout* or *bud*; feminine form of Germain
Germane, Germayne; **Famous namesakes:** Australian feminist author Germaine Greer

GERTRUDE German: Spear of strength
(Spanish) *Gertrudes, Gertrudis*; (Swedish) *Gertrud*; *Gertruda, Gertrut, Gesine, Truda, Trudchen, Trude*; **Old forms:** *Gertraud, Gertraude*; **Nicknames:** *Gesa, Trudie, Trudy, Trula, Gert, Gertie, Trudie*; **Famous namesakes:** Author Gertrude Stein, actress Gertrude Berg

GETHSEMANE (geth-SEM-ə-nee) Hebrew: Oil vat; the name of a garden on the Mount of Olives where Jesus prayed just before his arrest and crucifixion

GEVA (GAY-vah) Hebrew: Hill

GHADA (GAH-dah) Arabic: Charming girl

GHALYELA (GAL-ye-lah) African: Precious

> *"Everybody has a name anybody has a name and everybody anybody does what he does with his name feels what he feels about his name, likes or dislikes what he has to have with having his name, in short it is his name unless he changes his name unless he does what he likes what he likes with his name."*
> —Gertrude Stein

GIADA (JAH-dah) Italian: Variation of Jade
Famous namesakes: Chef Giada De Laurentiis

GIANA (JAH-nah) Italian: God is gracious; variant of Jane
Geonna, Gianara; Gianna; **Nicknames:** *Gia, Giannetta, Giannina*

GIGI (JEE-jee) French: Nickname for Georgia
Famous namesakes: Tennis player Gigi Fernandez

GILBERTA (jeel-BER-tə) German: Brilliant, pledge, trustworthy
Gilbarta, Gilberte; **Old forms:** *Gisilberhta*

GILDA English: Golden; also an abbreviation of Germanic names containing "gilde"; (Celtic) serves God
Gildan, Gildas, Gylda, Gyldan; **Famous namesakes:** Comedienne Gilda Radner

GILIA (gee-LIE-ah, gi-LIE-ah) Hebrew: Eternal joy
Geela, Gila, Gilah, Gilal, Gilala, Gilana, Gilat, Gilit; **Nicknames:** *Gili*

GILLIAN (JIL-ee-ən) English: Spelling variation of Jillian
Jillian; **Star babies:** daughter of Patty Hearst

GINA Greek: Well-born
Famous namesakes: Actress Geena Davis, actress Gina Lollabrigida; **Star babies:** daughters of Tony Danza, Sidney Poitier

GINATA Italian: Flower

GINGER English: Pep, liveliness. Ginger is also a nickname for Virginia. The pungent ginger root is used as a spice.
Famous namesakes: Dancer Ginger Rogers

> *"Sure he [Fred Astaire] was great, but don't forget that Ginger Rogers did everything he did— backwards and in high heels."*
> —Originally from a Frank and Ernest cartoon, famous from its use in a speech by Texas govenor Ann Richards

GINNY English: Nickname for Virginia
Ginnee, Ginney, Ginni, Ginnie, Jinnee, Jinney, Jinni, Jinnie, Jinny

GIORDANA (jor-DAH-nə) Italian: Variation of Jordan

GIOVANNA (jo-VAHN-nah) Italian: Variation of Jane
Jeovana; Geovana; **Nicknames:** *Gian, Gianina, Gianna, Giannina;* **Star babies:** daughter of Vanna White

GISELLE (ji-ZEL) German: Pledge, oath
(German) *Gisela, Gisella;* (Polish) *Gizela;* (Hungarian) *Gizella; Ghislaine, Gisel, Gisele,*

Guilaine, Jiselle; **Nicknames:** *Gilla, Gisa, Gizi, Gizike, Gizus*; **Famous namesakes:** Brazilian model and actress Gisele Bündchen

GITA (gee-tah) Hindi: Song

GITANA (hee-TAH-nah, gee-TAH-nah) Spanish: Gypsy

GITHA English: Gift

GIULIANA (joo-lee-AHN-ə) Italian: Variation of Juliana
Star babies: daughter of Luciano Pavarotti

GIUSEPPINA (joo-se-PEE-nə) Italian: Variation of Josephine

GIZA (GEE-zah) Hebrew: Cut stone
Gazit, Gisa

GLADYS (GLAD-is) Welsh: An old name of uncertain meaning; possibly a derivation of the Latin name Claudia, meaning *lame*
Gladis, Gwladys; **Nicknames:** *Glad*; **Famous namesakes:** Singer Gladys Knight

GLAFIRA Russian: Elegant, slim
Nicknames: *Glasha*

GLAN Welsh: From the shore

GLAW (GLOW) Welsh: Rain

GLEDA (GLAY-də) English: Happy

GLENDA (GLEN-də) Welsh: Fair, good, or from the glen
Glinda, Glynda; **Famous namesakes:** Actress Glenda Jackson

GLENNA Gaelic, Irish: From the glen
(Welsh) *Glynnis*; *Ghleanna, Glyn, Glynis, Glynna, Glynnes, Glynnis, Glen, Glenn, Glenne, Glennis, Glenys, Glyn, Glynae, Glynn*;
Famous namesakes: Actress Glenn Close

GLIONA Irish: Variation of Cleone

GLORIA Latin: Glory, renown, and respect
Gloriana, Gloriane, Glorianna, Gloribel, Gloriosa; **Famous namesakes:** Musician Gloria Estefan, feminist Gloria Steinem, fashion designer Gloria Vanderbilt

GLORIANN English: Glorious grace; modern blend of Gloria and Ann

GLYNNIS (GLEN-is) Welsh: Variation of Glenna

GOBNAIT (GAWB-net) Irish: Variation of Abigail

GODIVA (gə-DIE-və) English: Gift from God. Lady Godiva is the subject of a legend where she rode through the town of Coventry naked, covered only by her long, flowing hair.

GOEWIN (GO-win) Welsh: Sprightly; legendary daughter of Pebin

GOLBAHR Persian: Spring flower

GOLDA English, Hebrew: Golden, bright, and precious
Nicknames: *Goldie, Golds, Goldy*; **Famous namesakes:** Prime Minister of Israel Golda Meir, actress Goldie Hawn

GOLNAZ (gol-nahz) Persian: Cute like a flower

GOLSHAN Persian: Flower garden

GONCA (GON-jah) Turkish: Rosebud

GORAWEN (GOR-ah-wen) Welsh: Joy

GORDANA Scottish: From the wedge-shaped or three-cornered town or settlement, heroic; feminine form of Gordon
Gordania

GOTILDA Swedish: Strong
Nicknames: *Gota, Gote*

GRACE Latin, English: Lovely or graceful,
a virtue. The three mythological graces,
or charities, were nature goddesses: Aglaia
(brilliance), Thalia (flowering), and
Euphrosyne (joy). See also *Ance*
(German) *Gratia*; (Italian) *Grazia, Graziosa*;
(Spanish) *Engracia, Gracia, Graciana,
Graciela*; (Polish) *Grazyna*; (Hawaiian)
Kalake; *Gracella, Gracelynne*; *Graca, Graciene,
Gracinha, Grata*; **Nicknames:** *Gracelyn,
Gracie*; **Famous namesakes**: Princess Grace
Kelly, singer Grace Jones; **Star babies:**
daughters of Wynonna Judd, Meryl Streep
and Don Gummer

GRACELYN English: Graceful; a blend of
Grace and Lynn
Gracelynn, Gracelin, Gracelinn, Gracelynne

GRACIE English: Nickname for Grace
Famous namesakes: Comedienne Gracie
Allen; **Star babies:** daughters of Danny
DeVito and Rhea Perlman, Faith Hill and
Tim McGraw

GRÁINNE (GRAWN-ya) Irish: Possibly
derived from the Gaelic word *grán*, meaning
grain; name of an ancient Irish grain goddess
and often associated with *gráidh*, meaning *love*
Graina, Graine, Grania; *Granya*

GRANIA (GRAWN-ya) Celtic: Spelling
variation of Gráinne

GREENLEIGH (GREEN-lee) American:
Green meadow; possibly a varaint of Greeley,
but more likely a modern blend of the
color green and the English ending *–leigh*
(meadow)
Greenley, Greenlie, Greenlea

GREER Scottish: Variation of Gregoria
Grier; **Famous namesakes:** Actress Greer

Garson; **Star babies:** daughters of Kelsey
Grammer, Brooke Shields

GREGORIA Latin: Watchful; feminine form
of Gregory
(Scottish) *Greer*; *Gregoriana*

GRETA (GRET-ə) Swedish: Nickname for
Margaret
*Gretal, Grete, Gretel, Gretta, Grette, Griet,
Grietje*; **Famous namesakes:** Swedish actress
Greta Garbo; **Star babies:** daughters of David
Caruso, Phoebe Cates and Kevin Kline

GRETCHEN German: Diminutive form of
Margaret

GRISELDA (gri-ZEL-də) German: Gray
battle maiden. Italian author Giovanni
Boccaccio used the name for an exceptionally
patient wife, thus the expression "patience of
Griselda."
(French) *Griselle*; (Gaelic) *Giorsal*; (Scottish)
Grizel, Grizela; *Gricelda, Griselde, Grisella,
Grissel, Grizelda, Gryselda*; **Nicknames:** *Zelda,
Zelde*

GUADALUPE (gwah-dah-LOO-pay)
Spanish: This name of a Spanish city also refers
to a chain of mountains in Spain and a city
in Mexico. The Virgin Mary is Mexico's Lady
of Guadalupe. Christopher Columbus signed
his contract to go to the New World at the
Royal Monastery of Our Lady of Guadalupe in
Spain, now a popular destination for pilgrims;
(Arabic) valley of the wolf
Guadaloupe, Guadaloupa, Guadolupe;
Nicknames: *Lupe, Lupita, Guada, Lopina,
Lupeta, Lupina*

GUDA Swedish: Supreme

GUDNY Swedish: Unspoiled

GUDRUN (GUWD-roon) Norse: Divinely
inspired wisdom; derived from the Old Norse

roots *guð* (God) and *run* (secret wisdom). Gudrun was the wife of Sigurd in Norse legend.
Gudrid, Gudruna

GUENNOLA Celtic: White

GUIDA (GWEE-də) Italian: Guide

GUIDITTA (joo-DEET-ə) Italian: Variation of Judith

GUINEVERE (GWI-nə-veer) Welsh, Arthurian legend: White and smooth, or fair lady. Guinevere was King Arthur's beautiful queen in Arthurian legend. Jennifer derives from this name.
Guenevere, Gwenevere, Gwenhwyfar, Gwenhwyvar, Gwenyver; Old forms: *Gaenor, Gaynor*; **Nicknames:** *Gwen*

GULLVEIG Norse: Refers to Goldbranch, a sorceress of Norse mythology who had a great lust for gold

GUNHILDA Norse: Battle maiden (Swedish) *Gunilla, Gunnef; Gunhilde, Gunnel, Gunnhild, Gunnhilde*

GUNNA Scottish: White

GURI Hindi: Hindu goddess of plenty

GURICE Hebrew: Cub
Gurit

GURO Norse: Divinely inspired wisdom

GUSTAVA Swedish: Staff of the Goths; feminine form of Gustav
(Dutch) *Gust, Gusta, Gustaafa*; **Nicknames:** *Gustha, Gussie, Gussy*; **Diminutive forms:** *Gustel*

GWANWYN (GWAHN-win) Welsh: Spring

GWEN Welsh: Nickname for Gwendolyn
Star babies: daughter of Tammy Wynette

GWENDA (GWEN-də) Welsh: Spelling variation of Gwynn
Gwynda

GWENDOLYN (GWEN-də-lin) Welsh: Fair bow, a blend of the elements gwen (white, fair, or blessed) and dolen (bow or ring)
Guendolen, Gwendelyn, Gwendolen, Gwendolin, Gwendoline, Gwendoloena, Gwyndolen, Gwyndolin, Gwyndolyn; **Nicknames:** *Gwen, Gwendi, Wynne, Gwyn, Wendi, Wendie, Wendy*; **Famous namesakes:** Poet Gwendolyn Brooks

GWYNETH (GWIN-eth) Welsh: White, fair, or blessed
Gweneth, Gwenith, Gwenneth, Gwenyth, Gwynedd, Gwynith; **Famous namesakes:** Actress Gwyneth Paltrow

GWYNN Welsh: Fair, blessed
Gwenda, Gwenn, Gwenna, Gwyn, Gwynne; Gwen

GYPSY English: Wanderer; derived from Egyptian to describe tribes of nomads who migrated from India to Europe
Gipsy

HABIBA (hah-BE-bah) African: Sweetheart, beloved

HABIBAH (hah-BEE-bah) Egyptian: My sweetheart, my beloved
Habiba

HADAR (hah-DAHR) Hebrew: Beautiful, honored
Hadara, Hadarah

HADASSAH (hah-DAH-sah) Hebrew: Myrtle tree; also the biblical Queen Esther's Hebrew name
Nicknames: *Hada*

HADEYA Arabic: Gift, offering; also a spelling variant of Hadya, meaning quiet, well-behaved
(African) *Hadiya*; *Hedeya, Hadeyya, Hadya*

HADLEY (HAD-lee) English: From the heath or heather-covered meadow; a surname now used as a given name
Hadlee, Hadleigh, Hadlea, Hadlie

HADREA (HAY-dree-ə) Latin: Dark; from the Adriatic Sea region; feminine variant of Adrian and Hadrian
Hadria

HADYA (HAH-dee-yah) Arabic: Well-behaved, quiet; feminine variant of Hadi
Hadyah, Hadia, Hadiah

HAFSA (haf-SA) African: young lioness

HAGAR (HAY-gahr) Hebrew: Flight. In the Old Testament, Hagar was Sarah's Egyptian serving-maid who became the concubine to Abraham and the mother of Ishmael, considered to be the founder of the Arab people.

HAIBA (HAH-ee-bah) African: Charm

HAIDEE (HAY-dee) Greek: Haidee was created by Byron for a character in his poem *Don Juan*. He may have taken it from the Greek aidos, meaning modesty.
Haydee

HAILEY English: Spelling variation of Hayley

HAJNAL (HAWY-nawl) Hungarian: Dawn

HAKAN Norse: Of the chosen, tradionally used as a male name; (Swedish) highborn child

HAKIDONMUYA Native American: Time of waiting moon (Hopi)

HALCYONE (hal-SIE-o-nee) Greek: Time of peace, kingfisher. In Greek mythology, Halcyone threw herself into the sea after the death of her husband. Out of pity, the gods changed the pair into kingfishers, or halcyons, and caused the winds to cease blowing during the kingfisher's mating season. The expression "halcyon days" is derived from this myth and means a time of tranquility.

HALDIS Teutonic: Spirit of stone
Halldis; **Nicknames:** *Haldisa, Halldora*

HALEH Persian: Halo

HALEY (HAY-lee, HAL-ee) Scandinavian: Heroine, brave one; (English) variant of Halley and Hayley

HALFRID German: Peaceful heroine
(English) *Halfrith, Halfryta, Hallfrita*; *Halfrida*; **Nicknames:** *Halifrid*

HALFRIDA (hahl-FREE-də) German: Peaceful heroine; variant of Halfrid

HALIA (hah-LEE-ə) Hawaiian: Remembrance of a loved one

HALIMA (hah-LEEM-ah) Arabic: Gentle, patient; a fitting name for the woman who cared for the young prophet Mohammed after his mother's death
Halimah

HALIMEDA Greek: Thinking of the sea

HALLA Norse: Rock, stone

HALLDORA Norse: Spirit of stone; variant of Haldis

HALLE (HAL-ee) English: Variant of Halley or Hayley
Hallie, Halley; **Famous namesakes:** Actress Halle Berry

HALLEY English: From the meadow near the hall (implying large estate or home); a surname also used as a variant of Hayley
Halle, Hallie, Halie, Haley

HALLIE English: Variant of Halley and Hayley
Halle, Halley

HALONA (hah-LO-nah) Native American: Fortunate

HAMIDEH Persian: Praiseworthy, glorified; feminine form of Hamid, derived from hamd (giving thanks, usually to God)
Hamida

HANA Arabic: Bliss; (Persian) shrub henna
Hanaa; **Star babies:** daughter of Muhammad Ali

HANAKO (hah-nah-ko) Japanese: Flower child

HANITA (han-ee-tah) Hindi: Divine grace

HANNAH Hebrew: Favor, grace. Hannah was the biblical mother of the prophet Samuel.
(English) *Hannalee*; (Danish) *Hanne*; (Finnish) *Hanna, Hannele, Henna, Henni*; (Hungarian) *Hajna*; *Chana, Chanah, Hanah*; **Nicknames:** *Hana, Hannela*; **Famous namesakes:** Philosopher Hannah Arendt, sportscaster Hannah Storm; **Star babies:** daughters of Mel Gibson, Pat Benatar, Kristin Scott Thomas, Jilly Mack and Tom Selleck, Jessica Lange and Sam Shepard, Elizabeth Perkins, Helen Slater

HANNELA Hebrew: Nickname for Hannah

HANNELE Hebrew: Nickname for Hannah

HANZILA African: Road, path

HARA (HAHR-ah) Hindi: Another name for the Hindu deity Shiva

HARIMANNA German: Warrior maiden
Harimanne

HARLEY Anglo-Saxon, English: From the hare's meadow. Harley is a surname associated with the famous Harley-Davidson motorcycles. While traditionally a boy's name, it is now increasingly being used for both genders. (English) *Arleigh*; *Harleen, Harlie; Harlee, Harleigh, Harlie, Harlea*

HARLOW English: From the hill of the hares, from the army hill. Traditionally a boy's name, Harlow is now being used increasingly for both genders.
Harlowe; **Famous namesakes:** Actress Jean Harlow; **Star babies:** daughter of Nicole Richie and Joel Madden

HARMONY Latin: Unity, concord, musically in tune. Harmonia was the mythological daughter of Aphrodite.
(French) *Harmonie*; *Harmonee, Harmonia*

HAROLDA Teutonic: Commander; feminine variant of Harold
Haralda, Harelda, Harelde, Harolde

HARPER English: Minstrel. Harpers were more than entertainers when this name was created. They were a primary source of news and keepers of the historical record.

HARPINNA Latin: Mare of Oenomaus

HARRIET English: Nickname for Henrietta
Famous namesakes: Abolitionist Harriet Tubman

HASINA (hah-SEE-nah) African: Good (Swahili)

HATHOR (HAH-thor) Egyptian: The goddess of love, dance, and alcohol was depicted as a cow. At Thebes she was also Sakmet, the goddess of the dead and destruction.

HATSHEPSUT (haht-SHEP-soot) Egyptian: Princess Hatshepsut was the daughter of Thutmose I and Queen Ahmes

HATSUE (haht-soo-e) Japanese: Beginning, first time

HATTIE (HAT-ee) English: Nickname for Henrietta
Famous namesakes: Politician Hattie Wyatt Caraway

HAUSIS Native American: Old woman (Algonquin)
Nicknames: *Hausisse*

HAVEN (HAY-vən) English, Dutch: Place of safety, shelter

HAVVA Persian: Variation of Eve

HAWA African: Longing (Swahili)

HAYA Hebrew: To be, to live

HAYLEY (HAY-lee) English: From the hay meadow; an adapted surname traditionally used as a boy's name, now more common for girls
Hailey, Haleigh, Hallie, Haylie; Halley, Hayley, Haley, Haylee, Hayleigh, Haileigh, Hailee, Haylie, Haeley, Haelie, Haely, Hailea, Haily, Haylea; **Nicknames:** *Halle*; **Famous namesakes:** Actress Hayley Mills; **Star babies:** daughters of Stephen Baldwin, David Hasselhoff, Jeff Bridges

HAZAN (hah-ZAHN) Turkish: Autumn

HAZEL English: The hazel tree
Hazell; **Star babies:** daughter of Julia Roberts and Danny Moder

HEATHER English: A flowering evergreen plant that thrives on peaty, barren lands such as those found in Scotland

Famous namesakes: Actress Heather Locklear; **Star babies:** daughters of Jerry Garcia, Paul McCartney and Linda Eastman

HECUBA (HEK-yoo-bə) Greek: Wife of King Priam of Troy. Hecuba was the mother of Paris and Hector in Greek mythology.

HEDDA Teutonic: Pleasant, refuge from battle; a variant of Edda
Famous namesakes: Writer Hedda Hopper

HEDWIG (HED-vikh) German: Struggle, strife. The fictional Harry Potter named his owl Hedwig.
(French) *Hedvige*; (Czech) *Hedvika*; *Hedvig*; **Old forms:** *Haduwig, Hadwig*; **Nicknames:** *Hedy, Heddy*; **Diminutive forms:** *Hadu*

HEHET (HE-het) Egyptian: Goddess of the immeasurable

HEIDI (HIE-dee) German: Sweet or noble; a short form of Adelaide and Adelheid
Heida, Heide; **Star babies:** daughter of Larry Hagman

HEIDRUN Norse: In the Edda Saga of Norse mythology, Heidrun is the name of the goat that stands on the roof of Valhall. Instead of milk, she produces mead for the warriors of Odin.

HEKUBA (HEK-yoo-buh) Greek: Mother of Paris and Hector in Greek mythology

HELA Norse: Goddess of the underworld in Norse mythology

HELEN (HEL-ən) Greek: Nickname for Helena
Famous namesakes: Singer Helen Reddy

HELENA (he-LE-nah, hay-LAY-nah) Greek: Light. In Greek mythology, Helen was the daughter of Zeus by Leda and the most

beautiful woman in the world. By abducting her, Paris began the Trojan War. In Christopher Marlowe's play *Doctor Faustus*, the devil taunts Faustus with the image of Helen, whom he describes as "the face that launched a thousand ships," in reference to the entire Greek fleet that set sail to bring her home.
(French) *Helene*; (Spanish) *Ileanna*; (Russian) *Alyona, Yelena*; (Czech) *Helenka*; (Polish) *Halina*; (Ukrainian) *Olena*; (Romanian) *Ileana*; (Finnish) *Ilona*; (Hungarian) *Ili, Ilka, Ilke, Ilon, Ilonka, Iluska, Onella; Elynn, Helaine, Ilena, Ilene, Iliana, Yalena, Yalene*; **Nicknames:** *Helen, Lena*; **Famous namesakes:** Cosmetics entrepreneur Helena Rubinstein, author Helen Keller

HELGA Scandinavian, German: Blessed, holy
Elga, Helge; Olga

HELGE Norse: Spelling variation of Helga

HELIA Greek: Sun; feminine form of Helios

HELIKE Greek: Helike was an ancient Greek city that was destroyed by a massive earthquake and tidal wave. The entire city and all its inhabitants were lost beneath the sea. Helike is also the name of a nymph.
Helice; Helice

HELMI (HEL-mee) Finnish: Pearl

HELOISE (EL-o-ees) French: Spelling variation of Eloise
Famous namesakes: Self-help queen Heloise

HELSA Hebrew: Devoted to God

HELSIN Arthurian Legend: Mother of Lancelot

HEMERA (HEE-me-rə) Greek: Goddess of the day

HENGAMEH Persian: Uproar, wonder

HENICEA Greek: Daughter of Priam

HENLEY Irish: High field; surname

HENNA (HEN-ah) Finnish: Variation of Hannah

HENRIETTA (hen-ree-ET-ə) German: Keeper of the hearth, rules her household; feminine form of Henry. See also *Enriqua* (French) *Harriette, Henriette*; (Teutonic) *Enrika, Henuita*; (Swedish) *Henrika*; (Dutch) *Hendrika*; (Polish) *Henka, Henrieta*; (Finnish) *Riikka; Enrica, Enriqueta; Hanrietta, Hanriette, Harriett, Harrietta, Hatty, Henuite*; **Nicknames:** *Etta, Ettie, Etty, Harriet, Hattie, Heike, Hen, Henia, Henie, Hennie, Henny, Hettie*; **Famous namesakes:** English cookbook author Henrietta Green

HEPSIBA (HEP-zi-bə) Hebrew: She is my delight. Hepzibeth is another variant of this name.
Hephzibah; **Nicknames:** *Hepzibeth*

HEQET (HE-get) Egyptian: Mythical frog-headed goddess of Antinoopolis, associated with Khnum, a helper of women in childbirth.

HERA (HER-ə) Greek: Hera is the mythological wife of Zeus and was mainly worshipped as a goddess of marriage and birth.

HERLINDE German: Shield
(Spanish) *Erlina*; **Famous namesakes:** Photographer Herlinde Koelbl

HERMANDINA Greek: Well-born; variant of Hermione

HERMIONE (hər-MIE-ə-nee) Greek: Well-born, earthly; feminine form of Hermes and, in Greek mythology, the daughter of Menelaus and Helen. Kids and adults alike are sure to recognize the name as a character in J.K. Rowling's *Harry Potter* series.
Hermia; **Nicknames:** *Hermandina, Hermandine, Herminia*

HERMOSA (er-MO-sah) Spanish: Beautiful

HERO Greek: Hero. In Greek mythology, Hero was the lover of Leander, who would swim across the Hellespont each night to meet her. Hero is also the name of a character in Shakespeare's play *Much Ado about Nothing*.

HEROPHILE Greek: Daughter of Lamia and Poseidon, priestess of Apollo

HERSILIA Latin: A name from Roman mythology, Hersilia married a follower of Romulus.

HERTHA (HUR-thə) English: Of the earth (German) *Herta*; (Teutonic) *Heartha, Herthe*; (Finnish) *Hertta*

HERZELOYDE Arthurian Legend: Percival's mother

HESIONE (he-SIE-o-nee) Greek: Daughter of Laomedon

HESPER Greek: Evening star
(Latin) *Hesperie*; **Nicknames:** *Hespera, Hesperia*

HESPERIA (hes-PEER-ee-ə) Greek: Nickname for Hesper

HESTER Greek: Nickname for Esther; (Persian) star, myrtle leaf. Esther was a young Hebrew woman in the Bible who married the Persian ruler Xerxes and risked her life to save her people. (Persian) *Hetty*

HESTIA (HES-tee-ə) Greek, Persian: Goddess of hearth and home

HETTY Persian: Variation of Hester

HIALEAH (hie-ah-lee-ah) Native American: Pretty prairie (Seminole)

HIBERNIA Latin: An old name for Ireland

HIBISCUS Latin: Flower. The hibiscus is the state flower of Hawaii.
Hibiskus

HILA Hebrew: Praise; feminine form of Hillel; (Persian) sparrow-hawk

HILARY Latin: Cheerful, joyful; derived from the Latin word hilarius
(French) *Hilaire*; (Irish) *Hiolair*; *Hilaeira, Hillary*; **Old forms:** *Hilaria*; **Famous namesakes:** Politician and First Lady Hillary Clinton, actress Hilary Duff, actress Hilary Swank

HILDA German: Defending battle maiden; nickname for Hildegard
Hilde, Hildy

HILDEGARD (HIL-de-gahrd) German: Defending battle maiden. In Scandinavian mythology, Hildegard was a Valkyrie sent by Odin to escort battle heroes to Valhalla. Hildegard gained popularity in Germany in medieval times through Saint Hildegard of Bingen.
Nicknames: *Hilda, Hildagarde, Hilde*

HILDUR Norse: Battle maiden

HILMA German: Nickname for Wilhelmina

HIPPODAMIA (HIP-o-da-MIE-ə) Greek: In Greek mythology, she was the wife of Pirithous. The battle between Centaurs and Lapiths began at their wedding.
(Latin) *Hippodameia*

HIPPOLYTE (hi-PAHL-ə-tee) Greek: Greek mythological queen of the Amazons, a tribe of women warriors
Nicknames: *Hippolyta*

HIRAKA (heer-ah-kah) Japanese: Mighty one; a little diamond
Nicknames: *Kay*

HISOLDA Irish: Fair; variant of Isolde

HJORDIS Norse: Sword goddess
Hjördis

HOLDA German: Merciful. Holda was a Germanic goddess whose cult survived in the folklore of Germany, Austria, and Switzerland. She was considered the patron of the spinner.

HOLLAND English: Place name in the Netherlands; English surname
Famous namesakes: Actress Holland Taylor

HOLLIS English: Holy or holly tree; variant of Holly

HOLLY English: Holy or holly tree; a beautiful seasonal name for girls born at Christmas, and the name of Audrey Hepburn's memorable character Holly Golightly in *Breakfast at Tiffany's*
Hollee, Hollie; Holley; **Nicknames:** *Hollis, Hollyn;* **Famous namesakes:** Actress Holly Hunter; **Star babies:** daughter of Michael Bolton

HOMA Persian: Phoenix

HONEY English: Sweet

HONORA Latin: Honor; feminine form of Honorius
(Spanish) *Honoratas; Honorata, Honoria, Honorina, Honorine, Honour, Onora;*
Nicknames: *Honor*

HOPE English: The feeling that a desire will be fulfilled, one of the three Christian virtues; a name first commonly used by the Puritans

HORATIA (hə-RAY-shee-ə) Latin: Keeper of the hours

HORTENSE Latin: From the Roman family name Hortentius, which is derived from *hortus*, the Latin word for garden
(Spanish) *Hortencia;* (Polish) *Hortensja; Ortensia, Ortensiana, Ortensie;* **Nicknames:** *Hortendana*

HOURI Persian: Fairy

HUBERTA German: Bright in spirit; feminine form of Hubert
Huberte

HUETTE (HYOO-et) German: Intelligent, thoughtful; feminine form of Hugh
(French) *Hugette; Huetts, Hughetta, Hughette, Hugiet, Hugolina, Huguetta, Ugolina*

HUI (HWEE) Chinese: Wise

HULDA Norse: Sweet, beloved
(German) *Hulde*

HUMILITY English: Humble, without false price; a virtue name

HUMITA (hoo-MEE-tah) Native American: Shelled corn (Hopi)

HUNTER English: To hunt; an occupational name
Famous namesakes: Actress Holly Hunter

HURIT Native American: Beautiful (Algonquin)

HYACINTH (HIE-ə-sinth) Greek: A flower known for its beautiful scent and color. In Greek mythology, Hyacinthus was beloved and accidentally killed by Apollo. In tribute, Apollo had the flower that bears his name spring from his blood.
(French) *Hyacinthe, Jacinthe*; (Spanish) *Jacinta, Jakinda; Giancinta, Giancinte, Jacenia, Jacinda, Jacintha*; **Nicknames:** *Jaxine*

HYADES (HIE-ə-deez) Greek: A cluster of stars in the constellation Taurus

HYPATE Greek: Exceptional
Hypatia

HYPERMNESTRA (hip-erm-NES-trə) Greek: One of the Danaides, fifty daughters of Danaus

HYPSIPYLE (hip-SIP-ə-lee) Greek: Mythical queen of Lemnos

HYRIA Greek: Mythical daughter of Amphinomus

IAERA Latin: Dryad nymph, mother of Bitias and Pandarus

IANTHE (YAHN-thə) Greek: Violet flower; mythological sea nymph and daughter of Oceanus
Iolantha, Iolanthe

ICA Greek: Light

IDA (IE-də) German: Diligent, hard-working; (Hindi) hindu goddess of prayer and devotion; (Greek) name of a mountain in Asia Minor and a Greek nymph, mother of Teucer, Troy's first king; (English) prosperous (Welsh) *Idelle*; (Finnish) *Iida; Idaia*; **Star babies:** daughter of Dolph Lundgren

. . . what men
Unborn shall read o'er
ocean wide
And find Ianthe's name again
—Walter Landor, "Well I Remember How You Smiled"

IDABELLE English: Modern blend of Ida and Belle
Idabella

IDAIA German: Spelling variation of Ida

IDALIA Greek: Glorious sun; (German) elaboration of Ida, diligent
Idalie; Idaliah

IDALINA Teutonic: Possibly a variant of Ida or a blend of Ida and Lina
Idaline

IDALIS English: Origins are unclear, but Idalis may be either a variant of Adelle or Alise, or possibly a blend of Ida and Alise
Idalise, Idelis

IDEASHIA English: Modern blend of Ida and Aisha
Ideashiah

IDELISA Celtic: A modern blend of Ida and Lisa

IDELLE (ie-DEL) Welsh: Variation of Ida
Idella

IDETTA German: Hard-working; variant of Ida using a feminine French suffix
Idette

IDOIA (ee-DOI-ah) Spanish: From the Spanish location Idoia, an important place of worship of the Virgin Mary
Idoya

IDOLINA (ee-do-LEE-nah) Spanish: Idol, worshipped image

IDONA German: Variant of either Ida (diligent worker) or Idony (renewed)
Idone

IDONIA Spanish: Happy, good girl

IDONY (ie-DO-nee) Scandinavian: Renewed, rejuvenated. In Norse mythology, she was the goddess of spring and immortality charged with guarding the gods' apples of youth.
Idun, Iduna, Idunn

IDURRE (ee-DOO-re) Basque: Reference to the Virgin Mary

IESHA English: Spelling variation of Aisha
Iesha, Ieshea, Iesha

IFE (ee-FE) African: Love (Nigeria)

IGNACIA (ig-NAH-syah) Latin, Spanish: Fiery, passionate
Ignatia; Ignaci, Ignaciah, Ignacie, Ignacya, Ignasha, Ignashia; **Nicknames:** *Ignia, Nacha*

IGONE (EE-gon-e) Basque, Spanish: Refers to Christ's Ascension

IGRAINE (ee-GRAYN) English: Graceful; the legendary King Arthur's mother over whom a war was fought between her first husband, Gorlois, and her second, Arthur's father, Uther Pendragon
Igrayne, Ygraine

IKERNE (ee-KAYR-nay) Basque: Visitation

ILANA (ee-LAH-nah) Hebrew: Tree
Ilane; **Nicknames:** *Ilanit*

ILDIKO (EEL-dyee-KO) Hungarian: Warrior

ILIA (IL-ee-ah) Latin: Mythical vestal virgin who broke her vow of celibacy and became the mother, by the god Mars, of the twin boys Romulus and Remus

ILIANA (ee-lee-AHN-ah) Spanish: Variation of Eleana; (Greek) light; variant of Helena

ILMA (EEL-mah) Finnish: Air
Ilmatar

ILONA (EE-lo-naw) Hungarian: Variation of Helena

ILORI (il-lor-EE) African: Special treasure

ILSE (IL-sə) German: Spelling variation of Else

ILUMINADA (ee-loo-mee-NAH-dah) Spanish: Illuminated

ILYSSA English: Variation of Elise

IMALA (EE-mah-lah) Native American: Strong-willed, independent
Imalah

IMBER Polish: Ginger

IMELDA (ee-MEL-dah) Spanish: Powerful fighter; the name of a fourteenth-century Spanish saint
Famous namesakes: First Lady of the Philippines Imelda Marcos

IMENA (ee-MAY-nah) African: Dream

IMMACULATA Latin: Immaculate or without stain; given to commemorate the Virgin Mary's Immaculate Conception as Maria Immacolata
(Spanish) *Immaculada*

IMOGENE (IM-ə-jeen) Latin: Image, likeness. There is evidence that Imogen as a name is not derived from the Latin, but was simply a made-up name from a mistake in the use of the Gaelic *inghean*, meaning maiden.
Emogene, Imogen, Imogenia

IMPERIA Latin: Imperious, commanding

INA Irish: Pure or virginal; variant of Agnes

INARA (in-NAR-ə) Arabic: Heaven sent, enlightened
Enara

INARI (ee-NAHR-ee) Finnish: Place name for Lake Inari in Finland

INCA Scandinavian: Ing's abundance (Ing was the Norse mythological god of the earth's fertility). Inca also refers to Quechuan people living in the Cuzco Valley in Peru.

INDIA English: From the Sanskrit for river. India is a country in southern Asia. Fictional India Wilkes was Ashleigh's sister in Margaret Mitchell's *Gone with the Wind*.
Inda, Indee, Indi; **Star babies:** daughters of Marianne Williamson, Catherine Oxenberg, Philip Michael Thomas

INDIANA English: Place name for Indiana, one of the United States fondly known as the Hoosier State

INDIGO (IN-di-go) English: Deep blue-violet

INDIRA (in-DEER-ah) Sanskrit: Splendid, beautiful; another name of Lakshmi, the wife of the Hindu god Vishnu; (Hindi) mythological wife of Vishnu
Famous namesakes: Indian Prime Minister Indira Gandhi

INDRANI (in-DRAH-nee) Hindi: Mythological Indra's wife and consort, in some accounts she is called the goddess of wrath.

INEZ (ee-NAYS, ee-nes) Spanish: Variation of Agnes
Ines

INGE (ING-gə) Scandinavian, German: One who is foremost; an independent name and a short form of several Scandinavian and German names having *Ing–* as their first element. In Norse mythology, Ing was another name for the fertility and agriculture god Frey.
Inga

INGEBORG (ING-e-borg, ING-ge-borg) Scandinavian: Ing's protection, fortress of Ing; refers to the Norse god of fertility and agriculture
Ingaborg

INGELISE Scandinavian: Combination name pairing Inga and Liese

INGRID (ING-grit, ING-grid) Scandinavian: Beautiful; feminine version of the Norse fertility god Ing's name
(Finnish) *Inka, Inkeri*; *Inger*; *Inga, Inge*;
Famous namesakes: Swedish actress Ingrid Bergman

INIGA Latin: Fiery, passionate

INIKO (ee-NEE-ko) African: Born during troubled times

INIS (IN-əs) Irish: Island

INKERI (EEN-ker-ee) Finnish: Variation of Ingrid
Nicknames: *Inka*

INO Greek: Greek mythical daughter of Cadmus, foster mother of Dionysis, and stepmother of Prixes. It was from Ino that Prixes fled on the ram with the golden fleece. Zeus saved Ino from a tragic fate by turning her into Leucotha, the white sea goddess.

INOCENCIA (ee-no-SEN-see-ah) Spanish: Innocence
Inocenta

INOLA (in-o-lah) Native American: Black fox (Cherokee)

INTISARA Arabic: Triumphant
Intisar; Intesara, Entesara

IOLA Greek: Violet, dawn. In Greek mythology, the hero Hercules loved Iola; (Welsh) deemed worthy, valued by God
Iole

IOLANA (ee-o-LAH-nah) Hawaiian: To soar like the hawk; also the Hawaiian for Yolanda, a variant of Violet
Iolani

IONA (ie-ON-ə) Scottish, English: Place name for an island off the west coast of Scotland
Ionanna, Ionna

IONE (ie-O-nee) Greek: Amethyst, violet flower; possibly meaning from Ionia, an ancient region in Asia Minor
Iona, Ionessa, Ionia

IRAN Persian: Place name for Iran, an ancient Middle Eastern country in Asia

IRATZE (ee-RAHT-say) Basque: Reference to the Virgin Mary

IRELAND English: Place name for Ireland, a small country in northwestern Europe
Irelyn; **Star babies:** daughter of Kim Basinger and Alec Baldwin

IRENE (IE-reen) Greek: Peace; Irene was the Greek goddess of peace. Another famous bearer was an eighth-century Byzantine empress, the first woman to lead the Empire. She originally served as regent for her son but later had him killed and ruled alone.
(Russian) *Arina, Irina;* (Hungarian) *Irenke; Eirene, Irayna, Irena, Iriana, Irinia, Iryna;* **Nicknames:** *Irini, Rena, Rina*

IRIS Greek, Hebrew: Rainbow. Iris was the Greek mythological goddess of the rainbow. This name can also be given in reference to the English word (which derives from the same Greek source) for the name of the iris flower or the colored part of the eye. See also *Irsia*
(Finnish) *Iiris; Irisa*

IRMA (UR-mə) German: Strength, universal, or complete; a short form of many names begining with the element Irm or Erm, probably derived from *irm*, the root of the name Irmin, a German mythological god of war
(Latin) *Ermina; Erma, Ermelinda, Ermelinde, Irmgard, Irmina, Irmine;* **Nicknames:** *Irmuska;* **Famous namesakes:** Humorist Erma Bombeck

---

"When my kids become wild and unruly, I use a nice, safe playpen. When they're finished, I climb out."
—Erma Bombeck

IRMAK Turkish: River

IRSIA Persian: Rainbow; variant of Iris

IRUNE (ee-ROO-nay) Basque: Reference to the Holy Trinity

IRVETTE English: Sea friend; (Irish) attractive; (Welsh) white river
Irvetta; Irveta, Irvetah

ISA (EE-sah) German: Nickname for Isabel
Star babies: daughter of Michael Bolton

ISABEL (ee-sah-BEL, IZ-ə-bel) Spanish: Devoted to God. Isabel is generally considered a medieval Spanish form of Elizabeth, though some sources suggest Isabel actually derives from an old Semitic name meaning daughter of Baal. It is a royal name in Spain and Portugal.
(Hebrew) *Isibeal*; (French) *Isabelle*; (Italian) *Isabella*; (Scottish) *Iseabail, Isobel*; (Armenian) *Zabel*, *Isabela, Izabella, Ysabel, Ysabelle*; **Nicknames:** *Bel, Bella, Belle, Chavela, Chavelle, Isa*; **Star babies:** daughter of Annette Bening and Warren Beatty

ISABELLA Italian: Variation of Isabel
Nicknames: *Isa, Iza, Belicia, Belita*; **Star babies:** daughters of Andrew Lloyd Webber, Nicole Kidman and Tom Cruise, Lorenzo Lamas and Shauna Sand, Lori Loughlin

ISABIS (is-AH-bəs) African: Something that is beautiful

ISADORA Greek: Gift of Isis; derived from the name of the Egyptian fertility goddess and the Greek *doron*, meaning *gift*
(Spanish) *Isidora*; *Isadore*; **Famous namesakes:** Dancer Isadora Duncan

ISAURA (ee-SAWR-ə) Greek: From Isaurus, an ancient Asian country
Isaure

ISHA (EE-shah) Sanskrit: Master

ISHARA (ee-shar-rah) African: (Swahili) A good sign
Nicknames: *Shar*

ISHTAR (ISH-tahr) Assyrian: Star; the Babylonian and Assyrian goddess of love, war and fertility.

ISI (is-ee) Native American: Deer (Choctaw)

ISIS (IE-sis) Egyptian: Most powerful of the female Egyptian goddesses, she was consort and sister to Osirus, mother of Horus, and is usually depicted as a motherly woman with arms wide open. Isis was worshipped at the Island of Philae, and was later worshipped over the entire Roman Empire.
Auset; Aset

ISLA (IE-lah) Scottish: From Islay, a name of an island off the Scottish coast

ISMENE (is-MEE-nee, is-MAY-nay) Greek: Accounted wise, Greek mythical daughter of Oedipus and Jocasta and sister of Antigone
Ismini

ISOKE (ee-SO-keh) African: Gift from God

ISOLDE (i-SOL-də) Celtic, German: Fair one. Legendary Isolde of the White Hands (Iseut aux Blanches Mains) fell in love with the knight Tristan after drinking a love potion. Her story is the subject of Wagner's opera *Tristan und Isolde*.
(German) *Yseult*; (French) *Iseut*; (Irish) *Iseult*; *Hisolda, Isold, Isolda, Isole, Isotta, Isoud, Isoude, Ysolde*

ITA Gaelic: Thirsty
Itah

ITSASO (eet-SAH-so) Basque: The sea

ITXARO (eet-CHAH-ro) Basque: Hope

IULALIA (ee-oo-LAH-lee-ah) Hawaiian: Variation of Eulalie

IVALYN English: A name of unclear origins; possibly a variant of Ivana or Evelyn, possibly a blend of Ivy and Lynn

IVANA Czech: God has been gracious; feminine form of Ivan
(Russian) *Ivanna*; **Nicknames:** *Iva, Ivah, Vania, Vanya*; **Diminutive forms:** *Ivanka*; **Famous namesakes:** Socialite Ivana Trump

IVONNE French: Spelling variation of Yvonne

IVORY English: White, pure; a reference to the creamy-white color of ivory or to the hard tusk used for carving fine art and jewelry

IVY English: Botanical name for any one of a large number of climbing or creeping ornamental plants or vines
(Spanish) *Ivette*; *Ivey, Ivie*

IVYANNE English: Variant of Ivana or a modern blend of Ivy and Anne
Ivyanna

IZASKUN (ee-SAHS-koon) Basque: Reference to the Virgin Mary

IZUSA (ee-ZOO-sah) Native American: White stone
Izusah

JACELYN English: Modern blend of Jaye or Jacey and Lynn

JACENIA Greek: Spelling variation of Hyacinth

JACEY (JAY-see) English: Modern name, possibly based simply on the initials J.C. or a variation of Jacinda
Jacee, Jaci, Jacy, Jaicee, Jaycee, Jaycie; Jacie, Jayci

JACINDA (jə-SIN-dah) English: Spelling variation of Hyacinth

JACINTHE French: Variation of Hyacinth

JACKIE English: Nickname for Jacqueline
Jacki, Jacqui

JACOBA Hebrew: Supplanter or seizing by the heel; feminine form of Jacob
Jakoba, Jakobe

JACQUELINE (zhak-LEEN, JAK-ə-leen, JAK-ə-lin) French: Supplanter; feminine form of Jacques, Jacob, and James
(Hebrew) *Jakobah; Jacalyn, Jackleen, Jacklynn, Jaclyn, Jacqualine, Jacqueleen, Jacquelyn, Jacquelyne, Jacquelynne, Jaklyn, Jaquelin, Jaquelina, Jaqueline, Jaquetta*; **Nicknames:** *Jackie, Jacqui*; **Diminutive forms:** *Jacquenetta, Jacquenette, Jaquenette*; **Famous namesakes:** First Lady Jacqueline Bouvier Kennedy, English actress Jacqueline Bisset

JADE Spanish: Jewel, a green gemstone
(English) *Jadira*; (Italian) *Giada; Jaida, Jayde*; **Nicknames:** *Jady*; **Star babies:** daughters of Mick Jagger, Jesse Ventura

JADEN (JAY-dən) American: Unisex name; originally a male biblical name meaning God has heard
Jaiden, Jayden, Jadyn, Jaidyn, Jaidynn, Jaydyn, Jaydynn

JAE (JAY) English: Spelling variation of Jayna

JAEDA (JAY-də) Arabic: Goodness, long-necked beauty
Jada, Jawda, Jaydra, Jayeda; Jaide; **Famous namesakes:** Actress Jada Pinkett Smith

JAFFA (JAFF-ah) Hebrew: Beautiful
Jafit, Jafita, Yaffa; Jafa, Yafa, Yafit

JAGODA (yah-GO-dah) Slavic: Strawberry

JAHIA (JAH-hee-ah) African: Prominent
Jahiah

JAIDA English: Spelling variation of Jade

JAIME (HIE-may) Spanish: Supplanter; feminine form of James
(Scottish) *Jaimie; Jaimee, Jaimelynn, Jaimi, Jamee, Jamey, Jami, Jamia, Jamie, Jamilyn, Jaymee, Jaymie*

JAIMELYNN Scottish: Blend of names Jaime and Lynn

JAINA (JAY-nə) Hebrew: Spelling variation of Jane

JAIONE (hie-O-nay) Basque: Reference to the nativity

JALA (jah-lah) Arabic: High, great, imposing, illustrious
Jalaa

JALEH Persian: Rain

JALEN (JAY-lən) American: Variant of Jalena
Jaylen, Jaylin, Jaylinn, Jaylyn, Jaylynn, Jalyn, Jalynn, Jailen; **Famous namesakes:** Basketball player Jalen Rose

JAMILA (jah-MEE-lah) Arabic, African: Beautiful
(African) *Jameelah, Jamelia, Jamille; Jamilah, Jamilia, Jamilla, Jemila; Jamilieh, Jamile;* **Star babies:** daughter of Muhammad Ali

JAN Hebrew, Slavic: Gift from God. Jan is a feminine form of John and a variant of Jane. In Roman mythology, Jana was the wife of Janus.
(Hebrew) *Jana*

JANA Irish: Variation of Jane
Jannah, Jana; **Nicknames:** *Janie, Janey*

JANAI English: God has answered; variant of Jane or Jean
Jenae, Jenai, Jenay, Jenaya, Jennae, Jennay; **Nicknames:** *Jenee*

JANAIS English: God has answered; modern variant of Jane
Janae

JANALEE (YAH-nah-lee) Polish: Feminine form of John and a variant of Jane. Jana was the wife of Janus in Roman mythology.

JANALYN Polish: Feminine form of John and a variant of Jane
Jannalynn

JANAYA English: God has answered; modern variant of Jane
Janaye

JANE Hebrew: God is gracious; feminine form of John and a variant of Joan. See also *Shona*
(Hebrew) *Jans;* (Latin) *Joana;* (English) *Johnelle, Johnetta, Johnette;* (French) *Jeena, Jehane;* (Italian) *Ciana, Gianina, Gianna, Giannina, Giovana, Giovanna;* (Spanish) *Yoana, Zaina, Zanetta, Zanita;* (Gaelic) *Sheena, Sine, Siobhan;* (Irish) *Jana, Sinead;* (Welsh) *Sian;* (Russian) *Zhanna;* (Polish) *Janah, Janceena, Janica, Janka, Janna, Jannah, Jannalee, Jasia;* (Finnish) *Jaana; Jaina, Jaine, Janiece, Janis, Jannae, Janne, Jayne, Jenice, Jeniece, Jenise, Jeovana, Jeovanna, Joan, Johnna, Johnnie, Jonalyn, Jonalynn, Jonay, Jonell, Jonna, Zanna;* **Old forms:** *Janita, Jansje;* **Nicknames:** *Janee, Janey, Janicia, Janie, Jayni, Jaynie, Joanie, Joeanna, Joeanne, Joni, Jonni, Juanetta, Juanisha, Juanita;* **Diminutive forms:** *Jenette, Jonetta, Jonette, Jonnelle;* **Famous namesakes:** Actress Jane Fonda, author Jane Austen, journalist Jane Pauley, naturalist Jane Goodall, singer Janis Joplin; **Star babies:** daughter of Jim Carrey and Melissa Womer

> *"'It's giving girls names like that,' said Buggins, 'that nine times out of ten makes 'em go wrong. It unsettles 'em. If ever I was to have a girl, if ever I was to have a dozen girls, I'd call 'em all Jane.'"*
> —H.G. Wells, referring to the name Euphemia

JANELL English: God is gracious; variant of Jane
Janella; Janelle

JANET Hebrew: Gift from God; originally a diminutive of Jane, from the French variant Jeanette
(Scottish) *Janneth*; (Welsh) *Sioned*; (Russian) *Zaneta; Jannet*; **Diminutive forms:** *Janetta, Janette*; **Famous namesakes:** Singer Janet Jackson, Attorney General Janet Reno

JANETTE Hebrew: Diminutive form of Janet

JANICA Polish: Variation of Jane

JANICE Hebrew: God is gracious; variant of Jane
Janise, Jannis; Janiece, Janis, Jenice, Jeniece, Jenise; **Famous namesakes:** Singer Janis Joplin

JANICIA English: God is gracious; variant of Jane

JANNA (JAHN-nah) Hindi: Paradise
(Persian) *Jannat*

JANNAH (YAHN-ah) Polish: Variation of Jane

JARA (YAH-rə) Slavic: Spring

JARITA (jahr-ee-tah) Hindi: Mythical bird

JASLYNN English: Modern variant of Jasmine; blend of Jocelyn and the musical term jazz

JASMINE Persian: Flower known for its sweet fragrance
(Arabic) *Yasmina*; (French) *Jasmin*; (Danish) *Gelsomina*; (Hindi) *Yasiman*; (Turkish) *Yasemin*; *Jasmeen, Jasmyne, Jazmaine, Jazmina, Jazmine, Jazzmine, Jazzmyn, Jessamina, Jessamine, Jessamyn, Yasmia, Yazmin*; **Famous namesakes:** Actress Jasmine Guy; **Star babies:** daughters of Michael Jordan, Martin Lawrence

JAVANEH Persian: Young

JAVIERA (hah-vee-ER-ah) Spanish: Spelling variation of Xaviera

JAXINE (jak-SEEN) English: Variant of Jacinta, which is a Spanish form of Hyacinth; also a contemporary blend of Jack and Maxine

JAYA (jay-ah) Hindi: Victory
Old forms: *Jayanti*

JAYLYNN English: Blend of Jay and Lynn; feminine variant of Jay
Jaylene

JAYNA English: God has been gracious; variant of Jane that has become an independent name in much the same way the name Jay became independent from its origin, Jacob
Jae, Jaena, Jaenette

JAZLYN English: Modern variant of Jasmine; blend of Jocelyn and the musical term jazz
Jazlynn; **Nicknames:** *Jazzy*

JEAN Scottish: Variation of Jeanne

JEANETTE French: Diminutive form of
Jeanne
Jenette; **Famous namesakes:** Congresswoman
Jeanette Rankin

JEANINE (zha-NEEN, jə-NEEN) French:
Gift from God; diminutive form of Jeanne,
which is the French form of Jane or Joan
(Hebrew) *Janina; Janene, Janine, Jannina,
Jeannine, Jeneen, Jenina, Jenine, Jennine,
Jineen; Janine, Jeannine, Ganeen, Jenine*

*Jeannine, I dream of lilac time.
Your eyes, they beam in
lilac time.
Your winning smile, and
cheeks blushing like the rose,
Yet, all the while, you sigh
when nobody knows.*

*Jeannine, my queen of
lilac time,
When I return, I'll make
you mine,
For you and I, our love-dream
can never die,
Jeannine, I dream of lilac time.*
—Gene Austin, from the motion
picture *Lilac Time* (1928)

JEANNE French: Gift from God; variant of
John, Jean, or Jane
(Scottish) *Jean; Jeana, Jeanae, Jeanay, Jeane,
Jeanee, Jeanna*; **Nicknames:** *Jeanie, Jeannie,
Jenelle*; **Diminutive forms:** *Jeanelle, Jeanetta,
Jeanette, Jeanice, Jeanina, Jeannell, Jeannette,
Jenella*; **Star babies:** daughter of William Hurt
and Sandrine Bonnaire

JEMIMA (jə-MIE-mə) Hebrew: Little dove; in
the Bible, one of Job's three daughters, who were
known as the most beautiful women of their
time (the other two were Keziah and Keren)
Jemimah

JEMINA (je-MEE-nah) Hebrew, Finnish:
Listened to

JEN English: Nickname for Jennifer

JENAE English: God has answered; modern
variant of Jane or Jean, and a variation of
Janai

JENAYA English: Spelling variation of Janai

JENDAYI (jen-DAH-yee) African: Grateful,
thankful (Zimbabwe)

JENELLE English: Gift from God; variant
of Jeanne
Jenella

JENICA (zhie-NEE-kah, je-NEE-kah)
Romanian: God is gracious; a contemporary
Romanian form of Jane

JENNA English: Modern variant of Jenny
and Jennifer
Jena, Jennah; **Star babies:** daughter of Dustin
Hoffman and Anne Byrne

JENNALEE English: Spelling variation of
Jennifer

JENNALYN English: Spelling variation of
Jennifer

JENNARAE English: Spelling variation of
Jennifer

JENNIFER Welsh: Fair one; variant of
Guinevere
(English) *Jenita*; (Finnish) *Jenna; Genna,
Jenalee, Jenalyn, Jenalynn, Jenarae, Jenifer,*

Jennabel, Jennady, Jennalee, Jennalyn, Jennarae, Jennasee, Jennessa, Jennika, Jennilee, Jennilyn, Jennyfer; **Nicknames:** Jen, Jena, Jeni, Jenilynn, Jennah, Jenni, Jennie, Jennis, Jenny, Jennyann, Jennylee, Jinni, Jinny; **Diminutive forms:** Jenetta, Jennelle; **Famous namesakes:** Tennis player Jennifer Capriati, actress Jennifer Aniston, singer Jennifer Lopez; **Star babies:** daughters of Billy Crystal, Jack Nicholson and Sandra Knight, David Lynch, Roseanne and Bill Pentland, Bob Saget, Bill Gates

JENNY English: Nickname for Jennifer
Jenni, Jennie; **Famous namesakes:** Diet guru Jenny Craig; **Star babies:** daughter of Tony Orlando

JENSINE (YEN-seen) Danish: God is generous

JERI (JER-ee) English: Nickname for Geraldine

JERILYNN English: Rules by the spear. Blend of Jeri, which is a diminutive form of Geraldine and the suffix –lyn.

JERSEY English: A place name for the Channel Isle of Jersey in England, and a familiar abbreviation for New Jersey

JERUSHA (jə-ROO-shə) Hebrew: Inheritance

JESARA English: Rich, God beholds; a modern variation of Jessica

JESSAMINE French: Jasmine flower known for its sweet fragrance

JESSICA Hebrew: Rich, God beholds (Hawaiian) Iekika; **Famous namesakes:** Actress Jessica Lange, actress Jessica Tandy; **Star babies:** daughters of Jeff Bridges, Kate and Robert Capshaw, Roseanne and Bill Pentland, Bruce Springsteen

JESUSA (hay-SOO-sah) Spanish: Derived from Mary de Jesus, mother of Jesus Christ and a name for the Virgin Mary

JETTA Latin: Jet black
Jette

JEWEL Latin: Precious gem
Famous namesakes: Singer Jewel

JILL English: Youthful; familar form of Jillian or Gillian
Gill, Jilly, Jyl, Jyll; **Famous namesakes:** Actress Jill St. John, actress Jill Eikenberry

JILLIAN (JIL-ee-ən) English: Youthful; derived from the Latin name Julian
Gillian, Gillien, Jilian, Jillanne, Jillayne, Jillene, Jillesa, Jilliane, Jilliann, Jillianna, Jillianne, Jyllina; Gillian; **Nicknames:** Gill, Jill, Jilly, Jyl, Jyll; **Famous namesakes:** Actress Jillian Bach; **Star babies:** daughter of Vanessa Williams and Ramon Hervey

JIMENA (hee-MAY-nah) Spanish: Heard

JIMI English: Modern feminine form of Jimmy, a familar form of James
Jimmi

JINA (JEE-nah) African: Named child (Swahili)

JINX Latin: Spell
Jinxx, Jynx

JO English: A familiar form of Joanna and other names beginning with Jo–

JOAN Hebrew: Spelling variation of Jane

JOANNA Hebrew: Gift from God; variant of Joan, a feminine form of John (Hebrew) Johanna; (German) Hanna, Johannah; (Polish) Joanka; Joann, Joanne, Ohanna; **Nicknames:** Jo; **Star babies:** daughter of Julie Andrews and Blake Edwards

JOBINA Hebrew: Persecuted; feminine form of Job

JOCELYN French: Originally a boys' name, derived from the Germanic name Gautelen (English) *Joceline; Jocelin, Jocelina, Jocelyne, Jocelynn, Josalind, Josalyn, Josalynn, Joscelin, Josceline, Joscelyn, Joscelyne, Josilyn, Joslin, Joslyn, Jozlyn;* **Famous namesakes:** Australian film director Jocelyn Moorhouse

JOCHEBED (yo-HEV-ed) Hebrew: God's glory

JODY English: Nickname for Judith *Jodi, Jodee, Jodie;* **Famous namesakes:** Actress Jodie Foster

JOELLE (zho-EL, jo-EL) Hebrew, French: Lord is God; feminine form of Joel *Joeliyn, Joell, Joella, Joellen, Joelliana, Joelliane;* **Famous namesakes:** Actress Joelle Carter

JOELLEN French: Spelling variation of Joelle *Joeliyn, Joellyn*

JOHANNA (yo-HAH-nah) German: Variation of Joanna **Nicknames:** *Hanna*

JOHNELLE English: Variation of Jane

JOHNETTA English: Variation of Jane

JOHNNA English: Spelling variation of Jane

JOHNNIE English: Spelling variation of Jane *Joni, Jonni, Jonnie, Johnny*

JOLENE English: Beautiful; variant of Jolie *Joleen, Jolina, Joline*

JOLIE (zho-LEE, JO-lee) French: Beautiful *Jolee, Joleen, Joleigh, Joli, Jolien;* **Nicknames:** *Jolena, Jolene, Jolina, Joline, Jolleen, Jollene;*

Famous namesakes: Actress Angelina Jolie; **Star babies:** daughter of Quincy Jones

JONALYN English: Spelling variation of Jane

JONATI Hebrew: Dove

JONELL English: Spelling variation of Jane *Jonelle, Jonnelle*

JONETTA English: Diminutive form of Jane *Jonette*

JONI English: Nickname for Jane **Famous namesakes:** Singer Joni Mitchell, artist and author Joni Eareckson Tada

JONNA English: Spelling variation of Jane

JORCINA English: Farmer; variant of Georgia and Georgina *Jorcine*

JORDAN Hebrew: To flow downward. Jordan, the river in Palestine where Jesus was baptized, has been used as a given name since the Crusades. (French) *Jordane;* (Italian) *Giordana;* (Spanish) *Jordana; Jordanna, Jordanne, Yardena, Yordana; Jordyn, Jordynn;* **Diminutive forms:** *Jori;* **Star babies:** daughters of Bono, Sarah Brown, Leeza Gibbons, Cheryl Ladd

JORIE English: Nickname for Marjorie *Joree, Jorey, Jori, Jorey, Jory*

JOSEPHINE Hebrew: May God give increase; feminine form of Joseph (Italian) *Giuseppina;* (Spanish) *Josefa, Josefina;* (Irish) *Seosaimhthin;* (Hungarian) *Jozsefa; Josebe, Josepha, Josephina, Josetta, Yosebe, Yosepha, Yosephina;* **Nicknames:** *Fifna, Fifne, Fina, Josee, Josie, Josina;* **Diminutive forms:** *Fifi, Fifine, Josette;* **Famous namesakes:** Singer Josephine Baker;

Star babies: daughter of Linda Hamilton and James Cameron

JOSETTE (zho-ZET, jo-ZET) French: Diminutive form of Josephine

JOSIE English: Nickname for Josephine
Jozie, Jozy

JOSLIN French: Spelling variation of Jocelyn

JOSUNE (ho-SOO-nay) Spanish: Named for Jesus

JOURNEY American: Travel

JOVITA (ho-VEE-tah) Spanish: Feminine form of the Roman name Jove

JOY English, French: Joyous, merry; derived from *joie*, a word with Middle English and Old French lineage. Joy is also used as a familiar form of Jocelyn and Joyce.
(Latin) *Joya*; *Joi, Joia, Joie*

> *I have no name.*
> *I am but two days old.*
> *What shall I call thee?*
> *I happy am,*
> *Joy is my name.*
> *Sweet joy befall thee!*
> —William Blake, from
> *Songs of Innocence*

JOYANN English: Blend of the names Joy (rejoicing) and Ann (graceful)
Joyanna, Joyanne, Joyceanne

JOYCE English: Joyous, merry; derived from the Latin word *jocosa*, meaning joyous; a possible variant of Jocelyn
(Hawaiian) *Ioke*; *Joycelyn, Joycelynn*

JOYELLE (zhoi-EL, joi-EL) French, English: Rejoicing

JUANA (HWAHN-ah) Spanish: God's gift; feminine form of Juan, the popular Spanish form of John

JUDAH (JOO-də) Hebrew: Praised
Nicknames: *Jude*

JUDE Latin: Nickname for Judah

JUDITH Hebrew: Woman of Judea, praised one. Judith is a feminine form of Judah. Judea was the name of an ancient country in southern Palestine.
(French) *Judithe*; (Italian) *Guiditta*; (Scandinavian) *Judit*; (Hungarian) *Juci, Jucika*; *Yehudit*; **Nicknames:** *Joda, Jodee, Jodi, Jodie, Jody, Judi, Judie, Judy*; **Famous namesakes:** Dancer and choreographer Judith Jamison, actress Judith Ivey

JUDY Hebrew: Nickname for Judith
Judee, Judi, Judie; **Famous namesakes:** Actress Judy Garland, singer Judy Collins, actress Dame Judi Dench, author Judy Blume

JULIA Latin: Youthful, Jove's child; feminine form of Julian or Julius
(Italian) *Giulia, Guilia*; (Spanish) *Julina*; (Russian) *Ulyana, Yulia, Yuliya*; (Hungarian) *Juliska*; *Guilie, Iulia, Iulius, Julee, Juleen, Julene, Julesa, Juli, Julita*; **Nicknames:** *Ulya, Yulya*; **Diminutive forms:** *Yulenka*; **Famous namesakes:** Actress Julia Ormond, actress Julia Roberts, chef Julia Child; **Star babies:** daughters of Shaun Cassidy, Tony Randall

JULIANA Latin: Youthful; feminine form of Julian
(Italian) *Giuliana*; *Julianna, Julianne, Julieann, Julieanna, Julieanne, Julienne*; **Famous namesakes:** Musician Juliana Hatfield, actress Julianna Margulies; **Star babies:** daughter of Shelley Long

JULIET French: Youthful, Jove's child; variant of Julia. Juliet is the star-crossed lover in the Shakespearian tragedy *Romeo and Juliet*. (French) *Juliette*; (Italian) *Julietta*; (Spanish) *Julieta*; **Famous namesakes:** Actress Juliette Binoche; **Star babies:** daughter of Janine Turner

JUN (JUN) Japanese: Obedience

JUNE Latin: Young. In Roman mythology, Juno was a protectress of women and marriage. In modern times, June is known as the bridal month.
Junae, Junel, Junia, Juno; **Diminutive forms:** *Junelle, Junette*; **Famous namesakes:** Actress June Allyson

JUSTINE Latin: Fair, just, upright; feminine form of Justin
Jestina, Jestine, Justa, Justeen, Justeene, Justene, Justina, Justyne; **Famous namesakes:** Actress Justine Bateman; **Star babies:** daughter of Louis Malle and Alexandra Stewart

JYOTI (jyo-tee) Hindi: Light

KABIRA African: Powerful

KACEY English: Alert, vigorous; a phonetic form of the initials K.C. or variant of the Irish name Casey
K.C., Kacee, Kaci, Kacie, Kacy, Kasey, Kayce, Kaycee, Kayci, Kaycie

KACIA English: Alert, vigorous; variant of Casey

KADIA English: Rhyming variant of Katy or Cady
Kadee, Kadi, Kadian, Kadie, Kadienne

KAESHA English: Modern form of Kacie

KAFI African: Quiet

KAI (KIE) Native American: Willow tree, graceful (Navajo); (Hawaiian) the sea

KAIA (KY-yə) Greek: From the earth; mythological womanly personification of the earth and mother of the Titans; (Hawaiian) the sea
(Greek) *Gaea*; (Finnish) *Kaija*; **Star babies:** daughter of Cindy Crawford and Rande Gerber

KAILANI (kah-ee-LAH-nee) Hawaiian: Sea and sky
Kalanie

KAINDA (kah-EEN-dah) African: Hunter's daughter

KAIRA Scandinavian: Nickname for Katherine

KAISA (KY-sah) Finnish: Variation of Katherine

KAISLA (KAH-EES-lah) Finnish: Reed

KAITLYN Irish: Spelling variation of Caitlin
Kaitlan, Kaitleen, Kaitlin, Kaitlynn, Katelin, Kateline, Katelinn, Katelyn, Katelynn, Katlin, Katlyn, Katlynn, Katlynne

KAJSA (KIE-sə) Swedish: Nickname for Catherine

KAKALINA (kah-kah-LEE-nah) Hawaiian: Variation of Katherine

KALA (KAH-lah) Hawaiian: Variation of Sarah; (Hindi) black

KALAMA (kah-LAH-mah) Hawaiian: Flaming torch

KALANI (kah-LAH-nee) Hawaiian: Highborn, noble

KALANIT Hebrew: Flower

KALARA Latin: Shines
Kalate

KALEA (kah-LE-ah) Hawaiian: Bright, joy
Kaleah

KALEI (KAH-le-ee) Hawaiian: The flower
wreath

KALENA (kah-LE-nah) Hawaiian: Variation
of Katherine

KALI (KAH-lee) Hawaiian: Hesitation. In
Hindu mythology, Kali is the wife of Shiva
and a goddess symbolizing the essence of
destruction.

KALIFA (kah-LEE-fah) African: Chaste, holy
(Somali)

KALIKA Greek: Rosebud
(African) *Kali*; *Kalyca*; **Nicknames:** *Kalie, Kaly*

KALINA Polish: A flower

KALINDA (kah-LIN-dah) Hindi: The
sun; a Hindu mythological reference to the
mountains of Kalinda
Kalindi, Kalynda; Calinda

KALLAN Scandinavian: Flowing water, a
stream; (Gaelic) powerful in battle

KALLISTA (kə-LIS-tə) Greek: Spelling
variation of Callista
Kalista, Kallysta; **Nicknames:** *Kallie*

KAMALA (kah-mah-la) Hindi: One who is
like a lotus

KAME (kah-me) Japanese: Tortoise; denotes
long life

KAMEA (kah-MAY-ah) Hawaiian: The one
and only
Kameo

KAMEKO (kah-may-ko) Japanese: Child of
the tortoise

KAMI (kah-mee) Japanese: Divine aura

KAMILA Arabic: Spelling variation of
Camila; (Czech) a Roman family name,
possibly meaning noble
Kamilah, Kamilla, Kamille, Camila, Kamille

KANELI (KAH-ne-lee) Finnish: Cinnamon

KANERVA (KAH-ner-vah) Finnish: Heather

KANIKA (kah-NEE-kah) African: Black

KANYA (KAHN-yah) Hindi: Virgin; the
younger daughter

KARA Greek: Pure; (Latin) beloved, darling;
variant of Cara

KARAMIE Arabic: Hospitable

KAREN (KER-ən, KAR-ən) Danish, English:
Pure, innocent; variant of Katherine
(German) *Karin*; (Scandinavian) *Kariana,
Karianna, Karianne*; (Finnish) *Kaarina*;
*Caren, Carin, Caryn, Carynn, Karan, Karena,
Kariann, Karina, Karon, Karrah, Karren,
Karrin, Karyn*; **Nicknames:** *Kari, Karie, Karri,
Karrie*; **Famous namesakes:** Musician Karen
Carpenter, actress Karen Allen

KARIMA (kah-REE-mah) Arabic: Generous,
noble-born lady or daughter; feminine
variant of Karim
Karimah

KARINA (kah-REE-nah) Arabic:
Companion or accomplice; (English) pure;
abbreviation of Katherine
*Kareen, Kareena, Karin, Qareen, Qareena,
Qarin*

KARINTHA English: Beauty

> *"Karintha is a woman. She who carries beauty, perfect as dusk when the sun goes down."*
> —Jean Toomer, *Cane*

KARISMA English: Divinely favored

KARLA German: Variation of Carla
Star babies: daughter of Otis Redding

KARLESHA Contemporary: Variation of Carla

KARLINA (kahr-LEE-nah) German: Spelling variation of Caroline

KARLOTTA German: Variation of Charlotte

KARLY (KAHR-lee) German: Nickname for Carla

KARMA Sanskrit: Fate, destiny; Buddhist and Hindu concept of the inevitable effect of one's life actions
Carma

KAROLINA (kah-ro-LEE-nah) German: Variation of Caroline

KASEY Irish: Spelling variation of Casey

KASMIRA Slavic: Commanding peace

KASSIA (KA-shə) Greek: Spelling variation of Cassia

KASTANJA (KAHS-tahn-yah) Finnish: Chestnut

KASTEL American: Dew
(Finnish) *Kastehelmi*; *Kastelle*

KAT English: Nickname for Catherine

KATELIJN (kah-tə-LIEN) Dutch: Variation of Katherine

KATHERINE Greek: Pure, innocent. Katherine is a traditional name for women. It has variations in many languages and has been used since the third century AD. Early Latin forms Katerina and Caterina evolved into Katharine, Katherine, Catharine, and Catherine. Katherine is also a royal name: In England, it was borne by the formidable and popular Katherine of Aragon (1485–1536), first wife of Henry VIII, as well as by the wives of Henry V and Charles II. See also *Karina* (Greek) *Kasienka, Kolena, Kolina*; (French) *Carine*; (Scandinavian) *Karielle*; (Danish) *Kasen*; (Dutch) *Katelijn*; (Polish) *Kaska*; (Finnish) *Kaisa, Katja*; (Hawaiian) *Kakalina, Kalena*; (Yiddish) *Reina*; *Katheryn*; *Karalee, Karalie, Katharine, Katharyn, Kathelyn, Katherina, Kathrina, Kathrine, Kathryn, Kathryne, Kathrynn, Kethryn*; *Kathrin, Katherin, Katharin, Katrine*; **Nicknames:** *Kaira, Kaisu, Karah, Kathe, Käthe, Kathy, Kay, Kath, Kathye, Kat, Katie, Katy, Kate*; **Famous namesakes:** Actress Katharine Hepburn, actress Katharine Ross; **Star babies:** daughters of Sting, Tony Danza

> *"The name we give to something shapes our attitude toward it."*
> —Katherine Paterson

KATHLEEN Irish: Pure or innocent; variant of Catherine. Bing Crosby crooned the famous ballad, "I'll Take You Home Again, Kathleen." *Cathleen, Cathlin, Kathleena, Kathlene, Kathlynn*; **Nicknames:** *Kathy, Kathye, Kath, Leen*; **Famous namesakes:** Actress Kathleen Turner, Hollywood producer Kathleen Kennedy

KATHY English: Nickname for Katherine
Cathy, Kathie, Kathye; **Nicknames:** *Kath*; **Famous namesakes:** Actress Kathy Bates

KATIE English: Pure, innocent; a familiar form of Catherine, Katherine, and their spelling variants that can stand as an independent name as well
Katy; **Nicknames:** *Kat, Kate*; **Famous namesakes:** News anchor Katie Couric, lifestyle guru Katie Brown, actress Katie Holmes, actress Kate Hudson, actress Kate Jackson, actress Kate Mulgrew; **Star babies:** daughter of George Lucas

KATRINA Scandinavian: Variation of Catherine

KATYA (KAH-tyah) Russian: Nickname for Catherine
Katia; **Star babies:** daughter of Hunter Tylo

KAVITA (ku-vee-tah) Hindi: Poem

KAY Scandinavian, Greek: Pure, keeper of the keys; an abbreviation of Katherine and other names beginning with K. Sir Kay was one of King Arthur's knights.
Kaye

KAYA (KAH-yah) Literature: The name of a Native American character in the *American Girl* series of children's literature.

KAYANA English: Blend of Kay and Anna (English) *Kayanna*

KAYLA Hebrew: Uncertain meaning; most commonly given meanings are *the laurel crown* and *Who is like God?* which stems from the name Michael
Caila, Cayla, Kaela, Kaelah, Kaila, Kailah, Kaylah

KAYLEY English: Uncertain meaning. Kayley could likely derive from a Gaelic word meaning slender, but may also be a variant of Kay.
Caileigh, Cailley, Caleigh, Callee, Calli, Caylee, Cayley, Caylie, Kaelee, Kaeleigh, Kaeley, Kaeli, Kaelie, Kailee, Kailey, Kalee, Kaleigh, Kaley,

Kalie, Kaylea, Kaylee, Kaylei, Kayleigh, Kayli, Kaylie; **Nicknames:** *Kaelene, Kaelin, Kaelyn, Kaelynn, Kailan, Kailene, Kailin, Kailyn, Kailynne, Kalan, Kalen, Kalin, Kalyn, Kalynn, Kaylan, Kayleen, Kaylen, Kaylene, Kaylin, Kaylyn, Kaylynn*

KEALA (kay-AH-lah) Hawaiian: The pathway

KEANNA Irish: Ancient; feminine form of Kian or Keane

KEARA (KEER-ə) Irish: Dark-haired; feminine form of Kieran
Keira, Kera, Keriam, Keriana, Keriann, Kerianna, Kerianne, Kerilyn, Kerra, Kerri, Kerrianne, Kerrie

KEARNEY (KEER-nee, KAHR-nee) Irish: Victorious

KEELY Celtic: Beautiful
Famous namesakes: Actress Keely Shaye Smith

KEELYN Irish: Lively, aggressive; variant of Kelly
Keelia, Keelin

KEESHA English: Nickname for Lakeisha

KEIKI (KAY-kee) Hawaiian: Child

KEILANI (KAY-lah-nee, kay-LAH-nee) Hawaiian: Glorious chief

KEISHA (KEE-shə) English: Nickname for Lakeisha
Famous namesakes: Actress Keisha Castle-Hughes, actress Keisha Knight-Pulliam

KELBY Norse: Farm near the spring

KELDA Norse: Fountain or from the ship's island

KELEBEK Turkish: Butterfly

KELILAH (keh-LEE-lah) Hebrew: Laurel crown
Kelula; *Kelila*

KELLAN Gaelic: Blend of Kelly and Ellen

KELLSEY Irish: Brave

KELLY Irish: Warrior or bright-minded; originally a boy's name
Keeley, Keilah, Kelleigh, Kellen, Kelley, Kelli, Kellie, Kellye, Kellyn; *Kelli*; **Famous namesakes:** Actress Kelly Ripa, actress Kelly McGillis; **Star babies:** daughter of Larry King

KELLYANNE Gaelic: Blend of Kelly and Anne; (Irish) lively, aggressive

KELSEY Scottish: From the island, possibly from the island of ships; (English) spelling variant of Chelsea. See also *Kellsey*
Kelcey, Kelcie, Kelcy, Kellsie, Kelsee, Kelsi, Kelsie, Kelsy; **Nicknames:** *Kelsa*; **Star babies:** daughters of Kelly McGillis, Gabrielle Carteris

KENDALL English: Valley of the Kent. This surname has become a unisex name and likely refers to a river in England.
Kendal, Kendyl, Kyndall; **Star babies:** daughter of Bruce Jenner

KENDRA English: Blend of Ken (royal obligation, clear water) and Sandra (protector of man) or Andrea (manly or masculine); also feminine form of Kendrick (fearless leader); (Anglo-Saxon) water baby

KENISHA English: Modern creation, possible blend of Kenya and Aisha

KENNA English: Born of fire, good-looking; feminine form of Kenneth
Kenina

KENNEDY Irish: Helmet-head; a traditionally male name now used for either gender
Kennadi, Kennady, Kennedi

KENYA English: A country in Africa
Star babies: daughter of Nastassja Kinski and Quincy Jones

KENZINGTON English: Handsome, fiery; surname

KEREN Hebrew: Ray, beam, light, glory, horn, beauty; abbreviation of Kerenhappuch. In the Bible, Keren was one of Job's three daughters.
Kelyn, Keran, Kerrin; *Keryn*

KERI Irish: Spelling variation of Kerry

KERIANA Irish: Spelling variation of Keara

KERRY Gaelic, Irish: Dark haired; a county in Ireland
Keri; *Carrie, Cari, Kari, Karrie, Kerrie*

KERSTIN Swedish: Variation of Christina

KESAVA (kay-SAH-vah) Hindi: She of the beautiful hair

KEVIA English: Beautiful child; feminine form of Kevin
Kevina; *Kevya*; **Nicknames:** *Keva*

KHALILA (khah-LEE-lah) Arabic: Dearly beloved, darling, sweetheart, friend; feminine form of Khalil
Kalila; *Khaleela, Khaleelah*

KHANDAN Persian: Smiling

KHEPRI (ke-PREE) Egyptian: The scarab-beetle god identified with Re (Ra) as a creator god; often represented as a beetle within the sun-disk

KHINA Persian: Sweet voice, song

KIANA (kee-AH-nah) Hawaiian: Variation of Diana

KIANDRA Irish: Spelling variation of Keana

KICHI (kee-chee) Japanese: Lucky
Kicki

KIELO (KEE-E-lo) Finnish: Lily of the valley

KIERCE Contemporary: Uncertain meaning; perhaps a feminine variation of the Irish name for boys
Keerce

KIKKA German: Mistress of all

KILIWA (kee-LEE-wah) Hawaiian: Variation of Sylvia

KIMBERLY English: An English surname with an original meaning now unknown, but which almost certainly refers to a meadow. Some speculation exists that it is derived from a word referring to a royal meadow camp. Traditionally a boy's name, Kimberly is now more popularly used for girls.
Cimberleigh, Cymberly, Cynburleigh, Cyneburhleah; Kimber, Kimberlee, Kimberleigh, Kimberley, Kimberli, Kimberlie, Kimberlyn, Kimblyn, Kymberleigh, Kymberley, Kymmberly, Kymbra, Kymbrely; **Nicknames:** *Kim, Kimber, Kimbra, Kimm, Kimmi, Kimmy, Kym*

KIMI (kim-mee) Native American: Secret (Algonquin)

KIMIA Persian: Alchemy

KIMIMELA (kim-mee-meh-lah) Native American: Butterfly (Sioux)

KIRBY English: Church village, Teutonic residence. The Kirby coat of arms came into

existence centuries ago. The process of creating coats of arms (often called family crests) began in the eighth and ninth centuries.

KIRIE Latin: Light

KIRSTEN Scandinavian, English: Christian
Nicknames: *Kirstie, Kirsty*

KIRSTIE (KIRS-tee) Scottish: Nickname for Kirsten
Kirsty; **Famous namesakes:** Actress Kirstie Alley

KIT English: Nickname for Catherine

KITTY English: Nickname for Catherine
Famous namesakes: Singer and actress Kitty Carlisle Hart

KIVI (KEE-vee) Hebrew: Protected

KLARA Swedish: Variation of Clara

KLARIKA (KLAH-ree-kah) Latin: Clear
Klarisza; **Nicknames:** *Klari*

KOBRA Persian: Major

KOKO (ko-ko) Native American: Night (Blackfoot)

KRISTIN German: Variation of Christina

KRISTINE Latin, Danish: Follower of Christ; variant of Christine
(Polish) *Krystyn; Kristeena, Kristena, Kristian, Kristiana, Kristiane, Kristianna, Kristianne, Kristyne, Krystiana, Krystianna, Krystine;*
Nicknames: *Kris, Krissie, Krissy, Kristie, Kristy*

KUKKA (KOOK-ah) Finnish: Flower

KYLA Gaelic, Hebrew: Victorious; a narrow strait or channel.
Kylah, Kylea, Kyleen, Kyley, Kyli, Kylianne, Kylin

KYLIE Gaelic, Celtic: Victorious; a narrow strait or channel.
Kylee, Kyleigh; *Kiley*; **Star babies:** Singer Kylie Minogue

KYNA Gaelic: Intelligent

KYOKO (kee-yo-ko) Japanese: Child of the capital city

KYRA (KIE-rə, KEE-rə) Latin, Greek: Light; feminine form of Cyrus and variant of Cyra
Kira; **Famous namesakes:** Actress Kyra Sedgwick

KYRABEL English: Modern blend of Kyra and Belle

LACEY French: Derived from a French nobleman's surname brought to Britain and Ireland after the Norman conquest
Lacee, Lacene, Laci, Laciann, Lacie, Lacina, Lacy, Lacyann, Laycie; **Nicknames:** *Lace*;
Famous namesakes: Actress Lacey Chabert;
Star babies: daughter of Jackie Zeman

LACHESIS (la-KES-is) Greek: In Greek mythology, Lachesis was the second of the three fates. Her job was to measure the thread of life spun by Clotho.

LADA Russian: An Eastern European goddess of spring and love, Lada was worshipped throughout Lithuania, Poland, and Russia.

LADAN Persian: A flower

LAHJA (LAH-yah) Finnish: Gift

LAILA (LAY-lə) Arabic, Finnish, Persian: Born at night, nightfall. Qays, a seventh-century Arab poet, named the central character in his poems Laila.
Laylah, Leilah, Leyla; *Leila, Lailah, Layla*; **Star babies:** daughter of Muhammad Ali

LAJILA (lah-jee-lee) Hindi: Shy, modest
Lajili

LAKEISHA (lə-KEE-shə) American: Popular modern name, possibly an elaboration of Aisha (woman) using La– as a prefix, but may also be a variant of Letitia (joyful)
Lakesha, Lakeshia, Lakiesha, Lakisha, Laquisha; *LaKisha, LaKeesha, LaKysha*;
Nicknames: *Kecia, Keesha, Keisha, Kisha*

LAKEN (LAY-kən) American: Nature name, taken from lake, a body of water
Laiken, Layken, Laikyn

LAKSHMI (LUKSH-mee) Hindi: A good sign; a goddess of good fortune and wife of Vishnu
Laxmi

LALA Slavic: Tulip

LALASA Hindi: Love
Lalassa, Lallasa

LALEH Persian: Tulip

LALIA (LAY-lee-ə) Greek: Talkative, chatterer
Lalage

LALITA (lah-LEE-tah) Sanskrit: Pleasant, playful. In Hindu mythology, Lalita is playmate to the god Krishna.

LAMPETO Latin: Amazon leader mentioned in mythology

LAN (LAN) Vietnamese: Orchid

LANA (LAH-nə) Latin: Woolly, soft wool; (English) abbreviation for names such as Helen, Alana, and Svetlana; (Irish) content, pretty and peaceful; (Hawaiian) floating, frequently a part of Hawaiian names as well as a name itself
Lanna; **Famous namesakes:** Actress Lana Turner

LANAI (lah-NIE) Hawaiian: Terrace

LANDA Spanish: Reference to the Virgin Mary

LANDRADA (lahn-DRAH-dah) Spanish: Counselor
Nicknames: *Landra*

LANDRY English: Ruler of the place

LANE English: Path or small roadway
Laina, Laine, Lainie, Laney, Lanie; **Famous namesakes:** Actress Diane Lane, fictional reporter Lois Lane

LANGLEY English: From the long meadow; a surname and traditionally a boys' name, now being used for both genders. Langley, Virginia, is the famous home of the CIA.
Langlea, Langleah, Langly; **Star babies:** daughter of Mariel Hemingway

LANKA (lahn-kə) Hindi: From Lanka

LAODAMIA Greek: In Greek mythology, she was the wife of Protesilaus, the first Greek to be slain by the Trojans. Granted the chance for one last meeting with her dead husband, she decided she could not live without him and followed him into the underworld.

LAPIS (LAP-əs) Egyptian: A beautiful azure-blue stone that has been used in jewelry and for its medicinal value since ancient times

LARA (LAHR-ə) Latin: Famous, shining. Lara was a mythological Roman nymph who betrayed the love affair of Jupiter and Juturna, and was struck speechless as a result; (Greek) cheerful, happy; variant of Larissa, Laura, and Laraine
(Hawaiian) *Lala*; *Larae, Lari, Laria*; *Larah, Lariah, Larra, Larya, Laryah*; **Famous namesakes:** Actress Lara Flynn Boyle; **Star babies:** daughter of Bob Saget

LARALAINE Latin: Modern blend of Lara/Laura and Elaine

LARAMAE Latin: Modern blend of Lara/Laura and Mae/May

LAREINA (lah-RAY-nah) Spanish: The queen

LARINA Greek: Seagull; (Danish) feminine form of Lars
(Danish) *Larine*

LARINDA (lə-RIN-də) Latin: Protection; derived from lares, individual Roman household gods who were protectors of home and fields.

LARISSA Greek: Cheerful. In Greek mythology, Larissa was the mother of Pelasgus. Larissa is also the name of a city in Greece and is a moon of the planet Neptune. See also *Lara*
(Spanish) *Larisa*; (Russian) *Laryssa*; *Larisse*; **Nicknames:** *Lara, Risa*

LARK English: Lark, a songbird
arke; **Star babies:** daughter of Mia Farrow and Andre Previn

LARKIN English: Songbird; also an adapted surname meaning belonging to Laurence

LASAI (lah-SIE) Basque: Carefree

LASSIE Scottish: Little girl; the name of the beloved and brave canine heroine of Eric Knight's classic novel *Lassie Come Home*.
Lassey, Lassi, Lassy; **Nicknames:** *Lass*

> Lassie wi'the lint-white locks,
> Bonie lassie, artless lassie,
> Wilt thou wi' me tent
> the flocks,
> Wilt thou be my Dearie, O?
> —Robert Burns, "Lassie wi'
> the Lint-white Locks"

LASYA (lah-see-yah) Sanskrit: Dancer
Lasiya; **Nicknames:** *Seya*

LATA (lah-tah) Hindi: Beautiful vine

LATASHA English: Joyful, glad; modern
variant of Letitia

LATONIA Latin: Feminine form of Anthony

LATOYA (lə-TOI-ə) American: Victorious
one; possibly derived from Victoria
Famous namesakes: Singer LaToya Jackson

LATRICE (la-TREES) American: Noble
woman
Latricia

LAURA Latin: The laurel or sweet bay tree,
symbolic of honor and victory; old name
with many variants
(German) *Lorita*; (French) *Laure, Laurie*;
(Spanish) *Laurinda, Laurita, Lora*; (Scottish)
Lorna; (Welsh) *Lowri*; (Russian) *Lavra*;
Lauica, Laurissa, Lorah, Loria, Lorinda, Loris;
Nicknames: *Lori*; **Famous namesakes:**
Author Laura Ingalls Wilder, actress Laura
Linney, actress Laura Dern, First Lady Laura
Bush

LAURALEE English: Spelling variation of
Lorelei

LAUREL Latin, English, French: The laurel
tree or sweet bay tree is symbolic of honor
and victory. This is an old name with many
variants.
Laural, Lauralyn, Laurella, Laurelle, Lauriel

LAUREN (LOR-ən, LAWR-ən) Latin: Laurel,
symbolic of honor and victory. Lauren is also
a feminine form of Laurence, meaning from
Laurentium, a city in ancient Italy.
*Laureen, Laurena, Laurene, Laurenne, Laurina,
Lauryn, Loreen, Loreene, Loren, Lorena,
Lorene, Lorenia, Lorenna, Lorin, Lorren,
Lorrin, Lorrina, Loryn*; **Famous namesakes:**
Actress Lauren Holly, actress Lauren Bacall,
model Lauren Hutton

LAURENTIA Latin: Crowned with laurel
or from Laurentium, a city in ancient Italy
known for its laurel trees
(Italian) *Lorenza*; (Spanish) *Laurencia*;
Larentia

LAVEDA Latin: Purified
Lavare, Lavetta, Lavette

LAVERNE Latin: Spring, springlike
La Vergne, La Verne, Lavern, Laverna, Verna;
Diminutive forms: *Vernita*

LAVINIA (lə-VIN-ee-ə) Latin: Women of
Rome. In Roman legend, Lavinia was the
daughter of King Latinus and the wife of
Aeneas, a Trojan hero in Greek and Roman
mythology. According to legend, Aeneas
founded the city of Lavinium and named it in
honor of his wife.
(Spanish) *Levina, Luvenia, Luvina*; *Lavena,
Lavina*

LAYLA Arabic: Spelling variation of Leila
Star babies: daughter of Tanya Tucker

LEA (LAY-ə, LEE-ə) Hawaiian: Mythological
goddess of canoe builders
Famous namesakes: Actress Lea Thompson

LEAH (LEE-ə) Hebrew: Weary. In the Bible's Old Testament, Leah was the first wife of Jacob, and ancestress to the twelve tribes of Israel. Leah and her sister Rachel were considered symbols of the active (Leah) and the contemplative (Rachel) lives.
(French) *Léa*; **Famous namesakes:** Actress Lea Thompson, chef Leah Chase

> *"If anyone should want to know my name, I am called Leah. And I spend all my time weaving garlands of flowers with my fair hands"*
> —Dante Alighieri, *The Divine Comedy*

LEAL African: Faithful

LEANDRA (lee-AN-drə) Greek: Lioness; feminine form of Leander
Leodora; *Leoine, Leoline, Leona, Leonelle, Leonette, Leonice*

LEANN English: Origin unclear, possibly a variant of Liana, which is a short form of Juliana (young), or a modern blend of the names Lee and Ann.
Leana, Leanna, Leianna, Leanne, Leeann, Leeanne; **Famous namesakes:** Singer LeAnn Rimes

LECHSINSKA (LESH-een-skah, LEK-seen-skah) Polish: A woodland spirit of legend

LEDA (LEE-də) Greek: The mythological queen of Sparta and mother of Castor and Pollux, Leda was seduced by Zeus, who came to her in the form of a swan. That union resulted in the birth of her daughter, Helen of Troy.
Leta, Leyda, Lyda

LEE English: Meadow; an adapted surname now used as a given name for girls and boys.
Lea, Leia, Leigh, Ley; **Famous namesakes:** Actress Lee Merriweather, actress Lee Remick

LEELA (lee-lah) Sanskrit: Playful
Lila

LEHANA African: One who refuses

LEIGH (LEE) English: Spelling variation of Lee

LEIGHTON (LAY-tən) English: From the meadow town or settlement; surname

LEILA (LAY-lə) Arabic: Born at night. Music fans will surely recognize Layla from the popular Eric Clapton song.
Laila, Laili, Lailie, Layla, Laylie; **Star babies:** daughters of Greta Sacchi and Vincent D'Onofrio, Deborah Roberts and Al Roker

LEILANI (lay-LAH-nee) Hawaiian: Child of heaven, heavenly flowers
Nicknames: *Lani, Leia*

LELIA Latin: A Roman clan name of uncertain meaning; (Greek) well-spoken; a variant of Eulalia
Laelia, Lelah

LEMMIKKI (LEM-meek-ee) Finnish: Sweetheart

LEMPI (LEM-pee) Finnish: Love

LEMUELA Hebrew: Dedicated to God; feminine form of Lemuel

LENA Latin: A common pet form in several languages for names like Helena, Elena, Caroline, Magdalena, and Marlene
Leena, Lina; **Famous namesakes:** Actress Lena Olin, singer Lena Horne

LENAE (lə-NAY) English: Light; blend of Lena and Renee

LENIS Latin: Mild
Lenet, Leneta, Lenita

LENORA English: Light; variant of Leonora

LEOCADIA (lay-o-CAH-dee-ah) Spanish: Name of an island in Greece and a fourth-century Spanish saint
(French) *Leocadie*

LEODA German: Of the people
Leota

LEONA (lee-O-nə) Latin: Lioness; feminine form of Leon
(French) *Leone, Leonie*; (Spanish) *Leonita*; *Leoine, Leoline, Leonce, Leonda, Leondra, Leondrea, Leonela, Leonelle, Leonlina, Lonna*; **Nicknames:** *Loni, Lonnie*

LEONORA Greek: Light; a variant of Helena. See also *Lenora*
(German) *Leonore*; (French) *Léonore*; (Spanish) *Leonor; Lenore*; **Nicknames:** *Leola, Nora, Norah*

LEONTYNE (LEE-ən-teen) English: Like a lioness
Leontin, Leontina, Leontine; **Famous namesakes:** Opera diva Leontyne Price

LEOPOLDA (lee-ə-POL-də) German: Of the people
Leopoldina, Leopoldine

LEORA Greek: Light; a nickname for Eleanor
Liora

LEPEKA (le-PE-kah) Hawaiian: Variation of Rebecca

LESLIE Scottish, Gaelic: From the gray fortress, smaller meadow, or garden of hollies. Leslie was derived from a Scottish place name, became a surname, and is now used as a first name for both sexes.
Leslee, Lesley, Lezlie

LETA Latin: Joyful
Lita

LETHE (LEE-thee) Greek: Forgetfulness. In Greek mythology, Lethe was the River of Oblivion that caused the dead to forget about their past lives.
Leitha, Letha, Lethia

LETITIA Latin: Joyful, glad
(Italian) *Letizia*; (Spanish) *Leticia*; *Laetitia, Lateisha, Latesha, Laticia, Latisha, Letisha*; **Nicknames:** *Latasha, Lettie, Letty*

LEUCIPPE Greek: A mythological nymph

LEUCOTHEA (loo-CO-thee-ə) Greek: This mythological sea nymph was known as the White Goddess after she followed her son into the sea. Dionysus rescued her and she became Leucothea.
Leucothia

LEVANA Latin: To rise; Levana was a Roman mythological goddess and protectress of newborns.

LEVENE English: Nickname for Levina

LEVIA (le-VEE-ə) Hebrew: Lioness of the Lord
Leviah

LEVINA English: Flash, lightning
Levyna; **Nicknames:** *Levene*

LEXIE English: Nickname for Alexandra
Lexi, Lexina, Lexine, Lexy

LEYA (LAY-ah) Spanish: The law; (Hindi) lion

LIA Greek: Bringer of good news; also an abbreviation of names like Amalia and Rosalia

LIADAN (LEE-din) Irish: Gray lady

LIAN (LEE-an) Chinese: Graceful willow

LIANA French, Spanish: Lily
(French) *Liane*; *Leana, Leann*

LIANNA English: Spelling variation of Eliana

LIBBY English: Consecrated one, my God is bountiful, God of plenty; used alone or as a pet form or variant of Elizabeth

LIBERTY English: Freedom
(Latin) *Libera, Libertas*; (French) *Liberte*; **Star babies:** daughter of Jean and Casey Kasem

LIEALIA French: Spelling variation of Lela

LIESL (LEES-uh, LEEZ-ul) German: Diminutive form of Elizabeth

LIGIA Greek: Clear voice
Liegia

LIL Irish: Nickname for Lilian

LILA English: A pet form of Lilian or Delilah; (Persian) lilac; (Sanskrit) playful
Lyla; *Lilah*; Star babies: daughter of Kate Moss

LILAC Persian: Lilac

LILIAN Latin: Lily; symbolic of innocence, purity, and beauty
(Hebrew) *Lilah*; (Greek) *Lilika, Lilis*; (German) *Lilli*; (French) *Liliane*; (Italian) *Liliana*; (Finnish) *Lilja*; *Lila, Lilch, Lilia, Lilianna, Lilianne, Lilla, Lillian, Lilliana, Lilliane, Lilliann, Lillianna, Lillis*; **Old forms:** *Lillium*; **Nicknames:** *Lil, Lili, Lilie, Lillie, Lilly, Lily, Lilli*; **Famous namesakes:** Author Lillian Hellman

LILITH (LIL-ith) Assyrian: Of the night

LILO (LEE-lo) Hawaiian: Generous one. Lilo was the tiny heroine in the Disney film *Lilo and Stitch*.

LILY English: The lily is a flower symbolic of innocence, purity, and beauty.
Nicknames: *Lil, Lili, Lilie, Lillie, Lilly, Lilli*; **Famous namesakes:** Actress Lily Tomlin; **Star babies:** daughters of Chris O'Donnell and Caroline Fentriss, Amy Madigan and Ed Harris, Kathy Ireland, Meredith Vieira

LILYBETH English: Blend of Lily and Elizabeth
Lilybet; *Lilibeth*

LIMA Latin: Mythological goddess of the threshold
Limentina

LIN (LIN) Chinese: Forest or beautiful jade; also a spelling variation of the English name Lynn.

LINA (LEE-nə) Latin: A popular variant in several languages of names ending with *–line* or *–lina*; (Arabic, Persian) tender
Leena, Lena

LINDA Spanish, English: Pretty; may also refer to the linden, an ornamental shade tree also used for medicinal purposes
Lynda, Lyndall, Lyndee; **Nicknames:** *Lindi, Lindie, Lindy, Lyndi*; **Famous namesakes:** Actress Lynda Carter, journalist Linda Ellerbee

LINDEN English: The linden tree; this name describes a group of beautiful and often ornamental shade trees

LINDSAY (LINDZ-ee) English, Scottish: Island of linden trees
Lindsey, Linsey, Lyndsay, Lyndsey, Lyndsie, Lynsey, Lynzee, Lynzie; **Star babies:** daughter of Billy Crystal

LINKA Hungarian: Mannish

LINNEA (li-NAY-ə, LIN-ee-ə) Scandinavian: Lime tree or small mountain flower
Linna, Linnae, Lynae; **Nicknames:** *Nea*

LIOR (lee-OR) Hebrew: The light is with me, God's gift of light to me
Liora

LIRIT (li-REET) Hebrew: Lyrical, poetic, musical
Lirita

LISA English: My God is bountiful; variation of Elizabeth
(Finnish) *Liisa; Lesa*; **Famous namesakes:** Actress Lisa Kudrow

LISETTE (lee-ZET, li-SET) French: Diminutive form of Elizabeth
Lysette, Lisette, Lizette, Lizete

LISSA English: Honey. Lissa is an abbreviation of Melissa, Lissandra, and Alyssa. Lissa is also the name of a mother goddess in African mythology.
Lyssa

LITONYA (li-TON-yah) Native American: Darting hummingbird (Miwok)

LIV Norse: Life; also a familiar form for names like Olivia or Livana
Famous namesakes: Actress Liv Tyler, actress Liv Ullmann

LIVANA (lee-VAH-nah) Hebrew: White or the moon
Levana; **Nicknames:** *Leva, Liv, Liva*

LIZ English: Nickname for Elizabeth

LOANE Celtic: Light

LODEMA English: Guide
Lodima, Lodyma

LOGAN Gaelic: From the hollow; Logan has become a unisex name in addition to a being a surname.

LOIS (LO-is) English: Uncertain meaning, possibly a variant of Louise or from a Greek word meaning better. The biblical Lois was a grandmother of Timothy.
Loes

LOKELANI (lo-ke-LAH-nee) Hawaiian: Small red rose

LOLA Spanish: Nickname for Dolores
Famous namesakes: Singer Lola Falana; **Star babies:** daughter of Annie Lennox

LONDON English: Place name for the capital of the United Kingdom
Londyn, Londynn, Loundyn, Loundynn

LONI (LAH-nee) English: Lioness; a variant of Leona; (Hawaiian) sky
Lonnie; **Famous namesakes:** Actress Loni Anderson

LORANNA German: Variation of Loriann

LOREA (lor-AY-ah) Spanish: Flower

LOREEN English: Spelling variation of Lauren

LORELEI (LAWR-e-lie) German: Temptress whose singing lures men to destruction; also a rocky cliff on the Rhine River dangerous to boat passage
Lauralee, Lauralie, Loralei

LORELLE Latin: Little laurel
Lorella, Lorilla

LORENA English: Spelling variation of Lauren

LORETTA Latin: Little laurel; diminutive form of Laura

(French) *Laurette*; *Lauretta, Loreta, Lorette*;
Famous namesakes: Singer Loretta Lynn,
actress Loretta Swit, actress Loretta Young

LORI English: Nickname for Laura
Famous namesakes: Actress Lori Loughlin,
actress Lori Singer

LORIANN English: Refers to the laurel tree
or sweet bay tree, symbolic of honor and
victory; modern variant of Lora and Laurie
(German) *Loranna*; (Spanish) *Laurana*;
Lorian, Loriana, Lorianne

LORIEL English: Modern variant of Lora
and Laurie, referring to the laurel tree or
sweet bay tree symbolic of honor and victory.

LORILLA Latin: Spelling variation of Lorelle

LORILYNN English: Modern variant of Lora
and Laurie, referring to the laurel tree or
sweet bay tree symbolic of honor and victory.

LORIN French: Spelling variation of Lauren

LORNA Scottish: Variation of Laura

LORRAINE (lə-RAYN) French: From
Lorraine, the name of a province in France
and a French royal family
(English) *Lareina*; *Laraine, Larraine, Lauraine,
Loraina, Loraine, Lorayne, Lorraina*; *Lorine*;
Nicknames: *Lori, Lors, Lora*; **Famous
namesakes:** Author Lorraine Hansberry,
actress Laraine Newman; **Star babies:**
daughter of Rebecca Broussard and Jack
Nicholson

LORRELLA Teutonic: Form of Laurel

LOTTE (LAW-tə) German: Nickname for
Charlotte

LOTUS Greek: The lotus flower

LOU (LOO) German: Nickname for Louise

LOUELLA English: Blend of names Louise
(renowned warrior) and Ella (all)
(Spanish) *Luella*

LOUISE German, French: Renowned
warrior; feminine form of Louis
(German) *Louisa, Luise*; (Italian) *Luigina,
Luisa*; (Spanish) *Luiza*; (Gaelic) *Liusaidh*;
(Irish) *Labhaoise*; (Scandinavian) *Lovisa*;
(Finnish) *Loviisa*; (Hungarian) *Lujza*; *Louisane*;
Nicknames: *Lou, Loulou*; **Famous namesakes:**
Actress Mary-Louise Parker, author Louisa
May Alcott; **Star babies:** daughter of Prince
Edward Sophie, Countess of Wessex

LOURDES (LOOR-des) Spanish: Reference
to the Virgin Mary; taken from a town in
France that became famous as a shrine for
Catholic pilgrims after a peasant girl was said
to have had visions of the Virgin Mary at a
grotto there
Louredes; **Nicknames:** *Lorda, Lola*; **Star
babies:** daughter of Madonna

LOVE English: Love, affection
Nicknames: *Lovelyn*

LOVELYN English: Variant of Love

LUANA (loo-AN-ə) German: A blend of
Louise and Ann
Luane; *Louann, Louanna, Louanne, Luann*

LUBA Russian: Nickname for Lubov
Lyuba

LUBOV (LYOO-bawsh, loo-BOF) Russian:
Love
Lubava; **Nicknames:** *Luba, Luba*; **Diminutive
forms:** *Lyubochka*; **Famous namesakes:**
Russian actress Lubov Orlova

LUCERIA Latin: Circle of light
(Russian) *Lukeriya, Lusha*

LUCERNE (loo-SERN) Latin: Circle of light, lamp; also a city in Switzerland
Lucerna

LUCIA (loo-CHEE-ah) Italian: Variation of Lucy

LUCIANA (loo-see-AH-nah) Spanish: Variation of Lucy

LUCILLE (loo-SEEL) French: Variation of Lucy
Lucila, Lucile, Lucilla; **Nicknames:** *Luci, Lucie, Lucy*; **Famous namesakes:** Actress Lucille Ball

LUCINA (loo-SIE-nə) Latin: Illumination. Lucina was a mythological Roman goddess of childbirth and giver of first light to newborns. (Spanish) *Lucena*; *Lucinna*

LUCINDA Latin: Spelling variation of Lucy
Nicknames: *Cyndee, Cyndi, Cyndy*

LUCINE (LOO-seen) Armenian: Moon

LUCJA (LUWTS-yah) Polish: Bright; Polish form of Lucille

LUCRECE French: From the Latin name Lucretia. Lucrece goes back to the Renaissance era (Lucrezia Borgia was sister to Cesare Borgia).

LUCRETIA Latin: Unknown meaning; feminine of the clan name Lucretius. See also *Lucrece*
(Italian) *Lucrezia*; (Spanish) *Lucrecia*; **Famous namesakes:** Antislavery and women's rights leader Lucretia Mott

LUCY Latin: Light; a vernacular form of Lucia, the feminine form of Lucius
(French) *Lucette, Lucie, Lucienne, Lucile, Lucille*; (Italian) *Lucia, Luciana, Lucilla*; (Spanish) *Lucila, Lucita*; *Luci, Lucinda*;
Nicknames: *Lou, Lu, Lulu*; **Famous**

namesakes: Actress Lucille Ball, actress Lucy Liu; **Star babies:** daughter of Mimi Rogers

LUCYNA (luw-TSI-nah) Polish: Bright; Polish form of Lucille

LUDMILA (lood-MEE-lah) Russian: Loved by people
Lyudmila; **Nicknames:** *Luda*

LUIGHSEACH (LEE-shahk) Irish: Torch bringer

LUISA (loo-EE-sah) Spanish: Variation of Louise

LUJZA (loo-EE-sə) Hungarian: Variation of Louise
Famous namesakes: Hungarian actress Lujza Blaha

LULU English: Pet form of names such as Louise, Louella, or even Lucy; (African) pearl; (Native American) rabbit
Star babies: daughter of Edie Brickell and Paul Simon

LUMI (LOO-mee) Finnish: Snow

LUNA (LOO-nah) Latin: Moon
Lunetta

LUNDI (LOON-dee) French: Monday

LUPERCA Latin: In mythology, the goddess of herds and fruitfulness. Luperca, the wife of Lupercus, changed into the she-wolf who nursed Romulus and Remus.

LUR (LOOR) Spanish: Earth

LURLEEN German: Temptress; a modern variant of Lorelei
Lurlene, Lurlina, Lurline

LUSHA Russian: Variation of Luceria

LUZ (LOOS) Spanish: Light; Maria de la Luz (Mary of the Light) is another name for the Virgin Mary

LY (LEE) Vietnamese: Lion

LYCORIAS Greek: A mythological sea nymph

LYDIA Greek, Swedish: From Lydia (Russian) *Lidia, Lidija, Lidiya*; *Lydea*; **Nicknames:** *Liddie, Liddy*; **Star babies:** daughter of Bill Paxton

LYNAE Scandinavian: Spelling variation of Linnea

LYNETTE English, Welsh: Variant of ancient Welsh name Eiluned (shape or form) or Lynn (waterfall). In Arthurian legend, Lynette accompanied Sir Gareth on a knightly quest. *Lanette, Linette, Linnette, Luned, Lynelle, Lynessa, Lynet, Lynley, Lynnet, Lynnette*; **Nicknames:** *Lynna, Lynne, Lyn, Lynn*

LYNN English: Waterfall or lake
Lin, Linn, Linne, Lyn, Lynna, Lynne; Lin

LYRA (LIE-rə) Greek: Of the lyre or song; lyrical
Lyric, Lyrica, Lyris

LYRIC English: Nickname for Lyra
Star babies: daughter of Kenny and Tami Anderson

LYS (LEES) French: Lily

LYSANDRA Greek: Liberator; feminine form of Lysander, and sometimes used as a variant of Alexandra
Lisandra, Lisanne, Lissandra, Lizandra, Lizann

LYSIPPE Latin: Lets loose the horses. In Greek mythology, Lysippe was an Amazon queen revered for her intelligence and bravery. She was killed in battle, a heroine of her people.

MAARIT (MAH-reet) Finnish: Variation of Margaret

MAAT (MAH-aht) Egyptian: Mythical goddess of orderly conduct, order, truth, and justice, she was represented as a woman with an ostrich feather on her head.

MAB (MAYV) Irish: Happiness. Mab was known as the fairies' midwife, but she delivered dreams, not children.

> *"O, then, I see Queen Mab*
> *hath been with you.*
> *She is the fairies' midwife,*
> *and she comes*
> *In shape no bigger than*
> *an agate-stone*
> *On the fore-finger of an*
> *alderman."*
> —Mercutio to Romeo in Shakespeare's tragedy *Romeo and Juliet*

MABEL English: Lovable; abbreviation of Amabel
(Welsh) *Mabli; Mabelle; Mable;* **Famous namesakes:** Actress Mabel Albertson; **Star babies:** daughter of Tracey Ullman and Allan McKeown

MABINA Celtic: Nimble
Mabbina

MACHA Irish: In Irish mythology, Macha was one of the three aspects of the goddess of war and destruction, along with Bodb and Morrigan.

MACHARA Scottish: Plain

MACKENNA Scottish: Child of the handsome one
Makenna, Mckenna; **Nicknames:** *Kenna, Mac*

MACKENZIE Scottish: Child of the fair or wise one
Mckenzie; MacKenzie, McKenzie, Makenzie; **Nicknames:** *Kenzie*; **Famous namesakes:** Actress Mackenzie Phillips

MACY French: Possibly from an Old French word meaning Matthew's estate, though the name may also derive from the surname Mace, a medieval English first name of unknown meaning, or a similar Gaelic place name meaning *long, low hill.*
Macee, Macey, Maci, Macie; **Famous namesakes:** Singer Macy Gray

MADA Arabic: The end of the path

MADDIE English: A familiar form of Madeleine and Madison
Maddi, Maddy

MADEIRA (mə-DEER-ə) Portuguese: Sweet wine. Wine production is the principal industry of the Madeira Islands in the Atlantic Ocean off Africa's coast.

MADELEINE (ma-də-LEEN, MAD-ə-lin, MAD-ə-lien) French: High tower or woman from Magdala, a village on the Sea of Galilee and home to the biblical Mary Magdalene (Hebrew) *Madalen, Madalyn, Madelaine*; (English) *Madelina*; (German) *Maddalen, Maddalena, Maddalene, Maddalyn*; (Italian) *Maddelena*; (Spanish) *Madalynn, Madena, Madia, Madina*; (Irish) *Madailein, Maighdlin*; (Scandinavian) *Malena*; (Swedish) *Malin*; (Slavic) *Madlenka; Madalene, Madeleina, Madelena, Madelene, Madeline, Madelon; Madelynn*; **Nicknames:** *Maddie, Maddy, Madie, Mady*; **Famous namesakes:** Actress

Madeleine Stowe, author Madeleine L'Engle, actress Madeline Kahn

MADGE Greek: Nickname for Margaret

MADISON English: This surname, derived from Matthew or Matilda, has become a popular name for girls
Madisen, Madisyn, Maddison, Maddisen, Maddisyn; **Nicknames:** *Maddi, Maddie, Maddy, Madi, Mady*; **Star babies:** daughter of Sissy Spacek

MADLENKA (MUD-len-kə) Slavic: Variation of Madeleine

MADONNA Latin: My lady. Madonna is a respectful form of address similar to the French *madame,* also used in reference to the Virgin Mary, mother of Jesus Christ, especially in art depicting her with infant Jesus in her arms.
Famous namesakes: Singer Madonna Ciccone

> *"With a name like mine, you either become a nun or famous."*
> —Madonna "Madge" Ciccone

MADORA Greek: Variant of Medea

MADRE (MAH-dray) Spanish: Mother
Madra, Yadra

MADRI Hindi: Name from Indian mythology, wife of Pandu

MAE English: Spelling variation of May
Famous namesakes: Actress Mae West

MAERTISA English: Famous

MAESEN (MAY-sən) English: Stone worker; feminine form of Mason
Mason, Maesyn

MAEVE (MAYV) Irish: Intoxicating; the name of a great Irish warrior queen *Meadhbh*; **Old forms:** *Medb*

MAFUANE (mah-foo-AH-nay) African: Soil

MAGDA (MAHG-dah, MAHK-dah) Hebrew: Nickname for Magdalene

MAGDALENE (MAG-də-lən, MAG-də-leen) Hebrew, French: Woman from Magdala. The biblical Mary Magdalene came from Magdala, a village on the sea of Galilee whose name meant *tower* in Hebrew. She was healed by Jesus and remained with him during his ministry and the crucifixion, and was a witness to his resurrection.
(Spanish) *Magdalena*; (Finnish) *Matleena*; *Magdala*, *Magdalen*; **Nicknames:** *Alena*, *Leena*, *Magda*

MAGENA (mah-GEH-nah) Native American: Moon

MAGGIE Scottish: Pearl; a familiar form of Margaret
Maggy; **Star babies:** daughters of Faith Hill and Tim McGraw, Pat Sajak

MAGNA Norse: Great; feminine form of Magnus

MAGNILDA German: Strong battle maiden *Magnhilda*, *Magnild*, *Magnilde*

MAGNOLIA French: Flower known for its sweet scent, can be used as a reference to girls from the American South

MAHALA (mah-HAYL-ah) Hebrew: Tender, loving; (Arabic) powerful, slowly, gently, progresses in good works; (Native American) woman
Nicknames: *Mahalia*; **Famous namesakes:** Singer Mahalia Jackson

MAHI (mah-hee) Hindi: The earth

MAHIN Persian: Greatest

MAHINA (mah-HEE-nah) Hawaiian: Moon, moonlight

MAHLA Persian: Friendly

MAHOGANY English: Dark wood of the mahogany tree

MAHTA Persian: Moonlight
Mahtab

MAHUBEH Persian: A flower

MAHWAH (mah-wah) Native American: Beautiful (Lenni Lenape)

MAIA (MAY-ə, MIE-ə) Greek: Meaning unknown. In Greek and Roman mythology, she was the goddess of spring and growth. Maia was the eldest of the Pleiades, the group of seven stars in the constellation Taurus, who were the daughters of Atlas and Pleione. She and Zeus had a son Hermes, a god of fertility; (Hebrew) close to God
Maya

MAIBE (MAH-ee-bah) Egyptian: Grave; also means juices of quinces prepared into medicine

MAIDA (MAY-də) English: Maiden
Mayda, *Mayde*

MAILE (mah-EE-ray) Hawaiian: Derived from the name of a type of vine that grows in Hawaii

MAIR (MIE-er) Welsh: Variation of Mary

MAISIE Scottish: Pearl; abbreviation of Margaret

"Proud Maisie is in the wood"
—Sir Walter Scott, "Proud Maisie"

MAITANE English: Dearly loved
Nicknames: *Maitena*

MAITE (mah-EE-tah) Spanish: Lovable; blend of Maria and Teresa

MAITI Irish: Strong battle maiden; variant of Matilda and Maitilda

MAITLAND English: From the meadow land, possibly from Matthew's land; surname

MAIZAH African: Discerning

MAJA (MIE-ah) Swedish: Nickname for Margaret

MAJELLA Irish: Surname of Saint Gerard Majella; commonly used as a first name for girls in Ireland

MAJESTAS Latin: Royal bearing, dignity; Majestas was a Roman goddess of honor.
Nicknames: *Majesta*

MAKALA (mah-KAH-lah) Hawaiian: Myrtle

MAKAWEE (mah-kah-wee) Native American: Generous, abundant, freely giving and motherly (Sioux)
Macawi, Macawee

MAKENNA Scottish: Spelling variation of MacKenna

MALAK (MAH-lak) Arabic, Hebrew: Angel, messenger
Malaika

MALANA (ma-LAH-nah) Hawaiian: Buoyant

MALCAH Hebrew: Queen
Malkah

MALIA (mah-LEE-ah) Hawaiian: Variation of Maria
Star babies: daughter of President Barack and Michelle Obama

MALIKA Arabic, African: Queen; feminine form of Malek, meaning king; (Hungarian) industrious

MALIN (MAW-lin) Swedish: Variation of Madeleine

MALINA Hebrew: From the tower; variant of Magdalene; (Hawaiian) peace

MALLORY (MAL-ə-ree) French: Unfortunate, ill-fated. This surname became popular as a girls' name due to the female character Mallory on the popular TV series *Family Ties*, and as a tribute to Mallory Square, the location of Key West's famous Sunset Celebration.
Star babies: daughter of Rick Derringer

MALMUIRA Scottish: Dark-skinned
Nicknames: *Malmuirie*

MALVA Greek: Soft
Nicknames: *Malvina, Malvine, Malvinia*

MAMIE (MAM-ee) English: Bitter; familiar form of Mary and Miriam
Famous namesakes: Actress Mamie Van Doren

MANAR Arabic: Light; derived from Nour, meaning light
Manara; Manara

MANDALYN English: Nickname for Amanda

MANDANA Persian: Name of a Persian princess

MANDARA (mahn-DAH-rah) Hindi: From the mandara tree

MANDISA (mahn-DEE-sah) African: Sweetness
Star babies: daughter of Danny Glover

MANDY English: Familiar form of Amanda, worthy of love
Mandi, Mandie; **Famous namesakes:** Actress Mandy Moore

MANNING English: Son of a hero; surname

MANON (mah-NON) French: Variation of Maria

MANOUSH Persian: Sweet sun

MANSI (man-see) Native American: Plucked flower (Hopi)

MANTO Latin: Roman mythological nymph and prophetess, Manto was the mother of Ocnus, founder of the city of Mantua

MANUELA (mahn-WAY-lah) Spanish: Variation of Emmanuella

MAOLA Irish: Handmaiden
Nicknames: *Maoli*

MAOLMIN Gaelic: Polished chief

MARA (MAY-rə, MER-ə, MAHR-ə) Hebrew: Bitter. The biblical Naomi claimed the name Mara as an expression of grief after the deaths of her husband and sons. Mara is also a variant of Mary and abbreviation of Tamara.

MARALAH Native American: Born during an earthquake

MARCAIL Scottish: Variation of Margaret

MARCELLA (mahr-SEL-ə) Latin: Warring; feminine form of Marcellus, a name believed to have its root in Mars, the name of the mythological Roman god of war; also related to the name Mark
(French) *Marcelle, Marcellia, Marchelle*; (Spanish) *Marcela, Maricel, Maricela, Maricelia, Maricella, Marisela*; *Marcelina, Marcelinda, Marcellina, Marcelline, Marcelyn, Marcena, Marcine, Marsila, Marsile, Marsilla*; **Nicknames:** *Cella, Marci, Marcia, Marcy, Marsha, Marsil*; **Diminutive forms:** *Zella*; **Famous namesakes:** Tennis player Marcella Mesker

MARCENYA (mar-sen-YAH) American: Modern name of uncertain derivation

MARCIA (MAHR-shə) Latin: Nickname for Marcella
Marsha, Marsia, Martia; **Famous namesakes:** Actress Marcia Gay Harden

MARCY Latin: Nickname for Marcella
Marci, Marcie

MARDEA African: Last

MARELDA (mah-REL-də) German: Famous battle maiden
Old forms: *Maganhildi*

MAREN (MAH-ren) German: From the sea, though also a possible variant of Mara and Mary
(Italian) *Marea*

MARGARET Greek: Pearl. Medieval virgin Saint Margaret was beloved in many cultures. (German) *Margit*; (French) *Margaux, Margeaux, Margelaine, Margot, Marguerite*; (Italian) *Margherita*; (Spanish) *Margarita*; (Gaelic) *Mairearad, Mairghread, Marsali*; (Irish) *Mairead*; (Scottish) *Marcail*; (Welsh) *Marged, Margred, Mererid*; (Scandinavian) *Margareta*; (Danish) *Margarethe, Mettalise*; (Dutch) *Margriet*; (Czech) *Marjeta, Marketa*; (Polish) *Margisia, Margita*; (Finnish) *Maarit, Maija, Marketta*; (Armenian) *Margaid, Margarid*; *Margaretta, Margeret, Margerie, Margery, Margrit, Marjory*; **Nicknames:** *Ghita, Gitta, Greta, Gretal, Grete, Gryta, Madge, Maggi, Maggie, Maggy, Mai, Maiju, Maikki, Maj, Maja, Majori, Majorie, Margalo, Marge, Margo, Margolo, Marji, Marjo, Meg, Meta, Peg, Pegeen, Peggy, Peigi, Reetta, Rita*; **Diminutive forms:** *Gretchen, Gretel, Margosha*; **Famous namesakes:** Prime Minister Margaret Thatcher, author Margaret Mead, actress Meg Ryan, author Marge Piercy, author Margaret Atwood

MARGELAINE French: Variation of Margaret
Nicknames: *Marge, Margie*

MARGHERITA Italian: Variation of Margaret

MARGO (MAHR-go) French: Nickname for Margaret
Margaux

MARI Welsh: Bitter; a variant of Mary and favored prefix for blending with other names

MARIA Latin, Italian, Spanish: Bitter; variant of Mary and the most popular Spanish name in the world. This name is often given in honor of the Virgin Mary, Christ's mother. (French) *Manon, Marie*; (Spanish) *Malita, Mariquita*; (Scandinavian) *Mia*; (Slavic) *Marika*; (Russian) *Marisha*; (Finnish) *Maaria,* *Marita, Marja, Miia, Riia*; (Hungarian) *Mariska*; (Hawaiian) *Malia*; **Nicknames:** *Maree, Mimi*; **Diminutive forms:** *Manette*; **Famous namesakes:** Journalist and California first lady Maria Shriver, opera singer Maria Callas, educator Marie Montessori

MARIAH English: Bitter; a variant of Mary **Famous namesakes:** Singer Mariah Carey; **Star babies:** daughter of Kerry Kennedy and Andrew Cuomo

MARIAMNE Hebrew: Rebellious; variant of Miriam and the name of biblical King Herod's wife

MARIAN Latin: Bitter; derived from Mary (English) *Maryann*; (French) *Marianne*; (Dutch) *Marien*; (Hungarian) *Marianna*; *Mariana, Marianda, Mariane, Mariann, Marion, Maryan, Maryanna*

MARIANA Latin: Spelling variation of Marian
Marianna

MARIANNE French: Variation of Marian

MARIBELL Latin: Beautiful Marie; a blend of the names Mary or Marie and Belle
Maribel, Maribella, Maribelle, Marybell; Marybelle

MARICA Latin: A nymph

MARICRUZ (mah-ree-CROOZ) Spanish: Mary of the Cross

MARIE French: Variation of Maria
Famous namesakes: Singer Marie Osmond

MARIELLE French: Diminutive of Maria (English) *Mariel*; (Italian) *Mariella, Mariela, Mariele*; **Famous namesakes:** Actress Mariel Hemingway

MARIETTE French: Bitter; pet form of Marie
Marietta; **Famous namesakes:** Actress Mariette Hartley

MARIGOLD English: Mary's gold; also the name of a small golden, yellow, or orange flower
Nicknames: *Mari*

MARIKO (mah-ree-ko) Japanese: True or straight and benefit or reason

MARILIS (mə-RIL-is) Greek: Flower; an abbreviation of Amaryllis

MARILLA Celtic: Shining sea; a variant of Muriel and possible variant of the names Amaryllis or Amarilla

MARILYN English: Blend of Marie or Mary and Lyn.
Maralyn, Marilynn, Marylin, Marylyn, Marylynn; **Nicknames:** *Marlyn, Marlynn*; **Famous namesakes:** Actress Marilyn Monroe

MARINA Latin: Of the sea
(Russian) *Marinochka*; *Marnee, Marnell, Marni, Marnie*; **Old forms:** *Marnisha*; **Nicknames:** *Marinda, Marinella*

MARIPOSA (mah-ree-PO-sah) Spanish: Butterfly

MARISA (mə-RIS-ə) Latin, English: Of the sea; variant of Maris or Maria
Mareesa, Marissa; **Nicknames:** *Marise*; **Famous namesakes:** Actress Marissa Tomei; **Star babies:** daughter of John Wayne

MARISHA (mah-REE-sha) Russian: Variation of Maria
Nicknames: *Reesha, Risha*

MARISOL Spanish: Bitter sun; a blend of Mary and Sol

MARJA (MAHR-yah) Finnish: Variation of Maria

MARJAANA (MAHR-jah-ah) Finnish: A blend of the names Marja and Jaana

MARJAN (mar-YAN, mar-jan) Polish: Bitter, a variant of Mary; (Persian) coral
Marjaneh

MARJETA Czech: Variation of Margaret

MARJOLAINA French: Flower

MARJORIE (MAHR-jə-ree) English: Pearl; variant of Margaret
Margeree, Margery, Margerie, Marjerie, Marjery, Marjorey, Marjory; **Nicknames:** *Jorie, Joree, Jorey, Jori, Jorey, Jory, Marge, Margey, Margi, Margie, Margy, Marje, Marji, Marjie, Marjy*

MARKA African: Rebel

MARLA English: Nickname for Marlene

MARLENE (mahr-LE-nə, MAHR-leen) German, English: Blend of Maria and Magdalene referring to Mary Magdalene of the Bible. The name was first used by the German actress and singer Marlene Dietrich, whose real name was Maria Magdalene von Losch.
Marlenne, Marlin, Marline; **Nicknames:** *Marla, Marlaina, Marlayne, Marleena, Marleene, Marleina, Marlena, Marlina, Marlinda, Marlisa, Marliss, Marlys, Marlyssa*

MARLEY English: Near the meadow by the lake; surname; also a variant of Marlene, woman from Magdala
Marleigh; Marlea, Marleah, Marlee, Marly; **Famous namesakes:** Actress Marlee Matlin

MARLINDA German: Nickname for Marlene

MARLISA (mahr-LIS-ə) English: Nickname for Marlene
Marlissa

MARLOWE English: Marshy; from the hill by the lake
Marlow, Marlo; **Famous namesakes:** Actress Marlo Thomas

MARMAR Persian: Marble

MARNIE Hebrew: Rejoicing; variant of Marina
Marnee, Marnell, Marni

MARPESIA Greek: Snatcher; An Amazon queen who ruled with Lampedo, and together they excelled at building the Amazon empire. The Caucasus Mountains were once called the Marpesians after her.

MARQUISE (mahr-KEE) French: Royalty; a French royalty title
Marquisa, Marquisha

MARSHA Latin: Nickname for Marcella
Marcia, Marsia, Marsita, Martia; **Famous namesakes:** Actress Marsha Mason

MARTHA Aramaic: Lady. The biblical Martha was sister to Lazarus and Mary.
(French) *Marthe*; (Spanish) *Marta*; (Russian) *Marfa*; (Czech) *Marticka*; (Polish) *Masia*; (Finnish) *Martta*; *Marit*; **Nicknames:** *Marti, Mattie, Mart, Marti, Martie, Marty, Pat, Patti, Patty*; **Famous namesakes:** Dancer Martha Graham, First Lady Martha Washington

MARTINA Latin, Spanish, Swedish: Warlike; feminine form of Martin
(French) *Martine*; *Marteena, Martella*; **Famous namesakes:** Tennis player Martina Navratilova and tennis player Martina Hingis

MARVINA Celtic: Friend of the sea; feminine form of Marvin

MARY Hebrew, English: Bitter; Anglicized variant of Miriam; the mortal mother of Jesus Christ, generally known as the Virgin or Mother Mary, also the name of other important biblical characters, including Mary Magdalene.
(Gaelic) *Mairi*; (Irish) *Maire, Mayra*; (Scottish) *Maira*; (Welsh) *Maeryn, Mair*; (Russian) *Maruska*; **Diminutive forms:** *Mamie*; **Famous namesakes:** Philosopher Mary Wollstonecraft, author Mary Shelley (Wollstonecraft's daughter), Queen Mary (known as Queen of Scots), Artist Mary Eugenia Surratt; **Star babies:** daughter of Meryl Streep and Don Gummer

MARYANN English: Variation of Marian

MARYVONNE French: Blend of Marie and Yvonne

MASIKA (mah-SEE-kah) Egyptian: Born during the rain

MASTANEH Persian: Joyful

MATILDA (mə-TIL-də) German: Mighty battle maiden
(German) *Matilda*; (French) *Mathilde*; (Czech) *Matylda*; *Mathild, Matilde*; **Nicknames:** *Maiti, Tilda, Tilde, Tille, Tilly, Tilly*; **Famous namesakes:** English actress Tilda Swinton, French actress Mathilda May; **Star babies:** daughters of Elizabeth Perkins, Heath Ledger and Michelle Williams

> "Who'll come a-waltzing
> Matilda my darling,
> Who'll come a-waltzing
> Matilda with me?"
> —Traditional Australian folk song

MATRIKA (mah-TREE-kah) Hindi: Divine Mother

MATRYONA Russian: Lady; derived from the Latin word matrona
Nicknames: *Matryosha, Matryoshka*

MATSUKO (maht-soo-ko) Japanese: Pine tree child

MATTHEA Hebrew: Gift of God; feminine form of Matthew
Matea, Mathea, Mathia, Mattea, Matthia

MATUTA Latin: Derived from Matuta Mater, the Roman goddess of dawn

MAUDE (MAWD) French, Irish: Strong in war; variant of Mathilda
Maud; **Famous namesakes:** Actress Maude Adams

MAURA (MOR-ə, MAWR-ə) Irish: Bitter; variant of Mary. Also a feminine variant of the Latin Maurus and English Maurice, meaning dark-skinned
(Spanish) *Mora, Morisa, Morissa; Mora, Morah;* **Famous namesakes:** Actress Maura Tierney

MAUREEN Irish: Bitter; a variant of Mary
Maurine; Maura, Maurene, Maurisa, Maurita, Moreen, Morene, Morine; **Nicknames:** *Mo;*
Famous namesakes: Actress Maureen O'Hara, actress Maureen O'Sullivan, tennis star Maureen "Little Mo" Connolly

MAURISA Latin: Moorish, dark-skinned; feminine form of Maurice
(Italian) *Maurizia; Maurissa; Morisa, Morissa*

MAVA Hebrew: Pleasant

MAVIE Celtic: Variation of Mavis

MAVIS (MAY-vis) English: From the name of the type of bird, also called the song thrush, ultimately derived from Old French.
(Celtic) *Mavelle, Mavie*

MAVRA Latin: Moorish, dark-skinned

MAXINE Latin: Greatest; feminine form of Max
(Italian) *Massima; Maxime, Maxina;*
Nicknames: *Maxie*

MAY Latin: In Roman mythology, Maia was goddess of spring growth. The name of the month May comes from Maia. See also *Maia* (Hebrew) *Mayah;* (French) *Mai;* (Spanish) *Maya; Mae, Maelee, Maelynn; Maye;*
Nicknames: *Maylee, Mayleen, Maylene, Maylin;* **Star babies:** daughter of Madeline Stowe and Brian Benben

MAYA Sanskrit: Illusion, fantasy or God's power; also a variant of Maia
Famous namesakes: Poet Maya Angelou

MAYLEA (mey-le-AH) Hawaiian: Wildflower

MAZEL Hebrew: Luck

MEADOW English: An open, uncultivated field

MEDB (MAYV) Celtic: Original form of Maeve

MEDEA (mə-DEE-ə) Greek: In Greek mythology, Medea was one of the great sorceresses, and helped Jason win the Golden Fleece. She fled her home to be with him, but he deserted her.
Nicknames: *Madora, Medora*

MEDESICASTE Greek: Mythical daughter of Priam, she was taken captive by the Achaeans after the sack of Troy.

MEDITRINA Latin: Healer; mythical goddess of wine and health

MEDUSA (mə-DOO-sə) Greek: Sovereign female wisdom. Medusa was imported into Greece from Libya where she was worshipped by the Libyan Amazons as their Serpent-Goddess. Medusa (Metis) was the destroyer aspect of the Great Triple Goddess also called Neith, Anath, Athene, or Ath-enna in North Africa.

MEEDA Irish: Thirsty; an Anglicized variant of Mide
Ide, Mide

MEENA (mee-nah) Sanskrit: Precious stone
Mena; **Famous namesakes:** Actress Mena Suvari

MEGAN (MEG-ən) Welsh: Pearl; a variant of Marged, Megan is now commonly used as an independent name
Maegan, Meegan, Meeghan, Meggan, Meghan; Maygan, Maygen, Meaghan; **Nicknames:** *Meg, Meggie*; **Famous namesakes:** Actress Meg Ryan

MEGARA (ME-gə-rə) Greek: Mythological wife of Hercules
Nicknames: *Magaere*

MEHETABEL (mə-HET-ə-BEE-əl) Hebrew: God's best, God's favor

MEHLI (may-lee) Hindi: Rain

MEIRA (me-EE-rah) Hebrew: Light

MELANIE (MEL-ə-nee) Greek: Dark; the name of a Roman saint who became a great religious philanthropist
(French) *Melaina*; (Polish) *Mela, Melka; Melana, Melanee, Melania, Melanne*; **Famous namesakes:** Actress Melanie Griffith; **Star babies:** daughters of Peter Gabriel, Vanessa Williams and Ramon Hervey

MELANIPPE (mel-an-NIP-ee) Greek: Sister of Hippolyte and daughter of Ares. Heracles captured her and demanded Hippolyte's girdle in exchange for her freedom.

MELANTHA Greek: Dark flower
Melanthe, Melantho

MELE Hawaiian: Song

MELEK (me-LEK) Turkish: Form of Malak

MELIA (mə-LEE-ah) Greek: Sweet; Greek mythological nymph of clouds and rain, daughter of Oceanus; (Hawaiian) plumeria.

MELIKA Persian: A plant, melic grass

MELINA (mə-LEE-nah) Greek: Honey

MELINDA English, Greek: Modern blend of Melissa or Melanie and Linda, this name may also derive from the Latin word *melitus*, meaning *sweet*.
Malinda, Melynda; **Nicknames:** *Mindi, Mindie, Mindy*; **Star babies:** daughter of John Wayne

MELISSA Greek: Honeybee; a mythological Greek nymph who fed honey to the infant god Zeus and was later transformed into a bee (French) *Melisande*; (Spanish) *Melisenda, Meliza; Melisa, Melise, Melisha, Melisse, Mellisa*; **Nicknames:** *Lissa, Lyssa, Missy, Mel, Lissa*; **Famous namesakes:** Singer Melissa Manchester, singer Missy Elliott

MELITA (mə-LEE-tah) Greek: Honey

MELLONA Latin: Roman goddess, patroness of bees and beekeeping

MELODY Greek: Melody, song
(French) *Melodie*; *Melodee, Melodi*

MELOSA (may-LO-sah) Spanish: Honey, sweet
Nicknames: *Melosia*

MELPOMENE (mel-PAH-mə-nee) Greek: Mythical muse of tragedy

MELVINA Irish, English: Chieftan; feminine form of Melvin
Melva

MEMDI Native American: Henna

MENACHEMA Hebrew: Consolation
Menachemah

MENGLAD Norse: A Norse goddess sometimes identified with Freya

MEOQUANEE (me-o-kwah-nee) Native American: Wears red (Chippewa)

MERCEDES Spanish: Mercies; given in honor of the Virgin Mary
(French) *Mercède*; (Italian) *Mercede*; *Mercedez, Mercia, Mercie, Mercilla, Mercina*; **Star babies:** daughter of Joanne Whalley and Val Kilmer

MERCER English: Merchant; a name used for both genders

MERCY English: Merciful; virtue name
Mercie

MEREDITH Welsh: Magnificent chief or protector
Meridith; **Old forms:** *Maredud, Meredydd*; **Nicknames:** *Mer, Meri*; **Famous namesakes:** Actress Meredith Baxter

MERI (ME-ree) Finnish: Sea; (English) mirthful, joyous; variant of Merry, Meredith, Merilee, and similar names

MERIDEL English: Mirthful, joyous; variant of Merry and possibly Meredith

MERLA (mer-LAH) French: Blackbird; feminine form of Merle
Merlina

MEROPE Greek: Daughter of Oenopion, king of Chios; Orion fell in love with her, but Oenopion refused to give her up and blinded Orion.

MERRILEE English: Modern blend of Merry and Lee
Merilee

MERRILL (MER-əl) English: Shining sea; also a feminine variant of Merle, meaning blackbird
Merrille

MERRY English: Cheerful, happy; also a variant of Mary, Mercy, Meredith and similar names
Merri, Merrie; Meri

MERULA Latin: Blackbird

MERVEILLE (mer-VIE) French: Miracle
Marvel, Marvella, Marvelle

MERYL (MER-əl) Celtic: Spelling variation of Muriel
Famous namesakes: Actress Meryl Streep

MESSINA (me-SEE-nah) Latin: Middle child. Messina is also a city in Italy.

MI-NA (mih-nah) Native American: Firstborn daughter (Sioux)

MIA (MEE-ah) Scandinavian: Variation of Maria
Famous namesakes: Actress Mia Farrow, soccer player Mia Hamm; **Star babies:** daughter of Kate Winslet and James Threapleton

MICA Hebrew: Who is like the Lord; a diminutive of Michaela. Mica is also a type of mineral known for its ability to be separated into thin, even transparent, leaves.
Meeca, Meica, Michah, Mika, Myka, Mykah

MICHAELA (mə-KAY-lə) Hebrew, Latin, English: Who is like the Lord; feminine variant of Michael. Though the popular perception is that Michaela is a relatively new name, and a version of Michelle, the exact opposite is true and Michaela is the original. Michaela has a long history, and many spellings are well grounded in various ethnic traditions. One of the first was the biblical Michal: King Saul's daughter and the first wife of David.
(Latin) *Micaela, Mikayla, Mikella, Mikelle, Mikki, Mychaela*; (English) *Mikaela*; (French) *Michela, Michele, Michèle, Micheline, Michelle, Mychele, Mychelle*; (Spanish) *Micaella, Miguela, Miguelita, Miquela, Quela*; (Slavic) *Miesha, Mischa, Misha*; (African) *Machelle*; (Hawaiian) *Makelina*; *Mical, Michaelina, Michaeline, Michaelyn, Michalin, Michella, Mikele*; *Macaela, Macaila, Macayla, MacKayla, Mahalya, Makaila, Makayla, Makyla, Mckaila, Mckayla, Mechaela, Meeskaela, Mekea, Micaila, Micayla, Michael, Michele, Michell, Michella, Mihaila, Mihaliya, Mikaila, Mikhaila, Mikhala, Mishaela, Mishaila, Miskaela, Mychele, Mychelle, Myshell, Myshelle*; **Nicknames:** *Mia, Mica, Micah, Michal, Micole, Mika, Chelle, Chelly, Meeca, Meica, Mickey, Micki, Mickie, Micky, Myka, Mykah, Schelley, Shellee, Shelley, Shellie, Shelly*; **Famous namesakes:** Cinematographer Michaela Denis; **Star babies:** daughter of Kerry Kennedy and Andrew Cuomo

MICHELLE French: Variation of Michaela
Michele, Michella, Michell, Mychele, Mychelle, Myshell, Myshelle; **Nicknames:** *Chelle, Chelly, Meecha, Micha, Misha, Schelley, Shellee, Shelley, Shelli, Shellie, Shelly*; **Famous namesakes:** First Lady Michelle Obama,

actress Michelle Pfeiffer, Olympic skater Michelle Kwan; **Star babies:** daughters of Anne Rice, Deborah Norville, Kate Capshaw and Steven Spielberg

MICHIE (mee-chee) Japanese: Gateway; gracefully drooping flower

MICHIKO (mee-chee-ko) Japanese: Child of beauty

MIDORI (mee-dor-ee) Japanese: Green
Famous namesakes: Japanese figure skater Midori Ito

MIEKO (mee-e-ko) Japanese: Beautiful, blessed child

MIGISI (mih-gee-see) Native American: Eagle (Chippewa)

MIGNON (mee-NYON) French: Cute, attractive
Diminutive forms: *Mignonette*; **Famous namesakes:** Opera singer Mignon Dunne

MIKA (MEE-kah) Native American: Raccoon (Osage and Omaha-Ponca)

MIKIL Hawaiian: Quick, nimble

MIKKI English: Variation of Michaela
Micki, Mickie, Mickey, Micky

MILA (MEE-lah) Russian: Favor of the people; a short form of Ludmila; (Persian) stork

MILAGROS (mee-LAH-gros) Spanish: Miracle; taken from the Virgin Mary's title *Nuestra Senora de los Milagros* (Our Lady of Miracles)
Milagritos, Milagrosa; **Nicknames:** *Mila*

MILCAH Hebrew: Counsel

MILDRED English: Gentle counselor; Saint Mildred was a seventh-century abbess known for her generosity to the poor.
Mildraed, Mildrid, Mildryd

MILENA Czech: Gracious

MILEY (MIE-lee) Irish: Smiley
Milee; **Nicknames:** *Lee*; **Famous namesakes:** Singer Miley Cyrus

MILIANA Latin: Industrious; a feminine form of Emiliano

MILILANI (MEE-lee-AH-nee) Hawaiian: Praise, exalt; also a town in Hawaii

MILKA (MEEL-kə) Slavic: Industrious

MILLA (MEE-lah) Finnish: Freeborn, noble; a pet form of Camilla

MILLICENT (MIL-ə-sənt) German: Noble, strong
(German) *Milicent*; *Melicent*; **Nicknames:** *Millie*; **Famous namesakes:** Congresswoman Millicent Fenwick

MILOSLAVA (mee-lah-SLAH-vah) Slavic: Lover of glory

MIMI French: Nickname for Wilhelmina
Famous namesakes: Actress Mimi Rogers; **Star babies:** daughter of Donna Summer

MIN Chinese: Clever, quick

MINA (MEE-nə) German: Nickname for Wilhelmina; (Persian) the gemstone, lapis lazuli
Minna

MINDEL Yiddish: Bitter

MINDY English: Nickname for Melinda
Mindee, Mindi, Mindie

MINERVA (mi-NUR-və) Latin: Goddess of wisdom

MINKA Teutonic: Resolute
Famous namesakes: Actress Minka Kelly

MINNA (MI-nah) German: Nickname for Wilhelmina

MINNEHAHA (min-neh-hah-hah) Native American: Laughing water (Sioux); the name of the girl Hiawatha loved

MINNIE French: Nickname for Wilhelmina
Famous namesakes: Disney's beloved cartoon Minnie Mouse, comedienne Minnie Pearl

MINOU Persian: Paradise

MINTA Greek: Mint
(Finnish) *Minttu*; *Mintha*

MIRA (MEER-ə) Latin: Wonderful; derived from the Latin word mirandus; (Hindi) prosperous; a name born by India's Saint Mira Bai, a poet and devotee of Krishna
Nicknames: *Myrelle, Myrilla*; **Famous namesakes:** Actress Mira Sorvino

MIRABELLE French: Wonderful
Mirabella

MIRANDA Latin: Wonderful; derived from the Latin word mirandus. Miranda is the young girl in Shakespeare's *The Tempest*, raised and educated on an isolated island by her magician father Prospero.
(Spanish) *Mireya*; (Slavic) *Miriana*; *Mirande*; **Nicknames:** *Randa, Randi, Randie, Randy*; **Famous namesakes:** Actress Miranda Richardson

MIREILLE (mee-RAY) French: Variation of Miriam

Virtue Names

Looking for a name that represents a quality important to you and your partner?
Browse the below list for some virtuous monikers.
(For more virtue names, see pages 89, 240, and 321.)

Names Meaning "Fair" or "Just"

BOYS
Adel (Arabic)
Justin (Latin)
Nemesio (Spanish)
Zadok (Hebrew)

GIRLS
Adeleh (Persian)
Dice (Greek)
Justine (Latin)
Mackenzie (Scottish)

Names Meaning "Honest" or "Trustworthy"

BOYS
Achates (Greek)
Adib (Arabic)
Amin (Arabic)
Hemen (Hebrew)
Renjiro (Japanese)
Truman (English)

GIRLS
Alecta (Greek)
Aliz (Hungarian)
Amina (Arabic)

Ruth (Hebrew)
Vera (Latin)
Veronica (Latin)

Names Meaning "Loyal" or "Faithful"

BOYS
Amnon (Hebrew)
Dillon (Gaelic)
Fidel (Latin)
Fido (Spanish)
Leal (English)
Loyal (French)

GIRLS
Faith (English)
Fidelity (Latin)
Iman (Arabic)
Sadiki (Egyptian)
Usko (Finnish)
Wafa (African)

Names Meaning "Kind" or "Generous"

BOYS
Chanan (Hebrew)
Corliss (English)

Dorby (Polish)
Elden (English)
Fen (English)
Generoso (Spanish)
Gennadi (Russian)
Hashim (Arabic)
Karim (Arabic)
Latif (Arabic)
Maher (Irish)
Tayeb (Arabic)
Terence (Latin)

GIRLS
Adette (German)
Agatha (Greek)
Aldonza (Spanish)
Aliz (German)
Bahija (Arabic)
Esma (Anglo-Saxon)
Cordelia (Latin)
Generosa (Spanish)
Karima (Arabic)
Lilo (Hawaiian)
Lina (Arabic)
Makawee (Native American)
Sarama (African)
Yetta (English)
Declan (Irish)

MIRIAM Hebrew: Rebellious; an original variant of Mary
(French) *Mireille*; (Finnish) *Mirjami*; (Yiddish) *Mirel*; *Mariam*; **Nicknames:** *Mariamne, Mirit, Mitzi*; **Famous namesakes:** Singer Miriam Makeba

MIRKA (MEER-kə) Slavic: Peaceful

MISAE (mih-sah-eh, mih-say) Native American: White sun (Osage)

MISCHA (MEE-shah) Russian: Who is like the Lord; variant of Michaela
Meecha, Micha, Misha; **Famous namesakes:** Actress Mischa Barton

MISOKA (mee-so-kah) Japanese: Born on the last day of the month

MISTY English: Misty
Misti, Mistie, Mystee, Mysti

MITENA (mih-ten-ah) Native American: Born at the new moon (Omaha)

MITRA Persian: Name of a deity worshipped by ancient Iranians (goddess of loving kindness)

MITSU (meet-soo) Japanese: Shine

MITZI (MIT-see) German: Nickname for Miriam
Famous namesakes: Actress Mitzi Gaynor

MIYA (mee-yah) Japanese: Beauty
Star babies: daughter of Muhammad Ali

MNEMOSYNE (ni-MAWS-ə-nee) Greek: In Greek mythology, the goddess of memory

MOANA (MWAH-nah) Hawaiian: Ocean, sea

MODESTA (mo-DE-stah) Latin: Modest, a virtue
(English) *Modesty*

MODRON Celtic: Divine mother. A Celtic goddess by this name was linked with legendary Morgan Le Fay, sister to King Arthur. Both women were closely associated with the mythical island of Avalon.

MOERAE Greek: Fate, destiny
Moirae

MOIRA (MOI-ra) Irish: Bitter; a variant of Maire, an Irish form of Mary
Moire; **Famous namesakes:** Actress Moira Kelly

MOLARA (mo-LAHR-ah) Basque: Reference to the Virgin Mary

MOLLY Irish, English: Bitter; from the Gaelic Maili or Maille, a pet form of Mary
(Irish) *Maille, Mallaidh*; *Molli, Mollie*; **Famous namesakes:** Actress Molly Ringwald

MONA Irish: Little noble one, also used in several languages as a short form of Monica; The *Mona Lisa* painting by Leonardo da Vinci may be the most famous portrait in the history of art. The name *Mona Lisa* is a shortened form of *Madonna Lisa* (my lady, Lisa); (Native American) gathered of the seed of a jimson weed
Moina, Moyna

MONAHAN Irish: Monk; a surname adaptation traditionally used for boys
Monaghan

MONCA Irish: Wise

MONCHA Irish: Alone; possibly derived from the name of a Celtic goddess

MONICA Latin: Advisor, counselor; fourth-century saint known mainly by the writings of her son, Saint Augustine
(German) *Monika*; (French) *Monique*; *Moniqua*; **Famous namesakes:** Actress Monica Potter, Italian actress Monica Bellucci

MONIFA (MO-nee-fah) Egyptian: Lucky

MONIR Persian: Shining
Moneer

MONTANA Latin: Mountain; a northwestern American state
Star babies: daughter of Judd Hirsch

MONTSERRAT (mon-ser-RAHT, mahn-ser-AT) Latin: Jagged mountain. Montserrat is the name of a mountain near Barcelona, Spain.
Famous namesakes: Spanish soprano Montserrat Caballe

MOR Gaelic: Great
Nicknames: *Morag, Morella*

MORELA (mo-REH-lah) Polish: Apricot

MORGAN Welsh: Circling sea; a traditionally Welsh male name, used in legend by the powerful sorceress sister or stepsister of King Arthur
Morgen; **Nicknames:** *Morgaine, Morgana, Morgandy;* **Famous namesakes:** Actress Morgan Fairchild; **Star babies:** daughters of Clint Eastwood and Dina Ruiz, Keith Carney and Amy

MORGAUSE Welsh: Queen, half-sister of legendary King Arthur and Morgan Le Fay, wife of King Lot, mother of the important knights Agravaine, Gawain, Gareth, and Gaheris, she also was said to have raised Arthur's son, Mordred, and in some versions was his mother.
Margawse, Morgawse

MORIAH Hebrew: God teaches, seen by Yahweh; biblical name of the mount of the Jerusalem's Temple of Solomon
Moriel, Morit

MORNA Celtic: Dearly loved
Merna

MORRIGAN Celtic: A war goddess in Irish mythology

MORRIN (MOR-rin) Irish: Long-haired

MORVARID Persian: Pearl
Morvareed

MORVEN (MOR-vən, MWAWR-ven) Gaelic: Big gap

MORWENNA (mor-WEN-nah) Welsh: Maiden
Morwyn

MOSELLE Hebrew: From the water
Mozelle

MOYA Celtic: Bitter; a variant of Mary

MUIRE Irish: From the moor; a surname adapted to given name use

MUNA (MOO-nah) Arabic: Desire, aspiration; (Native American) overflowing spring (Hopi)
Mona

MURIEL Irish: Shining sea; also a variant of Mary; (Arabic) myrrh
(Irish) *Muireall; Merryl, Meryl, Myrla; Meriel;* **Old forms:** *Muirgheal*

MUSADORA Greek: Gift of the Muses
Musidora

MUSETTE (moo-SET) French: A song
Musetta

MUT (MOOT) Egyptian: Mythical mother, ancient Egyptian war goddess, consort of Amon and part of the Theban Triad group of gods. Mut was worshipped at Thebes.

MUTA Latin: Roman personification and goddess of silence

MYFANWY (mə-VAN-wee) Welsh: My woman

MYRA (MIE-rə) English: Derived from the Latin word for myrrh, and possibly a variant of the name Myrna. Myra may also have been invented by the English poet Fulke Grenville. **Nicknames:** *Myrina*

MYRINA English: Myrrh; a variant of Myra

MYRNA Arabic: Myrrh, an aromatic gum resin obtained from several Asian or African trees and shrubs, used in making perfume and incense. Considered very precious in ancient times, it was a kingly gift for one of the Magi to give to the the newborn Jesus. **Famous namesakes:** Actress Myrna Loy

MYRTLE (MUR-təl) English: A botanical name for an evergreen shrub. Myrtle was considered sacred to the Roman goddess of love, Venus, who used it as one of her symbols. (Latin) *Myrta*; (Greek) *Myrtia, Myrtisa*; **Nicknames:** *Myrtice, Myrtis*

MYSTIQUE (mis-TEEK) French: Air of mystery; Betty Friedan's bestselling book, *The Feminine Mystique*, is credited with launching the second wave of the feminist movement. *Mistique*

NABILA (nah-BEE-lah) Arabic: Born into nobility

NABIRYE (nah-BEER-yay) Egyptian: Mother of twins

NACSHA (nas-cha) Native American: Owl (Navajo)

NADA Arabic: Dew, giving (Persian) *Nadia; Nadya; Nadah, Nadia*

NADIA Russian, Slavic: Hope (Slavic) *Nadege*; (Polish) *Nadzia, Nadzieja, Nata, Natia; Nadya*; **Old forms:** *Nadezda, Nadezhda*; **Nicknames:** *Nadusha*; **Diminutive forms:** *Nadenka, Nadyenka, Nadyuiska*; **Famous namesakes:** Romanian gymnast Nadia Comaneci

"Loving a child doesn't mean giving in to all his whims; to love him is to bring out the best in him, to teach him to love what is difficult."
—Nadia Boulanger, the first woman to conduct the Boston Symphony Orchestra

NADINE (na-DEEN, nay-DEEN) French, Latin: Hope; diminutive of Nadia and a familiar form of Bernadette (German) *Nadina; Nadeen*

NADZIEJA (nah-JAY-ah) Polish: Variation of Nadia

NAEEMAH (nah-EE-mah) Egyptian: Benevolent *Na'ima*

NAHEED Persian: Immaculate

NAHLAH Arabic: Drink of water, to quench *Nahla*

NAIA (nah-ee-ah) Hawaiian: Dolphin

NAIARA (nie-AH-rah) Basque: From the name of the Spanish city Nájera *Naiaria*

NAIDA (NIE-də, NAY-də) Greek: Water nymph *Naia, Naiadia*

NAILAH (NAH-ee -ah, nah-EE-lah) African, Egyptian: Successful
Nala

NAIMA (nah-EEM-ah, NIE-mah) African: Graceful

NAIRNA Scottish: Dwells at the alder tree river
Nairne

NAJA African: Strong

NAJILA (nah-JEE-lah) Arabic: Brilliant eyes
Nicknames: *Najla*

NAJLA Arabic: Star; variation of the word Najee which means star

NAKEISHA (nə-KEE-shə) American: Her life

NALANI (nah-LAH-nee) Hawaiian: Silence of the heavens

NALDA (NAHL-dah) Spanish: Strong

NALIN (nah-lin) Native American: Young maiden (Apache)

NAMID (NAH-meed) Native American: Star dancer (Chippewa)

NAMPEYO (nam-pay-yo) Native American: Snake girl (Hopi). The name of one of the most celebrated of Hopi potters in the twentieth century

NANA Hawaiian: Name of a spring month, name of a star

NANCY English, French: Grace; variant of Ann often regarded as an independent name
(Irish) *Nainsi*; (Hungarian) *Nancsi, Nusa, Nusi*; *Nancey, Nanci, Nancie; Nancey, Nancie, Nanci*;
Nicknames: *Nannie, Nan*; **Famous namesakes:** First Lady Nancy Reagan, figure skater Nancy Kerrigan; **Star babies:** daughter of Robert Duvall

NANETTE (nah-NET) French, Hebrew: Favor, grace; variant of Anne
(French) *Nanine, Nynette; Nanelia, Nanelle, Nanetta, Nannette, Nanon, Ninette*;
Nicknames: *Nan, Nana, Nann, Nanny*

NANI (NAH-nee) Hawaiian: Beauty

NANNA Norse: Wife of Balder

NAOMI (nay-O-mee, nie-O-mee) Hebrew: Pleasant. In the Old Testament, Naomi was the mother-in-law of Ruth. After the death of her husband and sons and upon her return to Bethlehem, Naomi took the name Mara, meaning bitter.
(French) *Noemie*; (Spanish) *Noemi; Naamah, Neomi, Nyomi*; **Famous namesakes:** Actress Naomi Watts; **Star babies:** daughter of Stephen Kind and Tabitha Spruce

NAPIA Latin: Of the valley
Napea

NARA Greek: Contented, happy; (Japanese) oak
Narra

NARCISSA (nar-SIS-ə) Greek: Daffodil; feminine form of Narcissus, the beautiful boy of Greek mythology who fell in love with his own reflection in a pool and, unable to find consolation, died of sorrow.
(Spanish) *Narcisa*; (Russian) *Narkissa*; (Turkish) *Nergis*

NARDA Latin: Fragrant; (Persian) anointed
Nardia

NAREEN Celtic: Contented
Nareena, Nareene

NARISSA Greek: Sea nymph, daughter of Nereus. In Greek mythology, the Nereids were mermaids and deities of the seas.

NARMADA Hindi: Gives us pleasure

NASCIO (NAH-syo) Latin: Goddess of childbirth

NASHOTA (nah-SHO-tah) Native American: Twin

NASIMA Arabic: Breeze, fresh air; feminine form of Nasim. Sham el Nasim (smell the breeze) is an Egyptian spring festival that takes place the day after Easter in commemoration of Pharaonic spring and Nile festivals, and is celebrated by Muslims and Christians alike.
Naseema, Naseemah, Nessima, Nesima, Nesimah, Nessimah, Nesime, Nesimeh

NASRIN Persian: Wild rose
Nasreen

NASTASIA Russian: Variation of Anastasia
Nastasiya; *Nastassja*; **Nicknames:** *Nastya, Nastia, Nastiya,* **Diminutive forms:** *Nastunya*; **Famous namesakes:** German actress Nastassja Kinski

NATA Russian: Nickname for Natalia and Renata; (Native American) speaker

NATALIA (nah-TAHL-ee-ah) Spanish: Variation of Natalie
Nicknames: *Nati*; Star babies: daughter of Kobe Bryant

NATALIE French: Born on Christmas; popular name from the Latin Natalia. See also *Natasha*
(Italian) *Natala, Natale*; (Spanish) *Natalia*; (Russian) *Natalya*; *Natalee, Natassia, Nathalee, Nathalia, Nathalie*; **Nicknames:** *Nat, Tasha, Nata, Natty, Nat,* **Diminutive forms:** *Natashenka, Tashia, Tassa, Tosha*; **Famous namesakes:** Actress Natalie Wood, actress Natalie Portman; **Star babies:** daughter of George Foreman

NATANE (nah-TAH-ne) Native American: Daughter (Arapaho)

NATASHA Russian: Nickname for Natalya; Natasha Rostova is one of the main characters in Leo Tolstoy's novel *War and Peace*.
Natascha; **Nicknames:** *Tasha*; **Famous namesakes:** Canadian actress Natasha Henstridge, British actress Natasha Richardson, British actress Natascha McElhone; **Star babies:** daughters of Michael Caine, Candace Cameron and Valeri Bure, Vanessa Redgrave

NATESA (nah-TAY-shah) Hindi: Dancer

NATHAIRA Scottish: Snake
Nathara

NATHANIA (nah-THA-nee-ə) Hebrew: God's gift; feminine form of Nathaniel

NATI Hindi: Humble, bowing

NAUNET (NOW-net) Egyptian: Mythical goddess of the ocean

NAUSICAA (nah-O-shi-kə) Greek: Princess who finds Odysseus shipwrecked on Scheria. She is one of the most charming figures in *The Odyssey*.

NAUTIA Latin: From the sea

NAVEENA Native American: New

NAVIT (nah-VEET) Hebrew: Pleasant

NAWA (NOW-wah) Egyptian: Storm; Those storms that recur roughly at the same time each year have names, taken from the historic Coptic language.
Nawah, Nawwah

NAYANA (nay-yah-na) Hindi: Having beautiful eyes

NAYO (NAH-yo) African: She is our joy (Nigerian)

NAZNEEN Persian: Exquisitely beautiful, charming; a name used for a beloved woman or child

NAZY Persian: Cute
Nazilla; **Nicknames:** *Nazneen*

NEBULA Latin: Misty

NECEDAH (ne-CEE-dah) Native American: Yellow (Winnebago)

NECI Latin: Ardent, intense

NEDA (NE-də) English: Wealthy protector, feminine form of Ned; (Slavic, African) born on Sunday
Nedda

NEDIVAH Hebrew: Giving
Nediva

NEEJA Hindi: Lily

NEEMA (ne-E-mah) African: Born in prosperity (Swahili)

NEENAH (nee-nah) Native American: Running water (Winnebago)

NEFERTITI (nef-ər-TEE-tee) Egyptian: The beautiful woman has come; name of ancient Egyptian queen
Nefertari

NEHAMA Hebrew: Comfort; also a surname
Nechama

NEILA (NEE-lah) Gaelic: Champion; feminine variant of Neil
Neala, Neelie, Nielsine; Neela; **Nicknames:** *Nealie, Neely, Nia*

NEILIKKA (NE-EE-leek-ah) Finnish: Clove

NEITH (NEETH) Egyptian: The divine mother, great creator-goddess. In ancient Egyptian mythology, Neith is shown wearing a red crown; her emblem is a shield with two crossed arrows worn on her head. Neith was later associated with Athena by the Greeks. See also *Athena, Matrika*
(Latin) *Athene*; **Old forms:** *Mut, Net*

NEJMA Arabic: Star
Negma (Egyptian variant)

NELDA English: One who lives by the alder tree

NELIDA (nay-LEE-dah) Spanish: A diminutive form of Cornelia, Elena, and Reinalda

NELKE German: Carnation; flower name

NELL Greek, English: Light; familiar form of Eleanor, Cornelia, Prunella, and similar names (Russian) *Nelya*; *Nella, Nelma*; **Nicknames:** *Nelli, Nellie, Nelly*; **Famous namesakes:** Actress and singer Nell Carter

NELWIN English: Bright friend, Nell's friend
Nellwyn, Nelwina, Nelwyna

NEMESIS (NE-mə-səs) Greek: Retribution; the Greek goddess of vengeance

NEOLA Greek: Youthful

NEOMA Greek: New moon
Neomea, Neomenia, Neomia

NEORAH Hebrew: Enlightened
Neira, Nera

NEPHTHYS (nef-TEES) Egyptian: Mythical nature goddess; sister of Isis
Old forms: *Nebt het*

NEREA (ne-RAY-ah) Basque: Mine
Neria

NERIDA Greek: Sea nymph, mermaid. In Greek mythology the Nereids were the fifty daughters of Nereus and Doris who dwelled in the Mediterranean Sea.
Nereida, Nereyda, Nerice, Neried, Nerina, Nerine, Neris, Nerita

NERISSA (ne-RIS-ə) Greek: From the sea; also a character in Shakespeare's *Merchant of Venice*

NERYS (NER-is) Welsh: Lady

NESSIA Greek: Pure; (Scottish) from the headland
Nessa, Neysa

NET Egyptian: Original form of Neith

NETA (NE-tə) Hebrew, Spanish: Plant or shrub

NETTIE French: Familiar form for names such as Annette, Antoinette, Nanette, and others
Netty

NEVAEH (ni-VAY-ə) American: Heaven spelled backward

NEVE Irish: Anglicized spelling of Niamh
Famous namesakes: Canadian actress Neve Campbell

NEYLAN Turkish: Fulfilled wish

NIA English: Nickname for Neila

NIABI (nee-ab-ee) Native American: Young deer, fawn (Osage)

NIAMH (NEEV) Irish: Radiance, brightness. The daughter of the sea god Manannan, she was known as "Niamh of the Golden Hair," a beautiful princess riding on a white horse.
Neve; **Famous namesakes:** Irish actress Niamh Cusack

NICHELE English: Modern blend of Nichole and Michelle
Nichel, Nichelle

NICOLE Greek, French: Victorious; feminine form of Nicholas
(English) *Nicola*; (French) *Nicolette*; (Italian) *Colletta, Nicoletta*; (Spanish) *Coleta, Coletta, Nicanora, Nicolasa*; *Nichole, Nikolia*; **Nicknames:** *Nicci, Nicea, Nicia, Nicki, Nickie, Niki, Nikki, Nikkie*; **Famous namesakes:** Actress Nicole Kidman; **Star babies:** daughter of Lionel Richie

NIDIA Latin: Refuge, nest
Nydia

NIEVES (nee-AY-vays) Spanish: Snows; a name given in honor of Nuestra Señora de las Nieves (Our Lady of the Snows)
Nieva; **Nicknames:** *Neva, Nevada*

NIJLON Native American: Mistress (Algonquin)

NIKE (NIE-kee) Greek: Mythological personification of victory; also a major brand of athletic shoes and sports equipment

NIKI Greek: Nickname for Nicole

NIKITA (nee-KEE-tah) Russian: Masculine name used as feminine; popularized by the film and television show *La Femme Nikita*

NILIA Latin: From the Nile
Nila, Nile, Nilea

NIMAH Arabic: Blessing, grace
Neima, Neimah, Nima

NINA (NEE-nah) Russian: Dreamer, possibly from old Slavonic word *ninati* that means *to dream*; (Spanish) little girl; (Native American) strong
(Finnish) *Niina*; **Diminutive forms:** *Ninacska, Ninochka*; **Famous namesakes:** Jazz singer Nina Simone; **Star babies:** daughter of Robert De Niro and Helena Springs

NINEL Russian: Inversion of the name Lenin, the name of the first Soviet prime minister
Nicknames: *Nelya*

NINON (nee-NO) French: Diminutive form of Anne

NIOBE (nie-O-bee) Greek: Fern; Niobe was the daughter of Tantalus in Greek mythology.

NIPA (NEE-pah) Hindi: Stream

NIRA Hebrew: Plow or God's field
Niria

NIRETA Greek: From the sea

NIRVELI (neer-VAY-lee) Hindi: From the water

NISSE (Ni-sə) Scandinavian: Friendly elf
Nissa, Nysse

NITA (NEE-tah) Hebrew: To plant; (Native American) bear (Choctaw)

NITSA Greek: Peace

NITUNA (nee-TOO-nah) Native American: Daughter

NITZANAH Hebrew: Blossom
Nizana; **Nicknames:** *Nitza*

NIXI Latin: Goddess of childbirth

NOA (NO-ə) Hebrew: Motion; feminine form of Noah. In the Old Testament, Noa was the daughter of Zelophehad; **Famous namesakes:** Israeli actress Noa Tishby

NOE Hawaiian: Mist, misty

NOELANI (no-e-LAH-nee) Hawaiian: Mist of heaven

NOELLE (no-EL) French: Christmas; feminine variant of Noel
Noel, Noele, Noell, Noella; **Famous namesakes:** Actress Noelle Evans

NOKOMIS Native American: Grandmother (Chippewa)

NOLA Celtic: Nickname for Finola
Nuala

NOLANA Gaelic: Noble and renowned; feminine form of Nolan
Nolene

NOLITA Latin: Unwilling; also name of hip Manhattan neighborhood north of Little Italy
Noleta

NOMA Norse: Fate; (Hawaiian) example
Norn

NONA (NO-nah) Latin: Ninth, born ninth
Nonna

> Nona . . . Here's a name for those parents who plan on having more than one child.

NORA Greek: Light; diminutive of Eleanor; (Irish) honor; familiar form of Honora
(Irish) *Noreen, Noreena*; (Finnish) *Noora*; *Norah, Norina, Norine*; **Famous namesakes:** Singer Norah Jones

NORABEL English: Beautiful light; a modern blend of Nora and Belle

NORBERTA German: Bright heroine; feminine form of Norbert
Norberte; **Old forms:** *Norberaht*

NORDICA German: From the north
Norda, Nordika

NOREEN Irish: Variation of Nora

NORMA Latin: From the north; feminine form of Norman

NOVA (NO-və) Latin: New; (Native American) chases butterfly (Hopi)
Novea, Novia

NOX Latin: Night
Nyx

NUALA (NOO-la) Irish: Nickname for Finola

NUBIA (NOO-bee-ə) Egyptian: From Nubia (ancient name for Ethiopia)

NUDARA Arabic: Pure gold or silver; feminine variant of Nudar

NUMEES Native American: Sister (Algonquin)

NUNA (NOO-nah) Native American: Land

NUNZIA (NOON-zee-ah) Italian: Messenger
Nunciata

NURAY Turkish: Bright moon

NURIT (noo-REET) Hebrew: Plant
Nirit, Nureet, Nurita

NURU (noo-ROO) African: Born during the day

NUTTAH Native American: My heart (Algonquin)

NYCHELLE (ni-SHEL) Contemporary: Compound name of Nicole and Michelle
Nichelle

NYLA Arabic: Winner

NYMPHA (NIM-fah) Greek: Nymph, bride

NYSSA Greek: Goal
Nysa, Nyse

OAKLEY English: From the oak tree meadow; a surname and variant of Ackerley
Oaklea, Oaklee, Oakleigh, Oaklie, Oakly

OANA Romanian: God is gracious

OBA (oh-BAH) African: River goddess

OBELIA Greek: Pointed, from the Greek *obeliskos*, a pointed pillar
Obelie

OCEANA (OSH-nə) Greek: Feminine form of Oceanus. In Greek mythology, Oceanus was a Titan father of rivers and water nymphs.

OCTAVIA (ahk-TAYV-ee-ə) Latin: Eighth, traditionally given to the eighth child born into a family; the feminine form of Octavius
Octaviana, Octavie, Ottavia; Octaviacia, Octiana, Otavita, Ottava, Ottaviana;
Nicknames: *Tava, Tavia*

ODA Norse: Pointed; familiar form of any of the names with the roots of *aud* or *odd*

ODDVEIG Norse: Woman of the spear, derived from *oddr* (pointed) and *veig* (woman), this name has been used for many centuries

A Celebrity by Any Other Name . . .

Can you imagine these famous personalities with their given name?
While many shed their last name altogether most hold on to some aspect
of their first name.

Changed Name	Birth Name
Kareem Abdul-Jabbar:	Ferdinand Lewis Alcindor, Jr.
Muhammad Ali:	Cassius Marcellus Clay, Jr.
Woody Allen:	Allen Stewart Konigsberg
Julie Andrews:	Julia Elizabeth Wells
Fred Astaire:	Frederick Austerlitz
Lauren Bacall:	Betty Joan Perske
Tony Bennett:	Antonio Dominic Benedetto
Milton Berle:	Milton Berlinger
David Bowie:	David Robert Hayward-Jones
George Burns:	Nathan Brinbaum
Nicholas Cage:	Nicholas Coppola
Michael Caine:	Maurice J. Micklewhite
Truman Capote:	Truman Streckfus Persons
Chevy Chase:	Cornelius Crane Chase
Chubby Checker:	Ernest Evans
Cher:	Cherilyn Sarkisian
Eric Clapton:	Eric Clapp
Andrew Dice Clay:	Andrew Silverstein
Alice Cooper:	Vincent Damon Furnier
David Copperfield:	David Kotkin
Elvis Costello:	Declan Patrick McManus
Joan Crawford:	Lucille LeSueur
Rodney Dangerfield:	Jacob Cohen
Ted Danson:	Edward Bridge Danson III
Tony Danza:	Anthony Iadanza
Bo Diddley:	Elias Bates
Kirk Douglas:	Issur Danielovitch Demsky

Mike Douglas:	Michael Delaney Dowd, Jr.
Bob Dylan:	Robert Zimmerman
Gloria Estefan:	Gloria Maria Fajardo
Whoopi Goldberg:	Caryn Johnson
Pee Wee Herman:	Paul Rubenfeld
Hulk Hogan:	Terry Jean Bollette
Engelbert Humperdinck:	Arnold Gerry Dorsey
Elton John:	Reginald Kenneth Dwight
Michael Keaton:	Michael Douglas
B.B. King:	Riley B. King
Larry King:	Larry Zieger
Spike Lee:	Shelton Lee
Little Richard:	Richard Penniman
Madonna:	Madonna Louise Ciccone
Lee Majors:	Harvey Lee Yeary
Malcolm X:	Malcolm Little
Meat Loaf:	Marvin Lee Adair
Marilyn Monroe:	Norma Jean Mortensen
Demi Moore:	Demi Gynes
Nancy Reagan:	Anne Frances Robbins
Robert Redford:	Charles Robert Redford, Jr.
Ginger Rogers:	Virginia McMath
Roy Rogers:	Leonard Slye
Mickey Rooney:	Joe Yule, Jr.
Winona Ryder:	Winona Horowitz
Soupy Sales:	Milton Supman
Susan Sarandon:	Susan Abigail Tomalin
Charlie Sheen:	Carlos Irwin Estevez
Martin Sheen:	Ramon Estevez
Sinbad:	David Atkins
Sting:	Gordon Matthew Sumner
Donna Summer:	La Donna Andrea Gaines
Tina Turner:	Annie Mae Bullock
Christopher Walken:	Ronald Walken
John Wayne:	Marion Michael Morrison
Stevie Wonder:	Steveland Judkins

ODE (o-DE) African: Born on the road, during travel (Nigeria)

ODEDA (oh-de-dah) Hebrew: Stands strong, brave
Odede; Odeada

ODELETTE Greek, French: Little spring, little singer or ode
Odelet, Odeletta, Odelina, Odelle

ODELIA Greek, French: Melody, ode; (Hebrew) praise God; (German) prosperous battle, Odila is the more common spelling for this German name. See also *Odette, Otylia* (German) *Ordella, Otthild, Otthilda, Otthilde*; (French) *Odile*; (Czech) *Othili, Ottilie; Odele, Odelina, Odelinda, Odiana, Odiane, Odila, Odilia, Otilie, Ottila, Ottilia, Ottillia*

ODELLA Anglo-Saxon: Woods on the hill
Odelyn, Odelyna

ODESSA Greek: Wrathful. Odessa is the feminine version of Odysseus, which has taken on the connotative meaning of wandering, traveling adventure in honor of the famous voyage in Homer's epic *The Odyssey.*

ODETTE (o-DET) French: Variant of Odelia and Odile, the name of the bewitched heroine and love of Prince Siegfried in Tchaikovsky's classic ballet *Swan Lake.*

ODIANA German: Spelling variation of Odelia

ODINA (o-DEE-nah) Native American: Mountain (Algonquian)

ODYSSEIA Greek: Wrathful, wandering; feminine form of Odysseus
Nicknames: *Dessa*

OENONE (ee-NO-nee) Greek: In Greek mythology, daughter of the river-god Cebren, she was abducted by Paris and became his first wife and mother of Corythus.

OGIN (o-GEEN) Native American: Wild rose
Ogina, Ogyna

OHANNA Hebrew: Spelling variation of Joanna
Ohana, Ohannah

OIHANE (oy-AH-nay) Basque: From the forest

OKALANI (oh-kah-LAH-nee) Hawaiian: Heaven, heavenly
Okalana, Okalanah

OKSANA (ahk-SAH-nah) Ukrainian: Variation of Xenia
Oksanna, Oxana; **Diminutive forms:** *Ksanochka, Oksanka;* **Famous namesakes:** Skater Oksana Baiul

OLA (OO-lah) Scandinavian: Ancestor's relic, related to the masculine name Olaf; (Greek) possibly a familiar form of Olesia
Olah

OLABISI (o-LAH-bee-see) African: Joy multiplied (Nigeria)

OLALLA Greek: Spoken sweetly

OLATHE (o-LAY-thah) Native American: Beautiful (Shawnee)

OLAUG Norse: Dedicated to our ancestors

OLDWIN English: Special friend
Oldwyn; Oldwyn; **Nicknames:** *Oldwina*

OLEANDER (o-lee-AN-der) English: Botanical name from an evergreen shrub known for its fragrant white, lavender, or pink flowers and its poison. See also *Oliana*

OLENA (oh-LAY-nah) Ukrainian: Variation of Helena

OLETHA (o-LEE-thah) Scandinavian: Nimble, light-footed
Yaletha; *Oleta*

OLETHEA Latin: Honest, truthful; variant of Alethea

OLGA (OL-gah) Russian, Romanian, Hungarian: Blessed, holy; feminine form of Oleg and variant of Helga. Saint Olga was a princess of Kiev who introduced her subjects to Christianity.
Olenka; **Nicknames:** *Olya, Olina*; **Famous namesakes:** Soviet gymnast Olga Korbut

OLIANA (oh-lee-AH-nah) Hawaiian: variation of Oleander

OLINA (o-LEE-na) Hawaiian: Joyous; (Czech) familiar form of Olga

OLINDA Latin: Fragrant, perfumed; (Spanish) guardian of the property; (Greek) possible variant of Yolanda, violet flower

OLITA English: Variation of Alida

OLIVIA Latin, Spanish, Swedish: Olive tree (Irish) *Alvy, Oilbhe, Olive*; **Nicknames:** *Livia, Livie, Lyvia, Olivie*; **Famous namesakes:** British actress Olivia de Havilland, Australian singer and actress Olivia Newton-John; **Star babies:** daughters of Reggie Arrizu and Sheila Arrizu, Denzel Washington, Lori Loughlin and Massimo Giannulli

OLKA Polish: Variation of Alexandra
Ola

OLWEN (AHL-wen) Welsh: White footprint, white tracks; Olwen was the Celtic mythological daughter of Ysbaddaden and wife of Culwch, who completed many difficult tasks and saved her from her monstrous father.
Olwyna, Olwina, Olwyn

OLYMPIA Greek: From Mount Olympus, home to the gods
(French) *Olympe*; (Italian) *Olimpia*; **Nicknames:** *Pia*; **Famous namesakes:** Actress Olympia Dukakis

OMA Hebrew: Reverent, devoted; (German) grandmother, probably derived from the Latin meaning; (Latin) mother and another name for the Roman fertility goddess Bona Dea; (Arabic) mother, people, nation
Omah

OMENA (O-me-nah) Finnish: Apple

OMPHALE (OM-fə-lee) Greek: Legendary queen of Lydia

ONEIDA (o-NIE-dah) Native American: Standing rock; one who is a member of the Oneida tribe

ONELLA Hungarian: Variation of Helena

ONI (o-NEE) African: Born on holy ground, blessed place (Yorba)

ONNELI (ON-ne-lee) Finnish: Happiness

ONORA Irish: Spelling variation of Honora

OONA Irish: Unity; Gaelic form of Agnes
Una, Oonagh; **Famous namesakes:** Actress Oona O'Neill Chaplin (daughter of Eugene O'Neill and wife of Charlie Chaplin)

OPAL English: A jewel. An opal is a semiprecious stone known for its beautiful iridescent colors
(Sanskrit) *Opala*; (Hindi) *Upala*; *Opalina, Opaline, Opel*

OPHELIA (o-FEEL-yə) Greek: Help. It
is likely that the most famous Ophelia is
Polonius' daughter in Shakespeare's *Hamlet*
(French) *Ophelie*; (Spanish) *Ofelia*

OPS (AHPS) Latin: Another name for the
Roman Sabine, goddess of the earth and of
abundance and wealth

ORA (AWR-ə) Latin, Spanish: Golden,
variant of Aura and Aurelia; (Greek) gentle
breeze; (Hebrew) light
Orah

ORABELLA English: Answered prayer;
variant of Arabella
Orabel, Orabelle; **Nicknames:** *Bel, Belle, Bella,
Ora, Orra*

ORALEE Hebrew: The Lord is my light; also
a variant of Aurelia

ORANE (or-EN) French: Variation of Aurelia

ORBONA Latin: Roman goddess invoked by
parents to grant them children

OREA Greek: From the mountains
Oreah, Oria, Oriah

ORELLA Latin: Message from the gods,
delivered from the oracle, a name for the
oracle herself
Orela

ORIANA (or-ee-AH-nah) Latin, Italian:
Golden

ORIDA Native American: Expected one

ORIEL (or-ee-EL) French: Bird; related to
the oriole, known for its brilliant orange-gold
markings

ORKIDEH Persian: Orchid

ORLENA French: Gold
Orlene

ORMA African: Free

ORNA Irish: Little green one
(Gaelic) *Odharnait*; *Ornat*

ORPAH (OR-pə) Hebrew: Fawn. Oprah
Winfrey's name is actually a misspelling of
this uncommon Old Testament name.
Ofra, Ophrah, Oprah; **Famous namesakes:**
Canadian cellist Ofra Harnoy

ORQUIDEA (or-KEE-day-ah) Spanish:
Orchid
Orquidia

ORTENSIA Latin: Spelling variation of
Hortense

ORTYGIA Greek: Island known from Greek
mythology as the birthplace of Apollo and
Artemis

ORVA English: Brave friend; (French) golden

OSANE (o-SAH-nay) Basque: Cure, health

OSANNA Latin: Praise God
Osana; *Oksanna*

OSEYE (o-SE-ye) African: Happy
Osey

OSYKA Native American: Eagle (Choctaw)

OTRERA Latin: Queen of the Amazons
and mother of Penthesilea and Hippolyta in
Greek mythology

OTYLIA (o-TEEL-yah) Polish: Rich,
prosperous; variant of Odelia

OVIA Latin: Egg
Oviah

OWENA (oh-WEN-ah) Welsh: Noble-born, young fighter

PADMA (PAHD-mah) Hindi: Lotus

PAIGE French: Page, attendant
Page; **Famous namesakes:** Actress Paige Davis, actress Paige Moss; **Star babies:** daughter of Sinbad

PAISLEY Scottish: A particularly patterned, usually colorful fabric first produced in Paisley, Scotland
Paislee, Paisleigh, Paislie

PALES Latin: A goddess of shepherds and flocks in Roman mythology

PALLAS (PAL-əs) Greek: Another name for Athena, goddess of wisdom

PALMA Latin: Palm tree; also a place name
(Spanish) *Palmira; Palmyra*

PALOMA (pah-LO-mah) Spanish: Dove
Nicknames: *Aloma;* **Famous namesakes:** Jewelry designer Paloma Picasso; **Star babies:** daughter of Emilio Estevez and Carey Salley

PAMELA English: Invented by the sixteenth-century poet Sir Philip Sidney, Pamela is possibly derived from the Greek words *pan*, meaning *all*, and *meli*, meaning *honey*.
Pamelina, Pameline, Pamella, Pammeli;
Nicknames: *Pam;* **Famous namesakes:** Actress Pam Dawber, actress Pamela Anderson

PAMINA Italian: Meaning unknown; a character from Mozart's opera *Die Zauberflöte*

PAMUY Native American: Water moon (Hopi)

PANDITA (pahn-DEE-tah) Hindi: Studious

PANDORA (pan-DOR-ə) Greek: All gifted. According to mythology, Pandora was the first woman endowed with gifts from the gods. Pandora's box contained all the evils of the world.

PANPHILA Greek: All-loving

PANSY English: Flower name from the French word *pensée*, meaning *thought*
(Finnish) *Orvokki; Pansie; Pansey;* **Old forms:** *Pensee*

PANTEHA Persian: Name of a princess

PANTHEA Greek: All the gods; related to the Greek word *pantheon*, which means *temple to all gods*
Panthia, Pantheya

PAOLA (POW-lah) Italian: Variation of Paula

PAPINA (pah-PEE-nah) Native American: Vine which grows on oak tree (Miwok)

PARAND Persian: Silk

PARCA Latin: Named for the furies; myth name for the jewel

PARIS English: Original meaning uncertain, though the modern meaning refers to the French capital
Famous namesakes: Heiress Paris Hilton; **Star babies:** daughter of Michael Jackson

PARISA Persian: Like a fairy

PARKER English: Park keeper
Famous namesakes: Actress Parker Posey

PARTHENIA (par-THEE-nee-ə) Greek: Chaste
Parthenie

PARVANEH Persian: Butterfly

PARVATI (PAHR-vah-tee) Hindi: Daughter of the mountains. Parvati is a Hindu goddess.

PASCALE (pas-KAL) French: Born at Easter (Greek) *Pesha*; (Spanish) *Pascuala*; (Russian) *Parasha, Pasha, Praskovia*; *Pascala, Pascaline, Pasclina*; **Famous namesakes:** Canadian actress Pascale Bussières

PASTORA (pah-STO-rah) Spanish: Shepherdess
Pastore

PATIENCE Latin, French: Patient; a virtue name similiar to Hope and Prudence (Spanish) *Paciencia*; *Patiencia, Patientia*

PATRICIA Latin: Noble, patrician; feminine form of Patrick
(French) *Patrice*; (Italian) *Patrizia*; (Irish) *Padraigin*; **Nicknames:** *Pati, Trisa, Trish, Trisha, Pat, Patsy, Patti, Patty*; **Famous namesakes:** Singer Patti LaBelle, singer Patsy Cline, actress Patty Duke, First Lady Pat Nixon

PAULA Latin, Spanish, Swedish: Small; feminine form of Paul
(French) *Paulette, Pauline*; (Italian) *Paola*; (Swedish) *Paulina*; (Russian) *Pavlina, Polina*; (Ukrainian) *Pavla*; (Finnish) *Pauliina*; (Hungarian) *Palika*; **Nicknames:** *Pauleta*; **Diminutive forms:** *Pauletta, Paulita*; **Famous namesakes:** Singer Paula Abdul, Czech model Paulina Porizkova

PAULINE French: Variation of Paula
Famous namesakes: British actress Pauline Collins; **Star babies:** daughters of Princess Stephanie of Monaco, Wynonna and Arch Kelley III

PAVATI Native American: Clear water (Hopi)

PAX Greek: Peace; a Roman goddess of mythology
Star babies: son of Angelina Jolie and Brad Pitt

PAZ (PAHZ) Hebrew: Gold; (Spanish) peace
Paza; **Nicknames:** *Pazia, Pazit*

PEACE English: Peace, tranquility, contentment

PEARL English: Pearl; birthstone for the month of June that is said to impart health and wealth
Pearla, Pearle, Pearlina, Pearline; **Famous namesakes:** Singer Pearl Bailey

PEDRA (PAY-drah) Spanish: Rock; feminine form of Pedro, a popular Spanish form of Peter

PEG Greek: Nickname for Margaret

PEGAH Persian: Dawn

PELAGIA Greek: Dweller by the sea

PELICIA Greek: Weaver

PELLKITA Latin: Happy
Pellikita

PEMBE (PEM-be) Turkish: Pink

PENELOPE (pə-NEL-o-pee) Greek: Bobbin worker, weaver; faithful wife of Odysseus during the Trojan War
Penelopa, Pennelope; **Nicknames:** *Penny, Pennie*; **Famous namesakes:** Parenting expert Penelope Leach, actress Penelope Ann Miller

PENINAH (pe-NIE-nə) Hebrew: Pearl
Penina, Penine

PENTHESILEA (pen-thə-sil-EE-ə) Greek: Amazon queen killed by Achilles

PENTHIA Greek: Born fifth
Penthea

PEONY (PEE-ə-nee) Greek: Flower known for its medicinal powers; from Greek *paionia* and Paion, the physician of the gods

PEPITA (pay-PEE-tah) Spanish: He shall add; dimunitive of Jose, popular Spanish form of Joseph

PEPPER American: A pungent spice; indicative of a lively personality

PERDITA (per-DEE-tə) Latin: Lost; Perdita was the mother to ninety-nine dalmatians in the Disney film *101 Dalmatians*

PEREGRINE (PER-ə-grin, PER-ə-green) Latin: Wanderer, voyager. The peregrine is a favored bird in the ancient sport of falconry.
Peregrina; **Nicknames:** *Perry*

PERFECTA (per-FAYK-tah) Spanish: Perfect

PERO Greek: The beautiful daughter of Neleus and Chloris and mother of Asopus

PERPETUA (per-PE-twah) Latin: Continual

PERSEPHONE (pər-SEF-ə-nee) Greek: Goddess of the underworld, daughter of Zeus and Demeter
Persephonie

PERSIA (PER-zhə) Contemporary: Place name of a country now known as Iran
Persis

PERZSIKE Hebrew: Devoted to God
Nicknames: *Perzsi*

PETA (peh-tah) Native American: Golden eagle (Blackfoot)

PETRA (PET-rə) Greek: Rock; a feminine variant of Peter
(French) *Pierrette*; (Italian) *Pietra*; (Swedish) *Petronella*; (Danish) *Pedrine, Petrine*; (Polish) *Petronela*; *Parnella, Petrina, Petronelle, Petronia, Petronilla, Petronille, Pierretta*

PETUNIA (pə-TOON-yə) English: Lovely trumpet-shaped flower

PEYTON (PAY-tən) English: Warrior's village; a name used for both genders. *Peyton Place* was the name of a popular TV show in the 1960s.
Payton, Payten, Payden, Paiden, Paydyn, Paidyn

PHAEDRA (FAY-drə) Greek: Bright; daughter of Minos

PHEDORA Greek: Supreme gift
Pheodora

PHIALA Irish: Fifth-century Irish saint

PHILIPPA (FIL-ip-ə, fil-I-pə) Greek: Lover of horses; feminine form of Philip
(Spanish) *Felepita, Felipa*; (Polish) *Filipa, Filipina*; *Philipa, Philippine, Phillipa*;
Nicknames: *Pippa*

PHILLINA Greek: Loving
Phila, Philida, Philina, Phillida

PHILOMELA (fi-lə-MEE-lə) Greek: Nightingale
Philomel

PHILOMENA (fil-ə-MEEN-ə) Greek: Greatly loved
(French) *Philomene*; (Italian) *Filomena*; *Filomenia, Filomina, Philomina*

PHOEBE (FEE-bee) Greek: Sparkling, the shining one. In Greek mythology Phoebe was goddess of the moon, daughter of Leda, and mother of Leto.
(Greek) *Pheobe*; *Phebe*; **Famous namesakes:** Actress Phoebe Cates

PHOENIX (FEE-niks) Greek: Dark red. In mythology, the phoenix was a beautiful bird that built its own pyre and then was reborn from the ashes.
Star babies: daughter of Melanie Brown and Jimmy Gulzar

PHYLLIS (FIL-is) Greek: Green bough
Philis, Phillis, Phylis; **Famous namesakes:** Comedian Phyllis Diller

PIA (PEE-ə) Latin, Italian, Spanish, Swedish: Pious
Famous namesakes: Actress and singer Pia Zadora, Journalist Pia Lindstrom; **Star babies:** daughter of actress Ingrid Bergman

PICABO (PEEK-ə-boo) Native American: Shining waters
Famous namesakes: Skier Picabo Street

PIEDAD (pee-ay-DAHD) Spanish: Mercy

PIERRETTE (peer-ee-ET) French: Variation of Petra

PILAR (pee-LAHR) Spanish: Pillar
Pelar, Peleria, Piliar, Pillar; **Nicknames:** *Pili, Piluca, Pilucha*

PILI (PEE-lee, PI-lee) African: Born second

PILUMNUS Latin: Goddess of birthing

PINGA (PEEN-gah) Hindi: Tawny

PINJA (PEEN-yah) Finnish: Pine tree

PIPER (PIEP-ər) English: A surname which was originally given to a person who played on a pipe (flute).
Famous namesakes: Actress Piper Laurie; **Star babies:** daughter of Gillian Anderson and Clyde Klotz

PIPPA (PIP-ə) English: Nickname for Philippa

PIRJO Finnish: Variation of Bridget

PLACIDA (PLAH-cee-dah) Spanish: Tranquil; feminine form of Placido
Old forms: *Placidia*

POCAHONTAS (po-kə-HAHN-təs) Native American: Playful; Chief Powhatan's daughter who successfully argued for the life and release of Captain John Smith. Pocahontas was later held for ransom by Jamestown, Virginia, settlers, and eventually married one of them.

POLLY English: Bitter; variant of Molly, diminutive of Mary
Famous namesakes: Actress Polly Bergen, actress Polly Walker

POMONA Latin: Apple; Roman goddess of fruit trees and fertility

POPPY Latin, English: Flower name popular in the southern United States
Famous namesakes: Author Poppy Z. Brite; **Star babies:** daughter of Jamie Oliver

PORTIA (POR-shə) Latin: From a Roman family name of obscure meaning; name of a character in Shakespeare's *The Merchant of Venice* who disguises herself as a man in order to defend her husband, Antonio, in court
Famous namesakes: Australian actress Portia de Rossi

POTINA (po-TEE-ə) Latin: The Roman goddess who blessed mothers' milk.

PRABHA (prab-ha) Hindi: Light

PRESLEY English: From the priest's meadow; surname
Preslea, Preslee, Presleigh, Preslie; **Famous namesakes:** Singer Lisa Marie Presley; **Star babies:** daughter of Tanya Tucker

PRIMA (PREE-mə) Latin: First
Primalia; **Star babies:** daughter of Connie Sellecca and John Tesh

PRIMAVERA Italian, Spanish: Spring

PRIMROSE Latin, English: Flower name derived from the Latin phrase *prima rosa*, meaning *first rose*.

PRISCILLA (pri-SIL-ə) Latin: Archaic, ancient, she was banished; feminine variant of the Roman name Priscus
(Hungarian) *Piri, Piroska*; **Nicknames:** *Cilla*; **Diminutive forms:** *Prisca*; **Famous namesakes:** Actress Priscilla Kinsler, singer and songwriter Priscilla Ederly, actress Priscilla Presley

PROSPERA Latin: Prosper
Prosperia

PRUDENCE English: Derived from the Latin word *prudens*, meaning *good judgement*; virtue name
(Spanish) *Prudencia*; **Old forms:** *Prudentia*; **Famous namesakes:** Author Prudence Foster

PRUNELLA (proo-NEL-ə) Greek: Plum
(French) *Prune*; *Prunelle, Prunellia*; **Famous namesakes:** British actress Prunella Scales

PUEBLA (PWAY-blah) Spanish: The town; a state in Mexico

PURA (POOR-ah) Spanish: Pure
Nicknames: *Pureza, Purisima*

PYRENA Greek: Ardent, burning
Pyrene, Pyrenie

QETURAH (ke-TOO-rə) Hebrew: Incense

QIANRU (chee-an-roo) Chinese: Pretty smile

QUEEN English: Highest royal title for a woman
Queena, Queenie, Queeny; **Old forms:** *Cwen, Cwene*; **Famous namesakes:** Singer and actress Queen Latifah

QUENBY Scandinavian: Womanly, from the woman's estate
Quinby; Quinby

QUERIDA (ke-REE-də) Spanish: Beloved

QUESTA (KWES-tə) Latin: Seeker

QUIANA English: Divine
Quianna

QUIES Latin: Tranquil, restful; from Latin word *quiescere* meaning to rest

QUILLAN (KWIL-ən) Gaelic: Cub

QUINLAN (KWIN-lən) Gaelic: Graceful, strong, well made; also a variant of Quinn
Quinnlan, Quinlyn, Quinnlyn, Quinnlynn

QUINN (KWIN) Irish: Intelligent, wise; surname
Famous namesakes: Actress Quinn Cummings

QUINTA (KEEN-tə) Spanish: Born fifth
Quintina

QUITERIE (kee-TER-ee-e) Basque: Calm, tranquil
Quiteira

RAANANA Hebrew: Unspoiled, beautiful
Raananah

RABIA (RAH-bee-ah) African: Spring

RACHEL Hebrew: Ewe. In the Bible's Old
Testament, Rachel was the favorite wife
of Jacob and the mother of Joseph and
Benjamin. See also *Rahele*
(Spanish) *Raquel*; (Gaelic) *Raonaid*;
(Scottish) *Raoghnailt*; (Swedish) *Rakel*;
(Russian) *Rahil*; (Polish) *Rahel*; (Finnish)
Raakel; *Rachele, Rachelle*; **Nicknames:** *Rae*;
Famous namesakes: British actress/model
Rachel Ward; **Star babies:** daughters of
Natalie Appleton, Kathleen Turner and Jay
Weiss

RADELLA English: Elfin counselor

RADINKA (rah-DEEN-kah) Slavic: Lively

RAE (RAY) English: Doe; familiar form of
Rachel or feminine form of Ray
Famous namesakes: Actress Rae Dawn
Chong

RAFA Arabic: Happy, lightening, to shine, to
flutter (as in bird fluttering)

RAFIYA (RAH-fee-yah) African: Dignified

RAHA (ra-hah) Persian: Free

RAHELE Persian: Traveler

RAHIMA Arabic: Grace, merciful

RAIMUNDA (rie-MOON-dah) Spanish:
Wise defender

RAINEY English: Familiar form of Regina.
Rainey sometimes also is used in reference to
wet weather.
Raini, Rainie, Rainy

RAISA (rah-EE-sah) Russian: Easy, light
Famous namesakes: Soviet first lady Raisa
Gorbachev

RAIZE (RAY-zu) Yiddish: Rose
Raise; **Nicknames:** *Raizel, Raizi, Raysel*

RAJA (RAH-jah) Arabic: Hope
Rajaa, Ragaa

RAMIRA (rah-MEE-rah) Spanish: Judicious

RAMLA (RAHM-lah) African: Prophetess

RAMONA (rə-MON-ə) Spanish: Wise
defender; feminine form of Ramon
Nicknames: *Mona, Ramonia*; **Star babies:**
daughter of Jonathan Demme

RANA (RAH-nah) Arabic: Behold, attractive,
beauty; (Persian) elegant

RANIA (RAN-yah) Egyptian: Delightful
Ranya

RANICA Hebrew: Lovely tune
Ranice, Ranit, Ranita

RAPHAELLA (rah-fie-EL-ə) Hebrew: God
has healed
Rafela; *Rafaella, Rafaela, Raphaela*

RAQUEL (rah-KELL) Spanish: Variation of
Rachel
Famous namesakes: Actress Raquel Welch

RASHA Arabic: Gazelle

RASHIDA (rah-SHEE-dah) Egyptian:
Righteous
Rasheeda

RAUHA (ROW-hah) Finnish: Peace

RAVAN Persian: Spirit, soul

RAVEN English: Raven, blackbird
Ravyn

RAYKA Persian: Beloved
Ryka

RAYNA (RAY-nah) Czech: Pure, clean; variant of Catherine
Raina, Raine; **Star babies:** daughter of Mike Tyson and Monica Turner

REAGAN (RAY-gən, REE-gən) Irish: Little ruler
Raygen, Reaghan, Regan

REBA Hebrew: Fourth born, a square, one that lies or stoops down
Famous namesakes: Singer Reba McEntire

REBECCA Hebrew: Captivating, to tie, beautiful, desirable. Rebecca is the Latin form of the Hebrew name Rivka. The biblical Rebecca was the wife of Isaac and the mother of Jacob and Esau.
(Hawaiian) *Lepeka*; *Rebekah*; *Rebekah*; **Nicknames:** *Becca, Becki, Becky*; **Famous namesakes:** Actress Rebecca De Mornay, author Rebecca West; **Star babies:** daughter of Dustin Hoffman and Lisa Gottsegen

REESE English: Passionate, enthusiastic
Reece, Rice; **Famous namesakes:** Actress Reese Witherspoon

REGINA (rə-JEEN-ə) Latin: Queen
(French) *Reine*; (Spanish) *Reina*; (Norse) *Rana, Rania*; (Hindi) *Rani*; *Regine, Reginy*; **Nicknames:** *Rainey, Rainy, Reg, Reggie, Gina*; **Famous namesakes:** Actress Regina Taylor

> *Mother of heaven, Regina of the clouds,*
> *O sceptre of the sun, crown of the moon,*
> *There is not nothing, no, no, never nothing,*
> *Like the clashed edges of two words that kill.*
> —Wallace Stevens
> (1879–1955)

REIJA (RAY-ee-ə) Finnish: Vigilant, watchful

REINA (RAY-nah) Spanish: Variation of Regina

REMEDIOS (ray-MAY-dee-os) Spanish: Remedies

RENATA (re-NAH-tə) Latin: Reborn
Renatta, Rennatta; **Nicknames:** *Renny*

RENEE (rə-NAY) French, Latin: Reborn, to rise again
(German) *Renate*; *Rene, Renella, Renelle*; **Nicknames:** *Rena*; **Famous namesakes:** Actress Renee Zellweger, opera singer Renee Fleming; **Star babies:** daughter of Rachel Hunter and Rod Stewart

RENITA (re-NEE-tə) Latin: Dignified
Renyta, Renetta, Renetta, Renitah

RETA Greek: Speaker; (African) shaken

RETTA (RET-ə) English: Unknown meaning. This uncommon name likely began as a nickname for Henrietta, Margareta, or Loretta.
Reta, Rheta, Rhetta

REZ Hungarian: Copper-haired

RHEA (REE-ə) Greek: A brook or stream; in mythology, the mother of Zeus
Famous namesakes: Actress Rhea Perlman

RHIANNON (ree-AN-ən) Welsh: Great queen. In Welsh mythology, Rhiannon was the goddess of fertility and the moon. Stevie Nicks of the band Fleetwood Mac was inspired by the ethereal sound of Rhiannon when she wrote her smash hit of the same name.
Nicknames: *Rhianna*

RHODA (RO-də) Greek: Rose

RHODOS Latin: Daughter of Poseidon
Nicknames: *Rhode*

RHONWEN (RON-wen) Welsh: Slender, fair

RIA (REE-ah) Spanish: From the river's mouth

RICA (REE-kah) Spanish: Rich

RICARDA Spanish, Italian: Strong ruler; feminine form of Ricardo, a popular Spanish and Italian form of Richard

RICHAEL Irish: Saint

RIDHAA African: Goodwill

RIGMORA Swedish: Name of a queen
Rigmor

RIHANNA (ree-ayn-ah) Arabic: Sweet basil
Rihana; **Nicknames:** *Ray*

RIINA (REE-nah) Finnish: Nickname for Catherine

RILEY Irish: Brave. Originally a boy's name, Riley has become increasingly popular as a name for girls.
Rylie, Rylee, Ryleigh, Reilly; **Star babies:** daughter of Howie Mandel

RILLA (RIL-ə) German: Brook
Rille, Rillia, Rillie

RIMA (REE-mah) Arabic: White antelope

RIMONA (ri-MO-nah) Hebrew: Pomegranate

RINA (REE-nə) Hebrew: Song
Rena, Rinna, Rinnah

RIONA (ree-O-nah) Irish: Royal

RIPLEY English: From the shouter's meadow
Star babies: daughter of Thandie Newton

RITA (REE-tə) Greek: Pearl; a popular form of Margaret or Margarita
Famous namesakes: Actress Rita Moreno, actress Rita Hayworth

> *"I want to have children while my parents are still young enough to take care of them."*
> —Rita Rudner

RIVA Latin: Regain strength

RIVE (REEV) French: From the shore

ROBERTA English: Famous
Nicknames: *Bobbi, Robertia*; **Famous namesakes:** Singer Roberta Flack

ROBIN English: Bright with fame. An abbreviation of Robert that has become a unisex name, it's also the name of a bird. (Scottish) *Robena, Robina*; *Robyn*;
Diminutive forms: *Robinetta, Robinette*;
Famous namesakes: Actress Robin Givens, actress Robin Wright

ROCIO (ro-SEE-o) Spanish: Dew drops

RODERICA German: Famous ruler; feminine form of Roderick
(Spanish) *Roderiga*

ROHANA Hindi: Rising

ROLANDA German: Renowned in the land; feminine form of Roland
(Spanish) *Roldana*; *Orlanda, Rahlaunda*

ROMA Latin, Italian: From Rome, the capital of Italy
Famous namesakes: Irish actress Roma Downey

ROMAINE (ro-MAN) French: From Rome
Romana

ROMIA Italian: From Rome

ROMY (RO-mee) German: Bitter rose
Famous namesakes: Actress Romy Schneider;
Star babies: daughter of Ellen Barkin and Gabriel Byrne

RONA Norse: Mighty strength

RONIYA Hebrew: Joy of the Lord
Ron, Rona, Ronela, Ronella, Ronia, Ronit

RONJA (RAHN-yə) Scandinavian, Finnish: A character from a children's book by Astrid Lingren

RONLI Hebrew: Joy is mine
Ronili

RORY Irish: Red; a traditionally male name

ROSABELLE Latin: Beautiful rose

ROSALBA Latin: White rose

ROSALIE Italian: Rose
Rosalia; Rosalee

ROSALIND (ROZ-ə-lind) English: Beautiful rose
Rosaleen, Rosalina, Rosalinda, Rosalinde, Rosaline, Rosalyn

Jaques: Rosalind is your love's name?
Orlando: Yes, just.
Jaques: I do not like her name.
Orlando: There was no thought of pleasing you when she was christened.
—William Shakespeare, *As You Like It*

ROSAMARIA Spanish: Compound name of Rosa and Maria

ROSAMUND (ROZ-ə-mund) German: Noted protector or guardian
Rosamonde, Rosamunde, Rosemond, Rosemonde, Rosemunda

ROSANNA English: Blend of Rose and Anna
Rosana, Rosanne; **Famous namesakes:** Actress Rosanna Arquette

ROSARIO (ro-SAH-ree-o) Spanish: Rosary; refers to devotional prayers honoring the Virgin Mary
Nicknames: *Charo*

ROSE English, French: The rose is a flower known not only for its exceptional beauty and fragrance, but also as an enduring symbol of love. See also *Rozenn*
(Italian) *Rosa*; (Polish) *Rozalia*; (Finnish) *Roosa*; (Hungarian) *Rozsa*; *Roesia, Rohais*;
Nicknames: *Rosie*; **Diminutive forms:** *Rosetta*; **Famous namesakes:** Actress and model Rose McGowan

> "I looked on child rearing
> not only as a work of
> love and duty but as
> a profession that was
> fully as interesting
> and challenging as any
> honorable profession in
> the world and one that
> demanded the best that I
> could bring to it."
> —Rose Kennedy

ROSEMARY English, Latin: Blend of Rose and Mary; also refers to the herb (French) *Rosemarie*; *Rosemaria*

ROSHANAK (ro-shah-NAK) Persian: Small light

ROWAN (RO-ən) English: Little red-haired one; can also refer to the flowering Rowan tree *Rowen*; **Nicknames:** *Ro*; **Star babies:** daughter of Brooke Shields

Author Anne Rice named her beautiful leading character Rowan in *Lasher* (The Vampire Chronicles).

ROWENA English: Famous friend; (Celtic) fair-haired *Rowynna*

ROXANNE Persian, French: Dawn. In Edmund Rostand's play *Cyrano de Bergerac*, Cyrano and Christian court the beautiful Roxanne. *Roxane*; **Old forms:** *Roxana*; **Nicknames:** *Roxie, Roxy*; **Famous namesakes:** Actress Roxanne Hart

ROYA Persian: Dream, vision

ROYALE (roy-AHL) French: Regal

ROZENN (ro-ZEN) French: Rose; a name from Brittany, a region of France

RUBY Latin: A deep red, translucent precious stone. The name is derived from the Latin word *rubeus*, and can also be used as a pet name for Roberta and Robin. *Rubie*; **Famous namesakes:** Actress Ruby Dee; **Star babies:** daughters of Matthew Modine, Rod Stewart and Kelly Emberg, Suzanne Vega

RUFINA (roo-FEE-nə) Latin, Italian, Spanish: Red-haired (Spanish) *Rufa*

RUNO (ROO-no) Finnish: Poem

RUTH Hebrew: Friend. The Old Testament Book of Ruth centers on a young, loyal Moabite woman who refused to desert her mother-in-law even after her husband's death. She became an ancestor of King David. (Gaelic) *Rut*; *Ruti*

RYBA (REE-bah) Czech: Fish

SAADA (sah-AH-dah) African: Helper

SABA (SAY-bə) Greek: From Sheba; Muslim origin means *eastern wind*

SABAH (sah-BAH) Arabic, Egyptian: Morning *Saba*

SABIA Irish: Sweet

SABIHA (sab-ə-HA) African: morning, beauty

SABINA (sə-BEE-nə) Latin: Sabine. The Sabines were an ancient people of central Italy. Parents may recall the romantic *Griffin & Sabine* trilogy novels by Nick Bantock. (German) *Sabine*; *Savina*; **Nicknames:** *Bine, Bina*; **Famous namesakes:** Dutch actress Sabine Koning

SABRA (SAH-brah) Hebrew: Unclear meaning, possibly *to rest* or *cactus*; (African) patience

SABRINA (sə-BREEN-ə) Latin: From the border. Sabrina is the Latin word for the Severn River in Wales. In Celtic legend, Sabrina was the name of a princess who was drowned in the Severn. *Sabria, Xabrina*; **Nicknames:** *Zabrina, Zavrina*

SACAJAWEA (sak-ah-jah-wee-ah) Native American: Bird woman. The famous Sacajawea was a Shoshone woman named Boinaiv (grass maiden), who was renamed after Crow warriors captured her as an adolescent and sold her to a French-Canadian fur trader. The trader, Charbonneau, was hired as a guide for the Lewis and Clark expedition but it was Sacajawea, traveling with her newborn son, who was an invaluable asset on the journey. *Sacagawea*

SACHIKO (sah-chee-ko) Japanese: Good fortune, happiness **Nicknames:** *Sachi*

SADBH (SIEV) Irish: Good, sweet. This is the name of several Irish princesses, including the daughters of Conn of the Hundred Battles, Queen Medb of Connacht, and King Brian Boru. *Sadhbh*

SADIE (SAY-dee) Hebrew: Nickname for Sarah *Sada*; **Famous namesakes:** Actress Sada Thompson; **Star babies:** daughter of Adam

Sandler, Michael Ontkean, Elvira /Cassandra Peterson

SADIRA Arabic, Persian: Prominent point of a valley

SAETH Welsh: Arrow

SAFARA African: Her place

SAFFRON (SAF-rən) English: A spice **Star babies:** daughter of Simon Le Bon

SAFIYA (SAH-fee-yah, sah-FEE-yah) Egyptian: Pure or good friend

SAGA Norse: Legend, myth

SAGE Latin: Wise one *Saige*; **Star babies:** daughter of Lance Henriksen and Jane Pollack

SAGIRA (sah-GHEER-ah) Egyptian: Little

SAHKYO (sahk-yo) Native American: Mink (Navajo)

SAIDA (sah-EE-dah) Arabic, Persian: Happy, fortunate; feminine variant of Said *Saidah; Saidah*

SAILOR English: Sailor; an occupational name *Sayler, Saylor, Sailer*; **Star babies:** daughter of Christie Brinkley and Peter Cook

SAKARI (sah-KAH-ree) Hindi: Sweet

SAKHMET (SAK-met) Egyptian: A lion-headed goddess worshipped in Memphis, the wife of Ra

SAKINAH Arabic: God-inspired peace of mind; Sakinah stems from the word sekoon, meaning tranquility. (Persian) *Sakineh; Sekina*

SAKRA Hindi: From India

SAKURA (sah-koo-rah) Japanese: Cherry blossom

SALACIA Latin: Goddess of salt water

SALALI (sal-al-ee) Native American: Squirrel (Cherokee)

SALIMA Arabic: Peaceful, safe; feminine form of Salim and a spelling variant of Salama
Saleema, Zulima; Selima, Saleema, Zulima

SALLA (SAH-lah) Finnish: Place name of a mountain in Lapland

SALLY Hebrew: Nickname for Sarah
Sallee, Salli, Sallie, Salley; **Nicknames:** *Sal*; **Famous namesakes:** Actress Sally Field, Actress Sally Struthers, Astronaut Sally Ride; **Star babies:** daughter of Carly Simon and James Taylor

SALMA (SAHL-mah) Arabic: Peaceful; stems from *salam*, meaning *peace*; (Persian) sweetheart
Famous namesakes: Mexican actress Salma Hayek

SALOME (sə-LO-may) Hebrew: Peaceful
Saloma, Selima; **Star babies:** daughter of Alex Kingston

SALVADORA (sahl-bah-DOR-ah, sahl-vah-DOR-ah) Spanish: Savior; refers to Christ
Salbatora, Salvatora, Xalbadora, Xalvadora

SALVIA Latin: Whole, safe; Latin name indicating the medical value of the herb sage
Salva, Salvina, Salvinia

SAMANTHA Hebrew: Told by God; possibly a feminine form of Samuel; (Aramaic) listener
(Greek) *Amantha; Xamantha*; **Nicknames:** *Sam, Sami, Sammi, Sammie, Sammy*; **Famous namesake:** Singer Samantha Fox

SAMARA (sə-MAH-rah) Hebrew: Under God's rule

SAMIA Arabic: Elevated; feminine form of Sami

SAMINA (sah-mee-nah) Arabic: Healthy, plump, and voluptuous. In certain parts of the Middle East, a woman's weight is symbolic of her social status, wealth, and health, and in that regard, "more" is considered better. Slenderness is not desirable in those social strata.
Saminah

SAMIRAH Arabic: Companion, one who is entertaining

SAMUELA Hebrew: Told by God; feminine form of Samuel

SANAM Persian: Idol

SANAZ Persian: A flower

SANCIA Latin: Sacred
(Spanish) *Sancha*

SANCTA Latin: Sacred, a feminine variant of Archard

SANDHYA (san-dee-hah) Hindi: Twilight

SANDRA Italian: Nickname for Alexandra
Sandie, Sandy; **Famous namesakes:** Actress Sandra Bullock

SANNA (SAH-nah) Finnish: Variation of Susan
Sanni

SANURA (sah-NOO-rah) African: Kitten (Swahili)

SANY Hindi: Born on Sunday

SAOIRSE (SEER-sha) Irish: Freedom

SAPPHIRA (sə-FIE-rə) Hebrew, Greek: Beautiful. Sapphira was the biblical wife of Ananias, who conspired to deceive others and died after lying. Variant of Saphire
Sapphire

SARAH (SER-ə, SAR-ə) Hebrew: Princess; Sarah was the wife of Abraham in the Old Testament. Originally named Sarai, God changed her name after he told Abraham of Sarah's pregnancy.
(Spanish) *Sarita*; (Irish) *Saraid*; (Finnish) *Saara, Sari*; (Hungarian) *Sarika*; (Hawaiian) *Kala*; *Sara, Zarah*; **Old forms:** *Sarai*; **Nicknames:** *Sadie, Sallie, Sally*; **Famous namesakes:** Actress Sarah Jessica Parker, Duchess of York Sarah Ferguson; **Star babies:** daughters of Jimmy Buffett, Kiefer Sutherland, Andie MacDowell, Marlee Matlin

SARAMA African: Nice

SARANNA (sə-RAN-ə) English: Princess; a modern blend of Sarah and Anna

SARDA African: Hurried

SARELIA Latin: Of the spring, fertile; variant of Cerelia and possibly a variant of Cyril, in which case it will mean lady
Sarilia

SARILA Turkish: Waterfall

SARINA (sah-REE-nə) Contemporary: Princess; a form of Sarah

SARISHA Hindi: Sophisticated

SARITA (sah-ree-tah) Hindi: A flowing river.

SASHA (SAH-shah) Russian: Nickname for Alexandra
Sacha; **Star babies:** daughters of President Barack and Michelle Obama, Kate Capshaw and Steven Spielberg, Vanessa Williams and Rick Fox

SASSANDRA African: Name of a river located on the Ivory Coast

SATINE (SA-tən) English: Smooth fabric

SATU (sah-too) Finnish: Fairy tale

SATURNINA (sah-toor-NEE-nah) Spanish: Gift of Saturn; derived from the name of the Roman god

SAURA (SOW-rah) Hindi: Of the Saura; sun worshipper

SAVANNAH (sə-VAN-ə) American: From the open plain. This well-known spelling variation of the Spanish *Savanna* is especially recognizable in the United States as a city in Georgia.
(Spanish) *Savanna*; *Sabana*; **Star babies:** daughters of Steven Seagal and Arissa Wolf, Jimmy Buffett

SAWNI (saw-nee) Native American: Echo (Seminole)
Suwannee

SAXONA English: Swordsman; feminine form of Saxon
Saxonia

SCARLETT English: Red; recognizable for Scarlett O'Hara, the strong-minded heroine of Margaret Mitchell's epic *Gone with the Wind*
Scarlet; **Famous namesakes:** Actress Scarlett Johansson

SCHOLASTICA Latin: Scholar. Based upon centuries of tradition, Saint Scholastica is considered the twin sister of Saint Benedict of Nursia, founder of monastic communities and compiler of the Rule of Saint Benedict.

SCHUYLER (SKIE-lər) Dutch: Scholar *Skyla*; **Diminutive forms:** *Skye*

SCOTLYNN English: Variation of a place name, Scotland

SCOTTI English: From Scotland *Scota; Scottee, Scottie, Scotty*

SCOUT American: To listen; name of the young heroine in *To Kill a Mockingbird* **Star babies:** daughters of Tom Berenger, Demi Moore and Bruce Willis

SCYLLA (SIE-lə) Greek: A nymph of Greek mythology turned into a sea monster

SEBASTIANE Latin: Revered or the Roman term for a person from the ancient city of Sebastia; feminine form of Sebastian (French) *Sebastienne*; (Italian) *Sebastiana*; **Nicknames:** *Bastiana*

SEBILLE Arthurian Legend: A fairy

SEGULAH Hebrew: Precious; treasure

SEGUNDA (say-GOON-dah) Spanish: Born second (Latin) *Secuba*

SEINA (SAY-nah) Spanish: Innocent

SELA (SEE-lə) Hebrew: Rock. Sela was the biblical capital of Edom. Its variant Selah is found several times in the Book of Psalms, possibly indicating a pause. *Selah, Sele, Seleta*; **Famous namesakes:** Actress Sela Ward

SELAS African: Trinity

SELENA Spanish: Variation of Celine *Selina*; **Famous namesakes:** Tejana singer Selena Quintanilla-Pérez

SELINA Greek: Spelling variation of Celine *Selena*

SELMA Teutonic: God's protection; a feminine contraction of Anselm *Zelma*; **Old forms:** *Anselma*

SEMADAR Hebrew: Berry

SEMELE (SE-mə-lee) Greek: In Greek myth, the mother of Dionysus

SEMIRA Hebrew: Height of heavens

SENALDA (say-NAHL-dah) Spanish: Sign

SENECA (SEN-ə-kə) Latin: Discipline; the name of a Roman philosopher and statesman. Seneca also refers to a Native American tribe in New York.

SENONA (say-NO-nah) Spanish: Lively

SEPTEMBER English: The ninth month, born in the ninth month

SEPTIMA Latin: Born seventh

SERAPHINA (ser-ə-FEE-nə) Hebrew: Fiery. Seraphim are angels of heaven, each with three pairs of wings and known for their strong love. (Italian) *Serafina; Seraphine*

SEREN (SE-ren) Welsh: Star

SERENA (sə-REEN-ə) Latin: Tranquil, serene *Serene, Serina*; **Famous namesakes:** Tennis player Serena Williams

SERIHILDE German: Armored battle maiden
Serhild, Serhilda, Serihilda, Serilda, Serilde, Zereld, Zerelda, Zerelde

SERLINA Latin: Beautiful dawn; variant of Zerlina

SERPUHI (SER-poo-hee) Armenian: Holy
Serbuhie, Surpouhie

SETAREH Persian: Star

SEVILLA (say-VEE-yah) Spanish: Place name of a city in Spain

SHABAHANG Persian: Evening star

SHABNAN Persian: Raindrop
Shabnam

SHADA (SHAH-dah) Native American: Pelican

SHADI (shah-DEE) Persian: Happiness
Shadee; **Nicknames:** *Shadan*

SHAELAN Irish: A surname of unknown meaning, Shaelan may be a variant of Shea meaning hawklike, majestic.
Shaelyn, Shaelynn, Shealan, Shealyn, Shealynn, Shaylan, Shaylyn, Shaylynn, Shaelin, Shaelinn, Shealin, Shealinn, Shaylin, Shaylinn

SHAHLA (SHAH-lah) Persian: Dark-eyed woman

SHAHNAZ (sha-nahz) Persian: King's pride

SHAILA (shie-lah) Hindi: A small mountain
Shyla

SHAKIRA (shah-KEER-ah) Arabic: Grateful; feminine variant of Shakir
Shakeera, Shakeerah, Shakirah; **Famous namesakes:** Colombian singer Shakira

SHALOM (shah-LOM) Hebrew: Peace

SHANATA (sha-nah-tah) Hindi: Tranquil

SHANESSA Irish: God is gracious

SHANI (SHAH-nee) African: Wonderful

SHANIECE (shah-NEES) American: Gift of God
Shanice

SHANNON Irish: Old and wise; from the Shannon, the longest river and chief waterway of Ireland
Shanahan, Shannen; **Famous namesakes:** Astronaut Shannon Lucid, gymnast Shannon Miller, actress Shannen Doherty

SHANTA (shahn-ta) Hindi: Peaceful or calm
Shanti

SHAQUANA (sha-KWAH-nə) American: Truth in life

SHARADA (shah-RAH-dah) Hindi: Lute; goddess or learning

SHARIFAH (sah-REE-fah) Arabic: Illustrious, noble, honorable, respectable, honest; feminine form of Sherif
Sharifa, Sherifa, Cherifa, Charifa, Cherifah, Charifah

SHARLENE English: Spelling variation of Charlene; variant of Charlotte

SHARON Hebrew: A plain; an area of ancient Palestine where many roses grew
Shareen, Sharelle, Sharin, Sharona, Sharoni, Sharyn; **Nicknames:** *Shari, Sherri, Sherrie, Sherry;* **Famous namesakes:** Actress Sharon Stone

SHASA African: Precious water

SHASTI Hindi: Goddess of childbirth

SHAWN Irish: God has been gracious; feminine variant of Sean, a popular Irish cognate of John
Seana, Shauna, Sina; **Famous namesakes:** Musician Shawn Colvin, actress Sean Young

SHAWNEE (shaw-nee) Native American: Southern people, a tribal name (Algonquian)

SHAYNA Yiddish: Spelling variation of Sheina

SHAZIA Persian: Princess

SHEA (SHAY) Irish: Hawklike or majestic; an Irish family name that has become a popular name for girls
Shayla; Shae, Shay, Shaye; **Nicknames:** *Shaylee*

SHEBA (SHEE-bə) Hebrew: Oath

SHEILA Irish: Blind; an Irish variant of Cecilia, also an affectionate Australian slang term for a woman or girl
Sheela, Sheelagh, Sheelah, Sheilagh, Sheilah; **Famous namesakes:** Singer Sheila E., actress Sheila Kelley

SHEINA (SHAY-nah) Yiddish: Beautiful
Shaine, Shayna, Shayne

SHEIRAMOTH Hebrew: From heaven

SHELBY English: From the village or estate on the ledge; a surname that is more often used as a given name for girls than for boys.
Shelbey

SHELLEY English, Anglo-Saxon: From the ledge meadow. Traditionally a boys' name, Shelley is now used for both genders and is a popular nickname for Michelle
Shelly; Shellea, Shelleah, Shelleigh, Shelli, Shellie; **Nicknames:** *Shell*; **Famous**

namesakes: Actress Shelley Long, actress Shelley Winters

SHEMARIAH Hebrew: Protected by God

SHENANDOAH (shen-an-do-ah) Native American: Beautiful daughter of the stars (Algonquian); the name of a river and valley in the Blue Ridge Mountains of Virginia, renowned for its pristine beauty

SHERIDAN (SHER-i-dən) Irish: Untamed
Sheriden, Sheridon; **Nicknames:** *Sheri*

SHERRY English: Variant of Cheryl, Cher, and Sharon
Shari, Sherri, Sherrie; **Famous namesakes:** Puppeteer Shari Lewis

SHEYDA Persian: Lovesick
Shayda

SHIFRA Hebrew: Beautiful

SHILOH (SHIE-lo) Hebrew: The peaceful one, he who is to be sent. In the Bible, Shiloh is a prophetic name for the Messiah. Shiloh is also significant as the site of a crucial battle in the American Civil War.
Shilo; **Star babies:** daughters of Angelina Jolie and Brad Pitt, Tom Berenger

SHIRA Hebrew: Song
Shiri; Shirah

SHIRIN (SHIR-een) Persian: Sweet
Shireen

SHIRLEY English: From the bright meadow; surname
Sherlee, Sheri, Sherlie, Sherrlie, Sheryl, Shirely, Shirlea, Shirlee, Shirleen, Shirleigh, Shirlene, Shirlindam, Shirline, Shirlley, Shirly, Shirlyn, Shurlee; **Nicknames:** *Shirl*; **Famous namesakes:** Actress Shirley MacLaine

SHLOMIT (SHLO-meet) Hebrew: Tranquil

SHOHREH (sho-RAY) Persian: Famous
Famous namesakes: Iranian-American
actress Shohreh Aghdashloo

SHOLEH Persian: Flame

SHONA (SHO-nə) Gaelic: God is gracious; a
variant of Jane and Joan

SHOSHANA (sho-SHAH-nə) Hebrew: Lily
(Armenian) *Shousnan*

SHREYA (SHRAY-ah) Hindi: Auspicious

SIAN (SHAHN) Welsh: Variation of Jane
Shan; **Nicknames:** *Shanee, Siani*; **Star babies:**
daughter of Dave Evans

SIANY Irish: Good health

SIBLEY Greek: Nickname for Sybil

SIDDALEE American: Meaning unknown, but
possibly related to Siddel, an Old English male
name meaning *from the wide valley*. Siddalee is
a character in books by Rebecca Wells. Sidda is
also a school of yoga meditation.

SIDERA Latin: Luminous; the stars
Nicknames: *Sidra*

SIDONIA (sə-DON-yə) Latin: From Sidonia
(French) *Sidonie*

SIEGFRIEDA German: Victorious peace;
feminine form of Siegfried

SIENA (see-EN-ə) Italian: A city in the
Tuscany region of Italy
Sienna

SIERRA (see-ER-ah) Spanish: Saw-toothed
Ciera, Cierra, Siera; **Star babies:** daughter of
James Worthy

SIGNY (SIG-nee) Norse: New victory
(Swedish) *Signe*

SIGOURNEY Contemporary: Meaning
unknown
Famous namesakes: Actress Sigourney
Weaver

SIGRID (SIG-rid) Norse: Beautiful victory
(Finnish) *Siiri*

SIGUN Norse: Daughter of Volsung
Sigune, Sigyn

SIIRI (SEE-ree) Finnish: Variation of Sigrid

SIKA African: Money

SILE (SHEE-la) Gaelic: Youthful
Sileas

SILVER English: Precious metal, white metal

SIMA Scottish: Listener; (Persian) face

SIMBRA African: Lioness

SIMCHA Hebrew: Joy

SIMI (see-mee) Native American: Valley
of the wind (Chumash); a place name
in California, known for its fine wine
production

SIMIN Persian: Silver

SIMONE (see-MON) Hebrew, French:
Hearkening, listening; feminine form of
Simon
(Italian) *Simona*; *Shimona, Simeona*; **Famous
namesakes:** Scottish actress Simone Lahbib

SINA Irish: God has been gracious; a variant
of Shawn and Seana
Famous namesakes: German track star Sina
Schielke

SINCLAIR English: Saint Claire

SINEAD (shi-NAYD) Irish: Variation of Jane *Sineaid*; **Famous namesakes:** Singer Sinead O'Connor

SINI (SEE-nee) Finnish: Blue **Nicknames:** *Sinikka*

SINOBIA Greek: Stranger *Sinovia*

SINOPA (sin-o-pah) Native American: Young fox (Blackfoot)

SIOBHAN (shi-VAWN) Irish: God has been gracious (English) *Chevonne*; (Scottish) *Siubhan*; **Diminutive forms:** *Siobhainin*

SIONED (SHO-ned) Welsh: Variation of Janet

SIRAN (SEE-ran) Armenian: Beautiful

SIRENA Greek: A siren. The mythological sirens of Greek mythology lived on islands and lured sailors to destruction on the rocks with their sweet singing.

SISIKA (si-SEE-kah) Native American: Bird

SISKO (SEES-ko) Finnish: Sister

SISSY German: Nickname for Elizabeth **Famous namesakes:** Actress Sissy Spacek

SISTINE Italian: Refers to the Sistine Chapel in the Vatican

SITA (see-tah) Hindi: Goddess of the harvest

SITALA (si-TAH-lah) Native American: One who remembers (Miwok)

SITARA Hindi: The morning star

SIV Norse: Wife of Thor in Norse mythology

SKENA Scottish: From Skene

SKYE English: Sky; also a short form of Schuyler

SKYLA English: Sky; also a variant of Schuyler

SLANIA French: Health

SLOAN Scottish: Warrior, fighter; surname *Sloane*

SNOW English: Snow

SOCORRO (so-COR-ro) Spanish: Help **Nicknames:** *Coco*

SOHA Persian: Star

SOINTU (SOYN-too) Finnish: Sound

SOKANON Native American: Rain (Algonquin)

SOLANA (so-LAH-nah) Spanish: Sunlight

SOLANGE (so-LANZH) French: Dignified; a saint's name meaning *angel of the sun* *Sollange*

SOLEDAD (so-lay-DAHD) Spanish: Solitude *Soledada*

SOLITA (so-LEE-tə) Latin: Accustomed *Solyta*; **Nicknames:** *Sol*

SOLVEIG (SOOL-vay) Norse: Compound of the old Norse words for *house* and *strength* **Famous namesakes:** Actress Solveig Dommartin

SONA (so-NAH) Hindi: Gold

SONIA Russian: Variation of Sophia
Sonja, Sonje, Sonya; **Famous namesakes:**
Skater Sonja Henie; **Star babies:** daughter of
Nastassja Kinski and Ibrahim Moussa

SONNET (SAH-nət) Italian: A lyric poem
Star babies: daughter of Forest Whitaker

SOPHIA (so-FEE-ə) Greek: Wisdom
(Greek) *Zsofie*; (Spanish) *Sofia*;
(Scandinavian) *Sonje*; (Dutch) *Sofie*;
(Russian) *Sonia, Sonya*; (Polish) *Zofia*;
(Hungarian) *Zsofia, Zsofika*; *Zofie*;
Nicknames: *Sofi, Sophie*; **Famous namesakes:**
Actress Sophia Loren; **Star babies:** daughters
of Rebecca De Mornay and Patrick O'Neal,
Jennifer Flavin and Sylvester Stallone

SOPHRONIA (so-FRO-nee-ə) Greek: Wise,
sensible; feminine form of Sophronius
Sofronia; **Nicknames:** *Fronia*

SORAYA Persian: Name of a constellation
Famous namesakes: Wife of Reza Pahlewi,
Shah of Iran

SORCHA (SOR-kah) Irish: Shining bright

SORINA Danish: Strict; feminine form of
Soren

SORJA (SOR-yah) Finnish: Slender

SOROUSHI Persian: Messenger

SORREL (SOR-əl) English: An herb

SOUZAN Persian: Fire

SOYALA (so-yah-lah) Native American: The
winter solstice (Hopi)

STAR English: Star
Starla, Starr; **Famous namesakes:** TV
commentator Star Jones

STARLEEN English: Star girl
Nicknames: *Star*

STELLA Latin: Star. See also *Estee*
(French) *Estelle*; (Spanish) *Estela, Estella,
Estrella, Estrellita, Trella*; **Diminutive
forms:** *Estelita*; **Famous namesakes:** Drama
instructor Stella Adler, actress Stella Stevens;
Star babies: daughters of Elisabeth Shue,
Harvey Keitel, Melanie Griffith and Antonio
Banderas

> *That Stella (o dear name)
> that Stella is
> That virtuous soul, sure
> heir of heavenly bliss.*
> —Sir Philip Sidney,
> *Astrophil and Stella*

STEPHANIE (STEF-ə-nee) Greek: Crowned
in victory; feminine form of Stephen
(German) *Stefanie*; (French) *Etiennette*;
(Russian) *Panya, Stepanida, Stesha*; (Czech)
Stepanka; (Hawaiian) *Kekepania*; *Stefana,
Stefania, Stephana, Stephania*; **Nicknames:**
*Fanetta, Fanette, Stef, Steffi, Steffie, Steph,
Stephie, Stevie*; **Famous namesakes:**
Actress Stefanie Powers, actress Stephanie
Zimbalist, tennis player Steffi Graf, singer
Stevie Nicks; **Star babies:** daughter of Jon
Bon Jovi

STERLA Latin: Little star
Sterlla

STOCKARD English: Origins unclear, but
may refer to hardy tree, lumber. This unusual
name has become recognizable with the
popularity of actress Stockard Channing.
Stockhard, Stockhart, Stokkard

STORM English: Tempest
Storme; **Nicknames:** *Stormie, Stormy*; **Star babies:** daughter of Nikki Sixx

SUE English: Nickname for Susan

SUEANNE English: Lily; blend of the names Sue and Anne

SUELLEN English: Lily; blend of the name Sue and Ellen

SUKI (soo-kee) Japanese: Fond of
Sukie

SUMA Hindi: Flower

SUMMER English: Born in summer
Sommer; **Famous namesakes:** Swimmer Summer Sanders

SUNDAY Contemporary: Traditionally regarded as the first day of the week
Sundae; **Nicknames:** *Sunny*; **Star babies:** daughter of Nicole Kidman and Keith Urban

SUNNA Norse: Sun god
Nicknames: *Sunny*

SUNNIVA Irish: Gift of the sun. Saint Sunniva was the daughter of a tenth-century Irish king and fled her homeland to avoid marriage to a pagan king.
(Swedish) *Synnove*; **Old forms:** *Sunngifu*; **Nicknames:** *Sunn, Synne*

SUNNY English: Sunny, cheerful
Sunni, Sunnie

SUNSHINE English: Light from the sun

SUOMA (SOO-o-mah) Finnish: Finland

SURI Persian: Red rose
Star babies: daughter of Katie Holmes and Tom Cruise

SUSAN Hebrew: Lily; short form of Susannah and commonly used as an independent name. See also *Zuzu* (German) *Susanne*; (French) *Suzanne*; (Italian) *Susanna*; (Spanish) *Suelita, Susana*; (Irish) *Sosanna*; (Scottish) *Siusan*; (Slavic) *Suzan*; (Czech) *Zusa, Zuza, Zuzana*; (Polish) *Zuzanny*; (Finnish) *Sanna, Sanni*; (Hungarian) *Zsuska, Zsuzsanna, Zsuzsi*; *Suzanna, Suzannah, Suzetta*; **Old forms:** *Susannah*; **Nicknames:** *Sue, Sueanne, Suellen, Susie, Susy, Suzy, Zsa Zsa*; **Diminutive forms:** *Suzette*; **Famous namesakes:** Activist Susan B. Anthony, actress Susan Sarandon, actress Susan Dey

SUTRANI (soo-trah-nee) Sanskrit: The teachings of masters

SUVI (soo-vee) Finnish: Summer

SUZANNE (soo-ZAWN, soo-ZAN) French: Variation of Susan

SUZU (soo-zoo) Japanese: Bell

SVETLANA (svyet-LAH-nah) Russian: Luminescent
Nicknames: *Sveta*; **Famous namesakes:** Russian gymnast Svetlana Boguinskaia, opera singer Svetlana Strezeva

SWANHILDA Teutonic, Norse: Battle swan. In Norse mythology, Svanhild was the daughter of Sigurd and Gudrun.
Svanhild, Svenhilda, Svenhilde, Swanhild, Swanhilde; **Nicknames:** *Sunhild*

SYBIL (SIB-əl) Greek: Prophetess. In Greek and Roman legend, Sibyl was a name given to female prophets or fortune-tellers.
(Irish) *Sibeal*; (Scandinavian) *Sibella, Sibylla*; *Cibil, Cybil, Cybill, Sibyl, Sibyll, Sybilla, Sybyl*; **Nicknames:** *Sibley, Sib, Sibbie, Sibby*; **Famous namesakes:** Actress Cybill Shepherd

SYDNEY French, English: Uncertain meaning. The name may derive from a French place name for Saint Denis. Another theory states that this name comes from Old English for *wide island*. Sydney is easily recognized as the name of Australia's oldest and largest city.
Cidney, Cydnee, Cydney, Sidney, Sydnee

SYLVIA Latin: From the forest; Rhea Silvia was the mother of the twins Romulus and Remus in Roman mythology.
(French) *Sylvie*; (Italian) *Silvia, Sylvana*; (Polish) *Sylwia*; (Hawaiian) *Kiliwa*; *Silva, Sylva, Sylvania, Sylvina, Sylvonna*; **Famous namesakes:** Poet Sylvia Plath, journalist Sylvia Poggioli

SYONA (sie-YO-NAH) Hindi: Beautiful, happy

TABARA (tah-bar-ah) African: Prosperous

TABIA (tah-BEE-ah) Egyptian: Talented

TABITHA Aramaic: Gazelle; (Greek) good woman
Tabita; Tabatha, Tabetha; **Nicknames:** *Tab, Tabi, Tabbi, Tabbie, Tabby*; **Famous namesakes:** The daughter of Samantha in the American television sitcom *Bewitched*

TABLITA Native American: Tiara (Hopi)

TABORRI Native American: Voice that carries

TACINCALA Native American: Deer

TACITA Latin: Silent
Nicknames: *Tacy*

TADEWI (tah-deh-wee) Native American: Wind (Omaha)

TAFFY Welsh: Loved one
Famous namesakes: Folk singer Taffy Nivert

TAHIRAH (TAH-hee-rah) Arabic, Egyptian: Virginal; feminine form of Tahir

TAHKI Native American: Cold (Algonquin)

TAIFA African: Nation, tribe

TAIJA (tay-jah) Sanskrit: Made of light
Nicknames: *Tai*

TAIKA (tigh-ee-kah) Finnish: Magic; (Lithuanian) peace

TAIMA (tah-EE-mah) Native American: Thunderclap

TAIMI (TAH-ee-mee) Finnish: Young tree

TAINI (tah-ee-nee) Native American: New moon (Omaha)
Tainee

TAKALA (TAH-kah-lah) Native American: Corn tassel (Hopi)
Takalah

TAKIYAH (TAH-kee-yah, tah-KEE-yah) African: Righteous

TAKOUHI (TA-koo-hee) Armenian: Queen

TALA Persian: Gold; (Native American) wolf

TALAR Welsh: From the headland in the field

TALAYEH Persian: Golden ray of sun

TALE (TAH-le) African: Green

TALIAH (TAHL-yah) Hebrew: Dew of heaven; may be an abbreviation of Natalia
Tahlia, Tal, Talia, Taliya, Talya; **Nicknames:** *Tally*; **Famous namesakes:** Actress Talia Shire

TALIBAH (tah-LEE-bah) Egyptian: Seeks knowledge

TALIHAH Arabic: Scholar, knowledgeable person; a term used to describe an avant-garde researcher in a particular field

TALIKA Sanskrit: Applause
Nicknames: *Tally*

TALISE (tah-LEES) Native American: Beautiful water

TALITHA (TAL-i-thə) Aramaic: Young girl
Taletha

TALOR (tahl-OR) Hebrew: Morning dew
Talora, Talori

TALULA (tah-LOO-lah) Native American: Leaping water (Choctaw)
Tallulah; Tallula, Talulah, Talulla; **Nicknames:** *Tula, Lula;* **Famous namesakes:** Actress Tallulah Bankhead

TAMA (TAH-mah) Native American: Beautiful or fox

TAMAKO (tah-mah-ko) Japanese: Precious stone; girl

TAMALA African: Dark tree

TAMARA Hebrew: Palm tree. A variant of Tamar, this name is used as a symbolic name due to the beauty and fruitfulness of the tree.
Tamar, Tamarah, Tamra, Tamryn;
Nicknames: *Tami, Tammie, Tammy, Toma, Tomka;* **Famous namesakes:** Olympic skier Tamara McKinney

TAMASHA (tah-MAH-shah) African: Pageant

TAMIKA (tah-mee-kah) Japanese: People
Tami

TAMIRA (tə-MEER-ah) Hebrew: Tall, upright in values

TAMMY English: Nickname for Tamara
Tami, Tammi, Tammie; **Famous namesakes:** Singer Tammy Wynette

TAMSIN (TAM-sin) English: Twin; variant of Thomasina

TANA Greek: Fire or star goddess

TANDY Native American: Flower

TANESHA (tah-NEE-shah) American: Born on Monday
Tanishia; Tanisha

TANGERINE English: From Tangiers; also a type of fruit known for its deep orange color
Tangerina

TANI (tah-nee) Japanese: Valley

TANIS (TAH-nees, TAN-əs) Spanish: Camp of glory, military glory; feminine abbreviation of Estanislao, the Spanish variant of Stanislaus; (Native American) daughter
Tannis

TANYA Russian: Uncertain meaning, though some suggest praiseworthy. Tanya is a popular pet name for Tatiana, the feminine form of the ancient Roman family clan name Tatius, and easily stands on its own as an independent name.
Tania; Tahnya, Tanja, Tonnya, Tonya, Tonyah;
Famous namesakes: Musician Tanya Tucker

TAPATI Hindi: Daughter of the sun god

TARA (TAHR-ə, TER-ə) Irish, Gaelic: Rocky hill; place name of an Irish hill that served as an ancient seat of kingship. Tara is widely recognized as the name of the O'Hara's plantation in Margaret Mitchell's *Gone with*

the Wind; (Sanskrit) star; a goddess of Hindu
and Buddhist mythology
(English) *Taralynn, Tarin*; (Gaelic) *Teamhair*;
Tarrah; **Famous namesakes:** Olympic figure
skater Tara Lipinski; **Star babies:** daughters of
Johnny Cash, Oliver Stone

TARANEH Persian: Song

TAREN Greek: Innocent

TARIA (TAHR-ee-ə, TAHR-yah) Latin:
Happy, lucky
Tariah; **Nicknames:** *Tari, Tarry*

TARIAN Welsh: Shield

TARIKA Turkish: The spiritual way
Nicknames: *Tara*

TARINA (TAH-ree-nah) Finnish: Story

TARISAI African: Look, behold

TARLA (tar-lah) Hindi: Flowing and dazzling

TARSHA Native American: Brave

TARU (TAH-roo) Finnish: Legend

TARUH Arabic: Happy, remote, forsaken;
one who examines things carefully then offers
them up for discussion

TARYN (TER-ən, TAHR-ən) Contemporary:
Rocky hill
Taren, Tarin, Tarren, Tarynn

TASHA Sanskrit: To have good luck
Nicknames: *Tash*

TASINA SAPEWIN (tah-see-nah-sap-eh-
win) Native American: Black blanket (Ogala);
the wife of Crazy Horse

TATE English: Cheerful

Tait, Taite, Tayte; **Nicknames:** *Tatelyn, Tayten*

TATELYN English: Cheerful; a variant of Tate
Tatelynn, Taytelyn, Taytelynn

TATIANA (tah-TYAH-nah) Russian:
Feminine form of Tatius, an ancient Roman
clan name of uncertain meaning
(Scandinavian) *Taina*; *Tatianna*; **Nicknames:**
Tanya, Tania; **Diminutive forms:** *Tiahna,
Tiane, Tianna, Tiauna, Tionna*; **Famous
namesakes:** Opera singer Tatiana Troyanos;
Star babies: daughter of Caroline Kennedy

TATUM (TA-təm) English: Light-hearted
Famous namesakes: Actress Tatum O'Neal

TAURA (TOR-rə, TAWR-ə) English: Bull;
feminine form of Taurus, an astrological
name
Taurina

TAVIA Latin: Nickname for Octavia

TAWNY English: Golden brown; the warm
sandy color of a lion's coat
Tawnee, Tawney, Tawni, Tawnia, Tawnie

TAYANITA (tay-ah-nee-tah) Native
American: Young beaver (Cherokee)

TAYEN Native American: New moon

TAYLA African: She has been seen

TAYLOR English: Tailor. Once a surname
and boys' name, Taylor and its variants are
growing in popularity as names for girls.
Tailor, Tayler; **Famous namesakes:** Singer
Taylor Dayne; **Star babies:** daughters of
Michael Crichton, David Hasselhoff, Garth
Brooks

TAYSIR Arabic: Makes easier, simplifies

TCHERNAVA Russian: Brunette, dark

TEAGAN (TAY-gən) Irish: Little poet
Tegan, Teige

TEAL English: The bird teal; also the blue-green color.
Nicknames: *Teela*

TEFNUT (TEF-noot) Egyptian: God of atmospheric moisture. With Shu, Tefnut formed the first pair of the Heliopolitan Ennead.

TEGWEN (TEG-wen) Welsh: Fair, blessed

TELEA (tehl-lee-ah) Greek: Perfection
Teleia; **Nicknames:** *Telly*

TELEZA (tah-LE-zah) African: Slippery (Malawi)
Telleza

TELLUS Latin: Earth

TELYN Welsh: Harp

TEMIMA Hebrew: Whole, honest
Teme

TEMIRA (tə-MEER-ah) Hebrew: Tall, slender

TEMPEST English: Turbulent, stormy
Tempeste; **Famous namesakes:** Actress Tempest Bledsoe

TEMPLA Latin: Sanctuary, temple
Temple

TENDAI (ten-DAY) African: Be thankful to God

TERENTIA Latin: Tender, good; feminine form of the Roman clan name Terentius. Terentia was the name of Cicero's first wife

TERESA Spanish: Variation of Theresa
Nicknames: *Tere, Teresita*

TERIANN English: Modern blend of the familiar form of Theresa and Ann
Teriana

TERIKA English: Modern blend of the familiar form of Theresa and Erica

TERILYNN English: Modern blend of the familiar form of Theresa and Lynn

TERPSICHORE (terp-SIK-ər-ee) Greek: Delight of dance; a mythological muse of dance and lyric poetry

TERRA Latin: The planet earth. In mythology, Terra is the Roman earth goddess equivalent to the Greek Gaia.
Teralyn, Terrah

TERRENE Latin: Smooth
Terrin, Terryn, Teryn

TERRY English: Nickname for Theresa
Teri, Terri; **Famous namesakes:** Author Terry McMillan, actress Teri Garr

TERTIA Latin: Third
(Italian) *Terza*

TESS English: Nickname for Theresa
Famous namesakes: British TV host Tess Daly

TETHYS (TEE-thəs) Greek: The mythical Tethys and her husband Oceanus had thousands of children who became the world's lakes and rivers.

THADDEA (THAD-ee-ə) Greek: Meaning uncertain, possibly brave or wise; feminine form of Thaddeus
Thaddia

THADINA Hebrew: Given praise
Thadine

THAIS (TAH-ees, THA-ees) Greek: Beloved. Saint Thais is the famous Egyptian courtesan portrayed in Massenet's opera *Thaïs*. According to legend, she was a reputed sinner in Egypt who was converted to Christianity by Saint Paphnutius, brought to a convent, and lived out the rest of her days in seclusion. (Russian) *Taisiya*; *Thaisia*, *Thaisis*

THALASSA (tha-LAHS-ə) Greek: The sea, a mythological woman of the sea
Famous namesakes: Author Thalassa Ali

THALIA (TAHL-yə) Greek: To bloom. In Greek mythology, Thalia was the joyous muse of comedy.
Talia, *Thaleia*

THANDIWE (tahn-DEE-we) African: Loved one

THEA (THEE-ə) Greek: Goddess, godly; also an abbreviation of names like Althea and Dorothea. The mythological Thea was the Greek goddess of light and mother of the sun, moon, and dawn.
Teah, *Tia*, *Tiah*; *Tea*; **Famous namesakes:** British musician Thea Gilmore

THEKLA (THEK-lə) Greek: Divine fame; name borne by an early martyr
(Polish) *Tekli*; *Tecla*, *Tekla*, *Thecla*

THELMA Greek: Nursing
Telma; **Famous namesakes:** Actress Thelma Ritter

THEMA Greek: Goddess of justice, often portrayed holding scales
Themis

THEODORA Greek: Gift of God; feminine form of Theodore
(Italian) *Teodora*; (Russian) *Fedora*, *Fedosia*, *Feodora*; (Polish) *Teodory*; *Theadora*;
Nicknames: *Teddi*, *Tedra*, *Tedre*, *Theda*, *Dora*, *Thea*

THEODOSIA (thee-o-DOZ-ee-ə, thee-o-DO-zhah) Greek: Gift of God; feminine form of Theodosios
(Polish) *Teodozji*

THEOLA Greek: Divine

THEONE Greek: God's name
Theona

THEOPHILIA Greek: Loved by God

THERESA (tə-REE-sə, tə-RAY-zə) Greek: Reaper. Saint Theresa of Avila is one of the principal and most beloved saints of the Catholic Church, known for her simple goodness and nature of her love for God. (German) *Tresa*; (French) *Therese*; (Italian) *Teresa*; (Spanish) *Teresita*; (Irish) *Toireasa*; (Scandinavian) *Terese*; (Swedish) *Teresia*; (Romanian) *Tereza*; (Hungarian) *Teca*, *Terezia*, *Treszka*; *Tassos*, *Teresina*, *Terisita*, *Thera*;
Nicknames: *Teri*, *Terri*, *Terrie*, *Terry*, *Tess*, *Tessa*, *Tessia*, *Tessie*, *Tosia*, *Tracee*, *Traci*, *Tracy*, *Zyta*;
Famous namesakes: Albanian missionary Mother Teresa of Calcutta, actress Theresa Russell; **Star babies:** daughter of Jerry Garcia

THETIS (THEE-tis) Greek: Thetis is the mother of Achilles in Greek mythology. She held her son by the heel and dipped him into the river Styx in an attempt to make him immortal. Because his heel did not touch water, it was his one vulnerable spot.

THI (TEE) Vietnamese: Poem

THISBE (THIZ-bee) Greek: Where the doves live. Thisbe was considered the fairest maiden in all of Babylon, and was the lover of Pyramus, the most handsome youth.

THOMASINA (tom-ə-SEE-nə) Hebrew: Twin; feminine form of Thomas
Thoma, *Thomasin*, *Thomsina*, *Tomasina*, *Tomasine*; **Nicknames:** *Tommie*

THORA Norse: Thunder goddess; feminine form of Thor
Thyra, Tora, Tyra

THURAYYA Arabic: Star; refers to the Pleiades

TIA (TEE-ə) Spanish: Aunt
Famous namesakes: Actress Tia Carrere

TIARA (tee-AHR-ə) Latin: Crowned
Nicknames: *Tita*

TIBERIA Latin, Italian: From the Tiber River

TIERNEY Irish: Regal, lordly; surname
Famous namesakes: Actress Maura Tierney

TIERRA (tee-ER-ah) Spanish: Earth

TIESHA (TEE-shə, tie-EE-shə) American: Unknown; (English) variant of Leticia or Latisha; (Latin) variant of Tisha

TIFFANY Greek: God's appearance; a common English variant of the Greek name Theophania
Theophaneia, Theophania, Theophanie, Tifany, Tiffani, Tiffanie, Tiffeny, Tiffney, Tiphanie; **Nicknames:** *Tiff, Tiffi, Tiffy*

"Change it to what? Tiffany? It's been an advantage. It's unforgettable. I'm the only one."
—Swoosie Kurtz

TIKVA (tik-VAH) Hebrew: Hope

TILLY English: Nickname for Matilda

TIMEA (TEE-may-ah) Hungarian: Honor

TIMOTHEA Greek: One who honors God; feminine form of Timothy
Timothia; **Nicknames:** *Thea, Timmie, Timmy*

TINA Persian: Clay; Tina is also an English familiar form of Christina or Christine
Famous namesakes: Singer Tina Turner

TIPONI Native American: Figurine of authority (Hopi)

TIPPER Irish: Water wall; nickname and variant of the Irish surname Tabar
Famous namesakes: Second Lady Tipper Gore

TIRA (TEER-ə) Hebrew: Encampment, enclosure

TIRTHA (TEER-tə) Hindi: Ford

TIRZAH (TIR-zə) Hebrew: Delightful

TIVA (tih-vah) Native American: Dance (Hopi). Hopi dances are not just beautiful, but an integral part of the culture.

TIVONA (tee-VO-nə) Hebrew: Nature lover

TOIBE Hebrew: Goodly; the Yiddish form of the name means dove

TOMIKO (to-mee-ko) Japanese: Treasured child, fortunate child

TONI English: Nickname for Antonia
Tony; **Famous namesakes:** Author Toni Morrison

TONIA Latin, English: Praiseworthy; an abbreviation of Antonia
Nicknames: *Tonisha*

TONISHA English: Praiseworthy; a variant of Tonia, which is a short form of Antonia

TOPAZ Latin: Yellow or pale blue precious stone

TORI English: Nickname for Victoria
Torey, Torie, Torree, Torrey, Torri; **Famous namesakes:** Actress Tori Spelling, musician Tori Amos

TOURMALINE (TOOR-mə-lin, toor-mə-LEEN) Singhalese: Green or blue gemstone

TOVA (TO-vah) Hebrew: Good
Toba, Tovah; **Nicknames:** *Tobi, Tobey, Tobelle*

TOVIA (TOV-yah) Hebrew: God is good

TRACY Greek: Nickname for Theresa
Tracee, Tracey, Traci, Tracie, Trasey, Trasy; **Nicknames:** *Trace*; **Famous namesakes:** Actress Tracey Gold, entertainer Tracey Ullman, tennis player Tracy Austin, singer Tracy Chapman

TREASA (TRA-sa) Irish: Strong
Treise

TRESSA Gaelic: Strength

TREVA Celtic: Prudent

TRILBY English: One who sings musical trills, a soft hat. Early editions of George Du Maurier's novel *Trilby* showed a character wearing a felt hat with a narrow brim. The runaway success of the novel and stage production of the story created an immediate demand for the hat.

TRINA (TREE-nə) Scandinavian: Nickname for Catherine

TRINITY Latin: Three beings in one

TRISHA Hindi: Thirst

TRISNA Hindi: Desired
Trishna

TRISTANA Welsh: Full of sorrows; feminine form of Tristan
Triste, Tristen, Tristina, Tristyn; **Old forms:** *Trista*

TRIXIE Latin: Nickname for Beatrice
Star babies: daughter of Damon Wayans

TRUDY German: Spear of strength; diminutive of Gertrude commonly used as an independent name
Famous namesakes: Producer (and wife of Sting) Trudy Styler

TSIFIRA Hebrew: Crown

TUCCIA Latin: One of the six Vestal Virgins

TUESDAY English: The third day of the week, born on a Tuesday
Old forms: *Tiwesdaeg*

TUIJA (TOO-ee-ah) Finnish: Cedar

TULA (TOO-lah) Native American: Mountain peak (Choctaw)

TULIA Latin: Bound for glory
Tulla, Tullia

TULLY Celtic: Peaceful

TUSA (TOO-sah) Native American: Prairie dog (Zuni)

TUULI (TOO-lee) Finnish: Wind; The variant Tuulikki is a Finnish forest goddess
Tuulikki; **Nicknames:** *Tuulia*

TUWA (TOO-wah) Native American: Earth (Hopi)

TWYLA English: Woven
Twila; **Famous namesakes:** Choreographer Twyla Tharp

TYNE (TIEN) English: River
Tyna; **Famous namesakes:** Actress Tyne Daly

TYRA Scandinavian: Spelling variation of
Thora
Famous namesakes: Model and actress Tyra
Banks

TZIGANA (zee-GAH-nah) Hungarian:
Gypsy
Tzigane, Zigana

TZURIA (tzoo-ree-ə) Hebrew: God is
strength
Tzuriya, Zuria

TZVIYA (tsvee-yə) Hebrew: Doe, female
gazelle
Civia, Tzivia, Zibia, Zibiah, Zivia

UALANI Hawaiian: Heavenly rain
Ualana, Ualaney, Ualania, Ualanie

UDELE Anglo-Saxon: Wealthy, successful
Udela; Udella, Yudelle; **Nicknames:** *Uda,
Udah*

ULA (OO-lah) Celtic: Jewel of the sea;
(Spanish) sweet-spoken; a pet form of the
Greek name Eulalie; (Scandinavian) wealthy

ULLA (OO-lə) Scandinavian: Variation of
Ulrike

ULRIKE (uwl-REE-kə) German: Noble,
powerful; feminine form of Ulrich
(Scandinavian) *Ulla; Ulrica, Ulrika;*
Nicknames: *Uli*

ULTIMA Latin: Final, the last one

ULU (oo-LOO) African: Second daughter
(Nigeria)

ULULANI (OO-loo-LAH-nee) Hawaiian:
Divine inspiration

ULYANA Russian: Variation of Julia
Nicknames: *Ulya*

UMA (OO-mah) Hindi: Mother; another
name for the Hindu goddess Devi
Famous namesakes: Actress Uma Thurman

UMAYMA (oo-MAY-mah) Egyptian: Little
mother

UME (oo-me) Japanese: Plum blossom

UMIKO (oo-mee-ko) Japanese: Ocean girl

UNA (OO-nah) Latin: One, unity, together.
In Edmund Spenser's epic poem *The Faerie
Queene*, Una is the knight Redcrosse's
virtuous fair lady whose parents are held
captive by a dragon. (Native American)
remember (Hopi); (Welsh) white wave. See
also *Oona*
Ona; **Famous namesakes:** Actress Una Merkl

UNDINE Latin: Little waves, ripple,
mermaid. In German mythology, undines
were female water-spirits created without a
soul, but if one married a mortal man and
bore him a child, she was granted a soul and
made human.
Undina, Undinia; Ondine, Ondina

UNELMA (OO-nel-mah) Finnish: Dream,
fantasy

UNIQUE (yoo-NEEK) Latin: Only one,
special, unduplicated

UNITY English: Standing together, acting as
one
Unita

UNN Norse: Beloved girl
Unne

UPALA (oo-pah-lah) Hindi: Variation of Opal

URANIA (yə-RAY-nee-ə) Greek: Heavenly; mythological muse of the astronomy
Urainia

URBANA (ur-BAH-nah) Latin: Urban, lives in and belongs to the city; implies sophistication
Urbania; Urbanah

URBI (OOR-bee) African: Princess (Nigeria)

URENNA (oo-REN-nah) African: Father's pride (Nigeria)

URI (YOOR-ee) Hebrew: Light, flame

URIKA (oo-REE-kah) Native American: Useful to the tribe (Omaha)
Ureka, Urica

URIT (yoor-EET) Hebrew: Bright, light
Urice; Urita

URITH German: Deemed worthy
Uritha

URSULA (UR-sə-lə) Latin: Little bear. Saint Ursula was a British princess who was martyred for her faith during her return from a pilgrimage to Rome.
(French) *Ursule*; (Spanish) *Ursulina*; (Polish) *Urszula, Urszuli; Urseline, Ursola, Urzula, Vorsila*; **Nicknames:** *Sula, Ulla, Ursa*; **Famous namesakes:** Swiss actress Ursula Andress

USHA (OO-shah) Sanskrit, Hindi: Dawn, mythological daughter of heaven and sister of night
Ushas

UTE (OO-tə) German: Wealthy
Uta; **Famous namesakes:** German cabaret singer Ute Lemper, German actress Uta Hagen

UTINA (oo-TEE-nah) Native American: Member of my tribe, kin

VACHYA (vach-ya) Hindi: Well-spoken
Vac

VADIT Hebrew: Rose
Varda, Vardit, Vared

VALA Welsh: Chosen

VALDA Norse: Renowned ruler; (Teutonic) spirited in war
Valdis, Velda

VALENCIA Latin, Spanish: Brave, strong; place name of a Spanish city
Star babies: daughter of Marlon Jackson

VALENTIA (və-LEN-shee-ə) Latin: Strong; to be brave
Valencia; **Nicknames:** *Val, Vally*

VALENTINA Latin, Italian: Brave, strong; feminine form of Valentinus.
(Slavic) *Valeska*; **Nicknames:** *Valen, Valene, Valyn*; **Diminutive forms:** *Valechka*; **Famous namesakes:** First Russian female cosmonaut Valentina Tereshkova; **Star babies:** daughter of Angelica Bridges and Sheldon Souray

VALERIE Latin, French: Strong; derived from ancient Roman family name Valerius
(Italian) *Valeria*; *Balara, Balera, Balere, Valari, Valeraine, Valere, Valora; Valery, Valarie*; **Nicknames:** *Val*; **Famous namesakes:** Actress Valerie Perrin, actress Valerie Harper

VANAMO (VA-nah-mo) Finnish: A flower

VANESSA Greek: Butterfly; from Phanessa, the mystic goddess of an ancient Greek brotherhood; (Latin) named for Venus (Spanish) *Vanesa*; *Venessa*; **Old forms:** *Phanessa*; **Nicknames:** *Vania, Vanna, Vanny*; **Famous namesakes:** British actress Vanessa Redgrave, singer and actress Vanessa Williams

VARSHA (var-shah) Hindi: Rainshower

VARTOUHI (VAR-too-hee) Armenian: Rose lady
Vartoughi

VASARA (VAH-sah-ruh) Lithuanian: Summer

VASHTI (VASH-tee) Persian: Beautiful

VASILISA (vah-see-LEE-sah) Russian: Royal; feminine form of Basil
Nicknames: *Vassa*

VAYU Hindi: Vital force

VEDA Sanskrit: Knowledge; vedas are sacred scriptures that date back to 3,000 BC.

VEDETTA Italian: Guardian, scout
Vedette

VEGA Latin, Swedish: One of the brightest stars in the sky; also a surname; (Arabic) falling star, messenger
Famous namesakes: Musician Suzanne Vega

VELEDA Teutonic: Inspired intelligence. The historical Veleda was a first-century Germanic prophetess regarded as divine.

VELIKA (VEL-ee-kə) Slavic: Great, famous

VELLAMO (VEL-lah-mo) Finnish: Protector

VELVET English: Soft, rich fabric. Velvet has become an adjective to describe almost anything which has a soft, rich feel or texture.

VENETIA (ve-NE-shə) Italian: Place name for a northern Italian city
Venita; *Venice*

VENICE (VEN-əs) Italian: Place name of a town in Italy and also an area in southern California

VENTURA Spanish: Good fortune

VENUS (VEE-nəs) Latin: Goddess of love and beauty and the equivalent of the Greek goddess Aphrodite. From the ancient Greek "Venus de Milo" statue to Sandro Botticelli's "Birth of Venus," and even to a 1980s pop music song, Venus is an enduring symbol in the art and music of the world. The second planet from the sun is named for her. (Welsh) *Gwener*; (Russian) *Venera*; **Famous namesakes:** Tennis player Venus Williams

VERA Latin: True; (Russian) faith (Latin) *Veradis, Veradisia*; (Spanish) *Verdad*; (Russian) *Verochka*; (Czech) *Viera*; (Finnish) *Veera*; *Verena*; **Nicknames:** *Vreni*; **Diminutive forms:** *Verushka*; **Famous namesakes:** Fashion designer Vera Wang

VERBENA Latin: Sacred herb with fragrant flowers and leaves
Verbana, Verbenia

VERDA Latin: Unspoiled

VERENA (ve-RE-nah) German: Sacred wisdom; also a variation of Vera, meaning true
Verene, Verina

VERNA Latin: Spelling variation of Laverne
Famous namesakes: Actress Verna Bloom

VERONA (ver-O-nə) Italian: Place name of a town in Italy; also a variation of Verena

VERONICA Latin, Greek: Honest image. This name stems from a legend of a maiden who handed Christ her handkerchief on the way to Calvary, whereupon his likeness miraculously appeared on the cloth. (German) *Veronika*; (French) *Veronique*; (Polish) *Weronikia*; *Veronicha*; **Famous namesakes:** Actress Veronica Lake, French singer Veronique Sansone; **Star babies:** daughter of Rebecca DeMornay and Patrick O'Neal

VESPERA Latin: Evening star
Vesperia, Vespira

VESTA Latin: Goddess of the hearth

VETA Latin, Spanish: Life

VEVINA Irish: Sweet lady; Vevina was used by Scottish poet James MacPherson in his Ossianic poetry.

VIANNE French: Blend of Vivian and Anne. Juliette Binoche played a character with this name in the film *Chocolat*.

VICENTA (vee-SEN-tah) Spanish: Victor, conquering; feminine form of Vicente

VICTORIA Latin: Triumphant; feminine form of Victor. During the reign of England's Queen Victoria, Britain reached new heights in industrial and colonial power and diplomatic influence. The term *Victorian* today recalls her strong position on personal moral issues.
(Spanish) *Vittoria*; (Swedish) *Viktoria*; (Polish) *Wikitoria, Wikta, Wiktorja*; (Hawaiian) *Wikolia*; *Victoriana, Victorina, Victorine, Victriva*; **Nicknames:** *Torey, Tori, Toriana, Torree, Torrey, Torri, Torrie, Tory, Vic, Vicky, Vickie*; **Famous namesakes:** Actress Victoria Principal, singer Victoria "Posh" Adams; **Star babies:** daughters of Lorenzo Lamas and Shauna Sand, Tommy Lee Jones and Kimberlea Cloughley

VIDA (VID-ah) Hebrew: Nickname for Davina

VIDONIA (vee-DO-nee-ah) Portuguese: Vine branch

VIENNA Latin: Place name for the capital city of Austria

VIGILIA Latin: Alert, vigilant

VIJAYA (vi-jay-yah) Hindi: Victory

VIKA Scottish: From the creek

VILJA (VEEL-yah) Finnish: Grain

VIMALA (vee-mah-la) Hindi: Pure and attractive

VINA (VEE-nah) Spanish: From the vineyard

VINCENTIA Latin: Triumphant

VIOLA (vee-O-lə, vie-O-lə) Latin, Swedish: Violet, the name of a purple flower and also for that shade of purple. Viola is also an instrument in the violin family and the name of Shakespeare's heroine in *Twelfth Night*. (French) *Yolande*; (Polish) *Jolanta*

VIOLET English: Lovely purple flower (French) *Violette, Yolanthe*; (Italian) *Violetta*; (Spanish) *Yolanda*; **Nicknames:** *Vi*; **Famous namesakes:** Ugandan author Violet Barungi; **Star babies:** daughter of Ben Affleck and Jennifer Garner

VIRAG (VEE-rahg) Hungarian: Flower

VIRDISIA Latin: Young and budding
Virdia, Virdis, Virdisa, Viridianai

VIRGINIA Latin, English: Virginal, chaste; also name referring to Queen Elizabeth of England, "The Virgin Queen," who did not marry and for whom the state of Virginia is named. See also *Gina*
Virgena, Virgene, Virginee; Verginia, Verginya, Virgenya, Virginya; **Old forms:** *Virgina;* **Nicknames:** *Ginna, Ginnie, Ginny, Gigi, Ginger, Ginia, Ginya, Virge, Virgie, Virgy;* **Diminutive forms:** *Ginnette;* **Famous namesakes:** Author Virginia Woolf

VIRTUS Latin: Virtue
Virtua

VITA Latin: Life
(Hungarian) *Vicuska; Vitia*

VIVECA Scandinavian: With living voice from Middle Latin phrase *viva voce*; life, alive; (Teutonic) war castle, a place of refuge (Danish) *Vibeke;* **Famous namesakes:** Actress Vivica Fox

VIVIAN Latin, English: Full of life, lively. In Arthurian legend, Vivian was the Lady of the Lake and enchantress of Merlin.
(French) *Viviane, Vivienne;* (Italian) *Viviana;* (Spanish) *Bibiana;* (Finnish) *Viivi; Vivianne, Vivien;* **Nicknames:** *Bibi, Vavay;* **Famous namesakes:** British actress Vivien Leigh; **Star babies:** daughter of Debbie Allen

VIVIENNE (viv-ee-EN, VIV-ee-en) French: Variation of Vivian
Star babies: daughter of Angelina Jolie and Brad Pitt

VLADA (VLAHD-ah) Russian: To rule; feminine form of Vlad
Diminutive forms: *Vladka*

VOLVA Norse: A prophetess

VOR Norse: An omniscient goddess

VORSILA Greek: Spelling variation of Ursula

VOSGI (VOS-gee) Armenian: Gold
Vosgie, Voshkie, Voski

WACHIWI (wah-CHEE-wee) Native American: Dancing girl (Sioux)

WAKANDA (wah-KAHN-dah) Native American: Inner, magical power

WALBURGA German: Strong defender; Saint Walburga was an eighth-century English missionary to Germany.
(Finnish) *Vappu; Walburgha; Walpurga, Walpurgis*

WALDA German: Divine power; feminine form of Waldo and Oswald
Welda; Waldah, Waldina, Wellda

WALLIS (WAHL-is) English: From Wales; feminine form of Wallace
Waleis

WANDA German: Wanderer
(Polish) *Vanda, Wandy; Vande, Wande, Wandis, Wende, Wendelin, Wendelina, Wendeline; Wande;* **Famous namesakes:** Singer Wanda Jackson

WANETA (wah-NAY-tah) Native American: Charger
Wanita

WANETTA English: Pale, fair-faced; could also be given as a phonetic spelling of the Spanish name Juanita
Waneta, Wanita; **Nicknames:** *Wann*

WANGARI (WAHN-gah-ray) African: Leopard

WARDA English: Guard; feminine form of Ward

WASHTA (WAH-shtay) Native American: Good (Sioux)

WATSEKA (wat-seh-kah) Native American: Pretty woman (Potawatomi)

WAUNA (WAH-oo-nah) Native American: Call of the snow geese flying (Miwok)

WAVERLY English: Quaking aspen
Waverley, Waverlee, Waverlie, Waverlea, Waverleigh

WAYLAHSKISE (way-lah-skee-seh) Native American: Graceful (Shawnee)

WAYNOKA (way-no-kah) Native American: Sweet water (Cheyenne)

WEAYAYA (wee-ah-yah-yah) Native American: Sunset (Sioux)

WELCOME English: Received gladly, happily greeted

WENDA English, Welsh: Wanderer, stranger; variant of Wendy, Gwyneth, Guenevere, and Wanda

WENDELLE English: Wanderer, stranger. See also *Wenda*

WENDY English: A literary name that first appeared in James Barrie's *Peter Pan*. He took it from his childhood nickname *fwendy*, meaning *friend*. Some think it may also be a diminutive of the Welsh name Gwendolyn.
Nicknames: *Wendi*

WENONA (we-NO-nah) Native American: Spelling variation of Winona

WENYA (wen-yah) Chinese: Polite elegance

WESLEE (WEZ-lee) English: From the western meadow; feminine form of Wesley
Weslie, Weslia, Weslea, Wesleigh

WESLIA English: From the western meadow; a variant of Wesley
Weslie, Weslea, Wesleigh, Weslee, Wesley

WESTLEY English: From the western meadow; surname
Weslyn, Westlyn; Weslea, Weslee, Wesleigh, Westlea, Westleah, Westleigh

WHITLEY English: From the white meadow
Whitlea, Whitleigh, Whitlee

WHITNEY English, Anglo-Saxon: From the white island
Famous namesakes: Singer Whitney Houston

WICAHPI (wih-kah-pee) Native American: Star (Sioux)
Wicapi

WICAPI WAKAN (wih-kah-pee-wah-kan) Native American: Holy star (Sioux)
Wicahpi Wakan

WIEBKE (VEEP-kə, WEEB-kə) German: War

WIHAKAYDA Native American: Youngest daughter (Sioux)

WILDA Anglo-Saxon: Willow; (German) untamed, wild
Wildah, Willda, Wylda

WILEEN (wil-EEN) English: Variation of Wilhelmina

WILHELMINA German: Resolute protector; feminine variant of Wilhelm (English) *Wileen*; (Italian) *Guillelmina, Gulielma*; (Spanish) *Guillermina*; (Swedish) *Vilhelmina*; (Danish) *Wilhelmine*; (Finnish) *Miina, Valma*; *Wilhemina*; **Old forms:** *Wilhelma*; **Nicknames:** *Billie, Hilma, Mimi, Mina, Minetta, Minna, Minnie, Minny, Vilma, Willa, Wilma, Wilna*; **Diminutive forms:** *Minette, Willette*

WILLA English: Nickname for Wilhelmina
Famous namesakes: Author Willa Cather

WILLOW English: Slender, graceful; from the willow tree noted for graceful branches and leaves
Star babies: daughters of Gabrielle Anwar, Will Smith and Jada Pinkett Smith

WILMA German: Nickname for Wilhelmina

"Native Americans regard their names not as mere labels, but as essential parts of their personalities. A native person's name is as vital to his or her identity as the eyes or the teeth."
—Wilma Mankiller, first female elected as chief to the Cherokee Nation

---

WILONA Anglo-Saxon: Desired, longed for
Wilone; *Wylona*

WINEMA (we-NEH-mah) Native American: Female chief (Miwok)

WINFREY (WIN-free) English: Friend of peace
Famous namesakes: Oprah Winfrey

WINIFRED Welsh, German, Teutonic: Reconciled, blessed. Winifred was a martyred Welsh princess and traditionally considered the patron saint of virgins.
Nicknames: *Winnie*

WINIFRID German: Peaceful friend; (Welsh) variant of Guenievere
(Welsh) *Winnifred*; *Winfreda, Winifreda, Winifride, Wynfreda, Wynifred, Wynnifred*

WINNIE Welsh: Nickname for Winifred. Few children will hear the name Winnie without thinking of the beloved bear Winnie the Pooh and his friends in the Enchanted Forest.

WINOLA German: Gracious friend
Winolah, Wynola

WINONA (wi-NO-nah) Native American: First born; a nourisher or mother; mother of the legendary Hiawatha, unifier of the Iroquois tribe.
Wenona; **Nicknames:** *Winny, Winn, Nonna*; **Famous namesakes:** Winona Ryder

WINTER English: Seasonal name, born in the winter
Wynter

WITASHNAH (wih-tash-nah) Native American: Pure, untouched (Sioux)

WREN (REN) English: A small bird

WYANET (wie-AH-net) Native American: Legendary beautiful

WYNNE (WIN) Celtic: White or fair, light-skinned; also a familiar form of Guinevere, Gweneth and similar names
Wyn; **Nicknames:** *Wynnie*

XABRINA Latin: Spelling variation of Sabrina

XAMURRA (shah-MOOR-ah) Basque:
Gentle
Xamura; **Nicknames:** *Sha, Murra*

XANAY (shah-nay) Native American: One
that walks upon the earth
Shanay; **Nicknames:** *Shay*

XANDRA (ZAHN-drah) Spanish: Nickname
for Alexandra

XANTHE (ex-AHN-thə, ZAHN-thə) Greek:
Blond, yellow, golden
Xantha, Xanthia, Zanthe

XENIA (ZEEN-yə) Greek: Welcoming,
hospitable. Pop culture character Xena,
warrior princess, will have many associate this
name with strength and independence.
(Russian) *Aksiniya, Ksenia, Oksanochka*;
(Ukrainian) *Oksana; Xena, Zena, Zenda, Zene,
Zenia, Zenina, Zenna*; **Nicknames:** *Xia, Zina*;
Diminutive forms: *Oksanka*

XIOMARA (zhoh-MAHR-ah) Spanish:
Ready for battle
Ziomara; **Nicknames:** *Xi, Xio*

XYLEENA (zie-LEE-nə) Greek: Lives in the
forest, loves the forest
Xylia, Xyliana, Xylina, Xylinia, Xylona, Zylina

YAAKOVA Hebrew: Supplants

YAEL Hebrew: Mountain goat; in the Old
Testament, the name of a woman who killed
the captain of the Canaanite army
Jael; Yaela, Yaella

YAFFA Hebrew: Spelling variation of Jaffa
Jafa, Jafit, Yafa, Yafit

YALETHA Scandinavian: Spelling variation
of Oletha

YAMKA (YAHM-kah) Native American:
Blossom (Hopi)

YANAHA (yah-NAH-hah) Native American:
She meets the enemy, brave (Navajo)

YARA Arabic, Persian: Courage, strength

YARDENA Hebrew: Spelling variation of
Jordan

YARKONA (yahr-KO-nah) Hebrew: Green

YARONA Hebrew: Sing

YASMIN (YAZ-min, yas-MEEN) Arabic,
Hindi: Fragrant flower
Yasmine, Yasmeen; **Nicknames:** *Jazz*; **Star
babies:** daughter of Chrissie Hynde and Jim
Kerr

YEDDA English: Beautiful voice; possible
variant of Yetta

YEDIDA Hebrew: Friend
Jedidah, Yedidah

YESENIA (ye-SAY-nee-ah) Spanish:
Meaning unknown; gained popularity in the
'70s as a title character of a Spanish-language
soap opera
Llesenia

YETTA English: Generous, giving; possible
diminutive of Henrietta

YNES (ee-NEZ) French: Variation of Agnes

YOCHEVED Hebrew: God's glory
Yochebed

YOKI Native American: Rain (Hopi)

YOLANDA (yo-LAHN-dah) Spanish: Variation of Violet

YONA Hebrew: Dove; feminine variant of Jonah
Jonina, Jonita, Yonina, Yonita; Yonah

YOREH (yo-RE) Hebrew: Autumn rain

YOSEBE Hebrew: Spelling variation of Josephine

YOSHI (yo-shee) Japanese: Good, respectful
Yoshie, Yoshiko, Yoshio, Yoshiyo

YSEULT (i-SOOLT) French: Fair one; variant of Iseut and Isolde

YSOLDE Arthurian Legend: Spelling variation of Isolde

YUKI (yoo-kee) Japanese: Snow

YULE Norse: Born during Yuletide

YULIA (YOO-lee-ah) Russian: Variation of Julia

YURIKO (yoo-ree-ko) Japanese: Lily child or village of birth

YVETTE (ee-VET, i-VET) French: Diminutive form of Yvonne

YVONNE (ee-VON, i-VAWN) French: Archer; feminine variant of Yves (German) *Evon, Evonna, Evonne*; (Polish) *Iwona*; *Evony, Ivonne*; **Diminutive forms:** *Yvette*; **Famous namesakes:** Actress Yvonne Craig

ZABANA Native American: Meadow; variation of Savannah (Taino)

ZADA (ZAH-dah) Arabic: Huntress, fortunate

ZAHAR Hebrew: Dawn
Zaher, Zahir

ZAHARA (zah-har-rah) African: Flowers; abundant beauty
Star babies: daughter of Angelina Jolie and Brad Pitt

ZAHAVAH Hebrew: Gold or golden; variant of Zehava
Zahava

ZAHRA (ZAH-rə) Arabic: White, flowering, beauty; (African) flowering (Swahili)
Zara; Zahraa, Zahrah; **Famous namesakes:** Maltese children's author and illustrator Trevor Zahra, journalist Zahra Kazemi

ZAIDA (zah-EE-dah, ZAY-də) Arabic: Lucky, bountiful; also used in auction language, meaning to outbid another
Zayda; Zayda

ZAIDEE (ZAY-dee) Arabic: Wealthy. See also
Zada
Zaidi

ZAINA (zah-EE-nah) Spanish: Variation of Jane

ZAINABU (zah-ee-NAH-boo) African: Beautiful (Swahili)

ZALIKA (zah-LEE-kah) African, Egyptian: Well-born, noble (Swahili)
Zaliki

ZALTANA (zahl-TAH-nah) Native American: High mountain
Zaltanah

ZAMIRA (zah-mir-rah) Hebrew: Singer
Nicknames: *Mirah*

ZAMORA (zah-MOR-ah) Spanish: Place name of a Spanish city

ZANDRA (ZAHN-drah) Spanish: Nickname for Alexandra

ZANETA Russian: Variation of Janet

ZANNA (ZAH-nah) Hebrew: God is gracious; variant of Jane and possibly a variant of Susanna

ZANOBIA (zah-NO-bee-ə) Arabic: Father's ornament, petite and voluptuous
Zanouba, Zanoubia; **Famous namesakes:** Queen of Palmyra, Zenobia, lived in the third century and was known as the "warrior queen." She led her people in a war against Rome, much like Boudica did in England. Zenobia claimed to be a descendent of Cleopatra (of Egypt) and, indeed, came from a long history of Syrian and Abyssinian queens, including the Queen of Sheba.

ZANTA African: Beautiful girl

ZARA (ZAH-rə) Hebrew: Spelling variation of Zahra
Star babies: daughter of Princess Anne and Mark Phillips

ZARAHLINDA Hebrew: Beautiful princess; spelling variant of names Sarah and Linda

ZARIA (ZAHR-ee-ə) Arabic: Rose, visitor

ZAYNA Arabic: Beauty, ornament

ZDENKA Czech: Follower of Saint Denis, martyred Bishop of Paris; variant of Zdenek

ZEHAVA Hebrew: Gold or golden
Zahavah, Zehave, Zehavi, Zehavit, Zahava, Zehovit, Zehuvit

ZEHIRA Hebrew: Careful, protective

ZELDA (ZEL-də) Teutonic: Nickname for Griselda
Famous namesakes: Author Zelda Fitzgerald (wife of F. Scott Fitzgerald); **Star babies:** daughter of Robin Williams and Marsha Garces

ZELENA Greek: Variation of Celine

ZELENE English: Variation of Celine

ZELENKA (ze-LEHN-kah) Czech: Green, new, fresh, innocent

ZELIA (zay-LEE-ah) Spanish: Sunshine, daylight

ZELLA (ZEL-ə) German: Diminutive form of Marcella

ZELMA (ZEL-mə) English: Spelling variation of Selma

ZEMIRAH Hebrew: Joyous melody, song of praise
Zemira, Zimra, Zimria, Zymirah

ZEMORA Hebrew: Branch, extension
Zemorah

ZENA (ZEE-nə) African: News, but predominantly when the name is used, it is a variant of Xenia, meaning welcoming

ZENAIDA (zə-NAY-də) Greek: White dove, symbol of purity and adoration; also related to Zeus
(Russian) *Zinaida*; *Zenaide*; **Nicknames:** *Zina*; **Diminutive forms:** *Zinochka*

ZENDA Persian: Womanly; also Greek variant of Xenia, meaning welcoming

ZENOBE Greek: Born of Zeus; originally a male name, after the Greek mythological youngest son of Cronus and Rhea.

ZENOBIA (zə-NO-bee-ə) Greek: Sign; Queen Zenobia was third century ruler of the wealthy Arabian desert city of Palmyra. (Spanish) *Cenobia, Senobia*; (Russian) *Zinovia*; **Nicknames:** *Zena*

ZEPHYR (ZEF-ər) Greek: West wind, the gentle wind
(Greek) *Zephira*; (English) *Zephrine*; (Polish) *Zefiryn*; *Zephyra, Zyphire*; **Nicknames:** *Zephan*

ZERA (ZAY-rah) Hebrew: Seeds, beginnings
Zerah

ZERLINA Latin: Beautiful dawn. Zerlina is a young girl pursued by the Don in Mozart's opera *Don Giovanni*.
Serlina; Serlina

ZETA (ZAY-tə) Greek: Born last, the last letter of the Greek alphabet; (English) rose

ZEUXIPPE Latin: Greek mythological queen of Athens, she was the mother of Erechtheus, Butes, Procne, and Philomela

ZHANNA (ZHAHN-nah) Russian: Variation of Jane

ZIA (ZEE-ə) Arabic: Light, splendor, beautifully adorned
Zya; **Nicknames:** *Zi Zi*

ZIBA Persian: Beautiful

ZIBIA Hebrew: Spelling variation of Tzviya
Zibiah

ZIGANA (zee-GAH-nah) Hungarian: Spelling variation of Tzigana

ZIHNA (ZEE-nah) Native American: Spins, spinning (Hopi)

ZILLAH (ZIL-ə) Hebrew: Shadow; an Old Testament name
Zilla

ZIMRA Hebrew: Spelling variation of Zemirah

ZINA (ZEE-nə) English: Welcoming, hospitable; variant of Xenia

ZINAIDA (zee-nah-EE-dah) Russian: Variation of Zenaida

ZINERVA Italian: Fair, light-skinned

ZINNIA (ZIN-ee-ə) English: A flower

ZIPPORAH (zi-POR-ə, ZIP-or-ə) Hebrew: Bird; the name of Moses' wife in the Old Testament
Sippora, Tzippa, Tzzipporah, Zippora

ZITA (ZEE-tah) Arabic: Mistress; also the diminutive form for names ending in sita or zita, such as Rosita

ZITKALA (zit-KAH-lah) Native American: Bird (Sioux)
Famous namesakes: Sioux teacher and writer Zitkala Si

ZIVA Hebrew: Brilliant, radiant
Zivah

ZIVIA Hebrew: Spelling variation of Tzviya

ZLATA (ZLAH-tah) Slavic: Golden, guilded

ZOE (ZO-ee) Greek: Life, energy
(Russian) *Zoya, Zoyechka, Zoyenka*; *Zoel,*

Zoelle, Zoey, Zoia; *Zoey, Zoie, Zoyee, Zowy*; **Old forms:** *Zoelie*; **Famous namesakes:** Actress Zoe Caldwell; **Star babies:** daughters of Rosanna Arquette, Amanda Bears, Lisa Bonet and Lenny Kravitz, Woody Harrelson, Henry Winkler

ZOFIA (ZAW-fyah) Polish: Variation of Sophia
Zofie

ZOHAR (ZO-hahr) Hebrew: Sparkling, shining
Zoheret; *Zohara, Zohera*

ZOHREH Persian: The planet Venus

ZOLA (ZO-lə) Italian: Piece of the earth
Zoela, Zolah, Zoila

ZONA Latin: Sash or belt, mark of distinction
Zonah, Zonia

ZORA (ZO-rə) Slavic: Dawn; variant of Aurora; (African) a bargain (Hausa)
Famous namesakes: Author Zora Neale Hurston

> *"Perhaps love is a compelling necessity imposed on man by God that has something to do with suffering."*
> —Zora Neale Hurston, *The Woman in Gaul*

ZORINA (SAW-re-nah) Slavic: Golden
Sorina, Zorana

ZOYA (ZO-yah) Russian: Variation of Zoe

ZSA ZSA (ZHAW-zhaw) Hungarian: Familiar name for Susan; many people will think immediately of glamorous actress Zsa Zsa Gabor

ZSOFIA (ZHO-fee-aw) Hungarian: Variation of Sophia
Zsofie; **Nicknames:** *Zsofika*

ZSUZSANNA (ZHOO-zhawn-naw) Hungarian: Variation of Susan
Zuska

ZSUZSI (ZHOO-zhee) Hungarian: Variation of Susan

ZUDORA Hindi: Laborer, worker
Zudorah

ZURI (ZOO-ree) African: Beautiful (Swahili)

ZURIA Hebrew: Spelling variation of Tzuria

ZURINA (soor-EE-nah) Basque: White, fair-skinned
Nicknames: *Zuri, Zurie*

ZUWENA (zoo-WE-nah) African: Good (Swahili)
Zwena

ZUZELA (zoo-zeh-lah) Native American: Name of one of Sitting Bull's wives

ZUZU (ZOO-zoo) Czech: Lily; familiar form of Zuza and Susan. Fans of *It's a Wonderful Life* will remember the young girl and her glorious flower petals.

ZYLINA Greek: Lives in the forest; variant of Xyleena

ZYMIRAH Hebrew: Spelling variation of Zemirah

ZYTKA (ZIT-kah) Polish: Strong; a familiar form of Brygida
Nicknames: *Zyta*

Boys' Names

AAGE Norse: Ancestors

AARNE (AHR-nay) Finnish: Variation of Arnold

AARON Hebrew: The anglicized form of Aharon, meaning *high mountain*, *lofty*, or *inspired*. In the Bible, Moses' brother Aaron was Israel's first high priest and is remembered for his staff which blossomed miraculously. Popular in English-speaking countries since the Protestant Reformation; (Arabic) forest, thicken, strength (Arabic) *Haroun, Harun*; (Spanish) *Eron*; (Scandinavian) *Aaren*; (Swedish) *Aron*; (Slavic) *Arron*; (Finnish) *Aaro*; *Ahren, Harun al Rachid*; **Old forms:** *Aharon*; **Star babies:** son of Robert De Niro

ABALARDO Celtic: Noble

ABALLACH Arthurian legend: Father of Urien's wife Modron. Aballach is likely a variant of Avallach, a reference to the island of Avalon.

ABASI (ah-BAH-see) Egyptian: Stern (Swahili) *Abasy*

ABAYOMI (ah-BAH-yo-mee) African: Brings great joy (Nigeria)

ABBAN (AB-awn) Irish: Little abbot. This was the name of a sixth-century Irish saint, the son of King Cormac of Leinster. *Aban*

ABBAS (ah-BAHS) Hebrew: Father; (Arabic) lion, grim-faced, stern; the name of one of Mohammed's uncles *Abba; Abbe, Abbey, Abbie, Abo;* **Nicknames:** *Ab;* **Famous namesakes:** Algerian political leader Ferhat Abbas, Khedive of Egypt Abbas Hilmi, Arabic poet Abbas Ibn Al Ahnaf

ABBEY English: Diminutive variant of Abbas, Abbott, Abelard, and Abner *Abbie, Abby, Aby;* **Famous namesakes:** Activist Abbie Hoffman

ABBOT Hebrew, English: Father or head of a monastic community. This surname is likely derived from the Hebrew name Abba and may bring to mind the famed Abbott and Costello comedy team. (English) *Abbott; Abot, Abott;* **Nicknames:** *Abbey, Abbie, Abby, Abe*

ABDAL (AHBD-al) Arabic: Servant or slave of Allah. This name rarely stands alone but is generally followed by adjectives that are all attributes of Allah in the Muslim faith, and serve to identify God by one of his ninety-nine names. For example, Hakim means *wise*, so Abdel Hakim means *servant of the wise*. To avoid repetition, meanings of those names/ adjectives are listed as separate entries. *Abdel, Abdul, Abd El, Abd-al*

ABDERUS (ab-DEE-rəs) Greek: A friend of Hercules

ABDU (ab-DOO) African: Servant of God

ABEBE (ah-BE-bə) African: Asked for (Nigeria)

ABEL (AY-bəl) Hebrew: Son or breath. In the Bible, Abel was the son of Adam and Eve who was killed by his brother Cain in a fit of jealousy. (Russian) *Avel;* (Finnish) *Aapeli; Abell*

> "A good name is better than precious ointment."
> —Hebrew Ecclesiastes, 7:1

ABELARD (AH-be-lahrd) German: Resolute, noble, and steadfast (Spanish) *Abelardo*

ABHAINN Scottish: River, from the river

ABHAY (ah-BHAY) Hindi: Fearless

ABIMELECH (ah-BIM-ə-lek) Hebrew: Anglicized version of Avimelech, meaning father is king. *Avimelech*

ABIOLA (ah-BEE-o-lah) African: Born in wealth

ABIR (ah-BEER) Hebrew: Strong

ABIRAM (AH-bee-ram) Hebrew: Father of heights *Aviram*

ABISHA (ə-BIE-shə) Hebrew: God's gift

ABLENDAN (a-BLEHN-den) Anglo-Saxon: Dazzling, blinding

ABNER Hebrew: My father is light; In the Bible, Abner was King Saul's cousin and commander of his army. *Avner*; **Nicknames:** *Ab, Abbey, Abbie, Abby*

ABRAHAM Hebrew: Father of a multitude; Abraham was the first of the Old Testament patriarchs. God changed his name from Abram when He appointed him to be the father of the Hebrew nation. (Arabic) *Ibrahim*; (Italian) *Abramo*; (Spanish) *Abran*; (Irish) *Abracham*; *Avraham*; **Nicknames:** *Abe, Bram*; **Famous namesakes:** President Abraham Lincoln; **Star babies:** son of Matt Groening

ABRAM Hebrew: Exalted father; the biblical patriarch Abraham's name before God changed it

ABSALOM (AB-sə-lahm) Hebrew: Father of peace. In the Bible, the favored son of King David was renowned for his handsome appearance and ability to win loyalty and allegiance. (German) *Axel*; (Spanish) *Absalon*; *Avsalom, Avshalom*; *Absalon, Abshalom, Avshalom, Avsholom*; **Nicknames:** *Ab, Salom*

ABU Arabic: Father

ABU BAKR (AH-boo-BAHK-ur) Arabic: Father of a young camel. Abu Bakr was Mohammed the Prophet's companion **Famous namesakes:** Mohammed's father-in-law, first Caliph to initiate the Islamic conquests

ACCALON Arthurian legend: Morgan Le Fay's lover and partner

ACCIUS (AK-she-əs) Latin: Renowned Roman poet and playwright

ACE Latin, English, Anglo-Saxon: Unity. In English, Ace has become a term for one who is superior, one who excels. *Acey*; *Acer, Acie*

ACEL (ah-SEL) French: Adherent of a nobleman

ACENNAN (AH-cee-nahn) Anglo-Saxon: Brings forth, gives birth to

ACHAK Native American: Spirit (Algonquin)

ACHATES (ə-KAY-teez) Greek: Loyal friend; faithful companion of Aeneas whose story is chronicled in Virgil's *Aeneid*

ACHELOUS (a-kə-LO-əs) Greek: A mythological river god, Achelous was the eldest of the many sons of Oceanus and Tethys

ACHIILES (ə-KIL-eez) Greek: Achilles was the son of the mortal Peleus and the Nereid Thetis. He was the mightiest of the Greeks who fought in the Trojan War and was the hero of Homer's Iliad.

> "But sure the eye of Time beholds no name. So bless'd [Achilles] as thine in all the rolls of fame."
> —Alexander Pope's translation of *The Odyssey of Homer*

ACHIM (AH-khim) German: Nickname for Joachim

ACIS (AY-sis) Latin, Greek: Son of Faunus, a god of the forest similar to Pan, and a nymph, he later became the lover of Galatea, the Nereid

ACKERLEY English: From the oak tree meadow; a possible reference to acre of oak trees
Ackley, Aekerley, Aekley, Oakley; Ackerlea

ACRISIUS (a-KRISH-ee-əs) Latin, Greek: A mythological king of Argos, Acrisius locked his daughter Danae away in an attempt to avoid a prophesy. Zeus appeared to her as a shower of gold and fathered Perseus.

ACTAEON (ak-TEE-ən) Greek: From Attica. The hunter Actaeon stumbled upon the goddess Artemis while she bathed, so she turned him into a stag. His own hunting dogs then became his killers.
Actaeonis, Acteon

ACTON English: From the town or settlement near the oak trees
Actun

ADAIAH (ah-DIE-ə) Hebrew: God's witness, adorned by God; a son of Haman in the Bible
Adaia, Adaya, Adayah

ADAIR (ah-DER) Scottish: From the oak tree ford; surname. See also Athdar
(Gaelic) *Athdara*; (Irish) *Adare*

ADALARD (AH-dahl-ahr) German: Highborn and courageous. See also Adel
(English) *Allard; Adalhard, Adelard, Adelhard*;
Old forms: *Aethelhard, Alhard*

ADALRICH (AH-dahl-rikh) German: Highborn ruler, noble commander
Adalric, Adalrik, Adelric

ADALSON English: Son of a specific person now unknown, possibly Adam or any of the English names beginning with *Ad–*

ADAM Hebrew, English: Son of the red earth. In the Bible, Adam was first man created by God.
(English) *Addis*; (Spanish) *Adan*; (Gaelic) *Adhamh*; (Czech) *Damek*; (Finnish) *Aatami*; (Hawaiian) *Akamu; Addam, Adem*; **Star babies:** sons of Leonard Nimoy, Maurice Gibb

ADAMSON Hebrew, English: Son of Adam

ADDAI (ah-DIE) Hebrew: Man of God

ADDIS English: Variation of Adam

ADDISON English: Son of Adam; surname
Addeson, Adison, Adisson; **Nicknames:** *Ad, Addie, Addy*

ADDY (AD-ee) Teutonic: Variant of Adelard and Adam

ADE (ah-DAY) African: Royal (Nigeria)

ADEBEN (ah-de-BEN) African: Twelfth born (Ghana)

ADEL (ah-DEL) Arabic: Righteous, fair, just; stems from *adl*, meaning *justice*

ADHAMHNAN (OOM-nawn) Irish: Little Adam
Adamnan

ADIB (ah-deeb) Arabic: Polite, learned, cultured, honest; stems from Adab, a name meaning *manners*, which is also synonymous with culture and literature; masculine form of Adiba
Adeeb; **Famous namesakes:** Iranian national poet Adib Boroumand

ADIL (a-DEEL) Arabic: Similar, bundle, equal, like, brother-in-law; (Turkish) negotiation

ADIN (AY-din) Hebrew: Pleasure given. Adin was a biblical exile who returned to Israel from Babylon.

ADIR (ah-DEER) Hebrew: Powerful, mighty

ADISA (ah-DEE-sah) African: One who is clear

ADISH (AH-dish) Persian: Fire

ADIV (ah-DEEV) Hebrew: Delicate, gentle

ADKEN English: Made of oak; strong; variant of Aiken

ADKINS English: Made of oak, strong; son of Aiken
Atkinson, Atkinsone, Attkins

ADLAI (AD-lay, AD-lie) Hebrew: Refuge of God, justice of the Lord. Many will associate this name with politician Adlai Stevenson.
Adley; **Nicknames:** *Ad, Addey*

ADLER German: Eagle
Adlar

ADMETUS (ad-MEE-təs) Greek: A king of Pherae who was favored by Apollo, who gave him the gift of allowing another to take his place when it was time to die. His wife Alcestis offered, but the gods intervened and allowed both to continue life together.

ADNAN (AHD-nahn) Arabic: Abiding, stays in one place, he who loves land and makes it similar to Paradise, pleasurable. The latter meaning is derived from Gannat Adan (Paradise), the gardens of eternal abode.

ADNEY English: Lives on the noble's island; surname
Addaneye, Addney, Adny

ADOFO (ah-DO-fo) African: Fighter, warrior (Ghana)

ADOLPH (AH-dawlf, AY-dahlf) German: Noble wolf
(French) *Adolphus*; (Spanish) *Adolfo*; (Teutonic) *Adolf*; (Finnish) *Aatu*; **Old forms:** *Adalwolf*; **Nicknames:** *Dolph, Dolphus*

ADOM (ah-DOM) African: Receives help from the gods (Ghana)

ADON Hebrew: Lord, master

ADONAI (AH-do-nie) Hebrew: My Lord

ADONIS (ə-DAH-nəs) Greek: Extremely handsome. In Greek mythology, Adonis is a beautiful young man beloved of Aphrodite.

ADRIAN (AY-dree-ən) Latin: Dark; from the Adriatic Sea region
(Irish) *Aidrian*; (Dutch) *Arjan*; (Russian) *Adrik*; (Polish) *Adok*; (Hungarian) *Adojan*; *Adrien, Adrion, Adron, Andrion, Hadrien*; **Old forms:** *Hadrian*; **Star babies:** son of Edie Brickell and Paul Simon

ADRIEL (AY-dree-el) Hebrew: Of the flock of God, a member of God's congregation; (Native American) beaver, symbol of skill
Adriyel

ADRIK Russian: Variation of Adrian

ADVENT French: Born during Advent
Avent

AEGIS (AY-jəs, EE-jəs) Greek: Shield. In Greek mythology, Aegis was the goat-skin shield of Zeus and his daughter Athena.

AEKERMAN English: Man of oak, strong; a surname
Ackerman

AELLE (A-lə, EL-ə) Anglo-Saxon: Name of several Anglo-Saxon kings, including the first king of Deira in northern England
Aella, Aelli

AENEAS (i-NEE-əs) Greek: Praiseworthy; the Trojan warrior from Virgil's *Aeneid* (Spanish) *Eneas*; (Gaelic) *Aneas*

AENEDLEAH English: From the awe inspiring one's meadow; variant of Ansley

AENESCUMB English: Lives in the valley of the majestic one

AESIR (AY-zir, AY-sir) Norse: Of the gods

AESON (AY-sən) Greek: Mythological father of Jason. When Aeson was very old, Medea gave him the gift of a second youth.

AETHELRED (A-thəl-red) Anglo-Saxon: Noble counsel; an early Anglo-Saxon king of Wessex and Kent, son of Aethelwulf, brother of Aethelbald and Aethelberht
Ethelred

AETHELWULF (A-thəl-wuwlf) Anglo-Saxon: King or the West Saxons and father of King Alfred the Great
Ethelwulf

AFANEN Welsh: Raspberry

AGENOR (ah-JEE-nər) Greek: Mythological son of Poseidon, father of Europa and Cadmus

AGER (AH-her) Basque: Gathers

AGNI (AHG-nee) Hindi: Fire; in Hinduism, a fire god

AGRICAN (AH-gri-kahn) French: From the field
Famous namesakes: Agrican, king of Tartary

AHAB Hebrew: Uncle. Ahab was an Old Testament king and the husband of Jezebel, and the name was later given to a sea captain in Herman Melville's novel *Moby-Dick*.

AHANU (ah-HAH-noo) Native American: He laughs (Algonquin)

AHEARN Celtic: Lord of the horses (English) *Hearn, Hearne; Aherin, Ahern, Aherne*; **Nicknames:** *Aghy*

AHMAD (ah-MAHD, akh-MAHD) Arabic, Persian: Much praised, laudable; one of the Prophet Mohammed's many names
Amad, Amadi, Emad; Ahmed; **Famous namesakes:** Turkish writer Ahmed Mithat, Turkish head of state and writer Ahmed Vefik, football player and sports announcer Ahmad Rashad

AHMED (akh-MET, akh-MED) Arabic: The most praised
Ahmad

AHMIK (AH-mik) Native American: Beaver

AHTI (AH-tee) Finnish: God of water, sea, ocean

AIDAN (AY-dən) Irish, Gaelic: Little, fiery. Aidan is a modern English spelling of the early medieval Gaelic name Áedán. It was relatively common in early medieval Ireland, and was the name of at least two sixth- and seventh-century Celtic saints. In the late Middle Ages, the saint's name was spelled Aodhán, but the name appears to have dropped out of common use after the tenth century or so. Its modern popularity dates to a revival in the nineteenth or twentieth century.

AIDEN Gaelic: Spelling variation of Aidan

AIKEN (AY-kin) Anglo-Saxon: Made of oak, strong; a surname
(English) *Adkyn, Aiekin, Akker, Aeker, Aikin; Aitken;* See also *Adken;* **Famous namesakes:** Singer Clay Aiken

---

*"O Lord my God, that glib-tongued Aiken,
My very heart and soul are quakin'"*
—Robert Burns, "Holy Willie's Prayer"

AILBE German: Intelligent or noble

AILILL (AL-yil) Gaelic: Sprite; borne in Irish myth by the king of Connaught

AILIN (AY-lin) Irish: Variation of Alan

AIMO (IE-mo) Finnish: Generous amount

AINMIRE (AHN-meer) Irish: Great lord

AINSLEY Scottish, English: From his own meadow
Ainsleigh, Ainslie, Ansley, Aynsley

AINSWORTH (AYNZ-werth) English: From Ann's estate; a surname
Answorth

AITOR (ie-TOR) Basque: Good father; this name was created by Basque writer Agosti Xaho for his work "The Legend of Aitor."

AKAMU (ah-KAH-moo) Hawaiian: Variation of Adam

AKANDO (ah-KAHN-do) Native American: Ambush

AKBAR (AK-bahr) Persian: Big

AKECHETA Native American: Warrior (Sioux)

AKIBA (ah-KEE-bə, ah-KEE-və) Hebrew: Replaces, supplants; a variant of Akiva. Akiba was a Jewish rabbi, said to have lived in Jerusalem in the time of the Second Temple and to have devoted himself to the study of the law. Many sayings are transmitted in Akiba's name.

AKIL (ah-KEEL) Arabic: Masculine form of Akilah
Akeel

AKIO (ah-kee-o) Japanese: Bright boy

AKIVA (ah-KEE-vah) Hebrew: Replaces, supplants; variant of Yaakov (see Jacob); Akiva was the name of many renowned Talmudic scholars throughout history.
Akiba; Akavia, Akaviah, Akavya; **Nicknames:** *Kiba, Kiva*

AKKER English: Variation of Aiken

AKRAM (AHK-rahm) Arabic: More generous, more noble, more precious. Akram is the comparative form of the root word and adjective *karam*, meaning *generosity* and *nobility*.

AKUB Hebrew: Replaces

ALAIN (ah-LAYN) French: Variation of Alan
Alen

ALAIR Latin: Happy

ALAN Celtic: Handsome
(French) *Alain*; (Spanish) *Alano*; (Gaelic) *Ailean, Ailin*; (Scottish) *Ailein*; *Ailen, Allan, Allen*; **Nicknames:** *Al*; **Famous namesakes:** Astronaut Alan Shepard, actor Alan Alda, poet and writer Edgar Allan Poe

ALARD (AL-ard) Teutonic: Resolute

ALARIC (AL-ə-rik) German: Noble leader
(Spanish) *Alarico*; (Swedish) *Alrik*; (Danish) *Ulrik*; (Czech) *Oldrich*; *Alarick, Alarik, Aurick, Aurik, Udo, Ulric*; **Old forms:** *Ulrich*

ALAWN Welsh: Harmony

ALBA Italian: White; a place name

ALBAN Latin: White; from Alba, a city on a hill

ALBARIC French: Blond ruler

ALBERN English: Noble warrior, courageous; (Teutonic) noble bear
Alburn; **Old forms:** *Aethelbeorn*

ALBERT German: Noble, bright; Prince Albert was Queen Victoria's consort noted for enthusiastic support of the application of science to the modern industrial age. Albert Einstein developed the Theory of Relativity. (German) *Albrecht, Elbert*; (Italian)

Alberto; (Spanish) *Berto*; (Scottish) *Ailbert*; (Hungarian) *Béla*; *Aethelbeorht, Aethelberht, Aethelbert, Alburt, Dalbert, Delbert*; **Old forms:** *Adalbert, Adelbert*; **Nicknames:** *Al, Bertie, Bert*; **Famous namesakes:** Actor/director Albert Brooks, French philosopher Albert Camus

ALBIN Latin: White; related to Alba, a place
Albinus

ALBINUS Latin: White, pure; the name of a scholarly monk who encouraged Bede's creation of the *Ecclesiastical History of the English*

ALBRECHT (AHL-brekht) German: Variation of Albert
Famous namesakes: German artist Albrecht Dürer

ALBUS Latin: White; fictional character from *Harry Potter* series, Albus Dumbledore

ALCINOUS (al-SI-no-əs) Greek: A mythological king who entertained Odysseus

ALCOTT English: From the old cottage; surname
Alcot, Allcot, Allcott, Alkott

ALDEN English: Spelling variation of Alvin

ALDER English: From the alder tree

ALDFRITH (AHLD-vreeth) Anglo-Saxon: King of Northumbria known for his love of scholarship

ALDIS English: From the old house
Aldous, Aldus; Aldys, Aldisse

ALDO German, Italian: Old or wise, an elder; may also be a familar form of Aldous

ALDOUS (OLD-us) English: Spelling variation of Aldis

ALDRED (AL-drəd) Anglo-Saxon: Old counsel, old or wise advisor; a surname; (English) wise or red-haired man *Eldred, Eldrid; Alldred, Eldrid, Elldred*

ALDRICH (AL-dreech, AL-drək) Anglo-Saxon, English: Old and wise leader, noble ruler; a surname; (Teutonic) battle counsel (French) *Audric; Aldric, Aldrick, Aldrik, Aldrin, Eldrian, Eldrick, Eldridge*

ALDTUN English: From the old town, settlement

ALED (AH-led) Welsh: Offspring; a river in Denbighshire

ALEJANDRO (ah-lay-HAHN-dro) Spanish: Variation of Alexander

ALEKANEKELO (ah-le-kah-ne-KE-lo) Hawaiian: Variation of Alexander

ALEKSEI (ah-LYEK-syay, ah-LEK-say) Russian: Defender, helper; from the Greek word *alexein* (Ukrainian) *Alexio, Alexei;* **Old forms:** *Alexius;* **Nicknames:** *Alyosha;* **Diminutive forms:** *Alyoshenka;* **Famous namesakes:** Russian author Aleksey Tolstoy, Figure skater and Olympic champion Alexei Yagudin

ALERON (AH-lə-ron) French: Winged

ALEX English: Nickname for Alexander **Star babies:** son of Bob Hoskins

ALEXANDER Greek: Defends mankind; from the Greek word *Alexandros.* Alexander the Great was the king of Macedon, conqueror of much of Asia during 356-323 BC. See also *Zindel* (French) *Alexandre;* (Spanish) *Alejandro;* (Russian) *Aleksandr;* (Czech) *Aleksander, Ales;* (Polish) *Aleksy, Oles;* (Ukrainian) *Lyaksandro;* (Finnish) *Aleksanteri, Aleksi;* (Hungarian) *Elek,*

Sandor; (Persian) *Eskander;* (Turkish) *Iskender;* (Hawaiian) *Alekanekelo; Alexandrukas;* **Old forms:** *Alexandras, Alexandros;* **Nicknames:** *Alec, Aleck, Aleko, Alex, Alik, Leksi, Sacha, Sander, Sandro, Sandy, Santeri, Santtu, Sasha, Shura, Zander;* **Diminutive forms:** *Sashenka, Shurik;* **Famous namesakes:** Inventor Alexander Graham Bell, Russian swimmer Alexander Popov; **Star babies:** sons of Melanie Griffith and Steven Bauer, William Hurt

The Name
What is my name to you?
'T will die:
a wave that has but rolled
to reach
with a lone splash a
distant beach;
or in the timbered night a cry . . .

'T will leave a lifeless trace among names on your tablets: the design of an entangled gravestone line in an unfathomable tongue.

What is it then? A long-dead past, lost in the rush of madder dreams, upon your soul it will not cast Mnemosyne's pure tender beams.

But if some sorrow comes to you, utter my name with sighs, and tell the silence: "Memory is true— there beats a heart wherein I dwell."
—Alexander Pushkin

ALEXANDRE French: Variation of Alexander
Famous namesakes: French author
Alexandre Dumas

ALF Norse: Nickname for Alfred; Swedish:
Variation of Alfred

ALFRED (AL-frəd) Anglo-Saxon: Sage, elf
wisdom, implying an almost supernatural
understanding
(Italian) *Alfredo*; (Swedish) *Alf*; *Aelfraed*,
Aelfric, *Alfrid*, *Elfred*; *Ahlfred*, *Ailfred*, *Ailfrid*,
Ailfryd, *Alfeo*, *Alfredas*, *Alfrey*, *Alfredos*, *Avery*;
Nicknames: *Al*, *Alf*, *Alfey*, *Alfie*, *Alfy*, *Fred*,
Freddie, *Freddy*, *Fredo*; **Famous namesakes:**
Director Alfred Hitchcock, poet Alfred, Lord
Tennyson

ALFRID English: Spelling variation of Alfred

ALGAR (AL-gar) Anglo-Saxon: Elf-spear,
spearman; possible diminutive of Algernon
(German) *Alger*; (Celtic) *Ansgar*; (Norse)
Alfgeir; *Elgar*; **Famous namesakes:** Politician
Alger Hiss

ALGERNON (AL-jər-nahn) French:
Moustached
Algrenon

ALI (ah-LEE, AH-lee) Arabic, Persian:
Greatest, Lion of God; a variant of Allah,
one of the attributes of God. Storybook
hero Ali Baba was the main protagonist in *A
Thousand and One Nights: Ali Baba and the
Forty Thieves*. Boxing champion Muhammad
Ali (née Cassius Marcellus Clay) was named
a United Nations Messenger of Peace by
Secretary-General Kofi Annan.
Aly; *Aly*; **Famous namesakes:** Viceroy and
ruler of Egypt, Mohamed Ali (1769–1849),
was an Albanian born in Kavala. He founded
the Mohammed Ali Pasha Dynasty and
is sometimes alluded to as the founder of
modern Egypt.

ALICESON (AL-i-sən) English: Son of
Alice; Originally one of the few male names
to reference a woman, variants of Aliceson are
much more widely used for girls today.
Alycesone

ALIM (ah-LEEM) Arabic: Wise, learned,
omniscient, informed, knowing; one of the
attributes of God; (Hebrew) wise, learned
Abd al Alim; *Abdul Alim*, *Abdel Alim*, *El Alim*,
Al Alim

ALISTAIR Gaelic: Defender of mankind; an
Anglicized form of Alasdair, a Gaelic variant
of Alexander
(Irish) *Alsandair*; (Scottish) *Alastair*; *Alaster*,
Alistaire, *Alister*, *Allister*; **Nicknames:** *Alai*,
Alis; **Famous namesakes:** British broadcaster
Alistair Cooke

ALLARD English: Variation of Adalard

ALLEN Celtic: Spelling variation of Alan

ALOIN (ahl-əWAHN) French: Noble friend
Aluin

ALON (ah-lon) Hebrew: Oak tree
Allon

ALONZO (ah-LON-zo, ah-LAHN-zo)
Spanish: Variation of Alphonse
Nicknames: *Lonzo*; **Famous namesakes:**
Basketball player Alonzo Mourning

ALPHONSE (al-FAWNS) French: Ready and
noble, ready for battle; derived from the Old
German name Adelfuns. The variant Alfonso
is a royal name in Spain and Portugal.
(German) *Alphonso*; (Italian) *Alanzo*, *Alonso*,
Alonzo; (Spanish) *Alfonso*, *Foncho*, *Lonzo*;
(Swedish) *Alfons*; *Alphonsus*; **Old forms:**
Adelfuns; **Nicknames:** *Fonsie*, *Fonso*, *Fonzell*,
Fonzie, *Fonzo*, *Alphie*, *Alfy*, *Alphy*; **Famous
namesakes:** French author Alphonse Daudet,
Czech poster artist Alphonse Marie Mucha

> **Alphonse and Gaston** were two courteous comic strip characters created by Frederick Burr Opper, one of the most highly respected cartoonists of late 19th- and early 20th-century America.

ALRIC German: Rules all; the historical Gothic king who plundered Rome in AD 410. (English) *Alhrick, Alhrik*

ALSON English: Son of a specific person now unknown, possibly Alice or any of the English names beginning with *Al–*

ALSTON English: From the nobleman's town, possibly from the elf's town; surname *Aethelstun; Alsten, Alstin*

ALTAIR (ahl-tah-EER, ahl-TAYR) Arabic: Bird, poultry. Altair is the main star in the constellation Aquila, which is known as Orion in the western world.

ALTAN (ahl-TAHN) Turkish: Dawn

ALVAN Hebrew: Spelling variation of Alvin

ALVAR English: Army of elves (Spanish) *Alvaro, Alverio*

ALVER Latin: White

ALVIN English: Elf friend, noble friend, implies supernaturally good or wise friend (German) *Alvaro*; (Spanish) *Aluino*; (Teutonic) *Alcuin, Alwin, Alwyn, Aylmer, Aylwin; Adalwen, Adalwin, Adalwine, Aelfdane, Aelfdene, Alden, Aldin, Aldwin, Aldwyn, Alvan, Alvar, Alvyn, Audwin, Audwine, Aylwyn, Eldwin, Eldwyn, Elvern, Elvin, Elvyn, Elwen, Elwin, Elwyn*; **Nicknames:** *Alvy, Elvey, Elvy*; **Famous namesakes:** Popular singing chipmunk

ALVIS (AHL-vis) English: All-knowing

AMADEO (ah-mah-DAY-o) Spanish: Variation of Amadeus
Star babies: son of John Turturro

AMADEUS (ahm-ə-DAY-əs) Latin: Loved by God. Easily recognized as the name of Wolfgang Amadeus Mozart, an Austrian composer considered one of history's best and most creative musical geniuses (French) *Amado*; (Italian) *Amadeo, Amedeo*; *Amadou*

AMADO (ah-MAH-do) Spanish: Variation of Amadeus

AMASA (ah-MAY-sə) Hebrew: Burden. The biblical Amasa is King David's nephew.

AMAUD (ah-MO) French: Eagle ruler

AMAURY (a-mo-REE) French: Name of a count

AMBROSE (AM-broz) Greek: Immortal; Saint Ambrose was a fourth-century bishop of Milan.
(Italian) *Ambrosi*; (Spanish) *Ambrosio*; (Welsh) *Emrys*; (Swedish) *Ambrosius*; (Czech) *Ambroz*; (Hungarian) *Ambrus*

AMERY German: Divine; (Teutonic) hard working; (Irish) ridge; long hill

AMES English: Friend, love; surname adapted to first name use
Aimes, Aymes

AMIN (ah-meen) Arabic, Persian: Honest, trustworthy, guardian, faithful, loyal, steadfast, safe. Amin is also a word used in religious celebrations, as in *amen* (yes, be it so).
Famous namesakes: Afghan political leader Hafizollah Amin, Lebanese president Amin Gemayel, author Samir Amin

AMIR (a-MEER) Arabic, Persian: Prince, commanding; (Hebrew) strong, powerful

Aamir, Aamer, Amer, Amire, Amiri, Ameer, Amyr; **Famous namesakes:** Indonesian poet Amir Hamzah, Indian poet Amir Khusrau; **Star babies:** son of Mike Tyson

AMIRAM Hebrew: My people are mighty

AMIT (u-mit) Sanskrit: Immeasurable

AMITABHA (AH-mee-TAH-bhah) Hindi: One with immeasurable splendor

AMJAD (ah-MAHD) Arabic: Commendable; (Persian) most excellent, glorious

AMMAR (ah-MAHR) Arabic: Builder, constructor
El Ammar, Al Ammar; **Famous namesakes:** Former Palestinian president Yasser Arafat was known as Abu Ammar, the Builder Father

AMMIEL Hebrew: People of the Lord. Several biblical characters carry this name, including one of the spies sent to Canaan by Moses and Bathsheba's father.
Amiel

AMNON Hebrew: Faithful; biblical son of King David
Aminon

AMON (AH-mən) Egyptian: The great god of Thebes of uncertain origin. This god is also the Hermopolitian Ogdoad and is represented as a man, sometimes ithyphallic. Identified with Ra as Amon-Ra, sacred animals, the ram, and the goose, Amon was part of the Theban Triad, along with Mut and Khonsu; (Hebrew) hidden, possibly builder; name of one of the kings of Judah
Amun; Amen, Ammon, Amun

AMORY English: Variation of Emery

AMOS (AY-məs) Hebrew: Burden carried; the name of one of the twelve minor prophets of the Jewish faith.
Star babies: son of Andrea Bocelli

AMOUR (ah-MOR) French: Love

AMPHION (am-FIE-ən) Greek: Mythological son of the god Zeus and Antiope, he was a king of Thebes known for his supernatural musical abilities

AMPHITRYON (am-FI-tree-ən) Greek: The mythological husband of Alcmene

AMR (AH-mer) Arabic: Flourishing, thriving

AMREN Welsh: Legendary son of Bedwyr

AMSDEN English: From Ambrose's valley

AMYCUS (AM-i-cəs) Greek: Mythical son of Poseidon and the nymph Melia, he was king of the Bebryces and famous for his boxing skills

AN (AHN) Vietnamese: Peace

ANAKIN (AN-a-kin) Contemporary: The name of the character who eventually became Darth Vader in the *Star Wars* movie saga.

ANAKONI (an-ah-KO-nee) Hawaiian: Variation of Anthony

ANAND (ah-nund) Hindi: Happiness

ANASTASIUS Greek: Resurrection
(Italian) *Anastagio*; (Spanish) *Anastacio, Anastasio*; (Slavic) *Stasio; Anstice*

ANATOLE (ah-nah-TOL) French: Sunrise, the east
(Italian) *Anatolio*; (Russian) *Anatoli, Anatoly*; (Polish) *Anatol*; **Old forms:** *Anatolius*; **Nicknames:** *Tolya*

ANCAEUS (an-SEE-əs) Greek: An Argonaut and the mythological son of Zeus

Noble Names for Leaders

Certain your baby is destined for greatness? Peruse this list of names that mean "noble" or "leader."

Boys' Names	Girls' Names
Alaric (German)	Adalina (Teutonic)
Albert (German)	Adena (Hebrew)
Aldrich (Anglo-Saxon)	Alberta (German)
Alphonse (French)	Alfonsa (Spanish)
Barnett (English)	Alice (German)
Baron (Teutonic)	Allyn (Gaelic)
Bryce (Anglo-Saxon)	Aubrey (French)
Caeser (French)	Audrey (Anglo-Saxon)
Cedric (English)	Bricelyn (English)
Coyle (Irish)	Brylee (American)
Derek (English)	Delma (German)
Donald (Scottish)	Dereka (English)
Duke (Latin)	Donelle (Latin)
Earl (English)	Earlene (English)
Eric (Norse)	Edlyn (English)
Errol (German)	Elmira (English)
Eugene (Greek)	Elsa (German)
Herrick (German)	Erica (Norse)
Hiram (Hebrew)	Ethel (Anglo-Saxon)
Howard (English)	Farica (Teutonic)
Lonzo (Spanish)	Freda (German)
Melvin (Celtic)	Frederica (German)
Malloy (Irish)	Freya (Norse)
Nolan (Irish)	Kendra (English)
Patrick (Latin)	Latrice (African)
Quentin (Latin)	Milla (Finnish)
Rajah (Sanskrit)	Patricia (Latin)
Richard (German)	Rikka (Teutonic)
Sherif (Arabic)	Sherifah (Arabic)
Thanos (Greek)	Zalika (African)

ANCHISES (an-KIE-seez) Greek: Mythological father of Aeneas, belonging to the royal family of Troy

ANCIL (ahn-SEEL) French: Adherent of a nobleman
Ansel, Ansell

ANDERS Scandinavian: Variation of Andrew
Ander, Anderson, Andersson

ANDRE (awn-DRAY) French: Manly, brave
Famous namesakes: André Previn

ANDRES (ahn-DRAYS) Spanish: Variation of Andrew

ANDREW Greek, English, Scottish: Manly, brave; from the Greek Andreas. In the Bible, Andrew is the first of the twelve apostles chosen by Jesus and the brother of Peter. Andrew is a patron saint of Greece, Scotland, and Russia. (Greek) *Andreus, Andries, Aniol*; (English) *Andrian, Andric, Andriel*; (German) *Andreas*; (Italian) *Andino*; (Spanish) *Andreo, Andres*; (Portuguese) *Andre*; (Gaelic) *Aindreas*; (Scottish) *Kendrew*; (Welsh) *Andras*; (Scandinavian) *Ander, Anders, Anderson*; (Danish) *Anker*; (Slavic) *Andrei, Andrej, Andrik*; (Russian) *Andrusha*; (Czech) *Ondrej*; (Polish) *Andrzej, Jedrej, Jedrek, Jedrick, Jedrik*; (Finnish) *Antero*; (Hungarian) *Andor, Endre*; *Andrea, Andrey, Androu; Andruw*; **Nicknames:** *Andy, Dru, Tero, Drew*; **Famous namesakes:** Former president Andrew Jackson, Former president Andrew Johnson, Prince Andrew, the Duke of York, actor Andy Garcia, actor Andy Griffith, artist Andy Warhol, baseball player Andruw Jones, composer, Andrew Lloyd Webber, film director Andrei Tarkovsky; **Star babies:** son of Faith Daniels

ANGEL (ahn-HEL, AYN-jəl) Greek, Spanish: Messenger from God
(Italian) *Angelino, Angelo; Angell*

ANGUS (ANG-gəs) Scottish, Gaelic: One choice, one strength; the god of love in Celtic mythology
Aengus, Aonghus, Oengus, Ungus; Aengus, Anghus; **Nicknames:** *Gus*; **Star babies:** sons of Gordon Elliott, Amanda Pays and Corbin Bernsen, Donald Sutherland

ANLON (AHN-lun) Irish: Champion
Anluan

ANOKI (ah-NO-kee) Native American: Actor

ANSCOM English: From the valley of the majestic one; surname
Anscomb; Anscombe

ANSELM (AN-selm) Teutonic: God's protection. Saint Anselm was a twelfth-century archbishop of Canterbury and an influential theologian and church leader. (English) *Ansel, Ansell*; (Spanish) *Anselino, Anselmo, Anzelmo, Chemo, Selmo*; **Famous namesakes:** Photographer Ansel Adams

ANSLEY English: From the awe-inspiring one's meadow; surname
Aenedleah, Ainslie, Ansleigh; Ainslea, Ainslee, Ainsleigh, Ainsly, Annslea, Annsliegh, Annsley, Anslea, Anslie, Ansly

ANSON English, Anglo-Saxon, German: Anne's son; surname adapted to first name use
Hanson

ANTAEUS (an-TEE-əs) Greek: Mythological giant killed by Hercules

ANTHONY Latin: Roman clan name of uncertain etymology; popular definitions include highly praiseworthy and priceless (German) *Anton*; (French) *Antoine, D'anton, Danton*; (Italian) *Antonio*; (Spanish) *Tonio*; (Swedish) *Antonius*; (Basque) *Antton*; (Hungarian) *Antal*; (Hawaiian) *Akoni, Anakoni*; *Antoin, Antonin, Antoniy, Antony*; **Nicknames:** *Tony*; **Diminutive forms:** *Antonino*; **Famous namesakes:** Actor Anthony Hopkins, actor Anthony Perkins, actor Anthony Quinn, actor Antonio Banderas, composer Antonin Dvorak; **Star babies:** sons of Joan Collins, Jerry Lewis, Gregory Peck, Veronica Lake, Angela Lansbury

ANTON (ahn-TOHN) Russian: Variation of Anthony
Nicknames: *Antosha, Tosha, Toshka*; **Star babies:** son of Beverly D'Angelo and Al Pacino

ANTRANIG (AN-tra-neeg) Armenian: First born

ANTTI (AHN-tee) Finnish: Form of Andrew

ANWAR (AHN-wahr) Arabic: Luminous; President of Egypt Anwar el Sadat presided over Egypt from 1970 until his assasination in 1981. At Camp David, he signed the first peace treaty with Israel in 1978 and obtained the Nobel Peace Prize of the year.
Famous namesakes: Actress Gabrielle Anwar, Indonesian poet Chairil Anwar

APIS (AY-pis) Egyptian: Seen as the bull with a solar disk between its horns, Apis was associated with the gods Osiris and Ptah. See also Serapis.

APOLLO (ə-PAH-lo) Greek: Manly beauty. In Greek mythology, Apollo was one of the most important gods. He was the son of Zeus and Leto, and the twin brother of Artemis. Apollo was the god of music, prophecy, colonization, medicine, archery (though not war), poetry, dance, and intellectual inquiry. He was also a god of light and the sun.

AQUILINO (ah-kee-LEE-no) Spanish: Eagle

ARAGORN Literature: Central character in J.R.R. Tolkien's *The Lord of the Rings*, Aragorn is the heir of the Numenorean kings, and the one who finally returns to take back the throne.

ARAMIS (ahr-ah-MEE) French: Fictional swordsman from Alexandre Dumas' *Three Musketeers*

ARASH (ah-RASH) Persian: Hero

ARCAS Greek: Son of Zeus and the nymph Callisto, whom Hera turned into a bear. When hunting one day, Arcas prepared to kill the bear, not realizing it was his mother. Zeus intervened and transformed the two of them into the constellations Ursa Major and Ursa Minor, forever honoring them.

ARCHARD Anglo-Saxon, German: Sacred; (French) powerful
(German) *Eckerd, Ekhard*; *Archerd, Ekerd, Erkerd*; **Old forms:** *Erchanhardt*

ARCHER Latin, English: Bowman; an occupational name and English surname adapted to first name use
Archere

ARCHIE English: Nickname for Archibald
Nicknames: *Arch*

ARDAL (AHR-dahl) Irish: High honor
Ardghal, Artegal, Arthgallo

ARDELL Latin: Eager, industrious; (English) from the hare's dell
Ardel

ARDEN Latin: Fervent
Ardin

ARDLEY English: From the home lover's meadow
Ardaleah, Ardleigh; Ardlea, Ardsley, Ardsly

ARDOLF English: Home loving wolf
Ardolph, Ardwolf

AREF Persian: Wise

ARES (AYR-eez) Greek: God of war; son of Zeus and Hera

ARGO (AHR-go) Greek: Mythological name of Jason's ship

ARGUS (AR-gəs) Greek: Shining; a mythological figure whose hundred eyes, following his death, were said to be transferred by Hera to the tail of the peacock.

ARI (AHR-ee) Hebrew: Lion
Arie

ARIBERT (ah-ree-BAYR) French: Variation of Herbert

ARIC Norse: Spelling variation of Eric
Aaric, Arick, Arik, Arrick

ARIEL (AR-ee-əl, ER-ee-əl) Hebrew: Lion of God, a biblical name for Jerusalem; Shakespeare's name for a mischievous spirit in *The Tempest*.
Arye, Aryeh; Arel, Aryel, Aryell; **Famous namesakes:** Former Israeli Prime Minister Ariel Sharon

ARIF (ah-REEF) Arabic: Knowing, knowledgeable, acquainted, expert
Areef

ARION (ə-RI-ən) Greek: A Greek poet and musician

ARISTO (ə-RIS-to) Greek: Best

ARJAN (AHR-yahn) Dutch: Variation of Adrian

ARJUN (ur-juwn) Hindi: White, clear

ARKADI (ahr-KAH-dee) Russian: Native of Arcadia, an ancient pastoral region in Greece
Old forms: *Arkadios*; **Diminutive forms:** *Arkasha*

ARLEDGE English: Lake of the hares; a surname and variant of Harlake
Arlidge, Arlledge, Arrledge

ARLEN Irish, Gaelic: Pledge
Arlyn

ARLEY (AHR-lee) English: From the hare's meadow; variant of Harley
Arlea, Arleigh, Arlie, Arly

ARLO English: Spelling variation of Harlow
Famous namesakes: Folk singer Arlo Guthrie

ARMAN (ahr-mahn) Persian: Ideal

ARMAND (ar-MAWN) French: Variation of Herman
Famous namesakes: Actor Armand Assante

ARMAS (AR-mas) Finnish: Dear

ARMO (AHR-mo) Finnish: Mercy, grace

ARMON Hebrew: High fortress
(Italian) *Armond, Armondo*; (Teutonic) *Armino, Armonno; Armen, Armin*

ARMSTRONG English: Strong-armed

ARNAN Hebrew: Roaring stream

ARNETT English: Little eagle
Arnatt, Arnet, Arnott; Ornet, Ornette

ARNOLD Teutonic: Strong as an eagle
(Italian) *Arnaldo*; (Danish) *Arend*; (Finnish)
Aarne, Aarno; **Nicknames:** *Arnie, Arny*;
Famous namesakes: Actor and politician
Arnold Schwarzenegger, golfer Arnold Palmer

ARRIGO Italian: Variation of Harry

ARSALAN (ar-za-lahn) Persian: Lion
Arzalan

ARSEN (AHR-sen) Armenian: Variation of
Arsenios

ARSENIOS Greek: Strong and virile
(Greek) *Arsenio*; (Russian) *Arseni, Senya*;
(Armenian) *Arsen*; *Arsene*; **Famous
namesakes:** Actor and TV personality
Arsenio Hall

ARSHIA Persian: Throne
Arshya

ART English: Nickname for Arthur

ARTAY Persian: Strong

ARTEMII (ahr-TYEH-mee) Russian:
Healthy, wholesome
Nicknames: *Artem*

ARTHUR English: Noble, courageous;
possibly related to the obscure Roman family
name Artorius. Other possible sources include
an Irish Gaelic word meaning *stone*, and *artos*,
the Celtic word for *bear*. Most English speakers
will associate this name with legendary King
Arthur. Also, from the Icelandic, meaning a
follower of Thor, the Norse god of war.
(French) *Artus*; (Italian) *Arturo*; (Portuguese)
Artur; (Gaelic) *Artuir*; (Finnish) *Arttu,
Artturi*; **Nicknames:** *Art, Artie, Turi, Art,
Artie, Arty*; **Famous namesakes:** Musician
Art Garfunkel, tennis player Arthur Ashe,
playwright Arthur Miller

ARTIE English: Nickname for Arthur

ARUB Arabic: Eloquent, speaks perfectly
correct grammatical language, close to. Arub
is derived from *korb* (closeness) and in this
context may mean *loves his wife*. In colloquial
Egyptian Arabic, this word is sometimes used
to describe someone who is wily.

ARUN (ar-roon) Hindi: Sunrise

ARVAD Hebrew: Wanderer
(Hungarian) *Arpad*

ARVEL (AHR-vel) Welsh: Cried over
Arvil

ARVIN German, English, Teutonic: Friend of
the people
Arvis, Arvon, Arwin, Arwyn; **Nicknames:**
Arvie

ARWIN English: Spelling variation of Arvin

ARWOOD English: Spelling variation of
Garwood

ARYE Hebrew: Spelling variation of Ariel

ASA (AY-sə) Hebrew: Healer, physician;
name of one of the kings of Judah

ASAD (ah-SAHD) Arabic, Hindi, Persian:
Form of Abbas
Famous namesakes: Former president of
Syria Hafez El Asad

ASAPH Hebrew: Collector; biblical singer in
King David's choir
Asaf, Asif, Asiph

ASCOT English: From the eastern cottage.
An ascot is commonly known as a broad neck
scarf or tie which is considered sophisticated
and is usually worn with formal wear. Berkshire,
England hosts the famous Ascot horse races.
(English) *Ascott*; *Estcot, Estcott*

ASGARD (AZ-gahrd) Norse: Mythical city of the gods

ASH English: Ash tree; the root of several English names and therefore a familiar variant of them, including Ashley and Ashton (Norse) *Ask*; *Ashe*

ASHBURN English: Lives near the ash tree brook; surname
Aesoburne

ASHBY English, Scandinavian: From the ash tree farm; surname
Aescby; **Nicknames:** *Ash*

ASHER Hebrew: Happy, blessed. In the Bible, Jacob blessed his eighth son, Asher, with a life of abundance.
Anschel, Anshel

ASHFORD English: From the ford near the ash trees; surname
Aescford, Aisford; *Ashenford*; **Nicknames:** *Ash*

ASHKAN (ash-kahn) Persian: Name of the third dynasty of Persian kings

ASHKII (ash-kee-ee) Native American: Boy (Navajo)

ASHLEY English: From the ash tree meadow
Aescleah, Aisley, Ashly; *Ashleigh*; **Star babies:** sons of Barry Gibb, George Hamilton

ASHLIN English: Lives near the ash tree pool
Aesclin

ASHRAF (ASH-rahf) Arabic: Most honorable, noble. Ashraf is the superlative form of Sherif.

ASHTON English: From the town or settlement near the ash trees; surname
Aesctun, Aiston, Ashtin; **Nicknames:** *Ash*;
Famous namesakes: Actor Ashton Kutcher

ASHUR (AH-shuwr) Assyrian: Warlike; name used by an Assyrian god of war
Ashour

ASIM (ah-SEEM) Arabic: Spelling variation of Kasim
Asem, Kasim, Kasem

ASLAN (AHS-lahn) Turkish, Persian: Lion. Parents and children will recognize Aslan as the majestic golden lion who rules Narnia in the classic C.S. Lewis book *The Lion, the Witch and the Wardrobe*, part of the Chronicles of Narnia series.

ASPEN (AS-pən) American: Type of tree noted for heart-shaped leaves that flutter in the slightest breeze; Place name and ski resort town in Colorado
Aspyn, Aspin

ASWAD (ahs-WAHD) Arabic: Black

ASWIN (AS-win) Anglo-Saxon: Spear-friend, implies a close and trusted companion
Aescwine, Aescwyn, Ashwin, Ashwyn; *Aswyn, Aswynn, Aswynne*

ATA (AH-tah) Egyptian: Twin; (Turkish) ancestor

ATASH (ah-tash) Persian: Fire

ATEN (AH-tən) Egyptian: God of the sun-disk, worshipped as the great creator-god by Akhenaten in the Eighteenth Dynasty

ATHDAR Gaelic: From the oak tree ford; variant of Adair
Athdair, Athdara, Athdare

ATHELSTAN (A-thəl-stan) Anglo-Saxon: First West Saxon king to have effective rule over all England
Aethelstan; *Ethelstan*

ATHERTON English: From the town or settlement near the spring; surname
Aethretun

ATIF (AH-teef) Arabic: Compassionate, affectionate
Ateef; Atef

ATIRA (ah-TEE-rə) Hebrew: Pray

ATLAS (AT-ləs) Greek: Carried. In mythology, Atlas was forced by Zeus to carry the heavens on his shoulders forever as a punishment after he and the other Titans fought an unsuccessful war against Zeus and the Olympian gods.

ATMORE English: From the moor; surname
Attmore

ATTIS (A-tis) Latin: A solar and vegetation god, said to be a handsome child
Atys

ATUM (AH-təm) Egyptian: The original sun-god of Heliopolis who was later identified as Ra (Re). Atum was a primordial god that was represented in the form of a human and a serpent. He was the supreme god in the Heliopolitan Ennead (group of nine gods) and formed with Re to create Re-Atum.

ATWATER English: From near the water; surname
Attewater

ATWELL English: Lives near the well; surname
Attewell, Attwell

ATWOOD English: Lives near or in the woods; surname
Attewode; Atwoode; **Nicknames:** *Woody*

ATWORTH English: At the farmstead; surname
Atteworthe

AUBERON (O-bər-ahn) English: Rules with elf-wisdom, highborn; possible variant of Aubrey
Auberron, Oberron, Oeberon

AUBREY (AWB-ree) French, English, Teutonic: Elf ruler, implying leadership with supernatural wisdom
Aubry

AUDEL English: From the ancient valley or dell; surname
Audell

AUDEN English: Old friend; possible variant of Aidan
Audyn

AUDLEY (AWD-lee) Anglo-Saxon, English: From the ancient meadow; surname
Audie; Audlea, Audlee

AUDRICK German: Variation of Eric

AUDUN (OW-doon, OW-dun) Norse: Friend of wealth. Audun the Westfjorder was a central character in Grettir's Saga

AUGUST Latin: Spelling variation of Augustine
Star babies: son of Lena Olin

AUGUSTINE (AW-gə-steen, aw-GUS-tən) Latin: Majestic. Saint Augustine was the first archbishop of Canterbury.
(Spanish) *Agustin*; (Irish) *Aguistin*; (Polish) *Augustyn*; (Finnish) *Aukusti*; (Hungarian) *Agoston; Agustine, August, Augustin, Austen*;
Nicknames: *Augusty, Austin*

AUGUSTUS Latin: Majestic dignity, grandeur

AUHERT (o-HAYR) French: Noble

AULEY Irish: Variation of Olaf

AURA (OR-ə) Greek: Soft breeze

AURELIUS (aw-REL-ee-əs) Latin: Golden, blond
(French) *Aurelien*; (Italian) *Aurelio*; (Spanish) *Aureliano*; (Polish) *Aurek, Aureli*; *Aurelian*; **Famous namesakes:** Roman emperor Marcus Aurelius Antoninus

AURIVILLE (or-ee-VEE) French: From the gold town

AUSTIN English: Nickname for Augustine
Austyn; **Star babies:** sons of David Lynch, Sela Ward, Rebbie Jackson and Nathaniel Brown, Tommy Lee Jones, Paula Zahn, Michelle Phillips

AVALLACH Celtic: Related to the island of Avalon in Arthurian legend and Celtic mythology
Aballach

AVAON Welsh: Legendary son of Talyessin

AVATARA (ah-vah-tah-rah) Hindi: Descending

AVEDIS (AHV-a-des) Armenian: Brings good news

AVENELLE (ah-ven-EL) French: Lives near the oat field
Avenall, Aveneil

AVERILL Anglo-Saxon, English: Boar or boar warrior; born in April
Averell, Averil, Haverill; *Averel, Averyl, Avrel, Avrell, Avrill, Avryll, Haverell*; **Nicknames:** *Ave*

AVERY (AYV-ree, AY-vər-ee) Anglo-Saxon: Elf ruler, implying leadership with supernatural wisdom
Averey

AVI (ah-VEE) Hebrew: Aramaic variation of *abba*, meaning *father*.

AVIRIT Hebrew: Air

AVISHAI Hebrew: Gift from God
Avisha; *Abishai, Avshai*

AVITAL Hebrew: Father of dew; one of King David's sons
Abital, Avitul

AVIV (ah-VEEV) Hebrew: Spring, youth

AVONMORE Irish: From the great river

AXEL German, Hebrew, Scandinavian: Variation of Absalom
(Finnish) *Akseli*; *Aksel, Axl*; **Nicknames:** *Ax, Axe*; **Famous namesakes:** Singer Axl Rose

AXTON English: English surname related to a place, possibly the swordsman's town

AYDIN (IE-den) Turkish: Enlightened

AYERS English: Heir to a fortune; Ayers rock is an impressive and memorable landmark in Australia.

AYLMER (AYL-mer) English: Spelling variation of Elmer
Aillmer, Allmer, Aylmer

AYLWARD English, Teutonic: Awesome guardian, noble protector
Old forms: *Aethelweard, Athelward*; **Nicknames:** *Aegelweard, Ward*

AYO (AH-yo) African: Happiness

AZ Hebrew: Mighty

AZAD (ah-zahd) Persian: Free

AZARIAH (ah-zə-RIE-ə) Hebrew: Help of God; the name of numerous biblical characters
Azaria, Azaryah, Azaryahu, Azuriah; Azria, Azriah, Azuria, Azariahu, Azorya

AZIBO African: Youth (Nigeria)
Azy

AZIEL Hebrew: God is my strength

AZIM (ah-ZEEM) Arabic: Resolute, steady, determined; adjective that stems from Azm or Azima, meaning determination
Azmi; Azem, Azeem

AZIZ (ah-ZEEZ) Arabic: Cherished, beloved (Egyptian) *Azizi*

AZRAEL (ahz-ree-AYL) Hebrew: God is my help. In both Muslim and Jewish tradition, Azrael is the angel who parts the soul from the body at death.
Azriel

AZZAM (AH-zam) Arabic: Determined, resolved

BABAK (BAH-bak) Persian: Little father

BAC Scottish: Bank

BACCHUS (BAK-əs) Latin: Roman mythological god of wine, poetry, and revelry; equated with the Greek god Dionysus
Baccus

BADR (BAH-der) Arabic: Full moon. Badr is a site southwest of Medinah, Saudi Arabia, where Mohammed achieved victory over a Quoraychite caravan.

BADRU (BAH-droo) Egyptian: Born during the full moon

BAHAM Arabic: Lamb, calf, kid, to wean, brave, hero, difficult task

BAHIR (bah-HEER) Arabic: Dazzling, brilliant, splendid; masculine form of Bahira
Baheer

BAHRAM (BAH-rahm) Persian: Name of a Persian king; also the planet Mars

BAILEY English: Steward or law enforcer, from occupation of bailiff; surname adapted to first name use
Bayley; Baileigh, Bailie, Bayleigh; **Star babies:** sons of Anthony Edwards, Tracey Gold

BAINBRIDGE Gaelic, English: Lives near the pale bridge, a bridge over white water
Bainbrydge, Bainhrydge; **Old forms:** *Banbrigge;* **Nicknames:** *Bain*

BAIRD English, Celtic, Scottish: Minstrel; a medieval musical entertainer
Bard; Bayrd

BAKARI (bah-KAH-ree) Egyptian: Noble oath

BAKER English: Spelling variation of Baxter

BAKLI Norse: Son of Blaeng

BALARAMA (ba-lah-RAH-mah) Hindi: Powerful and blissful

BALDER (BAWL-der) Norse: Brave; the mythological son of Odin
Baldr, Baldur; **Old forms:** *Baldhere*

BALDRIK (BAL-drək) German: Bold (Anglo-Saxon) *Baldlice;* (Danish) *Balduin; Baldric*

BALE English: Spelling variation of Vail

BALEN Latin: Brave; (Arthurian legend) brother of Balaan

BALIN (BAH-leen) Hindi: Mighty warrior; (Arthurian legend) brother of Balaan

BALINT (BAH-leent) Hungarian: Variation of Valentine

BALMORAL (bal-MOR-əl) Scottish: From the majestic village. Balmoral Castle in Aberdeenshire, Scotland, has been the Scottish home of the royal family since it was purchased for Queen Victoria by Prince Albert in 1852.

BALTAZAR (bahl-tah-ZAHR) Spanish: Protect the king; the name traditionally given to one of the three wise men of the New Testament
(Greek) *Baltsaros*; (German) *Baltasar*

BAMDAD (bahm-dahd) Persian: Early morning

BANAN (BAWN-an) Irish: White

BANBHAN (BANV-awn) Irish: Piglet

BANCROFT English: From the bean field; surname
Benecroft; *Banfield*; **Nicknames:** *Ban, Bank, Binky*

BANNING Gaelic: Little blond one; (English) son of the slayer

BAPTISTE (bap-TEEST) Greek, French: Baptizer; named for John the Baptist

BARACK (bah-RAHK) Arabic: Blessing
Barak; **Famous namesakes:** President Barack Obama

BARAK (BER-ək, BAR-ək) Hebrew: Flash of lightning. In the Bible, the faithful fighter Barak cooperated with Deborah to win victory in battle against overwhelming odds.
Barrak

BARAM (bah-RAM) Hebrew: Son of the nation

BARAN Teutonic: Noble fighter or Ram; (Gaelic) noble warrior

BARCLAY (BAR-klay) Anglo-Saxon, English, Scottish: From the birch tree meadow. Barclay is the name of one of the largest banks in England. Also a surname; see Berkeley and Bartley
Bercleah

BARD English: Spelling variation of Baird

BARDEN English: Lives near the boar's den
Bardan

BARDOLF English: Ax-wielding wolf, ferocious;
Bardalph, Bardolph, Bardulf, Barwolf; Bardou, Bardoul, Bardulph; **Old forms:** *Bardawulf*

"Bardolph is fortune's foe"
—Shakespeare's *Henry V*

BARDON English: Minstrel, a singer-poet.

BARI (BAHR-ee) Arabic: Beneficent, righteous, godly, creator; attributes of Allah

BARLOW English: Lives on the bare hill

BARNABAS (BAHR-nə-bəs) Hebrew: Son of exhortation, from the Aramaic *barnebhu ah*. The biblical Barnabas was the missionary companion of the apostle Paul.
(German) *Bamey*; (French) *Barnabe, Bernabe*; **Nicknames:** *Barnaby, Barney, Barny*

BARNETT English: Nobleman, leader
Barnet

BARNEY English: Nickname for Barnabas

BARNHAM English: From the baron's house

BARNUM English: From the nobleman's home

BARON (BER-ən) English, French, Teutonic: Warrior; a title of nobility used as a given name; (Hebrew) derived from phrase Bar Aaron, meaning son of Aaron
Barrin, Barron; **Star babies:** son of Donald Trump

BARRA Celtic: Marksman

BARRETT German: Mighty as a bear or a variant of Barnett
Barret

BARRI (BAHR-ee) Welsh: Mound, summit

BARRIC (BAHR-ik) English: From the barley or the grain farm; surname
Barrick, Beric

BARRINGTON English: A town in England; refers to a fenced-in place; (Irish) fair-haired
Nicknames: *Barry*

BARRIS Welsh: Son of Harry
Barrys

BARRY Gaelic: Like a spear
Famous namesakes: Actor Barry Pepper, baseball player Barry Bonds, Australian actor Barry Humphries; **Star babies:** son of Dick Van Dyke

BART English: Nickname for Bartholomew
Famous namesakes: Football player Bart Starr

BARTHOLOMEW (bahr-THAHL-ə-myoo) Hebrew: Farmer, son of the earth; one of Christ's twelve apostles

(Hebrew) *Bartel*; (Spanish) *Bartoli, Bartolo, Bartolome, Toli*; (Gaelic) *Parlan, Parthalan*; (Swedish) *Bartholomeus*; (Danish) *Bardo*; (Czech) *Bartolomej*; (Finnish) *Perttu*; (Hungarian) *Bartalan*; (Aramaic) *Barthelemy*; *Bartley, Bartol*; **Nicknames:** *Bart, Barta, Barth, Bartlett, Batt, Bartlet, Bartlitt*

BARTLETT English: The farmer's son. This surname is also a variant of Bartholomew. John Bartlett's *Familiar Quotations* is one to the most referenced resources for speech writers and students in the English language.
Bartlet, Bartlitt

BARTLEY English, Scottish: From Bart's meadow, from the birch-tree meadow; probable variant of Barclay or Berkeley
Bartleah, Bartleigh

BARTON English: From the barley town of settlement; surname
Beretun; Barten, Barrton; **Nicknames:** *Bart*

BARTRAM Danish: Glorious raven. The raven was consecrated to the Norse war god Odin and was the emblem of the Danish royal standard.
(English) *Barthram*

BARUCH (BER-ook, BAHR-ook) Hebrew: Variation of Bennett

BASHIR (ba-SHEER) Arabic: Messenger, brings good news, herald; Eid el Bishara is the Feast of the Annunciation
Bashar, Basheer; Basheer, Bachir; **Famous namesakes:** Lebanese military commander and politician Bashir Gemayel

BASIL (BAZ-il) English: Kingly: Saint Basil the Great was a fourth-century bishop who was one of the fathers of the early Christian church. This was also the name of two Byzantine emperors.
(Greek) *Basile, Bazyli*; (Spanish) *Basilio*;

(Swedish) *Basmus*; (Dutch) *Basilius*; (Russian) *Vasily, Vassily*; **Nicknames:** *Vasya*; **Diminutive forms:** *Vasek*; **Star babies:** son of Dave Foley and Tabitha Southley

BAXTER English: Baker; an occupational surname transferred to first name use in 19th century
Baker; **Old forms:** *Backstere, Baecere*; **Nicknames:** *Bax*

BAYARD (BAY-erd) French, English: Auburn-haired. Bayard was a sixteenth-century French knight and national hero renowned for valor and purity of heart.
Baylen; **Nicknames:** *Bay*

BEACAN (BEH-gawn) Celtic: Small
Beagan, Becan; **Nicknames:** *Bec*

BEACHER English: Lives by the beech tree

BEAGEN Gaelic: Little one

BEALE (BEEL) English: Handsome; a variant of Beau
Beal, Beall

BEARACH (BYAR-ak) Celtic: Sharp

BEATHAN (BEE-thun) Scottish: Son of the right-handed

BEATTY Gaelic: Blesses
(Gaelic) *Biadhaiche*; *Beatie, Beattie*

BEAU (BO) French: Handsome
Famous namesakes: Beau Bridges

BEAUFORT (BO-fərt) French: From the beautiful fortress

BEAUVAIS (bo-VAY) French: From Beauvais

BEB Egyptian: Osiris' firstborn

BEBHINN (BAY-vin) Gaelic: Harmony

BECK English: Brook
Bek; **Famous namesakes:** Musician Beck

BECKETT English: Little mouth; a surname
Star babies: son of Melissa Etheridge

BECKHAM English: Place of the small stream; well-known surname thanks to the soccer star David Beckham
Beckam

BEDRICH (BED-rik) Czech: Variation of Frederick

BEECHER English: Lives by the beech tree; surname

BEHDAD Persian: Given honor

BEHNAM (bay-nahm) Persian: Reputable

BEHRUZ (bay-rooz) Persian: A good day
Behrooz, Behrouz

BEHZAD (be-zahd) Persian: Of noble family

BELA Hebrew: Destruction; also a Hungarian variant of Albert

BELDEN English: Lives in the beautiful glen valley
Beldan, Beldane, Beldene, Beldon

BELLAMY French: Handsome friend
Bellami

BELLEROPHON (bə-LER-ə-fən) Latin: Son of Glaucus; legendary hero noted for killing the Chimera

BELTRAN (bel-TRAHN) Spanish: Variation of Bertram

BEN English: Nickname for Benjamin
Famous namesakes: Inventor and statesman
Ben Franklin, actors Ben Affleck, actor Ben
Stiller; **Star babies:** sons of Rowan Atkinson,
Jeff Daniels, Neil Young

BENEDICT (BEN-ə-dikt) Latin: Blessed;
name was borne by several popes and
Saint Benedict, founder of the monastic
Benedictine Order
(German) *Bendix*; (Italian) *Benedetto*,
Benito; (Spanish) *Benedicto*; (Swedish)
Bengt; (Czech) *Benes*; (Hungarian) *Benedek*;
Nicknames: *Beni*

BENEN (BE-nen) Latin, Irish: Kind, well-
born
(Irish) *Beanon, Beinean, Binean*; **Old forms:**
Benignus

BENGT (BENKT) Swedish: Variation of
Benedict

BENJAMIN Hebrew, Spanish: Son of the
right hand. In the Bible, Benjamin was the
patriarch Jacob's youngest son. His mother,
Rachel, died giving birth to him and in her
last moments of life named him Benoni,
meaning *son of my sorrow*. His father did not
want him to have such an ominous moniker
and renamed him Binyamin.
(Italian) *Beniamino*; (Spanish) *Venjamin*;
(Russian) *Veniamin, Venamin*; **Old forms:**
Benyamin, Binyamin; **Nicknames:** *Ben,
Benji, Benjy, Bennie, Benno, Benny*; **Famous
namesakes:** Statesman and inventor Benjamin
Franklin, English composer Benjamin Britten,
actor Benjamin Bratt; **Star babies:** sons of
Annette Bening and Warren Beatty, Harrison
Ford, Carly Simon and James Taylor

BENNETT (BEN-ət) Latin: Blessed
(Hebrew) *Baruch*; *Bennet*; **Nicknames:** *Bence,
Benci, Benn*

BENOIT (ben-WAW) French: Blessed
Benoist; **Nicknames:** *Ben*; **Famous
namesakes:** French director Benoît Jacquot

BENONI (ben-O-nie) Hebrew: Son of my
sorrows

BENROY Hebrew: Royal mountain

BENSON English: Son of Benjamin;
surname

BENT Danish: Blessed

BENTLEY English: From the meadow of
coarse or bent grass
Bentleigh; *Bentlea*

BENTON English: Settlement near the bent
or coarse grass; surname
Bentun; **Nicknames:** *Ben*

BEOWULF (BAY-ə-wulf) Anglo-Saxon:
Intelligent wolf; mythical hero whose story
is told in one of the oldest works of English
literature, the epic poem *Beowulf*

BERDE (BER-dah) Danish: Glacier

BERG German, Swedish: Mountain

BERGIN Irish: Spearlike

BERGREN Swedish: From the mountain
brook
(English) *Bergen*; (Swedish) *Bergron*;
Berggren, Bergin

BERK (BERK) Turkish: Solid

BERKELEY (BURK-lee) Anglo-Saxon,
English, Irish: From the birch tree meadow;
also a well-known univeristy in California.
See Barclay and Bartley
(Irish) *Berk*; *Berkley*; **Diminutive forms:**
Berke

BERLIN English: Son of Bert; the capital of Germany
Berlyn; **Famous namesakes:** Composer Irving Berlin

BERN Scandinavian: Nickname for Bernard

BERNARD (bər-NAHRD) German: Strong and brave as a bear
(English) *Barnard, Burnell*; (German) *Bernhard*; (Italian) *Bernardo*; (Irish) *Beamard*; (Dutch) *Barend*; (Basque) *Benat, Bearnard, Berinhard, Bernelle, Burnard*; **Old forms:** *Bernardyn*; **Nicknames:** *Bern, Berne, Bernie, Bernon, Nardo*

BERNARDO (ber-NAHR-do) Spanish: Variation of Bernard
Nicknames: *Dino*

> "A name? . . . Ah, God, I've been called by a million names all my life. I don't want a name. I'm better off with a grunt or a groan for a name."
> —Bernardo Bertolucci,
>   *Last Tango in Paris*

BERNIE Scandinavian: Nickname for Bernard

BERT English: Bright; Bert is commonly given as a nickname for names such as Albert and Robert
Bertie, Burt, Butch; **Famous namesakes:** Actor Burt Lancaster, actor Burt Reynolds

BERTO (BAYR-to) Spanish: Variation of Albert

BERTOLD (BERT-hawlt) German: Bright ruler, shines
Berthold; **Nicknames:** *Bert*; **Famous namesakes:** German author Bertolt Brecht

BERTON English: From the fortified town
Bertin; **Nicknames:** *Bert*

BERTRAM Teutonic: Bright, shining raven
(French) *Bertrand*; (Italian) *Bertrando*; (Spanish) *Beltran*

BERWICK English: From the barley grange
Berwyk

BES Egyptian: A dwarf-deity with leonine features. Bes is a domestic god, protector against snakes and various terrors. He was venerated as the helper of women in childbirth.

BEVAN (BEV-ən) Welsh: Son of Evan; young warrior
Beven, Bevin, Bevyn

BEVERLEY English: From the beaver stream, beaver meadow; traditionally a boys' name, now more popularly used for girls, especially in the United States.
Beverly; Beverlea; **Nicknames:** *Bev, Leigh*

BHARAT (bah-raht) Hindi: The supporter

BHASKAR (bas-kahr) Hindi: Sun

BHIMA (BI-mah) Hindi: The fear-inspiring

BICKFORD English: From the hewer's ford
Nicknames: *Bick*

BIENVENIDO (bee-EN-vay-NEE-do) Spanish: Welcome

BIJAN (bee-szan) Persian: A name from Persian mythology, character in Shahnameh

BILL English: Nickname for William
Famous namesakes: Comedian Bill Cosby, Microsoft founder Bill Gates, actor Billy Crystal, musician Billy Joel

> "You know the only people who are always sure about the proper way to raise children? Those who've never had any."
> —Bill Cosby

BINAH Hebrew: Understanding
Binah

BING German: From the kettle-shaped hollow
Binge

BION (BIE-ən) Greek: A great force; powerful man

BIRK English, Scottish: Birch tree, where the birch trees grow; surname
Birch, Birche

BIRKETT English: From the birch covered coastland; surname
Birkhead, Birkhed, Burkett; Birket, Birkit, Birkitt, Burkett, Burkitt; **Nicknames:** *Birk, Burk*

BIRKEY English: From the island of birch trees; surname
Birkee, Birkie, Birky

BIRLEY English: From the meadow with the cattle byre (shed); surname
Byreleah; Birlea, Birlie, Birly, Byrlea, Byrlie

BIRNEY English: From the island with the brook; surname
(Irish) *Burney; Bureig, Burneig*

BISHOP English: Overseer

BJORN (BYORN) Scandinavian, Swedish: Bear
Biorn; **Famous namesakes:** Swedish tennis champion Bjorn Borg

BLAINE Irish, Scottish: Thin
Blainey, Blane, Blaney, Blayne

BLAIR Gaelic, Irish: Child of the fields

BLAISE (BLAYZ) Latin, French: Stammerer. Blaise Pascal was a brilliant seventeenth-century child prodigy, mathematician, scientist, and philosopher who invented the calculating machine and hydraulic press before dying at age thirty-nine.
(French) *Blaisdell;* (Spanish) *Blas;* (Swedish) *Blasius;* (Czech) *Blazej; Blais, Blaize, Blase, Blayze, Blaze*

BLAKELY Scandinavian: Black or white; dark-haired, can also mean the reverse: fair, pale
Nicknames: *Blaec, Blake*

BLANCO (BLAHN-ko) Spanish: Blond, white

BLEDDYN (BLETH-in) Welsh: Wolf

BLEIDD (BLAYTH) Welsh: Wolf

BLISS Anglo-Saxon: Intense joy; a name used since medieval times, but more often for girls

BLYTHE (BLIETH) English: Merry

BO Scandinavian: Nickname and abbreviation for Bogart and Beau

BOAZ (BO-az) Hebrew: Swift; an honorable and wealthy man of the Bible who married the loyal Moabite Ruth
Boas

BOB English: Nickname for Robert
Nicknames: *Bobbie, Bobby*; **Famous namesakes:** Actor Bob Newhart, comedian Bob Hope, musician Bob Dylan, game show host Bob Barker, hockey player Bobby Hull, hockey player Bobby Orr

BOCLEY English: Lives at the buck meadow; surname
Bocleah; Boclea, Bocleigh

BODEN (BO-dən) Anglo-Saxon: Messenger

BODHI (BO-dee) Hindi: Wise or enlightening
Star babies: son of actress Amy Brenneman

BOGART (BO-gahrt) German: Bowstring

BOGDAN (BAWG-dahn) Polish, Russian: God's gift
(Czech) *Bohdan*; **Nicknames:** *Bogdasha, Danya, Bogdashka*

BOGUMIL (baw-GUW-meew, baw-GUW-meel) Polish: God's love

BOGUSLAW (baw-GUW-swahf) Polish: God's glory
(Czech) *Bohuslav*

BOHUMIR Czech: God is great

BOJAN (BOY-ən) Slavic: Battle

BOLDIZSAR (BOL-dee-zhahr) Hungarian: Prince of splendor; one of three wise men who brought gifts to the Christ child.
Nicknames: *Bodi*

BOLTON English: The specific meaning of this name is unclear, though the ending –*ton* likely indicates that it refers to a town or settlement.
Bollton, Bolten, Boltin; **Famous namesakes:** Singer Michael Bolton

BOND English: Tied to the land, farmer; surname. Many will associate this name immediately with fictional secret agent James Bond.

BONIFACE (BAWN-ə-fəs) Latin: Does good; patron saint of Germany
(Spanish) *Bonifacio*; **Old forms:** *Bonifacius*

BOONE English: Good, a blessing
Famous namesakes: American frontier hero Daniel Boone

BORA (BORA) Turkish: Hurricane

BORAK (bor-AHK) Arabic: Lightning. Al Borak was the legendary magical horse that bore Mohammed from earth to the seventh heaven.

BORDEN English, Anglo-Saxon: From the boar valley
Bordan

BOREAS (BOR-ee-əs) Greek: North wind

BORG German, Norse, Swedish: From the castle; familar form of Burkhard

BORIS Russian, Slavic: Fighter; Saint Boris is the patron saint of Moscow.
Nicknames: *Borya, Borka*; **Diminutive forms:** *Boryenka*; **Famous namesakes:** Russian poet Boris Pasternak, author of the novel *Doctor Zhivago*, tennis star Boris Becker

BORISLAV Slavic: Glory in battle
(Polish) *Boryslaw*

BORNA Persian: Young

BOTROS (BOO-tros) Arabic: Variation of Peter
Butrus, Boutros; **Famous namesakes:** Secretary-General of the United Nations and Egyptian diplomat Boutros Boutros-Ghali

BOURKE English: Fortified hill

BOURNE English: From the brook

BOWEN Welsh, Gaelic: Blond, son of Owen
Bow, Bowyn; **Nicknames:** *Bowie*

BOYCE English: Lives near the wood

BOYDEN Anglo-Saxon: Blond or messenger
Nicknames: *Boyd*; **Famous namesakes:** Actor
Boyd Gaines, actor Billy Boyd

BOYNE (BOI-nə) Gaelic: White cow
Boin, Boine

BOYNTON (BOINT-ən) Gaelic: From the
white river

BOZIDAR Czech: Divine gift

BRAD English: Broad; a nickname for
Bradley and other names beginning with
Brad–.
Famous namesakes: Actor Brad Pitt

BRADAN (BRAY-dən) English: From the
broad valley

BRADBURN English: From the broad brook
Bradbourne; **Nicknames:** *Brad*

BRADEN (BRAY-den) Irish: Salmon; a
variant spelling from Gaelic and the surname
Ó Bradáin. Folklore tells of Finn MacCool, a
well-known Irish hero who burned his thumb
while cooking the Salmon of Knowledge.
He put the burned thumb in his mouth
and acquired the fish's gift of prophecy and
wisdom. See also Bradan
*Braddon, Bradene, Bradon, Bradyn, Braeden,
Braedon, Brayden, Braydon*; **Nicknames:**
Bradd, Brad

BRADFORD English: From the broad ford
Nicknames: *Brad, Ford*

BRADLEY English: From the broad
meadow; a surname adapted to widespread
first name use
*Bradleah, Bradlee; Bradlea, Bradleigh, Bradlie,
Bradly, Bradney*; **Nicknames:** *Brad, Bradd, Lee*

BRADSHAW English: Broad clearing in the
wood
Nicknames: *Brad, Shaw*; **Famous namesakes:**
Hall of Fame quarterback Terry Bradshaw

BRADWEN Welsh: Legendary son of Moren

BRADY English: From the wide island; a
surname evocative of the popular TV show *The
Brady Bunch*; (Gaelic, Irish) spirited; broad
*Bradig; Bradee, Bradey, Bradie, Braedy,
Braidie, Braidy, Braydie*; **Famous namesakes:**
Baseball player Brady Anderson

BRAHMA (BRAH-mə) Hindi: The creator;
first born of Brahman

BRAINARD English, Teutonic: Bold raven
Brainerd

BRAM Irish: Raven, also an abbreviation
of Abraham. Bram Stoker was the author of
Dracula.

BRAN (BRAN) Welsh, Celtic: Raven; a figure
in both Welsh and Irish mythology

BRANDEIS (BRAN-dies) German: Dwells
on a burned clearing

BRANDER Norse: Firebrand

BRANDON (BRAN-dən) English: From the
beacon hill or broom hill; sometimes used as
a variant of Brendan
(Italian) *Brando; Brandan, Branddun,
Branden, Brandin, Brandyn, Brannan,
Brannen, Brannon, Branson*; **Star babies:** sons
of Richard Marx, Kenneth Edmonds, Tracy
Austin

BRANDT (BRANT) German: Fiery torch; dweller on land cleared by burning (Norse) *Brandr*; *Brantley, Branton, Brantson*; *Brandy*; **Nicknames:** *Brand, Brant*; **Famous namesakes:** Politician Willy Brandt

BRANIMIR Czech: Great protection

BRANISLAV Czech: Spelling variation of Bronislaw

BRANT English: Proud; variant of Brandt. Mohawk Indian Joseph Brant was a renowned strategist who fought for the British during the American Revolution and a devout scholar who translated Christian religious works into his native Indian tongue.

BRANTON English: Spelling variation of Brandt

BRASIL Celtic: Battle
Breasal

BRAWLEY English: From meadow at the slope of the hill; surname
Braleah, Brawleigh; *Bralea, Brauleigh, Braulie, Brauly, Brawlea, Brawlie, Brawly*; **Star babies:** son of Nick Nolte

BRAXTON English: Brock's town

BRECK Gaelic: Freckled
Brecc; *Brec, Brek, Brech*

BREDE Norse: Broad

BREN German: Flame

BRENDAN (BREN-dən) Irish, Gaelic: Prince; the name of Irish saints, one of whom is said to have sailed to North America in the sixth century
Brandan, Breandan, Brenden, Brendon, Brennan, Brennen, Brennon; **Nicknames:**
Brenn; **Famous namesakes:** Irish playwright Brendan Behan, actor Brendan Fraser

BRENDON Irish: Spelling variation of Brendan

BRENT English: Hilltop
Brentan, Brenten, Brentley, Brenton; **Nicknames:** *Brendt*

BRETT English, Celtic: Brit, a person from Britain or Brittany; derived from a French surname of that meaning, but co-opted by English as a first name for both girls and boys (Scottish) *Bretton*; *Bret, Brittain, Brittan, Britton*; *Brit, Briton, Britt*; **Famous namesakes:** Quarterback Brett Favre, baseball player Bret Saberhagen; **Star babies:** son of Jimmy Connors

BRETTON Scottish: Variation of Brett
Brittain, Brittan; **Nicknames:** *Brit, Britt*

BREWSTER English: One who brews ale; may also be a variant of Webster
Brewstere

BRIAN Celtic, Norse: Popular name of uncertain meaning, but generally thought to be of Celtic origin; possible definitions include strength, ascension, or valor. The name is widespread in Ireland, partially due to the renown of Brian Boru, a high king and great national hero who crushed the Vikings' attempts to take his country.
Briant, Brien, Brion, Bryan, Bryant, Bryon; **Famous namesakes:** Actor Brian Dennehy, Singer Bryan Adams; **Star babies:** son of Jim Henson

BRICE English: Spelling variation of Bryce

BRICK English: Bridge.

BRIGHAM (BRIG-əm) English: Bridge.

BRIGHTON English: From the bright town; a seaside town in Southern England; surname
Bryton

BRITTON English: Brit, a person from Britain; derived from a French surname of that meaning, but co-opted as a first name by English speakers; variant of Brett
Bretton, Briton, Brittain, Brittan

BROCK English: Badger; variant of Brook (Gaelic) *Bhruic; Broc, Brocleah, Brocleigh, Brocly*; **Nicknames:** *Brok*

BRODERICK Welsh: Brother, son of Roderick, or from the broad ridge (Scottish) *Brodric, Brodrick;* (Scandinavian) *Broderic, Broderik, Brodrik;* **Nicknames:** *Brody, Rick*

BRODY (BRO-dee) Irish, Scottish: From the muddy place; a castle in Scotland (Scottish) *Brodie*

BROMLEY English: From the broom-covered meadow (broom is a shrub related to heather, with showy yellow flowers); surname *Bromleah, Bromleigh, Bromly; Bromlea, Bromlee, Broomlie*

BRONE Irish: Sorrow
Bron

BRONISLAW (braw-NEE-swahf) Polish: Protecting glory
(Czech) *Bronislav; Branislav*

BRONSON English: Brown's son.

BROOK English: Near the small stream; a surname originally used for boys that is used often now for girls as well, especially when spelled with the "e" at the end
Brooke, Brooks; Brookes

BRUCE French, English, Scottish: Surname since medieval times. Robert de Bruce, a knight from Normandy followed William the Conqueror to England. His descendants settled in Scotland and began to give this as a first name.
Famous namesakes: Actor Bruce Willis, singer Bruce Springsteen

BRUHIER Arabic: Name of a Sultan
Famous namesakes: Canadian actress Catherine Bruhier

BRUNO (BROO-no) German, Italian: Brown, dark-haired

BRUTUS (BROO-təs) Latin: Heavy, foolish

BRYANT Celtic: Spelling variation of Brian
Famous namesakes: Newsman Bryant Gumbel

BRYCE (BRIES) Anglo-Saxon: Son of a nobleman. Bryce Canyon in Utah became a national park in 1924 and has formations more than ten thousand years old.
(French) *Brys;* (Scottish) *Brycen, Bryceton, Bryston; Brice, Bryson*

BRYNN (BRIN) Welsh: From the hill

BUCK English: Male deer
Boc; **Star babies:** son of Roseanne Barr

BUCKLEY English: Buck's meadow or meadow of deer; surname; (Irish) boy *Bucklea, Bucklee, Buckleigh, Bucklie;* **Nicknames:** *Buck*

BUD English: Short for buddy, or possibly a child's pronunciation of brother; Bud has been used as a nickname since medieval times.
Budd, Buddy; **Famous namesakes:** Comedian Bud Abbott, actor Buddy Ebsen

BUIRON French: From the cottage; a common family name in France

BULUT (boo-LOOT) Turkish: Cloud

BURCET French: From the little stronghold

BURCH English: Birch tree; variant of Old English Birk
Birch, Birche

BURDETTE English: Bird
Burdett

BUREL French: Coarse hair; a common family name in France sometimes given as a first name in English-speaking countries
Burnell, Burrell

BURGESS English, Celtic: Lives in town
Burgeis; **Famous namesakes:** Actor Burgess Meredith

BURLEY English: From the castle's meadow; from the fortified meadow; from the meadow of knotted wood; surname
Burhleag, Burly; Burlea, Burlee, Byrley

BURNEY English: From the island with the brook; variant of Birney

BURTON English: From the fortified town
Nicknames: *Burt*

BUSBY Norse: Dwells at the village
Nicknames: *Buzz*; **Famous namesakes:** Choreographer Busby Berkeley

BYRNE (BURN) English: From the brook
Byrnes

BYRON English: The cattle herder or from the cow sheds; (Teutonic) from the cottage
Biron, Byram; **Famous namesakes:** Golfer Byron Nelson, actor Byron Mann; **Star babies:** son of Mel Harris

> *"'Tis pleasant, sure, to see one's name in print; A book's a book, although there's nothing in't."*
> —Lord Byron

CABLE French: Rope, ropemaker; also an English surname
Cabe, Cabell

CADDOCK Welsh: Battle sharp
Caddoc

CADE English: Round or barrel
Caden, Kade; **Star babies:** son of Keith Carradine

CADELL (KAH-dell) Welsh: Battle
Cadel

CADMAN (KAD-mən) Anglo-Saxon, Welsh: Warrior
Cadmon, Caedmon

CADMUS (KAD-məs) Greek: From the east
Kadmus

CADWALLON (kad-WAL-on) Welsh: Battle dissolver
Cadwallen

CAESAR (SEE-zər) Latin: Long-haired. Julius Caesar was one of ancient Rome's greatest politicians and military leaders, building Rome to be the center of a huge empire. The name Caesar came to be generic for any ruler in the empire and was later translated to Czar in Russian and Kaiser in German.
(French) *Cesar*; (Italian) *Ceasario, Cesare*; (Spanish) *Cesario, Cesaro*; **Famous namesakes:** Actor Cesar Romero, comedian Sid Caesar, labor union organizer Cesar Chavez

CAFFAR (KAR-fer) Irish: Helmet

CAGNEY Irish: Tribute; a surname
Famous namesakes: Actor James Cagney

CAI (KAY, KIE) Welsh: Variation of Gaius

CAILEAN (KAY-lin, KA-len) Gaelic: Child
*Caelan, Cailen, Cailin, Caillen, Calan,
Caley, Kaelan, Kaelin, Kalan, Kalen, Kalin*;
Nicknames: *Kael*

CAIN Hebrew: Acquired; in the Bible, Cain
was the son of Adam and Eve.

CAINE French: French place name unrelated
to the biblical Cain.

CALDER English: Cold brook; surname
Caldre, Calldwr

CALDWELL English: From the cold spring;
surname
Caldwiella

CALEB Hebrew: Bold or dog; an Israelite
who joined Moses from Egypt to live long
enough to enter the promised land.
Kaleb; **Nicknames:** *Cale, Kale*; **Star babies:**
sons of Jack Nicholson, Julianne Moore

CALHOUN (kal-HOON) Gaelic, Irish: From
the narrow forest; a surname

CALIGULA (kə-LIG-yoo-lə) Latin: Name
given to Gaius Ceasar when he was a child

CALIX (KAY-liks, KA-liks) Latin: Chalice

CALLAGHAN (KAL-ə-han) Irish: Strife
Callahan, Ceallach, Ceallachan, Keallach;
Nicknames: *Cillian*

CALLOUGH (KAL-luh) Irish: Bald
Calbhach, Calvagh

CALLUM (KAL-um) Scottish: Variation of
Columba

CALVERT English: Cow herder; surname
Calbert

CALVIN Latin: Bald
(Italian) *Calvino*; **Nicknames:** *Cal, Cal,
Kal*; **Famous namesakes:** Former president
Calvin Coolidge, baseball player Cal Ripken
Jr., designer Calvin Klein, Swiss religious
reformer John Calvin

CAMDEN Scottish, Gaelic: From the
winding valley; a surname adapted to first
name use, and a place name of a section of
London.
(Anglo-Saxon) *Camdene*; *Camdan, Camdin,
Camdyn, Kamden*; **Nicknames:** *Cam*

CAMERON Gaelic, Scottish: Crooked nose;
the name of a great Highland clan
Camron, Camshron, Kameron, Kamron;
Nicknames: *Camey, Kam, Cam*; **Star babies:**
sons of Emma Samms, Jimmy Buffett,
Michael Douglas and Diandra Luker

CAMILLO Latin: Meaning uncertain, possibly
indicates an attendant at a religious ceremony
or sacrifice; masculine form of Camilla
Camillus, Camilo

CAMLIN Celtic: Crooked line

CAMPBELL (KAM-bəl) Gaelic, Scottish:
Crooked mouth; name of a famous Highland
clan
Cambeul; **Nicknames:** *Cam, Camp*; **Famous
namesakes:** Actor Campbell Scott

CAN (JAHN) Turkish: Soul

CANAN (jah-NAHN) Turkish: Beloved

CANUTE (kə-NOOT) Norse: Spelling variation of Knut

CARADOC (KAH-rah-dok) Welsh: Beloved
Caradog

CARDEN Celtic: From the black fortress

CAREY (KER-ee) Welsh: Near the castle
Cary; **Famous namesakes:** Actor Cary Grant

"Cary Grant, born Archie Leach, was a poor boy who could barely spell "posh." That's acting for you—or maybe Hollywood."
—*Christian Science Monitor*

CARL English: Strong, manly; See also Karl
Famous namesakes: Actor Carl Reiner, astronomer Carl Sagan

CARLETON (KAHRL-tən) English: From Charles' town or settlement; surname
Carletun, Charleston, Charleton, Charlton; **Nicknames:** *Carl*

CARLIN Irish: Little champion
Carling, Cearbhallan; **Nicknames:** *Car, Carlie, Carly*; **Famous namesakes:** Comedian George Carlin

CARLISLE (KAHR-liel) English: From the walled city
Carlyle

CARLOS (KAHR-los) Spanish: Variation of Karl
Nicknames: *Lito, Litos, Carlito, Carlitos*;
Famous namesakes: Musician Carlos Santana, Brazilian musician Antonio Carlos Jobim

CARLSON English: Carl's son

CARMEL Hebrew: Garden, orchard, vineyard; Mount Carmel in Israel is considered a paradise.
(Italian) *Carmelo, Carmine*; *Karmel*;
Nicknames: *Carmi*

CARMICHAEL Gaelic, Scottish: Friend or follower of Saint Michael
Caramichil

CARR Scottish: From the marsh or mossy ground
Karr

CARRICK Gaelic: Rocky cliff
Carraig

CARRINGTON English: Origin is not entirely clear, but it refers to a town, possibly Charles' town; English surname
Carington

CARROLL Irish: Champion; (German) manly; variant of Carl
Carol, Carolus, Carrol, Cearbhall; **Famous namesakes:** Actor Carroll O'Connor, author Lewis Carroll

CARSON English, Scottish: Son of Carr
Carrson; **Famous namesakes:** Television host Carson Daly, actor and comedian Johnny Carson

CARSTEN (KAHR-sten) German: Variation of Christian
Carston, Karsten

CARSWELL English: Near the well where the watercress grows; surname
Caersewiella

CARTER English: Drives a cart; from a surname and occupational name
Cartere; **Famous namesakes:** Former president Jimmy Carter; **Star babies:** son of Alan Thicke

CARVELL French, English: Spearman's estate or marshy estate

CARWYN Welsh: Loved, blessed

CASEY Irish: Vigilant
Cacey, Kasen, Kasey; **Nicknames:** *Cace*; **Star babies:** son of Beau Bridges

CASIMIR (KAH-zi-meer) Slavic, Polish: Announcing peace
(Spanish) *Casimiro*; *Kazmer*; *Kasimer*, *Kasimir*, *Kazimir*; **Nicknames:** *Kazimierz*

CASPAR (kas-PAR) Persian: Keeper of the treasure. Caspar (sometimes known as Gaspar) is said to be the name of one of the three magi who traveled from afar to find the baby Jesus.
(English) *Jasper*; (French) *Gaspar*; (Polish) *Kaspar*; *Gaspard*; *Casper*

CASPIAN Irish: Borrowed from the sea

CASSIDY Irish, Gaelic: Clever or curly-headed
Caiside; **Nicknames:** *Cass*; **Famous namesakes:** Singer David Cassidy, actor Shaun Cassidy

CASSIUS (KASH-əs) Latin: Vain; a name recognized worldwide as belonging to the great boxer Cassius Clay, now known as Muhammad Ali

CAT Scottish: Spelling variation of Chait

CATHAL (KA-hal) Irish: Battle strong

CATON (cah-TON) Latin: Shrewd

CAWLEY Scottish: English cow meadow
Cauley

CECIL (SEE-səl, SE-səl) Latin: Blind
(Italian) *Cecilio*; *Cecilius*; **Famous namesakes:** Director Cecil B. DeMille, baseball player Cecil Fielder

CEDRIC (SED-rik) English: Battle leader
Cedrick, Cedrik, Keddrick, Kedric, Kedrick; *Sedric, Sedrick*; **Famous namesakes:** Ced, Rick

CENOBIO (say-NO-bee-o) Spanish: Spelling variation of Zenobio
Cenovio

CESAR (SAY-sahr) Spanish: Variation of Caesar
Famous namesakes: Activist Cesar Chavez

CHAD English: Warrior; a medieval given name from abbreviations of surnames Chadwick and Chadwell. Chad is also a seventeenth-century saint and an African country.
Famous namesakes: Actor Chad Lowe

CHADBURN English: From the wildcat brook; originally a surname
Chadburne, Chadbyrne

CHADWICK English: From the warrior's town; originally a surname
Chadwik, Chadwyk

CHAGAI Hebrew: Festive
Chagi

CHAIM (HIEM) Hebrew: Life
Chayim, Hayyim, Hyman

CHAIT Scottish: Catlike
Cat

CHAKRA (CHAH-krə) Hindi: Symbol of the sun

CHALMERS Scottish, Teutonic: Rules the home
Chalmar, Chalmer

CHANAN (HAH-nahn) Hebrew: Variation of Hanan

CHANCE French: Variation of Chauncey
Star babies: son of Larry King

CHANCELLOR English: Record keeper
Chaunceler, Chancelor; **Nicknames:** *Chaucer, Chaucor, Chauncory*

CHANDLER French, English: Maker of candles
Chanler

CHANDRA (CHAN-drə) Hindi: Shining moon
Chander

CHANE (SHAYN) French: Oak-hearted
Chaney, Chayne, Cheney, Cheyne

CHANNE English: Nickname for Channing

CHANNING English, French: Of uncertain origin, possibly related to French meaning canal or indicating a church official. The spelling is suggestive of a paternal meaning such as Chan or Cana's child.
Channon; **Nicknames:** *Chann, Channe*

CHANOCH (CHAY-nok) Hebrew: Dedicated

CHAPIN French: Clergyman

CHAPMAN English: Merchant
Nicknames: *Chap*

CHAPPEL (shah-PEL) French: Chapel
Chappell

CHARLES French: Derived from the Germanic Karl, meaning manly; a royal name borne by ten kings of France and introduced to Great Britain by Mary, Queen of Scots, who named her son Charles James. His son and grandson were also named Charles, furthering the name's popularity.
(Gaelic) *Tearlach*; (Irish) *Carlus*; (Welsh) *Siarl*; (Basque) *Xarles*; (Polish) *Carel*; (Hawaiian) *Kale*; **Nicknames:** *Charley, Charlie, Charlot, Charly, Chas, Chaz, Chick, Chuck*; **Famous namesakes:** Prince Charles, English author Charles Dickens

---

"Every baby born into the world is a finer one than the last."
—Charles Dickens

CHARLESON English: Son of Charles

CHARLTON (KAHRL-tən, CHAHRL-tən) English: From Charles' town or settlement; surname; variant of Carleton
Charleton, Charltun; **Nicknames:** *Carl*; **Famous namesakes:** Actor Charlton Heston

CHARRO (CHAHR-o) Spanish: Cowboy

CHASE English: Huntsman
Chace, Chayce, Chayce, Chaice; **Nicknames:** *Chad*

CHASKA (CHAHS-kah) Native American: Firstborn son (Sioux)

CHASKE (chah-skay) Native American: First son (Sioux)

CHATHAM (CHA-təm) English: From the soldier's land

CHAUNCEY (CHAWN-see) English, Latin: Chancellor, fortune; a gamble.
(French) *Chance*; *Chancey, Chaunce, Chauncy, Choncey*

CHAVIVI Hebrew: Dearly loved

CHENEY French: Spelling variation of Chane

CHESS English: Nickname for Chester

CHESTER English: Lives at the camp of the soldiers; an old Roman (Rochester) settlement in Britain
Cheston; **Nicknames:** *Chess, Chet*; **Famous namesakes:** WWII admiral Chester Nimitz; **Star babies:** son of Rita Wilson and Tom Hanks

CHET English: Nickname for Chester

CHETAN (chay-TAHN) Native American: Hawk (Sioux)

CHETWIN English: From the small house on the twisted or winding path
Cetewind, Chetwyn, Chetwynne; **Nicknames:** *Chet*

CHEVALIER (shə-VAL-yay) French: Horseman, knight
(French) *Cheval, Chevell*; **Nicknames:** *Chevy*; **Famous namesakes:** French actor Maurice Chevalier

CHEVY French: Nickname for Chevalier
Famous namesakes: Actor and comedian Chevy Chase

CHIAMAKA African: God is splendid

CHIBALE (chee-BAH-le) African: Kinship

CHICO (CHEE-ko) Spanish: Boy; also an abbreviation of Ezequiel

CHIDI African: God exists

CHIKE (CHEE-kə) African, Egyptian: God's power

CHILTON English: From the town or settlement near the well; surname
Celdtun; Chelton, Chiltun; **Nicknames:** *Chill*; **Famous namesakes:** Musician Alex Chilton

CHIMALA (chee-mah-lah) Mayan: Beauty

CHONI Hebrew: Gracious
Honi

CHRIS English: A nickname for Christian or Christopher, though Chris easily stands as an independent name
Famous namesakes: Actor Chris O'Donnell, comedian Chris Rock

CHRISTIAN Latin: Follower of Christ. In the Middle Ages, Christian was more often used as a girl's name but is now commonly used for boys.
(Greek) *Christiano*; (German) *Carsten, Karsten, Krischan*; (French) *Cretien*; (Spanish) *Cristian, Cristiano*; (Scandinavian) *Kristian*; (Swedish) *Krist*; (Danish) *Christiansen*; (Dutch) *Kerstan; Christiann*; **Nicknames:** *Chris*; **Famous namesakes:** Actor Christian Slater, basketball player Christian Laettner, Danish author Hans Christian Andersen, designer Christian Dior; **Star babies:** sons of Mel Gibson, Eddie Murphy, Tyler England

CHRISTO Slavic: Nickname for Christopher

CHRISTOPHER Greek, Latin: One who carries Christ; a beloved story tells of this name given to a saint that carried the Christ child across a river and is now known as the patron saint of travelers. Others believe Christopher means to carry Christ in one's heart.
(German) *Christoph*; (French) *Christophe*; (Italian) *Cristoforo*; (Spanish) *Cristobal, Cristofer, Cristofor, Criston, Cristos, Cristoval*; (Gaelic) *Crisdean*; (Scottish) *Christie, Kester*; (Welsh) *Crist*; (Scandinavian) *Kristof, Kristoffer*; (Danish) *Christoffer, Christofferson*;

(Polish) *Krzysztof; Kristofer; Christobel, Christoffel, Christofor, Cristophe, Kristoff, Kristopher;* **Old forms:** *Christophoros;* **Nicknames:** *Christo, Christy, Cris, Risto, Stoffel, Chris, Topher;* **Famous namesakes:** Actor Christopher Walken, actor Christopher Reeve, Italian explorer Christopher Columbus; **Star babies:** sons of Pierce Brosnan, Gene Hackman, Hunter Tylo, Sean Combs, Dean Cain and Samantha Torres, Maria Shriver and Arnold Schwarzenegger

CHRISTOS Greek: Familar form of Christopher
Khristos

CHURCHILL English: Lives near the church by the hill; surname
Churchyll, Circehyll; **Famous namesakes:** Former British Prime Minister Sir Winston Churchill

CIAN (KEE-an, KEEN) Irish: Ancient. See also Kian
Cianan, Kean, Keanan, Keandre, Keane, Keenan, Keene, Keenon, Kenan, Keondre, Kienan

CIAR (KEER) Irish: Dark

CIARAN (KEER-an) Gaelic: Spelling variation of Kieran

CIBOR (CHEE-bawr) Polish: Honorable battle

CICERO (SI-sə-ro) Latin: Chickpea; best known for the statesman, orator, and author of ancient Rome
(Spanish) *Ciceron*

CIRO (SEE-ro) Spanish: Variation of Cyrus

CLARENCE Latin: Bright
Nicknames: *Clare*

CLARK English: Surname and occupational name for a clerk or secretary.
Clarke; **Famous namesakes:** Superman's alter ego Clark Kent

CLAUDE (KLOD, KLAWD) French: Lame; derived from an old Roman name
(English) *Claud;* (Spanish) *Claudio; Claudios; Claudion;* **Old forms:** *Claudius, Klaudius;* **Famous namesakes:** Artist Claude Monet, composer Claude Debussy, actor Claude Rains

CLAUDIUS (KLAW-dee-əs) Latin: Original form of Claude
Famous namesakes: Roman emperor Claudius Nero Germanicus

CLAY English: Nickname for Clayton
Famous namesakes: Singer Clay Aiken

CLAYBORNE English: From the brook near the clay
Claiborn, Claybourne, Clayburn; **Nicknames:** *Clay*

CLAYTON English: Mortal; place name and surname
Clayten; **Nicknames:** *Clay*

CLEMENS (KLE-mənz) Latin: Clemency, mercy
(Latin) *Clementius;* (Italian) *Clemente;* (Czech) *Kliment;* (Hungarian) *Kelemen, Kellman, Klemen; Clement, Klemens;* **Nicknames:** *Clem, Klemenis;* **Famous namesakes:** German author Clemens Brentano, author Samuel Langhorne Clemens (pen name Mark Twain), baseball player Roberto Clemente

CLEON Greek: Illustrious

CLEVELAND English: Hilly land, from the cliff; a geographical name, most notably in Ohio
Cleavon, Clevon; **Nicknames:** *Cleve;* **Famous namesakes:** Former president Grover Cleveland

CLIFFORD English: Lives near the ford by the cliff. Children will recognize this name for the beloved classic canine character Clifford the Big Red Dog.
Clyford; **Nicknames:** *Cliff*; **Star babies:** son of Ken Olin

CLIFFTON English: From the town or settlement near the cliff; surname
Clifton, Cliftun, Clyffton, Clyftun

CLIFLAND English: From the land near the cliffs; surname
Clyfland

CLINT English: Nickname for Clinton

CLINTON English: Surname; from the headland estate or hillside town
Clinttun; *Clintt, Klint, Klinton*; **Nicknames:** *Clint*; **Famous namesakes:** Actor Clint Eastwood, former president Bill Clinton

CLIVE English: Lives near a cliff
Clyve; **Famous namesakes:** Music mogul Clive Davis

CLOTAIRE (klo-TAYR) French: Glory, power

CLOVIS (KLO-vis) Teutonic, French: Renowned fighter; an early form of Ludwig or Louis
(Spanish) *Clodoveo*

CLUNY Gaelic, Irish: From the meadow
Clunainach

CLYDE Scottish: Place name referring to the River Clyde in Scotland

COALAN Celtic: Slender

COBY (KO-bee) English: Uncertain meaning; possibly derived as a nickname for Jacob but is used as an independent name
Kobe, Koby; *Cobey, Cobi*

COCHISE (ko-CHEES) Native American: Hardwood; renowned chief of the Chiricahua Apache from 1812–1874

CODY English: Pillow
Codey, Codi, Codie; *Kodee, Kodie, Kodey, Kody*; **Famous namesakes:** Frontiersman Buffalo Bill Cody; **Star babies:** sons of Robin Williams, Kathie Lee and Frank Gifford

COHEN (KO-en) Hebrew: Surname, priest

COLBERT French: Dark, dark-haired; (English) seaman
Colbey

COLBY English: Dark-skinned or from a coal town. The name Colby became more prominent following the 1980s television series *The Colbys*.
Kolby

COLE English: Dark; also a nickname for Nicholas
Famous namesakes: Composer Cole Porter

COLIN (KAHL-in) Gaelic: A child or cub; variant of Coilean. In some languages, Colin is a nickname for Nicholas.
(Irish) *Coilin*; *Coilean, Collin, Colyn*; **Famous namesakes:** Irish actor Colin Farrell, British actor Colin Firth, British conductor Sir Colin Davis; **Star babies:** son of Tom Hanks

COLLIER (KOL-yer, KAHL-yer) English: Coal miner or merchant; surname and occupational name
Colier, Collyer, Colyer

COLTON English: From the coal town or dark town
Coleton, Colten; **Nicknames:** *Colt*

COLUMBA Latin: Dove. Saint Columba established several monasteries in Ireland and a convent on the Scottish island of Iona.

(English) *Colver, Colvyr, Culver*; (French) *Colombain*; (Italian) *Columbo*; (Gaelic) *Colm, Colum*; (Celtic) *Calum*; (Irish) *Colman*; (Scottish) *Callum*; **Old forms:** *Columbanus*

CONAN Celtic: Intelligent
Nicknames: *Kyne*

CONNELLY Irish: Love, friendship; surname

CONNOR Irish: Wolf lover
Conner, Conor; Cahner; **Star babies:** sons of Patrick Duffy, Ruth Pointer, Nicole Kidman and Tom Cruise

CONRAD German, Slavic: Bold advisor, wise. Joseph Conrad, author of several books, including the classic *Heart of Darkness*, was said to spend hours searching for the right word for each sentence in his writing. (Spanish) *Conrado*; (Swedish) *Konrad*; (Dutch) *Koenraad*; **Nicknames:** *Con, Connie, Koen, Kort, Kuno, Kunz*

CONSTANTINE (KAHN-stən-teen) Latin: Constant, steadfast. Emperor Constantine the Great made Christianity the official religion of the Roman Empire. (Greek) *Kostas*; (Spanish) *Constantino*; (Russian) *Konstantin*; (Polish) *Konstancji*; **Nicknames:** *Conny, Konstantinus, Kostya*

COOPER English: Barrel maker
Star babies: sons of Tim Matheson, Hugh Hefner

CORBIN Latin: Raven-haired
Corben, Corbett, Corbyn, Corvin; **Nicknames:** *Corby*; **Famous namesakes:** Actor Corbin Bernsen

CORBY English: Nickname for Corbin

CORDELL English: Maker or seller of rope or cord; surname

Cordale, Corday, Kordale, Kordell; **Diminutive forms:** *Cord, Kord*; **Famous namesakes:** Football player Kordell Stewart

COREY Irish: From the hollow
Correy, Cory; **Famous namesakes:** Actor Corey Feldman

CORLISS English: Good-hearted, cheery
Nicknames: *Corley*

CORMAC Irish, Gaelic: Charioteer
Cormack, Cormic, Cormick; **Star babies:** son of Tim Roth

CORNELIUS (kor-NEE-lee-əs) Latin: Horn
(Spanish) *Cornelio*; (Czech) *Kornel*

CORT French: Nickname for Curtis

CORTEZ (kor-TEZ) Spanish: A surname, possibly meaning courteous. The Spanish explorer and adventurer Hernando Cortes conquered the Aztec civilization of Mexico.

CORVIN English: Raven-haired.

CORWIN English: Friend of the heart; close, very dear friend
Corwan, Corwine, Corwyn

COSMO (KAHZ-mo) Greek: Universe, order
Cosimo

COURTLAND English: Form of Courtney

COURTNEY French: Courteous or from the court
Courtland Courtnay; Cortland, Courtenay; **Famous namesakes:** Actor Courtney B. Vance

COWAN (KOW-un) Irish: Twin
Comhghan

COYAN French: Modest
Coyne

CRAIG Gaelic: Rock

CRANDALL English: From the dell or valley of the cranes; surname
Crandell

CRANLEY English: From the meadow of the cranes; surname
Cranleah, Cranly; Cranelea

CREIGHTON (KRIE-tən, KRAY-tən) English, Scottish: From the rocky town or settlement; surname
(Scottish) *Crayton; Crichton*

CRISPIN (KRIS-pin) Latin: Curly-haired. The third-century martyr Saint Crispin is known as patron of shoemakers.
Famous namesakes: Actor Crispin Glover

CRISTOBAL (kree-STO-bahl) Spanish: Variation of Christopher

CRISTOPHE Greek: Spelling variation of Christopher

CROMPTON English: From the winding town or settlement

CRONUS (KRO-nəs) Greek: Titan of Greek mythology overthrown by son Zeus

CROSBY Norse: At the cross, at the town crossroads
Famous namesakes: Entertainer Bing Crosby

CROSLEY English: From the cross meadow; surname
Crosleah, Crosleigh, Crosly; Crosslea, Croslee, Crossleigh

CRUZ (KROOZ) Spanish, Portuguese: Cross

CUARTO (KWAHR-to) Spanish: Born fourth
Cuartio

CULLEN Irish, Gaelic, Celtic: Handsome or holly; from an Irish surname MacCuilinn
Cullan, Cullin; **Nicknames:** *Cully*

CULVER English: Variation of Columba

CURRO (KOOR-ro) Spanish: Free; pet form of Francisco
Currito

CURTIS French, English: Courteous
(English) *Curtiss;* (German) *Kurt, Kurtis;* (Spanish) *Curcio; Curtice;* **Nicknames:** *Cort, Court, Curt;* **Famous namesakes:** Actor Tony Curtis

CY (SIE) English: Nickname for Cyril
Sy

CYAN (SIE-an) English: Greenish blue color

CYD (SID) Contemporary: Nickname for Sidney
Sid, Syd

CYPRIAN (SIP-ree-ən) Greek: From Cyprus
(Italian) *Cipriano*

CYRANO (SEER-ə-no) Greek: From Cyrene. Cyrano de Bergerac was the romantic hero of Edmund Rostand's play by the same name. The character was based on a French author with this moniker.

CYRIL (SEER-əl) Greek: Lordly; Saint Cyril and his brother Saint Methodius developed the Cyrillic alphabet.
(Spanish) *Cirilo;* (Russian) *Kiril, Kirill;* (Polish) *Cyrek, Cyryl; Cyr, Cyrill;* **Old forms:** *Kyrillos;* **Nicknames:** *Cy*

CYRUS (SIE-rəs) Persian: Sun or enthroned; Cyrus the Great conquered Babylon and founded the Persian Empire.
(Spanish) *Ciro;* **Nicknames:** *Cy;* **Star babies:** son of Cybill Shepherd

DABIR (dah-BEER) Arabic: Teacher, manager

DACEY Gaelic: Southerner
(Spanish) *Dacio*; *Dace, Dacian, Dacy, Deasach*

DAEDALUS (DED-ə-ləs) Greek: Cunning. In Greek mythology, Daedalus was a skilled Athenian craftsman and inventor. King Minos had him imprisoned in his own invention—the labyrinth. Daedalus and his son Icarus tried to escape with wings he created of wax, feathers and thread, yet Icarus flew too close to the sun and died.

DAEGAN Irish, Gaelic: Black-haired
Dagen, Deegan; **Nicknames:** Daeg

DAG (DAG) Norse, Scandinavian: Day; in Norse mythology, the son of Nott and Dellingr
Famous namesakes: Secretary-General of the United Nations Dag Hammarskjold

DAGAN (DAY-gən, DAH-gahn) Hebrew: Grain
Daegan, Daegen, Dagen, Dagin, Dagon, Daygan, Daygen, Daygin, Daygon

DAGOBERT (DAH-go-bayrt) German: Glorious day
(Spanish) *Dagoberto*; *Dagbert*

DAGON (DAY-gon) Hebrew: Fish; a fish-god of the ancient Philistines

DAGWOOD English: From the shiny forest. A dagwood is a large, multi-layered sandwich with numerous fillings. The sandwich is named after Dagwood Bumstead, the well-known character who eats giant sandwiches in the comic strip *Blondie*.

DAHY Irish: Quick and agile

DAI (dah-ee) Japanese: Large

DAIRE (DAW-ra) Irish: Fruitful or dark oak
Darach, Darragh, Dary

DAKARAI (dah-kah-RAH-ee) African: Happiness (Zimbabwe)

DAKOTA American: Allies; name of a group of tribes more familiarly known as the Sioux
Dakoda, Dakotah; **Star babies:** son of Melanie Griffith and Don Johnson, Melissa Gilbert

DAKSHA (DAHK-sha) Hindi: Brilliant

DALE English: Lives in the dell or valley; originally a surname
Dael, Dayle; **Nicknames:** *Daley*; **Famous namesakes:** NASCAR driver Dale Earnhardt

> *"The sweetest sound is the person's own name."*
> —Dale Carnegie

DALLAS Scottish: From the field with the waterfall; originally for a place name in Scotland, but also a major city in Texas
Dalles, Dallis

DALLIN Irish: Unseeing; (English) proud
Dalan, Dalen, Dallan, Dallen, Dallon, Dalon; **Nicknames:** *Dal*

DALTON English: From the town or settlement in the dale; closely related to the name Denton; surname
Daleton, Dallten, Dalten, Daltun; **Nicknames:** *Dale*

DALY Gaelic: Assembly; a common Irish surname
Daley

DALZIEL (dee-EL) Scottish: From the little field

DAMAE (də-MAY) Greek: Tame

DAMARIO (dah-MAH-ree-o) Spanish: Gentle or calf; masculine of the Greek *Damaris*, a biblical woman who heard Paul speak at the open-air supreme court of Athens.
Demario

DAMASKENOS Greek: From Damascus. Damascus is the capital of Syria and one of the world's oldest cities
Damaskinos

DAMEK (DAH-mek) Czech: Variation of Adam

DAMIAN (DAY-mee-ən) Greek: One who tames or subdues. Saint Damian is the patron saint of physicians.
(English) *Damen, Damion, Damon*; (French) *Damien*; (Italian) *Damiano*; (Irish) *Daman*; *Damone; Damien*; **Old forms:** *Damianos*

DAMON English: Variation of Damian
Daemon, Daman, Damen, Daymon; **Famous namesakes:** Actor Damon Wayans, actor Matt Damon

DAN English: Nickname for Daniel; (Hebrew) judge; biblical fifth son of Jacob and founder of one of the twelve tribes of Israel; an independent name and also an abbreviation of Daniel.
Nicknames: *Dannie, Danny*; **Famous namesakes:** Actor Dan Ackroyd, newsman Dan Rather

DAN Hebrew: Judge; biblical fifth son of Jacob and founder of one of the twelve tribes of Israel; an independent name and also an abbreviation of Daniel.

DANA (DAY-nə) English: From Denmark
Dain, Daine, Dane; **Famous namesakes:** Actor Dana Carvey, actor Dane Clark

DANAUS (da-NAY-əs) Greek: According to Greek mythology, Danaus was a father to fifty daughters, known as the Danaides.

DANB Norse: From Denmark

DANIEL Hebrew: God is my judge. The biblical prophet and writer of the Book of Daniel was a teenager when taken to Babylon after the destruction of Jerusalem. He survived two death sentences: a lions' den, and a fiery furnace. See also Danila (Italian) *Daniele*; (Spanish) *Danilo*; (Irish) *Daineal, Dainial*; (Welsh) *Deiniol*; (Slavic) *Danek*; (Russian) *Danya*; (Hungarian) *Dani*; (Persian) *Danyal*; *Danell, Danil, Dannel, Dantrell*; **Nicknames:** *Dan, Dannie, Danny*; **Diminutive forms:** *Danylko*; **Famous namesakes:** Actor Daniel Day-Lewis, actor Danny DeVito, actor Danny Aiello, actor Daniel Radcliffe, frontiersman Daniel Boone; **Star babies:** sons of Anna Nicole Smith, Dan Rather, Natasha Richardson and Liam Neeson, Patricia Heaton and David Hunt

DANILA Russian: A variant of Daniel. Danila-Craftsman is the hero of Russian tales about a man who made wonderful things out of malachite.
Danya, Danilka, Danilushka

DANTE (DAHN-tay) Italian: Enduring; a contracted form of Durante. Italian author Dante Alighieri wrote the epic poem *The Divine Comedy* with its graphic description of medieval Hell known as Dante's Inferno. (English) *Dontae, Donte*; (Spanish) *Dantae, Dantel, Daunte*; *Dontay, Dontaye*; **Famous namesakes:** Poet Dante Gabriel Rossetti; **Star babies:** son of Chazz Palminteri

DANTON French: Variation of Anthony
Famous namesakes: Jazz bassist Danton Boller, French revolutionary Georges Jacques Danton

DANYA (DAHN-yah) Russian: Variation of Daniel

DAPHNIS (DAF-nəs) Greek: A name of Greek mythology, Daphnis was a shepherd and flute player who was blinded by a lover after being unfaithful to her.

DAR Hebrew: Pearl

DARBY Norse: From the deer estate; (Irish) free man
Famous namesakes: Author Darby Costello

DARCY French: From the Arcy (Oise River) which flows into the Seine; (Irish) dark
D'arcy, Darce; **Famous namesakes:** Baseball player D'arcy Flowers, Canadian hockey player Darcy Regier

DARIEN (DER-ee-ən, DAR-ee-ən) English: A name of uncertain origin, perhaps is a variant or blend of names such as Darren, Darius, or Adrian
Darian, Darion, Darrien, Darrion

> Or like stout Cortez when with eagle eyes
> He star'd at the Pacific—
> and all his men
> Look'd at each other
> with a wild surmise—
> Silent, upon a peak in Darien.
> —John Keats, "On First Looking into Chapman's Homer"

DARIUS (DER-ee-əs, DAR-ee-əs) Persian: Rich. Darius the Mede assumed kingship of Babylon after its conquest by Cyrus.
(Latin) *Dario*; *Darrius*; **Famous namesakes:** Singer Darius Rucker; **Star babies:** son of Christiane Amanpour

DARNELL English: From the hidden place
Darnall, Darnel

DARREN Gaelic, English: Great
Daran, Daren, Darin, Daron, Darrin, Darron, Darryn, Daryn, Dearan, Derren, Derrin

DARRENCE (DER-ənts) English: Uncertain meaning or origin; perhaps is a blend of Darryl and Clarence
Darence, Darrance, Derrance

DARROLD (DER-əld) English: Uncertain meaning; possibly an invented name, as a blend of Daryl and Harold or Gerald
Darold, Derald, Derrold

DARRYL (DER-əl) English: From a French surname and place name D'Arel (from Arielle in Calvados); used as both a surname and given name since the eleventh century
Dareau, Darel, Dariel, Dariell, Darrel, Darrell, Darroll, Darryll, Daryl, Daryle, Daryll, Derell, Derrall, Derrell, Derrill, Derryl; **Nicknames:** *Darry*; **Famous namesakes:** Baseball player Daryl Strawberry

DARSHAN (dahr-shahn) Sanskrit: To perceive

DARTAGNAN (dar-tahn-YAHN) French: From Artagnan; one of the main characters in Alexandre Dumas' novel *The Three Musketeers.*

DARTON English: From the deer park

DARVIN English: Blend of Darrel and Marvin

DARWIN English: Friend of the deer. The original meaning has taken on the similar sounding but different meaning of *dear friend.*
Darwyn, Deorwine, Derwan, Derwin, Derwyn, Durwin, Durwyn; **Famous namesakes:** Naturalist Charles Darwin

DASAN (DAH-sahn) Native American: Ruler

DAVEN Scandinavian: Bright Finn

DAVIAN English: Spelling variation of David

DAVID Hebrew: Dearly loved. The Old Testament has many stories of David's life, including his well-known defeat of Goliath the giant. He went on to become king of Israel and write the Book of Psalms. See also Kawika
(Arabic) *Dawud*; (Italian) *Davide*; (Gaelic) *Daibhid, Daibhidh*; (Irish) *Daithi*; (Welsh) *Dafydd, Dewey, Dewi*; (Persian) *Davood*; *Daveon, Davian, Davidson, Daviel, Davion, Daviot*; **Nicknames:** *Dave, Davey, Davie, Davy*; **Diminutive forms:** *Dai, Davi*; **Famous namesakes:** Rock star David Bowie, show host David Letterman, frontiersman Davy Crockett; **Star babies:** son of Robert Redford

DAVIN (DAH-vin) Scandinavian: Bright Finn, intelligent

DAVIS English: David's son; a surname
Famous namesakes: Confederate president Jefferson Davis

DAVU African: The beginning

DAWSON English: David's son; a surname

DAX French: Geographical name; a town in the Gascony region of southwestern France dating from before the Roman occupation
Dack; **Famous namesakes:** Actor Dax Shepard

DAYLAN English: Rhyming variant of Waylon; a historical blacksmith with supernatural powers.
Daelan, Dalyn, Daylen, Daylin, Daylon; **Nicknames:** *Dayne*

DAYNE English: Nickname for Daylan

DEACON (DEE-kən) Greek: Servant; also a church official
Deakin; **Nicknames:** *Deke*; **Famous namesakes:** Football player Deacon Jones; **Star babies:** son of Reese Witherspoon and Ryan Philippe

DEAN English: From the valley
Deane, Deanne, Dene; **Famous namesakes:** Actor Dean Cain, actor Dean Martin, actor James Dean, baseball player Dizzy Dean

DEARBORN English: From the deer brook
Dearbourne

DECLAN (DEK-lən) Irish: Full of goodness. Saint Declan founded a monastery in Ardmore, County Waterford, and is believed to have preached in Ireland before the arrival of Saint Patrick.

DEEMS English: Judge's son

DEERWARD English: Spelling variation of Derward

DEKEL (DAY-kel) Hebrew: Palm tree

DEL French: Surname prefix meaning *of the*; also used as an independent name and an abbreviation of names beginning with *Del–*

DELANEY (də-LAYN-ee) Irish: Descendant of the challenger. Delaney could also be derived from the Norman surname *De l'aunaie*, meaning *from the alder grove* in French.

DELANO French: Surname of unclear origin; possibly from *de la nuit* meaning *of the night*
Famous namesakes: President Franklin Delano Roosevelt

DELBERT English: Spelling variation of Albert

DELION (dehl-lee-ahn) French: Lion; fearless
Delyon

DELLING Norse: Shining

DELMAR (DEL-mər) Latin: Of the sea
(French) *Delmer*, *Delmore*

DELMONT French: Spelling variation of
Dumont

DELROY French: Of the king
(Spanish) *Delrico*; *Delray*, *Delron*; **Famous
namesakes:** Actor Delroy Lindo

DELVIN English: Godly friend.
Delvon

DEMBE (DEM-be) African: Peace

DEMETRIUS (de-MEE-tree-əs) Greek: Of
Demeter. Demeter is the mythological Greek
goddess of harvest and fertility.
(French) *Dimitri*; (Russian) *Dmitri*; *Demetri*,
Demetrios, *Demitri*, *Dimitrios*; **Diminutive
forms:** *Dimka*

DEMOTHI (de-MO-tee) Native American:
Talks while walking

DEMPSEY Gaelic, English: Proud; surname
Dempsy; **Famous namesakes:** Actor Patrick
Dempsey, boxer Jack Dempsey

DEMPSTER English: Judicious

DENBY Norse, Anglo-Saxon, Scandinavian:
From the Danish settlement; surname

DENHOLM Scottish: A place name

DENIZ (deh-NIZ) Turkish: Sea

DENLEY English: From the valley meadow;
surname
Denlie, *Denlea*, *Denleigh*, *Denly*

DENMAN English: Resident of a valley

DENNIS Greek: Follower of Dionysius.
Dionysius is the Greek god of wine
responsible for growth of the vines,
equivalent to the Roman god Bacchus. Saint
Denis is the patron saint of France.
(French) *Denis*; *Dennet*, *Denys*; **Nicknames:**
Denney, *Dennie*, *Denny*, *Deon*, *Dion*; **Famous
namesakes:** Actor Dennis Quaid, actor
Dennis Hopper, sailor Dennis Conner

DENNISON English: Son of Dennis; a
surname
Tennyson; *Denison*; **Nicknames:** *Den*

DENTON English: From the town or
settlement in the den; a surname closely
related to the name *Dalton*
Denten, *Dentin*, *Dentun*; **Nicknames:** *Denn*,
Denny

DENVER English: Variant of the surname
Danvers meaning from Anvers; capital of the
state of Colorado.

DENZEL English: A Cornish place name
Denzell, *Denzil*; **Famous namesakes:** Actor
Denzel Washington

DEORSA Gaelic: Variation of George

DERBY English: Deertown

DEREK German: People's ruler; a short
form of Theodoric commonly used as an
independent name
(Dutch) *Dirck*, *Dirk*; *Darek*, *Daric*, *Darick*,
Darrick, *Darroch*, *Darrock*, *Dereck*, *Derick*,
Derik, *Derrek*, *Derrick*, *Derrik*, *Deryck*, *Deryk*;
Famous namesakes: Baseball player Derek
Jeter

DERMOT Irish: Free man or without envy
Dermod, *Diarmad*, *Diarmaid*, *Diarmid*,
Kermit; **Nicknames:** *Darby*

DERRY Irish: Red-haired or like an oak; name of an Irish city

DERWARD (DUR-wərd) English: Guardian of the deer
Deerward, Deorward

DERWEN Welsh: From the oak tree

DERWENT English: Place name referring to Derwent rivers in England and Australia

DERWIN English: Spelling variation of Darwin
Derwan, Derwyn, Durwin, Durwyn

DERYA (DER-yah) Turkish: Ocean

DESIDERIO (DEZ-ee-DER-ree-o) Italian, Spanish: Desired
(French) *Didier*; **Nicknames:** *Deri, Derito, Desi, Dezi*; **Famous namesakes:** Actor and musician Desi Arnaz

DESMOND Irish: From Desmond; an area of South Munster, one of the four provinces of Ireland in the Middle Ages
Deasmumhan, Desmon, Desmund, Dezmond; **Famous namesakes:** South African Bishop Desmond Tutu

DESTIN French: Destiny; also a beach in Florida
Destan, Deston

DESTRY French: Variant of a French surname; American classic western film *Destry Rides Again*

DEVAL (dayv-ahl) Hindi: Divine

DEVEN (DAY-ven, DEV-en) Hindi: For God

DEVEREL (dev-REL) French: Surname derived from place name
(French) *Devereau; Deveral, Devere, Devereaux, Deverell, Devery, Devry*

DEVIN Gaelic: Poet, poetic; possibly related to the Latin word for divine. The variant Devon is a county in England noted for beautiful farmland.
Devan, Deveon, Devon, Devyn; Deven; **Nicknames:** *Dev*; **Star babies:** sons of Denis Leary, Vanessa Williams

DEVLIN Irish, Gaelic: Fierce bravery
Devland, Devlon, Devlyn

DEVRY English: Spelling variation of Deverel

DEWEY Welsh: Variation of David
Dewi

DEWI (DE-wee) Welsh: Variation of David

DEWITT Welsh: Blond, white
(English) *Dwight*

DIALLO (DEE-ah-lo) African: Bold

DIAMOND English: Of high value, brilliant; can refer to the precious stone
Famous namesakes: Actor Lou Diamond Phillips

DICHALI (dee-CHAH-lee) Native American: Speaks a lot

DICK English: Nickname for Richard
Famous namesakes: Actor Dick Van Dyke, TV personality Dick Clark

DIDIER (deed-YAY) French: Variation of Desiderio
Famous namesakes: French actor Didier Flamand

DIEGO (dee-AY-go) Spanish: Variation of James

DIETRICH (DEE-trik) German: Form of Dietrich
Dedric, Dedrik; Dedric, Dedrick, Dieter

DIGBY Norse: From the settlement or town near the ditch or dike; surname
Dikibyr

DILLON Irish, Gaelic: Faithful; from a different source than the Welsh name Dylan
Dilan, Dillen, Dylon; Dillan; **Famous namesakes:** Actor Matt Dillon

DIMA (DEE-mah) Russian: Nickname for Dmitri or Vladimir
Nicknames: *Dimka, Dimochka*

DINESH (di-nesh) Sanskrit: Sun

DINO (DEE-no) English, Spanish: From the dene; (Italian) abbreviation of names ending like Bernardino.

DION Greek: An abbreviation of Dionysus; more often used as an independent name
Deion, Deon, Dionte, Dondre; **Famous namesakes:** Singer Dion (of Dion and the Belmonts), Football player Deion Sanders

DIONDRE (dee-ON-dray) French: Blend of Dion and Andre

DIONYSIUS (die-ə-NIE-səs) Greek: The Greek god of wine. The great theater in Athens is dedicated to Dionysius.
(Polish) *Dionizy; Dionysios, Dionysus;*
Nicknames: *Dennis, Deion, Deon, Dion*

DIXON English: Son of Dick
Dickson; **Nicknames:** *Dix*

DMITRI (DMEE-tree) Russian: Variation of Demetrius

Dmitrii; **Nicknames:** *Dima, Dimochka;*
Famous namesakes: Russian chemist Dmitri Mendeleev, who discovered the periodic table, Composer Dmitri Shostakovich

DOANE English: Rolling hills
Doan

DOBRY (DO-bree) Polish: Good, kind

DOHASAN (do-HAH-sahn) Native American: Little bluff (Kiowa); an important Kiowa leader who did much for his tribe, including establishing a peace between the Kiowa and the Osage
Dohosan

DOLAN Irish: Raven-haired

DOMINGO (do-MEENG-go) Spanish: Variation of Dominic

DOMINIC Latin: Of the Lord; a name traditionally given to a child born on Sunday
(French) *Dominique;* (Spanish) *Domenico, Domingo;* (Basque) *Txomin;* (Russian) *Dominik;* (Hungarian) *Domo, Domokos; Dominick;* **Nicknames:** *Nick;* **Diminutive forms:** *Dom;* **Famous namesakes:** Opera singer Placido Domingo, Basketball player Dominique Wilkins; **Star babies:** son of Stevan Seagal and Kelly LeBrock

DON English: Nickname for Donald
Nicknames: *Donnie, Donny;* **Famous namesakes:** Actor Don Johnson, Actor Don Rickles, Actor Don Cheadle

"Babies are such a nice way to start people."
—Don Herold

DONAHUE Irish, Gaelic: Dark warrior
Donaghy, Donnchadh

DONALD Scottish, Gaelic: Ruler of all
(Hawaiian) *Kona; Domhnall, Donal, Donall,
Donel, Donell, Donnel, Donnell*; **Nicknames:**
Don, Donnie, Donny; **Famous namesakes:**
Singer Donny Osmond, actor Donald
Sutherland, business tycoon Donald Trump,
Disney character Donald Duck

DONAT (DAW-naht) Polish: Variation of
Donato

DONATIEN Latin: Presence of God

DONATO (do-NAH-to) Latin, Italian: Gift
from God
(Italian) *Donatello, Donzel*; (Polish) *Donat*

DONN Irish: Brown. A mythical figure in
Irish literature and folklore, Donn was known
as king of the underworld.

DONNAN (DUN-nahn) Irish: Brown-haired
Nicknames: *Donn*

DONNELLY Irish: Dark
Donnally; **Nicknames:** *Don*

DONOVAN Irish: Dark-haired
Donavan, Donavon

DOOLEY Gaelic: Dark hero

DOR Hebrew: Generation

DOREN Hebrew: Gift
Doron

DORIAN (DOR-ee-ən) Greek: From Doris
(region in Greece), descendant of Dorus, also
used as a familiar form of Isidore. Dorian was
the main character in Oscar Wilde's novel *The
Picture of Dorian Gray* who was given his wish
that his portrait would age while he remained
young and handsome.
Dorien, Dorion; **Star babies:** son of Lindsay
Wagner

DORRAN (DOR-un) Celtic: Stranger, exile
*Doran, Doron, Dorrance, Dorrel, Dorrell,
Dorren, Dorrin*

DOUG Scottish: Nickname for Douglas

DOUGAL (DOO-gul) Scottish: Dark stranger
Doughall, Dugald, Dughall; **Nicknames:**
Dougie

DOUGLAS Scottish: From the dark
river. The Scottish Douglas clan had two
historical branches: Black Douglases and Red
Douglases. The lords of these clans figure in
Sir Walter Scott's writing.
(Celtic) *Doughlas; Douglass, Dubhglas*;
Nicknames: *Doug* **Famous namesakes:** Actor
Douglas Fairbanks, author Douglas Adams,
General Douglas MacArthur

DOVEV (do-VAYV) Hebrew: Speaks in a
whisper
Nicknames: *Dov*

DOW Irish: Black-haired

DOWAN Irish: Black; dimunitive of the
Gaelic *Dubh*

DOYLE Irish: Dark stranger
Famous namesakes: *Sherlock Holmes* author
Sir Arthur Conan Doyle

DRAKE English: Dragon
Famous namesakes: English explorer Sir
Francis Drake

DREW English: Manly, brave; variant of Andrew
Drue; *Dru*; **Famous namesakes:** Football player Drew Bledsoe

DRISCOLL Irish: Uncertain meaning, possibly messenger, mediator, or sorrowful
Driscol

DRU (DROO) American: Nickname for Andrew

DRUMMOND Scottish: At the ridge
Drummand

DRYDEN English: From the dry valley; surname
Dridan, Driden, Drygedene; **Famous namesakes:** Poet John Dryden

DRYSTAN (DRIS-tən) Welsh: Form of Tristan

DUANE Irish: Small and dark; an Anglicized variant of the Gaelic name *Dubhan*.
Dewain, Dewayne, Duayne, Dubhan, Duwayne, Dwain, Dwaine, Dwane, Dwayne

DUBLIN Irish: Place name for the capital of Ireland

DUDLEY English: From the people's meadow
Famous namesakes: Actor Dudley Moore

DUFF Gaelic, Celtic: Dark
Dubh; **Nicknames:** *Duffy*

DUGAN (DOO-gun) Gaelic: Swarthy
Duggan

DUKA African: All

DUKE Latin: Leader; a royal title
Famous namesakes: Jazz musician Duke Ellington, actor John "The Duke" Wayne

DUME African: Bull

DUMI African: Inspirer

DUMONT French: Of the mountain
Delmon, Delmont

DUNCAN Gaelic, Scottish: Brown warrior; an Anglicized variant of Donnchadh and a Scottish royal name. The eleventh-century King Duncan was killed by fellow Scot Macbeth of Moray. Shakespeare portrays a version of Duncan's story in his famous play *Macbeth*.
Donnchadh; **Nicknames:** *Dunn, Dunc, Dunky*; **Famous namesakes:** American businessman Duncan Hines, basketball player Tim Duncan; **Star babies:** son of Gordon Elliott

DUNHAM (DUN-um) Celtic: Dark-skinned man

DUNLEY English: From the hill meadow; surname
Dunleah, Dunleigh, Dunly; Dunlea, Dunlie, Dunnlea, Dunnleigh, Dunnley

DUNMORE Scottish: From the great hill fortress
Dunmor

DUNSTAN (DUN-stən) English: Hill of stone

DUNTON English: From the town or settlement on the hill

DURANGO Spanish: Strong

DURANT Latin, French: Firm, enduring; more commonly found as a last name
(French) *Durante, Dureau; Duran, Durand, Duron, Durrant, Durrell*; **Famous namesakes:** Historians Will and Ariel Durant, Entertainer Jimmy Durante, Boxer Roberto Duran

DURRELL English: Spelling variation of Durant

DURWARD English: Keeper of the gate
Nicknames: *Ward*

DURWIN English: Spelling variation of
Darwin
Durwyn

DUSTIN English: A fighter
Dustan, Duston, Dustyn; **Nicknames:** *Dusty*;
Famous namesakes: Actor Dustin Hoffman

DUVAL French: Of the valley

DUYGU Turkish: Emotion

DWIGHT English: Variation of Dewitt
Famous namesakes: President Dwight D.
Eisenhower, baseball player Dwight Gooden

DWYER Irish: Dark and wise

DYAMI (dee-AH-mee) Native American: Eagle

DYLAN (DIL-ən) Welsh: Of the sea. In
Welsh mythology, Dylan was the god of
the sea. The Welsh name is from a different
source than the Irish Dillon.
Dilan, Dyllan, Dyllon; **Nicknames:** *Dillie*;
Famous namesakes: Welsh poet Dylan
Thomas, musician Bob Dylan; **Star babies:**
sons of Stephanie Seymour, Pierce Brosnan,
Pamela Anderson and Tommy Lee, Joan
Cusack, Michael Douglas and Catherine Zeta-
Jones, Kenneth Edmonds

DYSON English: Variant of Dennison

EACHAN (EE-kun) Scottish: Brown horse
Eachann

EAMON (AY-mon, AY-mən) Irish: Variation
of Edmund
Eamonn

EARL English: Nobleman; a name based on
the English aristocratic title
Earle, Erle, Errol, Erroll; **Famous namesakes:**
Actor Errol Flynn, actor James Earl Jones

EARNAN (ARN-awn) Irish: Knowing

EARVIN (ER-vin) English: Spelling variation
of Irving
Ervin; **Nicknames:** *Erv*; **Famous namesakes:**
Basketball player Earvin "Magic" Johnson

EATON English: Town or settlement by the
river; surname
Eatun; *Eatton, Eton, Eyton*

EBAN Hebrew: Rock
Eben; *Even*

EBENEZER (eb-ə-NEE-zər) Hebrew:
Rock of help. In the Old Testament, Samuel
gave this name to a monument he erected to
commemorate a victory. Ebenezer Scrooge
is a miserly character in the famous story *A
Christmas Carol* by Charles Dickens.

EBERHARD German: Brave boar
(English) *Everet, Everett*; (Spanish) *Evarado,
Everardo*; (Swedish) *Evert*; *Eberhardt,
Eburhardt, Everard, Everhard, Evrard*;
Nicknames: *Ever*

EBI Persian: Paternal

ED English: Nickname for Edward
Nicknames: *Eddie, Eddy*; **Famous
namesakes:** Actor Ed Asner, actor Ed Harris,
actor Ed Begley Jr., jockey Eddie Arcaro

EDBERT English: Wealthy and bright

EDE Dutch: Variation of Edward

EDEL German: Noble

EDER Hebrew: Flock. Shepherds used the biblical tower of Eder to watch over their sheep.

EDGAR German: Prosperous spearman (French) *Edgard*; (Spanish) *Edgardo*; *Eadger*; **Old forms:** *Eadgard*; **Nicknames:** *Ed*; **Famous namesakes:** Author Edgar Allan Poe, French artist Edgar Degas

"Were I called on to define, very briefly, the term Art, I should call it 'the reproduction of what the Senses perceive in Nature through the veil of the soul.' The mere imitation, however accurate, of what is in Nature, entitles no man to the sacred name of 'Artist.'"
—Edgar Allen Poe

EDISON English: Son of Edward *Eddis*, *Eddison*, *Edson*; **Famous namesakes:** Inventor Thomas Edison

EDMUND English: Wealthy protector (French) *Edmond*; (Italian) *Edmondo*; (Spanish) *Edmundo*; (Gaelic) *Eamonn*; (Irish) *Eames*, *Eamon*; *Eadmund*, *Edmon*, *Tedman*, *Tedmund*, *Theomund*; **Nicknames:** *Ed*, *Eddie*, *Ned*, *Ted*, *Teddy*; **Famous namesakes:** English poet Edmund Spenser, senator Edmund Muskie; **Star babies:** son of Ben Kingsley

EDRIC (ED-rik) Anglo-Saxon: Wealthy ruler *Eddrick*, *Edrick*

EDSEL English: Rich, wealthy man's estate; most notable as the name of Edsel Ford and the car that bore his name.

EDUARDO (e-DHWAHR-do) Spanish: Variation of Edward

EDWARD English: Prosperous, guardian; the name of eight kings of England since the Norman Conquest. See also *Iolo* (Anglo-Saxon) *Edred*; (French) *Eduard*; (Italian) *Edoardo*, *Eduardo*; (Spanish) *Duardo*, *Duarte*; (Portuguese) *Edwardo*; (Swedish) *Edvard*; (Dutch) *Ede*; (Basque) *Edorta*; (Finnish) *Eetu*; (Hawaiian) *Ekewaka*; *Edwald*; **Old forms:** *Eadward*; **Nicknames:** *Ed*, *Eddie*, *Eddy*, *Edik*; **Diminutive forms:** *Ned*; **Famous namesakes:** Senator Edward Kennedy, actor Edward Norton; **Star babies:** sons of Mel Brooks, Mel Gibson

EDWARDSON English: Son of Edward

EDWIN English: Wealthy friend *Edlin*, *Edwyn*; **Old forms:** *Eadwine*; **Nicknames:** *Ed*, *Eddy*, *Eddie*; **Famous namesakes:** Astronaut Edwin "Buzz" Aldrin

EFIM (ye-FEEM) Russian: Fair speech **Nicknames:** *Fima*

EFRAIN (e-frah-EEN) Spanish: Variation of Ephraim

EFRAT Hebrew: Honored

EFREM Russian: Variation of Ephraim

EFRON Hebrew: Bird *Ephron*; **Famous namesakes:** Actor Zac Efron

EGAN (EE-gun) Irish, Gaelic: Fiery *Eagan*, *Eagon*, *Eghan*, *Egon*

EGBERT (EG-bərt) Anglo-Saxon: Bright edge of a sword

EGIDIO (ə-GID-ee-o) Italian: Variation of Giles

EGON German: Strong with a sword; (Gaelic, Irish) fiery

EGOR (YE-gor, EE-gor) Russian: Variation of George
Nicknames: *Egorka*, *Zhora*

EIMHIN (AY-vin) Irish: Swift; a name sometimes Anglicized as Evan and Ewan

EINAR (IE-nar) Norse, Scandinavian: Lone warrior
(Finnish) *Eino*

EISA Arabic: Arabic form of Jesus as referenced in the Koran
Issa

EJNAR (IE-nahr) Danish: Warrior

EKEWAKA (e-ke-WAH-kah) Hawaiian: Variation of Edward

EKON (AY-kon) African: Strong (Nigeria)

ELAN (EE-lan) Native American: Friendly

ELDEN English: Elf friend, noble friend, implies supernaturally good or wise friend; variant of Alvin or Alden
(English) *Eldan*; *Eldin, Eldon, Eldwin, Eldwyn*

ELDER English: From near the elder tree; has also come to mean older, wiser, and is a governing officer of a church
Aeldra; *Eldor*

ELDRED (EL-drəd) Anglo-Saxon: Old counsel, old or wise advisor; variant of Aldred
Eldrid

ELDRIDGE English: Old, wise leader; surname; variant of Aldrich

ELDWIN English: Spelling variation of Alvin

ELEK (EL-ek) Hungarian: Variation of Alexander

ELEUTHERIOS (e-lef-THER-ee-os) Greek: Liberator
Eleftherios

ELFRED English: Spelling variation of Alfred

ELGAR Anglo-Saxon: Elf-spear, spearman; variant of Algar
Elger, Ellgar, Ellger

ELGIN English: Noble; white

ELHANAN Hebrew: He whom God has graciously bestowed

ELI (EE-lie) Hebrew: Ascended. This Old Testament figure was a high priest of Israel and instructed the young Samuel.
(French) *Elie*; *Ely*; **Famous namesakes:** Quarterback Eli Manning; **Star babies:** son of Sally Field

ELIAS (e-LIE-ahs, e-LEE-ahs) Greek: Variation of Elijah

ELIEZER (el-ie-EE-zər) Hebrew: God is my helper. In the Old Testament, this name belongs to both a servant of Abraham and one of Moses' sons.
(Spanish) *Eliazar*; (Basque) *Elazar*; *Eleazar*

ELIHU (i-LIE-hyoo, i-LIE-hoo) Hebrew: Spelling variation of Elijah

ELIJAH (e-LIE-jə, e-LIE-zhə) Hebrew: The Lord is my God; a biblical prophet told about in I and II Kings of the Old Testament. See also *Ilias, Ilya*

(Greek) *Elias*, *Ilyas*; (English) *Ellis*; (Italian) *Elia*; (Persian) *Iliya*; *Elihu*, *Eliot*; **Nicknames:** *Eli*, *Ely*; **Famous namesakes:** Actor Elijah Wood; **Star babies:** sons of Tiffany, James Spader, Cher, Bono, Wynonna Judd

ELISHA (ee-LIE-shə) Hebrew: God is salvation; a prophet and successor to Elijah (Italian) *Eliseo*

ELISHAMA (e-LISH-ə-mə) Hebrew: God hears

ELKANAH (el-KAYN-ə) Hebrew: God has created. In the Old Testament, Elkanah is Samuel's father.

ELLERY (EL-ə-ree) English: Island with elder trees; may also be a derivation of Hilary, meaning joyful
Ellary

ELLIOTT (E-lee-ət, EL-yət) Hebrew: The Lord is my God; variant of Elijah
Eliot, *Eliott*, *Elliot*; **Famous namesakes:** Actor Elliott Gould, poet T.S. Eliot

ELLIS English: Variation of Elijah

ELMER English, Anglo-Saxon: Highborn and renowned; (Teutonic) awe-inspiring
Almer, *Aylmer*; *Aillmer*, *Allmer*, *Aylmer*, *Eylmer*; **Old forms:** *Aegelmaere*, *Aethelmaere*

ELMO Italian: Helmet, protection. Saint Elmo is the common name for Saint Erasmus, the patron saint of sailors. Saint Elmo's fire is said to protect sailors and is the glow that accompanies a steady discharge of electricity from objects (such as masts of sailing ships) during thunderstorms or when electrified clouds are present.
Famous namesakes: Elmo, the lovable Sesame Street character

ELMORE English: From the moor with the elm trees; surname
Elmoor

ELOI Latin, French: Chosen one; abbreviation of Eligius
(Spanish) *Eligio*, *Eloy*; (Czech) *Alois*; *Elois*, *Alois*; **Old forms:** *Eligius*

ELRAD (EL-rud) Hebrew: God is the ruler

ELROY English: Variation of Leroy

ELSDON English: Nobleman's hill; surname
Athelston; *Elsden*; **Old forms:** *Aethelisdun*, *Aetheston*

ELTON English: From the old town
Alton, *Eldon*; **Famous namesakes:** Musician Elton John

ELVIN English: Elf friend, noble friend; variant of Alvin.
Elveryn, *Elvyn*

ELVIO Latin, Spanish: Blond, fair

ELVIS English: Elf friend, noble friend; variant of Alvin. Elvis Presley was an early American star of rock and roll and is considered one of the greatest of all time. His popularity has grown well after his death, and his home Graceland is an international tourist attraction.
Alvis, *Elvys*; **Famous namesakes:** Singer Elvis Costello, skater Elvis Stojko; **Star babies:** son of Anthony Perkins

ELWIN English: Elf friend, noble friend; variant of Alvin.
Elwyn

EMAN Irish: Serious; Irish form of Emest

EMERIL Italian: Meaning unknown
Famous namesakes: Popular TV chef Emeril Lagasse

EMERSON (E-mər-sən) English: Surname; son of Emery
Famous namesakes: Racecar driver Emerson Fittipaldi

EMERY (EM-ə-ree) German, English: Industrious
(English) *Amory*; (Czech) *Imrich*; (Hungarian) *Imre*

EMIL (ay-MEEL) Latin: Derived from a Roman clan name meaning industrious
(French) *Emile*; (Italian) *Emiliano*; (Spanish) *Emilio*; (Finnish) *Eemeli*; **Famous namesakes:** Actor Emilio Estevez, French writer Emile Zola

EMILIO (e-MEE-lee-o) Spanish: Variation of Emil
Famous namesakes: Actor Emilio Estevez

EMMANUEL (i -MAN-yoo-əl) Hebrew: God is with us; another name for the Messiah, this name is in both the Old and New Testaments
(German) *Immanuel*; (Italian) *Emanuele*; (Spanish) *Emanuel, Mano, Manolito, Manolo, Manuel, Manuelo*; **Nicknames:** *Iman, Imani, Mannie, Manny*

EMMETT English: Industrious, strong

EMRYS (EM-ris) Welsh: Variation of Ambrose

ENAPAY (en-ah-pay) Native American: Goes forth bravely (Sioux)

ENCELADUS (en-SEL-ə-dus) Greek: A giant. In Greek mythology, he fought against the Olympians and Zeus.

ENDYMION (en-DIM-ee-ən) Greek: A handsome youth of Greek mythology

> *"A thing of Beauty is a joy forever"*
> —John Keats, "Endymion: A Poetic Romance"

ENEAS (e-NAY-us) Spanish: Variation of Aeneas

ENGELBERT (ENG-gəl-bert) German: Bright angel
Ingelbert, Inglebert; **Famous namesakes:** Singer Engelbert Humperdinck

ENGIN Turkish: Vast

ENOCH (EE-nək) Hebrew: Trained and dedicated. Enoch was father of Methuselah, the oldest living man named in the Bible. (Danish) *Enok*

ENRIQUE (en-REE-kay) Spanish: Variation of Henry

ENZO Italian: Variation of Henry
Star babies: son of Patricia Arquette

EOGHAN (O-in, YO-in) Gaelic: Youth
Eoghann

EPHRAIM (EE-frah-im, EE-frəm, EFF-rəm) Hebrew: Fruitful; in the Old Testament, a son of Joseph
(Spanish) *Efrain*; (Russian) *Efrem*; *Efraim, Efran, Efrayim, Efren, Ephram, Ephrem*

ERAN (EE-rahn) Hebrew: Watchful
Nicknames: *Er*

ERASMUS (e-RAS-mus) Greek: Beloved. Saint Erasmus, more popularly known as Saint Elmo, is the patron saint of sailors. (Spanish) *Erasmo*; (Scandinavian) *Rasmus*; **Nicknames:** *Elmo*

ERDEM (ER-dem) Turkish: Virtue

ERI Hebrew: My guardian

ERIC Norse, Scandinavian: Eternal ruler, forever strong. According to Norse legend, the Viking Leif Ericson (son of Eric the Red) landed on the shores of America 500 years before Christopher Columbus.
(German) *Audrick, Erich*; (Spanish) *Eurico*; (Scandinavian) *Erik*; (Polish) *Eryk*; (Finnish) *Eero, Erkki*; *Aaric, Aric, Arick, Arik, Arrick, Aurick, Eirik, Erick, Eriq*; **Famous namesakes:** English musician Eric Clapton, children's author Eric Carle; **Star babies:** sons of Kirk Douglas, Donald Trump

ERICKSON Scandinavian: Son of Eric, ever kingly
Ericksen, Ericson, Erikson

ERIN Gaelic: Peace; a poetic name for Ireland, and a name used mostly by girls

ERMANNO (er-MAHN-o) Italian: Variation of Herman

ERNEST (UR-nəst) English: Serious, resolute
(Spanish) *Ernesto*; *Earnest*; **Nicknames:** *Ernie*; **Famous namesakes:** Author Ernest Hemmingway, actor Ernest Borgnine; **Star babies:** son of Loretta Lynn

ERROL (ER-əl) Scottish: Spelling variation of Earl
Erroll; **Famous namesakes:** Australian actor Errol Flynn

ERWIN English: Friend of the wild boar, friend of the sea; (Welsh) white river; variant of Irving
(Hungarian) *Ervin*; *Earwin, Earwine, Earwyn, Erwyn*; **Famous namesakes:** German general Erwin Rommel, author Irwin Shaw

ESA (ES-ah) Finnish: Variation of Isaiah

ESAU (EE-saw) Hebrew: Hairy. In the Book of Genesis, Esau is Jacob's older twin brother and a skilled and adventurous hunter.

ESDRAS (EZ-drəs) Hebrew: Spelling variation of Ezra

ESPEN Scandinavian: Bear god

ESTEBAN (es-TAY-bahn) Spanish: Variation of Stephen
Estefan, Estevan, Estevon; **Nicknames:** *Teb*

ESTON English: From the eastern town; surname
Easton

ETHAN Hebrew: Strong, firm; an Old Testament name
Aitan; *Ethen*; **Old forms:** *Etan*; **Famous namesakes:** Actor Ethan Hawke; **Star babies:** son of John Wayne

ETIENNE (ay-TYEN) French: Variation of Stephen

ETU (ay-too) Native American: Sun

EUGENE (yoo-JEEN) Greek: Well born, noble
(Greek) *Jeno*; (Spanish) *Eugenio*; (Swedish) *Eugen*; (Dutch) *Eugenius*; (Russian) *Evgeni, Yevgeny*; (Czech) *Evzen*; (Ukrainian) *Yevhen*; (Hungarian) *Jenci*; **Old forms:** *Eugenios*; **Nicknames:** *Gene, Zhenechka, Zhenka, Zhenya*; **Famous namesakes:** Playwright Eugene O'Neill

EUSEBIUS (yoo-SEE-bee-əs) Greek: Pious; the name of several saints
Eusebios

EUSTACE (YOO-stəs) Greek: Fruitful, productive
Eustachy, Eustis; **Nicknames:** Stacey, Stacy

EUSTON Irish: Heart

EVAN (EV-ən) Scottish: Variant of John;
(Celtic) young warrior
(Irish) *Ewan*; *Evann, Evin, Evyn*; **Famous
namesakes:** Author Evan Thomas; **Star
babies:** sons of Diana Ross, Bruce Springsteen

EVANDER (ee-VAN-dər, ə-VAN-dər) Latin:
Good man; also a deity of Roman mythology
Famous namesakes: Boxer Evander Holyfield

EVANTON English: God is gracious

EVERETT (EV-ə-rit, EV-rit) English:
Variation of Eberhard
Everet, Evert; **Nicknames:** Ever

EVERLEY English: From the boar's
meadow; from Ever's meadow; surname;
may evoke thoughts of the melodious Everly
Brothers singing duo
Eferleah, Everleigh, Everly; Everlie, Everlea

EVIAN English: Variant of Evan; the French
town famous for Evian spring water. Evian is
also a blend of Evan and Ian meaning John-
John.

EWAN (YOO-ən) Scottish: Young
Euan, Ewen, Ewyn; **Famous namesakes:**
Scottish actor Ewan McGregor

EWELL English: Spelling variation of Yule
Euell

EZEKIEL (i-ZEE-kee-əl) Hebrew: God
strengthens. The biblical Ezekiel was a
prophet among the captives taken to Babylon
at the fall of Jerusalem. The Old Testament
Book of Ezekiel contains his prophecies.
(English) *Zeke*; (Spanish) *Esequiel, Ezequiel*;
Ezechiel, Haskel; **Star babies:** son of Beau
Bridges

EZNIK (YEZ-neek) Armenian: Name of a
fifth-century philosopher
Yeznik

EZRA Hebrew: Helper; an Old Testament
prophet and author of the Book of Ezra
Esdras, Esra, Ezrah; **Famous namesakes:** Poet
Ezra Pound; **Star babies:** son of Paul Reiser

FABIAN (FAH-bee-ahn, FAY-bee-ən) Latin:
Bean farmer; derived from the Roman clan
name Fabius, a name given several Roman
emperors and 16 saints
(English) *Faber*; (French) *Fabien*; (Italian)
Fabiano, Fabio; (Russian) *Fabi*; *Fabion,
Fabiyn, Favian, Favio*; **Famous namesakes:**
Singer and actor Fabian

FABIO (FAH-bee-o) Italian: Variation of
Fabian

FABRICE (fa-BREES) French: From the
Latin word for *craftsman*, one who works
with his hands
(Italian) *Fabrizio*; *Fabrizius*; **Old forms:**
Fabricius

FABUMI African: Gift of God

FACHNAN Irish: Meaning unknown. Saint
Fachnan became the first bishop of Kilfenora,
Ireland in the twelfth century.
Fachna, Faughnan

FADEY (FAH-dee) Russian, Ukrainian:
Brave, courageous; also can be a Russian form
of *Thaddeus*
Faddei; **Diminutive forms:** *Fadeyka,
Fadeyushka, Fadyenka*

FADIL (fah-DEEL) Arabic: Virtuous,
excellence, superior, benefit, favor, eminent,
grace, distinguished
Fadeel

FAFNER Norse: A mythical dragon
Old forms: *Fafnir*

FAGAN Irish: Ardent
Faegan, Fagen, Fagin, Faodhagan

FAHEY Irish: From the green field; surname
sometimes used as first name
Fahy; **Famous namesakes:** Actor and dancer
Jeff Fahey

FAHIM (fah-HEEM) African: Learned

FAING Scottish: From the sheep pen

FAIRFAX English: Blond; surname rarely
used as a first name

FAISAL (FIE-sahl) Arabic: Decisive, criterion
Faysal; **Famous namesakes:** Iraqi King Faysal
the First and the Second, King of Saudi
Arabia King Faysal Ibn Abd Al Aziz

FAKHIR Arabic: Proud, honorary
Fakher

FALCO Latin: Surname relating to falconry
(English) *Falcon, Falkner*; (German) *Falk, Falke*;
Falken, Falko; **Famous namesakes:** Austrian
musician Falco (of "Rock Me Amadeus" fame)

FALLON Irish: In charge; surname used as a
first name

FANE English, Welsh: Joyful, good-natured
Fain, Faine, Fayne

FAOLAN Gaelic: Little wolf

FARAJI (fah-RAH-jee) African: Consolation
(Swahili)

FARAZ (far-ahz) Persian: Above, on the top

FARHAD (far-hahd) Persian: Handsome
youth; a name from Persian mythology

FARID (fah-REED) Arabic, Persian: One of
a kind
Fareed; **Famous namesakes:** Egyptian movie
star and musician Farid el Atrash

FARIS (FAYR-əs) Arabic: Knight, horseback
rider
Fares

FARJAD Persian: Excellent

FARLEY English: From the bull's meadow or
the sheep's meadow; surname
Faerrleah, Fairlie, Farleigh, Farly; *Fairlea,
Fairlee, Fairleigh, Fairley, Fairly, Farlea, Farlee,
Farlie*

FARNELL English: From the fern hill; surname
Farnall, Fearnhealh, Fernald

FARNHAM English: From the fern land or
home; surname
Fearnhamm

FARNLEY English: From the fern meadow;
surname
Farnly, Fearnleah; *Farnlea, Farnleigh*

FAROUK (fah-ROOK) Arabic: Wise, one
who distinguishes truth from falsehood
Faruk, Faruq; **Famous namesakes:** King
Farouk of Egypt

FARQUHAR (FAR-qu-har) Gaelic: Very
dear; surname used as first name (mainly in
Scotland)
Fearchar, Fearcher

FARR English: Traveler, voyager
*Faer, Faerwald, Farmon, Farold, Farrs, Fars,
Farson, Firman*

FARREL Irish, Celtic: Brave, victorious;
surname sometimes used as a first name
Farrell, Farry, Ferrell; **Famous namesakes:**
Irish actor Colin Farrell

FARREN Irish: Adventurous; some spelling variants are also surnames
Faran, Farrin, Feran, Ferran

FARROKH Persian: Happy, fortunate. Farrokh Bulsara was better known as Freddie Mercury, the flamboyant lead singer of the band Queen.

FARZAD (far-zahd) Persian: Splendid birth

FARZAM (far-zahm) Persian: Worthy, befitting

FARZAN (far-zahn) Persian: Wise

FARZIN (far-ZEEN) Persian: Learned

FASTRED German: Firm counsel

FAUNUS (FAWN-əs) Latin: God of forests

FAUST (FOWST) Latin: Auspicious, lucky. Faust was a legendary German alchemist and astrologer who is said to have sold his soul to the Devil in exchange for knowledge and power.
(French) *Fauste*; (Italian) *Fausto*; **Old forms:** *Faustus*; **Famous namesakes:** Italian soccer star Fausto Rossini

FAVONIUS Latin: West wind

FAZEL Persian: Learned

FEARGHALL (FERG-al) Gaelic: Victorious, highest choice
Fergall, Fergal

FEICH Irish: Raven
Fay

FEICHIN (FE-cheen) Irish: Young raven

FELIPE (fe-LEE-pay) Spanish: Variation of Philip
Felip, Felipo, Felippe, Filip, Filipe; **Nicknames:** *Felo, Lipe, Lipo*

FELIX (FEE-liks) Latin, French: Happy or lucky
(French) *Felicien*; (Italian) *Felicio*; (Spanish) *Feliciano*; (Polish) *Feliks*; *Felice, Felician*; **Famous namesakes:** Boxer Felix Trinidad

FELTON English: From the settlement in the field; surname
Feldon, Feldtun, Feldun, Feltin

FENTON English: From the settlement or town on the moor (fens)

FEODRAS Greek: Stone

FERDINAND (FER-də-nand) German: Adventurer, traveler
(French) *Fernand*; (Italian) *Ferdinando*; (Spanish) *Fernando, Hernan, Hernandez, Hernando*; (Portuguese) *Fernão*; **Nicknames:** *Ferdy, Ferdie*; **Famous namesakes:** Portuguese navigator Ferdinand Magellan; **Star babies:** son of Ben Kingsley

FERGUS (FUR-gəs) Gaelic, Scottish: Strong man; the name of a warrior prince of Ulster in Irish mythology
Fearghus, Ferghus

FERGUSON Scottish: Son of the first choice, son of Fergus; surname
Fergusson

FERMIN (fayr-MEEN) Spanish: Strong

FERNANDO (fer-NAHN-do) Spanish: Variation of Ferdinand
Nicknames: *Nando, Nano*

FERRIS Celtic: Rock, highest choice; possibly derived from Fergus or may be an Irish variant of Peter. The name Ferris was brought to prominence by the 1986 movie *Ferris Bueller's Day Off.*
Faris, Farris

FIACRE Celtic: Eagle. Saint Fiacre was an Irish saint who built a hospice in France.
Fiacra

FIDEL (fee-DEL) Latin, Spanish: Faithful (Italian) *Fidelio*; *Fedele, Fidal, Fidello*; **Old forms:** *Fidelis*; **Diminutive forms:** *Fido*; **Famous namesakes:** Cuban leader Fidel Castro

FIE Scottish: Dark of peace; MacFie is a Scottish surname
MacFie

FIELDING English: From or lives in the field; surname
Felding

FILBERT German: Brilliant
Felabert, Philbert; Filibert

FILMORE Scottish: Famous; surname
Filmarr, Filmer; Fillmore; **Famous namesakes:** President Millard Fillmore

FINBAR Irish, Celtic: Blond, handsome
Finnbar, Finnobarr, Fionnbarr, Fynbar

FINEEN Irish: Fair at birth
Finghin, Finnin

FINIAN Irish: Fair. Finians were warrior-followers of third-century legendary Irish hero Finn Mac Cumhail.

FINLAY Gaelic: Small blond soldier
Findlay; **Famous namesakes:** Scottish actor Finlay Currie; **Star babies:** son of Amanda Pays and Corbin Bernsen

FINN Irish, English, Gaelic: Fair. In Irish mythology, Finn Mac Cumhail was a legendary hero similar to the English Robin Hood.
Finian, Fionan, Fionn

FINNEEN Irish: Beautiful child

FINNEGAN Irish: Fair; Irish surname given notoriety by James Joyce's novel *Finnegan's Wake*

FIORELLO (fee-o-REL-o) Italian: Little flower
Famous namesakes: New York City Mayor Fiorello LaGuardia

FIRMAN English: Traveler; more common as a surname

FIRTH Scottish: Narrow inlet of the sea; also a surname
Famous namesakes: British actor Colin Firth

FITCH English: Ermine; surname used as first name
Fitche, Fytch

FITZ English: Surname prefix meaning *son of*; sometimes a familiar form name for these *Fitz–* names

FLANN Irish: Ruddy; Flanagan is a common surname derived from *Flann*
Flainn, Flanagan, Flannagain, Flannagan, Floinn; **Diminutive forms:** *Flannan*

FLANNERY Irish: Red-haired; a surname

FLAVIAN Latin: Golden or blond; from the Roman family name Flavius
(Italian) *Flavio*; (Polish) *Flawiusz*; **Old forms:** *Flavius*

FLAVIO (FLAH-vee-o) Italian: Variation of Flavian

FLEMING English, Anglo-Saxon: From Flanders; surname
Famous namesakes: British novelist Ian Fleming

FLETCHER English, Scottish: Profession name, arrow maker
Nicknames: *Fletch*; **Famous namesakes:** Sailor Fletcher Christian; **Star babies:** son of Mia Farrow and André Previn

FLORIAN (FLOR-ee-ahn) Latin: Flowering, blooming
(French) *Florien*; (Spanish) *Florentino, Florinio; Floren, Florentin, Florentyn, Florus*

FLOYD English: Gray
Famous namesakes: Jamaican musician Floyd Lloyd

FLYNN Irish: Son of a red-haired man; surname sometimes used as first name
Flynn, Flin, Flinn, Flyn; **Star babies:** son of James Earl Jones

FONTAINE French: Fountain, water source; surname sometimes given as a first name
(Italian) *Fontana; Fonteine*

FONZO (FON-zo) Spanish: Nickname for Alphonse

FORBES Gaelic: Field

FORD English: River crossing; familiar form of many names with Ford as their suffix
Famous namesakes: President Gerald Ford

FORREST English: From a surname meaning forest in Old French, originally belonging to a person who lived near a forest. The name now has a strong association with the Tom Hanks character from the 1994 film *Forrest Gump*; (Latin) woodsman, from the woods
Forest, Forester, Forrester, Foster; **Famous namesakes:** Actor Forest Whitaker

FORTUNE French: Luck, fortune
Fortino, Fortun, Fortunato

FOSTER English: Keeps the forest, forest-ranger; more common as a surname

FRANCESCO (frahn-CHES-ko) Italian: Variation of Francis

FRANCIS Latin: Free one, Frenchman. Saint Francis of Assisi was an Italian priest who founded the Franciscan order.
(German) *Frantz, Franz*; (French) *Francois*; (Italian) *Francesco, Franco*; (Spanish) *Cisco, Farruco, Francisco, Frasco, Frascuelo, Frisco*; (Teutonic) *Franziskus*; (Gaelic) *Frang, Frannsaidh*; (Swedish) *Frans*; (Czech) *Frantisek*; (Polish) *Frandszk*; (Hungarian) *Ferenc, Ferko; Ferke, Frandscus, Franta; Frances*; **Nicknames:** *Feri, Franchot, Frankie, Franky, Pancho, Frank*; **Diminutive forms:** *Pacho, Paco, Paquito*; **Famous namesakes:** Director Francis Ford Coppola, Spanish explorer Francisco Pizarro

> *"For my name and memory, I leave it to men's charitable speeches, to foreign nations, and to the next ages."*
> —Sir Francis Bacon

FRANCOIS (frahn-SWAW) French: Variation of Francis
Famous namesakes: French President François Mitterand, French director François Truffault

FRANK English: Free man; a nickname for Francis or Franklin but not uncommon as an independent name
Famous namesakes: Singer Frank Sinatra, architect Frank Lloyd Wright, composer Frank Zappa

FRANKLIN English: Free man, landholder *Franklyn*; **Nicknames:** *Frank*; **Famous namesakes:** President Franklin Delano Roosevelt, President Franklin Pierce

FRANTISEK Czech: Variation of Francis

FRANZ (FRAHNTS) German: Variation of Francis

FRASER (FRAY-zher) Scottish: Origin unclear, possibly of the forest men or curly-haired; name of a major Scottish clan. *Frasier, Frazer, Frazier*

FREDERICK German: Peaceful ruler. Numerous royalty from Prussia, Germany, and the Holy Roman Empire have borne this name, including the thirteenth-century patron of the arts Frederick II of Germany, and the eighteenth-century Frederick II of Prussia who was known as *Friedrich der Grosse* (Frederick the Great). (German) *Friedrich*; (French) *Frederic*; (Italian) *Federico*; (Scandinavian) *Frederik, Fredrik*; (Czech) *Bedrich*; (Polish) *Fryderyk*; (Hungarian) *Fredek*; *Frederek, Fredi, Fredric, Fredrick, Friedrich*; **Nicknames:** *Fred, Freddie, Freddy, Frici, Frits, Fritz*; **Diminutive forms:** *Friedel*; **Famous namesakes:** Dancer Fred Astaire, abolitionist Frederick Douglass, actor Fred Savage, children's entertainer Mr. Fred Rogers

FREEMAN English, Anglo-Saxon: Free man, a man freed from bound servitude to an overlord; more common as surname **Famous namesakes:** Actor Morgan Freeman

FRESCO (FRES-ko) Spanish: Fresh

FREWIN (FROO-in) English: Noble friend *Freowine, Frewen, Frewyn*

FREY (FRAY) Norse: He who is foremost. Frey was the god of agriculture and fertility in Norse mythology. **Old forms:** *Freyr*

FREYNE (FRAYN) English: Foreigner *Fraine, Frayne*

FRIDOLF Scandinavian: Peaceful wolf *Fridolph, Friduwulf, Fridwolf*

FRIEDRICH (FREED-rikh) German: Variation of Frederick **Famous namesakes:** German philosopher Friedrich Nietzsche

FRITZ (FRITS) German: Nickname for Frederick

GABRIEL Hebrew: God is my strength. One of seven archangels, Gabriel appeared to Mary to give her the news of her pregnancy and impending birth of Jesus. He appears in Christian, Jewish, and Muslim texts. (Arabic) *Jabril, Jibril*; (Italian) *Gabriele*; (Spanish) Gabian, *Gabrio*; (Basque) *Gabirel*; (Russian) *Gavriil, Gavrila*; (Czech) *Gabek*; (Finnish) *Kaapo*; (Hungarian) *Gabi, Gabor, Gabrian*; **Old forms:** *Gavriel*; **Nicknames:** *Gabe, Gabie, Riel, Gab, Gabbi, Gabby, Gabi*; **Diminutive forms:** *Gavri*; **Famous namesakes:** Colombian author Gabriel García Márquez, Irish actor Gabriel Byrne; **Star babies:** sons of Jason Alexander, Jerry Hall and Mick Jagger, Isabelle Adjani and Daniel Day-Lewis, Mia Farrow

GACE French: Pledge **Famous namesakes:** French troubadour Gace Brulé

GADIEL (gah-dee-el) Arabic: God is my wealth, twisted rope, way, mood, country, state, tribe, plait of hair

GAETANO (gie-TAH-no) Italian: From *Gaeta* (French) *Gaetane*

GAILLARD (gay-AHRD) French: High-spirited; French surname rarely used as a first name
Famous namesakes: Musician Slim Gaillard

GAIR Scottish, Gaelic: Small one
Gare, Gear

GAIUS (GIE-əs) Latin: Meaning uncertain; a common Roman name given to Gaius Julius Caesar and his son, Gaius Octavius
(Welsh) *Cai, Kay; Caius*

GALAHAD (GAL-ə-had) Arthurian legend: The son of Lancelot, Sir Galahad is best known as the knight who achieves the quest for the Holy Grail.
Galahalt, Galahault

GALE (GAYL) English: Lively; now rarely given as a name for boys
Gail, Gayle; Gaile; **Famous namesakes:** Actor Gale Harold, football player Gale Sayers

GALEN (GAY-lən) Greek, English: Tranquil. For nearly 1,500 years, accepted medical practices were based on the research of second-century physician Galen.
(Spanish) *Galeno;* (Gaelic) *Gaelan, Galyn; Galan, Gaylen;* **Famous namesakes:** Actor Galen Gering

GALL Celtic, Gaelic: Stranger. Saint Gall was one of the numerous seventh-century Irish monks who brought Christianity and learning back to Europe after the Dark Ages.
Gael; Gale

GALLAGHER (GAL-ə-gər) Irish, Gaelic: Eager helper; surname
Old forms: *Galchobhar;* **Famous namesakes:** Actor Peter Gallagher, actor David Gallagher, comedian Gallagher

GALT (GAHLT) Norse: From the high ground

GALTON English: Steep, wooded land
Gallton, Galten

GALWAY Gaelic: Irish place name; surname
Galaway, Galloway; **Famous namesakes:** Critic Galway Kinnell, Irish flautist James Galway

GAMAL (ga-MAHL) Egyptian: Handsome, beautiful. President of Egypt Gamal Abdel Nasser ruled from the time of the revolution in 1952 until his death in 1970.
Gimal; **Nicknames:** *Gimi*

GAMBA (GAM-bah) African: Warrior (Zimbabwe)

GANDEN (gahn-den) Sanskrit: Joy: A paradise
Nicknames: *Gandi*

GANESH (gah-NAYSH) Sanskrit: Lord of the multitude

GANNON Irish, Gaelic: Fair-skinned
Gannie, Gionnan

GANYMEDE (GAN-ə-meed) Greek: Cup bearer to the gods, son of King Tros of Troy. According to Greek mythology, this young, beautiful young man became one of Zeus' lovers.

GARCIA (gahr-SEE-ah) Spanish: An old surname of uncertain etymology; possibly means fox
Famous namesakes: Actor Andy Garcia

GARDNER English: Keeper of the garden; surname used as first name
(Teutonic) *Gardener; Gardiner;* **Nicknames:** *Gard*

GARETH (GAR-əth) Welsh: Gentle, modest, and brave. Sir Gareth was a legendary knight of King Arthur's Round Table.
Famous namesakes: British musician Gareth Gates

GARFIELD English: From the spear field; surname
Garafeld; **Famous namesakes:** President James A. Garfield

GARLAND English: From a surname meaning triangle land in Old English
Garlan, Garlen, Garlyn; **Famous namesakes:** Musician Garland Jeffreys

GARNELL English: Spelling variation of Garner

GARNER French: Keeper of grain; surname used as a first name
Garnell; *Garnier, Garnar*; **Famous namesakes:** Actor James Garner

GARNET (GAHR-nət) English: Armed with a spear
Garnett; **Famous namesakes:** English military man Sir Garnet Wolseley

GARON Hebrew: A threshing floor; also from the Hebrew word for throat
Garan, Garen, Garin, Garion

GARRETT Anglo-Saxon, English: Rules by the spear; variant of Gerald. See also *Gareth* (English) *Garrick*; (Dutch) *Garritt*; *Gared, Garet, Garett, Garrad, Garrard, Garred, Garret, Garreth, Jarret, Jarrett*; **Nicknames:** *Garrey, Garry, Gary*; **Famous namesakes:** Actor Brad Garrett, comedian Garrett Morris; **Star babies:** son of Bo Jackson

GARRICK (GER-ik, GAR-ik) English: Variation of Garrett

GARRISON English: Spear-fortified town
Nicknames: *Gary*; **Famous namesakes:** Author and radio host Garrison Keillor

GARSON English: Son of Gar
Garrson, Garsone; **Famous namesakes:** Playwright Garson Kanin

GARTH Norse, Scandinavian: Garden; from a surname, indicating someone who lived near or worked in a garden
Famous namesakes: Musician Garth Brooks

GARTON English: From the wedge-shaped or three-cornered town or settlement; a surname and probable variant of Gordon
Garatun, Garton, Gartin

GARVEY Gaelic, Irish: Rough peace; surname
Gairbhith, Gairbith, Garbhan, Garvan, Garve, Garvin, Girven, Girvyn; **Old forms:** *Garbhach*; **Famous namesakes:** Baseball player Steve Garvey, civil rights activist Marcus Garvey

GARWOOD English: From the fir forest; surname
Arwood, Ayrwode; **Nicknames:** *Woody*

GARWYN (GAR-win) Welsh: White vehicle
Garwin

GARY English: Nickname for Garrett
Famous namesakes: Cartoonist Gary Larson, British actor Gary Oldman, actor Gary Sinise, actor Gary Cooper; **Star babies:** son of Jerry Lewis

GASPAR (gah-SPAHR) Spanish: Variation of Caspar

GASTON (gas-TAWN) French: From Gascony
Gascon; **Famous namesakes:** French actor Gaston Modot; **Star babies:** son of Jaclyn Smith

GAUTIER (go-TEE-ay) French: Variation of Walter
Famous namesakes: French clothing designer Jean-Paul Gauthier

GAVIN (GAV-in) Scottish, Welsh: White hawk
(English) *Gawain*; (Italian) *Gavino*; (Gaelic) *Gabhan*; *Galvin, Galvyn, Gavan, Gaven, Gavyn, Gawen, Gawyn*; **Old forms:** *Gaelbhan*; **Famous namesakes:** Actor Gavin MacLeod, British musician/actor Gavin Rossdale

GAWAIN (gə-WAYN) Arthurian legend: The eldest son of Lot

GEB (GEB) Egyptian: Mythical earth god, husband of Nut. Geb was a member of the Heliopolitan Ennead and is represented as a man.

GEDALIAH (ged-ə-LIE-ə) Hebrew: God has made great
Gedalya, Gedalyahu

GELASIUS Greek: Laughter; name of the pope who decreed February 14th Valentine's Day

GENEROSO (he-nay-RO-so) Spanish: Generous

GENET African: Eden

GENIUS Latin: Spirit present at one's birth. Since a genius is also one with especially high intelligence or talent, this may be a tough name to live up to.

GENNADI (gyeh-NAH-dee) Russian: Noble, generous
Genadi, Genadiy; **Nicknames:** *Gena*; **Famous namesakes:** Actor Gennadi Vengerov

GEOFFREY (JEF-ree) English: Spelling variation of Jeffrey

Nicknames: *Geoff*; **Famous namesakes:** Author Geoffrey Chaucer

GEORGE (JORJ) Greek: Farmer. In medieval legend, Saint George (the knight who became patron saint of England) slayed a fire-breathing dragon. The name has been borne by numerous heads of state in England, Greece, and the United States.
(Greek) *Iorgas*; (German) *Georg*; (Italian) *Giorgio*; (Spanish) *Jorge*; (Gaelic) *Deorsa*; (Welsh) *Sior*; (Scandinavian) *Joran, Jorg, Jorn, Jurgen*; (Swedish) *Goran, Gorin*; (Danish) *Joren, Jorgen, Joris, Jory*; (Russian) *Egor, Igoryok, Yuri, Yurik, Yurochka, Zhorah*; (Czech) *Jiri*; (Polish) *Jerzy*; (Ukrainian) *Yuriy*; (Finnish) *Jorma, Yrjö*; (Hungarian) *Gyorgy, Gyurgi, Gyurka*; (Armenian) *Kevork*; (Hawaiian) *Keoki*; *Georges, Georget, Georgio, Jirkar*; **Nicknames:** *Georgie, Gorka*; **Famous namesakes:** Author George Orwell, designer Giorgio Armani, first U.S. president George Washington, president George Bush and president George W. Bush, singer George Michael, actor George Clooney; **Star babies:** Five sons of George Foreman

GERALD (JER-əld) German: Rules by the spear
(English) *Jaryl*; (French) *Geraud*; (Spanish) *Geraldo, Jeraldo*; (Gaelic) *Gearald*; (Irish) *Gearoid*; (Scandinavian) *Jarel, Jarell*; (Dutch) *Gerrit*; (Polish) *Gerek*; *Geralt, Gerold, Gerrald, Gerrell, Gerritt, Jerold, Jerrald, Jerrold*; **Nicknames:** Jerry; **Famous namesakes:** President Gerald Ford, journalist Geraldo Rivera

GERALDO (he-RAHL-do) Spanish: Variation of Gerald
Famous namesakes: Journalist Geraldo Rivera

GERARD (jə-RAHRD) German: Spear strength, brave with a spear. Introduced to England through the Norman conquest,

Gerard has remained popular since the Middle Ages.
(German) Gerhard; (French) Gérard; (Italian) Gerardo; (Spanish) Jerardo; (Polish) Gerik; (Hungarian) *Gellert*; *Geraud, Gerrard, Girard, Jerard*; **Nicknames**: *Gerd, Gere, Gero, Gerry, Gert*; **Famous namesakes**: French actor Gérard Depardieu

GERMAIN (jər-MEN) French: Brotherly; derived from the Latin word *germen* meaning a *sprout* or *bud*. Saint Germain was a sixth-century bishop who founded the monastery known today as Saint-Germain-des-Prés in Paris.
(English) *Jermaine*; (Spanish) *German*; *Germano, Jermain, Jermane, Jermayne*; **Old forms**: *Germanus*; **Famous namesakes**: Singer Jermaine Jackson

GERO (JE-ro) German: Nickname for Gerard

GERONIMO (jə-RAH-nə-mo) Greek: Sacred name; variant of the Greek saint's name Jerome. Best known in America as the name of one of the last warriors of the Chiricahua Apache Indians

GERSHOM (GUR-shahm) Hebrew: Exiled; an Old Testament name
Gersham

GERVASE (JUR-vəs) Teutonic: Meaning uncertain, possibly servant of the spear or warrior. Saint Gervasius was an early martyr whose remains were found in Milan.
(English) *Jarvis*; (French) *Gervais, Gervaise*; (Spanish) *Gervasio, Gervaso*; (Gaelic) *Gervin*; *Gervasy*; **Old forms**: *Gervasius*

GETHIN (GE-thin) Welsh: Dark-skinned

GHADIR Persian: Sword

GIACOMO (JAH-ko-mo) Italian: Variation of Jacob

Famous namesakes: Italian composer Giacomo Puccini; **Star babies**: son of Sting

GIAN (JAHN) Italian: Variation of John
Nicknames: *Gianni*; **Star babies**: son of Francis Ford Coppola

GIANCARLO (jahn-KAHR-lo) Italian: Italian double name comprised of John and Charles

GIBSON English: Gilbert's son; surname *Gibbson*; **Nicknames**: *Gib, Gibby*; **Famous namesakes**: Australian actor Mel Gibson

GIDEON (GID-ee-ən) Hebrew: Feller of trees
(Russian) *Hedeon*; (Ukrainian) *Hadeon*; *Gedeon*; **Star babies**: son of Mandy Patinkin

GIFFORD English: Brave
Guifford, Giford; **Famous namesakes**: Sports anchor Frank Gifford, environmental conservation pioneer Gifford Pinchot

GIL Hebrew: Happiness
Gili, Gilli; **Famous namesakes**: Violinist Gil Shaham, Canadian actor Gil Bellows

GILBERT German: Trusted oath
(Italian) *Gilberto*; *Gilburt, Guilbert*; *Guilbert, Guillebert*; **Old forms**: *Giselberht*

GILES (JIE-əlz) Greek, English: Young goat; may be associated with the shield of Zeus. Saint Giles was a popular seventh-century saint who worked miracles and healed the lame.
(French) *Gilles*; (Italian) *Egidio*; *Ghiles, Gilian, Geli*; **Old forms**: *Aegidius*

GILFRED German: Oath of peace
Old forms: *Gilfried*

GILLES (ZHEEL) French: Variation of Giles
Famous namesakes: Canadian racecar driver Gilles Villeneuve

GILMORE Celtic, Scottish: Serves Mary; surname
Gilmer

GILROY Celtic, Scottish: Serves the red-haired lord

GINO Italian: Nickname for John

GIORGIO (JIYOR-jo) Italian: Variation of George
Nicknames: *Gio*; **Famous namesakes:** Italian designer Giorgio Armani

GIOVANNI (jo-VAHN-nee) Italian: Variation of John
Geovanni, Gian, Gianni; **Nicknames:** *Giannino, Nino*; **Famous namesakes:** Artist Giovanni Bellini

GIUSEPPE (joo-ZEP-pe) Italian: Variation of Joseph

GLEN Gaelic: From the glen or valley
Gleann, Glenn, Glyn, Glynn; **Famous namesakes:** Singer Glen Campbell, bandleader Glenn Miller, actor Glenn Ford

GLENDON Gaelic: From the dark glen valley

GODFREY (GAHD-free) German, English: Peace of God; from the Germanic name Gottfried
(German) *Gottfried*; (Italian) *Goffredo*; (Spanish) *Godofredo*; (Irish) *Gofraidh, Gothfraidh; Godfried, Gofried, Gottfrid*

GOODWIN English: Good friend or friend of God
Godwin, Godwine, Godwyn, Goodwine, Goodwyn, Gowyn

GORAN (GOR-ahn) Swedish: Variation of George
Famous namesakes: Actor Goran Visnjic

GORDON Anglo-Saxon, Scottish: From the wedge-shaped or three-cornered town or settlement; a surname and the name of one of Scotland's great clans. See also *Garton* (English) *Garatun, Gorton; Gordain, Gordan*; **Nicknames:** *Gordie, Gordy, Gordy*; **Famous namesakes:** Singer Gordon Lightfoot, hockey legend Gordie Howe

GORMAN Gaelic, Irish: Blue-eyed one
Gormain

GOTTFRIED (GAWT-freet) German: Variation of *Godfrey*

GOVAN Welsh: God of the forge. Govannon is a son of the goddess Don and the brother of Gwydion and Amaethon.
Govannon, Goveniayle

GOWAN (GO-wahn) African: Rainmaker (Nigeria)

GRAHAM (GRAY-əm, GRAM) Anglo-Saxon: From the grey or great home; surname (Scottish) *Graeme; Graeham, Grahem*; **Nicknames:** *Gram*; **Famous namesakes:** Author Graham Greene, Inventor Alexander Graham Bell, chef Graham Kerr

GRANGER French, English: Farmer; surname. Grange organizations have served U.S. rural agricultural communities for almost 150 years, providing not only farming resources, but also social and educational opportunities.
(English) *Grangere; Grainger*; **Nicknames:** *Grange*

GRANT French, Scottish: Great or bestow; a surname that increased in popularity as a first name due to Civil War general and president Ulysses S. Grant
Famous namesakes: Basketball player Grant Hill

GRANTHAM (GRAN-thəm) English: From the great or grey land or fields; surname; possible variant of Grantley
Grantland; **Nicknames:** *Grant*

GRANTLEY English: From the large meadow; from the grey meadow; surname
Grantlea, Grantleah, Grantlee, Grantleigh, Grantlie, Grantly; **Nicknames:** *Grant*

GRANVILLE French: Great or large town; surname used as a first name
Grenville; **Famous namesakes:** English artist Granville Danny Clarke

GRAYSON English: Son of the reeve or Gray-haired

GREELEY English: From the gray meadow; possibly from the green meadow; surname
Graegleah, Greely; Greelea, Greeleigh

GREGORY Greek: Watchful; the name of several saints and popes. Pope Gregory I fostered the development of Gregorian chants. Pope Gregory XIII established the Gregorian calendar in 1582 to replace the Julian calendar.
(German) *Gregor*; (French) *Gregoire*; (Italian) *Gregorio*; (Welsh) *Grigor*; (Swedish) *Greger*; (Russian) *Grigory, Grisha*; (Armenian) *Krikor*; *Gergely, Gergor, Greggory, Gregoly, Gregorie, Gregorior*; **Old forms:** *Gregorios*; **Nicknames:** *Gergo, Greg, Gregg, Gregos*; **Famous namesakes:** Actor Gregory Hines, actor Gregory Peck; **Star babies:** son of Ray Romano

GRIFFITH (GRIF-əth) Welsh: Strong lord. The fierce griffin of mythology and medieval legend was a creature with foreparts of an eagle and hindquarters of a lion.
(Latin) *Griffin; Gruffydd*

GUIDO (GWEE-do) Italian: Variation of Guy
Famous namesakes: Italian musician Guido Deiro

GUILLAUME (gee-OM) French: Variation of William
Famous namesakes: French actor Guillaume Depardieu; **Star babies:** son of Gérard Depardieu

GUILLERMO (gee-YER-mo) Spanish: Variation of William

GUNNAR (GOO-nahr, GU-nər) Norse: Warrior; in Norse mythology, the husband of Brynhild
(Danish) *Gunder*

GUSTAV (GOO-stahf) Scandinavian: Staff of the Goths; a name borne by several Swedish kings
(French) *Gustave*; (Spanish) *Gustavo*; (Finnish) *Kustaa, Kusti, Kyösti*; (Hungarian) *Gusztav; Gustaf, Gustaof, Gustavus*; **Famous namesakes:** Austrian painter Gustav Klimt

GUY (GEE, GIE) French: Guide
(Italian) *Guido; Guye, Gye*; **Old forms:** *Guyon*; **Famous namesakes:** French tennis player Guy Forget, musician Guy Lombardo

GUYON (goo-YON) French: Original form of Guy

GWYN (GWIN) Welsh: Fair, blessed
Gwen, Gwynn

HAAKON (HAH-kən) Scandinavian: Highborn son; related to the name *Hagan*
(Gaelic) *Hogan; Hakan, Hakon*

HABIB (hah-BEEB) Arabic, Persian: Beloved, darling, lover, dear. Habib is also used as a term of endearment by adding a letter *i* to the ending for the masculine version *Habibi*, or *ti* for the feminine version *Habibti*.

HACKETT German: Little wood cutter
Hacket; **Famous namesakes:** Actor Buddy
Hackett

HACKMAN German: Wood cutter
Famous namesakes: Actor Gene Hackman

HADAR (hah-DAHR) Hebrew: Beautiful,
honored

HADDAD (hah-DAHD) Arabic: Smith,
ironsmith, blacksmith. Often used as a family
name as well as a first name, Haddad was a
storm god for the Semites.
Famous namesakes: Football player Drew
Haddad

HADDEN English: From the heath, near the
hill of heather
Haddon, Haden, Hadon; Haddan, Haddin

HADI (hah-DEE) Arabic, Persian: Guiding to
the light, to follow the true religion

HADLEY (HAD-lee) English: From the
heath or heather-covered meadow; a surname
*Heathleah, Heathley; Hadlea, Hadlee,
Hadleigh, Hadlee*; **Nicknames:** *Leigh*

HADRIAN (HAY-dree-ən) Latin: Dark. In
the second century, Roman Emperor Hadrian
built a magnificent wall in Britain. Named
for him, the wall still stands as one of the
wonders of the world.

HADWIN English: Ally
Hadwyn; **Old forms:** *Haethowine*

HAEMON (HEE-mən, HAY-mən) Greek:
In Greek mythology, Haemon was the son
of Creon and betrothed of Antigone. He is
remembered for his defense of Antigone and
his arguments about wise leadership.

HAFEZ Persian: Protector

HAFGRIM Norse: Norse mythological
character who lived in Southfrey

HAFIZ (hah-FEEZ) Arabic: Guardian,
committed to memory, one who has
memorized the Koran. See also *Hafez
Mahfouz; Hafez*; **Famous namesakes:** Former
president of Syria Hafez el Asad, sultan of
Morocco Moulay Hafiz, Egyptian poet Hafiz
Ibrahim, lyrical Persian poet Chams al Din
Mohammad Hafiz

HAGAN (HAY-gen) Irish: Youthful
(Norse) *Hagen*

HAGAR (HAY-gahr) Hebrew: Stranger
Hager; Hagir, Hagor, Hayger

HAGLEY English: From the hedged
meadow; surname
Hagaleah, Hagalean, Hagly; Haglea, Hagleigh

HAGOP (HAH-gup) Armenian: Variation
of James

HAGOS African: Happy (Ethiopia)

HAHNEE (HAH-nee) Native American:
Beggar, supplicant

HAIDAR (HIE-dar) Hindi: Lion

HAIG (HAYG) English: From the hedged
enclosure
Hayg; **Famous namesakes:** Statesman
Alexander Haig

HAILEY Irish: Spelling variation of Haley

HAINES English: From the vine-covered
cottage; surname
Hane, Hanes, Haynes; Hanes

HAJI (HAH-jee) African: Born during the
hajj, or pilgrimage to Mecca (Swahili)

HAKIM (hah-KEEM) Arabic: Wise, learned; colloquially refers to the doctor
Hakeem; *Hakeem*; **Famous namesakes:** Basketball player Hakeem Olajuwon

HAKIZIMANA (ah-kee-zee-MAH-nah) African: God is our savior (Rwanda)

HAL English: A familiar form usually for Henry but also for Halden, Hall, and related names
Famous namesakes: Actor Hal Holbrook, Actor Hal Linden

> "Before I knew thee, Hal, I knew nothing"
> —Falstaff in Shakespeare's
> *Henry IV, Part I*

HALBERT English: Brilliant hero
Halbart, Halburt; **Old forms:** *Halebeorht*; **Nicknames:** *Hal, Bert*

HALCYON (HAL-see-ən) Greek: Time of peace, kingfisher (bird). In Greek mythology, Halcyone threw herself into the sea after the death of her husband, and out of pity the gods changed the pair into kingfishers, or halcyons. The gods made winds cease blowing during the mating season of the kingfisher. The expression *halcyon days* is derived from this myth and means a time of tranquility or prosperity.

HALDEN Scandinavian: Half Dane. When this name was coined, Danes were fierce invaders—the name may refer to a child left behind the invaders or to describe someone as formidable.
Haldan, Haldane, Halvdan

HALE English: From the remote valley, healthy; an English surname and a Hawaiian variant of Harry
Hayle

> "I only regret that I have but one life to lose for my country."
> —Revolutionary War hero Nathan Hale's final words

HALEY Irish: Ingenious
Hailey; Haleigh, Halley

HALFORD English: From the hall by the ford, from the valley ford
Haleford

HALI Greek: Sea
Halea, Halee, Halie

HALIAN (hah-lee-AHN) Native American: Youthful, young (Zuni)

HALIFAX English: From the holy or blessed field

HALIL (hah-LEEL) Turkish: Dear friend
Halill, Halyl

HALIM (hah-LEEM) Arabic: Gentle, patient, indulgent, also means forbearing

HALIRRHOTHIUS (hal-i-RO-thee-əs) Latin: The mythical son of Poseidon, he loved Alcippe, the daughter of Ares, for which Ares killed him.

HALITHERSES Greek: A soothsayer on Ithaca who supported Telemachus and Odysseus

HALL English: House, manor; (Norse) in Norse mythology, the son of Helgi the Godless
Haele

HALLAM (HAL-əm) English: Valley

HALLAN (HAL-ən) English: Lives at the hall, belongs to the hall
Hallen, Hallin, Hallon

HALLDOR Norse: Thor's rock, the name of a minor character in Norse legend

HALLEY English: From the meadow near the hall (implying large estate home); surname
Healleah

HALLIWELL English: Near or from the holy spring
Hallwell, Halywell; **Old forms:** *Haligwiella*

HALLWARD English: Guardian of the hall, watchman

HALSEY English: From Hal's island; surname
Halsig; Hallsey, Hallsy, Halsy; **Famous namesakes:** Admiral William F. Halsey

HALSTEAD English: Grounds of the manor, belonging to those grounds; surname
Halsted

HALSTEN Swedish: Rock or stone
Hallstein, Hallsten; **Nicknames:** Halle

HALTON English: From the town, estate on the hill
Haltan, Halten, Haltin

HALVOR Norse: Rock, defender. Saint Hallvard is revered as a martyr who died in defense of innocence.
Hallvard, Halvard

HAM Hebrew: Hot; the biblical name of one of Noah's sons

HAMAL (hah-MAHL) Arabic: Lamb, to bear, a cloud containing much water; Hamal is the sign Aries

HAMAR Scandinavian: Hammer
Hammer; Hamer

HAMIDI (hah-MEE-dee) African: Praised, admired (Kenya)

HAMILL (HAM-əl) English: Scarred, implying a survivor; surname
Hamel, Hamell, Hamil, Hammill

HAMILTON English, Scottish: From the proud town, estate; surname of one of the great families of Scotland
Old forms: *Hamelstun*

HAMISH (HAYM-ish) Scottish: Variation of James

HAMISI (hah-MEE-see) African: Thursday's child, born on the fifth day of the week (Swahili)

HAMLET French: Little village. Shakespeare's protagonist in *Hamlet* speaks some of the most famous lines ever written for the stage, including, "To be, or not to be."

HAMLIN German: Loves the little home. In fairy tales, the Pied Piper of Hamelin saves the citizens from rats, but when he is not paid for his efforts, he lures the children away as well.
Hamelin

HAMMER Scandinavian: Spelling variation of Hamar

HAMMETT Scandinavian: From the village

HAMMOND English: From the small town

HAMPTON English: A place name with an unclear original meaning, although it refers to a settlement or town; place name for area outside London and location of Hampton Court Palace; surname
Hampten, Hamptyn

HAMUND Norse: Meaning unclear; the name of Sigmund and Borghild's son in Norse mythology

HAMZA (HAHM-zah) Arabic: Powerful
Hamzah

HANAN (HAY-nən) Hebrew: Merciful, grace; the name of various biblical men
(Hebrew) *Chanan*

HANANEEL Hebrew: God has graciously given; a tower in the wall at Jerusalem

HANBAL (HAHN-bahl) Arabic: Pristine, pure
Hanbel, Hanbil

HANDEL (HAND-əl) German: Variation of John

HANFORD English: From the high ford; surname

HANIF (HAH-neef, hah-NEEF) Arabic: Believes without doubt

HANK Teutonic: Nickname for Henry

HANLEY (HAN-lee) English: From the high meadow; surname
Hanly, Heanleah, Henley, Handlea, Handleigh, Handley; Hanlea, Hanlee, Hanleigh, Henlea, Henlee, Henleigh

HANNIBAL (HA-nə-bəl) Phoenician: Grace of God; name of a famous Carthaginian general who fought the Roman Empire and is remembered for his tactical genius and his trek across the Alps on elephants

HANS (HAHNS) German, Scandinavian, Dutch: God has been gracious; variant of John
(Scandinavian) *Hanz*; (Swedish) *Hansel*; (Finnish) *Hanes, Hannu; Han, Hannah*;
Famous namesakes: Danish writer Hans Christian Andersen

HANSEL (HAHN-sel) Swedish: Variation of Hans

HANSON Scandinavian: John's son; also a variant of Anson
Hansen

HAOA (hah-O-ah) Hawaiian: Variation of Howard

HAPI (HAH-pee) Egyptian: The god of the Nile in innundation. In Egyptian mythology, Hapy was represented as a man with full, heavy breasts, a clump of papyrus on his head, and bearing heavily-laden offering tables. The name was also used by a different deity, one of the four sons of Horus, representing the north.
Hapy

HARB (HAHRB) Arabic: War
Famous namesakes: Egyptian economist Mohammad Talaat Harb

HARBIN (ar-BANH) French: Little shining warrior

HARCOURT French: From the fortified farm; surname used as first name
Harcort

HARDEN English: From the hare's valley; surname
Hardin, Hardyn, Heardind

HARDING English: Brave, hardy, reliable
Haryng

HARDWIN English: Variation of Baldwin

HARDY German: Daring, strong, bold
Hardie, Harti

HARE English: Rabbit

HAREL (HER-əl) Hebrew: Mountain of God
Harrell; Haral, Harell, Hariel

HARFORD English: From the hare's ford;
surname
Haraford; Harfurd, Harrford

HARGROVE English: From the hare's grove;
surname
Hargrave, Hargreaves

HARI (HAH-ree) Hindi: Tawny; Hindu deity
combining Vishnu and Shiva

HARITH (HAHR-ith, hah-REETH) Arabic:
Gardener, grower

HARKIN Irish: Deep red color

HARLAKE English: The hare's lake; surname
Harelache, Harlak

HARLAN English: From the land or farm of
the hares, from the army land; a surname and
possible variant of Harley
Harland, Harlen, Harlon; **Famous
namesakes:** Harland "Colonel" Sanders
(founder of KFC)

HARLEY English: From the hare's meadow.
Harley is a surname associated with the
famous Harley-Davidson motorcycles.
Traditionally a boy's name, now increasingly
being used for both genders
*Arleigh, Arley, Arlie, Hareleah, Harleigh; Arlea,
Arly, Harlea, Harlee, Harly*

HARLOW English: From the hill of the
hares, from the army hill; a surname
Arlo, Harlowe

HARMON English: Form of Herman
Famous namesakes: Actor Mark Harmon

HAROLD Norse, English: Army commander.
Harald has been popular since the Vikings
and was borne by several kings of Norway
(Spanish) *Haraldo, Heraldo*; (Irish) *Aralt*;
(Scottish) *Harailt*; (Scandinavian) *Harald*;
Arild; **Nicknames:** *Harry*

HAROUN (hah-ROON) Arabic: Lofty or
inspired, a variant of Aaron. The Caliph
of Bagdad, Haroun al Rachid, partially
inspired Shehrezad's *One Thousand and One
Nights*. He was a contemporary of France's
Charlemagne, and in his time Baghdad
was the world's largest city and its most
prominent cultural seat.
Harun al Rachid; Harun

HARPER English: Minstrel. More than just
entertainers when this name was created,
Harpers were a primary source of news and
keepers of the historical record.
Old forms: *Hearpere*; **Star babies:** son of Paul
Simon

HARPOCRATES (har-PAHK-rə-teez)
Greek: Greek form of the Egyptian god
Harpa-Khruti (Horus the child), a late form
of Horus in his aspect of being the son of Isis
and Osiris. Harporcrates was represented as
a naked child wearing the lock of youth and
holding one finger to his mouth. He became
the god of silence and secrecy.

HARRINGTON Irish: From Harry's town or
settlement; surname
Nicknames: *Harry*

HARRIS English: Son of Harry or diminutive of Harry
Harrison

HARRISON English: Son of Harry; surname
Famous namesakes: Actor Harrison Ford;
Star babies: son of Jack Wagner

HARRY English: Familiar form of Herald or Henry. Harry Potter is the young wizard in the extremely popular series of children's books by J.K. Rowling.
(Italian) *Arrigo*; (Welsh) *Harri*; (Hawaiian) Hale; **Famous namesakes:** President Harry Truman, actor Harry Hamlin, musician Harry Connick Jr.; **Star babies:** sons of Billy Bob Thornton, Harry Letterman and Regina Lasko, Richard Dreyfuss

HART English: Stag and a familar form of Hartley, Hartford, and similar names; (Teutonic) strong, brave, and a familiar form of Hartman, Hartwig, and similar names
Harte

HARTFORD English: Near the stag or deer's ford

HARTLEY English: From the stag's meadow; surname
Hartlea, Hartlee, Hartleigh, Hartly

HARTMAN German: Strong, brave; (English) surname adapted to first name use
Hardtman, Hartmann

HARTWELL English: From near the deer's well or spring

HARTWIG Teutonic: Strong advisor
Hartwyg

HARTWOOD English: From the stag's forest; surname
Harwood

HARUKO (hah-roo-ko) African: First born

HARVEY French: Eager for battle; based on the Old German name Herewig
(French) *Herve*; **Old forms:** *Herewig*; **Famous namesakes:** Actor Harvey Keitel, playwright and actor Harvey Fierstein

HASAD (hah-SAHD) Turkish: Harvester, gatherer
Hassad

HASANI (hah-SAH-nee) African: Handsome (Swahili)
Hasan

HASHIM (HAH-sheem) Arabic: Destroys evil, bountiful, generous
(Persian) *Hashem*; *Hashem*

HASIN (hah-SEEN) Hindi: Laughing, smiling
Hazen

HASKEL (HAHS-kel) Hebrew: Spelling variation of Ezekiel

HASLETT English: From the hazel tree land
Haslet; Hazlett, Hazlitt

HASSAN (hah-SAHN) Arabic, Persian: Handsome, good
Famous namesakes: Sultan of Morocco Hassan the First, second king of Morocco Hassan the Second, Arab poet Hasan Ibn Thabit; **Star babies:** son of the Calif Ali

HASSEL German: Bewitched place
Hasel, Hassall, Hassell, Hazell

HASTIN (hah-steen) Hindi: Elephant
Hastan, Hasten, Haston, Hastyn

HASTINGS English: House counsel; surname
Old forms: *Haestingas*

HATIM (HAH-teem) Arabic: Judge
Hateem, Hatem

HAUK Norse: Hawk

HAVELOCK Norse: Sea warrior, sailor in battle
Haveloc, Haveloch

HAVEN (HAY-vən) English: Place of safety, shelter
Havyn; **Old forms:** *Haefen*

HAVERILL (HAYV-rəl, HAY-və-rəl) Anglo-Saxon: Spelling variation of Averill
Haverell

HAVGAN Irish: White, pure
Havgen, Havgin

HAWK English: Hunting bird. When this name was created, hunting with hawks was considered an aristocratic sport. See also *Hauk*

HAWLEY English: From the hedged meadow; surname
Hawly; Hawlea, Hawlee, Hawleigh

HAWTHORNE English: Shrub related to the apple family, known for its pink and white flowers and its red fruit
Hawthorn

HAYDEN (HAY-dən) English: From the hedged valley; surname adapted to given name use
Haydon, Hayes; **Famous namesakes:** Actor Hayden Christensen

HAYES (HAYZ) English: Spelling variation of Hayden; (Irish) surname

HAYWARD English: Ward or guardian of the hedged area
Old forms: *Hagaward*

HAYWOOD English: From the hedged forest; surname adapted to given name use
Heywood

HEARNE English: Variation of Ahearn

HEATH (HEETH) English: An open area of land covered by heather or the heather itself; a familiar form for Heathcliff and related names
Famous namesakes: Actor Heath Ledger

HEATHCLIFF English: From the heath cliff or heath-covered cliff; the unforgettable romantic character from Emily Bronte's *Wuthering Heights*
Heathclyf, Hetheclif

HEATON English: From the high town or settlement; surname

HEBER (HEE-bər) Hebrew: Partner, ally; biblical ancestor of Abraham

HECTOR (HEK-tər) Greek, Spanish: Steadfast; from Greek legend, a hero of Troy in the Trojan war
(Italian) *Ettore*; **Famous namesakes:** Actor Hector Elizondo

HEDDWYN (HETH-win) Welsh: Blessed peace

HEDEON (he-DAY-on) Russian: Variation of Gideon

HEDLEY English: From the heathered meadows; surname
Hedlea, Hedleigh

HEDWIG (HED-vikh) German: Fighter, strong one

HEIMDAL (HAYM-dahl) Norse: White god. In Norse mythology, Heimdal is the son of Odin and one of the Wave Maidens, and he is

the guardian of the rainbow bridge.
Heimdall

HEINRICH (HIEN-rikh) German: Variation
of Henry
Nicknames: *Heiko, Heinz*

HELAKU (he-LAH-koo) Native American:
Full of sun, sunny day

HELGE Scandinavian: Blessed, holy
(Anglo-Saxon) *Halig*; (Russian) *Oleg*; *Helgi*

HELIOS (HEE-lee-əs) Greek: Sun; the name
of the young Greek sun god who drove a
four-horse chariot across the sky each day

HELKI (HEL-kee) Native American:
Touching (Miwok)

HELMER Teutonic: Warrior's wrath

HELMUT (HEL-moot) German: Brave
Helmutt; *Hellmut, Hellmutt, Hellmuth*;
Famous namesakes: Chancellor Helmut Kohl

HEMAN (HAY-mən) Hebrew: Faithful, loyal
Hemen

HENDERSON English, Scottish: Henry's
son
Henson

HENDRICK Scandinavian: Variation of
Henry

HENLEY Irish: Spelling variation of Hanley

HENOCH Hebrew: Leader, initiator; also a
variant of Enoch

HENRY German: Rules his household; from
the German Heinrich. Introduced by the
Normans, the name Henry has belonged to
eight English kings and is the name of Prince
Charles' younger son.

(German) *Heinrich, Hennings*; (French)
Henri; (Italian) *Arrighetto, Enrico, Enzo*;
(Spanish) *Enrique*; (Portuguese) *Henrique*;
(Teutonic) *Henerik, Henning, Hinrich*; (Irish)
Hannraoi, Hanraoi; (Scandinavian) *Hendrick,
Henrick, Henrik*; (Swedish) *Hendrik*; (Basque)
Endika; (Russian) *Genry*; (Polish) *Henryk,
Honok*; (Finnish) *Heikki*; (Hawaiian) *Hanale*;
Heike, Heinroch, Henrich; **Nicknames:** *Hank,
Harro, Heiko, Heinz*; **Famous namesakes:**
Philosopher Henry David Thoureau,
automobile pioneer Henry Ford, actor Henry
Fonda; **Star babies:** sons of Dennis Hopper,
Julia Louis Dreyfuss and Brad Hall, Meryl
Streep, Steve Zahn, Amanda Pays and Corbin
Bernsen, Heidi Klum and Seal

HENSON Scottish: Spelling variation of
Henderson

HEPHAESTUS (hə-FES-təs, hə-FAYS-təs)
Greek: Greek mythological god of fire and the
patron of craftsmen

HERALD English: One who proclaims; also a
variant of Harold

HERBERT German: Illustrious warrior; a
name introduced to Britain by the Normans
(French) *Aribert*; (Spanish) *Herberto,
Heribert, Heriberto*; *Hurbert*; **Famous
namesakes:** President Herbert Hoover

In 1979, Michael Herbert Dengler tried
to change his name to 1069, but a judge
nixed the numerals in favor of having
Dengler become Ten Sixty-Nine or One
Zero Six Nine.

HERCULES (HUR-kyə-leez) Greek: Glory of Hera. The mythological hero was the mortal son of Zeus. After committing a dreadful crime while under a spell of insanity, he was granted a chance to regain honor by completing twelve supposedly impossible tasks. He did all successfully, using both his mighty physical strength and his cleverness. On his deathbed, he was granted immortality and the status of god.
(Italian) *Ercole*

HERMAN German: Warrior
(French) *Armand*; (Italian) *Armando*, *Ermanno*; (Swedish) *Hermann*; *Harman*, *Harme*, *Harmen*, *Harmon*; **Nicknames:** *Harm*, *Herm*

HERMES (HUR-meez) Greek: Messenger of the gods; also the name of famous French design label Hermès

HERMOD Norse: In Norse mythology, Hermod was the son of Odin and Frigg, and welcomed fallen warriors to Valhalla.

HERNANDO (er-NAHN-do) Spanish: Variation of Ferdinand

HERRICK German: War leader
Herryk

HERSHEL Hebrew: Deer
Herschel, Hirsch

HERVE (AYR-vay) French: Variation of Harvey

HESPEROS (HES-per-əs) Greek: Evening star
Hespero

HESUTU Native American: Picks up yellow jacket's nest (Miwok)

HEWITT (HYOO-it) German: Smart little one; possibly little Hugh or Hugh's son
Hewett, Hewlett, Hewlitt

HEWSON English: Spelling variation of Hughson
Famous namesakes: Singer Paul Hewson (Bono)

HEZEKIAH (hez-ə-KIE-ə) Hebrew: God is my strength; an Old Testament name belonging to a king of Judah

HIAMOVI Native American: High chief (Cheyenne)
Hyamovi

HIAWATHA (hie-ə-WAH-thə) Native American: River creator; historical Iroquois leader (Onodaga tribe) who helped bring about a peace of the five nations of the Iroquois people
Haionwhatha

> *Thus was born my Hiawatha,*
> *Thus was born the child*
> *of wonder*
> —Henry Wadsworth Longfellow,
> *Song of Hiawatha*

HIBAH Arabic: Gift
Hyba, Hybah

HIEREMIAS Greek: God will uplift

HIERONYMUS Latin: Sacred name; famous Roman surname derived from the given name of a second-century BC king of Syracuse
Famous namesakes: Dutch painter Hieronymus Bosch

HILAL (hil-AHL) Arabic: New moon, born at the new moon
Hylal

HILARY English: Cheerful; derived from the Latin Hilarius. Sir Edmund Hillary led the first expedition to successfully climb Mount Everest.
(Greek) *Hilarion*; (Spanish) *Hilario*; (Basque) *Ilari*; *Hillary, Hillery, Ilarion*; **Old forms:** *Hilarius*

HILDEBRAND (HIL-de-brand) Teutonic: Battle sword
Hildbrand, Hildebrandt

HILDEMAR German: Famous warrior

HILDERIC German: Warrior or fortress

HILLEL (HIL-el) Hebrew: Greatly praised. Hillel is the name of the Jewish organization which supports college students. Rabbi Hillel began the Talmud.

HILLIARD (HILL-yerd) Teutonic: Brave defender, brave warrior
Hiliard, Hiller

HILMAR (HIL-mər) Swedish: Famous, high-born
Hilmer

HILTON English: From the town or settlement on the hill; surname
Hylton

HINTO (HEEN-to) Native American: Blue hair (Dakota)
Hynto

HINUN (hee-NOON) Native American: Storm spirit
Hynun

HIPPOLYTUS (hi-PAHL-ə-təs) Greek: Frees the horses; Greek mythical son of Zeus and Hippolyta, a queen of the Amazons
Hipolit

HIRAM (HIE-rəm) Hebrew: Exalted, noble
Chiram, Hyrum; **Nicknames:** *Hi*

HIRSCH Yiddish: Spelling variation of Hershel

HOBBARD German: Spelling variation of Hubert

HOBERT German: Bert's hill
Nicknames: *Hobie*

HOBSON English: Robert's son
Hobbs, Hobs, Hobsen

HODGSON English: Spelling variation of Rogerson

HOFFMAN German: Influential, powerful one
Hofman

HOLBROOK English: From the brook in the hollow of the valley
Holbrooke

HOLCOMB English: From the deep valley

HOLDEN English: From the hollow in the valley. Holden Caulfield is the young, disillusioned main character of J.D. Salinger's novel *The Catcher in the Rye*.
Holdin, Holdyn; **Star babies:** sons of Dennis Miller, Rick Schroder

HOLIC (HO-lik) Czech: Barber

HOLLAND French: Place name as another name for the Netherlands; surname
Hollan

HOLLEB (HOL-ep) Polish: Dove

HOLLIS English: From the grove of holly trees

HOLMES English: From the river islands; surname of the great fictional detective, Sherlock
Famous namesakes: Writer Oliver Wendell Holmes

HOLT Anglo-Saxon, English: From the woods or forest

HOMAYOUN Persian: Royal, fortunate
Homayoon

HOMER Greek: Security, hostage, promise; the ancient Greek poet responsible for giving the world *The Iliad* and *The Odyssey*
(Spanish) *Homero*; *Homar, Homeros, Homerus*; **Star babies:** sons of Bill Murray, Carey Lowell and Richard Gere

HONDO (HON-do) African: Warrior, soldier (Zimbabwe)

HONON Native American: Bear (Miwok)

HONORE (o-no-RAY) French: Honor; derived from the Latin *Honoratus*
(Spanish) *Honorato*; **Old forms:** *Honoratus*; **Famous namesakes:** French artist Honoré Daumier

HONORIUS (hə-NOR-ee-əs) Latin: Honor. Honorius was the name of an emperor of the West Roman Empire and also the name of four popes.

HONOVI Native American: Strong

HONZA Czech: Variation of John

HORACE (HOR-əs) Latin: Keeper of the hours, timekeeper; derived from the Roman family clan name Horatius, and the name of a famous Roman poet

(Spanish) *Horado*; *Horacio, Horaz*; **Old forms:** *Horatius*

HORATIO (hə-RAY-shee-o) Latin: Keeper of the hours; derived from the same root as Horace and a Roman surname, Horatio was adapted to a given name use centuries ago. In Shakespeare's *Hamlet*, Horatio is the prince's friend, and it is to him Hamlet addresses many famous speeches. "Alas, poor Yorick! I knew him, Horatio."

HOREMHEB (hor-EM-heb) Egyptian: Name of a pharaoh in ancient Egypt

HORST German: Thicket
(English) *Hurst, Hurste*

HORTON English: From the garden town or estate. Horton is a surname and the name of the elephant protagonist in the Dr. Seuss classic *Horton Hears a Who.*

HORUS (HOR-əs) Egyptian: God of the sky. This earliest royal god was in the shape of a falcon, with the sun and the moon as his eyes. Horus was identified with the king during his lifetime and was regarded as the son of Isis and Osiris. The many forms of Horus are Re-Harakhti, Harsiesis, Haroeris, Harendotes, Khenti-irti, Khentekhtay (the crocodile god), and Harmakhis (Horus on the horizons). The Sphinx of Giza is considered to be the representation of the latter form of *Horus. Harakhty*

HOSA (ho-sah) Native American: Small crow (Arapaho)

HOSEA (ho-ZAY-ə) Hebrew: Salvation. The biblical Hosea was an Israelite prophet, and the Old Testament Book of Hosea is named after him.
Hoseia, Hoshea, Hoseah

HOTAH Native American: Gray or brown
(Sioux)
Hota

HOTOTO Native American: The whistler
(Hopi)

HOUGHTON (HO-tən) English: From the
estate or settlement on the headland

HOUMAN Persian: Possessing a good soul,
good nature
Human

HOUSTON English: From the hill town; a
surname and place name for a major city in
Texas
Huston

HOWARD English: High watchman,
noble watchman; an English surname of a
historically powerful family
(Hawaiian) *Haoa*; **Nicknames:** *Ward*; **Famous
namesakes:** Businessman Howard Hughes,
actor and director Ron Howard

HOWE German: High
How

HOWELL Welsh: Eminent, prominent; an
Anglicized variation of Hywel
Howel, Hywel

HOWI (how-ee) Native American: Turtledove
(Miwok)

HOWIE English: Nickname for Howard,
Howland, and similar names
Howey; **Famous namesakes:** Football player
and broadcaster Howie Long

HOWLAND English: From the hilly land
Howlan

HOYT Irish: Spirit

HRYCHLEAH English: From the meadow's
edge; surname
Hrychlea, Hrycleigh

HUARWAR Celtic, Welsh: Son of Avlawn or
Halwn, mentioned in Arthurian legend

HUBERT German: Bright in spirit. Saint
Hubert is the patron saint of hunters.
(Italian) *Uberto*; (Spanish) *Huberto*; *Hobard,
Hobart, Hobbard, Hubbard*; **Nicknames:**
Bert, Hubie, Hugh; **Famous namesakes:** Vice
President Hubert Humphrey

HUD Arabic: Name of a Muslim prophet and
used by several Muslim leaders
Star babies: son of John Mellencamp

HUDSON English: Hugh's son; a surname
adapted to given name use and a place name
for the Hudson River and famous Hudson
Bay in Canada

HUEIL Celtic: Legendary son of Caw, enemy
of Arthur

HUEY English: Nickname for *Hugh*
Famous namesakes: Politician Huey Long,
singer Huey Lewis

HUGH (HYOO) German: Intelligent,
thoughtful
(German) *Hugo*; (French) *Hugues*; (Italian)
Ugo; (Welsh) *Hew, Huw*; (Norse) *Hugin*;
Hughes; **Nicknames:** *Huey, Hughie*; **Famous
namesakes:** English actor Hugh Grant,
Playboy founder Hugh Hefner

HUGHSON English: Hugh's son, child;
surname
Hewson

HUGI Norse: A minor character in Norse
mythology, a young giant living in Utgard.

HUGO (HYOO-go) German: Variation of Hugh
Famous namesakes: German fashion designer Hugo Boss

HULA (hoo-lah) Native American: Eagle (Osage)

HULBERT German: Brilliant, shining grace
Hulbard, Hulbart; **Old forms:** *Huldiberaht*

HUMBERTO (oom-BER-to) Spanish: Famous warrior; traditional Spanish name from Old German, introduced to Britain by the Normans
(Italian) *Umberto*; (Teutonic) *Humbert*

> *"Humbert Humbert. What a thrillingly different name."*
> —Vladimir Nabokov, *Lolita*

HUMILITY English: Modesty, a virtue

HUMPHREY (HUM-free) German: Peaceful strength
(Italian) *Onfrio, Onofredo*; (Welsh) *Wmffre*; (Polish) *Onufry*; *Humfrey, Humfrid, Humfried, Hunfredo, Hunfrid, Hunfried*; **Famous namesakes:** Actor Humphrey Bogart

HUNT English: Pursue; a surname adapted to given name use and a familiar form of Hunter, Huntley, and similar names

HUNTER English: To hunt; an occupational name
Star babies: son of Niki Taylor

HUNTINGTON English: From the hunter's town or settlement; surname
Huntingden, Huntingdon, Huntingtun; *Huntingtin*; **Nicknames:** *Hunter*

HUNTLEY English: From the hunter's meadow; surname
Huntly; Huntlea, Huntlee, Huntleigh; **Nicknames:** *Hunt, Lee*

HURLBERT English: Strong, shining army; closely related to the name Herbert
Herlbert, Hurlbart; **Old forms:** *Herlebeorht*

HURLEY Irish: Sea tide
Hurlee, Hurly

HUSLU (HOO-sloo) Native American: Bear

HUSSEIN (hoo-SAYN) Arabic: Good, handsome. The founder of Shiite Islam was named Hussein.
(African) *Hasan, Hassain*; (Persian) *Hossein*; *Husani, Hussain; Husain, Husayn*; **Famous namesakes:** King of Jordan Hussein Ibn Talal, former Iraqi president Saddam Hussein, sultan of Egypt Hussein Kamal; **Star babies:** son of the Calif Ali and brother of Hasan

HUTCHINSON English: Child of the hutch, child of the rural working class

HUTE (HOO-te) Native American: Star

HUTTON English: From the town or estate on the ridge; surname

HUXFORD English: From Hugh's ford
Huxeford

HUXLEY English: From Hugh's meadow; surname
Huxly; Huxlea, Huxlee, Huxleigh

HVERGELMIR Norse: In Norse mythology, the wellspring of cold in Niflheim and the source of all cold rivers.

HYACINTH (HIE-ə-sinth) Greek: Flower name, purple. In Greek mythology, Hyacinth was beloved and accidentally killed by Apollo. From his blood sprang the flower that bears his name.
(Spanish) *Jacinto, Jax*

HYATT English: From the high gate; surname.
Hiatt

HYDE English: A name with several meanings, the oldest is likely deer and from the deer hide, but also may refer to a measure of land, or to the act of concealing
Hid, Hide

HYDER English: Tanner; an occupational name

HYLAS (HIE-ləs) Greek: In Greek mythology, Hylas was the son of Theiodamas and devoted companion of Heracles, joining him on the voyage of the Argo. When fetching water from a spring, a nymph was so entranced by his beauty that she kidnapped him.

HYPERION (hie-PEER-ee-ən) Greek: He who goes before the sun. The mythological Hyperion is the titan son of Uranus and Gaia and the father of Helios, Selene, and Eos.

HYPNOS (HIP-nəs) Greek: Personification of sleep in Greek mythology. The term *hypnosis* derives from this name.

IAGO (ee-AH-go) Spanish: Spanish and Welsh variant of James; One of literature's famous villains, Shakespeare's Iago is a very clever man.

> "O brave Iago, honest and just/That hast such noble sense of thy friend's wrong!"
> —William Shakespeare, *Othello*, V.i.31

IAKONA (ee-ə-KO-nə) Hawaiian: Healer

IAN (EE-ən, IE-ən,) Scottish: Variation of John
Famous namesakes: British author Ian Fleming, actor Ian Ziering

IAPETUS (ee-ah-PET-əs) Greek: In Greek mythology, he is the Titan son of Uranus and Gaia, and father of Atlas, Menoetius, Prometheus, and Epimetheus. A moon of Saturn is named for him.

IASION (ie-A-zhe-ən, ie-A-see-ən) Greek: The mythological Iasion was the son of Zeus and Electra and, by Demeter, the father of Plutus.
Iasius

IB Phoenician: Oath of Baal

IBRAHIM (ee-brah-HEEM) Arabic: Variation of Abraham
Famous namesakes: Ibrahim viceroy of Egypt and son of Mohammed Aly Basha, name of Muslim Indian sultans

IBSEN (IB-sən, IP-sən) German: Archer's son; surname
Ibsan, Ibsin, Ibson; **Famous namesakes:** Norwegian playwright Henrik Ibsen

IBYCUS Greek: Greek lyric poet. The expression *cranes of Ibycus* derives from a myth that Ibycus' murder was avenged by cranes who saw the crime.

ICARIUS (ie-KA-ree-əs) Greek: In Greek mythology, Icarius was an Athenian who so warmly welcomed Dionysus to Attica that the god gave him the gift of wine. He was tragically killed when his shepherds mistook the wine for poison, but the gods honored his spirit by placing him in the stars.

ICARUS (IK-ə-rəs) Greek: In Greek mythology, he was the son of the inventor Daedalus, and both were imprisoned by King Minos. In an attempt to escape, his father created wings of feathers and wax, but warned his son not to fly too high or the wings would melt. Lost in the joy of flight, Icarus forgot his father's warning. The sea where he died is named for him.

ICELOS Greek: The mythological Icelos was the son of Hypnos responsible for creating the images of humans in dreams.

ICHABOD (IK-ə-bahd) Hebrew: The glory has gone; an Old Testament name most commonly recognized as the protagonist Ichabod Crane in Washington Irving's *The Legend of Sleepy Hollow*.

IDAL English: From the yew tree valley; a surname and variant of Udell

IDAS Greek: In Greek mythology, Idas was an Argonaut so special that princess Marpessa chose him over the god Apollo.

IDEN (IE-den) Anglo-Saxon: Woody pasture

IDI (EE-dee) African: Born during the Id al-Fitr festival, which marks the end of Ramadan

IDOGBE (i-DOG-bay) African: Brother of twins (Nigeria)

IDOMENEUS (ie-DOM-en-oos) Greek: Grandson of Minos, king of Crete, and leader of the Cretan troops during the Trojan War, Idomeneus was famous for his bravery in battle.

IDRIS Arabic: Name of an important Muslim prophet also called Enoch; (Welsh) eager lord
Idress, Idriss, Idryss

IESTYN (YES-tin) Welsh: Just, lawful, fair; variant of Justin

IGASHO (ee-GAH-sho) Native American: Wanderer
Igashu

IGGY Latin: Nickname for Ignatius
Famous namesakes: Singer Iggy Pop

IGNACIO (eeg-NAH-see-o) Spanish: Variation of Ignatius

IGNATIUS (ig-NAY-shəs) Latin: Fiery; Saint Ignacius of Loyola founded the Catholic Jesuit order.
(French) *Ignace*; (Italian) *Ignazio*; (Spanish) *Ignacio, Ignado, Nacho*; (Basque) *Inaki*; (Russian) *Ignat, Ignatiy*; (Czech) *Ignac*;
Nicknames: *Iggy*

IGOR Russian: Variation of Ingvar
Egor; **Nicknames:** *Iggy*; **Famous namesakes:** Russian composer Igor Stravinsky

IKAIA (ee-o-KEE-ah) Hawaiian: Variation of Isaiah

IKE English: Nickname for Isaac

IKER (EE-ker) Basque: Visit

ILAN (ee-LAHN) Hebrew: Tree
Elan

ILBERT German: Renowned fighter

ILIAS (ee-LEE-əhs) Greek: The Lord is my God; variant of Elijah

ILLAN Latin, Basque: Young, youthful

ILMARI (ELL-mah-ree) Finnish: Air

ILYA (EEL-yah) Russian: The Lord is my God; variant of Elijah

IMAD (EE-mahd) Arabic: Supportive, relied upon

IMMANUEL (i-MAN-yoo-el) Hebrew: God is with us; variant of Emmanuel

IMRAN (EEM-rən) Arabic: Host

IMRE (EEM-re) Hungarian: Variation of Emery

INACHUS (IN-ə-kəs) Greek: Greek god of the river that bears his name, Inachus was the son of Oceanus and Tethys, and the father of Io.

INAY Hindi: Godlike, supreme

INCE (EEN-tseh) Hungarian: Innocent

INCENDIO (een-SEN-dee-o) Spanish: Fire

INDRA (IN-drah) Hindi: In Hindu culture, Indra was the supreme ruler of the gods.

INDRAJIT (IN-drah-jeet) Hindi: Conqueror of Indra

INGEL German: Angel

INGELBERT (ING-gəl-bert) German: Bright angel; variant of Englebert

INGER Scandinavian: Son's army
Ingharr

INGLISS Scottish: English, from England
Ingliss, Inglys

INGMAR (ING-mahr) Norse, Swedish: Famous Ing or famous son; refers to Ing, another name for Frey, the handsome Norse fertility god
Ingemar; Inge; **Famous namesakes:** Swedish director Ingmar Bergman

INGRAM (ING-grum) English: Angel, angelic

INGVAR (ING-vahr) Scandinavian: Ing's soldier
(Russian) *Igor;* **Famous namesakes:** Swedish singer Ingvar Wixell

INIR Scandinavian: Honorable, good

INNES Scottish, Irish: From the island or river island
(Celtic) *Inness, Innis;* (Irish) *Inis, Inys*

INNOCENT Latin, English: Innocent; name of numerous popes
(Italian) *Innocenzio;* (Spanish) *Inocencio, Inocente, Sencio*

INTEUS (een-TAY-oos) Native American: Proud, without shame

IOAN (YO-an) Welsh: Variation of John
Famous namesakes: Welsh actor Ioan Gruffudd

IOKEPA (ee-o-KE-pə) Hawaiian: May God give increase; variant of Joseph

IOKIA (ee-o-KEE-ah) Hawaiian: Healed by the power of God
Iokiah

IOLO (EEO-lo) Welsh: Familiar form of Iowerth, the Welsh version of Edward

ION (EEN) Irish: Variation of John

IONAKANA (ee-o-nah-KAH-nah)
Hawaiian: Gift from God; variant of Jonathan

IOSIF (ee-YAW-sif) Russian: Variation of
Joseph

IPHIS Greek: In Greek mythology, Iphis
was a shepherd who fell in love with the
maiden Anaxarete, but killed himself when
she refused his love. When she remained
uncaring, Aphrodite turned her to stone.

IRA (IE-rə) Hebrew: Watchful
Irah; **Famous namesakes:** Composer Ira
Gershwin, actor Ira Aldridge

IRAM English: Bright

IRFAN Arabic: Gratitude

IRMIN German: Strong

IRVING (UR-ving) English: Friend from the
sea or handsome friend; (Irish) handsome;
(Welsh) white or white river
(Welsh) *Inek*; *Earvin, Ervin, Ervine, Irven,
Irvin, Irvine, Irvyn, Irwin, Irwyn*; **Nicknames:**
Irv, Erv, Irv; **Famous namesakes:** Composer
Irving Berlin

ISA (ee-sa) Arabic: Arabic form of Jesus;
(Hebrew) nickname for Isaiah and Isaac
Isah

ISAAC (IE-zək) Hebrew: He laughs. The
biblical Issac was the only son of Abraham
by his wife Sarah. The prediction of his birth
was amusing to the couple because they were
very old, so God gave them the name Isaac for
their son, meaning one who laughs. Isaac later
became a father to the twins Esau and Jacob.
(Greek) *Isaak*; (Arabic) *Ishaq*; (Swedish) *Isak*;
(Dutch) *Issac*; (Basque) *Ixaka*; (Czech) *Izaac,
Izak*; (Armenian) *Sahak*; *Itzhak, Yitzhak*;
Nicknames: *Ike, Isa, Zack, Zak*; **Famous
namesakes:** Physicist Sir Isaac Newton,

author Isaac Asimov, violinist Itzhak Perlman;
Star babies: sons of Mandy Patinkin, Annie
Potts

ISAIAH (ie-ZAY-ə) Hebrew: God is salvation.
The biblical Book of Isaiah is named for a
Hebrew prophet of the Old Testament.
(Spanish) *Isaias*; (Finnish) *Esa*; (Hawaiian)
Ikaia; *Essaiah, Isiah, Izeyah*; *Isa, Isai, Isaih*;
Famous namesakes: Basketball player Isiah
Thomas; **Star babies:** son of Mia Farrow

ISAM (i-SAHM) Arabic: Safeguard,
protection

ISEKEMU Native American: Slow-moving
water

ISEN (EE-zen, IE-zen) Anglo-Saxon: Iron

ISHAAN (ish-ahn) Hindi: Direction;
compass
Ishana

ISHAM English: From or belonging to the
iron one's home
Isenham

ISHMAEL (ISH-may-əl) Hebrew: God
hears. In the Bible, Ishmael was the elder son
of Abraham by Hagar, the Egyptian slave of
Abraham's wife Sarah. Ishmael is considered
the patriarch of Arabs and forefather of Islam.
(Spanish) *Ismael*

"Call me Ishmael."
—The famous opening sentence of
    Herman Melville's epic novel *Moby-Dick*

ISIDORE (IZ-i-dor) Greek: Gift of Isis;
name of several saints
(Spanish) *Cedro, Cidro, Isadoro, Isidoro, Isidro*;
Esidore, Ixidor, Ysidro

ISLAM (is-LAHM) Arabic: Submission (to the will of God). Islam is the name of the religion preached by the Prophet Mohammed.

ISRAEL Hebrew: Prince of God. Israel was the name given to the biblical Jacob after he wrestled the angel of God. It was later taken by the Jewish people as the name of the twelve tribes descended from Jacob's sons and the name of their modern nation.
Isreal, Izreal, Yisreal, Ysrael

ISSA (ee-SAH) African: God is salvation (Swahili)
Issah

ISTU (EES-too) Native American: Sugar pine tree

ISTVAN (ISHT-vahn) Hungarian: Variation of Stephen
Nicknames: *Pista, Pisti*

ITTAMAR Hebrew: Island of palms
Itamar

IULIO (ee-oo-LEE-o) Hawaiian: Variation of Julian

IVAN (ee-VAHN, IE-vən) Russian: Variation of John

IVANHOE English: Possible variant of Ivan (John). Ivanhoe is the medieval Saxon protagonist in Sir Walter Scott's work of that name.

IVES English: Young archer, a name closely related to Ivor and from the same Norse roots

IVO (EE-vo, EE-fo) Teutonic: Yew wood, specifically that which was used for archer's bows

IVOR Scandinavian, English: Archer; a popular Scandinavian name derived from Old Norse elements
(English) *Ivon*; (French) *Yves, Yvet, Yvon*; (Basque) *Ibon*; *Ivar, Iver*

IXION (IKS-ee-ahn) Greek: A pivotal character in Greek mythology, Ixion was given a second chance after committing a great crime. He was then tricked by Zeus into thinking he was sleeping with Hera, and impregnated a cloud which bore him a son, Centaurus.

IYE Native American: Smoke

IZOD Irish: Fair-haired, blond; famous clothing brand name

IZZY Hebrew: Familiar form of Isaac, Isidore, or Israel

JAAFAN African: Small river

JABARI (jah-BAHR-ee) African, Egyptian: Comforter (Swahili)

JABBAR Arabic: Mighty, colossal, omnipotent, oppressor

JABEZ (JAY-bez) Hebrew: Born in pain, implying a survivor

JABILO African: Medicine man

JABIN (JAY-bin) Hebrew: Perceptive; the name of two kings of Hazor in the Old Testament

JABIR (JAH-beer) Arabic: Consoler, one who comforts
Famous namesakes: Arab physician, philosopher, and alchimist Jabir Ibn Hayan

JABULANI (jah-boo-LAH-nee) African: Happy, jubilant

JACE American: Familiar form of Jason, Jacy, and similar names

JACINTO (hah-SEEN-to) Spanish: Variation of Hyacinth
Nicknames: *Jax*

JACK English: God has been gracious, has shown favor; derived from Jacques or John but is well-established as a name on its own
Famous namesakes: Actor Jack Nicholson, golfer Jack Nicklaus, comedian Jack Benny; **Star babies:** sons of Kirk Cameron, Denis Leary, Luke Perry, Ozzie Osbourne, Joan Whalley and Val Kilmer, Meg Ryan and Dennis Quaid, Tim Roth, Willem Dafoe, Antonio Sabato Jr. and Virginia Madsen, Ellen Barkin and Gabriel Byrne, Susan Sarandon and Tim Robbins, Christie Brinkley, Cheryl Tiegs

> **According to UK National** Statistics, Jack has been the most popular name for baby boys for nine straight years. It has been one of the most popular choices in recent years for parents in Northern Ireland, Scotland, the Republic of Ireland, and New Zealand; but much less so in the United States and Australia, where it barely makes the top fifty.

JACKSON English: Son of Jack or John; a surname
Jaxon, Jaxson; **Star babies:** sons of Maria Bello, Patti Smith, Katey Sagal, Spike Lee, Natalie Maines

JACOB Hebrew: Supplanter or seizing by the heel. Jacob appears in the biblical book of Genesis as the youngest son of Isaac and Rebecca and twin to Esau. Jacob's sons were the founders of the twelve tribes of Israel, and he received the name Israel from God later in life. James is a common variant of this name. (Hebrew) *Jacobe*; (Latin) *Jacobae*; (Greek) *Iakovos*; (Arabic) *Yacoub*; (English) *Jago*; (German) *Jakob*; (French) *Jacquan, Jacquel, Jacquelin, Jacques, Jacquez*; (Italian) *Giacomo*; (Spanish) *Jacobo*; (Dutch) *Jaap*; (Russian) *Yakov*; (Finnish) *Jaakko, Jouko*; (Hawaiian) *Iakopa*; *Jaccob, Jacobus, Jacoby, Jacque*; **Old forms:** *Yaakov*; **Nicknames:** *Jake*; **Star babies:** sons of Dustin Hoffman, Albert Brooks, James Caan

JACOBSON English: Jacob's child

JACOREY English: Modern blend of Jay or possibly Jacob and Corey
Jakari; Jacori, Jacory

JACQUES (ZHAHK) French: Variation of Jacob

JACY (JAY-see) English: Modern name possibly derived from the initials J.C. or as a familiar form of Jason; (Native American) moon

JADON (JAH-dən, JAY-dən) Hebrew: Jehovah has heard; originally a male biblical name now used for both genders
Jaden, Jaiden; Jaiden, Jayden, Jadyn, Jadynn, Jaidyn, Jaidynn, Jaydyn, Jaydynn; **Nicknames:** *Jad*

JADRIEN (JAY-dree-ən) Contemporary: Modern blend of Jay and Adrien
Jadrian, Jaydrian, Jaydrien

JAEL (JAY-əl) Hebrew: Mountain goat
Yael

JAFAR (jah-FAHR) Hindi: Little stream, creek or brook
(African) *Jafaru; Ja'Far*

JAGDEEP (jug-deep) Sanskrit: Lamp of the world

JAGER (YAY-gur) German: Hunter
Jaegar; Jaeger

JAGGER English: Peddler or carter. For many, the name will bring to mind English musician Mick Jagger, the sometimes controversial and rebellious vocalist of the Rolling Stones.
Jager; Jagar, Jaggar

JAHAN (jah-HAHN) Hindi: The world

JAHI (JAH-hee) African: Dignified (Swahili)

JAHNU (jah-NOO) Hindi: Name of a Hindu legendary sage who played a role in the story of Ganga, the river goddess

JAIDEN (JAY-dən) Hebrew: Spelling variation of Jadon

JAIME (HIE-may) Spanish: Variation of James
Nicknames: *Diego, Yago*

JAIRUS (JAY-rəs) Hebrew: God enlightens. In the New Testament, Jairus is the father of a child brought back to life by Jesus.
(Spanish) *Jair, Jairo*

JAJAUN English: Modern blend of Jay and Juan

JAKEEM Arabic: Raised up, uplifted
Famous namesakes: Superhero Jakeem J. Thunder (alias for Jakeem J. Williams)

JALAL Arabic, Persian: Glory of the faith, illustrious, majesty
(Hindi) *Jaleel; Jalil;* **Famous namesakes:** Persian poet of the thirteenth century Jalal El Din Rumni, actor Jaleel White

JALEN (JAY-len) American: Modern blend of Jay and Len
Jalan, Jalon, Jaylen, Jaylon; **Famous namesakes:** Basketball player Jalen Rose

JALO (YAH-lo) Finnish: Noble

JAMAL (jah-MAHL) Arabic: Handsome, beautiful. Jamal was the name of a main character in the movie *Finding Forrester*, starring Sean Connery and Rob Brown. See also *Gamal*
(English) *Jamar; Jahmal, Jahmar, Jamael, Jamil, Jemal; Jahmal, Jamaal, Jamahl, Jamall;*
Nicknames: *Jam;* **Famous namesakes:** Actor Malcolm-Jamal Warner

JAMES Hebrew: Supplanter; variant of Jacob. Two of Christ's disciples, son of Zebedee and son of Alphaeus, were named James. In Britain, James is a royal name associated with kings of England and Scotland. See also *Iago*
(Spanish) *Diego, Jaime, Yago;* (Scottish) *Hamish;* (Basque) *Jakome;* (Armenian) *Hagop;* (Hawaiian) *Kimo; Jayme, Jaymes;*
Nicknames: *Jamie, Jem, Jim, Jimmie, Jimmy;*
Famous namesakes: Poet James Joyce, president Jimmy Carter, actor Jimmy Stewart; **Star babies:** sons of Art Garfunkel, Jon Voight, Belinda Carlisle, Jerry Hall and Mick Jagger, Thomas Gibson, Annie Potts

JAMESON English: Son of James
(Scottish) *Jamieson; Jamison*

JAMIE Scottish: Nickname for James
Jaimie, Jamey, Jayme; **Famous namesakes:** British chef Jamie Oliver

JAMIL (jah-MEEL) Arabic: Spelling variation of Jamal
Gamil, Gameel, Jamel, Jameel, Jamiel

JAMIN Hebrew: Right hand. In the Old Testament, this is a son of Simeon.
Jamon

JAMSHID (jam-shid) Persian: King, a character in Persian mythology (Shahnameh)
Jamsheed

JAN (YAHN) Dutch: Variation of John
Famous namesakes: Actor Jan-Michael
Vincent, singer Jan Berry

JANSEN German: Variation of John

JANUS (JAY-nəs) Latin: Archway. In Roman
mythology, Janus is the god of beginnings and
endings, and is often shown with a double-
faced head looking in opposite directions. The
month of January is named after him.
(Polish) *Januarius, Jarek*

JAPHET (JAY-fet) Hebrew: Handsome
or beautiful; used by some as a variant of
Japheth

JAPHETH (JAY-fəth) Hebrew: Enlarged,
expands. In the Bible, Japheth was a son of
Noah and the father of the people of Europe
and Asia Minor.
Yaphet

JARAH (JAY-rə) Hebrew: Honey, he
gives sweetness. The biblical Jarah was a
descendant of Jonathan.

JARED Hebrew: Descending; a pre-flood
biblical name related to Jordan
(English) *Jarrod*; *Jerad, Jered, Yered*; *Jarod,
Jarrod, Jerod, Jerrod*; **Famous namesakes:**
Actor Jared Leto; **Star babies:** sons of Richard
Harris, Paula Zahn

JARETH (JER-əth) Contemporary: Modern
blend of Jared and Gareth
Jarreth

JARI (YAHR-ee) Finnish: Helmeted warrior;
abbreviation of Jalmari

JARL (YAHRL) Scandinavian: Nobleman;
royalty title similar to the English earl

JARLATH (JAHR-lath) Irish: Master, in
charge; derived from Iarfhlaith, a name of

uncertain origin but with the root laith
meaning lord

JAROMIR (YAHR-o-meer) Slavic: Spring
Nicknames: *Jarek, Jaro*; **Famous namesakes:**
Hockey player Jaromir Jagr

JARON (JER-ən) Hebrew: He who sings, cry
of joy; variant of Yaron

JARRAH Arabic: A vessel, an earthenware
jar, emmigrating people, tribe

JARRETT English: Spelling variation of
Garrett

JARVIS English: Variation of Gervase
Famous namesakes: British singer Jarvis
Cocker

JASON Greek: To heal. In Greek mythology,
Jason led a group of warriors called the
Argonauts on a search to find the Golden
Fleece. The name may also be a variation of
Joshua, meaning *the Lord is my salvation*.
(Polish) *Jacek*; *Jaison, Jasen, Jaysen, Jayson*;
Nicknames: *Jace, Jase, Jayce*; **Famous
namesakes:** Actor Jason Alexander, actor
Jason Robards; **Star babies:** son of Sean
Connery

JASPAR Arabic: Keeper of the treasure; a
variant of Caspar or Gaspar. Jaspar was a
magic figure in the tale of *Aladdin and the
Magical Lamp*.
(Hungarian) *Gazsi*; *Jasper*; **Famous
namesakes:** Musician Bobby Jaspar; lawyer
M. Henri Jaspar; **Star babies:** son of Wynton
Marsalis

JASPER French: Ornamental stone, brown,
beige, or red in color; also a variant of Caspar

JAVAD Persian: Liberal

JAVAN (YAH-vən, JAY-vən) Hebrew: Greece; the Biblical name of one of Noah's grandsons
Jahvon, Jaivon

JAVED Persian: Eternal

JAVIER (hah-vee-ER) Spanish: Variation of Xavier
Javiero, Javi

JAVOR Slavic: Maple tree

JAWHAR Arabic: Jewel, essence
Jawhara, Gawhara, Gawhar

JAX English: Nickname for John

JAXON English: Variation of John

JAY English: Originally a familiar form of names such as Jacob, James, and Jason, now a given name in its own right. The name also refers to several species of a large family of birds; (Hindi) various deities in Hindi classical mythological writings are named Jay.
Jae, Jai, Jaye; **Famous namesakes:** Comedian Jay Leno, author Jay McInerney

JAYCEE English: Name based on the way the initials J.C. sound, possible variant of Jayce

JAYDEE English: Name based on the way the initials J.D. sound

JAYYED Arabic: Masculine variant of Jaeda, meaning good
Jaied

JEAN (ZHAHN) French: Variation of John

JEAN-BAPTISTE (ZHAWN-bap-TEEST) French: French combination name honoring Saint John the Baptist

JEAN-PAUL (ZHAWN-POL) French: Double name composed of Jean (God is gracious) and Paul (little)
Famous namesakes: French fashion designer Jean-Paul Gauthier

JEDIDIAH (jed-i-DIE-ə) Hebrew: Beloved of God. In the Bible, the blessing name Jedidiah was given to King Solomon in infancy.
Jedadiah, Jedaiah, Jedediah, Jediah, Yedidiah, Yedidyah; **Nicknames:** *Jedd, Jedi*

JEDREK (YED-rik, JED-rik) Polish: Variation of Andrew

JEDRICK (YED-rik, JED-rik) Polish: Variation of Andrew

JEFF English: Nickname for Jeffrey
Famous namesakes: Racing driver Jeff Gordon, actor Jeff Bridges, actor Jeff Daniels, actor Jeff Goldblum

JEFFERSON English: Son of Geoffrey, a surname adapted to occasional given name use.
Famous namesakes: President Thomas Jefferson; **Star babies:** son of Tony Randall

JEFFORD English: Jeff's ford; surname

JEFFREY French, Anglo-Saxon: Peaceful. A variant of Geoffrey, the three-syllable spelling alternate Jeffery has been used since medieval times.
(French) *Geoffrey*; (Irish) *Sheary, Sheron*; *Geffrey, Jeffery, Jeffry, Jeoffroi*; **Old forms:** *Geoffroi*; **Nicknames:** *Geoff, Jeff*; **Famous namesakes:** English author Jeffrey Archer

JENO (YEH-no) Greek: Variation of Eugene

JENS (YENS) Scandinavian: Variation of John
Jensen, Jenson

JERARD (jə-RAHRD) English: Spelling variation of Gerard
Nicknames: *Jerry*

JEREMIAH (jer-ə-MIE-ə) Hebrew: The Lord exalts; the name of a major Old Testament prophet
(Greek) *Jeremias*; (Italian) *Geremia*; (Russian) *Yerik*; *Jeramie, Jeramy*; **Nicknames:** *Jere, Jeremy*

JEREMY English: The Lord exalts; variant of Jeremiah
Famous namesakes: Actor Jeremy Irons; **Star babies:** son of Jermaine Jackson

JERICHO (JER-i-ko) Arabic: City of the moon. In the Bible, Jericho was the City of Canaan that was destroyed when its walls collapsed.
(Spanish) *Jerico*

JERIEL English: Spelling variation of Yeriel

JERMAINE English: Variation of Germain
Famous namesakes: Singer Jermaine Jackson.

JEROME Greek, French: Sacred name. In the fifth century, Saint Jerome created the Vulgate, a Latin translation of the Bible
(Italian) *Geronimo*; (Spanish) *Jeronimo*; (Polish) *Hieronim*; **Old forms:** *Hieronymus*; **Nicknames:** *Jerry*; **Famous namesakes:** Choreographer Jerome Robbins, comedian Jerry Seinfeld

JERRETT English: Spear strong; variant of Garrett
Jerett
JERVIS English: Variant of the French name Gervaise spearman

JERZY (YE-zhi) Polish: Variation of George

JESSE (JES-ee) Hebrew: God exists, wealthy. The biblical Jesse was the father of King David. Jesse is also the name of famous American track-and-field star Jesse Owens.
Jessie, Jessy; **Nicknames:** *Jess*; **Famous namesakes:** Outlaw Jesse James, politician Jesse Jackson; **Star babies:** sons of Bob Dylan, Jon Bon Jovi

JESUS (JEE-zəs, hay-SOOS) Hebrew, Spanish: The Lord is my salvation; Jesus Christ is the central figure of the Bible's New Testament, and Christianity is founded on his life and teachings. The name is most commonly used by Spanish-speaking families and stems from the same Hebrew root as Joshua.

JETHRO Hebrew: Overflowing, abundance; In the Bible, Jethro was Moses' father-in-law.
Famous namesakes: Inventor Jethro Tull, Rock group Jethro Tull

JETT English: A black mineral or intense black color
Star babies: son of Kelly Preston and John Travolta

JIM English: Nickname for James
Nicknames: *Jimi, Jimmey, Jimmie, Jimmy*; **Famous namesakes:** Actor Jim Carrey, puppeteer Jim Henson

JIRAIR (ZHEE-rayr) Armenian: Industrious

JIRO (jee-ro) Japanese: Second son

JOACHIM (JO-ə-kim, YO-ah-khim) Hebrew: God will judge. Joaquin is a beloved Spanish form of this name
(Spanish) *Joaquin, Quin, Quino, Yoaquin*; (Russian) *Ioakim*; *Akim*; **Nicknames:** *Achim*

JOAQUIN (wah-KEEN) Spanish: Variation of Joachim
Nicknames: *Quin*; **Famous namesakes:** Actor Joaquin Phoenix

JOB (JOB) Hebrew: Persecuted. In the Old Testament Book of Job, God allows Satan to test Job's faith through a series of misfortunes. **Old forms:** *Jobe*

JOCELYN French: Transferred surname derived from the Germanic name Gautelen, which comes from the name of a Germanic tribe, the Gauts
Nicknames: *Jos*

JOCK Scottish: Variation of John

JOE English: Nickname for Joseph
Famous namesakes: Actor Joe Pesci, boxer Joe Louis, baseball player Joe DiMaggio, quarterback Joe Namath; **Star babies:** sons of Kevin Costner, Christine Lahti

JOEL (JOL) Hebrew: Lord is God; a biblical prophet and author of the Book of Joel
Old forms: *Yoel*; **Famous namesakes:** Actor Joel Gray

JOHANN (YO-hahn) German: God has been gracious; a variant of John. The German composer Johann Sebastian Bach is considered to be a great genius of Baroque music. He also fathered (and named) thirteen children with his wife, Anna.
Famous namesakes: German inventor and printer Johann Gutenberg, Austrian composer Johann Strauss

JOHN Hebrew: God has been gracious; John is the name of one of Christ's disciples, and another biblical John—John the Baptist—baptized Christ in the Jordan River. One of the most popular names in the world, variants of John have been created in almost every language. See also *Johann*
(Greek) *Ioan, Ioannis, Ivan*; (Arabic) *Yahya, Yohanna*; (English) *Jaxon*; (German) *Handel, Jansen, Johan, Johannes*; (French) *Jean, Johnn*; (Italian) *Gian, Giovani, Giovanni, Giovonni*; (Spanish) *Juan, Juancho, Juanito*;

(Portuguese) *Joao*; (Teutonic) *Hans*; (Gaelic) *Iain*; (Celtic) *Eoin*; (Irish) *Ion, Keon, Seán*; (Scottish) *Ian, Jock*; (Welsh) *Ieuan, Iwan, Sion*; (Scandinavian) *Jens, Jensen, Jenson*; (Swedish) *Jan*; (Danish) *Jantzen, Jen, Joen*; (Basque) *Iban*; (Slavic) *Ivano*; (Czech) *Hanus, Honza, Ianos, Jenda*; (Polish) *Janek*; (Finnish) *Hannes, Joni, Jouni, Juha, Juhana, Juhani, Juho, Jukka, Jussi*; (Hungarian) *Jena*; (Hawaiian) *Keoni*; (Estonian) *Jaan*; *Giannes, Giovanny, Giovany, Jon, Jonn, Jonnie*; **Nicknames:** *Gino, Jack, Jackie, Jacky, Jax, Johnnie, Johnny, Jonni*;
Famous namesakes: Actor Johnny Depp, actor John Wayne, musician John Lennon, composer Johannes Bach, president John F. Kennedy, president John Tyler, president John Adams, president John Quincy Adams; **Star babies:** sons of Tracey Ullman, Caroline Kennedy and Ed Schlossberg, Denzel Washington, Michelle Pfeiffer, Rob Lowe, Jane Seymour, Ally Walker

JOHNSON English: Son of John; most common as a last name
Johnston

JOLON (JO-lon) Native American: Valley of the dead oaks

JOLYON English: Downy-haired

JON English: Variant of John or abbreviation of Jonathan. Jon is sometimes used in the French fashion, hyphenated with a second name like Jon-Carlo or Jon-Paul.

JONAH (JO-nə) Hebrew: Dove. In the Bible, Jonah the prophet was swallowed by a great fish and safely emerged from his belly three days later. Sailors traditionally use this name to personify someone who brings bad luck.
(Greek) *Jonas*; (Finnish) *Joona*; *Yonah*

JONAS Greek: Variation of Jonah
Famous namesakes: Research scientist Jonas Salk

JONATHAN Hebrew: Gift from God. In the Bible, Jonathan was a son of Saul and close friend of King David. See also *Ionakana* (Finnish) *Joonatan*; *Jonatan*, *Yehonatan*; *Jonathon*; **Nicknames:** *Jon*; **Famous namesakes:** Actor Jonathan Taylor Thomas, English author Jonathan Swift, comedian Jonathan Winters; **Star babies:** son of Paulina Porizkova and Rik Ocasek

JOONA (YO-nah) Finnish: Variation of Jonah

JOOST (YOST) Dutch: Variation of Justin **Famous namesakes:** Dutch author Joost Elfers

JORAN (YOR-uhn) Scandinavian: Variation of George

JORDAN Hebrew: To flow downward. The river in Palestine where Jesus was baptized has been used as a given name since the Crusades. The name likely had a boost among parents of boys with the popularity of NBA star Michael Jordan.
(French) *Jourdan*; *Jordain*, *Jordell*, *Jorden*, *Jordon*, *Jourdon*, *Yarden*; **Nicknames:** *Jordi*, *Jordy*; **Star babies:** sons of Beau Bridges, Pia Zadora

JORDELL Hebrew: Spelling variation of Jordan

JORDY Hebrew: Nickname for Jordan

JORGE (HOR-hay) Spanish: Variation of George

JORGEN (YER-gen) Danish: Variation of George
Joris

JORMA (YOR-mə) Finnish: Variation of George
Famous namesakes: Musician Jorma Kaukonen

JORMUNGAND Norse: In Norse mythology, Jormungand was one of the three children of the god Loki and his wife, the giantess Angrboda. He was a serpent who remained deep in the ocean where he bit his own tail and encircled the world.

JOSÉ (ho-SAY) Spanish: Variation of Joseph **Nicknames:** *Che*, *Joselito*, *Pepe*, *Pepillo*; **Famous namesakes:** Actor José Ferrer, Spanish opera singer José Carreras

JOSEPH Hebrew: May God give increase. In the Bible, Joseph is the favored son of Jacob. He was sold by his brothers into slavery and later rose to become a supreme power in Egypt. The New Testament carpenter named Joseph was the husband of Mary, the mother of Jesus. See also *Iokepa* (Arabic) *Yusef*, *Yusuf*; (German) *Josef*; (French) *Josephe*; (Italian) *Giuseppe*; (Spanish) *Che*, *Jose*, *Joselito*, *Pepe*, *Pepillo*; (Gaelic) *Ioseph*, *Seosamh*, *Seosaph*; (Basque) *Txanton*; (Russian) *Iosif*; (Polish) *Josep*; (Hungarian) *Joska*, *Jozsef*, *Jozsi*; (Armenian) *Hovsep*; *Josephus*, *Yosef*; **Nicknames:** *Joe*, *Joey*, **Famous namesakes:** Actor Joseph Fiennes, author Joseph Conrad; **Star babies:** son of Kristin Scott-Thomas

JOSH Hebrew: Nickname for Joshua **Famous namesakes:** Actor Josh Hartnett, actor Josh Charles

JOSHA (JO-shuh) Hindi: Satisfied *Joshah*

JOSHUA Hebrew: The Lord is my salvation. In the Old Testament, Joshua led his army in the conquest of Jericho and eventually all of Canaan, and was a leader of the Israelites. The Book of Joshua bears his name. According to legend, Mormon pioneers named the rare desert trees in California's Joshua Tree National Park after the biblical figure. (Spanish) *Josue*; (Hawaiian) *Iokua*; *Jesiah*, *Josu*, *Yehoshua*; **Nicknames:** *Josh*, *Joss*

Names That Mean Brains

Looking for an intellectual moniker? Here's a list of names that have intellectual wisdom in their meanings.

Boys' Names

Al Alim (Arabic)
Albert (German)
Alden (Anglo-Saxon)
Aldo (German)
Aldred (English)
Alfred (Anglo-Saxon)
Alim (Arabic)
Alvin (English)
Aref (Persian)
Bodhi (Hindi)
Conrad (German)
Farzan (Persian)
Hakim (Arabic)
Hewitt (German)
Hugh (English, German)
Manu (Hindi)
Quinn (Celtic)
Rambert (German)
Raymond (French, German)
Reginald (English)
Sagan (Slavic)
Thaddeus (Hebrew)
Trevor (Celtic)
Zaki (Arabic)

Girls' Names

Alda (German)
Aldene (Italian)
Aldred (English)
Alka (Polish)
Auberta (Teutonic)
Bernardina (Teutonic)
Channing (English)
Eberta (Teutonic)
Dana (Persian)
Dara (Hebrew)
Darissa (Hebrew)
Elda (Anglo-Saxon)
Elberta (Teutonic)
Ethelda (Teutonic)
Monica (Latin)
Ramona (Spanish)
Sage (Latin)
Salvina (Latin)
Shanahan (Irish)
Shannon (Irish)
Sophronia (Greek)

JOSIAH (jo-SIE-ə) Hebrew: The Lord supports. The biblical Josiah became king of Judah at age eight after his father was killed and was known for his religious reforms. (Spanish) *Josias*; *Joziah*

JOTHAM (JO-thəm) Hebrew: God is upright; a biblical king of Judah during a time of military strife

JOVAN Latin: Father of the sky, majestic, Jove-like; derived from Jove
Jovani, Jovann, Jovanni, Jovanny, Jovany, Jovi, Jovin, Jovito, Jovon

JOVE Latin: A form of the name Jupiter, the supreme god in Roman mythology

JUAN (HWAHN) Spanish: Variation of John
Nicknames: *Chan, Juancho, Juancito, Juanito, Yoni*; **Famous namesakes:** Literary hero Don Juan, Spanish king Juan Carlos, Spanish explorer Juan Ponce de León

JUBAL (JOO-bəl) Hebrew: The ram; inventor of the harp and pipes

JUDAH (JOO-də) Hebrew: Praised. In the Bible, one of Jacob's twelve sons and the ancestor of the tribe of Judah. The Greek form Judas is associated with the biblical Judas Iscariot who betrayed Jesus. (Greek) *Judas*; *Yehuda, Yehudi*; **Nicknames:** *Jude, Jud, Judd*

JUDD English: To flow down; originally a familiar form of Jordan, but became more of a name in its own right centuries ago when it was used to refer to children who were baptized with water from the river Jordan. *Jud*; **Famous namesakes:** Actor Judd Hirsch, actor Judd Nelson

JUDE Hebrew: Praised; a variant of Judah. The Beatles' smash hit "Hey Jude" was one

of the first rock singles to break the standard running time, lasting over seven minutes—yet it still landed in the top spot on the charts in the United Kingdom and United States. **Famous namesakes:** Actor Jude Law

JUDSON American: Son of Judd

JULES (ZHUYL, JOOLZ) French: Variation of Julian
Famous namesakes: French author Jules Verne

JULIAN Latin: Youthful; form of Julius and family clan name of several powerful Roman emperors. In the New Testament, Roman centurion Julius saved Paul's life during a hazardous voyage. (French) *Jules, Julien*; (Italian) *Giuliano, Giulio*; (Spanish) *Juliano, Julio, Yulius*; (Hungarian) *Gyula, Gyuszi*; (Hawaiian) *Iulio, Julen, Jullian, Jullien*; **Old forms:** *Julius*; **Nicknames:** *Jules*; **Diminutive forms:** *Julito*; **Famous namesakes:** English actor Julian Sands, English musician Julian Lennon; **Star babies:** sons of Robert De Niro, Lisa Kudrow

JULIO (HOO-lee-o) Spanish: Variation of Julian
Nicknames: *Julito, Ulio*; **Famous namesakes:** Singer Julio Iglesias

JULIUS Latin: Youth; an old Roman family name most commonly recognized as the name of Gaius Julius Caesar, one of ancient Rome's greatest generals and leaders
Famous namesakes: Basketball player Julius "Dr. J" Irving, Julius Henry "Groucho" Marx; **Star babies:** son of Lucy Lawless and Rob Tapert

"Groucho is not my real name. I'm breaking it in for a friend."
—Groucho Marx

JUMOKE (joo-MO-kay) African: Beloved child (Nigeria)

JUNIUS (JOO-nyəs) Latin: Young, junior, similar to the name Julius
Junus

JUPITER (JOO-pi-tər) Latin: Jupiter is the supreme god of Roman mythology, the equivalent to the Greek god, Zeus. Jupiter is also the name of the largest planet in our solar system.

JURGEN (YOOR-gən) Scandinavian: Variation of George
Jorgen

JUSTICE English: Variation of Justin
Star babies: son of Steven Seagal

JUSTIN Latin, English: Just, lawful, fair; a form of the New Testament biblical name Justus. See also *Iestyn*
(English) *Justice*; (French) *Juste*; (Spanish) *Justino*; (Dutch) *Joost*; (Polish) *Justyn*; *Justain*, *Justis*; **Old forms:** *Justus*; **Famous namesakes:** Singer Justin Timberlake; **Star babies:** sons of Sean Combs, Andie MacDowell

JUWAN (joo-WAHN) American: True
Famous namesakes: Basketball player Juwan Howard

KACHADA Native American: White man (Hopi)

KADAR (KAH-dahr) Arabic: Strength, fate, destiny, predestination, powerful
Kadir, Qadir; Qadar, Kedar

KAELAN Gaelic: Spelling variation of Cailean

KAEMON (kah-ay-mon) Japanese: Joyful, righthanded; an old Samurai name

KAFELE (kah-FE-le) Egyptian: Would die for

KAGA (kah-gah) Native American: Chronicler

KAGAN Irish: A thinker
Kagen

KAHERDIN Arthurian legend: Brother of Isolde

KAHOKU (ka-HO-koo) Hawaiian: Star

KAI Welsh, Scottish, Finnish: Keeper of the keys; (Hawaiian) the sea
(Swedish) *Kaj*

KAIKURA African: Ground squirrel

KAILASA (kie-lah-suh) Hindi: Silver mountain

KAIMANA (kah-ee-MAH-nah) Hawaiian: Ocean's power, diamond

KAIMI Hawaiian: Seeker

KAINE Gaelic: Spelling variation of Kane

KAIPO (kah-EE-po) Hawaiian: Sweetheart

KAISER (KIE-zer) German: Emperor; variant of Caesar

KAISON English: Keeper of the keys; modern variant of Kai

KAJETAN (kah-YE-tahn) Polish: From the city of Gaeta

KAJIKA Native American: Walks without sound

KAKAR (KAH-kahr) Hindi: *Grass*

KALA (KAH-lah) Hindi: Black; Hindu god of time

KALANI (kah-LAH-nee) Hawaiian: The sky, chieftain

KALE (KAH-le) Hawaiian: Variation of Charles

KALEO (kah-LE-o) Hawaiian: One voice

KALEVA (KAH-le-vah) Finnish: Hero

KALF Norse: A name from a Norse medieval saga, the stepson of Asgeir

KALIQ (KAH-leek) Arabic: Creative (a godly quality); also referred to as *Al Khallak Khaliq, Khalek, Khaleq*

KALLE (KAHL) Swedish: Strong, manly; a Scandinavian variant of Karl

KAMAL (kah-MAHL) Arabic, Persian: Perfection, completion; (Hindi) lotus (Turkish) *Kemal*

KAMBIZ Persian: Fortunate

KAMRAN (kahm-rahn) Persian: Successful

KANA (KAH-nah) Hawaiian: A Maui demigod who could take the form of a rope and stretch from Molokai to Hawaii

KANE (KAYN) Gaelic: Battle, warrior. *Citizen Kane*, starring Orson Welles, is thought by many to be one of the greatest American movies ever made. *Kaine, Kayne*

KANGI (KAN-gee) Native American: Raven, crow (Sioux) *Kangee*

KANIEL Hebrew: Reed

KANNAN (kah-nun) Sanskrit: A form of Krishna

KANOA (kah-NO-ah) Hawaiian: Free

KANSBAR Persian: Treasure master

KAPIL (kah-pil) Hindi: From Kapila

KAPONO (kah-PO-no) Hawaiian: Righteous one

KARAM (kar-RAHM) Arabic: Hospitable

KARDEIZ Arthurian legend: Son of Percival

KARI Norse, Finnish: Gust of wind or curly-haired

KARIM (kah-REEM) Arabic, Persian: Generous, noble. The Koran lists Al Karim (The Generous) as one of the ninety-nine names of God.
Kareem; *Kharim*; **Famous namesakes:** Basketball player Kareem Abdul-Jabbar, Indian religious monarch Karim Al Alami, French writer, singer, and composer Karim Kacel

KARL German: Strong, manly. The writings of Karl Marx helped form the policies for the political and economic system known as Communism. See also *Carl, Kalle* (Italian) *Carlo*; (Spanish) *Carlos*; (Slavic) *Karol*; (Russian) *Karolek*; (Czech) *Karel*; (Finnish) *Kaarle, Kaarlo*; (Hungarian) *Karoly*; **Famous namesakes:** Actor Karl Malden, fashion designer Karl Lagerfeld

KARLHEINZ (KAHRL-hients) German: Strong, manly; a blend of Karl and Heinz

KASEKO (kah-SAY-ko) African: Mock

KASEY Irish: Spelling variation of Casey

KASIM (kah-SEEM) Arabic: Defender, divider, oath, portion, gift, division, protector; Kasim el Wagh is one who has a handsome face; (African) controller of anger (Egyptian) *Asim*; *Kaseem*; *Asim, Asem, Kasem, Kassem, Kassim, Kaseem, Qaseem, Qassim, Qasim*

KASIYA (kah-SEE-yah) Egyptian: Departs

KATEB (kah-teb) Arabic: Writer; from old Arabic

KATUNGI (kah-TOO-ngee) African: Rich

KAVEH (kah-ve) Persian: A name from Persian mythology, character in *Shahnameh*

KAVI (KAV-ee) Hindi: Poet

KAWA (kah-wah) Native American: Great (Apache)

KAWIKA (kah-VEE-kah) Hawaiian: Dearly loved; variant of David

KAY Welsh: Variation of Gaius. In Arthurian legend, Kay was a knight of the Round Table.

KAYAN Persian: Star

KAYONGA (kah-YO-ngah) African: Ash

KAZI African: Work

KAZMER (KAHZ-mer) Polish: Form of Casimir
Cazmer; **Nicknames:** *Kaz*

KAZUO (kah-zoo) Japanese: First-born son

KEAHI (ke-AH-hee) Hawaiian: Fiery one

KEALY Irish: Handsome

KEANAN Irish: Spelling variation of Cian

KEANU (kee-AH-noo) Hawaiian: Cool breeze over the mountains
Famous namesakes: Keanu Reeves

KEARNEY Irish: Victorious
Carney, Karney

KEATON English: Surname derived from a place name meaning *shed town* in Old English
Famous namesakes: Actor Buster Keaton, actor Michael Keaton

KEDRIC English: Battle or war leader; variant of Cedric
Cedric, Kedrick, Keddrick

KEEFE Irish, Gaelic: Handsome, cherished

KEEGAN Irish, Gaelic: Small and fiery
Aodhagan, Keagan, Keaghan, Kegan

KEELAN Gaelic: Slender. See also *Kellan*
Caolan, Kealan, Keilan, Keillan, Kelan, Kellen;
Nicknames: *Caley, Caly*

KEENAN Irish: Spelling variation of Cian
Famous namesakes: Actor Keenan Ivory Wayans, actor Keenan Wynn

KEI Arthurian legend: Arthur's brother
Ke

KEIJI (kay-jee) Japanese: Respect

KEIR (KEER) Gaelic: Dusky, dark-haired
Famous namesakes: Actor Keir Dullea

KEITARO (kay-tah-ro) Japanese: Blessed

KEITH Irish: Forest; Originally a Scottish place name, Keith was also the surname of a long line of Scottish earls.
Famous namesakes: English musician Keith Richards, actor Keith Carradine, baseball player Keith Hernandez

KEKOA (ke-KO-ə) Hawaiian: The brave one

KELBY Norse: Farm near the spring

KELE (KEL) Native American: Sparrow hawk (Hopi)
Kelle

KELL Norse: From the spring

KELLACH (KEL-akh) Irish: Strife

KELLAN Gaelic: Spelling variation of Keelan; (African) powerful

KELLMAN Hungarian: Variation of Clemens

KELLY Irish: Warrior or bright-minded (Gaelic) *Kellye*; *Kelle, Kelley, Kellee, Kelley*; **Famous namesakes:** Dancer and actor Gene Kelly

KELSEY English: From the island, possibly from the island of ships; (Irish) warrior (Norse) *Kelsig, Kiollsig*; **Famous namesakes:** Actor Kelsey Grammer

KELVIN Gaelic, English, Celtic: From the narrow river; possibly a place name for the River Kelvin in Scotland
Kelvan, Kelven, Kelvyn, Kelwin, Kelwyn; **Famous namesakes:** British physicist Lord Kelvin

KEME Native American: Secret (Algonquin)

KEMP English: Warrior, champion

KEMUEL (KEM-yoo-el) Hebrew: God has raised up. Kemuel is a biblical figure and relative of Abraham.

KEN English: Nickname of Kenneth and an abbreviation of names beginning with *Ken–*; the main squeeze of the world-famous Barbie doll; (Japanese) healthy, strong

Kenn, Kennan; **Nicknames:** *Kennie, Kenny*; **Famous namesakes:** Baseball player Ken Griffey Jr., producer Ken Burns, singer Kenny Rogers

KENDALL English: Valley of the Kent. This surname has become a unisex name and likely refers to a river in England.
Kendal, Kendale, Kendel, Kendell, Kendhal; **Nicknames:** *Ken, Kenny*

KENDI African: Loved one

KENDRICK Anglo-Saxon: This is a name with a disputed meaning, and there are several possibilities: royal power from the Old English name Cyneric, bold power from Old English Ceneric, high hill from the Welsh Cynwrig, or son of Henry from the Gaelic surname Mac Eanraig.
Kendric; **Nicknames:** *Kendrix*

KENELM English: Bold defender. Saint Kenelm was a ninth-century prince (or perhaps king) of Mercia.

KENJI (ken-jee) Japanese: Intelligent second son, strong and vigorous
Nicknames: *Kenjiro*

KENLEY English: From the king's meadow; a surname and variant of Kingsley

KENNARD English: Royal guard, chieftain

KENNEDY Gaelic: Helmet-head or misshapen head
Famous namesakes: President John F. Kennedy

KENNELLY Irish: Pledge

KENNER Gaelic: Brave chieftain

KENNETH Scottish, English: Born of fire, handsome

Nicknames: *Kenney, Kenny, Ken, Kennie, Kenny;* **Famous namesakes:** Actor Kenneth Branagh, composer Kenneth "Babyface" Edmonds

KENT English: Border, coast, bright white. Kent is a county in England known for its lovely countryside.

KENTARO (ken-tah-ro) Japanese: Sharp; big boy

KENTON English: From the royal settlement or town, likely related to the county Kent in England; surname
Kentan, Kentin, Kentun

KENTRELL English: Royal chieftain

KENWARD English: Bold guardian

KENWAY English: Bold warrior
Nicknames: *Ken*

KENYON Gaelic: Blond

KEOKI (ke-O-kee) Hawaiian: Variation of George

KEONI (ke-O-nee) Hawaiian: Variation of John

KEREM (ke-REM) Turkish: Kindness

KERMICHAEL Gaelic: From Michael's fortress

KERMIT Gaelic: Free man or without envy; a variant of Dermot. Kermit is a name made famous by Jim Henson's lovable green muppet Kermit the Frog who stars on *Sesame Street.*

KERR Gaelic: Marshland

KERRY Gaelic: Dark, dusky; refers to the county that lies along the southwestern coast of Ireland
Keary, Kerrigan; **Famous namesakes:** Football player Kerry Collins

KERWIN Irish: Little dark one
Kerwen, Kerwyn

KESIN (ke-SEEN) Hindi: Long-haired beggar

KESTER Scottish: Variation of Christopher

KETIL Norse: Sacrificial kettle
Kjell

KEVIN Irish: Handsome; name of a famous Irish hermit-saint
Cavan, Kavan, Kaven, Kevan, Keven, Keveon, Kevinn, Kevion, Kevon, Kevyn; **Nicknames:** *Kevis, Kev;* **Famous namesakes:** Actor Kevin Costner, actor Kevin Bacon, actor Kevin Spacey, actor Kevin Kline; **Star babies:** son of Tatum O'Neal and John McEnroe

KEYVAN Persian: World, universe
Kayvan

KHACHIG (KHA-chig) Armenian: Small cross

KHALFANI (kahl-FAH-nee) Egyptian: Shall rule

KHALID (KAH-leed, kah-LEED) Arabic: Eternal, immortal, glorious
Kalid; **Old forms:** *Khaldun;* **Star babies:** King of Saudi Arabia Khalid Ibn Abdel Aziz

KHALIL (khah-LEEL, khah-LIL) Arabic: Companion, friend, lover. The writings of Lebanese poet Khalil Gibran in *The Prophet* have been translated worldwide.
Kahliel, Kahlil, Kalil; **Famous namesakes:** Arab philologist Al Khalil Ibn Ahmad

KHAN (KAHN) Arabic, Turkish: Prince; a title used by central Asian tribal chieftains and ruling princes. Khan is also an inn built around a courtyard where caravans may rest. (Turkish) *Khanh*; *Khanh, Kan*; **Famous namesakes:** Indian singer Ustad Salamat Ali Khan

KHARIF Arabic: Autumn, fall; born during autumn
Karif, Kareef

KHASIB Arabic: Fertile
Kaseeb; *Khaseb*

KHAYRI Arabic: Generous, charitable, benevolent (act or organization); derived from Kheir, meaning goodness
Famous namesakes: Egyptian playwright Badie Khayri

KHAYYAT Arabic: Tailor
Famous namesakes: Artist and singer Isaac Khayat

KHONSU (KON-soo) Egyptian: God of the moon represented as a man. With Amon and Mut as father and mother, these three gods form the Theban triad.

KHOURY (KOOR-ee) Arabic: Priest. This name is very popular in Lebanon, both as a first name and as a family name.
Koury; **Famous namesakes:** Lebanese head of state Bichara Khalil El Khoury, Egyptian author and photographer Ayman Khoury

KHUFU (KOO-foo) Egyptian: Ancient king of Egypt and pyramid builder

KIAN (KEE-an, KEEN) Irish: Spelling variation of Cian; (Persian) surname of the second dynasty of Persian kings

KIBO (kee-bo) Japanese: Hope

KIEFER (KEE-fər) German: Barrel maker; possibly a variation of Cooper
Keefer, Keifer; Kieffer; **Famous namesakes:** Actor Kiefer Sutherland

KIERCE Irish: Dark-haired one; a surname and variant of Kieran

KILBY Teutonic: From the farm by the spring

KILDARE Irish: Church of the oak; a place name from County Kildare in the Irish province of Leinster
Kildaire

KIMBALL Welsh: Warrior chief. This name gained in popularity through Rudyard Kipling's novel *Kim*, a story about an orphan Irish boy growing up in India.
Kimble; **Nicknames:** *Kim*

KIMO (KEE-mo) Hawaiian: Variation of James

KIMONI African: Great man

KINDIN Latin: Born fifth

KING English: King is one of several titles occasionally used as given names.

KINGDON English: From the king's hall

KINGSLEY English: From the king's meadow; surname
Kenley, Kenly, Kinsley, Rexley; Kenlea, Kenlee, Kenleigh, Kenlie, Kingslea, Kingslie, Kingsly, Kinsey, Kinslea, Kinslee, Kinslie, Kinsly;
Famous namesakes: Actor Ben Kingsley, English novelist Kingsley Amis

KINGSTON English: From the king's village or estate. The Kingston Trio was a popular folk group from the San Francisco Bay area in the late 1950s and early 1960s.

Star babies: son of Gwen Stefani and Gavin Rossdale

KINNELL Gaelic: From the head of the cliff

KINNEY Scottish: The fire-sprung; possibly derived from Cionaodh, a compound of the elements cion meaning respect or affection and Aodh, the name of a pagan god of fire.

KINNON Scottish: Fair-born

KINNY Scottish: From the top of the cliff

KINSEY English: Victorious

KIP English: From the pointed hill
Kipp, Kippar; **Nicknames:** *Kippie*

KIRABO African: Gift from God

KIRBY English, Teutonic, Norse: Church village, Teutonic residence
Kerbie, Kerbey, Kirbey, Kirkbie, Kirkby;
Famous namesakes: Baseball player Kirby Puckett, actor Bruno Kirby

KIRILL (kee-REEL) Russian: Variation of Cyril

KIRK English, Scandinavian: From the church; a nickname for many male English names related to churches, such as Kirkland and Kirkwood
(Scottish) *Kerk, Kyrk*; *Kirke*; **Famous namesakes:** Actor Kirk Douglas, actor Kirk Cameron

KIRKAN Armenian: Watchful
Nicknames: *Kirk*

KIRKLAND English, Scottish: From the church land; surname
(Scottish) *Kirklin, Kirklyn*; **Nicknames:** *Kirk*

KIRKLEY English: From the church's meadow
Kirkly; Kirklea, Kirklee, Kirkleigh, Kirklie;
Nicknames: *Kirk*

KIRKWOOD English: From the forest near the church; surname
Kyrkwode; **Nicknames:** *Kirk*

KIVA Hebrew: Replaces, supplants; variant of Akiva
Kiba

KLAS Swedish: Victorious; a short form of Nicholas and Nikolaus

KLAUS (KLOWS) German: Nickname for Nicholas
Famous namesakes: German actor Klaus Kinski

KNIGHT English: Noble, soldier
Famous namesakes: Basketball coach Bobby Knight

KNOX (NAHKS) English: From the hills
Knocks; **Star babies:** son of Angelina Jolie and Brad Pitt

KNUT (NOOT) Norse: Knot; a name most likely recognized in America for the legendary football coach *Knute Rockne*
Canute, Cnut, Cnute, Knud, Knute

KOBE (KO-bee) English: Spelling variation of Coby
Famous namesakes: Basketball player Kobe Bryant

KOHANA (ko-hah-nah) Native American: Swift (Sioux)

KOI (ko-ee) Native American: Panther (Choctaw); (Hawaiian) urge, implore; the Hawaiian equivalent of Troy.

KOJO (ko-JO) African: Born on Monday

KOLB Armenian: From Kolb

KONA (KO-nah) Hawaiian: Variation of Donald

KONANI (ko-NAH-nee) Hawaiian: Bright

KONRAD (KAHN-rad) German: Bold advisor, wise; a spelling variation of Conrad **Nicknames:** *Kord, Kort, Kunz*

KOREN Hebrew: Shining, beaming

KORNEL Czech: Variation of Cornelius

KORT German: Bold advisor, wise; a nickname for Conrad and Konrad

KORUDON (ko-ROO-dun) Greek: Helmeted

KOUROSH Persian: The first Persian king

KRATOS (KRAH-tos) Greek: Strength, power

KRISHNA (KRISH-nah) Hindi: Black or dark; One of the greatest of the Hindu Gods.

KRISTIAN Scandinavian: Variation of Christian

KRISTOFF Scandinavian: Spelling variation of Christopher

KUDRET (koo-DRET) Turkish: Power

KULBERT German: Calm, bright

KUMAR (koo-MAHR) Hindi: Prince

KURON African: Thanks

KURT German: Variation of Curtis **Famous namesakes:** Actor Kurt Russell, author Kurt Vonnegut

KURUK Native American: Bear (Pawnee)

KYLE Gaelic, Irish: A narrow strait or channel *Kile, Kylan, Kylar, Kylen, Kyler, Kyrell*; **Nicknames:** *Kiley, Kye*; **Famous namesakes:** Actor Kyle MacLachlan, actor Kyle Chandler; **Star babies:** son of Clint Eastwood

KYLER Gaelic: A narrow strait or channel. This variant of Kyle could also be derived from a Dutch surname meaning *archer*.

KYNE English: Intelligent; variant of Conan

KYRKSEN Scottish: Dweller by the church

KYROS (KEER-os) Greek: Master

LABAN (LAY-bən) Hebrew: White; the Old Testament father of Rachel and Leah *Lavan*

LACHLAN Scottish: Land of lakes, land of lochs; originally a Scottish nickname for someone from Norway (Gaelic) *Lachlann*; (Irish) *Laughlin, Lochlain, Lochlann, Loughlin*; *Lakeland, Laochailan*; **Nicknames:** *Lach, Lache, Laec*

LACKO Slavic: Famous ruler

LADBROC English: Lives by the path by the brook

LADD English: Young boy *Lad, Ladde; Laddey, Laddie, Laddy*; **Famous namesakes:** Actor Alan Ladd

LADON (LAY-dən) Greek: Dragon of Hera

LAEFERTUN English: Spelling variation of Leverton

LAERTES (lay-ER-tees) Greek: A character in Greek mythology, father of Odysseus and king of Ithaca.

LAFAYETTE French: This is a surname used as first name. At the age of twenty, the French nobleman Marquis de Lafayette fought for four years in the American Revolution.

LAGMANN Norse: Lawyer

LAIDLEY English: From the meadow near the creek; surname
Laidly; *Laidlea, Laidlee, Laidleigh, Laidlie*

LAILOKEN Arthurian legend: A name from Celtic mythology of a Scottish lord and madman with prophetic abilities. Lailoken may have been the source for the character of Merlin.

LAINE English: Spelling variation of Lane

LAIRGNEN Celtic: Of Connaught

LAIS (LAYS) Hindi: Lion

LAIUS (LAY-əs) Greek: The mythological father of Oedipus

LAL (LAHL) Hindi: Beloved

LAMAR (lə-MAHR) French: Of the sea
Lamarr; **Famous namesakes:** Senator Lamar Alexander

LAMBERT (LAHM-bert) German, French: Light of land
Lambart, Lambrecht; **Famous namesakes:** Actor Christopher Lambert

LAMBI Norse: A name from a medieval Norse saga, son of Thorbjorn the Feeble

LAMONT (lə-MAHNT) Scandinavian, Scottish: Man of law; a clan name

Lamond; Lemond; **Famous namesakes:** Cyclist Greg LeMond

LAMORAT Arthurian legend: The brother of Percival

LANCE French: Assistant
(Italian) *Lanzo;* **Old forms:** *Lancelin, Lancelot, Launcelot;* **Famous namesakes:** Cyclist Lance Armstrong

LANCELOT French: Assistant. Sir Lancelot was one of King Arthur's greatest and bravest knights in the legends of the Round Table. The scandal that followed his love affair with Queen Guenevere, the king's wife, led to his downfall.
Launcelot

LANDER German: Landowner

LANDON Anglo-Saxon, English: Grassy plain
Landis; Landan, Landen, Landin; **Famous namesakes:** Actor Michael Landon

LANDRY Anglo-Saxon: Ruler of the place
Famous namesakes: Football coach Tom Landry

LANE English: Path or small roadway
(Scottish) *Lean, Leane; Laine, Layne*

LANG Anglo-Saxon: Long, tall
Nicknames: *Lange*

LANGDON (LANG-dən) English: Ridge, long hill
Lancdon

LANGFORD (LANG-furd) English: Lives near the long ford

LANGLEY English: From the long meadow. Langley, Virginia, is well-known as the home of the Central Intelligence Agency.
Langleah

LANGSTON English: From the farm of the tall man, town of the giant
Lankston, Lanston, Langsden, Langsdon, Langton; **Famous namesakes:** Poet Langston Hughes; **Star babies:** son of Laurence Fishburne

LANGUNDO (lahn-GOON-do) Native American: Peaceful

LANNY English: Nickname for Roland

LANSA Native American: Lance (Hopi)

LANSTON English: From the long estate

LANTZ Yiddish: Lancer

LANY Irish: Servant

LAOCOON (lay-AH-kə-wahn) Greek: In Greek mythology, Laocoon was the Trojan priest who warned his countrymen against the wooden horse left by the Greeks.

LAOIDHIGH Irish: Poet, poetic

LAOMEDON (lay-AHM-i-dən) Greek, Latin: The mythological father of Priam, King of Troy

LAPIDOS Hebrew: Torch
Nicknames: *Lapidoth*

LAPU Native American: Cedar bark (Hopi)

LARAMIE French: A place name and transferred surname. Laramie is a town in Wyoming named for the nineteenth-century French fur trapper Jacques La Ramee.

LAREN Scottish: Laurel; variant of Lawrence

LARES (LAYR-eez) Latin: The Lares were friendly mythological guardian spirits of households and fields.

LARGO (LAHR-go) Italian: Wide, broad; in music, *largo* indicates a very slow tempo

LARK English: Lark, a songbird; used predominantly for girls
Larke

LARNELL (lahr-NEL) English: Modern blend of the English names Larry and Darnell

LARRY English: Nickname for Lawrence **Famous namesakes:** Basketball player Larry Bird

LARS Scandinavian: Variation of Lawrence
Larsen, Larson, Larz

LARTIUS Latin: Lartius and his companion Herminius were legendary heroes who saved Rome.

LARUE (lah-ROO) French: Street; surname used as first name

LASALLE (lə-SAL) French: The hall; surname used as a first name

LASZLO (LAHS-lo) Hungarian: Nickname for Vladislav

LATHAM (LAY-thəm) Teutonic: Dwells by the barn

LATHAN (LAY-thən) English: A contemporary rhyming variant of Nathan

LATHROP English: From the farmstead with the barn; surname

LATIF (lah-TEEF) Arabic, Egyptian: Gentle, kind, pleasant, nice; spelling variant of Lutfi

LATIMER English: Intepreter

LATINUS Latin: King of Latium, the kingdom from which the Roman Empire gradually emerged

LAUDALINO Latin: Praise

LAUDEGRANCE Arthurian legend: The father of Guinevere

LAUGHLIN (LAHK-lin) Irish: Variation of Lachlan

LAUNDER English: From the grassy plain

LAUNFAL Arthurian legend: A knight in Arthurian legend

LAURENZ German: Laurel. Variant of Lawrence.

LAWFORD English: From the ford at the hill

LAWLER Gaelic: Soft-spoken

LAWLEY English: From the hill meadow; surname
Lawly, Lawlea, Lawleigh, Lawlie; **Diminutive forms:** *Law, Lawe*

LAWRENCE (LOR-ənts) Latin, English: Laurel. The laurel tree is symbolic of honor and victory. The name is also considered to mean *from Laurentium*, a city in ancient Italy known for its laurel trees. Saint Lawrence was a Roman deacon and martyr. See also *Laurenz, Laren*
(Latin) *Laurencho*; (English) *Loran, Lorin*; (German) *Lorenz*; (French) *Laurent*; (Italian) *Lauro, Lorenzo, Renzo*; (Gaelic) *Labhras*; (Scottish) *Labhrainn*; (Scandinavian) *Lars, Lorens*; (Swedish) *Larz*; (Danish) *Lauritz*; (Dutch) *Laurens*; (Czech) *Vavrinec*; (Polish) *Laiurenty*; (Finnish) *Lasse, Lauri*; (Hungarian) *Lenci, Lorant, Loreca, Lorenc, Lorencz*; *Laureano, Laurente, Laurian, Lawron*; **Old forms:** *Laurentius*; **Nicknames:**

Larry, Lauriano, Laurie, Lawrie, Lawson, Lorry; **Famous namesakes:** Actor Laurence Olivier, actor Laurence Fishburne, musician Lawrence Welk

LAWSON English: Laurel. Variant of Lawrence; surname meaning son of Lawrence.

LAWTON English: From the hill town or settlement, possibly the town near the lake or Lawrence's town; surname
Laughton; *Loughton*; **Nicknames:** *Law*

LAYNE English: Spelling variation of Lane

LAYTON English: From the meadow town or settlement; a surname and variant of Leighton

LAZARUS (LAZ-ər-əs) Hebrew: Help of God. In the Bible, Lazarus, Martha and Mary's brother, was brought back to life by Jesus Christ. The religious order of Saint Lazaro was established during the time of the Crusades.
(Italian) *Lazzaro*; (Spanish) *Lazaro*;
Nicknames: *Lazar*; **Famous namesakes:** Greek Lazarus the Painter

LEANDER (lee-AN-dər) Greek: Lion-man; a figure from Greek mythology and also the name of a sixth-century saint who became the bishop of Seville
(French) *Leandre*; (Spanish) *Leandro*; (Contemporary) *Leandrew*; *Liander, Liandro*; **Old forms:** *Leandros*

LEANNAN Gaelic: Lover
(Irish) *Lennon*

LEAR English: The story of King Lear existed up to four centuries before Shakespeare's play *King Lear*. Lear was a British king who reigned before the birth of Christ. Predated by references in British mythology to Lyr or Ler, Geoffrey of Monmouth recorded a story of King Lear and his daughters in his Historia Regum Britanniae of 1137.

LEARY Irish: Shepherd
Laoghaire; **Famous namesakes:** Comedian Denis Leary

LECH (LEKH) Polish: A Pole; name of the legendary founder of the Polish people.
Famous namesakes: Polish union organizer Lech Walesa

LEE English: Meadow; an adapted surname now used as a given name for boys and girls.
Lay, Leigh

LEGER (lay-GER) French: Name of a French saint and several French villages
Famous namesakes: French artist Fernand Léger

LEGOLAS (LEG-o-lahs) Literature: Character in *The Lord of the Rings* trilogy by J.R.R. Tolkien. Legolas is the son of the elf lord Thranduil and is an incredibly accurate archer. Legolas means green leaf in his language.

LEIB (LEEB) Yiddish: Lion
Leyb

LEICESTER (LES-tər) Latin: Name of the city in England founded in Roman times
Lester

LEIDOLF Norse: Wolf descendant

LEIF (LAYF) Scandinavian: Son, descendant. According to Norse legend, Viking Leif Ericson landed his longboat on North American shores some 500 years before Columbus arrived in the Caribbean.
Famous namesakes: Actor and singer Leif Garrett

LEIGH (LEE) English: Spelling variation of Lee
Lee

LEIGHTON (LAY-tən) English: From the meadow town or settlement; surname
Layton; Leyton

LEITH Celtic: Broad ridge
Leathan

LELAND (LEE-lənd) English: From the meadow land; surname
Leeland; Leighland, Leyland

LEMAN English: From the valley

LEMUEL (LEM-yoo-əl) Hebrew: Dedicated to God; an Old Testament name

LEN Native American: Flute (Hopi); (English) bold as a lion; an abbreviation of Leonard

LENNO Native American: Man

LENNON Irish: Variation of Leannan
Famous namesakes: John Lennon; **Star babies:** son of Patsy Kensit and Liam Gallagher

LENNOX Scottish, Gaelic: Surname and clan name, which was derived from the name of a district in Scotland, the Levenach. Lennox, a Scottish nobleman, appears in Shakespeare's *Macbeth*.
Lenox

LEO Latin: Lion; a popular name in ancient Rome and the name of thirteen popes. The lion is a figure in art and religious symbolism of many cultures symbolizing royalty, grandeur, and courage.

(English) *Lion*; (French) *Leon, Leonce*;
(Italian) *Leone*; (Russian) *Lev*; (Armenian)
Levon; **Nicknames:** *Levka, Lewa*; **Famous
namesakes:** Russian author Leo Tolstoy

---

*A hare, upon meeting
a lioness one day, said
reproachfully, "I have
always a great number of
children while you have only
one or two now and then."
The lioness replied, "That is
true, but my one child is a
lion."*
—An Ethiopian fable written by Lokman
(c. 1100 BC)

LEON (lay-ON) Spanish: Variation of Leo

LEONARD (LEN-ərd) German: Bold as a
lion; name of a medieval saint
(German) *Leonhard*; (Italian) *Leonardo*;
(Swedish) *Lennart*; *Leonaldo*; **Nicknames:**
Lenny, Leo; **Famous namesakes:** Composer
and conductor Leonard Bernstein, artist
Leonardo da Vinci, musician Lenny Kravitz

LEONIDAS (lee-o-NIE-dəs) Greek: Lion.
Leonidas was a Spartan king from the fifth
century BC who sacrificed his life defending
the pass of Thermopylae from the Persians;
also the name of a saint and martyr from
Alexandria
(Spanish) *Leonides*; (Russian) *Leonid, Lyonya*;
Leonide, Leontis

LEOPOLD (LEE-ə-pold) German: A bold
man, prince of the people
(Italian) *Leopoldo*; *Luitpold*; **Diminutive
forms:** *Poldi*

LERON (le-RON) Hebrew: The song is
mine; (French) the circle; derived from le
rond

LEROUX (lə-ROO) French: The red-haired
one; surname sometimes used as a first name

LEROY French: The king
(English) *Elroy*; (French) *Leroi*; *Learoyd*,
Leeroy; **Famous namesakes:** Artist Leroy
Nieman

LESLIE Scottish, Gaelic: From the gray
fortress, smaller meadow, or garden of hollies.
Leslie was derived from a Scottish place name,
became a surname, and is now used as a first
name for both sexes.
Lesley; **Famous namesakes:** Actor Leslie
Howard, actor Leslie Nielsen; **Star babies:** son
of Gene Hackman

LESTER English: Phonetic form of Leicester,
originally denoting a person who was from
that place

LEVERTON English: From the rush farm;
surname
Laefertun; *Levertun*; **Nicknames:** *Lev*

LEVI (LEE-vie) Hebrew: Joined; in the Bible,
Jacob's third son and father of the tribe of
priests
(Finnish) *Leevi*; *Levey*; **Nicknames:** *Lev*; **Star
babies:** sons of Dave Evans, Tyler England

LEVKA Russian: **Nickname** for Leo

LEWIS English: Renowned fighter; a form
of Louis
Nicknames: *Lew*; **Famous namesakes:**
Author Lewis Carroll

LI (LEE) Chinese: Strong

LIAM (LEE-am) Irish: Diminutive form of William
Famous namesakes: Irish actor Liam Neeson; **Star babies:** sons of Kevin Costner, Faye Dunaway, Calista Flockhart, Rachel Hunter and Rod Stewart

LIBBY English: My God is bountiful, God of plenty; masculine form of Elizabeth, can be used as a surname

LIBER Latin: Free

LICHAS Greek: In Greek mythology, Lichas was Heracles' servant. He brought the poisoned shirt from Deianira to Heracles, killing him.

LIDMANN Anglo-Saxon: Sailor

LIFTON English: From the hillside town

LINCOLN English: Lakeside colony. This name of an early Roman settlement in England is widely recognized in the United States as the surname of President Abraham Lincoln.
Nicknames: *Linc, Link*

LINDELL English: Lives in the linden tree dell or valley; surname
Lendall, Lendell, Lindael, Lindel; Lyndell, Lyndale; **Nicknames:** *Linn;* **Diminutive forms:** *Lin*

LINDEN English: The linden tree; this name describes a variety of popular ornamental shade trees
Lindon, Lyndon; **Nicknames:** *Lind, Lin, Lindy, Lyn;* **Diminutive forms:** *Lynd;* **Famous namesakes:** President Lyndon Baines Johnson

LINDLEY English: From the linden tree meadow; surname
Lindleigh, Lindly; Lindlea, Lindlee, Lindlie

LINDSAY (LINDZ-ee) English, Scottish: Island of linden trees
Lyndsie; Lindsey

LINFORD English: Linden tree ford

LINLEY English: From the meadow of flax; surname
Linleah, Linly; Lindlea, Lindleigh, Lindlee

LINN Anglo-Saxon: A short form of several names beginning with *Linn–*, not common as an independent name for boys

LINUS Latin: Flax. Linus is the Latin form of the Greek name Linos. In Greek legend, Linos was the son of the god Apollo and a music teacher to Heracles. Today, parents and kids will recognize Linus as the blanket-carrying Peanuts character.
Lino; **Famous namesakes:** Chemist Linus Pauling

LINWOOD English: Lives in the linden tree grove or forest; surname
Lynwood

LIONEL Latin: Young lion
(Spanish) *Leonel; Lionell, Lonell;* **Famous namesakes:** Actor Lionel Barrymore, musician Lionel Richie

LISIMBA (lee-SIM-bah) Egyptian: Lion

LIST Anglo-Saxon: Cunning

LIVINGSTON English: From Lyfing's town
Old forms: *Lyfing*

LIWANU (lee-WAH-noo) Native American: Growling bear (Miwok)

LLACHEU Arthurian legend: Name of one of King Arthur's illegitimate sons

LLEWELYN (loo-WEL-in) Welsh: Lionlike
Lewellyn, *Llewellyn*

LLOYD (LOID) Welsh: Gray
Floyd; **Famous namesakes:** Actor Lloyd
Bridges

LLYR (LEER) Welsh: God of the sea
(Irish) *Lir*

LOCKE English: Lives by tbe stronghold; a
surname referring to a lock or locksmith
Famous namesakes: John Locke

LOGAN Gaelic: From the hollow. Logan has
become a unisex name in addition to a being
a surname.
Logen, *Loghan*; **Star babies:** son of Robert
Plant

LOHENGRIN Arthurian legend: The son of
Percival. Lohengrin is also a romantic opera
by Richard Wagner.

LOIC (lo-EEK) French: Variation of Louis

LOMAN Irish: Bare

LOMBARD Latin: Long beard

LON Gaelic: Fierce; blackbird

LONATO (lo-NAH-to) Native American:
Flint

LOOTAH Native American: Red (Sioux)

LORAN (LOR-ən) English: Variation of
Lawrence

LORCAN (LOR-kan, LUR-kawn) Irish: Little
fierce one
Star babies: son of Peter O'Toole

LORENZO (lo-REN-tso, lo-REN-so) Italian:
Variation of Lawrence

LORIMAR English: Saddle maker

LORNE (LAWRN) Scottish: Variation of
Lawrence
Lauren, *Loren*, *Lorren*; **Famous namesakes:**
Canadian actor Lorne Greene, actor Loren
Dean, Saturday Night Live producer Lorne
Michaels

LORNELL Scottish: Form of Lawrence

LOT Hebrew: A covering, veil. The biblical
nephew of Abraham, Lot was miraculously
delivered from the destruction of Sodom and
Gomorrah.

LOTHAR (LO-tahr) German: Famous in
battle
(German) *Luther*; (Italian) *Geomar*, *Giomar*;
Loring, *Lothair*, *Lotharing*

LOUGHLIN (LAHK-lin) Irish: Variation of
Lachlan

LOUIS (LOO-is, loo-EE) German, French:
Famous warrior; popular French spelling of
Ludwig. See also *Ludwig*
(French) *Loic*, *Ludovic*; (Italian) *Ludovico*,
Luigi; (Spanish) *Luis*; (Irish) *Lughaidh*;
(Scottish) *Luthais*; (Swedish) *Ludvik*; (Polish)
Ludwik; *Lewis*; **Nicknames:** *Lutz*, *Lou*, *Louie*,
Louey; **Famous namesakes:** Musician Louis
Armstrong, writer and director Louis Malle;
Star babies: sons of Mel Gibson, Bill Pullman

LOUP French: Wolf; often used in combined
names like Jean-Loup
Famous namesakes: French author Paul-
Loup Sulitzer

LOWELL (LO-əl) French: Young wolf
Lovell; *Lowel*, *Lovel*; **Famous namesakes:**
Actor Lowell Sherman

LOXIAS Greek: Oracle; one of the titles of
Apollo

LOYAL French: True, faithful, unswerving

LUBOMIR (luw-BAW-meer) Polish: Loves peace

LUBOSLAW (LUW-bo-swahf) Polish: Loves glory
Ludoslaw

LUC (LOOK) French: Variation of Luke
Star babies: son of Dave Coulier and Jayne Modean

LUCAS English: Spelling variation of Luke
Lukas; **Star babies:** sons of Richard Marx, Willie Nelson, Mick Jagger

LUCKY English: Fortunate. Lucky is also used as a nickname for Lucas and its variants. **Famous namesakes:** Actor and model Lucky Vanous

LUDLOW English: Surname derived from the name of the ancient town of Ludlow, in North Wales. Llud, in Welsh, signifies whatever connects or keeps together. Llud was also a prince of the Britons.

LUDWIG (LOOT-vikh, LUD-wig) German: Famous fighter. Ludwig van Beethoven is one of the most famous composers in history. He broke the norm of composing solely for social, religious, or teaching purposes, and earned a new freedom in music composition for others.

LUFIAN Anglo-Saxon: Love

LUGHAIDH (LOO-ee) Irish: Variation of Louis

LUIGI (loo-EE-jee) Italian: Variation of Louis

LUIS (loo-EES) Spanish: Variation of Louis

LUKA (LOO-kah) Russian: Light; the Russian form of Lucas, and Luke

LUKAS German: Variation of Luke

LUKE Greek: Light giving. Luke was a first-century Christian who wrote one of the four Gospel accounts of the life of Christ and the book of Acts. He was known as the beloved physician. See also *Luka* (Anglo-Saxon) *Lucan*; (German) *Lukas*; (French) *Luc, Lucas, Lucien*; (Italian) *Lucca, Luciano, Lucio*; (Spanish) *Lucero*; (Polish) *Lucaas, Lucjusz, Lukasz*; (Hungarian) *Lukacs*; (Armenian) *Ghoukas*; *Loukas, Lucian, Lucious, Lucius, Luk, Luken, Lukyan*; **Famous namesakes:** Actor Luke Perry, actor Luke Wilson; **Star babies:** son of Rick Schroder

LUNAIRE (loo-NAYR) French: Moon-like, related to the moon

LUNDEN Anglo-Saxon: From London

LUNDY Scottish: Lundy Island sits off the Bristol Channel off the north coast of Devon in the United Kingdom, and many puffin live there.

LUTFI Arabic: Gentle, kind, pleasant, nice; can also be used as a family name
Loutfy, Loutfi, Lutfy

LUTHER German: Variation of Lothar
Famous namesakes: Civil rights activist Martin Luther King Jr., musician Luther Vandross

LUTZ (LUWTS) German: Famous fighter; a variation of Louis. A lutz is also a jump in figure skating, named after Austrian skater Alois Lutz.

LYCAON (lie-KAY-ən) Greek: A king of Arcadia

LYCOMEDES (lie-ko-MEE-deez) Greek: A king in the island of Scyros, to whose court Achilles, disguised as a maiden, was sent by his mother who was anxious to prevent her son from fighting in the Trojan War.

LYDELL English: From the open dell

LYEL Scottish: Loyal

LYFING English: Dearly loved

LYLE French: From the island
Lisle; **Famous namesakes:** Musician Lyle Lovett

LYMAN English: From the meadow

LYNN English: Waterfall or lake
Lyn

LYOVA Russian: Lion; a pet form of Lev
Lewa; **Nicknames:** *Lewa*

LYSANDER (lie-SAN-der) Greek: Liberator. Lysander is a main character in Shakespeare's *A Midsummer Night's Dream.*
(Spanish) *Lisandro*

LYTING Norse: A name from a medieval Norse saga, Lyting is the brother of Thorstein Torfi.

MABLEVI African: Do not deceive

MABON (MAB-on, MAY-bən) Welsh, Celtic: Legendary son of Modron

MACARIO (mah-KAH-ree-o) Spanish: Blessed; derived from ancient Greek and the name of several saints

MACAULEY Scottish: Righteous
Famous namesakes: Actor Macaulay Culkin

MACE English: Heavy staff; a medieval weapon used by knights in the Middle Ages
Spanish) *Macerio*

MACK Scottish: Son of; nickname often used for people with surnames like McGregor, McAllister, McAndrews, et cetera.
Mac

MACKAY Scottish: Son of fire

MACKENZIE Scottish: Child of the fair or wise one
Nicknames: *Kenzie, Mac*

MACKLIN Celtic: Son of Flann or form of Mack
Macklyn

MACNAB Gaelic, Scottish: Son of the abbot
McNab, McNabb; **Famous namesakes:** Quarterback Donovan McNabb

MACON English: To make; a variant of Mason and the name of cities in France and the state of Georgia

MACSEN (MAC-sen) Welsh: Variation of Maximilian

MADDOCK Welsh, Celtic: Beneficent
Maddoc, Maddog, Madoc, Madog; **Old forms:** *Madawc*

MADDOX English, Welsh: Son of Maddock; (Celtic) beneficent
Madox; **Star babies:** son of Angelina Jolie and Brad Pitt

MADU (MAH-doo) Egyptian: Of the people

MAGNUS (MAG-nəs) Latin: Great; the name of several kings of Norway and Sweden (Gaelic) *Maghnus, Manus*; (Finnish) *Mauno*; **Star babies:** son of Will Ferrell

MAHDI Arabic: Guided to the right path. Mahdi is the Muslim messiah, expected by some to return and restore the true religion. This is the title used for Mohammed's successor. (Persian) *Mehdi*

MAHER Arabic: Skilled, skillful *Mahir*; **Famous namesakes:** Comedian Bill Maher

MAHFOUZ (MAH-fooz) Arabic: One who is protected; the passive voice variant of Hafiz, which means custodian or guardian *Mahfooz*

MAHKAH (mah-kah) Native American: Earth (Sioux)

MAHMOUD Arabic: Praised, glorified. This variant is often used for Mohammed, the founder of the Islamic religion. *Mahmood, Mahmud*; **Famous namesakes:** Turkish sultan Mahmud Bigara

MAHPEE (mah-pee) Native American: Sky (Sioux)

MAITLAND English: From the meadow land, possibly from Matthew's land; surname

MAJID (mah-JEED) Persian: Great, superior *Majeed*

MAKAIO (mah-KAH-ee-o) Hawaiian: Variation of Matthew

MAKANI (mah-KAHN-ee) Hawaiian: Wind, breeze **Star babies:** daughter of Woody Harrelson

MAKIN Arabic: Strong, firm, solid *Makeen*

MAKSIM Russian: Variation of Maximilian **Star babies:** sons of Candace Cameron and Valeri Bure

MALACHI (MAL-ə-kie) Hebrew: Messenger of God; a minor prophet in the Old Testament and author of the biblical Book of Malachi *Malachy*

MALCOLM (MAL-kəm) Scottish, Gaelic: Servant of Saint Columba; a royal name in Scotland. A Shakespearean tragedy is based on the true story of Prince Malcolm who became king after Macbeth killed his father Duncan. **Nicknames:** *Colm*; **Famous namesakes:** British actor Malcolm McDowell, civil rights activist Malcolm X (née Little); **Star babies:** sons of Harrison Ford, Denzel Washington

MALEK (MAH-lik, mah-LEEK) Arabic: King, owner *Malik*; **Famous namesakes:** Eighth-century Arab musician Malek Ibn Abu Samah Al Tai

MALEKO (mah-LE-ko) Hawaiian: Variation of Mark

MALLOGAN English: My small cove

MALLORY (MAL-ə-ree) German: War counselor; (French) misfortunate

MALLOY Irish: Noble chief

MALONEY Irish: Serves Saint John; (Gaelic) devoted to God

MANASSEH (mə-NAS-ə) Hebrew: Forgetful. The Greek variant Manasses is a Civil War battlefield in Virginia. *Menashe*

MANFRED (MAHN-fred) German: Man of peace (English) *Manfrid*; *Manfried*; **Old forms:** *Manfrit*; **Nicknames:** *Mani, Mann*; **Famous namesakes:** German chemist Manfred Eigen, musician Manfred Mann

MANKATO (man-kay-to) Native American: Blue earth (Sioux)
Mahecate, Monecato

MANLEY English: From the man's meadow; a name with connotations of masculinity
Manly, Mannleah; Manlea, Manleigh

MANNING English: Son of a hero

MANNIS Gaelic: Great

MANO Hawaiian: Shark

MANSFIELD English: From the field by the small river; surname
Maunfeld

MANSOUR (mahn-SOOR) Arabic: Triumphant, supported by God
Mansoor, Mansur; **Famous namesakes:** Persian musician Mansour, Iranian tennis player Mansour Bahrami

MANTON Anglo-Saxon, English: From the man's (or possibly Mann's) town or settlement, from the hero's settlement; surname
Manten, Mannton; **Nicknames:** *Man*

MANU (mah-NOO) Hindi: Wise; a ruler of the earth

MANUEL (mahn-WEL) Spanish: Variation of Emmanuel
Nicknames: *Manny, Mano, Manolito, Manolo, Manuelo;* **Famous namesakes:** Shoe designer Manolo Blahnik

MANVILLE French: From the great town
Mandeville, Manneville, Manvel, Manvil

MANZO (mahn-zo) Japanese: Ten thousand-fold-strong third son

MARCEL (mar-SEL) French: Warlike, hammer; a variant of Mark

(French) *Marceau;* (Italian) *Marcello, Marcelo; Marcell, Marcellin, Marcely;* **Old forms:** *Marcellus;* **Diminutive forms:** *Marcelino;* **Famous namesakes:** French mime Marcel Marceau; **Star babies:** son of Dr. Dre

MARCUS Latin: Hammer; a popular name in Roman times, as evidenced by the names of two famous Romans: emperor and philosopher Marcus Aurelius and statesman Marcus Tullius Cicero.
Famous namesakes: Football player Marcus Allen, civil rights activist Marcus Garvey; **Star babies:** son of Michael Jordan

MARDEN English: From the valley with the pool; surname used as a given name
Mardon

MAREO (mah-ray-o) Japanese: Rare

MARINO Latin: Of the sea
Famous namesakes: Quarterback Dan Marino

MARIO (MAHR-ee-o) Latin, Italian, Spanish: A name of uncertain meaning, possibly derived from a Roman family name Marius, indicating the Roman war god Mars; derived from the Latin root *mas*, meaning *manly*; or used as a masculine variation of Mary, meaning *bitter* and most often given in honor of the Virgin Mary
(Spanish) *Mariano;* **Old forms:** *Marius;* **Famous namesakes:** Politician Mario Cuomo, racecar driver Mario Andretti, hockey player Mario Lemieux

MARK Latin: Warlike, of Mars (the god of war); The biblical Mark, sometimes called John Mark, was a missionary companion to Peter and Paul and writer of one of the four Gospel accounts of the life of Jesus; (Arthurian legend) Tristan's uncle (Latin) *Markel*; (German) *Markell, Marx*; (French) *Marc*; (Italian) *Marciano, Marcio, Marco, Marquise*; (Spanish) *Marcos*; (Irish) *Marcas*; (Welsh) *Mawrth*; (Scandinavian) *Marten*; (Dutch) *Markos, Markus*; (Czech) *Marek*; (Finnish) *Markku*; (Hungarian) *Marton*; (Hawaiian) *Maleko*; *Marq, Marque, Martel, Martell, Martyn*; **Nicknames:** *Markey, Marty*; **Famous namesakes:** Actor Mark Wahlberg, actor Mark Harmon, swimmer Mark Spitz, baseball player Mark McGwire, Roman general and statesman Mark Antony

MARLEY English: Near the meadow by the lake; surname *Marleigh, Marly; Marlea*; **Famous namesakes:** Musician Bob Marley

MARLOWE English: Marshy; from the hill by the lake **Famous namesakes:** Christopher Marlowe

MARMION (mahr-mee-ON) French: Small one; also title of popular narrative poem by Sir Walter Scott *Marmeon, Marmyon*

MARQUIS (mahr-KEE) French: A title name ranking below duke and above earl (Spanish) *Marquez*; (Portuguese) *Marques*; **Famous namesakes:** Baseball player Marquis Grissom

MARSH English: From the marsh

MARSHALL French: Horse-keeper, steward; an occupational name and a common family name in Scotland *Marshal*; **Famous namesakes:** Department store founder Marshall Field, football player Marshall Faulk, media theorist Marshall McLuhan

MARSTON English: From the town or settlement near the marsh; surname *Marsden, Marsten, Merestun*; **Star babies:** son of Hugh Hefner

MARTIN Latin: Warlike; another name originating from Mars, the Roman god of war (Italian) *Martino*; (Spanish) *Martinez*; (Gaelic) *Mairtin, Martainn*; (Polish) *Marcinek*; (Finnish) *Martti*; *Martel, Martial, Martinien, Morten*; **Old forms:** *Martinus*; **Nicknames:** *Marton*; **Famous namesakes:** Civil rights leader Martin Luther King Jr., actor Martin Short, director Martin Scorsese, theologian Martin Luther

MARVIN English: Friend of the sea *Marven, Marvyn, Marwin, Marwyn*; **Famous namesakes:** Composer Marvin Hamlisch, singer Marvin Gaye

MASAO (mah-sah-o) Japanese: Righteous

MASLIN (mahs-LEEN) French: Little Thomas *Masselin*

MASON French: Stone worker; from French word *maçon* *Macon, Masson*; **Famous namesakes:** Actor Mason Adams; **Star babies:** son of Cuba Gooding Jr., Laura San Giacomo, Josie Bissett and Rob Estes

MASOUD (mah-SOOD) Arabic: Fortunate, lucky (Egyptian) *Masud; Masud, Massoud*

MASSIMO (mah-SEE-mo) Italian: Variation of Maximilian

MATHER (MA-thər) English: Powerful army

MATIN Arabic: Strong, solid, firm, hard

MATOSKAH (mah-to-skah) Native American: White bear (Sioux)

MATT English: Nickname for Matthew
Famous namesakes: Actor Matt Damon, actor Matt LeBlanc, writer and producer Matt Groening

MATTHEW Hebrew: Gift of God. The biblical Matthew was one of Christ's apostles and author of the first gospel in the New Testament.
(Hebrew) *Machau, Matyas, Misi, Miska*; (German) *Matthias*; (French) *Mathieu, Matthieu*; (Italian) *Matteo*; (Spanish) *Matias*; (Portuguese) *Mateus*; (Welsh) *Mathias*; (Swedish) *Mats, Matteus, Mattias*; (Russian) *Matvey*; (Ukrainian) *Matviyko*; (Finnish) *Matti*; (Hawaiian) *Makaio; Mathew, Mayhew*; **Nicknames:** *Mate, Matej, Mateo, Mathe, Matro, Matt, Matusha, Matz*; **Famous namesakes:** Actors Matthew Broderick, Matthew Modine, Matthew Perry and Matthew McConaughey; **Star babies:** sons of Elvis Costello, Christopher Reeve, Rob Lowe, Connie Chung and Maury Povich, Eddie Money, Mia Farrow and André Previn

MAURICE (mo-REES, MOR-is) French: Moorish; dark-skinned
(Latin) *Mauritins*; (Greek) *Maur*; (English) *Morse*; (German) *Moritz*; (Italian) *Maurio, Maurizio*; (Spanish) *Maricio, Mauricio, Mauritio*; (Welsh) *Myrick*; (Russian) *Moriz*; (Finnish) *Mauri*; (Hungarian) *Moricz*; *Mauro, Merek, Moor, Moore, Morell*; **Old forms:** *Mauricius*; **Nicknames:** *Maury, Morie, Morrey, Morrie*; **Famous namesakes:** French actor and singer Maurice Chevalier, children's book author Maurice Sendak, musician Maurice Gibb

MAVERICK (MAV-er-ik, MAV-rik) Contemporary: Independent. When a nineteenth-century American named Maverick refused to brand his calves as other ranchers did, his name came to signify an independent man who avoids conformity. *Mavrick*

MAX Latin: Greatest; a nickname for names such as Maximilian and Maxwell, but also an independent name
Star babies: sons of Dustin Hoffman, Christina Aguilera

MAXFIELD English: From Mack or Max's field; surname
Maxfeld; **Nicknames:** *Max*; **Famous namesakes:** Painter Maxfield Parrish

MAXIMILIAN (mak-si-MIL-yən) Latin: Greatest; Maximilian I reigned as the Holy Roman Emperor from 1493 to 1519, while the Vienna-born Ferdinand Maximilian Joseph ruled as emperor of Mexico from 1864 to 1867.
(English) *Maxton*; (German) *Maximillian*; (French) *Maxence, Maxime*; (Italian) *Massimo, Maximiliano, Maximino, Maximo*; (Welsh) *Macsen*; (Russian) *Maksim, Maxim*; (Polish) *Maksym, Maksymilian*; (Hungarian) *Miksa; Maximos*; **Old forms:** *Maximus*; **Nicknames:** *Mac, Mack, Max*; **Famous namesakes:** Austrian actor Maximilian Schell; **Star babies:** son of Jeremy Irons

MAXWELL Anglo-Saxon, Scottish: From Marcus' pool or well; a surname
Nicknames: *Max*; **Star babies:** son of Andrew Dice Clay

MAYER (MIE-er) Latin, German: Great or mayor
Mayor; **Famous namesakes:** Businessman Oscar Mayer

MAYFIELD English: From the strong man's field; surname
Mayfeld

MAYNARD (MAY-nərd) Anglo-Saxon: Powerful, brave
Mayne, Maynor; **Famous namesakes:** Jazz musician Maynard Ferguson, economist John Maynard Keynes

MAYO Gaelic: Lives near the yew trees. This name of a county in Ireland is likely more recognized in the United States as that of the Mayo Clinic, one of the world's largest medical centers.

MEAD (MEED) English: From the meadow; a surname possibly related to the rich honey wine
(Irish) *Meade*; *Maed*

MECCUS Anglo-Saxon: Son of Gus

MEDUS Greek: Son of Medea by Aegeus. Medus conquered barbarians after having come to Colchis with his mother, and called his kingdom Media after himself.

MEDWIN Teutonic: Powerful friend
Medwine, Medwyn

MEHRDAD Persian: Gift from the sun

MEINHARD (MIEN-hahrd) German: Firm; See also *Maynard*
Meinke, Meinrad, Meinyard; **Nicknames:** *Meino*

MEIR Hebrew: Enlightens
Meyer

MEL English: A nickname for Melvin and other names beginning with Mel-.
Famous namesakes: Actor and director Mel Gibson, actor and filmmaker Mel Brooks, voice specialist Mel Blanc

MELBOURNE English: From the mill stream
Melborn, Melburn, Melbyrne; **Nicknames:** *Mel*

MELCHIOR Persian: King; According to tradition, Melchior was one of the three wise men who traveled a long distance to see the baby Jesus.
Melchoir, Melker

MELDON (MEL-dən) English: From the hillside mill

MELDRICK English: From the powerful mill
Meldrik

MELICERTES Greek: In Greek legend, the son of the Boeotian prince Athamas

MELRONE Irish: Servant of Saint Ruadhan

MELVILLE French, Anglo-Saxon: Busy, industrious town; surname used as first name
Mellville; **Nicknames:** *Mel*; **Famous namesakes:** Author Herman Melville

MELVIN English: Mill friend; (Celtic) leader or chief
Malvin, Malvyn, Melvon, Melvyn; **Nicknames:** *Mel*

MEMPHIS (MEM-fis) Contemporary: A city in Tennessee. Memphis was also the first capital of ancient Egypt.

MENACHEM (men-AH-kem) Hebrew: Comfort

MENDEL (MEHN-dəl) Hebrew: One who repairs

MENELAUS (me-nə-LAY-əs) Greek: In Greek legend, Menelaus was the son of Atreus and the brother of Agamemnon. He was married to Helen, and became the ruler of Helen's homeland, Lacedaemon.

MERCER English: Merchant
Mercher; **Nicknames:** *Merce*; **Famous namesakes:** Jazz musician Mercer Ellington

(son of Duke Ellington), choreographer Merce Cunningham

MEREDITH Welsh: Magnificient chief or protector
Meridith

MERLE (MURL) French: Blackbird
Merla; **Famous namesakes:** Singer Merle Haggard

MERLIN (MUR-lin) Anglo-Saxon, French: Falcon. In Arthurian legend, the wizard Merlin was King Arthur's mentor.
Marlan, Marlin, Marlon, Merlion, Merlyn; **Famous namesakes:** Football player Merlin Olsen

MERLOW English: From the hill by the lake
Merlo, Merloe

MERRICK Welsh: Dark-skinned, a Moor; variant of Maurice
Merrik

MERRILL (MER-əl) English: Shining sea; (Teutonic) famous
Merril

MERRITT English: Little famous one

MERTON (MUR-tən) English, Anglo-Saxon: From the estate by the lake

MERVIN English: Hill by the sea or a famous friend; sometimes used as a form of Merlin
Merwin, Merwyn; **Old forms:** *Mervyn*

MEYER Hebrew: Spelling variation of Meir

MICAH (MIE-kə) Hebrew: Who is like the Lord; a variant of Michael. Micah was a prophet and writer of the biblical book that bears his name.
Mycah; **Star babies:** son of Neil Diamond

MICHAEL Hebrew: Who is like the Lord. An archangel of Jewish and Christian scripture, Michael is portrayed as a warrior and leader of heaven's armies who defeats and casts out the dragon in the Book of Revelation. Michael has been such a popular name throughout history that a list of famous Michaels would contain hundreds of individuals, including emperors, politicians, writers, poets, actors, sports heroes, and more. See also *Miguel, Misha*
(Hebrew) *Mika, Mikel*; (Latin) *Mikelle*; (Greek) *Mikhalis, Mikhos*; (French) *Michel*; (Italian) *Michele*; (Spanish) *Migel, Migueo*; (Gaelic) *Micheil*; (Irish) *Mícheál*; (Welsh) *Mihangel*; (Scandinavian) *Mikael, Mikell, Mikkel*; (Basque) *Miquel*; (Slavic) *Miko*; (Russian) *Mikhail, Mischa*; (Polish) *Michal*; (Ukrainian) *Mychajlo*; (Finnish) *Mikko*; (Hungarian) *Mihaly*; *Maichail, Micah, Michail; Micael, Mical, Michiel, Mihail, Mikol, Mycah, Mychal, Mykal, Mykell*; **Nicknames:** *Mick, Mickey, Miikka, Mike, Micky, Mikey, Miky*; **Diminutive forms:** *Mishenka*; **Famous namesakes:** Singer Michael Jackson, actor Michael Douglas, basketball player Michael Jordan, actor Michael Caine, actor Michael J. Fox, swimmer Michael Phelps; **Star babies:** sons of Julio Iglesias, Kelly Ripa, Natasha Richardson and Liam Neeson

> *"Love one another and you will be happy. It's as simple and difficult as that."*
> —Michael Leunig

MICHELANGELO Italian: A blend of Michael and Angelo. Italian artist Michelangelo Buonarroti is one of history's greatest painters and sculptors. His works are famous throughout the world, including *David, Pietà,* and the Sistine Chapel.

MICHIO (mee-chee-o) Japanese: Road, husband

MIDAS (MIE-dəs) Greek: In Greek mythology, everything King Midas touched turned to gold.

MIGUEL (mee-GEL) Spanish: Who is like the Lord; a variant of Michael
Migel, Migueo; **Nicknames:** *Mico*

MIKHAIL (mee-khah-EEL) Russian: Variation of Michael
Famous namesakes: Soviet leader Mikhail Gorbachev, Russian-American dancer Mikhail Baryshnikov

MIKI (mee-kee) Japanese: Trunk of tree

MIKLOS Czech: Variation of Nicholas

MILAD Persian: Birth

MILAN Czech: The favored one or beloved one; also the name of Italy's second largest city
Famous namesakes: Czech author Milan Kundera

> "We don't know when our name came into being or how some distant ancestor acquired it . . . , [yet] we are ridiculously proud of it as if we had thought it up ourselves in a moment of brilliant inspiration."
> —Milan Kundera, *Immortality*

MILAP Native American: Charitable

MILBURN (MIL-bərn) English: From the mill stream

MILES Latin, Greek, English: Soldier; sometimes used as a variant of Michael
Myles; **Famous namesakes:** Jazz musician Miles Davis; **Star babies:** sons of Lionel Richie, Susan Sarandon and Tim Robbins, Elisabeth Shue

MILFORD (MIL-fərd) English: From the mill's ford

MILLARD (MIL-ərd) English: Miller, one who grinds grain; occupational surname used as first name
Famous namesakes: President Millard Fillmore

MILLER English: One who grinds grain; an occupational name
Millen; **Famous namesakes:** Playwright Arthur Miller, band leader and musician Glenn Miller

MILO (MIE-lo) English, Greek: Soldier; form of Miles
Mylo; **Star babies:** sons of Mel Gibson, Camryn Manheim, Ricki Lake

MILOS (MEE-los) Slavic, Czech: Pleasant

MILOSLAV (MEE-lah-slahv) Slavic: Lover of glory

MILTON English: From the mill town or settlement, possibly from the middle town or settlement; surname
Millton, Milten, Miltin, Miltun, Mylton; **Nicknames:** *Milt, Milty*; **Famous namesakes:** Comedian Milton Berle

MIN Egyptian: The primeval god of Coptos, who was later revered as a god of fertility. Closely associated with Amun, this god is represented as an ithyphallic human statue holding a flagellum.

MINH (MIN) Vietnamese: Bright, smart

MINORU (mee-no-roo) Japanese: Bear fruit, ripen

MINOS (MIE-nəs) Greek, Latin: In Greek mythology, Minos is the son of Zeus and the King of Crete.

MIRO (MEE-ro) Finnish: Variation of Miroslav

MIRON (MEE-rawn) Polish: Peace

MIROSLAV (mee-rah-SLAHF) Russian: Peaceful
(Finnish) *Miro*; *Miroslaw*

MISHA (MEE-shah) Russian: Who is like the Lord; a familiar form of Michael, also meaning bear cub in Russian
Nicknames: *Mishka*; **Diminutive forms:** *Mishenka*

MISHAN (mee-shahn) Hebrew: Support

MISU (MEE-soo) Native American: Rippling brook (Miwok)

MITCHELL Hebrew: Who is like the Lord; a variant of Michael
Mitchel; **Nicknames:** *Mitch*

MOCHNI Native American: Talking bird (Hopi)

MODESTUS (mo-DE-stəs) Latin: Modest
Modeste, *Modesto*

MOGENS (MONS) Danish: Powerful

MOHAMMAD Arabic: Praiseworthy, glorified. Mohammad was the founder of the Islamic religion; derived from *hamd*, meaning *giving thanks* (usually to God).
(Persian) *Hamed*; *Hamden, Hamdun, Hamid, Hammad, Humayd, Mahmoud, Muhammad*;
Nicknames: *Hamada, Hammouda*

MOHAN (mo-HAHN) Hindi: The deluder

MOHSEN (mo-SEN) Persian: One who does good

MOKETAVATO Native American: Black kettle (Cheyenne)

MOLIMO Native American: Bear walking into shade (Miwok)

MONGWAU Native American: Owl (Hopi)

MONROE Gaelic, Scottish: From the mount on the river Row
Munro, Munroe; **Famous namesakes:** President James Monroe

MONTAGUE (MAHN-tə-gyoo) French: Pointed mountain; Romeo's surname in Shakespeare's *Romeo and Juliet*
(Italian) *Montae*; *Montagew, Montaigu*

MONTANA Latin: Mountain; a northwestern U.S. state
(French) *Montagne*; **Famous namesakes:** Quarterback Joe Montana; **Star babies:** sons of Laurence Fishburne, Richard Thomas

MONTGOMERY English: From the wealthy man's mountain. Montgomery is also the state capital of Alabama.
(Italian) *Montay, Montes, Montez*;
Nicknames: *Monte, Montie, Monty*; **Famous namesakes:** Actor Montgomery Clift

MONTREAL French: Royal mountain; a city in Quebec
Montrell, Montrelle

MONTY English: Nickname for Montgomery
Famous namesakes: Game show host Monty Hall

MOORE Irish: Marshland; a moor

MORAD Persian: Desire, wish

MORDECAI (mor-də-KIE) Hebrew: Servant of Marduk. In the Old Testament, Mordecai was the cousin and caretaker of Esther.

MORELEY English: From the meadow on the moor; surname *Morlee, Morly; Moorley, Moorly, Morleigh, Morrley;* **Famous namesakes:** Newsman Morley Safer

MOREN Welsh: Legendary son of Iaen

MORGAN Welsh: Circling sea. Originally a surname and given name for boys, Morgan has become frequently used for girls also. **Famous namesakes:** Actor Morgan Freeman

MORIO (mo-ree-o) Japanese: Actively vigorous, defender

MORITZ (MO-rits) German: Variation of Maurice

MORRELL Latin: Swarthy

MORRIS Latin: Dark-skinned, a Moor; an English form of Maurice

MORTEZA Persian: Chosen

MORTIMER Latin: Dwells by the still water *Mortemer;* **Nicknames:** *Mort;* **Famous namesakes:** Author Mortimer J. Adler

MORTON English: From the town or settlement near the moors; surname *Morten, Mortin, Mortun*

MORVEN (MOR-vən, MWAWR-ven) Welsh: Lives by the sea; a district in North Argyll Scotland *Morvin, Morvyn, Moryn*

MOSES Hebrew: Saved from the water. Moses was the biblical prophet who received the Ten Commandments, led the oppressed Jewish people out of Egypt, and founded Israel. He was born in ancient Egypt in the town of Goshen. Just before his birth, Pharaoh had ordered that all male Hebrew infants be put to death. Moses' mother placed him in a basket made of papyrus and set it floating on the Nile, where it was found by Pharaoh's daughter, who raised Moses as her own child. (Arabic) *Musa;* (Spanish) *Moises; Mozes;* **Old forms:** *Mosheh;* **Nicknames:** *Moshe, Moss;* **Famous namesakes:** Basketball player Moses Malone, baseball player Moises Alou; **Star babies:** son of Gwyneth Paltrow and Chris Martin

The story of Moses was portrayed in Disney's movie, *The Prince of Egypt.*

MOSI (MO-see) African: Born first

MOSWEN (MOHS-wen) African: Light-colored skin

MOTEGA (mo-TE-gah) Native American: New arrow

MOUKIB Arabic: Last of the prophets

MUATA Native American: Yellow jackets inside a nest (Miwok)

MUDAWAR Arabic: Round

MUHUNNAD Arabic: Sword

MUIR Scottish: From the moor

MUKHTAR Arabic: Chosen

MUKKI Native American: Child (Algonquin)

MUNA Arabic: Desire, aspiration
Omneya

MUNDY Irish: From Reamonn

MUNI (MOO-nee) Hindi: One who teaches the truth

MURDOCK Scottish: Protector of the sea
Murdoc, Murdoch; **Famous namesakes:** Media magnate Rupert Murdoch

MURPHY Irish: Sea warrior
Murphey; *Murfee*; **Nicknames:** *Murph*

MURRAY Celtic: Protects the sea. Children may recognize this name as belonging to Murray, the red-shirted musician of The Wiggles; (Scottish) ancient Scottish clan surname and a place name now called Moray *Murry*; **Old forms:** *Murtagh*; **Famous namesakes:** Actor Bill Murray, actor F. Murray Abraham

MWAI (MWAH-ee) African: Prosperity

MYLES Latin: Spelling variation of Miles
Star babies: sons of Sherilyn Fenn and Toulouse Hardy, Eddie Murphy

MYRON Greek: Derived from myrrh. Myrrh, an aromatic gum resin obtained from several Asian or African trees and shrubs, is used in making perfume and incense; (Arabic) the name Myron (accent on the second syllable) is the Arabic name of the Confirmation Sacrament in Christianity.

NAAMAN (nah-ah-MAHN) Hebrew: Pleasant, sweet, beautiful. In the Bible, Naaman was the general of the army of Aram.

NAASIR (NAH-sir) African: Defender

NAB Scottish: Abbot

NABIL (nah-BEEL) Arabic: Noble
Nabeel

NACHMAN Hebrew: Compassionate

NADAV (nah-DAHV) Hebrew: Noble, generous. The biblical Nadav was the oldest son of Aaron, the high priest.
Nadiv

NADIM Arabic: Friend, companion, someone to confide in
Nadeem

NADIR Arabic: Rare, precious
Nader; **Famous namesakes:** Persian King Nadir Shah

NAFTALI (NAF-tə-lie) Hebrew: To wrestle or be crafty or a comparison; in the Bible, the sixth son of Jacob
Naftalie; **Nicknames:** *Naf*

NAHUM (NAY-əm) Hebrew: Compassionate; a biblical tribesman of Judah

NAISER African: Founder of clans

NAJIB Arabic: Generous, noble-born, excellent. Egyptian Naguib Mohammad was one of the Free Officers who planned and executed the overthrow of the British occupation of Egypt.
(Egyptian) *Naguib*; *Nagib, Nageeb, Najeeb*;
Famous namesakes: Egyptian novelist Naguib Mahfouz

NAJJAR Arabic: Carpenter
(Egyptian) *Naggar*

NAMIR (nah-MEER) Hebrew: Leopard

NANDA (NAHN-dah) Sanskrit: Joy

NANSEN (NAHN-sən) Scandinavian:
Nancy's son

NAOIS (NEE-sha) Celtic: Mythical warrior

NAPOLEON Italian: Man from Naples.
Napoleon will likely always be linked with
French emperor Napoleon Bonaparte, a
great military genius who created an
enormous empire.

NARAYAN (nah-rah-yan) Hindi: The house
of beings

NARCISSUS (nar-SIS-əs) Greek: Daffodil.
In Greek mythology, Narcissus fell in love
with his own reflection—giving us the term
narcissism.
Narcisse; **Nicknames:** *Narkis*

NARDO German: Nickname for Bernard

NARIUS Latin: Cheerful
(Italian) *Nario*; **Nicknames:** *Nari*

NARMER (NAHR-mahr) Egyptian: Name
of a king

NASH English: Cliff

NASIM Arabic, Persian: Breeze, fresh air.
Sham el Nasim, or Smell the Breeze, is an
Egyptian spring festival that takes place
the day after Easter in commemoration
of Pharaonic spring and Nile festivals,
and is celebrated by Muslims and
Christians alike.
Nassim, Naseem

NASSER (NAHS-ser) Arabic: Victorious,
supporting, protector. Gamal Abdel Nasser
was the first president of Egypt.

NASSOR (NAH-sor) Egyptian: Victor

NASTAS Native American: Curve like foxtail
grass (Navajo)

NAT Hebrew: Gift from God; a short form of
Nathan and Nathaniel
Famous namesakes: Singer Nat King Cole

NATAL (nah-TAHL) Spanish: Born at
Christmas

NATHAN Hebrew: Gift from God. The
biblical Nathan was a prophet during the
reigns of David and Solomon. Nathan Hale
was a courageous American patriot and
spy of the Revolutionary War, and one of
America's earliest heroes.
Nicknames: *Nate*; **Famous namesakes:** Actor
Nathan Lane; **Star babies:** sons of Mark
Hamill, Leeza Gibbons

NATHANIEL Hebrew: Gift from God or
born on Christmas; one of Christ's twelve
disciples
(French) *Nathanael*; *Natanael, Nataniel,
Nathanial, Nethanel*; **Nicknames:** *Nat,
Nate, Nathan*; **Star babies:** son of Jonathan
Davis

NAVEEN (nə-VEEN) Sanskrit: New
Navin; **Famous namesakes:** British actor
Naveen Andrews

NAVID Persian: Good news
Naveed

NAZAIRE French: Blessed; based on Hebrew
name

NEALON Celtic: Spelling variation of Neil

NEB Welsh: Legendary son of Caw

NECHEMYA (NEK-eh-MIE-ə) Hebrew: Comforted by the Lord
Nechemia, Nechemiah

NED English: Diminutive form of Edward
Star babies: son of Dave Foley and Tabitha Southley

NEEVE (NEEV) Gaelic: Diminutive form of Nevin

NEFEN German: Nephew
Nefin; **Nicknames:** *Nef, Neff*

NEHEMIAH (nee-hə-MIE-ə) Hebrew: Comforted by God; an Old Testament leader of the Jews responsible for numerous political and religious reforms
Nicknames: *Nemo, Nemos*

NEIL (NEEL) Gaelic: Champion. A dynasty of Irish kings was founded by Niall of the Nine Hostages.
(English) *Neal, Niles*; (Spanish) *Niguel*; (Scandinavian) *Nils*; *Neale, Neall, Nealon, Neill, Nigel*; **Famous namesakes:** Astronaut Neil Armstrong, singer Neil Diamond, singer Neil Young

NELEUS (NEE-loos) Greek: Mythic son of Poseidon and Tyro, twin brother of Pelias, and father of Nestor, Neleus became king of Pylos but angered Heracles, who killed him.

NELS Celtic: Nickname for Nelson

NELSON English: Son of Neil
Nellson; **Nicknames:** *Nels*; **Famous namesakes:** Political leader Nelson Mandela

NEMESIO (nay-MAY-see-o) Spanish: Justice

NEPTUNE (NEP-toon) Latin: The mythological god of water; Neptune is also is one of the two planets in our solar system that cannot be seen from Earth with the naked eye.

NEREUS (NEER-oos) Greek: A mythological name of uncertain meaning; god of the sea and the nereids

NESTOR (NES-tor) Greek: Traveler. Ruler of Pylos and a great warrior of Greek mythology, Nestor was known for his wisdom and longevity.
(Spanish) *Nestorio*

NEVILLE French, English: From the new town
Old forms: *Neuveville*; **Famous namesakes:** British Prime Minister Neville Chamberlain

NEVIN Gaelic: Holy man; worships the saints; (Teutonic) nephew
Nevan, Nevins, Nevyn; **Diminutive forms:** *Neeve*

NEWTON Anglo-Saxon, English: From the new town or settlement; surname; evocative of scientist Sir Isaac Newton
Newtun; **Nicknames:** *Newt*

NIALL (NEE-al, NIE-al) Irish: Champion or passionate; variant of Neil
(Scandinavian) *Nijel*; *Nigel*

NIAZ (nee-az) Hindi: Offering or gift

NICHOLAS Greek: Victorious. This New Testament name grew in popularity through Saint Nicholas, a fourth-century bishop known as the patron saint of sailors, travelers, bakers, merchants, and especially children. Saint Nicholas is now best known in the United States as Santa Claus, a name that comes from Sinterklaas, which is Dutch for Saint Nicholas.
(Greek) *Nicolaus, Niklaus, Nikolos*; (English) *Colson, Nickson*; (German) *Nickolaus, Nikolaus*; (French) *Nicolas*; (Italian) *Niccolo, Nicola*; (Spanish) *Nicanor*; (Gaelic) *Neacal, Niocol*; (Scottish) *Neakail*; (Scandinavian) *Neilson, Nielsson, Nilsen*; (Swedish) *Niklas, Nils*; (Danish) *Niels*; (Dutch) *Nicolaas*; (Slavic) *Miklas, Mikolas, Nicholai*; (Russian) *Nicolai, Nikolai*; (Czech) *Miklos*; (Polish) *Mikolaj*; (Finnish) *Niilo, Teemu*; *Nicholaus, Nickolas, Nikolajis, Nikolas*; **Nicknames:** *Cole, Coley, Colin, Klas, Klaus, Kolya, Nick, Nicky, Nico, Nicol, Nicoli, Nicolo, Nik, Nikki, Nikko, Niklos, Niko, Nikos, Nilo, Nilos*; **Famous namesakes:** Actor Nicholas Brendon, actor Nicolas Cage; **Star babies:** sons of Vanna White, Gene Simmons, Phil Collins, Marilu Henner

NICK English: Nickname for Nicholas
Famous namesakes: Actor Nick Nolte

NICODEMUS (nik-ə-DEE-məs) Greek: Victory of the people. In the Bible, Nicodemus was a Pharisee and a member of the Jewish court in Jerusalem. He later helped entomb Christ's body.
(Polish) *Nikodem*

NIGAN (NEE-gahn) Native American: Ahead

NIGEL (NIE-jəl) Gaelic: Champion; from the Irish Gaelic name Niall
Nijel; **Famous namesakes:** Actor Nigel Hawthorne

NIK Persian: Good

NIKHIL (ni-KEEL) Hindi: Whole, all

NIKITA Russian: Unconquered
Old forms: *Aniketos*; **Famous namesakes:** Soviet premier Nikita Kruschev

NIKITI Native American: Round or smooth

NILES Scandinavian: Son of Neil

NILS (NEELS) Scandinavian: Variation of Neil

NISHAN (NUWSH-an) Armenian: Sign

NISSIM (NISS-im) Hebrew: Miracle

NITIS (NEE-tes) Native American: Friend (Delaware)

NIXON English: Abbreviation of Nicholas, possibly meaning Nick's son. The mythological Nike was the Greek goddess of victory and root origin of Nicholas.
Nixen; **Famous namesakes:** President Richard Nixon

NIYOL Native American: Wind (Navajo)

NOAH Hebrew: To comfort. In the Old Testament, God chose Noah to build a great ark that kept him, his family, and enough animals to repopulate the earth alive during the Great Flood which lasted forty days and forty nights.
(Spanish) *Noe*; (Dutch) *Noach*; **Famous namesakes:** Actor Noah Wyle; **Star babies:** sons of Jason Alexander, Thom Yorke, Kim Alexis

NODIN (NO-din) Native American: Wind

NOEL (no-EL, NOL) French: Born on Christmas or Christ's birth
Natalio, Noell, Nohle; **Famous namesakes:** Singer Noel Gallagher

NOLAN Irish: Noble and renowned
Noland, Nolen, Nolyn; **Famous namesakes:**
Baseball player Nolan Ryan

NORBELL Scottish: Noble; surname

NORBERT German, English: Shining one
from the north; (Norse) hero
(Spanish) *Norberto*

NORCROSS English: From the northern
crossroads; surname
Northcross; **Nicknames:** *North*

NORMAN English, German, French: From
the north, northerner. The name Norman
appeared before the French Norman
Conquest, and therefore while both names
may come from the same root, they are not as
directly linked as may first appear.
(German) *Normand*; (Spanish) *Normando*;
(Teutonic) *Tormod*; **Nicknames:** *Norm*;
Famous namesakes: Artist Norman
Rockwell, author Norman Mailer

NORRIS French, English: From the north,
northerner; based on Old French surname
Famous namesakes: Author Frank Norris

NORTHCLIFF English: From the northern
cliff; surname
Northclif, Northcliffe, Northclyf

NORTHROP English: From the northern
farm; surname
Northrup

NORTON Anglo-Saxon, English: From the
northern town or settlement; surname
Northtun, Nortin; **Famous namesakes:** Actor
Edward Norton

NORVILLE Anglo-Saxon: From the north
village or estate; surname
(Scottish) *Norval*; *Norvel*

NORVIN English: Friend from the north;
surname
Norwin, Norwyn

NORWARD English: Northern guardian;
surname; (Teutonic) guardian of the north
road
Northward

NORWELL English: From the northern well
or spring; surname
Norwel; Northwell

NORWOOD English: From the northern
woods; surname
Northwode; Northwood; **Nicknames:** *North*

NOSHI Native American: Father
(Algonquin)

NOUR (NOOR) Egyptian: Light, luminous
Nur; **Famous namesakes:** Egyptian actor
Nour el Sherif

NUDAR Arabic: Pure gold or silver

NUNCIO (NOON-see-o) Latin: Messenger
Nunzio

NURI (NOOR-ee) Hebrew: My fire

NYLE English: Island; (Celtic) champion;
(Anglo-Saxon) desire

OAKDEN English: From the oak tree valley

OAKES English: Near the oaks
Okes

OAKLEY English: From the oak tree
meadow; a surname and variant of Ackerley
Oaklea, Oaklee, Oakleigh, Oaklie, Oakly

OBADIAH (o-bə-DIE-ə) Hebrew: Servant of God; a minor Old Testament prophet
Obediah, Ovadiah, Oved

OBERON (O-bər-ahn) German, French: Highborn and bear-like. The most famous Oberon is Shakespeare's king of the fairies in *A Midsummer's Night Dream*.
Auberon; Oberron, Oeberon

OBI (O-bee) African: Heart (Nigeria)

OCEANUS (o-SEE-ə-nəs) Greek: Father of the Oceanids. In Greek mythology, Oceanus was a Titan father of rivers and water nymphs.

OCHEN African: Twin

OCTAVIUS (ahk-TAYV-ee-əs) Latin: Eighth (French) *Octave*; (Spanish) *Octavio, Tavio*; *Octavian*; **Nicknames:** *Tavey*; **Famous namesakes:** Mexican poet Octavio Paz

ODAKOTA (o-dah-ko-tah) Native American: A friend (Sioux); variant of Dakota

ODDVAR Norse: The spear's point

ODED (O-bed) Hebrew: To restore

ODELL (o-DEL) English: Of the valley, or an old English place name and surname meaning woad hill. Woad is an Old World plant formerly grown for its leaves that yield a blue dye.
Odale, Odayle, Odel

ODILO Teutonic: Rich in battle

ODIN (OH-din) Norse: A chief deity of Norse mythology, Odin is the god of war and death, poetry, and culture.

ODION (o-dee-ON) African: First child of the twins

ODON (O-don) Anglo-Saxon: Wealthy defender; variant of Edmund
Odin; **Nicknames:** *Odi, Ody*

ODRAN Irish, Gaelic: Little pale green one
Odhran, Oran

ODYSSEUS (o-DIS-ee-əs) Greek: Wrathful; the clever and resourceful mythological hero of Homer's epic *The Odyssey*.
Ulysses

OEDIPUS (ED-i-pəs) Greek: Swollen foot. Oedipus was the king of Thebes in Greek mythology who unknowingly killed his father and married his mother. The story led to the term *Oedipus complex*, first used by Sigmund Freud.

OENEUS (EE-nee-əs, EEN-yoos) Greek: Mythological king of Calydon

OFER (O-fer) Hebrew: Fawn
Ofar

OGALEESHA (o-gal-ee-sha) Native American: Red shirt wearer (Sioux)

OGDEN (AWG-dən) English: From the oak tree valley; surname
Ogdon; Ogdan; **Famous namesakes:** Poet Ogden Nash

OHANZEE (O-han-zee) Native American: Shadow (Sioux)

OHIN (o-HEEN) African: Chief

OKAL African: To cross

OLAF (O-lahf, O-ləf) Scandinavian: Ancestral heritage. In use since the Viking age, this name was borne by several Norwegian kings, including Saint Olaf, the patron saint of Norway. See also *Olen* (Irish) *Auley, Auliffe*; (Finnish) *Olavi, Olli; Ola, Olav, Olave, Olin, Olof*; **Nicknames:** *Ole*

OLDRICH Czech: Variation of Alaric

OLEG (ah-LYEG) Russian: Variation of Helge *Olezka*; **Famous namesakes:** Russian fashion designer Oleg Cassini

OLEN Russian: Deer
Olian, Oliene, Olyan

OLIVER Latin: Peaceful or the olive tree, which symbolizes fruitfulness, beauty, and dignity; Extending an olive branch signifies an offer of peace; (Norse) affectionate (French) *Olivier*; (Spanish) *Oliverio*; (Portuguese) *Oliverios*; (Irish) *Oilibhear, Olliver*; **Nicknames:** *Ollie, Ol, Ollie, Olly*; **Star babies:** sons of Goldie Hawn and Bill Hudsen, Amanda Pays and Corbin Bernsen, Martin Short

"*I find the great thing in this world is not so much where we stand, as in what direction we are moving— we must sail sometimes against it—but we must sail, and not drift, nor lie at anchor.*"
—Oliver Wendell Holmes

OMAR Arabic: Life or thriving, long-living (African) *Omarr*; *Ommar*; *Omer*; **Famous namesakes:** Arab poet Omar Abi Rabeiah, actor Omar Sharif, actor Omar Epps, actor Omar Gooding

OMER Hebrew: Sheaf

OMID Persian: Hope

OMRI (OM-rie) Hebrew: Sheaves of grain

ONNI (O-nee) Finnish: Happiness

ONSLOW English: From the zealous one's hill
Onslowe

ONURIS (o-NOO-ris) Egyptian: God of This in Upper Egypt. The divine huntsman is represented as a man.

ORANG Persian: Wisdom
Aurang

OREL Russian: Eagle
Oral, Orrel

OREN (OR-en) Hebrew: Pine tree; (Gaelic) pale-skinned
Orin, Orren, Orrin; **Famous namesakes:** Senator Orrin Hatch

ORESTES (ə-RES-teez) Greek: From the mountain; the son of Agamemnon and Clytemnestra
Oreste

ORETA Greek: Virtue, the Greek concept of striving for excellence in all aspects of one's life; variant of Arete
Oretha, Oretta, Orette

ORFORD English: From the cattle ford

ORI Hebrew: My light

ORINGO African: He who likes to hunt

ORION (o-RIE-ən) Greek: Son of fire, dawning. The mythological Orion was a mighty hunter and son of Poseidon. The constellation Orion contains three conspicuous stars.
(Basque) *Zorian, Zorion*

ORLANDO Spanish, Italian: Renowned in the land; variant of Roland
Orlan, Orland, Orlondo; **Nicknames:** *Lando, Olo*; **Famous namesakes:** Actor Orlando Bloom

ORMAN English: Spearman

ORPHEUS (OR-fee-əs) Greek: A great musician and poet of Greek myth, Orpheus was greatly in love with his wife Eurydice, whom he lost twice to death.

ORRICK English: From the ancient oak tree
Orik

ORSON (OR-sən) Latin, English: Little bear, like a bear
(Italian) *Orsino; Ourson*; **Famous namesakes:** Actor and director Orson Welles

ORTON English: From the shore settlement or town; a surname
Oratun, Ortun; **Famous namesakes:** Playwright Joe Orton

ORVILLE French: Gold town
Orvelle, Orvil; **Famous namesakes:** Aviation pioneer Orville Wright, popcorn icon Orville Redenbacher

ORVIN English: Spear friend
Orvyn

OSBERT English: Divinely brilliant

OSBORN English: Divine bear
Osbourne, Osburn, Usbeorn; **Nicknames:** *Oz, Ozzie, Ozzy*; **Famous namesakes:** Singer Ozzy Osbourne

OSCAR English: God's spear; (Irish) deer friend
(Finnish) *Oskari*; (Hungarian) *Oszkar; Osckar, Oskar, Osker*; **Famous namesakes:** Writer Oscar Wilde

> *"When I like people immensely, I never tell their names to anyone. It is like surrendering a part of them."*
> —Oscar Wilde

OSIRIS (o-SIE-ris) Egyptian: God of the dead and the underworld. Osiris is regarded as the king who watches over the nether world and is rejuvenated in his son, Horus. As the symbol of eternal life he was worshipped at Abydos and Philae. As a god of inundation and vegetation, he is also represented as a mummified king.

OSMAN Arabic: Young of bustard, young of snake, Abu (father of) Osman means serpent. Othmani refers to someone of Ottoman descent. This name can be used as a first or last name.
Othman; **Famous namesakes:** Turkish Prince Osman the First was responsible for establishing the Ottoman Empire.

OSMAR English: Divinely glorious

OSMOND English: Divine protector
Osman, Osmont, Osmund; **Famous namesakes:** Singer Donny Osmond

OSRED English: Divine counselor

OSRIC English: Divine ruler
Osrick

OSWALD English: Divine power (Spanish) *Osvaldo*; (Scandinavian) *Osvald*; *Oswell*; **Nicknames:** *Waldo*, *Ossie*; **Famous namesakes:** British author Oswald Chambers

OSWIN English: God's friend

OTHMAN German: Wealthy

OTIENO (o-tee-E-no) African: Born at night

OTIS German: Wealthy; derivation of Otto **Famous namesakes:** Singer Otis Redding

OTTO German: Wealthy; a modern form of Odo used in numerous countries (Czech) *Ota*, *Otik*; *Odo*, *Otho*, *Oto*

OURAY (o-RAY) Native American: Arrow (Ute); renowned leader of the Uncomaghre Ute

OVADYA (o-vahd-YAH) Hebrew: Serves God

OWEN (O-ən) Celtic, Welsh: Young warrior (French) *Ouen*; (Welsh) *Owain*; *Owin*, *Owyn*; **Famous namesakes:** Actor Owen Wilson; **Star babies:** sons of Christopher Reeve, Stephen King, Phoebe Cates and Kevin Kline

OXFORD English: A place name, meaning from the ox ford. The prestigious Oxford University is the oldest university in the United Kingdom.

OXTON English: From the oxen town or settlement; surname *Oxtun*; **Nicknames:** *Ox*

OZ Hebrew: Powerful, courageous **Nicknames:** *Ozi*, *Ozzi*, *Ozzie*, *Ozzy*; **Famous namesakes:** Baseball player Ozzie Smith, singer Ozzy Osbourne

PAAVO (PAH-vo) Finnish: Variation of Paul

PABLO (PAH-blo) Spanish: Variation of Paul **Famous namesakes:** Artist Pablo Picasso, poet Pablo Neruda

PACE English: Peace *Paice*

PACO (PAH-ko) Spanish: Free one; a nickname for Francisco, a popular Spanish form of Francis

PADRAIG (PAW-drig, PAW-rig) Irish: Variation of Patrick *Padhraig*

PADRIG (PAH-drəg) Welsh: Variation of Patrick

PAGE French: Attendant *Padgett*, *Paget*, *Paige*

PALAEMON (pa-LEE-mən, pa-LAY-mən) Greek: A sea god of Greek mythology

PALBEN (PAHL-ben) Basque: Blond

PALINURUS Latin: The helmsman for Aeneas

PALMER English: Pilgrim bearing a palm branch *Palmere*

PALTI (PAL-tie) Hebrew: My deliverance

PAN Greek: The mythological god of shepherds and flocks, Pan is often depicted with a reed pipe and chasing nymphs through the forests while in the shape of a goat. Parents and children will both recognize the name as also belonging to Peter Pan, the flying boy who journeyed to Never-Never Land to escape adulthood.

PANCHO (PAHN-cho) Spanish: Free; a variant of Francisco. Pancho Villa was a rebel general during the Mexican Revolution.

PARIS Greek, French: Original meaning uncertain, though the modern meaning refers to the French capital. As a man's name, Paris is most recognized for a well-known character of Greek mythology. Paris fell in love with and abducted Helen of Troy, the beautiful wife of King Menelaus. This led to the Trojan War, during which Paris killed the Greek hero Achilles with a bow and arrow.
Star babies: sons of Blair Underwood, Pierce Brosnan

PARKER English: Park keeper
Parke; **Nicknames:** *Park*; **Famous namesakes:** Actor Parker Stevenson; **Star babies:** son of Rosie O'Donnell

PARKIN English: Little rock

PARNELL French: Little Peter
Parnall, Parnel, Pernel, Pernell; **Famous namesakes:** Nineteenth-century Irish nationalist Charles Parnell

PAROUNAG (PA-roo-nag) Armenian: Grateful

PARR English: Castle park

PARRISH English: Lives near the church
Parisch; Parish

PARTHENIOS (par-THEE-nee-əs) Greek: Virgin

PASCAL (pa-SKAL) French, Hebrew: Born at Passover or Easter. This name derives from both Hebrew and Latin, and is appropriate to celebrate the birth of a child born during either spring holiday.

(Italian) *Pasquale*; (Spanish) *Pascual, Pasqual; Pascale*; **Famous namesakes:** French philosopher and inventor Blaise Pascal

PATRICK Latin, Irish: Noble, patrician. Saint Patrick (whose original name was Sucat), adopted his name when he became a missionary to Ireland. He is now the patron saint of Ireland, and there are numerous legends about him. Of course his feast day of March 17 is commonly known as the holiday of shamrocks and wearing o' the green.
(French) *Patrice*; (Italian) *Patrizio*; (Spanish) *Patricio, Patrico*; (Gaelic) *Padhra, Padruig*; (Irish) *Paddy, Padhraig, Padraic, Padraig, Padriac, Paidi*; (Welsh) *Padrig*; (Polish) *Patryk*; **Nicknames:** *Pat*; **Famous namesakes:** Actor Patrick Stewart, actor Patrick Swayze, basketball player Patrick Ewing; **Star babies:** sons of Tom Berenger, John Wayne, Arnold Schwarzenegger

PATROCLUS (pa-TRO-cləs) Greek: In Greek mythology, Patroclus was Achilles' best friend, slain by Hector the great warrior during the Trojan War.

PATTON English: From the fighters' town or settlement; a surname and possibly a variant of Peyton or Patrick
Patten, Pattin; **Famous namesakes:** General George S. Patton

PAUL Latin: Little. The biblical apostle and evangelist Paul was an important leader in the church. His letters to early Christians comprise many New Testament books.
(Greek) *Pavlos*; (Arabic) *Boulus*; (Italian) *Paolo*; (Spanish) *Pablo, Paulino, Paulo*; (Gaelic) *Pol*; (Welsh) *Pewlin*; (Scandinavian) *Pal*; (Danish) *Poul*; (Dutch) *Pauel*; (Slavic) *Pavel*; (Russian) *Pavlo*; (Czech) *Havel*; (Polish) *Pawel, Pawelek, Pawl*; (Finnish)

Paavali, Paavo; (Hungarian) *Palko*; (Armenian) *Boghos*; **Old forms:** *Paulus*; **Nicknames:** *Paulie*; **Famous namesakes:** Artist Paul Cezanne, actor Paul Newman, musician Paul McCartney, musician Paul Simon

PAX Latin: Peace
Star babies: Son of Angelina Jolie and Brad Pitt

PAXTON English: From the peaceful town or settlement
Paxon, Paxtun; **Nicknames:** *Pax*; **Famous namesakes:** Actor Bill Paxton

PAYAM Persian: Message

PAYDEN English: From the fighter's den or valley; surname

PAZ (PAHZ) Hebrew: Gold; (Spanish) peace

PEDRO (PAY-dro) Spanish: Variation of Peter
Famous namesakes: Spanish conqueror Pedro de Alvarado, pitcher Pedro Martinez; **Star babies:** son of Frances McDormand and Joel Coen

PEGASUS (PEG-ə-səs) Greek: The offspring of Medusa and Poseidon, Pegasus was the winged horse of Greek mythology

PELLTUN English: From the town or settlement near the pool

PEMBROKE Welsh: Lives in the headland

PENATES (pə-NAY-teez) Latin: The inner ones. In Roman mythology, the Penates were the gods of the household.

PENLEY English: From the enclosed pasture meadow; surname
Penleigh, Pennleah; *Penlea, Penly, Pennlea, Pennleigh, Pennley*

PENTON English: From the enclosed town or settlement; surname
Pentin, Pentun

PER (PAYR) Swedish: Variation of Peter

PERCIVAL (PUR-si-vəl) French: Pierce the valley. In Arthurian legend, Percival was a knight of the Round Table who glimpsed the Holy Grail.
(German) *Parsifal*; *Parsefal, Perceval*; **Nicknames:** *Percy*

PERCY French: From Percy; also a nickname for Percival
Famous namesakes: English poet Percy Blysshe Shelley

PERKIN English: Little Peter
Perkins

PERRY English, Latin: Pear tree; also a nickname for the Latin Peregrine
Famous namesakes: Singer Perry Como, Actor Matthew Perry

PERUN Slavic: Thunder; In Slavic mythology, Perun was the god of thunder and lightning.

PESACH (PE-sah, PE-sahkh) Hebrew: To pass over; the Hebrew name of the Passover holiday commemorating the sparing of the Hebrews in Egypt
Pessach

PETER Greek: Rock; Peter was a biblical fisherman and one of Christ's twelve disciples. In Catholic tradition he is the first pope. See also *Takis* (Greek) *Panos, Petros*; (Arabic) *Botros*; (French) *Pierre*; (Italian) *Pero, Piero, Pietro*; (Spanish) *Pedro*; (Gaelic) *Peadair, Peadar*; (Welsh) *Pedr*; (Scandinavian) *Pedar, Petter*; (Swedish) *Per*; (Dutch) *Pieter*; (Slavic) *Pyotr*; (Czech) *Petr*; (Polish) *Pietrek, Piotr*; (Finnish) *Pekka, Pietari*; (Armenian) *Bedros*; **Nicknames:** *Pete, Petya*; **Famous namesakes:** English actor Peter Sellers, English musician Peter Gabriel, English musician Pete Townshend; **Star babies:** sons of Mikhail Baryshnikov and Lisa Rinehart, Sally Field, Princess Anne and Mark Phillips, Stephanie Seymour, Jack Wagner

PEVERELL French: Piper

PEYMAN Persian: Promise
Payman

PEYTON (PAY-tən) English: Warrior's village; a unisex name. *Peyton Place* was the name of a popular TV show from the 1960s; (Irish) a variant of Patrick; (Latin) regal or royal
Paden, Paegastun, Paton, Payton; Payton, Payten, Payden; **Famous namesakes:** Quarterback Peyton Manning

PHAETON (FAY-ə-thən) Greek: Shining one; the son of the sun-god Helios in Greek mythology

PHANTASOS Greek: Apparition; a son of Hypnos in Greek mythology and a personification of dreams

PHELAN (FAY-lən) Gaelic, Irish: Little wolf
Faolan, Felan

PHELPS English: Son of Philip
Famous namesakes: Swimmer Michael Phelps

PHERSON Scottish: Parson

PHILBERT German: Spelling variation of Filbert
Philibert

PHILEMON (fi-LEE-mən) Greek: Affectionate. One of Paul's epistles in the New Testament is addressed to Philemon.

PHILIP (FIL-ip) Greek: Lover of horses. Philip was one of Christ's twelve apostles. This name has also been borne by numerous kings of Spain, France, and Macedonia. (French) *Philippe*; (Italian) *Filippio, Filippo*; (Spanish) *Felipe, Filipo*; (Gaelic) *Pilib*; (Scottish) *Filib*; (Scandinavian) *Filip*; (Hungarian) *Fulop, Philipp, Phillip*; **Nicknames:** *Flip, Phil*; **Famous namesakes:** Britain's Prince Philip, painter Filippo Lippi, TV host Phil Donahue, football player Phil Simms

PHILO Greek: To love

PHINEAS (FIN-ee-əs) Hebrew: Meaning uncertain; suggested definitions include oracle, dark-skinned, mouth of brass, and a serpent's mouth
Phinees, Phineus, Pinchas; Phinnaeus, Pinchos, Pincus, Pinhas, Pinkas, Pinkus; **Nicknames:** *Pini*; **Famous namesakes:** Showman Phineas Taylor (P.T.) Barnum; **Star babies:** son of Julia Roberts and Danny Moder

PHOEBUS (FEE-bəs) Greek: Shining one. Phoebus was an epithet of Apollo in Greek mythology.

PHOENIX (FEE-niks) Greek: Dark red. In mythology, the phoenix was a beautiful bird that built its own pyre and then was reborn from the ashes.
Famous namesakes: Actor Joaquin Phoenix and his late brother River Phoenix

PHORCYS (FOR-sis) Greek: A sea god in Greek mythology

PICKFORD English: From the woodcutter's ford

PIERCE English: Rock; a variant of Piers, an older form of Peter
Pearce, Pearson, Peirce, Piers, Pierson; **Famous namesakes:** Actor Pierce Brosnan

PIERPONT (PEER-pont) French: Lives by the stone bridge; surname made famous by American banker J. Pierpont Morgan
Pierrepont

PIERRE (pee-YER) French: Variation of Peter
Famous namesakes: Canadian Prime Minister Pierre Trudeau, French fashion designer Pierre Cardin

PIETRO (pee-AY-tro) Italian: Variation of Peter

PIO (PEE-o) Latin: Pious; a name of numerous popes
Pious, Pius

PIPPIN French: Eighth-century king of the Franks, father of Charlemagne, Emperor of the Holy Roman Empire
Peppin

PITNEY English: From the stubborn island; surname
Pittney; **Nicknames:** *Pitt*

PLACIDO (PLAH-cee-do) Spanish: Tranquil
Famous namesakes: Opera singer Placido Domingo

PLATO (PLAY-to) Greek: Broad-shouldered. Plato was a renowned philosopher of Greece, a student of Socrates, and a teacher of Aristotle.
(Spanish) *Platon*

PLATT French: The flat land

PLUTO (PLOO-to) Latin: Wealth; a mythological Roman god of the underworld whose Greek name is Hades. Pluto is also the name of a dwarf planet and Mickey Mouse's dog.

POLLARD Teutonic: Short-haired

POLLUX (PAHL-uks) Latin: In Greek mythology, Pollux was the brother of Helen of Troy and a twin of Castor, with whom he forms the constellation Gemini.

POLYPHEMUS (pah-lə-FEE-məs) Greek: Mythic son of Poseidon and Thoosa, Polyphemus was a Cyclops, a giant semi-human monster with a single eye in the center of his forehead. He's best known for capturing Odysseus in Homer's epic *Odyssey*.

POMEROY French: An apple orchard

PONCE (PON-say) Spanish: Fifth
Famous namesakes: Spanish explorer Ponce de León

PONTIFEX (PAHN-tə-feks) Latin: Priest. In ancient Rome, the pontifex was an official that supervised religious activities.

PORFIRIO Greek: Purple stone
Porfiro, Prophyrios; **Famous namesakes:** Mexican president Porfirio Diaz

PORTER Latin: Gatekeeper

POSEIDON (po-SIE-dən) Greek: The Greek mythological god of the sea, earthquakes, and horses

POUYAN Persian: Searcher

POWELL Welsh: A contraction of Ap Howell, meaning *son of Howell*; a surname *Powel, Pouel, Pauwel*

PRENTICE (PREN-tis) English: Apprentice

PRESCOTT English: From the priest's cottage; surname *Prescot, Priestcot*

PRESLEY English: From the priest's meadow; a surname evocative of Elvis Presley *Preslea, Preslee, Presleigh, Preslie, Priestley, Priestlea, Priestleigh*; **Nicknames:** *Pres*; **Star babies:** son of Cindy Crawford and Rande Gerber

PRESTON English: From the priest's estate *Pfeostun, Prestin*; **Nicknames:** *Pres*; **Star babies:** son of Larry Hagman

PREWITT French: Brave *Pruitt*

PRIAM (PRIE-əm) Greek: In Greek mythology, Priam was king and ruler of Troy during the Trojan War.

PRIAPUS (prie-AY-pəs) Greek: A mythological god of fertility

PRICE Welsh: Son of Rhys *Pryce*

PRIESTLY English: From the priest's meadow; a surname and variant of Presley *Priestley, Priestlea, Priestleigh*; **Famous namesakes:** Actor Jason Priestly

PRIMO (PREE-mo) Italian: Firstborn

PRINCE Latin: Prince **Famous namesakes:** Musician Prince; **Star babies:** Two sons of Michael Jackson

PRINCETON English: From the town or place belonging to the prince or the royal family; an ivy league university in New Jersey

PROCTOR Latin: Administrator; an occupational name

PROMETHEUS (pro-MEE-thee-əs) Greek: A mythological deity, Prometheus stole fire from the gods and gave it to men.

PROSPERO (PRO-sper-o) Spanish: Successful

PROTESILAUS (pro-TES-i-LAY-əs) Greek: In Greek mythology, Protesilaus was the Thessalian king and the first to die in the Trojan War. Even though it had been foretold that the first Greek who touched Trojan ground would die, Protesilaus did not hesitate.

PROTEUS (PRO-tee-əs) Greek: A prophetic sea god of Greek mythology

PRYOR Latin: Servant of the priory, though as a title it refers to the head of a monastery *Prior*

PTAH (PTAH) Egyptian: Creator god of Memphis. This god coalesced with Sokaris and Osiris and is represented as a man in mummy form, possibly originally as a statue. He was the patron god of craftsmen and was equated by the Greeks with Hephaestus. See also *Hephaestus*

PUCK English: Elf; mischievous character in Shakespeare's *Midsummer's Night Dream*

PUTNAM English: Dwells by the pond

PYGMALION (pig-MAYL-ee-ən) Greek: A sculptor and king of Cyprus. According to Greek legend, Pygmalion carved a statue of a beautiful woman from ivory and adored it so much he named her Galatea and prayed for a wife like her. The goddess Aphrodite brought the sculpture to life for Pygmalion, and he and his bride shared a happy life together.

QABIC Arabic: Able, capable
Quabic

QABIL Arabic: Capable
Qabill

QADIM Arabic: Ancient
Quadim

QAMAR Arabic: Moon
Quamar; Quamir

QASIM Arabic: Divides
Quasim

QUADARIUS English: Modern blend name of Quan (possibly as a variant of Juan) and Darius
Quadarias, Qudarius

QUADE (KWAYD) Latin: Fourth, born fourth (English) *Quaid; Quartus; Quaden, Quadin, Quadre, Qwade*

QUAIN (KWAYN) French: Clever, quick

QUANAH (KWAH-nə) Native American: Fragrance, specific odor (Comanche)

QUANDRE (KWAWN-dray) English: Modern blend of Quan (possibly as a variant of Juan) and Andre
Quandray, Qudre

QUANMAINE English: Modern blend of Quan (possibly as a variant of Juan) and Jermaine
Quanmain, Quanmane

QUANTAVIUS (kwahn-TAYV-ee-əs) English: Modern blend of Quan (possibly as a variant of Juan) and Octavius
Quantavious

QUASHAWN English: Modern blend of Quan and Shawn
Quashan, Quashen, Quashon

QUENNEL French: From the little oak tree
Quenal, Quenall, Quenel, Quenell, Quennel

QUENTIN (KWEN-tin) Latin, French: Born fifth. Quentin is the name of numerous religious and political leaders throughout history. The famous prison in San Francisco derives its name from the martyred Saint Quintin; (English) from the Queen's place, town *Quenton, Quinton; Quenten, Quenton, Quentyn;* **Old forms:** *Quintus;* **Nicknames:** *Quent, Quint;* **Famous namesakes:** Filmmaker Quentin Tarantino

> "The children despise their parents until the age of forty, when they suddenly become just like them—thus preserving the system."
> —Author Quentin Crewe in a 1962 *Saturday Evening Post* piece about the British upper class

QUENTRELL English, French: A modern name of unclear origins, but probably related to Quentin

QUIGLEY (KWIG-lee) Gaelic, Irish: From the mother, the maternal side; may have been related at some point specifically to land belonging to the mother's side
Quiglea, Quiglee, Quigleigh

QUILLAN (KWIL-ən) Gaelic: Cub, small one
Quilan, Quilen, Quilin, Quillen

QUILLON (KWIL-ən) Latin: Sword, long knife
Quilon

QUIMBY (KWIM-bee) Norse: From the man's estate
Quinby; Quenby, Quenbey, Quemby

QUINCEY (KWIN-see) French: From the fifth child's estate
Quincy; **Famous namesakes:** President John Quincy Adams, music icon Quincy Jones

QUINDARIUS English: Modern blend of Quin and Darius

QUINLAN (KWIN-lən) Gaelic: Graceful, strong, well made; also a variant of Quinn
Quinlin

QUINN (KWIN) Gaelic, Scottish: Wisdom, intelligence. Quinn is derived from O'Cuinn, a Gaelic surname and is also a familiar form of Quincey and similar names
Quin; **Famous namesakes:** Actor Aidan Quinn, actor Anthony Quinn; **Star babies:** son of Sean Young

QUINSHAWN English: Modern blend of Quin and Shawn

QUINT (KWINT) French: Nickname for Quentin

QUINTAVIUS (kwin-TAYV-ee-əs) English: Modern blend of Quin and Octavius

QUINTRELL English: Unclear origin, but a variant of Quentin, Quincey, and Quinn

RA (RAH) Egyptian: Sun god of Heliopolis. From the fifth dynasty onward, Ra became a national god and combined with the supreme deity Amon. As head of the great ennead and supreme judge, this god was represented as falcon-headed and was often linked with other gods aspiring to universality, such as Amon, Amon-Ra, and Sobk-Ra.
Re

RAAMAH (RAY-mah, RAY-ah-mah) Hebrew: Thunderclap
Rama, Ramah

RAANAN Hebrew: Fresh, beautiful

RABI (rah-bee) Arabic: Spring; also means *my lord* if pronounced with accent on the first syllable

RACER English: One who races, loves to run or compete
Rayce; **Nicknames:** *Race*

RACHAM (rah-KHAHM) Hebrew: Sympathetic, filled with compassion
Rachaman, Rachamin

RADAMES (RAH-da-mays) Egyptian: An Egyptian prince and the name of the hero in Puccini's opera *Aida*

RADBERT English: Red-haired or brilliant counselor
Radburt

RADBURN English: Lives by the red stream
Radbourne, Radbyrne, Raedburne; Radborn, Radborne, Radbourn, Radburne

RADCLIFF English: Near the red cliff; surname
Radclyf, Radcliffe, Raedclyf; Ratcliff, Ratcliffe

RADFORD English: From the red or reedy ford; a variant of Redford
Radferd, Radfurd, Raeford

RADLEY English: From or near the red meadow; surname
Raedleah, Redley, Ridley

RADMAN (RAHD-mən) Slavic: Happy
Radmon

RADNOR English: From the red shore or the reedy shore

RADOLF English: Red wolf
Radolph

RADOMIL (RAHD-o-meel, RAHD-o-mil) Slavic: Peaceful bliss

RADORM Norse: In Norse mythology, the brother of Jolgeir

RADOSLAW (rah-DAW-swahf) Polish: Contented, at peace

RADWAN Hebrew, Arabic: Delightful

RAED Arabic: Leader, scout, explorer, major (military title)
Raiid

RAFE (RAYF) English: Nickname for Rafferty or Ralph

RAFFERTY Irish: Rich, prospering
Rafertey, Raferti, Raferty; **Nicknames:** *Rafer, Rafe, Raffer*; **Star babies:** son of Sadie Frost and Jude Law

RAFI (RAH-fee) Arabic: Exhalted; (Hebrew) nickname for Raphael

RAFIK (rah-FEEK) Arabic: Companion, friend
Rafeek, Rafiq

RAGHIB Arabic: Desires, wants

RAGNAROK (RAG-nuh-rahk) Norse: The final battle of the gods in Norse mythology, the end of the world, the beginning of a new one

RAI (rie-ee) Japanese: Thunder

RAIDEN (rie-den, ray-den) Japanese: Thunder; mythological thunder god
Raidon, Rayden, Raydon

RAINE (RAYN) English: Rule, also wise
Rane, Rayne; *Rain, Raines*

RAINIER (rə-NEER) French: Variation of Raynor
Famous namesakes: Prince Rainier of Monaco

RAJABU African: Born in the seventh month of the Islamic calendar (Swahili)

RAJAH Sanskrit: King, prince, the ruler
Raja, Rajan; **Nicknames:** *Raj, Raji*

RAJNISH (raj-neesh) Hindi: Hindu god of the night

RAKIN Arabic: Respectful, firm, steady, confident

RALEIGH (RAW-lee) English: From the roe deer meadow; surname and the capital city of North Carolina
Raleah, Raley, Rally, Rawley; *Ralea, Rawlea, Rawleigh, Rawlee*; **Famous namesakes:** English explorer Sir Walter Raleigh

RALPH English: Wolf counsel. An old name from Scandinavian and Germanic elements, Ralph is pronounced "Rafe" in many areas outside the United States. See also *Rolfe* (French) *Raoul*; (Spanish) *Raul*; (Scandinavian) *Rolf*; *Raff, Ralf, Rolph*; **Famous namesakes:** Actor Ralph Fiennes, actor Ralph Macchio, activist Ralph Nader, fashion designer Ralph Lauren

> "We find a delight in the
> beauty and happiness of
> children that makes the
> heart too big for the body."
> —Ralph Waldo Emerson

RALSTON English: Ralph's town or wolf's
town
Ralsten

RAM English: Male sheep. Ram is also a nickname for Ramsden, Ramsey, and related names.
Ramm

RAMA (RAH-mah) Sanskrit: Awesome,
godlike. Rama was the mythological seventh
incarnation of Vishnu.
Ram, Ramanan

RAMBERT German: Mighty or intelligent
Rambart

RAMI Arabic, Persian: Loving, thrower,
rifleman
Ramy; Ramey, Ramy

RAMIRO (rah-MEER-o) Spanish: Highest
judge
Ramario, Ramires, Ramos

RAMON (rah-MON) Spanish: Variation of
Raymond
Ramone; **Famous namesakes:** Spanish poet
Juan Ramón Jiménez

RAMSDEN English: From the ram's valley
Ramsden, Ramsdin

RAMSES (RAM-seez) Egyptian: Begotten
by or belonging to Ra, the sun god; the name
of several powerful Pharoahs of ancient Egypt

RAMSEY English, Teutonic: Ram's island or
raven's island; surname adapted to popular
first name use
Ramsay, Ramzey, Ramzi

RANCE English: Familiar form of Laurence
and Ransom

RAND English: Shield, defender

RANDALL English: Shield wolf; variant of
Randolph
*Randahl, Randal, Randale, Randel, Randell,
Rendall, Rendell;* **Nicknames:** *Randy;* **Famous
namesakes:** Actor Tony Randall, quarterback
Randall Cunningham

RANDOLPH English: Shield wolf, defender
and protector. The wolf is revered for its
strength, cunning, and fearlessness. Quite
possibly this name was derived as an
identifier for a family which used the emblem
of the wolf as part of its coat of arms.
Randolf, Ranolf; **Nicknames:** *Rando*

RANDON English: Possibly from the
shielded town or valley, possibly a form of
Randolph

RANDSON English: Rand or Randolph's
son, possibly child of the shield as a reference
to a young man in training for battle

RANDY English: A nickname of Randolph,
Randall, Rand, and related names
Famous namesakes: Actor Randy Quaid,
composer Randy Newman, pitcher Randy
Johnson, singer Randy Travis

RANEN Hebrew: To sing, to be joyful
Ranon

RANG English: Raven

RANGER French: Ward of the forest
Rainger

RANGEY English: From raven's island

RANGFORD English: From the raven's ford

RANI Hebrew: My song, my joy

RANJAN (RUN-jun) Hindi: Delighted, sun

RANKIN English: Little shield, child of the shield
Randkin; *Ransom*

RANSLEY English: From the raven's meadow; surname
Ranslea, Ranslee, Ransleigh, Ransly

RANSOM Latin: Redeem; (English) shield child, Rand's son

RAPHAEL (rah-fie-EL, RAF-ee-el) Hebrew: God has healed; the name of one of the archangels and of one of the greatest painters of the Renaissance
(Italian) *Rafaele, Rafaello*; (Spanish) *Rafael*; (Polish) *Rafal*; *Raphale, Rapheal, Raphello*; **Famous namesakes:** Composer Raphael Mostel, painter Raphael Sanzio; **Star babies:** sons of Juliette Binoche, Robert De Niro

RASHAD (rah-SHAHD) Arabic: Thinker, counselor; one who shows reason, good sense, integrity and maturity, also means nastartium (flower); a spelling variation of Rashid
Reshad; *Rashaad*

RASHAWN Contemporary: Modern blend of Ray or Ra and Shawn
Rashae, Rashane, Rashaun, Rayshaun, Rayshawn, Reshawn, Rishawn

RASHID (rah-SHEED) Arabic: Counselor, thinker, spiritual instructor. Rashid is also the name of Rosetta, a large town in Egypt. See also *Rashidi*
Rasheed; *Rashed*; **Famous namesakes:**

Journalist Ahmed Rashid, basketball player Rasheed Wallace

RASHIDA (rah-SHEE-dah) African: Rightly guided
Famous namesakes: Actress Rashida Jones

RASHIDI (rah-SHEE-dee) African: Rightly guided

RASMUS (RUS-moos) Scandinavian: Variation of Erasmus

RATMIR Russian: Peace protector

RAUL (rah-OOL) Spanish: Variation of Ralph
Raol, Raoul, Raulio; **Nicknames:** *Rulo*; **Famous namesakes:** Actor Raul Julia

RAVEN English: Raven, blackbird
Ravenel; *Ravin*

RAVI (RAH-vee) Sanskrit: Sun; also the name of the mythological Hindi sun god Ravi
Famous namesakes: Sitar player and composer Ravi Shankar

RAVID Hebrew: Ornament; also a form of Arvid

RAVIV (rah-VEEV) Hebrew: Rain, dew, reviving waters
Ravyv

RAWDON English: From the rough hill

RAWLEY English: From the roe deer meadow; a surname and variant of Raleigh
Rawlea, Rawleigh, Rawlee

RAWLING English: Raleigh's son, small Raleigh

RAWLINS French: Roland's child or diminutive for Roland

RAWLS English: Raleigh's son or a short form of Raleigh
Famous namesakes: Singer and actor Lou Rawls

RAY Latin: Radiant; (English) familiar form of Rayburn, Raymond, and related names; (French) regal, royal

RAYCE English: Spelling variation of Racer

RAYFORD English: Deer's ford

RAYHAN Arabic: God favors

RAYI Hebrew: Friend of mine

RAYMOND German: Wise protector (English) *Redmund*; (German) *Raimund*; (Italian) *Raimondo*; (Spanish) *Rai, Raimundo, Ramon, Ramone, Rayman, Raymon, Reymundo*; (Gaelic) *Reamonn*; (Irish) *Redmond*; (Polish) *Rajmund*; *Radmund, Raimond, Ramond, Raymund*; **Famous namesakes:** Actor Ray Romano, actor Raymond Burr; **Star babies:** sons of Jack Nicholson, Tina Turner

RAYNE English: Spelling variation of Raine

RAYNOR (RAY-nər) Norse: Warrior of judgment. The origin of this name seems to stem from both the Germanic name Reginar and the Norse name Ragnar.
(German) *Rainer, Reiner*; (French) *Rainier, Ranier*; (Scandinavian) *Ragnar, Regner*; *Rainor, Rayner, Raynord*

RAZI (RAH-zee) Aramaic: Secret
Raziel

READ English: Redhead; variant of Reid

READING English: Reid's son, diminutive of Reid, or the wandering redhead
Redding

REAGAN (RAY-gən, REE-gən) Irish: Little ruler
Reaghan, Regan, Riagan; Raegan, Raegin, Raegon, Raegyn, Raugan, Raigen, Raigin, Raygan, Reagen, Reigan, Reigen, Reighan, Rheagan; **Famous namesakes:** President Ronald Reagan

REBEL English: Modern name reflecting an independent personality

RED English: Color name and a variant for Redman, Redley, and related names
Redd; **Famous namesakes:** Actor Red Skelton, actor Redd Foxx

REDA Arabic: Fulfilled, contented
Ridah, Ridha

REDFORD English: From the red or reedy ford
Old forms: *Raedford;* **Famous namesakes:** Actor Robert Redford

REDLEY English: From or near the red meadow; variant of Radley

REDMAN English: Red-haired advisor, companion
Old forms: *Redamann*

REECE (REES) Welsh, English: Passionate, enthusiastic
Rees, Reese, Rhett, Rhys; Rice; **Nicknames:** *Rhy*

REEVE English: Steward, an occupational name referring to a caretaker. When this name was coined in medieval times, the reeve was very important and oversaw the running of the entire estate, including the lives of feudal serfs.
Reave, Reve

REEVES English: Reeve's son, belonging to Reeve
Reaves

REGIN Norse: A mythical blacksmith god, Regin was the son of Rodmar and the foster father of Sigurd.

REGINALD (REJ-i-nəld) English: Powerful, wise counsel
(French) *Renaud*; (Italian) *Rinaldo*; (Spanish) *Reynaldo, Reynardo*; (Gaelic) *Raghnall*; *Ragnol, Reynald, Reynold, Reynolds*; **Old forms:** *Regenweald*; **Nicknames:** *Reggie, Reg, Reggie*; **Famous namesakes:** Baseball player Reggie Jackson

REGIS Latin: Ruler
Famous namesakes: TV personality Regis Philbin

REID (REED) English: Redhead; a surname adapted a long time ago for given name use
Read, Reade, Redd, Reed

REIDAR Norse: Nest fighter
Reider

REIJO (RAY-yo) Finnish: Vigilant, watchful

REINHARD German: Strong and courageous counselor
(French) *Raynard*; *Rainart, Rainhard, Renke, Reynard*; *Reinhart*

REINHOLD (RIEN-hold) Teutonic: Variant of Reynard or Reinhart; the various roots of this name have the general meaning of stong, wise advisor, or advice; (Swedish) variant of Ragnar; (English) variant of Reynold
Famous namesakes: Actor Judge Reinhold

REMINGTON English: From the raven family settlement or town. This name will remind art lovers of Frederick Remington who specialized in scenes of western life.
Famous namesakes: Fictional detective Remington Steele

REMUS (REE-məs) Latin: Quick. In Roman mythology, Remus and Romulus were the twin brothers who founded Rome.

REMY French: From Rheims, France; (English) familiar form of Remington
Remi

RENDOR Hungarian: Peacekeeper, policeman

RENE (rə-NAY) French, Latin: Reborn, to rise again
(Italian) *Renato*; **Old forms:** *Renatus*; **Nicknames:** *Rennie, Renny*; **Famous namesakes:** French philosopher and scientist René Descartes

---

"Cogito ergo sum (I think, therefore I am)."
—René Descartes

RENFIELD English: From the raven's field, possibly from the roe deer field; surname
Ranfield

RENFRED English: Enduring peace; possibly a derivation from peaceful raven
Renfrid, Rinfred

RENFREW Welsh: From the raven woods

RENJIRO (ren-jee-ro) Japanese: Honest, true

RENNY Irish: Small but powerful; (French) form of Rene
Renne, Rennie

RENSHAW English: From the raven forest

RENTON English: From the roe deer town or settlement; surname
Rentin, Renten

RENWICK Teutonic: Place where the ravens nest
Renwyk

REUBEN (ROO-bən) Hebrew: Behold a son; in the Old Testament, the firstborn of Jacob and Leah, and patriarch of one of the twelve tribes of Israel
(Greek) *Rouvin*; (Spanish) *Ruben*; *Reuven*, *Rubin*, *Rueban*; **Nicknames:** *Rube*, *Ruby*; **Famous namesakes:** Cartoonist Rube Goldberg

REX Latin: King

REXFORD English: From the king's ford

REXLEY English: From the king's meadow; variant of Kingsley
Rex

REXTON English: From the king's town, settlement

REY (RAY) French: Regal, kingly; a variant of Roy; (Spanish) familiar form of Reynaldo

REYES (RAY-es) Spanish: Kings

REYNOLD (REN-əld) English: Spelling variation of Reginald

REZ Hungarian: Redhead, copper-haired

REZA Persian: Will, consent

REZIN (REE-zin) Hebrew: Delightful, a joy

RHADAMANTHUS (ra-də-MAN-thəs) Greek: A judge in the underworld of Greek mythology

RHEGED (RE-get) Anglo-Saxon, Welsh: From Rheged, a northern kingdom of England; name of Uriens, one of the most famous of kings in Arthurian legend and a historical figure who was one of the earliest Christian kings

RHESUS (REE-səs) Latin: A mythical king of Thrace and the name of a species of monkeys

RHETT (RET) Welsh: Passionate, enthusiastic; a variant of Reece. Rhett Butler is the dashing hero of Margaret Mitchell's *Gone with the Wind*.

RHODES (RODS) Greek: Where the roses grow; an island in Greece
(Spanish) *Rodas*; *Rodes*

RHYS (REES) Welsh: Spelling variation of Reece
Famous namesakes: British actor Rhys Ifans

RICE Welsh, English: Variant of Reece
Ryce

RICHARD German, English: Powerful, strong ruler. This Old German name was introduced to England by the Normans and borne by three kings of England. King Richard the lion-hearted was the first of them.
(Italian) *Ricardo*, *Ricco*; (Spanish) *Cardo*, *Richi*, *Rico*, *Riqui*; (Welsh) *Rhisiart*; (Scandinavian) *Rikkard*, *Rikki*; (Swedish) *Rikard*; (Dutch) *Rikke*; (Polish) *Ryszard*; (Finnish) *Riku*; *Ricard*, *Riccardo*, *Ricciardo*, *Rickard*, *Rickey*, *Rickie*, *Rickward*, *Ricman*, *Ricweard*, *Riocard*; **Old forms:** *Richart*, *Rikward*; **Nicknames:** *Dick*, *Ric*, *Rich*, *Rick*, *Ricky*; **Famous namesakes:** President Richard Nixon, actor Richard Dreyfuss, actor Richard Gere

RICHMAN English: Powerful
Rickman; *Richmen*, *Richmun*, *Rychman*; **Famous namesakes:** Actor Alan Rickman

RICHMOND German, English: Strong protector, powerful defender. Richmond is the capital city of Virginia and a town in Yorkshire, England.

RICK English: Familiar form of Cedric, Frederick, and Richard
Nicknames: *Ricky*; **Famous namesakes:** Actor Rick Moranis, entertainer Rick Springfield, entertainer Ricky Martin

RICKER English: Strong army

RIDDOCK Irish: From the smooth field
Reidhachadh, Riddoc, Riddick; **Famous namesakes:** Boxer Riddick Bowe

RIDER English: Horseman, knight
Ridere, Ryder; Ridder, Rydder

RIDGE English: From the ridge or cliff's edge
Rigg, Rydge

RIDGELY English: From the meadow's ridge or from the meadow near the ridge; surname
Ridgeley; Ridgelea, Ridgeley, Ridgeleigh

RIDLEY English: From or near the red meadow; variant of Radley
Famous namesakes: Film director Ridley Scott

RIEL (ree-EL) Spanish: Nickname for Gabriel

RIGBY English: From the ruling valley; surname
Rigbee, Rigbie, Rygby

RIGEL Arabic: Foot. Rigel is a blue star of the first magnitude that marks the hunter's left foot in the Orion constellation.
Rigl, Regl

RIGGS English: Son of Ridge, belonging to Ridge
Famous namesakes: Tennis player Bobby Riggs

RIGOBERT German: Wealthy, wonderful

RIKU (REE-koo) Finnish: Variation of Richard

RILEY Irish: Brave; though originally a boy's name, Riley has become increasingly popular as a name for girls.
(Irish) *Ryleigh; Reilley, Reilly, Ryley; Reilly*;
Star babies: son of David Lynch

RING English: Ring, circle
Nicknames: *Ringo*

RINGO English: Nickname for Ring
Famous namesakes: Beatle Ringo Starr

RIO (REE-o) Spanish: Variant of River; a familiar form of Spanish names ending with *–rio*. The Rio Grande is one of the longest rivers in North America, and Rio de Janeiro is the second largest city in Brazil.
Star babies: son of Sean Young

RIORDAN (REER-den) Irish, Gaelic: Royal bard
Riordain; **Old forms:** *Rioghbhardan*

RIPLEY Anglo-Saxon, English: From the shouter's meadow; surname
Hrapenly, Hrypanleah

RISHI (ri-shee) Hindi: Sage, wise man

RISLEY English: From the meadow of brushwood or shrubs; surname
Rislea, Rislee, Risleigh, Rislie

RISTO (REES-to) Finnish: Nickname for Christopher

RISTON English: From the town or settlement near the shrubs; surname
Risten, Ristun, Whriston, Wriston

RITTER German: Knight, abiding by the knight's code of ethics, chivalrous
Famous namesakes: Actor John Ritter

RIVER English: Body of water. See also *Rio*
Famous namesakes: Actor River Phoenix

RIYAD Arabic: Garden; stems from rayy, meaning rain, abundant or copious water. Riyadh is the capital of Saudi Arabia.
Riyadh

ROALD (RO-ahld) Swedish: Variation of Ronald
Famous namesakes: British author Roald Dahl, Norwegian explorer Roald Amundsen

ROANO Spanish: Reddish-brown skin

ROAR Norse: Praised warrior

ROB English: Nickname for Robert
Robb; **Famous namesakes:** Actor Rob Lowe

ROBERT English: Bright with fame; an all-time favorite boys' name since the Middle Ages and popular worldwide
(German) *Rupert, Ruprecht*; (Italian) *Roberto*; (Gaelic) *Riobart*; (Irish) *Riobard, Roibeard, Roibin*; (Scottish) *Rab*; (Finnish) *Pertti, Roope*; **Nicknames:** *Bob, Bobbie, Bobby, Rob, Robb, Robbie, Robbin, Robby, Robinet, Robin*; **Famous namesakes:** Actor Robert De Niro, actor Robert Downey Jr., actor Robert Duvall, actor Robert Redford, Scottish author Robert Louis Stevenson, Confederate general Robert E. Lee, poet Robert Frost, senator Robert Kennedy

> A name with meaning could
> bring up a child,
> Taking the child out of
> the parents' hands.
> Better a meaningless name,
> I should say,
> As leaving more to nature
> and happy chance.
> Name children some names
> and see what you do.
> —Robert Frost, *Maple*

ROBERTSON English: Robert's son, belonging to Robert
Roberts, Robinson

ROBIN English: Bright with fame; an abbreviation of Robert popular since the medieval days of Robin Hood. Robin is well known to children as the name of Winnie the Pooh's boy companion Christopher Robin.
Robbin, Roibin, Robyn; **Famous namesakes:** Actor Robin Williams, musician Robin Gibb

ROBINSON English: Variant of Robertson and name of the adventurous protagonist in Daniel Defoe's *Robinson Crusoe*

ROCCO Italian: Rock
Star babies: son of Madonna

ROCK English: Rock, solid
Roch, Rocke; **Nicknames:** *Rocky*; **Famous namesakes:** Actor Rock Hudson

ROCKFORD English: From the rocky ford; surname

ROCKLAND English: From the rocky land; surname

ROCKLEDGE English: From the rocky ledge; surname

ROCKLEY English: From the rocky meadow, fields; surname

ROCKWELL English: From the rocky well; surname
Famous namesakes: Artist Norman Rockwell, artist and author Rockwell Kent

ROCKY English: Familiar form of Rock. The well-known fictional prize fighter Rocky Balboa fought his way to the top.

ROD English: Staff, also a familiar form for several names, including Roderick and Rodney
Rodd

RODDY (RAH-dee) German: Nickname for Roderick
Famous namesakes: Actor Roddy McDowall

RODEN (RO-dən) English: From the red or deer valley
Rodan, Rodin, Roedan; **Famous namesakes:** Artist Auguste Rodin

RODERICK (RAHD-ə-rik) German: Famous ruler
(French) *Rodrigue*; (Spanish) *Roderigo, Rodrigo*; (Czech) *Radek*; *Roddric, Roderic, Roderik, Rodric, Rodrick, Rodrik*; **Nicknames:** *Rodd, Roddy, Rod*; *Rick*

RODION Russian: Rosy. Rodion Raskolnikov is the main character in Dostoyevsky's novel *Crime and Punishment.*
Nicknames: *Rodya, Rodenka, Rodka*; **Famous namesakes:** Russian composer Rodion Shchedrin

RODMAN German: Famous man

RODNEY English: From the famous one's island
Nicknames: *Rod, Rodd*

RODWELL English: Lives by the red spring

ROE (RO) English: Deer
Row, Rowe

ROGAN Irish: Spelling variation of Rohan

ROGER Teutonic: Famous spearman
(Italian) *Ruggero, Ruggiero*; (Spanish) *Rogelio, Rogerio, Rogerios*; (Scandinavian) *Rutger, Ruttger*; *Rogir, Rotger, Rudger, Rudiger*; *Rodger*; **Nicknames:** *Rog*

ROGERSON English: Roger's son, child; surname
Hodgson; **Old forms:** *Hodsone*; **Nicknames:** *Hod*

ROHAN Gaelic, Irish: Redheaded; (Sanskrit) ascending; (Persian) learned, scholarly
Rowen; *Rogan, Rowin, Rowyn*; **Old forms:** *Ruadhagan*; **Nicknames:** *Row, Rowe*

ROLAND (RO-lənd) German, French: Renowned in the land. Roland was a great legendary knight who served the medieval king Charlemagne.
(English) *Rolando, Rollins*; (Spanish) *Roldan*; *Orlin, Rollan, Rolland, Rollin, Rowland*; *Orlando, Orlondo*; **Nicknames:** *Lannie, Lanny, Rollie, Rollo, Lando, Olo*

ROLFE (RAWLF) German: Familiar form for either Ralph or Rudolph
Rolph

ROLIHLAHLA (ro-lee-ha-la) African: Pulling down the branch of a tree; troublemaker
Famous namesakes: Nelson Mendela's real first name

ROLLINS English: Variation of Roland

ROLON (ro-LON, RO-lun) Spanish: Famous wolf
Rollon

ROMAN Latin: One from Rome
(French) *Romain*; (Italian) *Romano*; (Portuguese) *Romao*; **Nicknames:** *Mancho, Roma*; **Star babies:** sons of Francis Ford Coppola, Debra Messing and Daniel Zelman

ROMEO Latin: Pilgrim to Rome; The most famous Romeo is likely the protagonist of Shakespeare's *Romeo and Juliet*, the tragic story of a young couple that falls in love despite the violent feud between their families, and whose death ends that feud. One of the most famous scenes in literature is the balcony scene, which begins with Juliet wishing Romeo is not who he is.

"What's in a name? That which we call a rose By any other name would smell as sweet. So Romeo would, were not he Romeo called."
—William Shakespeare, *Romeo and Juliet*

ROMNEY Welsh: From the winding river
Old forms: *Rumenea*

ROMULUS (RAWM-yə-ləs) Latin: Twin brother of Remus and the mythical founder of Rome, after whom the city derives its name

RONALD English, Scottish: Powerful, rules with counsel; from the same root as Reynold (Spanish) *Naldo, Renaldo*; (Swedish) *Roald*; *Ranald, Ronal*; **Nicknames:** *Ron, Ronn, Ronnie, Ronny*; **Famous namesakes:** President Ronald Reagan, clown Ronald McDonald; **Star babies:** son of Tina Turner

RONAN (RON-awn) Irish: Little seal

RONDEL French: Short poem of fourteen lines containing only two rhyming sounds

RONEL Hebrew: Song of the Lord
Ronell; **Nicknames:** *Roni*

RONSON English: Son of Ronald
Ronaldson, Ronsen

ROOK (RUWK) English: Raven
Ruck

ROONEY Irish, Gaelic: Red-haired
Famous namesakes: Actor Mickey Rooney, newsman Andy Rooney

ROOSEVELT (RO-zə-velt) Scandinavian: Rose field
Famous namesakes: President Theodore Roosevelt, president Franklin Delano Roosevelt

ROPER English: Rope maker; an occupational name
Rapere

RORY Irish: Red. The last high king of Ireland was Rory O'Connor, who died in 1198. Irish rebel chief Rory O'More is celebrated in poetry, drink, and music.
Rorey, Rorry, Ruairi; **Star babies:** son of Bill Gates

ROSARIO (ro-SAH-ree-o) Spanish, Portuguese: Rosary; refers to devotional prayers honoring the Virgin Mary

ROSCOE Scandinavian, English: Land or forest of the roe deer
Rosco

ROSS Scottish, Latin: From the headlands; (German) variant of Roswald; (English) variant of Roswell, Russell
Ros

ROSTISLAV Slavic: Seize glory

ROSWALD English: Rose field

ROSWELL English: From the horse well or spring

ROTH German, Scottish: Red, redhead; used as a surname and given name
Famous namesakes: Author Philip Roth

ROTHWELL Norse: Dwells near the red spring

ROURKE (RORK) Irish, Gaelic: Famous king; an ancient given name adopted as an Irish clan name

Roark, Rorke, Ruarc, Ruark; **Famous namesakes:** Actor Mickey Rourke

ROVER English: Wanderer
Old forms: *Rovere*

ROWAN (RO-ən) Irish, English: Little red-haired one; can also refer to the flowering Rowan tree
Roan, Roane, Ruadhan; **Nicknames:** *Row*

ROWDY English: Boisterous, loud. Many parents would consider this a perfect description of an excited young boy.

ROWE Irish: Nickname for Rohan

ROWELL English: From the roe deer's spring

ROWLEY English: From the rough or roughly cleared meadow; surname
Ruhleah; Rowlea, Rowlee, Rowleigh, Rowly

ROWSON (RO-sən) Anglo-Saxon: Rowe's son, the redhead's son
Roweson; **Old forms:** *Ruadson*

ROXBURY English: From the raven's town or estate

ROY French: Regal, kingly; (Gaelic) red-haired
Roi, Royal, Royall, Rui

ROYAL French: Spelling variation of Roy

ROYCE English, French: Roy's son or variant of Reece; (German) famous; (Latin) regal
(English) *Royse; Royse*; **Star babies:** son of Sinbad

ROYDEN English: From the rye or royal valley

RUDD English: Familiar form of several names including Rudolph and Rudyard

RUDOLPH (ROO-dahlf) Teutonic: Famous wolf; well-known by children for the fabled red-nosed reindeer
(Spanish) *Rodolfo, Rolo, Rudi, Rudolfo, Rudy*; (Scandinavian) *Rudolf*; (Swedish) *Rolf, Rolfe*;
Nicknames: *Rolphe*; **Famous namesakes:** Actor Rudolph Valentino, dancer Rudolf Nureyev

RUDY German: Nickname for Rudolph
Famous namesakes: Politician Rudy Giuliani, figure skater Rudy Galindo

RUDYARD English: From the rough enclosure
Nicknames: *Rudy*; **Famous namesakes:** Author Rudyard Kipling

RUFORD English: From the red ford
Rufford

RUFUS (ROO-fəs) Latin: Red-haired; several early saints had this name
(French) *Ruff, Ruffe*; (Spanish) *Rufio, Rufo*; (Polish) *Rufin; Rufeo*

RUGBY English: From the raven's estate, fortress. The popular sport of rugby was named after a school bearing this name.

RULE Latin: Command
(French) *Ruelle*

RUMFORD English: From the wide ford

RUNE (ROON) Norse: Secret

RUPERT German: Variation of Robert
Ruprecht; **Famous namesakes:** British actor Rupert Everett, media magnate Rupert Murdoch

RUSH French: Nickname for Russell
Famous namesakes: Conservative political pundit Rush Limbaugh

RUSHFORD English: Lives near the rush ford
Old forms: *Ryscford*

RUSHKIN French: Nickname for Russell

RUSLAN (roo-SLAHN) Russian: This name was used by Aleksandr Pushkin in his poem *Ruslan and Ludmila.*

RUSSELL French, English: Redhead; (Anglo-Saxon) fox, color of the fox (red) *Roselyn, Roslyn, Roslin, Rosselin, Rosselyn, Rousse, Roussel, Rousset, Rousskin, Russel;* **Nicknames:** *Rush, Rushe, Rushkin, Russ, Rust, Rusty;* **Famous namesakes:** Actor Russell Crowe

RUSTY English: Nickname for Russell

RUTHERFORD English: From the cattle ford
Rutherfurd; **Famous namesakes:** President Rutherford Hayes

RUTLAND Norse: From the red or root land
Rotland

RUTLEDGE English: From the red ledge or cliff; surname
Routledge

RUTLEY English: From the root meadow or red meadow; surname
Rutlea, Rutleigh, Rutlee, Rutlie

RYAN Irish, Gaelic: Kingly
Rayan, Rian, Rion, Ryen, Ryon; Rien, Ryne; **Famous namesakes:** Actor Ryan O'Neal, baseball player Ryne Sandberg

RYCE English: Spelling variation of Rice

RYCROFT English: From the rye field; surname
Ryecroft

RYDER English: Spelling variation of Rider

RYDGE English: Spelling variation of Ridge

RYE English: A specific grain used in breads, cereals, and whiskey; also a familiar form of many English names which conatin the root ry or rye

RYLAND English, Irish: From the land or fields of rye; surname
(Irish) *Rylan*

RYMAN English: Rye merchant

RYTON English: From the rye town or settlement; surname

SAA (SAH) Egyptian: A nature god

SAADYA (sah-ahd-yah) Hebrew: God's helper

SAAM Persian: A name from Persian mythology, a character in Shahnameh
Sam

SAAMAN Persian: Home, welfare
Saman

SAAR (sah-ahr) Hebrew: Wind

SABIH Arabic: Handsome
Sobhi

SABIN (SAY-bin) Latin: A Sabine. The Sabines were a rival tribe living in central Italy near the time that Rome was established by Romulus and Remus.
(Italian) *Savino;* (Spanish) *Sabino;* **Old forms:** *Sabinus*

SABIR Arabic: Patient, enduring, persevering
Saber; **Famous namesakes:** Kurdish poet Refiq Sabir, swimmer Sabir Muhammad

SABOLA (SAH-bo-lah) Egyptian: Pepper

SABRA (SAH-brah) Egyptian: Patient

SABRE (sah-BRAY, SAY-ber) French: Sword

SABURO (sah-boo-ro) Japanese: Third son

SACHIN (sah-chin) Sanskrit: Pure

SACHIO (sah-chee-o) Japanese: Fortunately born

SADEGH Persian: Sincere

SADIKI (sah-DEE-kee) African: Faithful

SADIQ Arabic: Friend
Sadeeq

SAGE English, French: Wise one
Sagan, Sagar; Saige, Sayge; **Star babies:** sons of Tracey Gold and Roby Marshall, Sylvester Stallone

SAGHIR Arabic: Short, small

SAHALE (sah-HAH-le) Native American: Falcon

SAHEN (SAH-hen) Hindi: Above

SAHIR Arabic: Wakeful; (Hindi) friend

SAID (sah-EED) Arabic, Persian: Happy, fortunate. Port Said is a large city on the Suez Canal in Egypt.
Saeed

SAKERI Hebrew: Remembered by God

SAKIMA (sah-KEE-mah) Native American: King

SALAH Arabic: Good, righteous

First Ayyubid Sultan of Egypt during the time of the Fatimid reign, Salah al-Din Yusuf Ibn Ayyub (1138–1193) became renown in the western world under the name of Saladin. Despite his fierce opposition to the Christian powers, Saladin achieved a great reputation in Europe as a chivalrous knight, so much so that there existed by the 14th century an epic poem about his exploits, and Dante included him among the virtuous pagan souls in Limbo.

SALEM Hebrew: Peace; in the Psalms, Salem is used as an abbreviated name for Jerusalem.
Old forms: *Shalom*

SALIM (sah-LEEM) Arabic: Safe
Salam; Selim

SALMALIN (sahl-mah-leen) Hindi: Claw

SALMONEUS Greek, Latin: King of Elis who pretended to be equal to Zeus by driving around in a bronze chariot and imitating Zeus' thunder and lightning.

SALTON English: From the willow tree town or settlement; surname
Salhtun; Saltin, Salten

SALVADOR (SAHL-vah-dor) Latin, Spanish: Savior; given in reference to Jesus Christ
(Italian) *Salvatore, Salvatorio;* (Spanish) *Salbatore, Salvadore, Salvino, Xabat, Xalbador, Xalvador; Salvator;* **Nicknames:** *Sal;* **Famous namesakes:** Artist Salvador Dali

SAMI Arabic, Persian: Elevated, exalted; (Finnish) asked of God; short form of Samuli

> *"Name is a fence and within it you are nameless."*
> —Samuli Paronen, Finnish writer

SAMMAN Arabic: Grocer, butter merchant

SAMSON (SAM-sən) Hebrew: Sun. The biblical Samson was an Israelite judge given superhuman strength by God. His power diminished when Delilah, his Philistine mistress, learned his strength was in his long hair and had his locks shorn.
(English) *Sampson; Sanson*

SAMU (SAH-moo) Finnish: Asked of God; short form of Samuli

SAMUEL (SAM-yoo-əl) Hebrew: Told by God. The biblical Samuel was a judge and prophet in early Israel who annointed Saul and David as kings. Two Old Testament books are named for him. See also *Samu* (Finnish) *Samuli*; (Hungarian) *Samuka*; (Yiddish) *Schmuel*; *Samoel, Schmaiah; Samual, Samuell, Samualle*; **Nicknames:** *Sam, Sammy, Sami*; **Famous namesakes:** Irish playwright Samuel Beckett, actor Samuel Jackson, opera singer Samuel Ramey, actor Sammy Davis Jr., baseball player Sammy Sosa; **Star babies:** sons of Bob Dylan, Sally Field, Jason Hervey, Jeremy Irons, Jessica Lange and Sam Shepard

> *"A self-made man may prefer a self-made name."*
> —Learned Hand, granting court permission for Samuel Goldfish to change his name to Samuel Goldwyn

SANDERS English: Alexander's son; surname

SANDERSON English: Alexander's son

SANDY English: Defender of man; abbreviation of Alexander
Famous namesakes: Pitcher Sandy Koufax

SANI (SAH-nee) Native American: The old one, age implying wisdom (Navajo)

SANJAR Persian: Emperor, king

SANJAY (sahn-jay) Hindi: Victorious

SANJIRO (sahn-jee-ro) Japanese: Admired, praiseworthy

SANJIV (sahn-jeev) Hindi: Long life
Sanjeev

SANTIAGO (sahn-tee-AH-go) Spanish: Saint James. Santiago is the capital and largest city of Chile.

SANTO (SAHN-to) Italian: Sacred, holy, saint
(Spanish) *Sancho, Santos*; **Diminutive forms:** *Santino*

SAQR Arabic: Falcon

SARAD (sah-RAHD) Hindi: Born during the fall

SARKIS (SAR-kis) Armenian: Variation of Sergio

SARSOUR Arabic: Bug; masculine version of Sarsoura

SASHA (SAH-shah) Russian: Nickname for Alexander

SASSON Hebrew: Joy

SATCHEL American: Small bag, sack
Nicknames: *Satch*; **Famous namesakes:**
Baseball player Satchel Paige; **Star babies:** son
of Woody Allen and Mia Farrow

SATURN (SA-tərn) Latin: Saturn was the
god of the harvest in early Roman mythology.
Saturn is also the second largest planet in our
solar system and has seven rings around it.
(Spanish) *Saturnin*; (Welsh) *Sadwm*;
(Basque) *Satordi*

SAUL (SAWL) Hebrew: Inquired of God;
name of the first king of Israel and the
Hebrew name of the apostle Paul before his
conversion to Christianity
Famous namesakes: Author Saul Bellow

SAVILLE (sah-VEE) French: From the
willow farm; surname
Sauville, Savill; Savile; **Famous namesakes:**
Designer Peter Saville

SAVION (SAY-vee-ən, ZAY-vee-ən)
Contemporary: Possibly derived from Xavier
Famous namesakes: Tap dancer Savion
Glover

SAWYER (SOI-ər) English, Celtic:
Woodcutter. This surname is familiar to many
as the main character of Mark Twain's classic
novel *The Adventures of Tom Sawyer*.
Sawyere, Sawyers; **Star babies:** son of Kate
Capshaw and Steven Spielberg

SAXON (SAK-sən) English, Teutonic:
Swordsman, knife. Saxons were among the
Germanic tribes who invaded and settled
fifth-century England.
Saxan, Saxton

SAYER Welsh: Carpenter; surname
Saer, Sayers, Sayre, Sayres; **Famous
namesakes:** British musician Leo Sayer

SAYYID Arabic: Master

SCHUYLER (SKIE-lər) Dutch: Shelter, scholar
Schylar, Schyler, Skyelar, Skylar, Skyler, Skylor

SCOTT English, Scottish: From Scotland, a
Gael; also a surname
Scot, Scottas; **Nicknames:** *Scottie, Scotty*;
Famous namesakes: Basketball player Scottie
Pippen, musician Scott Joplin

SCULLY Irish, Gaelic: Herald; surname
Old forms: *Scolaighe*

SEABERT English: Glory at sea
Saebeorht, Seabright, Seaburt, Sebert

SEAGHDA Irish: Majestic

SEAMUS (SHAY-mus) Gaelic: Supplanter;
variant of James
Seumas, Shamus, Shemus

SEAN (SHAWN) Irish: God has been
gracious; a very popular variant of John
*Seanan, Shaan, Shain, Shaine, Shan, Shandon,
Shandy, Shane, Shann, Shauden, Shaughn,
Shaun, Shaundre, Shawn, Shayne, Shonn*;
Famous namesakes: Actor Sean Astin,
actor Sean Connery, actor Sean Penn; **Star
babies:** sons of Mark Harmon, John Lennon
and Yoko Ono, Britney Spears and Kevin
Federline, Oliver Stone, Tatum O'Neal and
John McEnroe, Pierce Brosnan

---

*"The most important thing
in my father's life? World
peace. Me and my brother.
My mom."*
—Sean Taro Ono Lennon regarding his
father, John Lennon

SEARLE English, Teutonic: Armed, manly
Searlas, Searlus

SEATON (SEET-ən) Anglo-Saxon, English: The town or settlement near the sea; surname *Seeton, Seton*

SEB Egyptian: God of the earth

SEBASTIAN (sə-BAS-chən) Latin: Revered or the Roman term for a person from the ancient city of Sebastia; A third-century martyred centurion became Saint Sebastian, patron saint of soldiers.
(French) *Sebastien*; (Italian) *Sebastiano*; (Spanish) *Bastian, Sevastian*; (Hungarian) *Sebestyen, Sebo*; *Sabastian, Sebasten*; **Old forms:** *Sebastianus*; **Nicknames:** *Baz*; **Famous namesakes:** British track star Sebastian Coe; **Star babies:** son of James Spader

SEDGELEY English: From the sword meadow, referring possibly to a sharp vegetation in the meadow, possibly to a meadow owned by a swordsman, possibly a training meadow for swordsmen; surname *Sedgley, Sedgely, Sedgelea, Sedgleigh*

SEEGER English: Seaman; surname *Seager, Segar, Seger*; **Famous namesakes:** Musician Pete Seeger, musician Bob Seger

SEFU (SE-foo) Egyptian: Sword

SEGENAM Native American: Idle (Algonquin)

SEGUNDO (say-GOON-do) Spanish: Born second

SEIJI (say-jee) Japanese: Lawful, manages affairs of state
Famous namesakes: Japanese conductor Seiji Ozawa

SEITH Welsh: Seven

SEKANI (se-KAH-nee) Egyptian: Full of laughter

SELBY English: From the manor village or estate; a surname and possible variant of Shelby

SELIG German: Blessed, happy in life *Saelig, Sealey, Seeley, Seely, Selik, Zelig; Zelik, Zeligman, Zelyg*; **Old forms:** *Seelig*; **Famous namesakes:** Baseball commissioner Bud Selig

SENUSNET (se-NOOS-net) Egyptian: Name of a pharaoh

SEPPO (SAY-po) Finnish: Smith

SEPTIMUS Latin: Born seventh

SERAPHIM (SER-ə-fim) Hebrew: Fiery. Seraphim are angels of heaven, each with three pairs of wings and known for their strong love.
(Spanish) *Serafin*; *Serafim*; *Serafino, Sarafino*

SERAPIS (sə-RAH-pis, sə-RAY-pəs) Egyptian: Variant for the god Apis. Serapis was mainly worshipped in Alexandria, and was later worshipped by the Greeks as Zeus. He was never fully accepted by the Egyptians in the Ptolemaic period.

SERENO Latin: Calm
Old forms: *Serenus*

SERGE (SAYRZH) French: Variation of Sergio

SERGIO (SER-hee-o) Latin, Italian: Servant (French) *Serge*; (Russian) *Sergei, Seriozha, Seriozhenka*; (Polish) *Sergiusz, Serjuisz*; (Armenian) *Sarkis*; *Sergeo*; **Old forms:** *Sergios, Sergius*; **Famous namesakes:** Film director Sergio Leone

SETH Hebrew: Compensation. Seth was the third child of Adam and Eve, so named because God gave Eve another son after Abel had been killed; (Egyptian) the god of storms

and the desert, son of Geb and Nut, and brother of Osiris (and later, his murderer); In the Heliopolitan Ennead, this god was in the form of an animal with no zoological equivalent and is hence identified with many animals. The Greeks equated him with Typhon.
Set, Sutekh; **Star babies:** son of Sylvester Stallone

SETHOS (SE-thos) Egyptian: Name of a prince

SEVRIN Latin: Strict, restrained; a saint's name
(French) *Severin*; (Spanish) *Severo*; (Polish) *Seweryn*; *Severn, Severne*; **Old forms:** *Severus*

SEWARD (SOO-ərd) English: Sea guardian; a surname. William Henry Seward was the secretary of state during the American Civil War. While in office, he oversaw the purchase of Alaska from Russia. At the time, Alaska did not seem valuable to the United States, and the purchase was called "Seward's Folly."
Old forms: *Saeweard*

SEXTUS Latin: Bom sixth
Sixtus

SEYMOUR English: Marshy land near the sea

SHABAKA (SHA-bə-kə) Egyptian: Name of a king

SHAHAB Persian: Shooting star, meteor

SHAHAM Persian: The exact meaning of this name is unknown, though it is derived from the Persian word shah, meaning king.

SHAHIN Persian: Falcon
Shaheen

SHAKA (SHAH-kah) African: The name of the Zulu tribal leader sometimes compared to Attila the Hun. Shaka shaped an amalgamation of tribes into the great Zulu nation in the early nineteenth century. (Zulu); (Hindi) from the Shaka

SHAKIR Arabic: Grateful; masculine form of Shakira
Shakeer

SHAKOUR Arabic: Grateful
Shakur, Shakoor

SHALYA Hindi: Throne

SHAMBA Hindi: Son of Krishna

SHAMI Hindi: Husband

SHAMIL Persian: The north wind

SHAN Gaelic: Old, wise

SHANDLEY English: From the loud or boisterous meadow; surname
Scandleah; *Shandlea, Shandlee, Shandleigh*; **Nicknames:** *Shandy*

SHANE Irish: Variant of Sean, a popular Irish cognate of John. *Shane* was a successful Western motion picture of the 1950s.

SHANKARA (shan-kar-ah) Hindi: To bring luck or happiness

SHANNON Irish: Old and wise; from the Shannon, a river of Ireland
Shannen; **Famous namesakes:** Football player Shannon Sharpe

SHAQUILLE Arabic: Handsome; contemporary spelling of Shakil
Shakil, Shaqeel, Shaqueel, Shaquil; **Nicknames:** *Shaq*; **Famous namesakes:** Basketball player Shaquille O'Neal

SHARIF (shah-REEF) Arabic: Spelling variation of Sherif
Sherif, Charif, Cherif, Shereef, Shareef;
Famous namesakes: Egyptian actor Omar Sharif

SHAW English: From the shady grove; (Irish) surname.

SHEA (SHAY) Irish: Hawklike or majestic; an Irish family name and the name of New York's Shea Stadium
Shae, Shai, Shay, Shaye, Shey; **Star babies:** son of John Grisham

SHEARY (SHEER-ee) Irish: Variation of Jeffrey

SHEFFIELD English: From the crooked field; surname
Scaffeld

SHELBY English: From the village or estate on the ledge. Though appropriate for boys or girls, use for boys has declined while use for girls has risen in recent history.
(Anglo-Saxon) *Shelny; Selby; Selbey;* **Star babies:** son of Reba McEntire

SHELDON English, Anglo-Saxon: A farm in a deep valley.
Shelden

SHELLEY Anglo-Saxon, English: From the ledge meadow; a surname evocative of the poet Percy Bysshe Shelley
Shelly

SHELTON English: From the ledge town or settlement; surname
Scelftun

SHEM Hebrew: Renown, name, as in one of note. The biblical Shem was the eldest of Noah's three sons and therefore, according to lore, an ancestor of the human race.

SHEPHERD English: Shepherd
Shepard, Shephard; **Nicknames:** *Shep;*
Famous namesakes: Newsman Shepard Smith

SHEPLY Anglo-Saxon, English: From the sheep meadow (sheep being extremely important to the English economy and culture); surname
(English) *Sceapleigh; Shepley, Shipley*

SHERIDAN (SHER-i-dən) Irish: Untamed
Sheriden, Sheridon

SHERIF (sha-REEF) Arabic: Illustrious, noble, honorable, respectable, honest. Sharif is a term used to describe Mohammed's descendants.
Ashraf, Sharif; Sharif, Shereef, Shareef, Cherif, Charif; **Famous namesakes:** Egyptian actor Nour El-Sherif

SHERLOCK English: Blond; made famous by the Sherlock Holmes detective stories by Sir Arthur Conan Doyle

SHERMAN English: Cuts the nap of woolen cloth. In medieval times, the shireman served as governor-judge of an English shire or county.
(German) *Shermon*

SHERWIN English: Swift, quick as the wind
Sherwyn

SHERWOOD English: From the bright forest. Sherwood Forest in England has long been associated with the legendary hero Robin Hood.

SHESHA (she-shah) Hindi: King of serpents

SHILAH Native American: Brother (Navajo)

SHILOH (SHIE-lo) Hebrew: The peaceful one, he who is to be sent. In the Bible, Shiloh

is a prophetic name for the Messiah. Shiloh is also significant as the site of a crucial battle in the American Civil War.
Shilo

SHIMON Hebrew: Son of Simon
Old forms: *Shim'on*; **Famous namesakes:** Israeli prime minister Shimon Peres

SHIMSHON Hebrew: Bright sun

SHIRIKI Native American: Coyote (Pawnee)

SHIRON Hebrew: Songfest

SHIVA (SHI-vah) Hindi: God of the moon

SHIYE Native American: Son (Navajo)

SHIZHE'E Native American: Father (Navajo)

SHODA (sho-dah) Japanese: Flat and level field

SHU (SHOO) Egyptian: The god of air and the bearer of heaven. Shu was an ancient cosmic power who, with Tefnut, formed the first pair of gods in the Heliopolitan Ennead. He is represented as a man separating the sky from the earth.

SHUNNAR Arabic: Bird

SIAMAK Persian: Black-haired man

SIARL (SHARL) Welsh: Variation of Charles

SIBLEY Latin: Prophetic

SICHEII Native American: Grandfather (Navajo)

SIDNEY French, English: Uncertain meaning. Sidney may be from a French place name, Saint Denis. Another theory states that

this name stems from Old English meaning *wide island*. Sidney is favored for boys, while Sydney is used almost entirely for girls.
Cydney, Sydney; **Nicknames:** *Cyd, Sid, Syd*; **Famous namesakes:** Actor Sidney Poitier, hockey player Sidney Crosby

SIDONUS Latin: Follower of Saint Denis, the martyred Bishop of Paris
(Czech) *Zdenek*

SIEGFRIED (SIG-freed) German: Victorious peace; a dragon-killing hero of Germanic legend
Siegfred, Sigfrid, Sigfried, Sigifrid, Sigifrith

SIGMUND (SIG-mənd) German: Victorious protection
(Norse) *Sigurd, Sigvard*; (Polish) *Zygmunt*; *Sigismondo, Sigismund, Sigmond, Zsigmond*; **Nicknames:** *Zsiga, Siggy, Ziggy*; **Famous namesakes:** Austrian psychiatrist Sigmund Freud; **Star babies:** son of Jackie Jackson and Enid Spann

SIGWALT German: Victorious ruler
Sigiwald, Sigwald

SIJUR Norse: Victorious defender

SIKE Native American: He sits at home (Navajo)

SILAS English: Variation of Silvain

SILVAIN (sil-VAYN) Latin: Of the forest; referring to the mythological Roman god of trees
(English) *Selvyn, Silas, Sylvester*; (German) *Silvan, Silvester*; (French) *Silvestre*; (Italian) *Silvio*; (Spanish) *Silvanio, Silvano*; (Portuguese) *Silverio*; *Silio, Silos, Silvanos, Sylvan, Sylvanus*; **Old forms:** *Silvanus, Silvius*; **Nicknames:** *Sil, Sill*; **Famous namesakes:** French animator Sylvain Chomet

SILVESTER German: Variation of Silvain
Sylvester, Sly; **Famous namesakes:** Actor
Sylvester Stallone

SIMAO Hebrew: Obedient

SIMCHA Hebrew: Joy

SIMON Hebrew: Hearkening, listening.
There were several men named Simon in the
Bible, including Simon Peter, one of Christ's
twelve disciples. See also *Ximenes*
(Hebrew) *Siomon*; (Greek) *Symeon*; (French)
Simeon; (Gaelic) *Sim*; (Russian) *Semyon*;
(Finnish) *Simo*; *Simen, Simpson, Symon,
Ximen, Ximon, Ximun*; **Famous namesakes:**
British director Simon West, musician Paul
Simon, playwright Neil Simon; **Star babies:**
son of Phil Collins

SINCLAIR French, English, Scottish: Saint
Clair
Sinclaire; **Famous namesakes:** Author Sinclair
Lewis

SINDRI Norse: A mythical dwarf
Star babies: son of Björk

SINJON (SIN-jən) English: Holy, sanctified;
a name honoring Saint John
Sinjin; Sinjun

SINON Greek: A Greek spy who gained the
trust of the Trojans during the Trojan War by
pretending to be on their side

SIODHACHAN Irish: Little peaceful one

SION (SHON) Welsh: Variation of John

SIOR (SHOR) Welsh: Variation of George

SISYPHUS (SIS-e-phəs) Greek: Son of
Aelous

SIWILI Native American: Tail of the fox

SKAH Native American: White (Sioux)

SKANDA (skahn-dah) Hindi: God of war

SKEET English: Swift
Skeat, Skete, Sketes; **Famous namesakes:** Actor
Skeet Ulrich

SKIPPER English: Captain
Skippere; **Nicknames:** *Skip, Skippy*

SKYE English: Refers to the Scottish Isle of
Skye; a nature name referring to the sky

SLADE English: From the valley; surname
Slaed; Slayde; **Star babies:** son of David Brenner

SLATER English: Roof slater; surname for
one who installs slate roofs
Star babies: son of Angela Bassett and
Courtney B. Vance

SLAVIN Gaelic: Mountain; surname
Sleven, Slevin, Slevyn

SLAVOCHKA Slavic: Glory

SLOAN Gaelic, Scottish: Warrior, fighter;
surname
Sloane

SMEDLEY English: From the flat meadow
Smetheleah; Smedlea, Smedleigh, Smedly

SMITH English: Tradesman, blacksmith;
surname
Smyth, Smythe; **Famous namesakes:** Actor
Will Smith

SOBHI Arabic: Spelling variation of Sabih
Sobhy; **Famous namesakes:** Egyptian
comedian Mohammed Sobhy, Egyptian artist
and painter Magdi Sobhy

SOCRATES (SAHK-rə-teez) Greek:
Meaning unknown. Socrates was an ancient

and influential Greek philosopher and teacher.

SOHRAB (so-rahb) Persian: A name from Persian mythology and character in Shahnameh

SOL (SOL) Spanish: Sun

SOLOMON (SAHL-ə-mən) Hebrew: Peace; variant of Salem. Solomon (son of David and Bathsheba) succeeded his father as King of Israel. The Old Testament's Proverbs and Ecclesiastes are ascribed to him. (Arabic) *Sulaiman*; (Spanish) *Salomon*; (Turkish) *Suleyman*; (Yiddish) *Schlomo*; *Salamon*; **Nicknames:** *Sol*; **Famous namesakes:** Artist and writer Solomon Charles Levine

SOMNUS Latin: Sleep

SONGAA Native American: Strong

SONNY English: Son; a nickname and given name
Sonnie; **Famous namesakes:** Actor and politician Sonny Bono

SOREN (SO-ren) Danish: Strict; possibly a variant of Severin, Soren is the Danish form of Thor
Famous namesakes: Danish philosopher Soren Kierkegaard

SOROUSH Persian: Messenger

SORRELL (so-REL) French: Reddish-brown hair
Sorel

SOTERIOS Greek: Savior

SOUTHWELL English: From the southern well; surname

SOWI'NGWA Native American: Black-tailed deer (Hopi)

SPALDING English: From the split or divided field; a surname and well-known brand of sporting goods
Spelding; *Spaulding*; **Famous namesakes:** Humorist and author Spalding Gray

SPARTACUS (SPAHR-tə-kəs) Latin: From the city of Sparta

SPENCER English: Keeper of provisions
Spenser; **Nicknames:** *Spence*; **Famous namesakes:** Actor Spencer Tracy; **Star babies:** sons of Cuba Gooding Jr., Gena Lee Nolin

SQUIRE English: Shieldbearer
Squier; **Famous namesakes:** Actor Squire Fridell

STACY English: Productive; familiar form of Eustace
Famous namesakes: Actor Stacy Keach

STAMITOS Greek: Enduring
Stamatis

STANBURY English: From the stone fortress; surname adapted to first name use
Stanbeny; **Old forms:** *Stanburgh*

STANDISH English: From the stony park; a surname evocative of Pilgrim leader Miles Standish
Standisch

STANFIELD English: From the stony field; surname
Stanfeld; *Stansfeld*, *Stansfield*

STANFORD English: From the stony ford; a surname and the name of the prestigious Stanford University in California
Stamford; *Standford*

STANHOPE English: From the stony hollow; surname
Stanhop

STANISLAUS Slavic: Camp of glory, military glory; a name borne by Slavic kings and Saint Stanislaus, the patron saint of Poland
(Spanish) *Estanislao*; (Russian) *Stanislav*; *Stanislas, Stanislaw*; **Nicknames:** *Stannes, Stas, Stan*; **Famous namesakes:** Wrestler Stanislaus Zbyszko

STANLEY English: From near the stony meadow; a surname commonly used as a first name
Stanly; **Nicknames:** *Lee*; **Diminutive forms:** *Stan*; **Famous namesakes:** Director Stanley Kubrick; **Star babies:** son of M.C. Hammer

STANTON English: Stony town or village; surname
Stantun, Staunton; *Stanten*

STANWAY English: Stony road or path; surname
Stanweg

STANWICK English: Lives in or near the stony village; surname
Stanwic, Stanwik, Stanwyk

STANWOOD English: From the stony wood or forest; surname
Stanwode; **Nicknames:** *Stan, Woody*

STARBUCK English: Star deer, a prized deer. For many, this name likely conjures up images of piping hot java from the Starbucks coffee chain.

STAVROS Greek: Victorious

STEELE English: Hard or durable (as steel)
Steel

STEFAN (SHTE-fahn, STEF-ən) German: Variation of Stephen
Steffan, Steffon, Stefon, Stephon; **Famous namesakes:** Tennis player Stefan Edberg, basketball player Stephon Marbury

STEIN German: Stone; surname
(Swedish) *Sten*; *Steen, Steiner*; **Famous namesakes:** Actor Sten Eirik, actor Ben Stein

STEPHEN (STEEV-ən, STEF-ən) Greek: Crowned in victory. The New Testament portrays Stephen as an inspired leader of the church. A speech of his stirred an angry mob and he was stoned, becoming Christianity's first martyr.
(German) *Stefan*; (French) *Etienne, Stephane*; (Italian) *Stefano, Stephano*; (Spanish) *Esteban, Estebe, Estefan, Estevan, Estevon*; (Portuguese) *Estevao*; (Gaelic) *Steaphan, Stiabhan*; (Welsh) *Steffan, Steffen*; (Swedish) *Staffan*; (Russian) *Stepan, Stepka*; (Hungarian) *Istvan, Pista, Pisti*; *Steafan, Steffon, Stefon, Stephon, Stevan, Steven, Stevon, Stevyn*; **Old forms:** *Stefanos, Stephanos*; **Nicknames:** *Steve, Stevie*; **Famous namesakes:** Actor Stephen Baldwin, actor Steve Martin, author Stephen King, filmmaker Steven Spielberg

STERLING English, German: Of high quality, pure; refers to sterling silver, and may come from the star emblem found on early coins
Staerling, Starling, Sterlyn, Stirling; *Styrling*; **Famous namesakes:** Football player Sterling Sharpe

STETSON American: Cowboy hat

STEWART Scottish, English: Steward. A medieval steward was charged with the care of castle and estate affairs. Stuart and Stewart are clan names of the royal house of Scotland.
(English) *Stuart*; *Steward, Stewert*; **Nicknames:** *Stew*; **Famous namesakes:** Musician Stewart Copeland

STIG (STIG) Swedish: From the mount

STOCKLEY English: From the meadow of tree stumps; surname
Stocleah; *Stocklea, Stockleigh*

STORM English: Tempest, storm; nature name
Storme; **Famous namesakes:** Meteorologist Storm Field

STROM Czech: Stream, tree
Famous namesakes: Senator Strom Thurmond

STUART English: Variation of Stewart

SUFFIELD English: From the south field; surname
Suthfeld

SULAIMAN (soo-lah-ee-MAHN) Arabic: Variation of Solomon

SULLIVAN Irish: Dark eyes; surname
Sulliven; **Old forms:** *Suileabhan*; **Nicknames:** *Sully*

SULLY (SUL-ee) English: From the south meadow. Sully is the beloved monster from the animated movie *Monsters, Inc.* Sully is also a nickname for Sullivan.

SULO (SOO-lo) Finnish: Sweet

SULYA Hindi: God of the sun

SUMMER Contemporary: Born in summer
Sommer

SUNREET Hindi: Pure

SURI (SUR-ee) Hindi: Lord Krishna

SURTR Norse: A mythical giant

SUTCLIFF English: From the southern cliff; surname
Sutclyf, Suthclif, Suttecliff

SUTHLEY English: From the south meadow; surname
Suthleah

SUTTON English: From the southern settlement or town; surname

SVEN Scandinavian: Youth
Svein, Svend, Svens, Svewn, Sveyn; **Famous namesakes:** Director Sven Nykvist

SWAIN English: Knight's attendant
Swayn

TABBART German: Brilliant
Nicknames: *Tab*

TABER Irish: Well

TABIB Arabic: Physician
Tabeeb

TABOR (TAY-bə) Hebrew: Drum. In the Bible, Mount Tabor is a landmark mountain near Nazareth; (Hungarian) camp
Nicknames: *Tab*

TADD English: Nickname for Thaddeus

TADEO (tah-DAY-o) Spanish: Praise

TADLEIGH Irish: Bard

TAFT English: River
Nicknames: *Taffy*; **Famous namesakes:** President William Howard Taft

TAG Teutonic: Day; (Irish) handsome; a variant of Teague
Tage

TAGGART Gaelic: Son of a priest

TAHIR (TAH-heer) Arabic, African: Pure, purify
(Persian) *Taher*; *Tahu*; *Taher*

TAHKEOME Native American: Little robe
(Cheyenne)

TAIMA Native American: Thunderclap
Taima, Taiomah, Tama, Tamah

TAJ African: Exalted (Urdu); (Sanskrit) crown
Star babies: son of Tito Jackson

TAJO (TAH-ho) Spanish: Cut, steep cliff

TAKEO (tah-kay-o) Japanese: Strong like bamboo

TAKIS (TAH-kis) Greek: Contemporary Greek variant of Peter

TAKODA (tah-ko-dah) Native American: Friend to everyone (Sioux)

TAL Hebrew, English: Dew

TALBOT English: To destroy bad messages; the surname of an aristocratic Irish family who gave this name to their bloodhound, thus creating a breed of dogs name Talbot.
Talbert, Talbott, Talford; **Nicknames:** *Tally*

TALEB (TAH-ləb) Arabic: Seeker
Talib

TALIESIN (tal-ee-ES-in) Welsh: Brow. In Welsh mythology, Taliesin was a wizard and bard who acquired the gift of prophecy.

TALON French, English: Claw
Tallon

TALUS Greek: In Greek legend, Talus was the son of Perdix and twelve-year-old nephew and apprentice of Daedalus. He surpassed his uncle in skill, however, by inventing the saw, potter's wheel, and compass for drawing circles.

TAMAR (TAH-mahr) Hebrew: Palm tree; the daughter of Judah in the Bible's Old Testament
(Russian) *Tamryn*; *Tamarr*

TAMAS (tah-mahsh) Hungarian: Variation of Thomas

TAMIR Arabic: Owns palm trees, date dealer, full of dates

TANGUY (tahn-GEE) French: Warrior

TANISHIA African: Born on Monday

TANJIRO (tahn-jee-ro) Japanese: High-valued second son

TANNER English: Leather worker; occupational surname
Tannere

TANTON English: From the quiet river farm

TAPIO (TAH-pee-o) Finnish: Finnish god of the forest, hunting, and animals

TARAFAH Arabic: Twinkling of an eye, sight, glance, to blink; can be used to imply nobility of birth from both parents

TAREK Arabic: This name has several meanings including morning star, nocturnal visitor, and to knock at a door. In the year 711, a former slave, a Berber by the name of Tariq Ibn-Ziyad, led an army of about 7,000 Moors ashore at a point close to the huge rock which dominates the entrance to the Mediterranean. They called the rock

Jabal Tariq, or Tariq's Mount, and eventually western tongues changed the name to Gibraltar.
Tareq, Tarik, Tariq, Tareeq, Tarique, Tarick, Tareck; **Famous namesakes:** Egyptian writer Tarek Ali Hassan, director and producer Tarek El Kashef

TARIF Arabic: Unique, novel, rare, exquisite; often used to describe an interesting story

TARIQ (tah-REEK) Arabic: Spelling variation of Tarek. If emphasis is placed on the second syllable, Tariq additionally means way, road, or path.
Tarik; Tareeq

TARMO (TAHR-mo) Finnish: Energy

TARO (tar-o) Japanese: Big boy or first son

TARRANT Welsh: Thunder
Tarant, Tarynt

TASUNKE Native American: Horse (Dakota)

TATANKA PTECILA (tah-tahn-kah-pteh-see-lah) Native American: Short bull (Sioux)

TATE English: Cheerful; (Native American) he who talks too much; (Irish) measure of land
Tait, Tayt, Tayte

TAU African: Lion

TAURUS Latin: Bull. Taurus is a constellation picturing the forequarters of a bull and is a sign of the zodiac.
(Spanish) *Taurino, Tauro, Toro; Taurean*

TAVEY Latin: Nickname for Octavius

TAVIS (TA-vis) Scottish, Irish: Twin; possibly a variant of Thomas
Tavish, Tavon, Tevin, Tevis

TAVORIAN African: Misfortune

TAWEEL Arabic: Tall
Tawil, El Tawil, Al Taweel; **Famous namesakes:** Egyptian composer Kamal El-Tawil

TAYEB Arabic: Good, kind
Tayib; Tayyeb, Tayyheb

TAYLOR English: Tailor. Once a surname and boy's name, Taylor has become popular for both genders.
Taylan, Tayler, Taylon, Tylor; Tailor, Tayler; **Famous namesakes:** President Zachary Taylor

TEAGUE (TEEG) Celtic: A poet or philosopher
(Greek) *Tiege;* (Irish) *Tighe, Teaghue, Teauge;* **Nicknames:** *Tag*

TEARLACH Scottish: Variation of Charles

TEARLE English: Stern
Nicknames: *Tearley, Tearly*

TED English: Nickname for Theodore

TEDMUND English: National protector
Tedman

TEDRICK English: Variation of Theodore

TEEMU (TAY-moo) Finnish: Variation of Nicholas

TEETONKA Native American: Talks too much (Sioux)

TELAMON (TE-lə-mahn) Greek: In Greek mythology, Telamon was the son of Aeacus, King of Aegina. He was one of the Argonauts who accompanied Jason on the quest for the Golden Fleece, and was present at the hunt for the Calydonian boar.

TELFORD French: Ironworker
(Polish) *Telek*; *Telfer, Telfor, Telfour*

TELUTCI Native American: Bear making
dust (Miwok)

TEMPLETON English: Town near the
temple, very possibly related to strongholds
of the Knights-Templars; Templeton will
be recognized by children as the name
of Wilbur's rat friend in the classic book
Charlotte's Web.
Tempeltun; *Templeten*; **Nicknames:** *Temple,
Temp*

TENNYSON (TE-nə-sən) English: Spelling
variation of Dennison
Nicknames: *Tenny*; **Famous namesakes:**
English poet Alfred Tennyson; **Star babies:**
son of Russell Crowe

TERENCE Latin, English: Tender, good and
gracious; a Roman clan name
Tarrence, Terrance, Terrence; **Nicknames:**
Teris, Terry

TERIKA English: Masculine form of Teresa

TERO (TAYR-o) Finnish: Manly; short form
of Antero

TERRELL (TER-əl, tə-REL) English:
Powerful, thunder ruler; may be alluding to
Thor, the Norse god of thunder
*Terell, Terrall, Terrel, Terrelle, Terrill, Tirell;
Teral, Terryl, Teryl, Tarel, Tarrell, Terrel, Terall,
Terrel*; **Famous namesakes:** Football player
Terrell Davis, football player Terrell Owens

TERRIS English: Son of Terrell or Terry
Terriss, Terrys

TERRON English: Earthman; contemporary
rhyming blends of Ter– plus Darin.
Taren, Taron, Tarran, Tarrin, Terran, Terrin

TERRY English: Abbreviation of Terrance
and Terrell. Terry is also an Anglicized
phonetic form of the French given name
Thierry, from an older Germanic name
meaning powerful ruler.

TESHI African: Bright

TEVIN (TE-vin) Irish: Twin; possibly a
variant of Thomas

THAD Greek: Nickname for Thaddeus

THADDEUS (THAD-ee-əs) Greek: Meaning
uncertain, possibly brave or wise. Thaddeus
was one of the twelve apostles described in
the Bible's New Testament.
Thaddius, Thadeus; **Nicknames:** *Tad, Tadd,
Thad*

THAMYRIS Greek: In Greek mythology,
Thamyris was a poet who loved the beautiful
youth Hyacinthus.

THANE (THAYN) English, Scottish:
Follower; Shakespeare's Macbeth was Thane
of Cawdor.
Thayne

THANOS (THAN-os) Greek: Nobleman

THATCHER English: Roofer; an
occupational name
Thacher, Thacker, Thackere, Thaxter

THAW English: Melting ice

THAYER Teutonic: Nation's army

THEO Greek: Nickname for Theodore
Star babies: son of Kate Capshaw and Steven
Spielberg

THEOBALD (THEE-ə-bawld) Teutonic:
People's prince
(Irish) *Tibbot*; *Thibaud*; **Nicknames:** *Thilo*

THEODORE Greek: Gift of God; the name of saints, popes, and American president Theodore Roosevelt, for whom the teddy bear was originally named
(English) *Tedric, Tedrick*; (Italian) *Teodoro*; (Gaelic) *Teadoir*; (Welsh) *Tewdwr*; (Norse) *Theodrekr*; (Russian) *Fedor, Fedyenka, Feodor, Fyodor*; (Polish) *Teodor, Teos, Tolek*; (Hungarian) *Tivadar; Teodors, Theodon*; **Old forms:** *Theodoros*; **Nicknames:** *Fedya, Ted, Tedd, Teddie, Teddy, Teo, Teyo, Theo*; **Famous namesakes:** President Theodore Roosevelt, singer and actor Theodore Bikel, Russian author Fyodor Dostoyevsky

"The boy who is going to make a great man must not make up his mind merely to overcome a thousand obstacles, but to win in spite of a thousand repulses and defeats."
—Theodore Roosevelt

THEODRIC German: People's ruler; the original form of the more common names Derek and Dirk
Theodrik; **Old forms:** *Theodoric*; **Nicknames:** *Dedrick, Dieter, Thieny, Thierry*

THEOPHILE (tay-o-FEEL) French: Variation of Theophilus

THEOPHILUS (thee-AHF-ə-ləs) Greek: Divinely loved
(French) *Theophile*

THERON (THER-ən) Greek, French: Hunter, untamed
Therron

THILO German: Medieval short form of all German male names beginning with the prefix *Diet–* (as in Dietrich)

THOMAS Aramaic, Greek: Twin. In the New Testament, Thomas the apostle doubted the resurrection of Jesus. This name is also borne by several saints, including philosopher and theologian Saint Thomas Aquinas.
(French) *Thome*; (Italian) *Tommaso*; (Spanish) *Tomas*; (Irish) *Tomaisin*; (Welsh) *Tomos*; (Polish) *Tomasz, Tomek, Tomislaw*; (Finnish) *Tomi, Tommi*; (Hungarian) *Tamas; Thompson*; **Nicknames:** *Thom, Tom, Tommy*; **Famous namesakes:** Inventor Thomas Edison, president Thomas Jefferson; **Star babies:** sons of Dana Carvey, Jamie Lee Curtis and Christopher Guest

THOMKINS (TAHM-kinz) English: Little Tom

THOR Norse: Thunder; Mythological Thor was the Norse god of thunder and a son of Odin. His main weapon was a hammer named Mjollnir. The day Thursday was named for Thor. See also *Thorbert*
(Scandinavian) *Thoren, Thorian; Thorin, Tor*

THORALD Norse: Thor ruler

THORBERT Teutonic: Glorious as Thor

THORLEY English, Teutonic: From Thor's meadow; surname
Thurleah, Thurleigh, Torley; Thorlea, Thorlee, Thorleigh, Thorly

THORMOND English: Thor's protection
Thormod, Thormund

THORNLEY English: From the thorny meadow; surname
Thornly; Thornlea, Thornleigh

THORNTON (THORN-tən) Gaelic: Town of thorns. Thorn variants are English surnames occasionally used as given names. *Thorntun*; **Nicknames:** *Thorn*

THOROLF (TOR-rolf) Scandinavian: Thor's wolf

THORPE English, Teutonic: From the village *Thorp*; **Famous namesakes:** Athlete Jim Thorpe, Australian swimmer Ian Thorpe

THOTH (THAHTH) Egyptian: Moon god; associated with wisdom and sacred writing

THUNDER English: Stormy tempered

THURLOW English: From Thor's hill **Nicknames:** *Thurl, Thurle*

THURMAN Scandinavian: Thunder; a surname and variant of Thor

THURMOND English: Thor's protection

THURSTON Scandinavian, English, Teutonic: Thor's stone, thunder; surname adapted to first name use (Teutonic) *Thorsten*; (Norse) *Thorstein*; (Swedish) *Torsten*; *Thurstan, Thurstun*

TIASSALE African: It is forgotten

TIBBOT Irish: Variation of Theobald

TIBOR Slavic: Holy place

TIERNAN (TEER-nən) Celtic: Lord, chief *Tiernay*; **Nicknames:** *Tier*

TIHKOOSUE Native American: Short (Algonquin)

TILDEN English: From the fertile valley; surname *Tiladene*; *Tillden, Tildon*

TILFORD English: From the fertile ford

TILL (TIL) German: Medieval pet form of all German male names beginning with the prefix Diet- (as in Dietrich)

TILLMAN English: Virile; (German) mighty *Tilman*; **Nicknames:** *Till*

TILTON English: From the fertile town or estate; surname *Tillton*

TIMO (TEE-mo) Finnish: Variation of Timothy

TIMOTHY Greek: One who honors God. The biblical Timothy was a young Christian friend of Paul in the New Testament. (Greek) *Timotheos, Timun*; (English) *Timon*; (Spanish) *Timoteo*; (Irish) *Tiomoid*; (Welsh) *Timotheus*; (Polish) *Tymek, Tymon, Tymoteusz*; (Finnish) *Timo*; **Nicknames:** *Tim, Timmy*; **Famous namesakes:** Actor Timothy Hutton, actor Tim Robbins, comedian Tim Allen; **Star babies:** son of Tim Roth

TITOS Greek: Of the giants

TITUS (TIE-təs) Latin, Greek: Hero; an early Christian missionary and companion to Paul. See also *Titos* (Italian) *Tito*; *Tityus*; **Famous namesakes:** Tito Jackson

TOBIAS (to-BIE-əs) Greek: God is good; a form of Tobiah, an Old Testament Hebrew name (Hebrew) *Tobiah*; (English) *Tobin, Tobyn*; (Finnish) *Topias*; **Nicknames:** *Tobey, Tobie, Toby, Topi*

TOBY English: Nickname for Tobias *Tobey, Tobie*; **Famous namesakes:** Actor Tobey Maguire

TOCHO Native American: Mountain lion (Hopi)

TODD English, Scottish: Fox; a clever or wily person.
Tod; **Famous namesakes:** Designer Todd Oldham, skater Todd Eldredge

TOGQUOS Native American: Twin (Algonquin)

TOHOPKA Native American: Wild beast (Hopi)

TOIVO (TOY-vo) Finnish: Hope

TOKALA (to-kah-lah) Native American: Fox (Sioux)

TOLAND Anglo-Saxon, English: From the toll or taxed lands; surname
Tolan, Tolland

TOLMAN English: Collects taxes

TOM English: Nickname for Thomas
Thom; **Nicknames:** *Tommie, Tommy*; **Famous namesakes:** Actor Tom Cruise, actor Tom Hanks, designer Tommy Hilfiger

TOMKIN English: Little Tom

TOMLIN English: Little twin

TOMMASO (to-MAHS-o, to-MAHZ-o) Italian: Variation of Thomas

TOOANTUH Native American: Spring frog (Cherokee)

TORIN (TOR-ən) Irish, Scottish: Chief; also a variant of Torrance
Toryn

TORKEL Swedish: Thor's kettle
Torquil

TORMEY Irish: Thunder spirit
Tormaigh

TORMOD (TOR-mitch) Gaelic: Variation of Norman

TORRANCE (TOR-ənts) Gaelic, Scottish: From the knolls. Torr is a name for a craggy hilltop and also may refer to a watchtower.
Toran, Torean, Torence, Torion, Torran, Torrans, Torrence, Torrian; **Nicknames:** *Tor, Toren, Torey, Torr, Torrey, Torrie, Torry, Tory*

TORSTEN Teutonic: Spelling variation of Thurston

TORU (to-roo) Japanese: To deify or pass, absorb

TOSHI (to-shee) Japanese: Superior, fast, has advantage or is auspicious

TOSHIRO (to-shee-ro) Japanese: Talented, intelligent, or fast

TOVI (TO-vee) Hebrew: My goodness
Tohy

TOWLEY English: From the town meadow; surname
Townly, Tunleah; Townlea

TRACY French: From Thracia; a surname taken from a Norman French place name.
Tracey; **Nicknames:** *Trace*; **Star babies:** son of Ice-T

TRAHERN (tra-HERN) Celtic, Welsh: Strong as iron

TRAUGOTT Teutonic: God's truth

TRAVIS French: Crossing or crossroads (French) *Travers*; **Star babies:** son of Kyra Segdwick and Kevin Bacon

TREASACH Irish: Warlike
Treacy, Treasigh

TREMAINE English: House made of stone
Tramaine, Tremain, Tremayne

TRENT Latin: Swift rapid stream; a city in Italy; (French) thirty

TRENTON English: Rapid river or stream; the capital of New Jersey
Trenten, Trentin

TREVELYAN (tree-VEL-yahn) Welsh: From Elian's home or a fair town
Traveon, Travion, Travon, Trevan, Trevelian, Treven, Trevian, Trevion, Trevon, Trevonn, Trevyn

TREVES French: A place name and surname

TREVOR (TRE-vər) Welsh: Large village
Trevin; **Star babies:** son of Wayne Gretzky and Janet Jones

TREY (TRAY) English: Three; a variant of Traigh
Traigh; **Star babies:** son of Will Smith and Sheree Zampino

TRIPPER English: Traveler
Nicknames: *Trip, Tripp, Tryp, Trypp*

TRISTAN Celtic: Full of sorrows; a variant of Tristam. In Arthurian legend, Tristan was a knight of the Round Table and tragic hero of the medieval tale Tristram and Isolde. (Welsh) *Trystan; Tristen, Tristian, Tristin, Tristyn*; **Old forms:** *Tristam, Tristram*; **Star babies:** sons of Wayne Gretzky and Janet Jones, Natasha Henstridge

> **The character of** Walter Shandy in Laurence Sterne's novel *Tristram Shandy* believes that names are as important to a person's character as noses are to a person's appearance. Walter's solution to the problem of his new child's crushed nose is to name him Trismegistus, the name of the greatest king, lawgiver, philosopher, priest, and engineer of all time. Walter's rationale is that if one does not have a sizable nose, he at least has a chance in life if he has a significant name, and this is one of the best. In the end, however, his child is accidentally christened with the name Tristram, which Walter considers the worst name in the world.

TRISTRAM Arthurian legend: Original form of Tristan

TRITON (TRIE-tən) Latin, Greek: In Greek mythology, Triton is the son of Poseidon and Amphitrite and lived with them in a golden palace under the sea. Triton was represented as having the body of a man with the tail of a fish.

TROY Irish: A foot soldier. The ancient city of Troy was made famous in Greek legends. *Troi, Troye, Troyes*; **Famous namesakes:** Football player Troy Aikman; **Star babies:** sons of Jane Fonda and Tom Hayden, Leeza Gibbons

TRUESDALE English: From the beloved one's farm
Truesdell, Truitestall

TRUMAN English: Loyal, honest
Trumen; **Nicknames:** *True, Tru*; **Famous namesakes:** Author Truman Capote, president Harry S. Truman; **Star babies:** son of Rita Wilson and Tom Hanks

TRUMBLE English: Strong or bold
Trumbald, Trumhall

TRYGVE (TREEG-və, TRIG-vee) Norse: Brave, trustworthy
Nicknames: *Tryg, Trig*

TUBANSI African: Enduring

TUCKER English: Tucker of cloth
Tuckere

TUKETU Native American: Bear making dust (Miwok)

TULIO Latin, Spanish: Lively

TULLIS Latin: Rank
Nicknames: *Tulley, Tully*

TULLIUS Latin: Name of a king

TULLY Irish: Peaceful

TUPI (TOO-pee) Native American: To pull up (Miwok)

TUPPER English: Ram herder
Tuppere

TURNER Latin: One who turns bone, wood, or metal on the lathe; (French) champion in a tournament

TUTANKHAMUN (too-tahn-KAH-mən) Egyptian: Name of a pharaoh. King Nebkheperura Tutankhamun (King Tut) remains the most famous of all the Pharaohs of Ancient Egypt, but in fact he was a short-lived and fairly insignificant ruler during a transitional period in history. Little was known of him prior to Howard Carter's methodical detective work, but the discovery of his tomb and the amazing contents it held ultimately ensured this boy king of the immortality he sought.

Tutankhamon, Tutankhamoun; **Nicknames:** *King Tut*

TUVIYA Hebrew: The biblical Tuviya was a Levite during the reign of Jehoshaphat.
Tuvya

TYLER English: Tile layer or a variant of Taylor, an English surname frequently used as a given name.
Taylar

TYR (TEER) Scandinavian: Warrior. Tyr was a daring and brave god of war in Norse mythology.

TYRE Latin: From Tyre

TYREE Scottish: Island dweller

TYREECE English: Form of Terrence

TYREL English: Powerful, thunder ruler; a form of Terrell
Tyrell, Tyrelle; **Star babies:** son of Jesse Ventura

TYRONE (tie-RON) Irish: From Owen's territory; the name of a county in Ireland; (Greek) sovereign
Tyronne; **Nicknames:** *Ty;* **Famous namesakes:** Actor Tyrone Power

TYRUS English: Modern blend of Tyrone and Cyrus; may also be a reference to the ancient Phoenician city of Tyre. See also *Tyre*
Tirus, Tyrrus, Tirrus; **Nicknames:** *Ty*

TYSON French: Hot tempered, firebrand; (English) the son of Ty, which is a form of the Greek God of wine, Dionysus
(English) *Tyvan; Tyeson, Tyesone;* **Nicknames:** *Ty, Tyce, Tye, Tyeis*

TZURIEL (ZOO-ree-el, tsoo-ree-EL) Hebrew: Rock of Jehovah
Zuriel

UBERTO (oo-BER-to) Italian: Variation of Hubert

UDELL English: From the yew tree valley; surname
Idal, Iwdael, Udale, Udall, Udayle, Yudell

UDOLF English: Prosperous or wealthy wolf
Udolph

UGO (OO-go) Italian: Variation of Hugh
Famous namesakes: Venezuelan President Hugo Chávez

ULF Scandinavian: Wolf

ULFRED English: Peaceful wolf

ULGER English: Warring or fighting wolf

ULL Norse: Glory; in Norse mythology, the god of winter and skiers

ULLOCK English: Sporting wolf
Ullok

ULMER English: Famous wolf
(Norse) *Ulfmaerr; Ulmar, Ulmarr*

ULRICH (UWL-rikh) German: Noble leader

ULYSSES (yoo-LIS-eez) Latin: Wrathful; variant of the Greek *Odysseus*, best known as a main character of the poet Homer's two great epics. Ulysses S. Grant commanded the Union armies during the Civil War and became president of the United States in 1868.
(Spanish) *Ulises*

UMBERTO (oom-BER-to) Italian: Variation of Humberto
Famous namesakes: Italian author Umberto Eco

UMI (OO-mee) African: Life

UNAI (oo-NIE) Basque: Cowherd

UNWIN English: Not a friend, implies stranger
Unwine, Unwyn

UPCHURCH English: From the upper church

UPTON (UP-tən) Anglo-Saxon, English: From the upper town or settlement; surname
Uptun; **Famous namesakes:** Author Upton Sinclair

UPWOOD English: From the upper forest
Upwode

URBAN (UR-bən) Latin: Of the city
(Spanish) *Urbano; Urbain*

URI (YOOR-ee) Hebrew: Light, flame; an Old Testament name that is also a short form of Uriah and Uriel

URIAH (yoo-RIE-ə) Hebrew: Light, flame
Urian, Uriel; **Nicknames:** *Uri*

URIEL (YUR-ee-əl) Hebrew: Spelling variation of Uriah

URIEN Arthurian legend: Privileged birth. In Arthurian legend, Urien was a king of Gore and the husband of Morgan Le Fay.

UZIAH (oo-ZIE-ə, ə-ZIE-ə) Hebrew: God is my strength; an Old Testament name
Uziel, Uzziah, Uzziel

VADIM (vah-DEEM) Russian: Attractive *Wadim*; **Famous namesakes:** French Director Roger Vadim (née Roger Vadim Plemiannikov)

VADIN (vah-DEEN) Hindi: Speaker

VAHAN Armenian: Shield

VAHID Persian: The only one

VAIL English: Lives in the valley; familar to many as the name of a ski resort town in Colorado
Bale, Vale, Vayle

VAL Latin: Nickname for Valerian
Famous namesakes: Actor Val Kilmer

VALDEMAR (VAHL-də-mahr) Swedish: Variation of Walter

VALENTINE Latin, English: Valiant, strong; variant of Valentinus and the name of more than 50 saints and three Roman emperors (English) *Valen*; (Italian) *Valentino*; (Spanish) *Valentin*; (Hungarian) *Balint*; *Valentyn*; **Nicknames:** *Val*

VALERIAN Latin: Valiant, brave, healthy. Valerian has a similar origin and meaning as Valentine but is not from the same name. See also *Valiant*
(Latin) *Valerius*; (Italian) *Valerio*; (Russian) *Valerik, Valery*; *Valera, Valerijs, Vallen*; **Nicknames:** *Val*

VALFRID Swedish: Variation of Walfried

VALI Norse: Uncertain meaning; Vali was a son of Odin in Norse mythology.

VALIANT English: Brave, strong, and healthy; main character of the historical adventure comic strip *Prince Valiant*

VALO (VAH-lo) Finnish: Light

VANCE English: Marshland; surname
Famous namesakes: Secretary of State Cyrus Vance

VARDON French: From the green hill; surname
Varden

VARICK Teutonic: Defending ruler
(English) *Warrick*; *Vareck, Varek, Varik*; *Varrick*

VARTAN (VAR-tan) Armenian: Giver of roses
Famous namesakes: Armenian musician Vartan Gevorkian

VAUGHN (VAWN) Welsh, Celtic: Little
Vaughan

VAVRIN Czech: Laurel

VELI (VE-lee) Finnish: Brother

VERN English: This surname is also used as an abbreviation of Vernon or Lavern.

VERYL French: True
Verel, Verrall, Verrell, Verrill

VESA (VES-ah) Finnish: Sprout, young tree

VICTOR Latin, Spanish: To conquer
(Italian) *Vittorio*; (Spanish) *Victoriano, Victorino, Victorio, Victoro*; (Russian) *Viktor*; (Polish) *Wictor*; (Hungarian) *Vidor*; **Nicknames:** *Vic, Vick, Victorien*; **Famous namesakes:** French author Victor Hugo

VICTORIO (vik-TOR-ee-o) Spanish: Variation of Victor

VIDAL French: Variation of Vito
Famous namesakes: Hair stylist Vidal Sassoon

VIGGO (VEE-go) Scandinavian: War
Famous namesakes: Actor Viggo Mortensen

VINCE Latin: Nickname for Vincent
Famous namesakes: Musician Vince Gill

VINCENT Latin: To conquer; the name of
several early saints in France
(Italian) *Vincenzio, Vincenzo*; (Spanish)
Vicente; (Hungarian) *Vincze*; *Vincens, Vinci,
Vincien, Vinzenz*; **Nicknames:** *Vince, Vinnie*;
Famous namesakes: Artist Vincent Van
Gogh; **Star babies:** son of Sophie Marceau

> "If one feels the need
> of something grand,
> something infinite,
> something that makes
> one feel aware of God, one
> need not go far to find it. I
> think that I see something
> deeper, more infinite, more
> eternal than the ocean in
> the expression of the eyes of
> a little baby when it wakes
> in the morning and coos or
> laughs because it sees the
> sun shining on its cradle."
> —Vincent Van Gogh

VINSON English: Vincent's son, Vinn's son
Vinsone

VIRGIL (VUR-jəl) Latin: Flourishing; most
commonly recognized as the name of the
Roman poet-philosopher and author of the
time-honored epic *The Aeneid*.
(Latin) *Verdell, Vernell*; (Spanish) *Virgilio*

VISHNU (VISH-noo) Hindi: Protector of the
worlds in the Hindu sacred triad

VITALY (vee-TAH-lee) Russian: Variation of
Vito
Vitaliy; **Nicknames:** *Vitalik, Vitya, Vitia*;
Famous namesakes: Gymnast Vitaly Scherbo

VITO Latin, Italian: Life; also a surname
(French) *Vidal*; (Spanish) *Videl*; (Russian)
Vitaly; (Polish) *Wit*; *Vital, Vitale*; **Old forms:**
Vitus; **Famous namesakes:** Actor Danny
DeVito

VLAD (VLAHD) Russian: To rule
Diminutive forms: *Vladik*

VLADIMIR (VLAHD-ə-meer, VLAD-ə-
meer) Slavic, Russian: To rule the land
Nicknames: *Volodya, Dima*; **Famous
namesakes:** Russian president Vladimir Putin

VLADISLAV (vlah-dee-SLAHF) Russian,
Slavic: Rules with glory
(Slavic) *Ladislas*; **Nicknames:** *Laszlo*

VLAS Russian: Slow

VOITTO (VOEET-to) Finnish: Victory

VOLGA (VOL-gah) Russian: Name of a river
in Russia

VOLKER (FAWL-ker) German: People's
guard, defender
Famous namesakes: German director Volker
Schlondorff

VUKAN Romanian: Possibly a variant of
Vulcan, the Roman smith god. The historical
Vukan was the son of Stephen, the founder of
the Nemanyid dynasty in Serbia.

WACIAN Anglo-Saxon: To keep watch, alert

WADE (WAYD) Anglo-Saxon: River ford; also a name from Scandinavian mythology
Waed, *Wayde*; **Famous namesakes:** Baseball player Wade Boggs

WADLEY (WAHD-lee) English: From Wade's meadow, from the ford meadow; surname
Wadeley, *Wadelea*, *Wadlea*, *Wadleigh*

WADSWORTH (WAHDZ-wərth) English: From Wade's estate; surname
Famous namesakes: Poet Henry Wadsworth Longfellow

WAGNER German: Wagon maker; an occupational surname
Famous namesakes: Composer Richard Wagner

WAINWRIGHT (WAYN-riet) English: Wagon maker; an occupational name and surname
Famous namesakes: Folk musician Loudon Wainwright

WAITE (WAYT) English: Guard, watchman; surname
Wait, *Wayte*

WAKEFIELD English: From Wake's field, from the damp field; surname
Wacfeld

WAKELEY English: From Wake's meadow, from the damp meadow; surname
Wacleah; *Wakelea*, *Wakeleigh*, *Wakeley*

WAKEMAN English: Watchman; an occupational name and surname
Wacuman; **Diminutive forms:** *Wake*

WALCOTT English: Cottage by the wall, possibly a Welshman's cottage; surname
Walcot; *Wallcot*, *Wallcott*, *Wolcott*

WALDEN English: From the wooded valley. For many, this name is associated with *Walden*, a classic piece of American literature from Henry David Thoreau.
Waldon

WALDO English: Nickname for Oswald
Famous namesakes: Author and poet Ralph Waldo Emerson

WALFORD English: From the Welshman's ford

WALFRED German: Spelling variation of Walfried

WALKER English: Worker in cloth; a surname and occupational name
Famous namesakes: Author Walker Percy; **Star babies:** sons of Anne Curry and Brian Ross, John Michael Montgomery, Adrienne Barbeau and Billy Van Zandt

WALLACE English, Scottish: Welshman. Sir William Wallace was a Scottish hero who led a revolt against King Edward I of England.
Wallis, *Walsh*, *Welch*, *Welsh*; **Nicknames:** *Wally*; **Famous namesakes:** Poet Wallace Stevens

WALT German: Nickname for Walter
Famous namesakes: Poet Walt Whitman

WALTER German: Powerful warrior, ruler of an army
(French) *Gauthier*, *Gautier*; (Italian) *Galterio*; (Spanish) *Galtero*, *Gualterio*; (Irish) *Ualtar*; (Swedish) *Valdemar*; (Dutch) *Wouter*; (Finnish) *Valtteri*; *Walten*, *Walthari*, *Walther*; **Nicknames:** *Walt*; **Famous namesakes:** English author Sir Walter Scott, news anchorman Walter Cronkite

WALTON English: From the Welshman's town or settlement

WALWYN English: Welsh friend

WAMBLEESKA (wam-blee-ska) Native American: White eagle (Sioux)

WARD English: Guard, watchman; an occupational name and surname
Warde, Warden, Weard, Worden; **Famous namesakes:** Fictional TV dad Ward Cleaver, actor Ward Bond

WARDLEY English: From the watchman's or guardian's meadow; surname
Weardleah; *Wardlea, Wardleigh*; **Nicknames:** *Ward, Lee*

WARFIELD English: From the field by the weir (trap for catching fish); surname
Weifield; **Famous namesakes:** Football player Paul Warfield

WARFORD English: From the ford near the weir (a trap for catching fish)
Weiford

WARLEY English: From the meadow near the weir (a trap for catching fish)
Warleigh, Weirley

WARNER German, English: Defending warrior
Famous namesakes: Actor Warner Baxter

WARREN English: Warrior; surname or place name
Famous namesakes: President Warren Harding, actor Warren Beatty

WASHBURN English: From the flooding brook
Washbourne, Washburne; *Washborn*

WASHINGTON English: From the intelligent one's town or settlement; surname
Famous namesakes: Author Washington Irving, educator Booker T. Washington

WASIM Arabic: Handsome

WATSON English: Son of Walter, son of Watt
Watkins, Wattekinson, Wattesone, Wattikinson, Wattkins, Watts, Wattson; **Famous namesakes:** Golfer Tom Watson

WAVERLEY English: From the meadow of quaking aspen trees; evocative of Sir Walter Scott's Waverly novels
Waefreleah; *Waverly, Waverlea, Waverlee, Waverleigh*; **Famous namesakes:** Cookbook author Waverly Root

WAYLAND English, Scandinavian: The land by the path or road. The mythological Scandinavian Wayland was a blacksmith with supernatural powers similar to Vulcan.
Waylan, Waylin, Waylon, Wegland, Weyland; Waylen, Weylan, Weylin, Weylon; **Nicknames:** *Way*; **Famous namesakes:** Singer Waylon Jennings

WAYNE English: One who makes or drives wagons
Wain; **Famous namesakes:** Hockey player Wayne Gretzky, entertainer Wayne Newton

WEATHERLY English: From the wether sheep meadow; a surname and variant of Wetherly

WEBBER German: Weaver
Webb, Webbe, Weber; **Famous namesakes:** British theatrical composer Andrew Lloyd Webber, jazz drummer Chick Webb

WEBLEY English: From the weaver's meadow; surname
Webbeleah; *Webbley, Weblea, Webbly, Webly*

WEIRLEY English: Spelling variation of Warley

WELBORNE (WEL-bərn) English: From the spring brook; no connection to aristocratic birth
Welborn, Welburn

WELBY English, German: Well-farm; name of a popular TV doctor *Marcus Welby, MD*

WELTON English: Place of the well, town near the well; surname

WENCESLAS (WEN-səs-laws) Slavic: More glory. Saint Wenceslas was a tenth-century duke of Bohemia murdered by his brother. He is the patron saint of the Czech Republic. This was also the name of several Bohemian kings.
(Hungarian) *Vencel*; *Wenceslaus*; **Nicknames:** *Vaclav*; **Famous namesakes:** Czech President Václav Havel

WENDELL German: Wanderer
Wendale, Wendall, Wendel; **Famous namesakes:** Attorney and presidential candidate Wendell Willkie

WERNER German: Defending warrior
(Finnish) *Verneri*

WESLEY English: From the western meadow; surname
Wessley, Westleah, Westley; *Weslie, Weslea, Wesleigh, Weslee*; **Diminutive forms:** *Wes*; **Famous namesakes:** Actor Wesley Snipes, General Wesley Clark

WESTBROOK English: From the western brook; surname
Westbroc; *Wesbrook, Westbrooke*; **Nicknames:** *Brook, Brooke, Wes, West*

WESTBY English: From the western farm; surname
Wesby, Westbee, Westbie

WESTCOTT English: From the western cottage; surname
Westcot; *Wescot, Wescott*; **Nicknames:** *Wes*

WESTON English: From the western town or settlement; surname

Westen, Westin, Westun; **Nicknames:** *West, Wes*; **Star babies:** son of Nicolas Cage

WETHERLY English: From the wether sheep meadow (sheep being extremely important to the English culture and economy); surname
Weatherby, Weatherly, Wetherby, Wethrby, Wethrleah; *Wetherby, Wetherlea*

WHARTON (WOR-tən) English: From the town or settlement near the weir (a trap for catching fish). This variant of Warton is recognized as the name of the Ivy League Wharton School of Business.
Warton, Wartun; **Famous namesakes:** Author Edith Wharton

WHEATLEY English: From the wheat meadow; surname
Wheatlea; **Old forms:** *Hwaeteleah*

WHEELER English: Wheel maker
Old forms: *Hweolere*

WHITBY (WIT-bee) English, Scandinavian: From the white farm; surname
Hwitby, Whitley; *Whitbey, Whitbee, Whitbie*; **Nicknames:** *Whit*

WHITCOMB English: From the white valley; surname
Whitcumb; *Whitcombe*; **Nicknames:** *Whit*

WHITFIELD English: From the white field; surname

WHITFORD English: From the white ford
Hwitford

WHITLAW English: From the small white hill; surname
Old forms: *Hwithloew*

WHITLOCK English: Blond, white locks of hair
Old forms: *Hwitloc*

WHITMORE English: From the white moor *Whitmoor*; *Whittemore, Witmore, Wittemore*

WHITNEY English, Anglo-Saxon: From the white island. In recent years, Whitney has been used more for girls than boys.

WHITTAKER (WIT-ə-kər) English: From the white acre

WICKHAM (WIK-əm) English: From the village paddocks; surname *Wiccum, Wickam*; **Famous namesakes:** British actor Jeffrey Wickham

WICKLEY English: From the village meadow; surname *Wicleah*; *Wichlea*

WILBUR German: Resolute, brilliant (German) *Wilbart*; *Wilber, Wilbert, Wilburn, Wilburt*; **Famous namesakes:** Aviation pioneer Wilbur Wright

WILEY English: Spelling variation of Wylie *Wylie*; **Famous namesakes:** Actor Wiley Wiggins

WILFRED English, Teutonic: Desires peace (German) *Wilfredo*; *Wilford, Wilfrid*

WILL English: Nickname for William **Famous namesakes:** Actor Will Smith; **Star babies:** son of Colin Firth and Meg Tilly

WILLIAM German: Resolute protector; *will* meaning *strong* and *helm* meaning *helmet*. For centuries after the Norman conquest in 1066, large numbers of English boys were given the name William in tribute to William the Conqueror. The firstborn son of Prince Charles is named William. (German) *Wilhelm*; (French) *Guillaume*; (Italian) *Guglielmo, Guillermo*; (Gaelic) *Uilleam, Uilliam*; (Welsh) *Gwilym*; (Swedish) *Vilhelm*; (Dutch) *Willem*; (Czech) *Vilem*;

(Finnish) *Viljami*; *Guilerme*; **Nicknames:** *Bill, Billie, Billy, Pim, Will, Willie, Willy, Wim*; **Diminutive forms:** *Liam, Lyam*; **Famous namesakes:** President William Jefferson Clinton, playwright William Shakespeare, actor William Hurt

"Heaven lies about us in our infancy!"
—William Wordsworth

WILLY English: Nickname for William

WILSON English: William's son; a surname often used as first name *Willesone, Williams, Williamson*; *Wilsyn, Willsyn, Wilsen, Wylson*; **Nicknames:** *Will, Willie, Willy*; **Famous namesakes:** Musician Wilson Pickett; **Star babies:** son of Christine Lahti and Thomas Schlamme

WIM German: Nickname for William **Famous namesakes:** German film director Wim Wenders

WINDSOR English: Riverbank with a winch; surname of the British royal family

WINFIELD English: Friend's field; surname *Winefeld, Winefield, Wynfield*; *Winnfield, Wynfeld*; **Famous namesakes:** Baseball player Dave Winfield

WINFRED English, Teutonic: Friend of peace. This surname is rarely used, perhaps because it sounds so similar to Winifred. *Winefrith, Winfrid, Winfrith, Winfryd, Wylfrid, Wynfred, Wynfrith*

WINSLOW English: Friend's hill, friend's place; surname *Winslowe*; **Famous namesakes:** Painter Winslow Homer

WINSTON English: From the friend's (or friendly) town or settlement, or from Wine's town or settlement; surname
Winton, Wynston, Wynton; Winsten, Winstonn, Wynstan; **Famous namesakes:** British prime minister Winston Churchill, jazz musician Wynton Marsalis

WINTER English: Seasonal name, born in the winter
Wynter; Winters, Wynters

WINTHROP (WIN-thrəp) English: Wine's estate

WOLCOTT English: Lives in Wolf's cottage (Wolf is a person's name, not the animal); surname
Woolcott, Wulfcot

WOODLEY English: From the wooded meadow; surname
Wodeleah

WOODROW English: From the cottages in the wood; woody
Woodroe, Woodrowe; **Nicknames:** *Woody, Woody;* **Famous namesakes:** President Woodrow Wilson, filmmaker Woody Allen

WOODWARD English: Forester
Nicknames: *Woody*

WULFHERE Anglo-Saxon: An early king of the Mercia

WYATT English: Guide
Wiatt; **Famous namesakes:** American frontiersman Wyatt Earp; **Star babies:** son of Goldie Hawn and Kurt Russell

WYCLIFF English: From the white cliff; surname
Wyclyf, Wyclyffe, Wyclef; **Nicknames:** *Cliff, Wyc, Wake;* **Famous namesakes:** Musician Wyclef Jean

WYLIE English: Well-watered meadow; sounds like wily, meaning beguiling or clever; (Anglo-Saxon) enchanting
Wiley

WYMAN (WIE-mən) Anglo-Saxon, English: Fair-haired man, possibly fair-haired warrior

WYN (WIN) Welsh: Fair
Wynne

WYNDHAM (WIN-dəm) English: From the windy village, hamlet; surname adapted to first name use
Windham

WYNN English, Welsh: Friend, fair. The root *wynn* is part of many English given names and surnames, emphasizing the importance of a good friend in life.
(Welsh) *Winn; Wyne*

WYNONO Native American: Firstborn, eldest (Sioux)

WYTHE (WIETH) English: Near the willow tree; surname adapted to first name use
Wyth

XANDER Greek: Diminutive form of Alexander

XANTHUS (ZAN-thəs) Greek, Latin: Golden-haired. In Greek mythology, an immortal horse belonging to Achilles, given the power of speech by Hera so that he could warn Achilles that he was about to die.

XAVIER (ex-SAH-vee-er, ZAY-vee-ər, ex-ZAY-vee-ər) Basque: The new house; popularized by the sixteenth-century Jesuit missionary Saint Francis Xavier
(Spanish) *Javier, Javiero, Xever;* (Basque) *Xaiver; Xabief, Zavier;* **Famous namesakes:** Cuban musician Xavier Cugat

XENOS (ZEE-nos) Greek: Stranger; also a common variant of Xenophon
Xeno

XERXES (ZURK-seez) Persian: Ruler over heroes, monarch; name of a fifth-century BC king of Persia. He attempted an invasion of Greece that ended unsuccessfully at the battle of Salamis.

XIMENES (hee-MEN-es) Spanish: Hearkening, listening; variant of Simon

XIOMAR (zhoh-MAHR) Spanish: Famous in battle; variant of Geomar

XUTHUS (ZOO-thəs) Greek: Son of Helen

XYLON (ZIE-lən) Greek: From the forest

YAEL Hebrew: Spelling variation of Jael

YAFEU (yah-FAY-oo) African: Bold

YAGIL Hebrew: He will rejoice
Yagel, Yagyl

YAHTO Native American: Blue (Sioux)

YAIR Hebrew: Enlighten

YALE Welsh: From the fertile hill; associated with Ivy League Yale University

YAMAL (yah-mahl) Hindi: One of a pair of twins

YANCY Native American: Englishman, derived possibly from *yankee*
Yancey, Yansey, Yauncey, Yanci

YARDEN Hebrew: Spelling variation of Jordan
Yardeni

YARDLEY English: From the enclosed meadow
Yardly; Yardlee, Yardlea, Yardleigh, Yarley, Yeardley

YARON Hebrew: He who sings, cry of joy
Jaran, Jaren, Jaron, Jarren, Jarron; Yairon

YASHA (YAH-shah) Russian: Russian familar form for Jacob or James
Yashka, Yashko

YASIN Arabic: Rich, prophet

YASIR Arabic: Easy, simple, homely, small; masculine version of Taysir

YATES English: Lives near the gates, gate keeper
Yeats; **Famous namesakes:** Irish poet and dramatist William Butler Yeats, Irish painter and writer John Butler Yeats

YAVIN Hebrew: He understands
Javin, Yabin

YAW African: Born on Thursday

YEHUDI Hebrew: Praised; variant of Judah
Yehuda; **Famous namesakes:** British violinist and conductor Yehudi Menuhin

YEOMAN (YO-mən) English: Retainer, attendant; a man born free. In England a yeoman is considered next in order to gentry.
Yoman; Youman

YERIEL Hebrew: Established by God
Jeriel

YESHAYA Hebrew: Gift

YEVGENY (yev-GYE-nee, eev-GYE-nee) Russian: Variation of Eugene
Famous namesakes: Russian conductor Yevgeny Svetlanov, Russian conductor Yevgeny Mravinsky

YIFTACH Hebrew: He will open

YIGAL Hebrew: He shall redeem, be redeemed
Yigel

YORK English: From the boar estate; from the yew town; place name, York in England, New York in the United States; Duke of York is a title held by the English royal family (usually a younger son of king or queen)
Yorke, Yorick, Yoricke; **Famous namesakes:** Actor Dick York

YOSEF (YO-sef) Hebrew: Spelling variation of Joseph

YSBADDADEN (is-ba-THA-den) Celtic: In Celtic mythology, Ysbaddaden was a fierce giant who would die if separated from his daughter, Olwen.
Yspaddaden

YSIDRO (ee-SEE-dro) Greek: Spelling variation of Isidore

YUDELL English: From the yew tree valley; surname; variant of Udell

YULE (YOOL) English: Born at Yuletide or winter's soltice, late December, now taken to mean born at Christmas
Ewell, Yul; Euell; **Famous namesakes:** Actor Yul Brenner

YULI (YOO-lee) Basque: Youthful, young

YUMA (YOO-mah) Native American: Chiefs son

YURI (YOO-ree) Russian: Variation of George
Yurii; **Nicknames:** *Yurochka, Yura, Yore, Yorii, Yurick*; **Famous namesakes:** Russian Cosmonaut Yuri Gagarin

YUSUF (YOO-səf) Arabic: Variation of Joseph
Yousef, Youssef, Yousuf, Yusef

YUTO (yoo-to) Japanese: A town located in Hamana District, Shizuoka, Japan.

YUVAL Hebrew: Rejoice, be happy

YVES (EEV) French: Variation of Ivor
Yvon; **Famous namesakes:** French singer Yves Montand, French fashion designer Yves Saint Laurent

ZABDIEL Hebrew: Gift, present
Zabdil, Zabdyl; **Nicknames:** *Zabdi, Zabdy, Zabi, Zavdi, Zebdy*

ZACCHAEUS (za-KEE-əs) Hebrew: Clean, pure. The biblical Zacchaeus was a wealthy tax collector who became a disciple of Jesus.

ZACHARIAH (zak-ə-RIE-ə) Hebrew: Original form of Zachary

ZACHARY (ZAK-ə-ree) Hebrew: God remembers, remembrance of the Lord; derived from the name Zechariah. There are over thirty men with this name mentioned in the Bible, including the author of the Book of Zechariah. (Hebrew) *Zachaios*; (German) *Zacharia*; (Spanish) *Zacarias*; (Finnish) *Sakari, Sakarias, Saku*; (Persian) *Zakaria*; *Zacharias, Zachely, Zackary, Zackery, Zakari, Zakary, Zechariah*; **Old forms:** *Zachariah*; **Nicknames:** *Zac, Zach, Zack, Zak*; **Famous namesakes:** Actor Zachary Scott, president Zachary Taylor, actor Zachery Ty Bryan, actor Zac Efron; **Star babies:** sons of Cheryl Tiegs, Elizabeth Vargas

ZADIK (ZAY-dək) Hebrew: Righteous

ZADOK (ZAY-dok) Hebrew: Just, righteous
Zadoc

ZADORNIN (sah-DOR-neen) Basque: Saturn

ZAFIR Arabic: Victorious, successful
(Hindi) *Zafar*; *Zafeer*; **Famous namesakes:**
Bosnian journalist Zafir Behlic

ZAHID (zah-HEED) Arabic: Self-denying,
ascetic, abstemious; if accent is placed on
the second syllable, means moderate, little,
trifling, insignificant
Zahed

ZAHIR (zah-HEER, zah-HER) Arabic:
Sparkling, bright
Zuhayr; *Zaher*; **Famous namesakes:** Afghan
singer Ahmed Zahir, king of Afghanistan
Mohammed Zahir Shah

ZAHUR (zah-HOOR) African: Flower, from
the Arabic word for flourishing (Swahili)

ZAID (zah-EED) Arabic: Increases, grows
Zaied, Zaiid, Zayd

ZAIDE (TZAY-də, TZAY-dee) Hebrew: Elder
Zayde

ZAIM (Za-eem) Arabic: General, title of
authority

ZAKAI (zay-KIE) Hebrew: Pure, sinless,
innocent

ZAKI (ZAH-kee) Arabic: Smart, intelligent,
compassionate
Famous namesakes: Egyptian musician Zaki

ZALE (ZAYL) Greek: Power of the sea
Zail, Zaile, Zayl, Zayle

ZANDER (ZAN-dər) English: Nickname for
Alexander

ZANE (ZAYN) Hebrew, English: Everything
that is good and beautiful; also ornament or
decoration

Zain, Zaine, Zayne; **Nicknames:** *Zani*;
Famous namesakes: Author Zane Gray

ZANTE (ZAHN-tay) Greek: The island
Zakynthos

ZARED (ZAYR-ed) Hebrew: Ambush, trap
Zarad

ZAREK (ZAH-rek) Polish, Greek, Slavic:
God protect the king; biblical king of Babylon
who learned of his impending defeat by
literally reading the writing on the wall
Zarec, Zareck, Zaric, Zarik, Zaryk, Zereck, Zerick

ZAVIER (ZAY-vee-ər) Arabic: Spelling
variation of Xavier

ZAYIT (zie-EET) Hebrew: Olive

ZBIGNIEW (ZBEEG-nyef) Polish: Do away
with anger, be content

ZE'EV (zi-EV, zi-AYV) Hebrew: Wolf. In the
Bible, when Jacob blesses his son Benjamin,
he compares him to a wolf with this name.

ZEBEDIAH (zeb-ə-DIE-ə) Hebrew: God's
gift; biblical father of the apostles James and
John
Zebadiah; *Zebadia, Zebadya, Zebadyah,
Zebedia, Zebedya, Zebedyah, Zebidia,
Zebidiah*; **Nicknames:** *Zeb, Zebedee, Zebad*

ZEBULON (ZEB-yoo-lən) Hebrew: From
the high house, the honored one; biblical son
of Jacob
Zebulun, Zevulun; *Zabulan, Zebulan, Zebulen,
Zebulin, Zebulun, Zebulyn, Zevulon, Zhebule*

ZECHARIAH (ze-kə-RIE-ə) Hebrew:
Spelling variation of Zachary

ZEDEKIAH (ze-də-KIE-ə) Hebrew: The
Lord is mighty and just; biblical king of Judah
Zedechiah, Zedekiahs; **Nicknames:** *Zed*

ZEKE (ZEEK) Hebrew: Nickname for Ezekiel
Star babies: son of Neil Young

ZEKI (ze-KEE) Turkish: Clever
Zekie, Zeky

ZELENY Czech: Green, fresh
Nicknames: *Zel*

ZELOTES (ze-LO-teez) Greek: Name given to Simon, one of the apostles, probably in association with the sect of Zealots

ZEMARIAH (ze-MAHR-ee-ə) Hebrew: Song
Zemaria

ZENAS Greek: Welcoming
Zenios

ZENOBIO (zə-NO-bee-o) Greek, Spanish: Life of Zeus
Cenobio; Cenovio, Senobio, Senovio, Zenobios, Zenovio

ZENON (ZE-nawn) Greek: Derived from the name Zeus, ruler of the gods in Greek mythology. Greek philosopher Zeno was the founder of stoicism.
(Spanish) *Cenon, Senon; Zeno*

ZEPHANIAH (ze-fə-NIE-ə) Hebrew: Treasured by the Lord; a minor Old Testament prophet and author of the Book of Zephaniah
Nicknames: *Zephan, Zeph*

ZEROUN (DZE-roon) Armenian: Respected, honored for wisdom

ZESIRO (ze-SEE-ro) African: Older twin (Uganda)

ZETES (ZEE-teez) Greek: Son of Boreas, brother of Calais, one of the famous argonauts of Greek mythology

ZETHUS (ZEE-thəs) Greek: Mythical son of Zeus and Antiope, and twin brother of Amphion

ZEUS (ZOOS) Greek: Chief god of Greek mythology; Zeus ruled from atop Mount Olympus

ZEV Hebrew: Familar form of Zebediah, Zebulon and other similar Hebrew names

ZEVID (ZE-vid) Hebrew: Given a gift

ZIGOR (SEE-gor) Basque: Punishes, punishment

ZIKOMO (zee-KO-mo) African: Gratitude

ZIMRAN (ZIEM-rahn) Hebrew: Sacred, holy; one of Abraham's sons

ZIMRI (ZIM-ree) Hebrew: Worthy, to be praised

ZINAN (zee-nan) Japanese: Second-born son

ZINDEL Yiddish: Defends mankind; variant of Alexander

ZION (ZIE-ahn) Hebrew: Name of an ancient citadel located in the center of Jerusalem. Zion is also used to refer to a Jewish homeland and to heaven.

ZITOMIR Czech: Live well
Zitek

ZIVEN (ZEE-ven) Slavic, Polish: Full of life, vigorous
Zivon; **Nicknames:** *Ziv*

ZIYA (ZEE-ə) Arabic: Shining light
Zia

ZIYAD (zee-YAHD) African: Increasing

ZOHAR (ZO-hahr) Hebrew: Sparkling, shining
Zohair, Zohare; **Nicknames:** *Ziv*

ZOLTAN (ZOL-tahn) Hungarian: Life, energy, from the Greek *zoe*, meaning *life*
Zoltar; **Famous namesakes:** Hungarian composer Zoltán Kodály

ZORION (so-REE-ən) Basque: Variation of Orion
Zorian

ZUHAYR (zoo-HAYR) Arabic: Sparkling. Zuhayr is also the masculine, diminutive form of Zahra, changing the meaning to *small flower* or *blossom*.

ZURIEL (zoo-ree-EL) Hebrew: Spelling variation of Tzuriel

ZVI (TZVEE) Hebrew: Deer, gazelle
(Dutch) *Zwi*

ZYGMUNT (ZIK-muwnt) Polish: Variation of Sigmund

Your Name

Other names considered for you:

_____

_____

But we chose . . .

_____

Because:

_____

_____

_____

_____

_____

_____

_____

With love,

_____